The Barefoot Sisters
SOUTHBOUND

The Barefoot Sisters

SOUTHBOUND

Lucy and Susan Letcher
a.k.a. Isis and jackrabbit

STACKPOLE
BOOKS

For the hikers, maintainers, trail angels . . .
and especially for the dreamers.
—Isis and jackrabbit

Published by
STACKPOLE BOOKS
5067 Ritter Road
Mechanicsburg, PA 17055
www.stackpolebooks.com

Printed in the United States of America

10 9 8 7 6 5 4 3 2

First edition

Cover design by Caroline M. Stover

Library of Congress Cataloging-in-Publication Data

Letcher, Lucy.
  The barefoot sisters southbound / Lucy and Susan Letcher.
    p. cm.
  ISBN-13: 978-0-8117-3530-8
  ISBN-10: 0-8117-3530-3
  1. Hiking—Appalachian Trail. 2. Appalachian Trail—Description and travel.
  3. Letcher, Lucy. 4. Letcher, Susan. I. Letcher, Susan. II. Title.
  GV199.42.A68L47 2009
  917.404'43—dc22
                                                        2008032917

CONTENTS

CHAPTER 1

The Wilderness

jackrabbit

A sudden gust of wind lashed my face with rain and ice crystals. Just ahead of me on the trail, my sister Lucy picked her way through a maze of granite boulders dotted with sparse lichens. I imagined how the two of us would look to a passerby: two tall women in black pants and teal Gore-Tex jackets, wisps of blond hair plastered to the sides of our faces, bulging packs, bare feet. Crazy.

The low clouds and sleet lifted for a moment, revealing the final climb ahead. Perhaps half a mile and we would be standing on Baxter Peak, the highest point of Mount Katahdin. This would be the fourth time I'd reached that peak. The climb alone had always given me a sense of strength and accomplishment. But this time, the summit of Katahdin would be more than just another mountain. It would be the beginning of a long pilgrimage through pristine forests, hedgerows, national parks, mosquito-ridden swamps; through towns and cities, over back roads and major highways; into a Superfund site. It would be a journey across the rumpled spine of the eastern mountains and an equally demanding passage across our own interior landscapes. Although I did not know it at the time, my sister and I would devote more than fifteen months of our lives to the Appalachian Trail.

We stood for a moment before the venerable signpost marking the summit. Scored with graffiti and the constant onslaught of weather, it stands perhaps three feet high, a wooden A-frame painted Forest Service brown with recessed white letters:

KATAHDIN   5268 ft.
Northern Terminus of the Appalachian Trail

Below this were a few waypoints: *Thoreau Spring, 1.0, Katahdin Stream Campground, 5.2.* At the bottom of the list: *Springer Mountain, Georgia, 2160.2.* More than two thousand miles. It was simply a number, too large and incomprehensible to have any bearing on me. The farthest I had ever walked in a day was ten miles and that was with a daypack. Now I was contemplating a journey of months, covering thousands of miles. All of a sudden, there on the summit with the clouds screaming past us, it didn't seem like such a great idea.

I turned to my sister, half-expecting to see the same doubt mirrored in her face. But her eyes were shining, and she smiled with an almost feral intensity. It was a look I would come to know all too well over the next year and a half, and it meant, *I am going to do this and no one had better try to stop me.* "We're really doing this," she shouted over the wind's howl and the lashing rain. "We're hiking the Appalachian Trail!"

And with that, we turned to head down the mountain. We found the first white blaze on a rock near the signpost: a swath of white paint about two by six inches. There was nothing remarkable about it—it was just a streak of pigment on the rocks, worn by the weather—but we both stopped, briefly, to lay a hand on it. We knew that we would be following these blazes from rock to rock, tree to tree, all the way to Georgia.

The rain picked up as we descended below treeline. The cold stones underfoot gave way to mud that, ankle-deep in places, made a satisfying *squishploop* sound, and the rough roots of spruce and fir stretched across the trail. It was noticeably warmer in the forest, where the trees blocked the wind. Conifers on the high slopes gave way to maple, birch, and beech, their leaves still touched with the delicate yellow-green of spring. Clouds of blackflies crawled into our hair and into the cuffs of our clothing, leaving streaks of blood and lumpy welts wherever they bit.

As I walked, I thought about the last few weeks before this cold, rainy summer solstice. Ten days earlier, I had earned my diploma from Carleton College in Minnesota, with a double major in music and biology. The next day, I had flown to Bangor, Maine, driven an hour to my mother's house on the coast, and started packing. I had played the piano in all my spare time, not knowing when I would get a chance again. In the evenings, I took long walks with my sister; Lucy and I had barely seen each other in the past four years, except for vacations. Now we were planning to spend six months in each other's company.

We reached the campground just at dusk and pitched our tent under a picnic shelter. Both of us were too exhausted to say much. We hung the sopping-wet jackets and pants over the rafters to drip dry, cooked our supper over a smoky fire, and drifted off to sleep to the sound of rain drumming on the tin roof. My last thought, before I sank into dreaming, was this: *at least we don't have to worry about wet boots in the morning.*

My whole body groaned with the effort of lifting my full pack in the morning. Besides our regular gear (tent, sleeping bag and liner, sleeping mat, stove, water bottles, med kit, changes of clothing), we were carrying twelve days' worth of food. After Katahdin, the Trail traverses the "Hundred Mile Wilderness," a 119-mile stretch of remote forests with no access to towns. We wanted to be well-prepared. We'd left most of our gear at the foot of the mountain while we hiked Katahdin, since the steep, broken rocks are hard enough to negotiate even with a daypack.

I'd thought I was in good shape—in college, I'd been running every morning, and I had just gained my black belt in Tae Kwon Do. But backpacking was something else. A friend who had finished the Appalachian Trail several years earlier had told me, "nothing gets you in shape for the Trail, short of putting your pack on and walking." *Damn, she was right,* I thought grimly as I lurched down the trail.

We had decided to try hiking barefoot because it was the way we had always walked, since we were kids, in the mountains near our home on the coast of Maine. We loved the sense of connection to the ground that barefoot hiking gave us. Every surface felt different underfoot: granite, shale, pine needles, thick mud. We didn't want to sacrifice that link with the earth. I was not accustomed to hiking barefoot with so much weight on my back, though. At first, my passage was slow and painstaking. The rough-barked roots, mud, and soft spruce needles felt good underfoot, but sharp rocks and sticks seemed to lurk in unexpected places. The tiny triangular scales of spruce cones stuck into the pads of my feet. I kept my eyes on the trail, for the most part. *Unless I get better at this barefoot thing,* I thought, *I'm going to see every rock and tree root between here and Georgia.*

When I did glance up, the woods had a sort of minimalist beauty, with the bold straight trunks of spruce and pine splitting the middle ground into rectangles of green light. Everywhere the vista was different, but always a variation of the same theme: black spruce, red spruce, white pine, balsam fir, red maple, moose maple, paper birch. Mossy boulders, the soft orange of fallen spruce needles, dapples of light and shade. We passed small clear tarns and, in the midday calm, each one bore an inverted green-gold forest, a deep blue reflected sky shot through with small ripples.

At Daicey Pond Campsite in Baxter State Park, the official checkpoint for hikers starting the Appalachian Trail in Maine, we slung off our packs on the grass beside the ranger station and knocked on the camouflage-green door. A ranger in khakis and a Smokey the Bear hat handed us two questionnaires and motioned us to sit in the white plastic armchairs in front of his desk.

"You guys thru-hiking?" We had heard the term before—hiking an entire long-distance trail in one stretch—but all of a sudden it applied to us. Once again I thought of the impossibly large number of miles to Georgia on the sign atop the mountain. I thought of the impossibly heavy packs sitting outside. I grinned—an expression probably not unlike my sister's wild you-can't-stop-me smile of the day before—and answered in the affirmative.

We filled out the surveys, noting our ages (twenty-two and twenty-five), names and address (our mother's), emergency contacts. For "occupation" I put "student," for lack of a better idea. There was a space at the bottom of the form for "trail name." I knew hikers chose names like CB handles, something to identify themselves in the Trail community. My sister wrote "Isis" in her delicate script, a name she'd earned years earlier on another adventure. I hesitated for a moment, and blocked in "JACKRABBIT" in capitals. It was the only nickname that had ever stuck with me, given by a friend in Tae Kwon Do. "You jump like jackrabbit," he said in a fake Karate Kid accent, and it became the name I used in our impromptu Saturday sparring classes. It seemed only fitting to carry it with me on this journey, as a reminder of what I had learned and who I had become. It made me feel strong, invincible, in that moment. Susan could have doubts and second thoughts, but Jackrabbit was thru-hiking the Appalachian Trail.

The ranger asked about our plans and our previous wilderness experience. He seemed satisfied with our tales of adventure growing up in the Maine woods and exploring the seashore and lakes. We showed him the med kit, emergency blankets, twelve days' rations. He took the questionnaires and entered our names in a large book. As we left Daicey Pond, he came out on the lawn and wished us luck.

"I don't say this to many people, but I think you've got what it takes to make it. You guys know what you're doing out there. Just keep your heads about you, keep putting one foot in front of the other; that's about all you gotta do."

We thanked him and turned to go.

"Hey, you guys going barefoot?" We turned and nodded.

"As long as it's comfortable," Isis said.

"As long as it's fun," I added.

I thought the ranger was about to retract his confidence in our ability (and sanity), but he smiled. "There are a few that do that. I don't know how. Well, if it works for you, more power to you."

We stopped for lunch by a wide, slow stream. Clouds of blackflies settled around us immediately, but I hardly noticed them in my fatigue. The soles of my feet felt hot and dry, a little sore to the touch in places. I took out a small plastic container of moisturizer to rub onto my feet. It was an ointment my sister had made from beeswax, olive oil, and healing herbs, designed to keep our calluses from drying out and cracking. The color and texture of cold pea soup, it looked unappetizing, but had a pleasant scent of fresh herbs and honey. It seemed to work, soothing the dry ache in my soles.

Lucy (I couldn't quite get used to "Isis" yet) took our lunch from her food bag: little plastic bags of peanuts, sunflower seeds, and dried fruit. We had read that peanuts and sunflower seeds, in combination, provide a complete protein and a good amount of carbohydrates, and we reasoned that bags of nuts and seeds would take up much less space in our already-burgeoning food bags than a calorically equal amount of crackers and peanut butter. I dug into the bags, oblivious to the residue of beeswax and forest floor that still clung to my hands. This was my first step on the long descent into a general unawareness of filth that long-distance hikers cultivate. The A.T. (as we would quickly learn to call it) is not for the squeamish.

We spent that night at Abol Bridge Campground. A squat red building near the river housed the general store and campground office. Logging trucks, laden with spruces of pitifully small diameter, idled in the parking lot or roared past, ka-thumping over the railroad ties of the bridge. For $15, we rented a plot of almost-level gravel and a picnic table.

I felt a little foolish, at first, when I saw the store—why were we carrying twelve days' food? We didn't have a guidebook, and our maps had indicated nothing about accommodations at Abol Bridge. One look at the shelves, though, and I was glad we'd stocked up before we left. The only vegetarian options—and my sister and I are, nominally, vegetarians—were a few cans of wax beans, instant potato flakes, chips and pretzels, a couple boxes of saltines, and some post-dated Wonder Bread. Little that was packable, certainly, and nothing I'd want to survive on for ten days. We bought some fruit juice.

As dusk fell, we cooked macaroni over our Zip stove. Most camp stoves require fuel, but the Zip stove is a wood-burner. A tiny motor in the bottom turns a battery-driven fan that blows air into the firebox. Once the stove is lit, it will burn almost anything—we sometimes used it to incinerate squeezed-out teabags—but it needs constant feeding. In the line of scrubby trees between our campsite and the next, I gathered fallen twigs.

"D'you think this is enough, Isis?" The name sounded false and disorienting in the darkening campsite. All of a sudden, I thought about the act of naming and the power it contains. I knew who "Jackrabbit" was: the strong side of me. The one who had shattered pine boards with powerful kicks and strikes, vanquished opponents in the ring; the one aware and at home inside my body, who understood strength and forbearance, violence and peace. I recognized Jackrabbit, but who was Isis?

"Get a couple more twigs," she said. "The pine burns well; see if you can find more of that." Together, we broke the branches into thumb-sized pieces and fed them into the smoking belly of the stove.

Isis

B efore I take up the narrative of our Appalachian Trail adventures, let me step back a few years and tell you another story: how I got the name Isis. In more ways than one, my A.T. hike began with this earlier journey.

My trail name comes from my first backpacking trip, a four-day hike through the Andes to Machu Picchu. Scott Grierson, a friend of our family whose appetite for adventure has led him from the A.T. to the Amazon, was hoping to start an ecotourism project in Peru. He had some potential backers for the project—but they had heard enough stories of his previous journeys in the rain forest to be concerned about liability. Frustrated with the delays in funding, he decided to organize a trip that would prove he could bring ordinary tourists through the Peruvian mountains and jungles alive. He planned a three-week tour that started with the hike to Machu Picchu and concluded with a wild ride down the Urubamba River on three-foot-wide, half-submerged rafts made of balsa wood. A couple of his hiking buddies signed up immediately, but they hardly qualified as "ordinary tourists." That was where my sister and I came in.

Susan heard of the trip from Scott's mother, who played with her in a chamber music trio. Susan was seventeen at the time, a star athlete just out of high school, immortal and bored. She jumped at the opportunity to join Scott's expedition and test her championship track-and-field muscles against the Andes.

I'm not sure why I decided to go along. Susan would tell you that my older sister instincts kicked in, that I tagged along to try to protect her, but as far as I can recall, I was more worried about keeping up with her. A shy, studious sophomore in college, I had none of her physical advantages. All I had was a deep-rooted stubbornness, which had pulled me through many long nights of essay writing—that, and the knowledge that I had never yet encountered the limits of my body's strength. Of course, I had never really tried.

We spent two days acclimatizing in the high mountain city of Cuzco. While we sat in cafés sipping a thin, bitter tea that the Incas used to combat altitude sickness, Scott and his friends Karl and Hago regaled us with stories of their earlier travels. Most often, they reminisced about their A.T. hikes. Each of them had hiked the Trail at least once; Scott, who goes by the well-merited trail name of Maineak, had hiked it four times. He described to us the crenellated ridges of the Smokies, arching like narrow suspension bridges between the peaks, and the red autumn maples reflected in New England lakes at dawn. His adventures ranged from hiking four miles into town and back to bring pizza to friends at a campfire, to helping police and rangers track down a murderer. Susan and I listened wide-eyed.

Back at the hotel, our daydreams became plans.

"We could hike it together," Susan said, "if you wait for me to finish college."

"Let's do it!" I told her. "Assuming, of course, that I survive the current adventure."

The first eight miles of the Inca Trail out of Ollantaytambo led slowly up the side of a long, narrow valley to the saddle where we planned to make camp. All afternoon, I could see the distant furrow in the mountains that marked the campsite. I spun out my strength, step after step, trying to make it last just that far. Inca porters trotted past us, barefoot or shod in flip-flops made from old tires, each lugging a bundle three times his size. Folding chairs and cages full of live chickens hung from their backs. My own pack, which I had painstakingly pared down to thirty-five pounds (by bringing far too little food), felt like it was wearing holes in my hip bones and pulling my shoulder blades down through the soles of my boots.

Later in the day, the tourists who had hired the porters came sauntering up the trail, carrying only their cameras and water bottles. At that point I didn't have enough energy to waste on feeling jealous. *They're a different kind of animal,* I thought to myself. *They laugh and walk upright. I'm the kind of animal that just puts one foot in front of the other, until it gets to the place where it can rest.*

When we finally reached the saddle where we had planned to camp, we discovered that all the porters and tourists had already occupied all the clear, level ground. There might have been room to squeeze in a few more tents at the edges, but Scott and his friends didn't want to stay in such a crowded place. Our guide, Fernando, mentioned that he knew of a smaller, much less frequented site about a mile up the mountain. At the rate we'd been moving, we could get there an hour before dark.

I thought about telling them all that I couldn't do it. The trail turned at the saddle, and I could see the narrow track climbing away up the mountain's flank at a much steeper angle. I knew that neither muscle nor prayer would carry me up it at the two-thirds-of-a-mile-per-hour pace I had sustained so far. Still, I didn't want to prove myself a spoilsport on the first day of the trek; it seemed easier to face a physical impasse than to disappoint the others.

A hundred yards up the mountain I collapsed. The white trail wavered in front of me, and I couldn't see where to put my feet. Thinking I might be dehydrated, I sat down on a rock to take a drink. When I tried to stand up again, my legs buckled. Susan, who had waited for me, tried to help me up, but my knees seemed unwilling to engage. I don't know how long we waited. The sun slid toward the jagged rim of the mountains, and shadows crept out from behind the white rocks. The world looked slippery, as if Dali had painted it—the stones, my hands, the water bottle they held seemed to melt at the edges. Susan found some wild fruit that looked like unripe blackberries, and we ate it, not caring that it might be poisonous, so long as it gave us a few free calories.

Eventually Fernando came back to look for us. He took my pack and carried it for me, having left his own pack at the campsite up above. Susan led me by the hand. I had to stop and rest every five minutes. The stars were coming out as I stumbled into camp. Scott greeted us with cups of hot cocoa, mixed with rum from his "medical supplies" bag. Susan cooked our meager supper of one packet of ramen noodles each. Then we set up our tent and turned in, only to discover that the summer sleeping bags we had packed were far too thin. I lay half awake all night, sick with the thought that I'd already failed, wondering if I'd have the strength to stagger back down the mountain and catch a bus to Cuzco the next day, or if Fernando would have to carry me.

As it turned out, I didn't go back to Cuzco. I was fine the next day. I went slowly, but, for the rest of the trip, I had no trouble with the altitude. Hunger and sleeplessness waited in the back of my mind until, safely over the mountains, I had time to appease them. I had found the limits of my physical strength, but I had also found that my stubbornness could be applied to more than just late nights in a college library. Somewhere in the cloud forest, on the other side of a 14,000-foot pass called Huarmi Huañusca, "the place where the woman died," we sat around a campfire eating our evening's ration of ramen and listening to Scott's Trail stories.

"We're going to hike the A.T. someday. Maybe when we've both finished college," I told him.

Scott looked at us for a minute, as if calculating the gap between our enthusiasm and our experience. Finally he said, "If you're going to hike, you need trail names." He turned to me. "I'm going to call you Isis, because she's a goddess of death and resurrection."

The name proved prophetic; I collapsed the first day I carried a full pack on the A.T., too. Setting out from Katahdin Stream Campsite, I took the lead, afraid that if I let Susan—or Jackrabbit, as she'd decided to call herself—get ahead of me, I wouldn't see her again until Georgia. She was still the strong one, long-legged as her trail name implied.

Enthusiasm carried me four or five miles past Daicey Pond, and then the fifty-five pounds in my pack caught up with me. After a snack break, Jackrabbit got up first and started walking. I struggled to keep up with her, half running, feeling as though I couldn't breathe properly. It seemed that she never looked back to see if I was still behind her. We'd planned to hike fourteen miles that day, all the way to Hurd Brook Lean-to. I was pretty sure I wouldn't make it. I imagined my sister setting up camp, beginning to worry, while I staggered along in the darkness, miles behind her. This thought brought an enormous wave of self-pity washing over me. I started to cry. Not a good idea—crying made my already labored breathing ten times more difficult.

At the turn of the trail ahead of me, Jackrabbit had stopped to talk with two hikers. I hurried to catch up, to tell her I wouldn't make it as far as Hurd Brook and wanted to stay at Abol Bridge Campground, some four miles closer. The men she was talking to turned out to be northbounders: thruhikers who had started in Georgia, now nearly finished with their 2,160-mile journey. Thin, sun-browned and windburned, one heavily bearded and one with about five days' worth of stubble, they carried packs that seemed hardly big enough to fit one decent picnic. Their glances flickered past us, toward Katahdin, as they spoke. I asked them how far to Abol Bridge Campground.

"Abol Bridge? You're almost there," the bearded one answered. My shoulders slumped with relief, as far as they could in the complex interlacing of pack straps. I stared hard at the bend in the trail ahead of us, hoping to see the corner of a building through the trees.

"Yeah," said the other, "it's only a mile, mile and a half, I'd say."

They wished us a good hike and were gone, vanishing into the forest as easily as deer.

A whole mile, maybe even a mile and a half to go! Suddenly, the belt of my pack felt like a circle of fire around my hips. The blackflies and mosquitoes that had been swarming around us all day became a furious humming in my skull. I sat down in the middle of the trail.

"It would be easier to hike if you'd stop crying," Jackrabbit said. I started to sob. With a sigh, she sat down beside me. She opened her water bottle and offered me a drink. I refused to take my headnet off; I drank through the mosquito netting. After ten minutes of patient persuasion, Jackrabbit convinced me to lift the net up enough to eat a few bites of an energy bar. Then she pulled me to my feet. The last mile to Abol Bridge was just as slow and painful as I expected it to be, but, one step at a time, I made it. Jackrabbit walked beside me all the way.

Taking a shower at the campground that night, I discovered dark bruises as big as the palms of my hands, one over each of my hipbones, and a wide swath of rash across the small of my back. There were sores on my shoulders, and the tops of my hands and feet were so thoroughly stippled with mosquito bites that they felt like the skins of cucumbers. Strangely, this physical evidence of the pain I'd been feeling encouraged me.

So I'm not such a wimp as I thought I was, this afternoon, I said to myself. *All these bruises and I still made it this far. Maybe I will get to Georgia.*

It was three full days before I was able to take my mind off my pack weight, but I did keep going. As I walked, I ran through an inventory of all the food and gear I was carrying, telling myself the usefulness of each item in turn. When this didn't help, I went over all the food I'd eaten so far. *Half a pound of oatmeal, a quarter pound of peanuts, an energy bar and some couscous—my pack must be a whole pound lighter than yesterday,* I thought. As a last resort, I let my mind dwell on the pound of dark chocolate I had stashed away in the bottom of my food bag. Whatever else I had to lug along with it, there was at least one pound that was worth the effort.

jackrabbit

On the third day out, we camped at Rainbow Spring Campsite, a small clearing in the beech woods set back from the shore of Rainbow Lake. The trees there were still touched with the light green of spring. I could hear the waves lapping the shore as I set my pack down and began searching for twigs to feed the Zip stove.

A hiker came up the trail, a tall lanky man with short-cropped red hair and ears that stuck out a bit. His pack was huge, and he walked with two trekking poles. He had a frank, open face covered with freckles.

"Hi, I'm Matt," he said.

"Jackrabbit," I told him. Each time my trail name crossed my lips, it became more familiar, and this time, when I heard my sister say "Isis," it sounded natural.

"You thru-hiking, Matt?"

"Yes. At least, that's my plan." A tentative smile.

"Same for us," Isis said. "We're hoping to hike the whole thing, but we'll see how it goes."

"Definitely going as far as New Hampshire," I said.

"It's a good section of Trail." Matt slung off his giant green pack.

"You've done it before?"

"Yeah, I hiked Maine last September."

"And you still don't have a trail name?"

"Many suggestions were bandied about. I'm afraid none stuck."

"Such as?"

He smiled, and his ears turned pink. "Well, I went to the grocery store in Stratton and I bought a ton of food. They gave me a box to carry it out in, you know, one of those Mason jar boxes. There were a bunch of hikers hanging around on the steps outside the store, and when I came out with this box they all started shouting, 'Ball Jar! Ball Jar!' So for a while I signed that in registers. You know, those notebooks in the shelters. I'd write, 'what's in *your* jar?'" He shrugged. "But that didn't last very long."

I set up the tent, snapping the poles together and feeding them into their nylon sleeves, and we went for a swim in the bracingly cold water. The wind had whipped the surface into six-inch waves, so I didn't stay in long. As I sat on the bank watching Matt and Isis cavort in the lake, another hiker came up beside me.

"Hi, I'm Ashley," she said. She was about five four, compact and muscular, with dark hair and bright blue eyes.

"Jackrabbit. Pleased to meet you."

She dropped her pack and sat down beside me on the rocks. "Are you thru-hiking?"

"That's the plan. You?"

"Yup." She grinned widely. "Who are your companions out there?"

"That's Matt, way out in the waves," I said. "And that's my sister Isis."

She looked at me more closely. "You're not—are you the ones I saw on Katahdin, barefoot?"

"Well, unless it was our stunt doubles."

"And you're thru-hiking? Barefoot?"

"As far as we get. We figured we'd try to hike Katahdin barefoot, and if we could do that, then we'd try to get through the Wilderness, and if we manage that, well—"

"But why barefoot?"

I shrugged. "I like being barefoot. You can feel the trail with all your senses. We grew up hiking this way."

"Don't you worry about getting cut or anything?"

"You learn how to step carefully. And it just feels so good, on the forest floor, or in the mud—"

"Wow. When I first saw you, I thought it was pretty crazy. That's neat, though. I hadn't really thought about how it would feel."

As the light in the beeches turned golden, we gathered enough wood for a small fire. We sat on logs around the firepit and told stories while Isis cooked a pot of lentils and rice.

Matt was from Tennessee; he had just received his Masters in geology from the University of Maine. Ashley had just graduated from Virginia Tech with a biology degree. Both of them had already hiked long sections of the A.T.

"The best thing about this trail is how it brings people together," Ashley said. "People from all walks of life come out here, and they're just hikers. It doesn't matter whether they're students, or doctors, or lawyers, or garbage collectors—they're all the same on the Trail."

Matt, staring into the fire, smiled wistfully. "I don't know. I think the best thing the Trail has done for me is to teach me about change. It's all about flow out here. Impermanence. You meet people and you have a great time, but you know you might never see them again. Nothing lasts."

We were all quiet for a while. "Do you remember that plaque at the base of Katahdin?" Matt said. "Down by the parking lot?"

"Yeah, I think so."

"It says something like, 'cities may crumble, towns will come and go, but Katahdin will forever stand, a monument to the people of Maine.' But I can't help thinking that it all depends on the timescale you look at. Katahdin will crumble too, given enough time. Everything changes."

"Hmm." Ashley smiled. "But we might as well enjoy it while it lasts, don't you think?"

Isis

Late in the afternoon of our fourth day, we climbed our first mountain since Katahdin, a 700-foot rise called Nesuntabunt. At the summit I took out our usual snack of peanuts and sunflower seeds. In the planning stage of our hike, Jackrabbit and I had congratulated each other on the logistical brilliance of choosing nuts and seeds as our luncheon staple, instead of the bagels or crackers favored by most hikers we'd read about. Now, four days into our hike, I would have been happy never to see another peanut, but I still had five pounds of them in my pack and eighty miles to walk to the next grocery store.

Jackrabbit and I made a half-hearted attempt at the snack mix. After a few minutes I gave up and pulled out an extra ration of granola bars, giving myself the excuse that we had just hiked up a mountain and deserved a treat. I sat on a granite ledge of Nesuntabunt in the midsummer sun, trying to eat the granola bar slowly. It was the closest thing I had to bread. Seven hundred feet down, the surface of Nahmakanta Lake glinted with tiny whitecaps. To the north, Katahdin towered over the forest and lakes like a sphinx reclining on a green and azure cloth. I looked across all the miles we'd hiked, swamps and ledges, gravel roads, spruce woods, and the rough granite spine of the great mountain itself—and then my mind, with all the certainty of a compass needle, snapped back to the subject of bread. Bread: rosemary, oatmeal, potato, rye. The texture of a good crust, the smell of sourdough. Bread with butter, bread with cheese. All the way down the mountain, I daydreamed of the foods we didn't have.

That night, we camped with Matt at Wadleigh Stream Lean-to. It was far too buggy to consider sleeping in the open, three-sided structure, but I sat down to cook supper on the split log that formed a convenient bench across the front of the shelter. I knew from reading about the Trail that there were lean-tos every ten to fifteen miles along it, constructed by the local trail maintaining clubs. We'd passed a few of them already, but this was the first one I'd had time to take a close look at. The walls were made of spruce logs about eight inches in diameter, stacked and joined in the manner of a log cabin. Larger logs formed pillars at the ends of my bench, joining it to the two side walls. A gap of about three feet separated my seat from the elevated spruce-plank sleeping platform. At the back wall, the corrugated tin roof was only three or four feet above the platform; it rose steeply to a peak just above my head, then ended with a few feet of overhang. Suspended from the roof, just above me, were a half-dozen empty tuna cans. Each one was hung upside down by a string running through a hole in the bottom. A few inches below the can, a stick was tied crosswise to the end of the string. They looked like someone's early attempt to invent bells, with the clappers attached at the wrong angle. Matt was sitting next to me, cooking his supper, so I asked him about them.

"Those are mouse hangers," he told me. "You hang your food bags from the sticks and mice can't get around the cans."

"What about bears?"

"Well, the theory is that most bears around here are too shy to go after your food bag when you're sleeping five feet away from it."

I privately concluded that I wasn't ready to stake my food bag, or my sleeping self, on such a theory, and planned to keep on hanging my food from tree branches far from my tent at night. But I feigned nonchalance, asking Matt, "If we don't have to worry about bears, what sorts of animals are problems?"

"Mice, chipmunks, squirrels . . . and porcupines, of course, they're a real nuisance, though more for the trail maintainers than for us."

"Porcupines?"

"Yes. Do you know what you're sitting on?"

I jumped up to check if, in my fatigue, I had accidentally sat down in some spilled food or mud from someone's boot. It would be at least a week before I could wash my clothes, and I didn't want to get them grimy any faster than necessary.

Matt laughed. "I mean the bench. It's called a porcupine trap. Porcupines love salt, you see, and this lean-to has about twenty years' worth of hiker sweat soaked into its floorboards. If porcupines could reach the sleeping platform, they'd gnaw on the edge until there was nothing left of it. They're good climbers, but they're kind of dumb. They smell the salt, climb up to that log you're sitting on, and try to reach the platform. But it's too far for them; they fall down between the log and the platform and have to make their way out through those gaps under the ends of the side walls."

By that time, Jackrabbit had finished setting up the tent and joined us. "Lentils again?" She sighed. "I'd eat the *floor* if it tasted anything like bread."

"Want a cracker?" Matt asked. "I've got plenty." He held out a package of gray, rectangular rye crackers of a kind our mother used to buy for herself. As children, we had derisively called them "cardboard crackers," claiming that they had about as much flavor as the box they came in.

"Matt, you are a god!" said Jackrabbit. She took one cracker, carefully split it down the middle, and handed half to me. Then we both turned our attention to the pot of lentils, saving our cracker halves for dessert.

That half-cracker may have been what kept us from getting off the Trail in the middle of the next day. A passing northbounder told us the story:

"If you turn left at the next logging road," he said, "and walk a quarter of a mile, you come to a dock on a lake, with an air horn hanging off it. You honk the air horn, and someone comes and picks you up in a boat, and they take you to this place where there's pizza and showers and cold beer!"

It sounded so much like a hiker's fantasy that we thought he was just teasing us, seeing what he could pull over on the new southbounders. When we reached the logging road, though, we found a business card pinned to a tree, advertising a hunting lodge called White House Landing. At the bottom of the card someone had drawn an arrow pointing left, down the road, and written, "honk the air horn at the dock." We talked it over for about five minutes—pizza sounded delicious beyond imagining, just then—but Matt's cracker had dispelled enough of our food cravings that neither one of us was thinking with her stomach. Jackrabbit said that she didn't want to fall so far behind our newfound friends. Ashley was probably half a day ahead of us, and we might not catch up with her even in Monson if we took the afternoon off. I agreed, adding that it would feel like a bit of a cop-out, stopping for pizza and showers in the middle of the Wilderness, when we'd prepared ourselves for twelve days of continuous hiking. I was exhausted, I didn't like the way I'd started to smell, and even the thought of peanuts turned my stomach—but I wanted to complete this first section of the Trail in the way we'd set out to hike it.

We stopped for lunch on the shore of Pemadumcook Lake, a few miles farther on. The giant form of Mount Katahdin rose above the water, dwarfing the low hills we had crossed. As we unpacked our food bags, Ashley stepped out of the woods. She told us that she'd gotten off the day before at White House Landing, accompanying a fellow hiker who had twisted his knee. Ashley brought cheese and more crackers, which she shared with us. Even more than the food, her cheerful nature revived us. The clouds seemed to lift as she sang, "blue skies, smilin' on me, nothin' but blue skies, far as I see . . ." She broke off.

"Matt thinks that should be my trail name. Blue Skies. I sing that song all the time."

"It's perfect!" Jackrabbit and I both spoke at once.

"You think so? Then I have a name! I'm going to go write it in the first register I can find. See you at the campsite!" She strode off up the trail, singing.

jackrabbit

After a few days of barefoot hiking, I could tell that my feet were toughening—the little scales of spruce cones hardly bothered me, and the sharp sticks and hidden rocks were still perceptible, but no longer painful. In flat, low places the trail ran along bog bridges: split cedar logs lay lengthwise to form a track through marshy sphagnum moss. The old wood felt deliciously soft and smooth under my bare soles.

One thing was bothersome, though: the bugs. Blackflies wiggled their way into our hair and the cuffs of our clothing. Thick clouds of mosquitoes hung in the air, making an ominous whine that followed us everywhere. Whenever we stood still, even for a moment, they landed and bit straight through the thin cotton shirts we wore over our tank tops. At one point, the trail crossed a beautiful open bog with small dark pools of water and drifts of tall purple iris. I wanted to pause and look at the flowers, but the cloud of bloodsucking insects hovering over the surface of the water was audible even from a distance. Isis and I exchanged a glance and started running, our heavy packs bumping awkwardly. We didn't slow down until we reached slightly higher ground, several hundred yards from the swamp.

We stopped for the night at Antlers Tentsite, a space of open ground at the end of a skinny point, with a firepit of blackened stones. The lake glimmered all around through the branches of tall red pines. Matt and Ashley—now Blue Skies, I reminded myself—were there, setting up their tarps between trees.

"Hiya, sisters," Matt said. "Isis, right?" She nodded, smiling. "And I can't remember your trail name. Grasshopper?"

"Sorry, Matt, wrong phylum. I'm Jackrabbit. Long legs, big ears." And a jumping round kick that would flatten an opponent from ten feet away, but I didn't feel the need to explain that part of the name just then.

"Hi, guys," Blue Skies said. "Good hike today?"

"Yeah, the bugs were something else, though."

We exchanged a few more pleasantries while I laid out the ground cloth and set up the tent. I could see thunderheads building rapidly over the lake, so I gathered wood as quickly as I could and set a pot of water to boil on the Zip stove for macaroni.

The storm hit just as I finished cooking. I quickly put out the stove, drained the noodles, and shook the cheese packets into the pot, and we dove into the tent with our spoons and our dinner. We had leaned our packs against trees outside, with their waterproof covers, and the rest of our gear was in the tent. I felt slightly smug: *woman outwits nature, stays dry in storm.* The raindrops beat against the fly of the tent, sounding as fierce as hail. I sat back and scooped a heaping spoonful of the macaroni and cheese. But just then, I felt a trickle of water soaking my shorts.

"There's water coming in the back of the tent!" Isis said. "It's pouring in! My sleeping bag is getting wet!"

And so it was. A veritable river was flowing across the slick nylon. We tried to pile our gear against the edges where it was drier, but soon the whole floor was awash. Miserable, we perched on our haunches and finished off the pot of macaroni, watching our sleeping bags darken with dampness.

The storm blew over in a relatively short while, and in the late light everything glistened, wet. When we stepped outside to survey the damages, it was evident what had happened; the ground cloth, sticking out for several inches on all sides of the tent, had acted as a funnel. All the rain draining off the fly had poured right back under the tent.

Blue Skies came over while we were wringing out our sleeping bags. "You guys okay? What happened?"

"We had a bit of a problem with the ground cloth," I said.

Her forehead wrinkled. "If you cut the ground cloth to fit just inside the tent footprint, you won't have any drainage problems," she offered.

"Thanks." I gave a rueful smile. "Wish I'd known that half an hour ago."

"The same thing happened to me on my first solo backpacking trip, actually," she said.

"Live and learn."

"Yeah."

"I've got a lot of learning to do, I think. I'm just glad to be out here."

"Me too. It's so beautiful." She stared out across the lake for a moment. The storm still darkened the mountains on the far side, but the lake sparkled with late sunlight. "This is an awesome tent site. Have you seen the privy here?"

"Well, I haven't really needed—"

"Oh, you ought to check it out. It's really something."

"If you say so."

And it was something—larger than most of the outhouses I'd seen, it had a small table with a wash basin (no running water, of course), a chair, and a mirror. Rainbow-colored curtains hung in the screened windows, and the interior was blissfully free of mosquitoes. A sign on the door proclaimed it "Fort Relief."

I stole a look in the mirror. It was my face, all right, the same constellations of freckles, blue eyes, and high cheekbones, but hidden under layers of dirt and soot. Blackfly bites had left lumps and streaks of blood on my cheeks. Wild wisps of dark blond hair straggled out in all directions. In the enclosed space, I was powerfully aware of the odor I exuded: a rank, heavy mammalian perfume of four-day-old sweat. Funk. I out-stank the privy itself. Was it possible that two weeks ago I had marched across a stage in cap and gown and picked up my college diploma? I stared into the eyes of the grungy woman in the mirror and we winked at each other, sharing a secret joke.

A green spiral-bound notebook lay on the table, with "Antlers Tentsite Register" scrawled on the cover. I sat down in the chair to read it, enjoying the dry and mosquito-free interior of the privy. The register was full of dates, names, short comments about the weather, jokes, illustrations, quotes, deep thoughts. Blue Skies had signed with her new name and drawn a caricature of herself, grinning, wearing pigtails.

I picked up the pen and wrote: *6/25. Isis and jackrabbit tented here.* I looked back at what I'd written: Isis and jackrabbit. I was so unaccustomed to my trail name that I had written it in lowercase. *Well,* I thought, *why not?* I'd chosen the name Jackrabbit because it made me feel strong and invincible. Yet in the past few days I'd amply demonstrated that I was still capable of stupid mistakes. To write my name in lowercase might be a more accurate reflection of how I felt now: uncertain, confused, chagrined. *This is new territory,* I thought. *The skills I've mastered over the last four years are not the skills that will serve me here.*

Isis

By the time we reached Antlers Tentsite, every inch of my skin itched from bug bites and sweat. I couldn't do much about the bites, but the sweat, at least, could be washed away. Jackrabbit, who isn't a big fan of cold water, offered to set up camp while I took a dip.

I waded into the lake, my feet slipping on mossy stones, hoping to get out deep enough to go for a quick swim. I must have walked out a hundred yards from shore, but the water never reached past my knees. Finally, I sat down, leaned back, and lay still for a minute beneath the thin layer of water. Then I rinsed my hair and headed back to shore. Halfway there, I looked over my shoulder. Two of the biggest leeches I've ever seen were gliding along in my wake, and a third was detaching itself from the underside of a nearby rock, preparing to join in the chase. I've never run so fast through knee-deep water. Ten minutes later, when I came back to the shore to get water for supper (escorted by the cloud of mosquitoes I was almost accustomed to), the leeches were still there, oonching their slick bodies as far up the beach as they could go, waving their mouth ends toward me. It felt as though everything, in the water and sky, was after my blood.

That night, as I huddled, shivering, in the least soggy corner of my sleeping bag, the memories I was trying to walk away from came flocking back to my mind. In the fall before I started hiking, my first long-term boyfriend had broken off our relationship abruptly, over the phone, claiming that our difference in religion precluded any serious attachment. He was Lutheran, I am Wiccan. I suppose the incongruity would be obvious to anyone who wasn't in love. But we'd talked about our religions at great length, and it seemed to me that we'd found a way to mesh them. Eric ruefully admitted that he believed in the pagan Norse gods of his ancestors, and I told him that I worshipped a god of compassion and self-sacrifice, though I called her Inanna, not Jesus.

The day he broke up with me, I reminded him of those conversations, trying to hold him on the line. And then he said things I could not forgive. He said that when he and I were together, he'd forgotten everything he held dear: honor, family, faith. He said that his friends, understanding the awful ascendancy I had over him, had counseled him to break up with me over the phone, so I wouldn't be able to frustrate his purpose with spells. I started to protest, but he continued, saying that it was one thing for him to indulge in a sinful liaison while he was young—anyone could make that mistake—but he wanted to have children someday, and he couldn't imagine me the mother of his children. This was the man who had told me, only a week before, that if he was dying in the desert he'd rather find me than find water.

In the winter that followed, I fell into a deep depression. I could hardly look at food; I lost twenty pounds in a month. I lay awake until 2:00, sometimes 4:00 in the morning, turning our last conversation over and over in my mind, searching for any vestigial scrap of tenderness, or, alternately, sifting through all my memories of the good times, trying to find some hint in his words or behavior that could have prepared me for such a betrayal. In the mornings I worked at a bakery, a job I used to love for the scents of yeast and molasses, and the comforting, everyday magic of rising bread. But that winter, whether from carelessness or exhaustion, I burned my arms on the heavy baking trays and cut my hands with the onion knives almost every day. I still have scars from it.

By the time jackrabbit (with a lower-case j, she'd told me, like the animal) and I hiked Katahdin, I was still fifteen pounds underweight, but I hoped and believed that I'd put my depression behind me. I've spent enough of my life out of doors to know that one can't afford to be careless with knives and fire in the wilderness.

That night at Antlers Tentsite, though, the loss of Eric washed over me one final time in all its first intensity. The sky cleared after the storm and moonlight poured through the thin walls of the tent, bringing back memories of the night I met him. We walked past fields of purple lupine, its peppery scent mixing with the salt tang of the harbor. As the twilight deepened, a full moon rose red over the river, and when he rowed me out to the ship where I was working, we tried to follow the moon's wake, battling a rushing ebb tide. After he left me safe on the deck, I watched the tide, grown even stronger, catch him and sweep him far off his course. I followed the glint of his hair under the now-white moon, until he disappeared up the river.

A loon called, over the lake. I was curled in my sleeping bag, under the red pines; Eric was somewhere in the South Pacific. I knew I would never see him again, had known that ever since I hung up the phone eight months before. Still, in the warm, clear night, I felt that he was close beside me, and I could reach him if only I knew how to draw back the curtain between us. The wings of thousands of mosquitoes brushed against the tent, reminding me of the terrible delicacy of a lover's hands, how the faintest touch echoes in the caves of the pelvis and ribcage.

jackrabbit

We left Antlers Tentsite late in the morning, after building a fire to dry out our gear. It was a long day's hike, hampered by many little ups and downs and by patches of sharp gravel in the trail. Of all the surfaces for bare-foot hiking, gravel is the worst; it's nearly impossible to set your foot down without landing on many small, sharp uncomfortable points. Late in the day, as gloom settled around us, I wished I had a watch. It was impossible to tell whether night was truly coming or another cloud bank was moving over. I'd decided not to bring a watch on the Trail when we started, since the microscheduled world of classes and exams was all too fresh in my head, but I was beginning to regret it.

"Where do you think we are?"

Isis stopped and took out the map. "Well, that lake back there must have been Crawford Pond, so I guess this is Little Boardman Mountain."

"Are there any campsites near here? It seems like it's getting late."

"I already told you. There's nothing. I guess we'll just have to find a level piece of ground somewhere. We have enough water to cook with."

"I guess so." Part of me wanted to just keep going, hiking into the night, until we found familiar people again. I missed Blue Skies' cheerfulness and Matt's profound and sometimes ridiculous Zen proclamations. I was nervous about camping in the middle of the woods, with no one else around. But I was more nervous about trying to hike after dark with our single feeble flash-light, and I was bone tired.

The shadows thickened under the moose maple and witch hobble bushes. The woods here were full of tiny maple saplings, probably regrowing from a clear-cut. Here and there, the pale bark of birches shone between the ranks of gray trunks. I started looking for a place to spend the night.

"How about this?" It was a clearing maybe twice the size of our tent foot-print, right beside the path.

"That'll have to do."

We set up the tent and Isis cooked beans and rice. A fierce cloud of mos-quitoes whined around us as we ate, and we said little. We brushed our teeth, hung our food bags over the branch of a maple tree up the trail, and turned in for the night.

I lay awake for a long time, listening to the sounds of the night forest around us. Branches creaked, wind stirred the leaves, and small animals twit-tered and rustled. I strained my ears, waiting for the regularity of footsteps to signal an approaching threat: strange human? Bear? But the sounds blended into one patternless yet steady hush, and eventually I fell asleep.

Isis

On a cool, bright morning, we reached the 3,500-foot summit of Whitecap Mountain and looked back for our last clear view of Katahdin. Thirty miles distant as the crow flies (and almost seventy miles as the Trail winds around lakes and along streambanks), the great mountain still filled the horizon. It seemed impossible that we would walk beyond sight of it; I imagined us standing at the summit of Springer, at the southern end of our hike, and looking out through the winter forest to see the jagged edge of Katahdin shining across two thousand miles of air.

Cheered by the sunlight and the sight of Katahdin, we hiked fast. Soon I was daydreaming about catching up with Matt and Blue Skies, who we hadn't seen in two days. *Get real,* I told myself, *there are seventeen miles and some 3,000 feet of elevation gain between the place we started this morning and Chairback Gap Lean-to, where they must be staying tonight.* The longest day we had hiked, up to that point, was the perfectly flat eleven miles between Wadleigh Stream and Antlers Tentsite.

By the time the summer day drew to a close, I felt more than ready to spread out my sleeping bag on any patch of level ground. None presented itself, though; the trail was bordered by a stream on one side and dense spruce thickets on the other. I'd checked the map earlier, and we were nowhere near any designated campsites or shelters. How much farther would we have to walk?

Orange-edged sunbeams slanted through the branches. A wood thrush's song—silvery notes spiraling up and down the scale in endless variations—rippled through the canopy. I looked up; instead of trees the width of my waist, we stood in the shadows of trees around which both of us together could barely stretch our arms. Out of vast tracts of commercial forest, we had stepped into forest primeval: the Hermitage, owned by the Nature Conservancy, one of the last few patches of old-growth in the state.

This forest was so different from the young woods we had crossed that we could hardly recognize the species of the trees. Jackrabbit and I walked round and round one ancient deciduous tree that seemed to have sprung from another world, or another era of this one. Its deeply fissured, graygreen bark looked like a cross between beech and maple, but its high branches glowed a strange, pale gold in the twilight. Finally jackrabbit found a fallen leaf; the tree was a white birch, and the mysterious glow at its crown was the sun on limbs still slender enough to be wrapped in the familiar papery bark.

After the Hermitage, the ordinary woods, which only a few nights ago had felt so deep and mysterious and full of bears, seemed like a toy forest in which we were children pretending to go for a hike. It took a slow uphill mile for reality to sink in, but when it did, it was sobering. We were still four or five miles from the nearest shelter—half a day's hike, at our current pace. We were low on water, and we hadn't seen a flat patch of ground big enough for a tent since we'd left the Hermitage. It looked like we'd have to hike another mile and a half uphill, trying to beat the darkness, and camp at East Chairback Pond a quarter mile off the trail. It wasn't a designated campsite, so we'd probably be alone. I'd felt nervous enough on Little Boardman Mountain, camping right beside the A.T. This was much worse. What if something happened to us? A quarter mile seemed like a long ways to go just to see a pond; maybe no other hiker would come down there for days.

Under the thick mesh of spruce boughs, the ground was so dark I could barely see where I was putting my feet, so when the pond opened in front of us, reflecting all the light left in the sky, it took a moment for my eyes to adjust to its brightness. There was a person coming toward us, out of the woods. More people behind him. Then I saw the tents.

Our friends Blue Skies and Matt were camped there, along with three people who'd started just ahead of us, whose register entries we had been following for a week. There were Nor'easter and Creen, a couple from the Midwest who drew witty cartoons about Trail life and wrote their adventures in verse. We also met Waterfall, a solo hiker from Louisiana whose exuberant register entries had cheered us in some of the swampiest, most buggy places. She could describe thunderstorms in a way that made you want to step out of the shelter, turn your face to the sky, and feel the rain stream off your forehead and run down your shoulder blades.

Catching up to the people whose register entries had cheered and entertained us felt like meeting minor celebrities, people whose voices we'd heard on the radio, but who we'd never expected to share a campsite and a cup of tea with. Tired as we were from our first fourteen-mile day, we stayed up for an hour after dark, listening to each other's stories of how we came to the Trail, making our plans and wishes to hike together, while the pond beside us darkened and filled with constellations.

jackrabbit

In the morning, a thin mist drifted over the surface of the pond, evaporating where the sun touched it. The amber-colored water glinted with refracting sunbeams. I filtered two liters into our water bottles and packed up the tent while Isis cooked a pot of oatmeal.

We hiked out early and stopped at the top of the first mountain for a drink of filtered pond water: brownish and slightly musky, but refreshing. I turned to look over the land we had crossed. Blue-gray lakes in the valleys shimmered with cat's-paw winds. Huge cloud shadows lumbered across the green carpet of forest. My breath slowly returned to normal, but my legs were still aching and trembling. I wondered how many people had stood in this same spot and felt exactly what I felt then: Triumph. Exhaustion. Doubt. I thought again of the wooden sign on Katahdin. If eighty-five miles felt like this, how would two thousand miles feel?

Isis took out the map, a long strip of waterproof paper. The top part was a normal topographic map, showing perhaps thirty miles of the Trail corridor. We usually concentrated on a tiny strip along the bottom: the elevation profile. Today's profile looked like the seismograph for a medium-sized earthquake.

"You've got to be kidding me," I said. "Look at this, Isis. They even ran out of names for these lumps. There's Chairback, and Columbus, and then it just goes Third Mountain, Fourth Mountain . . ."

"Yikes."

"Fourth Mountain Bog. This ought to be interesting. I hope we don't have to run through it like that bog before Antlers."

"Ooh, that was awful." I remembered the sound of mosquitoes audible even before we reached the bog and the feeling of the cloud of insects hitting my skin as I ran.

As it turned out, Fourth Mountain Bog was beautiful. Cedar trees on either side of the trail leaned at crazy angles. A breeze swept through their open canopies, fending off the mosquitoes for once. Frogs winked and disappeared in the small pools, and insects jumped crazily across the bog bridges underfoot; the flowers of cranberry, cotton grass, pitcher plants, and sundew swayed in the wind. Red and green leaves stitched the surface of the pinkish green sphagnum moss like patterns on a quilt. Overhead, we could see clouds building up in clotted towers, signaling a storm, so we hurried for the next mountain.

For the third time that day, a spruce grouse exploded from the bushes just in front of Isis. Its thudding wingbeats split the silence and wakened my adrenaline. The small brown bird flapped up against Isis several times, desperate to distract her from the flock of chicks that ran peeping into the underbrush. We stopped and stood still until the bird gave up and disappeared under the bushes.

"I actually caught hold of its tail," Isis said.

"And you let go?" I asked, incredulous. "That's a lot of protein."

"Yeah, but it wouldn't really fit into our pot. Aren't you supposed to dip a bird into boiling water before you cook it, so you can pluck the feathers?"

"Hmm. Yeah. We could cook it on a spit, roast it."

"What about the little chicks, though?"

"They'd cook even faster!"

"Jackrabbit! Wait a minute, aren't we supposed to be vegetarians?"

"Any food we don't have to carry is good in my book."

"We're only five days out. After a month of this, you're going to be a total scavenger!"

We reached Cloud Pond Lean-to just after the rain began. Matt sat on the edge of the sleeping platform, his long lean form folded up with his arms around his knees. A pot of water simmered on his stove beside him. "Hey, sisters."

"Hey, Matt. Found a trail name yet?"

"Nope."

Blue Skies and Waterfall came up from the lake, carrying pots of water for cooking. They shook the rain from their ponchos and stepped into the shelter. Both of them had their hair in pigtails, and they looked like a pair of scruffy girl scouts.

"Hi, ladies." Blue Skies gave a tired grin. "Quite a day, wasn't it?"

"We were just talkin' about that profile map," Waterfall said in her soft Southern accent. "I could swear there was a mountain out there that wasn't on the map."

"Yeah, right between Third and Fourth," Isis said. "We should call it Mount Three and a Half."

"How about Mount Three and a Half Kicking-ass?" I said.

"How about a profile map that shows it like it is?" said Blue Skies.

Matt sighed in a knowing way. "Profile maps are evil."

"How so?" Isis asked as she slung her pack off.

"Well, they give you false expectations. They're never really accurate. Sometimes the map looks harder than the trail really is, and you think you're in great shape. Sometimes the map looks easy, and the trail's not, so you get frustrated." He paused to adjust his stove, which was hissing ominously. "I don't even carry the maps any more. Just a *Data Book*."

"What's a *Data Book*?" I asked. Matt, Waterfall, and Blue Skies all fell silent and stared at me. By their expressions, I had a sudden sense that my question had been akin to asking "what does 'subtract' mean?" in an algebra class.

Matt fished something out of the top of his pack and tossed it over to me. It was a thin volume with a photo of Katahdin on the cover. The title read *Appalachian Trail Data Book 2000*, and inside there were columns of numbers: the distances between shelters, springs, roads, and mountains, all the way to Georgia. I thumbed through it, watching the numbers grow. It hardly seemed possible that 2,160 miles of trail could be boiled down into sixty-seven pages. Into the quiet came the sound of rain on the roof and far-off thunder.

"Thanks." I handed it back to him.

"So you guys don't have a *Data Book*?" Blue Skies finally asked. "How did you plan your hike?"

"Well, we have the maps for Maine," Isis said. "We're going to buy the other maps as we go along, you know, just sort of wing it."

"Wing it. Wow. No mail drops or anything?"

"Mail drops?"

"That's when you send yourself a box of food and stuff in a town," Waterfall offered helpfully.

"Oh. No, we're just going to buy food in grocery stores as we go."

"Wow." Blue Skies digested this information, and I felt sure she was weighing our utter lack of knowledge and experience. I waited for her judgment to fall. Instead, she said, "When do you plan on finishing?"

"Oh, around Christmas," I said.

She brightened. "Maybe we can hike together, then. That's just about when I'm planning to finish."

When the storm had subsided, I set up our Zip stove on a log by the firepit and gathered twigs to cook supper. Under the thickly woven branches of hemlocks and spruces, the forest floor had stayed almost dry. Waterfall sat beside me, wearing a head net against the clouds of blackflies that had emerged after the rain. Frogs began calling as dusk settled.

"Are those loons?" Waterfall asked.

"What? Oh. No, those are frogs. Loons are mostly on bigger lakes. They sound like somebody laughing, kind of, but sad and wistful too. I hope we'll get to see one—they're beautiful birds, all black except a white ring around the neck."

"Wow. I've never even heard a loon, let alone see one. I'm hard of hearin', actually. My hearin' aid's all right for most things, but I have a hard time tellin' what's what with high sounds."

I noticed, for the first time, the tiny coil of plastic in Waterfall's right ear.

"I used to be embarrassed of it in high school. I wouldn't wear it, so people thought I was kind of a snob. They'd say somethin' to me, and I wouldn't hear, and they'd think I was ignorin' them. In college, things got a lot better. I just figured, I'll be me, and if people don't like me, it's their loss."

"Way to go. I think college is a good place for figuring out who you are, what you want."

"Are you just out of college?"

"Yeah. You?"

She laughed. "I've been out of school for quite a while. But thank you. No, I work as a technical writer in Baton Rouge."

"Technical writer? Do you write instruction manuals and cereal boxes and that kind of thing?"

"Pretty much. Most of what I do is actually editing. People bring reports to me and I make them readable." She laughed. "Oh, I make it sound so borin'. But really it's a pretty good job."

"So what brings you to the Trail?"

"Well, I discovered backpackin' when I was in school. I just love it. I feel so . . . so connected to everythin' out here. I feel like I can see what really matters when I'm on the Trail. It's so peaceful. I've had this dream of hiking the whole Trail for probably ten years now."

"And here you are."

She laughed again. "Here we all are. Isn't it great?"

I was tired, and wet, and hungry; my muscles ached and a new batch of bug bites were itching; but none of it mattered—in that moment it *was* great to be there, right there in the darkening wet forest, with people who had been strangers just days ago and who now felt like old friends.

Isis

In the morning I discovered how Cloud Pond got its name. Mist clung to the branches of cedars along the shore and hung so thickly over the water that its surface blended imperceptibly into sky. When we hiked out, the whole mountain seemed to be caught in the underbelly of a cloud. Legions of gnarled spruce trees took shape from the air as we approached them, their dark trunks streaked with rain. The moss beneath them glowed emerald, and by contrast, the spruce needles carpeting the trail turned a bright red-brown. The springy ground muffled our footsteps; the only sound in the world was the steady drip of water from the trees.

In this weather we came to the Barren Ledges, at the southern end of the Barren-Chairback range. From register entries at Cloud Pond and conversations with northbounders, we knew that this was one of the best views in the Wilderness. Below us to our left lay the wide Lake Onawa, dotted with islands, and on three sides of us rose the steep-sided, round-shouldered mountains of Maine. I walked out to the edge of a smooth granite outcropping and peered into the blowing fog.

Beside me, jackrabbit mused aloud, "I wonder if there's another ledge ten feet below us, or if it's a thousand-foot drop straight down to the shore of the lake?"

Although the shapes of the mountains we'd seen so far made a series of ledges seem far more likely than a drop-off below us, I felt a shiver run through my spine as we sat down for a snack on the rock's edge. A shiver, not of fear, but of something strangely akin to delight. I thought of Milan Kundera's definition of vertigo: a longing for empty air beneath our feet.

As we walked down the mountain the wind picked up. Close beside us in the mist, two tree trunks scraping together made an eerie moaning sound. Halfway down to the lean-to where we'd planned to eat lunch, we stepped out below the cloud layer and found ourselves in a forest of tall, straight spruce trees, interspersed with yellow birches. Between the gusts of wind surging through their branches, we could hear an occasional mutter of thunder in the distance. Just as we reached the shelter, the stand of hemlocks around it darkened as quickly as if someone were turning down the lights in a theater. I scrambled around picking up wood for our stove while jackrabbit went looking for water. The first fat drops of rain were already ringing on the shelter's tin roof by the time we sat down to lunch. Lightning flashed and a great peal of thunder echoed across the sky almost before our eyes had readjusted to the gloom. I made a pot of tea and pulled the last of my pound of chocolate out of the bottom of my food bag. By then the tin roof sounded like the whole percussion section of a jazz band.

We were on our second pot of tea when a very wet little dog bounded into the shelter, followed shortly by an equally sodden young man. When he saw that we were trying to dry the shivering dog with handkerchiefs, he gave us a sweet dimpled grin. He introduced himself as Tenbrooks, and the dog was Molly, names he'd chosen from a bluegrass song. Molly was a stray who had followed him out of a town somewhere in North Carolina. He'd always wanted a dog, so he picked up some dog food and took her to a vet for shots, and they'd been hiking together ever since. He was a flip-flopper, not a north-bounder: a new term for us. He explained that he'd started at the southern end of the Trail, hiked as far as central Virginia, and then hitchhiked up to Katahdin to walk south from there. He would complete his hike at the place where he'd gotten off the Trail in Virginia. He said he'd set out to do a regular northbound hike, but soon realized that he wouldn't have enough time to enjoy the Trail if he hurried to reach Katahdin before Baxter State Park's mid-October closing date.

The storm didn't clear until five o'clock by Tenbrooks' watch, so all three of us decided to stay at the lean-to for the night. The sun broke through the clouds; the ground steamed where its light fell into the clearing in front of the shelter. Jackrabbit went down the water trail to play her penny whistle—soon the strains of "The Sally Gardens" mingled with the quick stream's laughter. I asked Tenbrooks where he came from, and he answered with a story that sounded like an updated version of a fairytale. He was the youngest of seven sons, and most of his brothers were lawyers. His parents wanted him to go to law school too, but law didn't interest him at all. I asked what did interest him.

"Playin' bluegrass music and wanderin' in the woods," he answered. He threw his head back and laughed, spreading his arms wide as if to embrace the whole clearing, the hemlocks, and the sunbeams. "So here I am."

He looked so beautiful, with his strong arms outstretched and his clear eyes sparkling under thick golden lashes, that I wanted to kiss him. Only once, I told myself, and only for comfort. But I stayed where I was sitting, in the dappled shade of a hemlock. Beside this joyous child of fortune, I felt like an old woman, full of secrets and darkness—certainly not the princess who belonged in his story.

The next morning Tenbrooks and Molly left early, planning to hike fifteen miles into Monson. Jackrabbit and I had no intention of trying to hike a fifteen, but we still got out pretty early, for us. About half a mile out from the shelter, we paused to study our maps and discovered that the steep slate streambank beside us was part of the Slugundy Gorge. Half a mile farther on, we would traverse a landscape feature known as the Bodfish Intervale. We were still laughing about these names when jackrabbit slipped on the damp pine needles, landed on her bottom, and slid a few feet downhill.

"Are you hurt?" I asked, hurrying over to her.

"Of course not," she answered, arching her eyebrows. "I'm just practicing my Slugundy Slide for the Summer Olympics. It's an Extreme Hiking Maneuver," she explained.

"If that's a Slugundy, what's a Bodfish?" I asked, offering her a hand up.

She thought for a moment. "A Bodfish Squat," she said slowly, "is when you're on a ledge a few feet high, and you turn sideways and reach one leg down to the bottom while bending the other knee. The distance between the top of the ledge and the ground is the Bodfish Intervale."

A hundred yards farther, the trail turned and curved steeply down the bank toward a ford.

"I don't think I'm going to attempt a Bodfish," I told jackrabbit. "Too big an intervale for me." I sat down on a root, reaching both my feet toward the ground while steadying myself with both hands.

"This," I announced, "is known as the Nesuntabunt Five-wheel Drive."

Over the course of the day our lexicon of Extreme Hiking Maneuvers had grown to include the Piscataquis Pirouette, which involves grabbing a tree and pivoting around it on the way down a steep slope, and the Potaywadjo Posthole, in which one sinks up to one's knee (or beyond) in a particularly swampy section of trail.

In the early afternoon we turned a corner in the trail and came upon a most incongruous apparition. Seated on a stream bank, filtering water just as if he were a hiker, was a man who looked altogether too civilized to be there. He wore a button-down shirt in a shade suspiciously close to white, and a Tilley hat perched on his long, neatly combed hair. He was so thin that he looked fragile; his legs were like sticks beneath his khaki pants. I wondered how he could have walked, even from the nearest logging road, on those legs. Still, there was the water filter, and I noticed that he was leaning against what appeared to be a fairly substantial pack. I asked if he was hiking the Wilderness.

"I'm hiking the Appalachian Trail southbound," he answered. "And you?"

That night, our last night before Monson, we shared a shelter with him. His name was Alan. He was a chef from San Francisco, and he'd never backpacked before. After hearing about the A.T. from a Canadian uncle of his, he'd decided on the spot that he wanted to hike it. He had prepared for his trip far more than we had, spending months dehydrating fruits and vegetables from his local farmer's market and leaving carefully sealed and labeled packages of them for a friend to mail to him at various points along the Trail. But he'd had no time to practice hiking. It had taken him twenty days to get through the Wilderness, compared to our eleven. Still, he said, he had plenty of food, and he didn't want it to end yet.

Suddenly I realized that I didn't want the Wilderness to end, either. I didn't want to hear traffic or sleep in a room with four walls, where I might not be awakened by the light of dawn. I didn't want to leave that campfire, where a man we had met two hours ago shared tea and stories and dried strawberries with us, and walk back to a world where most people were, and would remain, strangers to each other.

jackrabbit

Isis and I stuffed our sleeping bags into their sacks and began rolling the air out of our inflatable mattresses. Alan had left already. It was a cool morning, and traceries of mist had risen out of the stream.

"I had such a neat dream last night," Isis said. "I dreamed we walked out to the road, and there was a guy in the parking lot there. He said, 'Hi. I'm Mr. Shaw. Need a ride to town?'" Shaw's Boarding House, the hiker hostel in Monson, was one of the legendary places that Maineak and his hiker friends had described to us at our campfires in the Andes.

I laughed. "That *is* a cool dream. It'd be nice if we can get a ride to town—it's like, what, three miles?"

"Something like that. And you know what our mom thinks about us trying to hitchhike."

We finished stowing our gear and set out. With my food bag nearly empty, I hardly noticed the weight of my pack. The trail, strewn with spruce needles, felt cool and soft underfoot. I marveled at how quickly I had become accustomed to walking barefoot with a pack. My feet wrapped themselves around roots and rocks, and I easily shifted my balance to avoid sharp edges. New ridges of muscle had grown above my arches, and all the surfaces of my feet felt alive and aware.

The woods were the same solid wall of green—spruce, pine, birch and moose maple—and the enormous blanket of the forest smothered sounds. Distant bird calls came back indistinct and fuzzy. We stopped for a snack by a stream where a handful of damselflies hung in the air, needle-thin insects with turquoise bodies and wide black wings. They flapped slowly above the green water, and their wing beats looked like windows of darkness opening in the air.

Traffic sounds began to filter through the trees, and we found ourselves in a gravel parking lot by the side of a two-lane highway. As we stepped out into the clearing, away from the shade of interlocking branches, the July sun dazzled our eyes. Cars whizzed past like strange insects. It was another world, a world of metal and heat and speed, cutting through the heart of the forest world we had known for the last eleven days. Part of me wanted to turn and run back into the woods.

A rust-stained red pickup pulled into the lot, and the driver jumped out. He was a wizened, thin man, probably in his seventies, wearing a John Deere baseball cap. He eyed us critically.

"You must be the barefoot girls," he said in a brusque Maine accent. "I had another hiker in this morning, said you'd be comin' along. I'm Keith Shaw. You want a ride to town?"

CHAPTER 2

Southbounders

Isis

Keith Shaw drove us into Monson without once glancing at the road. Jackrabbit, who sat next to him, had his full attention; he regaled her with the thirty-year history of his hunting lodge, including anecdotes about the first few A.T. hikers who'd stayed there, and mouth-watering descriptions of his wife's home cooking. He also took every opportunity to cast aspersion on the Pie Lady, the owner of Monson's other hiker hostel. "Now you can't believe everything you hear about that Pie Lady, but I've got some stories that would—" Every once in a while, jackrabbit interrupted him, exclaiming, "Mr. Shaw, watch out for that car," or "Mr. Shaw, I think we're in the bike lane." To which he would reply, "Ayuh. Now I remember one time a few years back when there was a bear in the backyard . . ."

We checked in at Shaw's Boarding House, took showers, and changed into the only remotely clean clothes we had left: our Gore-Tex rain gear. I happily dumped the last few bags of our peanuts into the "hiker box," an over-flowing cardboard box of spare gear and food in the common room of the hostel where hikers could leave extra items and pick up what they needed. Dressed in nothing but Gore-Tex, we set out to walk the two blocks to the laundromat. It was a hot, bright day, and I was just about to remark to jackrabbit how absurd we must look, when a young man drove by us and whistled. I looked around to see who he could have whistled at; we were the only human females in sight. Just then, a car full of teenage boys drove by, and they, too, whistled at us.

"Damn," said jackrabbit. "Does sweaty Gore-Tex exude some kind of pheromone?"

"Maybe it's just that it leaves so much to the imagination," I said. "These town kids must think hikers have great bodies, from all the exercise we get. If they could see the bruises and bug bites, they might be a bit less enthusiastic."

Most of the hikers in town had congregated at the laundromat, which was also a pizzeria. Blue Skies, talking on the pay phone just outside the door, looked up and waved to us as we passed. Inside the laundry room, we found Matt perched on top of a washing machine, reading a magazine. Nor'easter and Creen were loading their clothes into a dryer. Two lanky, bearded north-bounders (or nobos, as we were learning to call them) stood at the kitchen counter, debating whether to split three large pizzas, or just get one pizza each and then go find some ice cream. A young man in a tie-dyed t-shirt and a gray-haired man with a neatly trimmed beard and round glasses sat at a corner table, playing chess with a tiny, fold-up board. Even the hikers I didn't know were easy to distinguish from the locals, a blue-haired sexagenarian, several middle-aged men in plaid flannel shirts, and the sulky anorexic teenager sweeping the floor.

In our mud-spattered Gore-Tex, we must have been just as easy to recognize. As I was struggling to get the recalcitrant change machine to accept my crumpled dollar, the young man in the tie-dyed t-shirt tapped me on the shoulder. He handed me a crisp new bill.

"Are you a sobo?" he asked, using the A.T. lingo for southbounder.

"Yeah," I answered. "How 'bout you?"

"Yup. My dad and I are hiking together." He waved toward the man who'd been playing chess with him. "I'm Bugbiter, and he calls himself O.D.—short for Old Dude."

"I'm Isis." Each time I said the name Isis, I felt it become more my own. In our first few days in the Wilderness, I'd been a little embarrassed to introduce myself as a goddess, even though I was proud of the way I'd earned my trail name. Now, with a hundred and twenty miles behind me and new muscles already changing the shape of my legs, I felt that I was growing into Isis. Lucy, who'd spent the whole winter sick over the loss of Eric, seemed a distant memory.

An hour or so later, we sat out on the back lawn with Blue Skies and Waterfall, eating pizza. Tenbrooks had found a guitar to borrow; he leaned against an oak, his eyes closed and his face tilted toward the sun, serenading us with a wistful, bluesy rendition of "She'll Be Coming 'Round the Mountain." Molly curled beside him, her head on his leg.

"This pizza sure tastes good," said Waterfall, "but I already miss the Trail. This mornin' at breakfast I was thinkin', 'I could be up on top a mountain right now, watchin' the sun rise. I could've covered three miles by now.'"

"Yeah," said Blue Skies. "I feel out of place here. I was at the post office a few hours ago, picking up my mail drop, and I caught myself thinking, 'what am I doing inside a building, picking up a package for this Ashley person? I'm Blue Skies now. I belong in the woods, moving.'"

As they spoke, they glanced past the lawn, over the surface of the nearby lake, toward the dark fringe of pines on its far shore. Their eyes shone. It was an expression I'd often seen on the faces of nobos, looking north toward Katahdin. As southbounders, we didn't have any such lofty mountain as a goal. I knew that Springer, the Trail's southern terminus, was an inconsequential, wooded peak no higher than the mountains surrounding it. I squinted at the line of trees, across the bright water, and felt my lips curve in an eager smile. *The Trail itself is our goal,* I thought. *And we'll be there tomorrow. And the next day, and the day after that, for the next half year of our lives.*

jackrabbit

With one final injunction to avoid the Pie Lady at all costs, Keith Shaw dropped us off at the trailhead. His pickup pulled away in a cloud of dust, and we crossed the road to where the narrow path led into the woods.

My feet felt wonderfully alive on the soft moss and decomposing spruce needles of the trail. Their soles tingled with anticipation, glad to be moving again. It was a cool day, and the woods smelled sweet and fresh from recent rainfall. Everywhere was the pale green light of spring, filtered through maple and beech leaves still delicate with newness. We forded so many small streams that I lost count. They ranged from rivulets I could almost step across to wide, knee-deep torrents, and all the water was bone-chilling. Each time I stepped out of a stream, my feet and legs felt powerfully aware, reveling in the suddenly warm air.

Isis walked a little ways ahead of me, as she had since the second day out. She had a fear of being left behind, and on that day she hadn't been able to keep up with my pace. I was not always happy walking in the back, following her pace, but it seemed like a necessary compromise. Most of the time I was so absorbed in the sounds of the forest around me and the feeling of the trail underfoot that I barely noticed her presence just ahead. We almost always walked within sight of each other, but we seldom talked.

In midafternoon, under a canopy of second-growth birches as thin as my wrist, Isis stopped so suddenly that I nearly ran into her.

"What?" I said, slightly annoyed.

"Shh." She pointed to a bush beside the trail ahead. It took a moment for my mind to focus around what I saw there, and when it did, the hairs on the back of my neck stood up. Just beside the trail, there was a raccoon, crouching in an odd position. In broad daylight. It hadn't moved when we came into view.

Before we left for the Trail, a wildlife biologist friend had warned me: "Rabies is on the upswing in the East." Animals acting abnormally—nocturnal creatures out by daylight hours, wild animals that didn't spook or even appear to notice when humans came close—I knew these were danger signs. I tried to remember the symptoms of rabies: first, the hydrophobia, a fear of water and an inability to swallow. Then a rage, in which the animal staggers madly around, foaming at the mouth, biting anything it can get, and lastly a stupor leading to death. It seemed like a bad way to go.

I looked again at the raccoon up ahead. It still hadn't moved out of the patch of sunlight. Maybe it was in the last stages of the disease, too weak to move. Then again, maybe not. As I watched, the animal roused itself from the crouch and staggered across the trail with a sickly, lurching gait. It was hard to see clearly in the dappled shade, but there seemed to be a white string of drool hanging from its muzzle. The raccoon came to a stop on the other side of the trail, still close to the footpath.

"Now what?"

"Maybe if we throw something, you know, not at it but toward it, maybe it'll move." Isis picked up a section of a rotting birch log as she said this, and lobbed it to land in the bushes a few feet from the sick raccoon. The creature didn't stir. She threw another chunk of wood, closer this time, and still it didn't move.

"Maybe we should just run past it," she said. "It doesn't seem like it can move very fast."

"Okay, but I'd feel better if I had a staff or something."

We picked up some maple branches that lay by the trail and quickly peeled off the twigs, making ourselves stout five-foot poles. I could feel adrenaline coursing through my veins, heightening my perceptions. I could see every leaf on every twig, hear all the separate birdsongs and rustlings at once. Balancing the poles in our hands, ready to fend off an attack, we ran past the bush where the raccoon lay. Once again, it didn't move. I caught a glimpse of it as we ran by; its fur was tattered and mangy, and what I had thought was drool was instead a cluster of porcupine needles stuck through its lower lip.

"Maybe that's why it's sick," Isis said, when we had run a safe distance away and stopped to catch our breath. "You saw the porcupine needles, too, didn't you?"

"Yes," I said darkly. "But what would possess a raccoon to attack a porcupine in the first place?"

That night at Horseshoe Canyon Lean-to, we were still a little jumpy. The clouds had come over and the sky threatened rain, casting a palpable gloom over the clearing in front of the shelter. Matt and Blue Skies were already there. They sat on the porcupine trap cooking dinner, the quiet hiss of their stoves providing a backdrop to the watery calls of two wood thrushes in the trees outside. They waved as we walked up the side trail to the shelter.

"Hey, guys. What's up?"

We told them about the raccoon, our story coming out in a jumble of incoherent sentences. Matt looked alarmed.

"How close was this to the shelter?"

"Oh, come on!" Blue Skies said. "It's not like we're going to hike any farther tonight anyway."

"And that raccoon wasn't going very far, that's for sure," I added.

"I remember some stealth sites down by the river, a couple miles from here," Matt offered earnestly, but there were no takers. It was getting darker by the minute outside, and not just with evening; we would have rain that night, without a doubt. Somehow the thought of tenting in the rain, isolated and wet, was much less appealing than staying in the crowded, dry shelter, even with the threat of a rabid raccoon nearby.

We stepped over the porcupine trap and set our packs down on the shelter floor. Every night the system became a little more streamlined, and it took us less time to "move in": roll out our air mattresses and sleeping bags, put on another layer of warm clothing against the chill of night, take out the stove and pot and that night's food, hang our food bags on the mouse hangers, and stash our empty packs in a corner of the shelter. By now the process was almost automatic.

As we finished, the little dog Molly came bounding up the trail, her ears flopping.

"Molly will protect us from that raccoon, won't you, girl," Blue Skies said, as the dog ran up for a pat on the head.

Tenbrooks came up the side trail a moment later, rubbing his hands together. "Chilly evenin'," he said. "This'd be a good night for a fire, if that rain holds off."

"Good idea." Isis sprang into action. She unclipped the hatchet from its pouch in her pack, and set off toward a large spruce blowdown back in the woods.

O.D. and Bugbiter, the two hikers we'd met in the Monson laundromat, came up the path to the shelter. O.D. was a man in his mid-fifties, with short gray hair and a few days' worth of salt-and-pepper beard on his rounded cheeks. Bugbiter looked about eighteen, a kid with curly blond hair and a slightly bemused smile. He waved as they came in.

"Glad we got here before the rain," O.D. said.

Isis came back just then, barefoot and hauling a load of brush and spruce branches. I jumped over the porcupine trap to help break up the wood. As O.D. caught sight of our feet, he laughed with joy.

"Holy shit! It's you! You're real! Andy—Bugbiter—and I saw your footprints all through the wilderness, and I thought it was a practical joke, you know, somebody with a staff that had a bare footprint on the end or something . . . And then when I met you in town, you had shoes on . . . But it's really you." He grinned, his twinkling gray eyes flashing from his lined face.

"Yeah, that's us," Isis said.

"The barefoot sisters," he said. "The Barefoot Sisters."

We had chosen our trail names before we started hiking, but here was a name that had truly come to us on the Trail. At the moment he said it, I knew the name would stay with us. *Isis and jackrabbit, the Barefoot Sisters.*

O.D. and Bugbiter introduced themselves to Matt and Blue Skies and Tenbrooks.

"O.D.? There's gotta be a story behind that one," Tenbrooks said.

"It's 'cause dad's an old dude," Bugbiter said.

"Old Dude, Old Duffer, Obviously Deluded . . . stands for a lot of things," he said with a wry grin.

"And what about Bugbiter? What's the story there?"

"Well, I always get bitten more than anybody else . . . So one night in the Wilderness I was lying there, getting eaten alive as usual, and dad goes, 'You need a trail name.' So I go, 'How about Bugbiter?'" He shrugged eloquently. "I was tired, you know? It made sense at the time."

Waterfall came up the trail soon after them, and all of us filled up the shelter with damp gear and smelly bodies. It began to drizzle outside, sure enough, but by that time Isis had coaxed the damp spruce branches into flame. The little blaze crackled and sputtered in the firepit but did not go out. Rain made plinking sounds on the fiberglass roof and a gentle sort of hissing against the leaves outside.

We packed into the shelter in our sleeping bags and made room for one more; Alan, the man we had met at Leeman Brook just outside Monson, came in at dusk. The fire was still going, smoky but bright. In his light-colored clothing, he seemed to glow in flickering orange against the muted blue-gray backdrop of the rainy woods. He walked painstakingly, leaning on his poles, but I caught a glimpse of his wide smile when the coals flared up.

"I didn't think I'd make it here before dark," he said. "That was a long day for me, considering when I started."

Various voices rose from the interior of the shelter, offering congratulations. I remembered Alan saying that he'd taken twenty days to get through the Wilderness. I had marveled at his determination, but at the time, I hadn't imagined he would make it much farther. He had seemed too citified, too fastidious and well-mannered, to stay on the Trail very long. Here he was, though, still lugging his pack, and grinning broadly.

After we had all cooked and eaten supper, we lay in the shelter listening to the rain. The fire was still spluttering on the grate. Isis added some pine branches, which flared up to illuminate the clearing.

"We ought to tell some stories, with a campfire like that," Tenbrooks said.

"Ooh, I've got a scary one," came a young voice that I recognized as Bugbiter's. "Did you guys ever hear about the Purple Dolly?"

"No, no scary stories tonight," Blue Skies said from next to me. "We had enough of a scare from hearing about that raccoon."

"How about a song?" Alan said, and sounds of assent came from all around. He began a ribald Scottish ballad. His voice was a startlingly clear and rich tenor, and he rolled the words off his tongue with such joyful abandon that we all rolled with laughter. I silently revised my opinion of him. He was not as prudish as I had imagined, and the depth I had seen in his eyes was not just melancholy. There was more to him than I had seen before. We exploded in applause when he finished.

"That was awesome," Waterfall said. "Nobody's given you a trail name for that?"

"Well, a couple I met early on wanted to call me Songbird. I didn't like it, though. Too . . . delicate."

"I'm gonna call you Highlander, 'cause nobody but a real highlander could sing like that."

"Highlander. I like it. 'There can be only one,'" he said in a deep mock-heroic voice. "Does anybody else have a song?"

"Actually, I write songs," Waterfall said. Her voice was suddenly shy. "I don't usually sing 'em in front of people—" but with all of us cheering her on, she eventually gave in. Her soft, sweet soprano rose through the dark air of the shelter. We all grew quiet, and even the rain on the roof seemed to hush and listen.

The evening went by in song and stories. O.D. and Bugbiter sang an Irish drinking song, the newly minted Highlander recited a trove of Ogden Nash poems, Isis recited "The Raven," and I sang a song I had written in college. The fire died slowly, hissing, in the rain.

Tenbrooks had been silent all evening, but as the coals began to wink out, he started a story in his Southern drawl. "Once upon a time there was an old, old man, who knew he was dyin'. So he called his grandchildren to him, and he said to them all, 'Before I die, I want you to bring me the most beautiful thing in the world.'

"The oldest one went out first. He walked out across the land for days and days, and he saw many beautiful things. He saw the sun comin' up over marshes and woods, and the sun goin' down over hills and lakes. He saw birds of all colors, and flowers, and butterflies. At last he came to the sea, and at the edge of the sea he found a stone. It was round and green, and it sparkled just like the water. So he took it back to his grandfather and said, 'I have found you the most beautiful thing in the world.'

"And the old man looked at it, and said, 'That is beautiful indeed. Thank you for bringin' that to me. But that is not the most beautiful thing in the world.'

"So the middle child went out lookin'. She went up into the mountains, and she too saw beautiful things everywhere. She saw the stars reflected in rivers, and the moon goin' down among the silver peaks. At last she got up to the highest mountain of all, and she found a flower the color of moonlight growin' there. The wind came up and shook its petals off, and she gathered them up and took them to her grandfather.

"And he looked at them, and he said, 'These are truly beautiful. Thank you for bringin' them to me. But they are not the most beautiful thing in the world.'

"And so the youngest two, who were twins, went out lookin'. They walked together, through a giant forest where the sun came down like light from high windows. They slept out on a mountain, and watched shootin' stars, and saw the sunrise come up like a cup of fire poured into the sky. They saw deer runnin' in the forest and horses runnin' on the plains. One night the frost came. It was bitter cold and they were afraid, and they huddled together under a blanket of leaves.

"The next day they went back to their grandfather, and they said, 'We haven't brought you anythin'. We got cold and we were scared, and so we came back.'

"He said, 'Tell me about your journey.'

"So they told him about the shady forest, and the mountain with the shooting stars, and the sunrise, and the deer, and the horses. They told him what it was like to be afraid when the frost came. 'But we were never really scared,' they said, 'because we were together.'"

The coals had almost died in the fire now, and somewhere out in the wet darkness an owl hooted. In the cave of the shelter, we waited for the end of the story.

"The old man said, 'My children, truly this is the most beautiful thing in the world. Your story. It is beautiful that you have seen these things, and that you were together. It is beautiful that you have come back to tell me this.'

"And he passed on into the endless dream."

On the fourth of July, we crossed Moxie Bald Mountain late in the afternoon. It was the highest peak we'd seen in many miles. The summit, an open expanse of granite ledges, glowed pink in contrast with the steel gray of the sky. The rock felt cool and rough underfoot, and familiar; it was so much like the mountains of our childhood home on the coast. Stunted spruces grew here and there in the cracks between sheets of rock, with a few low-growing shrubs of rhodora, bearberry, huckleberry, and sweet fern. In the low places where rainwater pooled, sphagnum moss, cranberries, and small rushes grew. We could see all the way down to the valley, where Moxie Pond reflected the quiescent clouds. An island stood in the center of the pond, and in the flat calm all the trees on its shore were mirrored perfectly in the water.

"This would be a great place to watch the fireworks," Isis said.

"Do you think we could see the Greenville show from here?"

We heard someone calling from the next knoll of granite. "Hey, ladies! Good hike today?"

"Tenbrooks!"

He sat on a tilted rock ledge, dangling his legs over the side. Molly lolled on the rock beside him with her little pink tongue hanging out. I dropped my pack by the side of the trail and scrambled up the rock to join them. "You want to camp up here and watch the fireworks?"

"I was thinkin' about it." He brushed his dark blond hair back from his eyes and grinned. "Seems like we might get some natural fireworks, too, though, and this doesn't look like the best place to be if we do."

As if in answer to his comment, there was a low rumble of thunder in the southeast. Isis and I had been so preoccupied with the beauty of the lake down in the valley that we hadn't looked over in the other direction. When we did, there was a solid wall of towering clouds, still distant but moving closer every moment. Sheets of rain hung like dark veils from the underside of the storm, and I saw a flash of lightning illuminate one of the spires.

"Time to get out of here," Isis said, and I didn't argue.

We reached Bald Mountain Brook Lean-to just as the rain began and jumped into the crowded shelter.

"That was a close one," Tenbrooks shouted over the sound of rain drumming on the tin roof. "I love stayin' dry." Molly nuzzled up to him as if in agreement.

The shelter was a jumble of people, gear, and packs; Waterfall lay in the corner, writing in the shelter register, Matt and Blue Skies sat on the porcupine trap cooking dinner, and O.D. and Bugbiter lounged against the back wall, wrapped in their sleeping bags. There was the familiar rank atmosphere of unwashed bodies, wet gear, and old sweat, but in the few weeks we had been on the Trail, I had ceased to mind it. It was a warm, woolly mammal scent, like a barn full of horses, and in my mind, the shelter smell had come to represent security and companionship.

The rain let up after half an hour, and a troop of Boy Scouts, who had camped down by the brook, came out of their tents to cook supper on the fire ring. The gangly ten-year-olds jockeyed for position on the logs and rocks around the fireplace. In a short while, they had a roaring fire going. One of the leaders raked some of the coals to one side so they could cook.

The troop had brought inordinate amounts of food; cans of soup and ravioli bubbled in the coals next to a heap of foil-wrapped potatoes, and shish kabobs rested on the battered iron grill. I fed a few twigs into the Zip stove and stirred our pot of hamburger-less Hamburger Helper, trying not to stare at the Boy Scouts' feast. The famous hiker appetite had kicked in at last, after two weeks on the Trail, and I was constantly hungry; I couldn't carry enough food to make up for the effort of hiking. In Monson, I'd been astounded to see a northbounder consume an entire large pizza by himself. Now I felt sure I could do the same, if a large pizza happened to cross my path.

The Boy Scouts finished off their kabobs, but the stack of potatoes was almost undiminished, and six cans of stew and ravioli were untouched.

The scoutmaster turned to the shelter. "Hey, are you guys hungry?"

A chorus of affirmatives came from the thru-hikers. Isis climbed out and passed the potatoes back to the shelter, where we split the stack carefully into eight portions. Isis and I got the ravioli, since it was vegetarian; the other hikers split the stew. After half a pot of Hamburger Helper (which congealed suspiciously as it cooled and tasted of some unidentifiable preservative), the ravioli and the hot baked potato were like manna from heaven.

"Thank you so much!" I said between bites.

Matt put down his can of stew and smiled at the scoutmaster. "You guys are angels," he said.

"Oh, I wouldn't go that far! If you guys eat it, me and the boys don't have to pack it out."

"No, there's a tradition on the Trail. When anybody helps out hikers, especially by giving them food, it's called trail magic, and the people who do it are called trail angels. So you guys *are* angels."

"Jeez, I've never been called an angel before. Maybe I oughta feed hikers more often!"

"That's the spirit!"

After supper, as the woods began to fill with twilight, Tenbrooks went to his pack and took out a small bundle wrapped in plastic.

"Happy Independence Day," he said, and passed out sparklers. There were just enough to go around between the hikers and the Boy Scouts. We lit them in the coals of the fire and danced around the clearing. The brilliant cascades of sparks cast a warm golden light on our faces.

The scoutmaster waited until most of the sparklers had gone out, and then he leaned forward. A fountain of crackling white light erupted from the coals. He stood up, holding the sparkler high, and began to sing in a rich baritone: "O, beautiful for spacious skies, for amber waves of grain . . ."

The dancing stopped, as if on cue, and all of us, scouts and hikers, came to stand beside him, watching the coals and the last sparkler burn down. Our voices joined in, one by one, until the chorus swelled to fill the dark clearing with sound as the sparklers had filled it with light.

The last sparkler went out. "Time for bed," the scoutmaster said softly, and the boys trooped out of the clearing and down to their tents.

Before the man left for his own tent by the brook, he stopped to talk to Tenbrooks, who was sitting on the porcupine trap staring into the fire. "Thanks. This was the best Fourth I've had in a long time."

I could just see the gleam of Tenbrooks' smile. "Me, too."

As I drifted off to sleep, I heard Bugbiter slap another mosquito. "Man, why do they always go after me?"

"'Cause you taste better than an old duffer like me," O.D. said, and he rolled over in his mummy bag. He was snoring in a few moments.

"Do you think we can make it to Caratunk tonight?" I asked. We were a few miles into the day's hike, and the sun was still low in the morning sky.

"Hope so. Waterfall said there's a hostel there that's supposed to be awesome."

"What is it, like, fifteen total?"

"Yeah."

"Any big lumps in the way?" We had taken to speaking about bumps in the elevation profile this way; somehow "big lump" sounded less threatening than "mountain."

"Mmm, a few. Not too bad."

"What is that smell?" I wrinkled my nostrils and sniffed the air. A rank and salty odor drifted toward us on the wind. "D'you smell it too, Isis?"

"Yeah. Smells like a big mammal of some kind."

"Do you think it's a moose? Maybe a bear . . ."

But we stopped our speculation, because at that very moment the source of the smell hove into view.

It was a man, coming north on the trail. He was tall and looked to be in his mid-forties, with gray hair and a gray beard so tangled that it was impossible to tell where one ended and the other began. He wore a ratty white t-shirt, khaki shorts, a small overnight pack, and, improbably, red penny loafers with shiny new pennies. A cloud of palpable odor surrounded him.

"I am Starman," he said, when we came close. We gave our trail names, but he appeared not to hear, and continued speaking in a low, intense voice. His hazel eyes wandered disconcertingly. "I have considered changing my trail name to Shaman. Maybe I will."

Then he glanced down and noticed our feet. "Barefoot!" he said. "Well, I know some people who hike naked. One guy hiked the entire length of the

Trail in Maine with no clothing . . ." He regaled us with stories of naked hiking for perhaps ten minutes, his voice charged with concentration. Then, abruptly, he stopped in midsentence. "I must go!"

He strode off up the trail, leaving a slowly dissipating stench and a sensation of utter disorientation. When he was gone, I turned to Isis. "He was possibly the strangest person I've ever met."

She shrugged. "Certainly the most fragrant."

Most northbounders, at this stage in the Trail, were pretty odd looking: hairy and scruffy, pared down to muscle and bone. Starman was the strangest by far, though.

We stopped for a snack at Pleasant Pond Lean-to. A young hiker sat on the porcupine trap, thumbing through the register. He was rail-thin, with a mop of blond hair and slightly protruding eyes that gave him a studious look. He reminded me of the hero of a Thomas Hardy novel.

"Oh, hi," he said, glancing up as we set our packs down. "I'm Nightmare."

We introduced ourselves. "How'd you get a name like that?" I asked.

His face relaxed into a smile. "Last year I hiked the Presidentials in August with a couple friends. I don't know if you guys have done much hiking in the Whites. The weather there can be absolutely brutal, even in summer."

We had never done any hiking in New Hampshire, but we had heard the stories of snow in August, eighty-knot winds, and unpredictable, violent storms.

"Well, the thing was, the whole week we were there it was sunny and seventy-five degrees." He shrugged. "It was so warm and calm on Mount Washington that I stood outside in shirtsleeves eating a freakin' ice cream cone. Up there at the summit, we got to talking about my thru-hike, because I was planning it at that point. The other guys started ribbing me about weather karma, saying, 'next time you hike the Whites you're dead meat! Hiking with you is gonna be everybody's worst nightmare!' And so one of them, who'd hiked about half the Trail, said I should take that as my trail name. I like it. It keeps the riffraff away." He flashed us a maniacal bug-eyed look, and then burst out laughing.

"Speaking of riffraff, did you meet that guy—"

"Starman? Oh yeah. I could smell him before I saw him. I was filtering water at the lake, and he came right down and sat next to me. He started in about how filters are worthless and *Giardia* is a myth perpetuated by the government. He ranted on for about ten minutes, and then he stood up all of a sudden, and he said, 'I've got forty dollars and a decision to make!' And then he took off." Nightmare shook his head. "Takes all kinds."

We made good time all day, although, as usual, there were many small elevation changes that didn't show up on the profile map. The sun was still above the trees when we reached Caratunk, Maine, population 98: one street of high Victorian houses, a church, a school, and a post office. The Kennebec River, a clear dark torrent over rounded stones, framed the town on one side, and on the other side the hills rose up, covered with thick pine woods. A little ways out of town on the main road, a converted trailer served filling, greasy food. Most of the customers were logging truck drivers, who left their vehicles idling in the wide gravel parking lot as they ate. Isis and I filled up on town food—pizza, French fries, and onion rings. (It turned out that I still couldn't manage a large pizza by myself, especially after appetizers, but a pair of nobos turned up just in time to bolt down the last two slices.) We slept well that night at the Caratunk House, a luxurious Bed and Breakfast with hiker rates so reasonable that I thought I had misheard the owner. Matt, Tenbrooks, and Blue Skies tented in a field near the edge of town.

The next day we crossed the Kennebec. It was one of the strangest sections of the Trail, because we didn't walk at all—we paddled. The trail came out of the woods on a wide gravel beach, and there we found a tall, lean, red-haired man waiting with a canoe. "I'm Steve Longley," he said. "The ferryman."

"Pleased to meet you." We had heard rumors of the ferryman along the Trail, and a nobo had told us his story; apparently several hikers had drowned trying to ford the Kennebec, many years ago. The Appalachian Trail Conference, the A.T.'s managing organization, had searched for a safer crossing. The nearest bridges were twenty miles in either direction. Instead of rerouting the Trail, they had decided to hire Steve, a former raft guide, to carry thru-hikers safely over the river. From May to October, rain or shine, he had paddled his red canoe across the Kennebec for fifteen years, dispensing words of wisdom to his passengers.

"Stow your packs in the canoe." He caught sight of our feet, and a spark of interest glowed in his eyes. "You must be the Barefoot Sisters. I've heard a lot about you. Tell me, why do you do it?"

"Because it feels so good sometimes," Isis said. "You can feel the living earth under your feet."

Steve nodded shortly. "I figured it was something like that. People told me you must be crazy, or doing some kind of penance. I didn't think so. We all have our reasons for what we do."

"What about you?" I asked him. "Why do you cross the Kennebec over and over?" I knew that most raft-guiding jobs must pay better than this, and certainly there wasn't much excitement to be had in ferrying people across the same stretch of relatively flat water.

He regarded me with an inscrutable stare, and then turned to look out over the flow of small rapids. "Because it's never the same river twice."

We moved the red canoe into the current. Isis sat in the middle with our packs, and I paddled in the bow. Steve was in the stern, standing upright with his paddle in hand. The river was wide and low, barely four feet of brownish-gold water over the rounded cobbles. As I watched, the water level on the far bank crept upwards. "What's happening?" I called to Steve. "Why is the river rising?"

"Hydro dam release upstream." He kept the canoe steady without effort. "That's why we tell people not to ford the Kennebec. Depth changes fast, and that current's pretty strong." Looking over the side of the boat, I saw that six feet of rushing water now slid past underneath us. We were still in midstream, equidistant from the banks. I shivered, imagining what it would be like to get caught by that current while fording the river with a pack on.

"Never the same river twice," I said wryly.

"You can stow your paddle now." Steve guided the canoe toward a marshy landing area on the far bank. "It never is the same river. When you think you know something through and through, that's when it takes you by surprise. Remember that."

Isis

On our first night out from Caratunk, we stayed at Pierce Pond Lean-to with Tenbrooks, Blue Skies, and Matt. I dove into the pond from the small cliff in front of the shelter and managed to stay in the water long enough to lure jackrabbit and Blue Skies in before my teeth started to chatter. Luckily, Tenbrooks had a fire roaring in front of the shelter when we left the icy water. We sat on logs around the firepit, cooking, while the sun sank toward the lake's far shore, leaving a broad gold path across the water. The smell of wood smoke and the sound of waves lapping against the shore reminded me of the canoe camping trips of my childhood, when we'd sit around the fire late into the night, entertaining each other with wild tales of pirates and fairies, ogres and ghosts.

"Let's tell stories," jackrabbit said, voicing my thought.

She began with a retelling of the myth of Orpheus. Matt followed with a Chinese legend about a man who gave up all his material goods, one by one, in a quest for enlightenment, but could not bear to part with an embroidered shawl that had once been his daughter's. Tenbrooks sang the bluegrass song for which he and Molly were named, and I recited a Tennyson poem, "The Splendor Falls." The same threads of loss and nostalgia ran through all our stories. We all understood that this would be one of our last evenings together; Tenbrooks and Blue Skies were much stronger hikers than jackrabbit and I were, and I could tell that Matt, too, was eager to stretch his long legs and cover more miles in a day than we could hope to.

As I spoke the last lines of the poem, the loons started calling. Their wild laughter echoed back and forth over the water, rising in pitch as many voices joined in, then fading away to a single, mournful cry. We fell silent, watching reflected clouds ripple like red and gold pennants across the lake. When the sky darkened, and a pale evening star shone over the mountains, I turned toward Blue Skies and asked if she had a story to tell. She was sitting on a log beside the fire, hugging her knees and gazing out at the water. I'd always admired her strength—both the physical prowess that meant she'd soon be hiking far ahead of us and the steadfast good humor with which she met every challenge, from rainstorms to shin splints. But now, with her eyes wide and her face pale in the dusk, she looked small and frightened and very, very young.

"I don't know any stories," she answered, "except the one I'm in. And I don't even know where that one's taking me. I'm twenty-two. I've finished college. I'm not ready for the career track, and I haven't thought much about grad school. Sometimes I'm afraid that I'm on the Trail just because it gives me a sense of direction. I get up in the morning, I follow the white blazes, and I feel like I know where I'm going."

"Yeah," said Tenbrooks. "Me too."

"Yeah," said jackrabbit.

jackrabbit

The next day, Matt and Blue Skies joined us for lunch by a small clear pond with a gravel beach. We'd had a morning of easy walking, a level trail over comfortable forest floors and bog bridges. A fresh breeze kept the mosquitoes down.

Isis passed me some crackers and cheese, and I handed her the banana chips from my food bag. Matt offered around a Ziploc of what I took to be dried apricots, but the taste convinced me otherwise. I fought the impulse to spit out the unidentifiable brown lump—it was calories, after all. Calories I hadn't had to carry.

"What *was* that?" I asked when I had managed to swallow.

"Chicken-flavored soy chunk. Want some more? I've got plenty."

"Uh, no thanks."

Matt took his *Data Book* from the top of his pack and glanced through it. "Where are you guys headed tonight?" he asked.

"I'm not sure," Isis said. "We'll probably end up camping by that stream, what's it called . . . Jerome Brook. What about you?"

Matt gave a quizzical smile. "I bet we could all make it to Little Bigelow Lean-to. It's another eight miles, but it stays flat until the last part."

I did a quick calculation. "That would make seventeen miles today."

"Yeah," he said matter-of-factly. "A good day."

Isis protested. "That's more than we've ever done before."

"We did a fifteen into Caratunk."

"But that was with our packs almost empty! We've still got three days of food left."

"We'll see."

"Little Bigelow is a great place," Matt said. "Hope I'll see you there."

He and Blue Skies packed up and left, but Isis and I lingered by the shore, enjoying the warmth of the sun and the sensation of full bellies. When I got up, it felt as though all my muscles had stiffened. Isis groaned, too.

"We must've sat still for too long," I said.

"Hiker hobble," she said as we lurched toward our packs. "That's what the nobos call it. They say it never really goes away."

"Great. Two thousand miles of this to look forward to."

Back on the trail, I somehow settled into the rhythm of hiking and barely noticed the aches and pains in my muscles. It was bizarre, I reflected, that without the pack I could hardly walk, and with it I could go all day. I wondered if "all day" today would stretch to seventeen miles.

Several roads crossed the trail here, the worn asphalt incongruous amid the miles of forest. At one of the road crossings, we found two northbounders stopping for a water break. They were tall, broad-shouldered men with long dark hair and shaggy beards. They leaned on their trekking poles, their faces full of quiet satisfaction. Yellow spray paint on the pavement spelled out *2,000 MILES*.

I stopped at the edge of the road and took a drink, too. "Hey, congrats on reaching the two-thousand-mile mark."

"Thanks," the younger one said. Then he caught sight of our mud-brown, bugbitten bare feet, and he broke into a wild grin. "Hey, Jaybird! It's the Barefoot Sisters!"

The older man perked up and smiled broadly. "No shit," he said, managing to draw the expletive into two syllables. "It's an honor, a real honor. Y'all are famous. I been hearing 'bout y'all since I got to Maine . . . Listen, would y'all mind if I got a picture?"

We posed beside him on the gray pavement, slightly bemused, while his companion snapped a photo. I had never guessed that rumor of our presence would spread so fast, or that our story would cause so much interest. It was flattering to be treated like a celebrity, but also a little disconcerting. The attention felt undeserved. Here were people who had walked more than ten times as far as we had, people who had almost completed the Trail, and they were treating us like something special.

"This'll be a day to remember. Two thousand miles, and meetin' the Barefoot Sisters. Thank y'all."

Buoyed by the encounter with the northbounders, we hiked fast, reveling in our ability to skim over the trail. We jumped from rock to rock and root to root, and our feet instinctively formed themselves around the terrain and propelled us forward. Toward evening, though, our energy began to wane where the trail took a sharp turn uphill.

"Where are we?" I asked Isis.

"Well, judging from the map, once we start going uphill after this turn it's maybe another mile . . ."

And twenty minutes later we found the side trail to Little Bigelow Lean-to. We arrived just before dark, sore and tired but glowing with our accomplishment. Matt and Blue Skies were nowhere to be seen—probably tarping out behind the shelter, which was occupied by a crowd of northbounders.

"Hi, I'm jackrabbit," I said into the darkening shelter. I caught a few of the names that came back.

"So, how far did you hike today?" said a skinny blond man, who had given his name as "Patagonia."

I beamed with pride. "We had a big day today. Our first seventeen."

He made no effort to suppress his laughter. "Nice. Lipton and I did a twenty-seven."

I was trying to formulate a reply when a familiar voice came from the back of the shelter. "Hey, these guys started two weeks ago. How long have *you* been on the Trail?"

Tenbrooks! I hadn't seen him in the shadowy corner of the shelter. Molly roused herself from sleep and jumped out to give us doggy kisses.

"Hey, Tenbrooks. Hey, Molly girl. Good to see some familiar faces!"

"Hi there, jackrabbit. Glad you made it!"

I set up the tent while Isis gathered firewood to cook supper. Matt and Blue Skies emerged from the gloom of the woods behind the shelter and joined us at the firepit.

Blue Skies leaned close to Isis and whispered something.

"What?"

"It's Tenbrooks's birthday. Let's do something special."

We rummaged around in our food bags for treats we could give him. Someone produced a peanut butter cup, and someone else had a chocolate-covered granola bar. Isis rigged a candle of sorts from a scroll of flammable birch bark. We carried the impromptu cake to the shelter and sang.

"Thanks, guys," Tenbrooks said. "Is that a peanut butter cup? My favorite!"

"I hope it's a good year," Blue Skies told him, beaming.

"It's off to a good start," he said. The crowd of sobos started to disperse, but he stopped us. "Wait. Time to cut the cake." He divided the granola bar and the candy into ten tiny portions, just enough for everyone at the shelter.

The nobos warmed up to us after this. Lipton, a thin dark-haired woman with a raspy voice, told us about the highlights of the next section of Trail. "Have you guys heard about the Octagon? It's this ski lodge up on Sugarloaf where you can stay for free. It has a woodstove, and the views are pretty sweet. What else . . . oh, like, three days from here, there's a moose skeleton right by the trail."

"Right next to the trail?" Matt said.

"Yeah, if the thing had gotten any farther before it keeled over, it'd be *in* the trail. You can't miss it."

We talked for a while longer as the fire died, and then we wished the nobos luck and headed for our tent. In the morning, they were gone before we awoke.

Isis

We packed hurriedly in the still-cold morning. The gradual, two-mile ascent of Little Bigelow warmed us, and we stopped for a snack on one of the sunny, sheltered ledges near its peak. As we ate our granola bars, a section hiker who was standing nearby, enjoying the view, struck up a conversation with us. He told us that he'd met Waterfall a few miles back and had a wonderful time talking with her. When I told him that we planned to camp with her that evening, his face brightened.

"May I ask you a big favor? Your friend told me she really misses fruit, and I have an orange in my pack that I meant to give her. Could you bring it to her?"

"Sure," I said. I knew how unfailingly amiable Waterfall was—more than once, when jackrabbit and I had been hurrying to reach camp before dark, we'd passed her standing beside the trail, answering a dayhiker's questions. If a weekender was having trouble setting up his tent, Waterfall was the one who'd stop in the middle of cooking her dinner to offer him help. I smiled, thinking what a treat it would be to see her expression when she received this man's surprise gift.

He reached into his pack and took out two oranges.

"I've got an extra, if you'd like it."

"Awesome. Thank you!"

He reached into the bag again.

"I'll be off the trail in two days, and I don't think I'll have time to eat this," he said, pulling out an enormous bar of milk chocolate. "Would you . . ."

"Oh, yes please," I answered, feeling like a child who's just met Santa.

On the way up Avery Peak, the next mountain of the Bigelow Range, we walked into a sculpture garden of granite. Peach-colored boulders the size of houses leaned at crazy angles over the trail, with ferns clinging to their spines, and slender birch trees leaning from their crevices. I was so entranced that I didn't even hear the first rumbles of thunder.

"Isis, get under here!" Jackrabbit was crouched in the shelter of an over-hung cliff, waving at me. Startled at her tone of voice, I looked around, to see what she was hiding from. A soft breeze rustled the leaves of the birches, and a cloudless sky gleamed through their branches. Then I heard the rain. Drops the size of grapes spattered on the dry leaves of the forest floor. I turned around—a dark cloud seethed over the mountain's rim, moving so rapidly it looked like a time-lapse film. I ran for jackrabbit's impromptu shelter.

Safe under the cliff, we waited for the storm to abate, singing sea chanties over the roar of wind and thunder. The rain pelted down in huge, pale drops that hung in the moss and slid like rivers of moonstones over the forest floor. A few drops shook loose from a hemlock branch and pooled at our feet. Jackrabbit reached down and plucked one milky gem from the pool.

"Rain's changed to hail," she said, handing it to me.

Five minutes later, the sky shone blue again. We crept out from our over-hang and headed up the mountain, slipping on the hailstones that littered the ground. Underfoot, they felt like slick, cold pebbles, smooth as glass. About a mile from the peak, we met a gaggle of wild-eyed teenagers in shorts and t-shirts who were running down the trail. The first one skidded to a halt when he saw me.

"Did you—did you see that storm?" he asked. "We were up th-there. On th-the peak. Her hair stood straight up!" He gestured to a young woman whose hair, plastered down with sweat and rain, reached the small of her back. She gazed off into the trees, her eyes glazed. Her teeth were chattering.

"Do you have a car at the foot of the mountain?" I asked the boy. He nodded. "You'd better keep going," I told him. "Your friend needs to get to a warm place fast."

As the last kid in the group filed past, he looked up at me and stammered, "watch out—there's a—a big—a big *mud* up there!"

A quarter mile farther on, jackrabbit and I found the trail blocked by a deep, muddy puddle full of floating hail. We splashed through it nonchalantly, joking that such a big mud might terrify us—if we had boots to get soaked in it.

We were still laughing when we turned a corner in the trail and found ourselves at the base of a mud- and rockslide about fifty feet high. From where we stood, it looked almost vertical. Sure enough, a white blaze beckoned from a tree at the top. I looked at jackrabbit.

"A big mud," she murmured. "Bit of an understatement, if you ask me."

"I don't see any alternative," I said, waving a hand at the cliff that flanked the Big Mud on one side, and the impenetrable tangle of underbrush on the other.

I started to climb. For every three feet of ground I gained, I slid back two. When I tried to grab rocks to pull myself up, they came out in my hands. At one point, a twenty-pound lump of granite came loose under me. Trying to shove it aside so that it wouldn't hit jackrabbit, I lost my balance and slipped to the edge of the cliff. I dug my fingers and toes into the thick mud, scrabbling for something to hold on to. Finally, I caught a root and jerked to a halt. I clung to it, trembling, unwilling to move back out on the shifting slope.

"Are you all right?" jackrabbit called up to me.

"Yeah, I'm fine." I answered. *Do you hear that? You're fine. So act like it,* I told myself. I lifted my head and peered over the cliff's edge at the place I would have fallen. It was only a ten-foot drop, ending in a pile of brush that would have made a scratchy but springy landing pad. Laughing at my fear, I let go of my handhold and crawled back onto the slick, unsteady path.

Near the top of Avery Peak, the second thunderstorm hit. We decided to wait just below treeline, crouching among the shoulder-high spruce. Luckily, no hail fell this time, but the wind and rain made us shiver beneath our Gore-Tex. I thought of the section hiker's chocolate bar, stashed in the top of my pack. I'd intended to bring it to the shelter and share with our friends that night, but I thought a few bites of it would be just the thing to take my mind off the cold. I could still save most of it for our friends.

"Hey, jackrabbit, how 'bout a little chocolate while we wait?" I asked. In less than two minutes, we had finished the whole bar.

We reached the peak just as the sky cleared. To our right, three thousand feet below, Flagstaff Lake sparkled gold and deep blue, and the shadows of a few fluffy, fair-weather clouds freckled the verdant slopes of the mountains beyond it. Eastward, on our left, billowing thunderheads sailed into a bruise-colored sky, their undersides pulsing with lightning. Ahead of us, the trail curved along the crest of the Bigelows, bordered with blocks of lichen-covered stones. Small pools of rainwater jeweled the path, some reflecting the dark sky, others throwing nothing but sun to the eye in blinding, radiating flashes. All around us, reddish clumps of saxifrage and blooming cranberry glittered with droplets, and far ahead, where the trail dipped between Avery and West Peak, a forest of tiny alpine birches shook in the wind, the facets of their wet leaves catching the light at a thousand angles. Behind them, a wall of cloud rose from the shadowy eastern valley, caught the wind, and streamed off the backs of the peaks, evaporating as it rose.

In this magical place I forgot myself; it wasn't until we were scrambling down the back of South Horn, the last peak in the range, that I realized I was still cold. I looked at jackrabbit; she, too, was shivering, and her lips were almost white.

"Let's stop and put on some warmer clothes," I said.

"No," she answered, her teeth chattering. "Let's keep going. If we stop moving we'll get even colder, and anyway, we're almost to the shelter."

This seemed logical enough, and an argument would've taken too much energy. I stumbled on, feeling colder and colder as the sun sank behind thick spruce branches.

At the shelter, I gave Waterfall her orange, along with the section hiker's greeting.

"You carried an orange all that way for me? That was real sweet of you." She flung her arms around my shoulders.

"No trouble," I muttered, shrugging out of the embrace that felt prickly with warmth. I unpacked my camp sneakers and went down to the pond to rinse my feet. Sitting with my legs in the water—its chill was soothing now— I watched a thin mist lift from the pond's edges as the sun set. I would have been happy to stay there all night, watching the stars wheel by, but a dull memory tugged at the back of my mind. Jackrabbit—what about jackrabbit? She was waiting for me at the shelter—it was my night to cook dinner, wasn't it? As the sky changed from lilac to indigo, I rubbed green salve into my feet, put on my sneakers, and headed back to the lean-to. I found jackrabbit right where I'd left her, perched on the edge of the porcupine trap hugging her knees. When she saw me, she scowled.

"Where have you been all this time?"

"What do you mean, where have I been? I told you I was going to wash my feet."

"It took you forty-five minutes to wash your feet? It's your turn to cook. I've been waiting for you to make dinner."

"Okay, okay, I'll make it now. Help me gather some wood for the stove, and it'll be done in no time."

"No! I won't help you. It's your night to cook, and besides, I'm so tired I'm not even hungry anymore!"

"Fine, then. I won't make dinner. You can eat gorp."

Ignoring the bag of gorp I flung in her direction, jackrabbit crawled into her sleeping bag and flopped down on her mat with her back to me. I ate a few handfuls of gorp, and then, feeling a vague guilt over the fact that I'd failed to make dinner for jackrabbit, I put the food away and got into my own bag.

We had four smooth, downhill miles to hike to the town of Stratton, but it took us all morning to get there. Every half-mile we had to stop, sit down on a rock, and eat something. The third time we stopped, jackrabbit said, "I think that was a bad idea, skipping dinner last night."

"No kidding. What came over us?"

"I don't know, but I think I was kind of a bitch."

"Yeah, you were, but I was, too. I got so cold, I couldn't think."

"Does hypothermia make you grumpy? It might've been that."

"I think it does. Yeah, I remember something like that from first aid classes. You get irritable, then disoriented, then you start to think you're too hot instead of too cold, so you pull off all your clothes and jump in a snow-bank and die."

"Good thing there weren't any snowbanks around last night," jackrabbit laughed. "Don't worry. Now that we know the symptoms, we'll look out for each other. If one of us starts to get hypothermic, the other will do something about it."

"Does that mean that next time you get bitchy, I can tie you up in a sweater and stuff you in your sleeping bag?"

She jumped into a Tae Kwon Do fighting stance, then winked at me from behind her raised hands. "You could try."

jackrabbit

As we climbed the shoulder of Sugarloaf Mountain, south of Stratton, the trail came out of the woods onto a steep slope of tumbled scree and small shrubs. Traversing the inside of a cirque, we could see the sweep of the mountain above, gray-green and wreathed in dark clouds that lowered as we watched. The trail was strewn with small sharp stones, and landslides had cut across it in places, so we walked carefully.

A hiker was making his way down the path toward us. His scruffy beard and thin frame, and the loping grace in his stride, marked him as a north-bounder. When he saw us, his face lit up with recognition.

"The Barefoot Sisters! I heard all about you."

We smiled and said hello. I was becoming less startled by the attention we were attracting—he was probably the tenth hiker to recognize us—but no less uncomfortable. We had explained numerous times that we were barefoot because we enjoyed it, because we loved to feel the trail underfoot and expe-rience hiking with all our senses, but every time we were met with the same incredulity, and often with a kind of hero-worship that I found embarrassing.

The northbounder was staring at our feet. Bugbitten, begrimed, and slightly pink from the cold, they were far from impressive.

"Amazing. Absolutely amazing. Can I take a picture?"

"Sure." Isis started to climb the embankment on the upper side of the narrow trail so we would both fit in the frame, but the northbounder shook his head.

"Just the feet," he said. "I just want a picture of your feet."

When he was down the trail and out of earshot, we laughed ourselves silly.

"We ought to give our feet trail names, since they attract so much atten-tion," Isis said. "Remember the cowboys on *Prairie Home Companion*? I'm going to call mine Dusty and Lefty."

As we made our way along the narrow trail, I wondered why anyone would want a picture of our feet alone. It was a little disconcerting. Had we become a sideshow attraction in the A.T. carnival? I wanted to be remem-bered as a person, not a pair of disembodied feet walking the Trail.

At the summit of Sugarloaf, it was impossible to see more than a few feet ahead in the driven mist. The wind screamed across the broken stones, sucking the warmth from our bodies. Goose bumps instantly rose on the exposed flesh of our legs and arms.

"Where is this Octagon supposed to be?" I yelled to Isis over the roaring wind.

"I don't know. Let's go upwind first."

I agreed—it would be easier to backtrack that way if we didn't find it. We struggled against the onslaught of streaming clouds. In a few minutes, a tower came into view. It looked like there was a tiny room in the base of it, but the whole building was surrounded by a chain-link fence. The gate was pad-locked.

"Is this it?" I yelled.

"There's no way in!"

"I'm getting too cold."

"So put your Gore-Tex on!"

"We must be almost there."

As we sagged against the fence, catching our breath, I caught a faint scent of wood smoke.

"We should go back," Isis said. "What if it's not there? We can go on and find a campsite . . ."

"It's there, I know it is."

We headed into the wind again, and there it was, probably less than fifty feet from the first tower. The building was hidden by clouds until we stood on the back porch. Isis threw the door open and we tumbled onto the rough wooden floor inside. My ears rang with the sudden silence.

The "Octagon" turned out to be a hexagon, with plate glass windows on almost every side. The view right then was a uniform pearly gray. The lodge was a large building, closer to the size of a house than the cramped confines of a shelter. The entry we had used opened into a high-ceilinged room, taking up half the hexagon, with a map of the ski area covering one wall. Steps led up to a higher platform in the other half of the building, where we found some familiar faces.

"O.D.! Bugbiter! It sure is good to see you guys."

"Hey, jackrabbit, Isis. Good to see you, too." They sat on benches in front of a gigantic woodstove. The radiating heat felt delicious.

"Did you guys bring in all this wood?" A pile of gnarled spruce skeletons lay next to the stove, probably enough to keep it going for three days.

O.D. shrugged. "My kid has way too much energy. We got here early, and he was still rarin' to go."

The teenager struck a muscleman pose. "I am the unstoppable Bugbiter-tron!"

As the mist outside darkened, we sat around the fire talking. "Can I ask you something?" O.D. said.

"Go ahead."

"Well, out in the real world, I'm a physical therapist. And I was wondering . . . could I have a look at your feet?"

"Sure." I held up my grimy right foot for inspection. The sole had a leathery callus, stained yellowish brown from the forest floor, and the arch and ankle bulged with muscle. In the heat from the stove, veins stood out from the surface as though from a weightlifter's biceps.

O.D. shook his head. "That's truly amazing. I have never seen a foot with muscles like that. I see so many people with fallen arches, or sprained ankles, and they have these little feet that are nothing but bones. Wow. You guys are something else."

Bugbiter tossed a log on the fire. "Dad, aren't people *supposed* to walk barefoot? I mean, didn't we evolve, and, like, come out of the trees barefoot?"

"Good point."

"You should try it some time," Isis said.

Bugbiter looked slightly alarmed. "I like my boots. What you do is cool and all, but I just don't think I could hack it. I kick rocks and stuff all the time."

"You have to develop an awareness. When you start out, you always have to think about where you're putting your feet. After a while it just becomes second nature."

The morning dawned clear and calm. In all directions, ridges of saw-toothed mountains shone bluish behind the plate glass windows, under a peach-colored sky. The distinctive shape of the Bigelows, two small peaks and two large ones, loomed across the valley, and far beyond them on the horizon was a silver knife-blade shape that might have been Katahdin. Innumerable other peaks dotted the landscape, with lakes shining like small silver coins in the valleys.

"Looks pretty impressive, doesn't it?" O.D. said.

"Yeah," I said. "Feels like quite an accomplishment."

He grinned. "Look over there." He pointed off to the south. Ranks of bare, imposing summits, jagged ridges, and deep-shadowed valleys stretched off to the horizon. In the early light, the mountains looked like agitated storm waves on the ocean. "That's where we're going."

Isis

The day after Sugarloaf, we hiked eleven miles over some of the roughest terrain we'd seen. The trail was so steep in one place, where it descended through a tangle of spruce roots and rocks beside a small waterfall, that we had to take off our packs and hand them down to each other. At the base of the waterfall, we came to a lovely quiet stream, with maples and cedars leaning over its clear pools, in which the peaks of surrounding mountains lay reflected. We sat down for a late lunch on a boulder in the middle of the stream, where we were soon joined by a tall, gray-haired hiker with braces on both his knees. He pulled a heavy-looking camera out of a pouch on his hip-belt, focused on the reflections in the stream, and waited for a fallen leaf to drift into the sky beside the highest mountain.

As he returned the camera to its pouch, he asked if we were hiking the whole Trail. When I answered in the affirmative, he sighed.

"You kids are so lucky," he said. "If I had hiked when I was your age, I would've lived my life differently."

"How so?" I asked him.

"I went straight from college into an accounting firm. I did well, got promoted. Married my college sweetheart. What's left of all that? Alimony payments and a house too big for one old man. I started hiking fifteen years ago just to do something with my vacation time after the divorce. Now I'm retired, I've got more time, but my knees aren't what they used to be. I've hiked all the way here from Georgia in a bunch of hundred-fifty, two-hundred-mile sections. And I love it. If I'd realized, when I was twenty-one, how little money it took to make me happy, I would've been a nature photographer."

That evening at Poplar Ridge Lean-to, I met a man with a very different perspective. He, too, was a section hiker, a paramedic from Atlanta. In the flickering light of our Zip stove, his round, clean-shaven cheeks and the bald spot in the middle of his light brown hair gave him the appearance of a jolly Medieval monk.

"I'm on vacation," he said, "but I'd like to know what you girls are doing in the woods, at this point in your lives. Do you have jobs?"

Jackrabbit answered that we were thru-hiking southbound. "I just finished college; my sister's been out for a few years."

His jaw dropped. "Do you know what you're missing out on?" he asked. "The job market is at an all-time high. Kids your age, you go into technology, and you're making eighty thousand dollars your first year! With paid vacations and business trips to Las Vegas! All you have to know is how to turn on a computer."

The language he was speaking, of job markets and computers and casinos, seemed so alien to the world of white blazes and wood fires and lean-tos in which we were living, that neither jackrabbit nor I could come up with any response.

Mistaking our silence, he continued, "If you're not intelligent enough to work in technology, you could always go into nursing. It's steady employment with good benefits, and there's always a demand for nurses. You'd never be out of a job."

jackrabbit

We crossed the Saddleback Range, with its expanses of high heath bogs and open granite, on a splendid day. The sky was clear blue from horizon to horizon, and a light breeze kept us cool. Like Moxie Bald, these mountains reminded me of home. I remembered that today we would cross the 216-mile mark: one-tenth of the Trail. It was a small accomplishment compared to the nobos we had seen, but it still felt worthy of celebration. As I hiked, I formulated a piece of doggerel to write in the next register:

> Two-sixteen today: I'm a tenth of the way
> and no closer to figuring out
> what to do with my life—all the A.T.'s advice
> has been about doing without.

Climbing down into the spruce woods, off the open ridges, I suddenly felt a jab of pain in my right hip. It was as though a hot needle tore into the joint with each step. I stopped and stretched, trying to breathe deeply and subdue the pain. My sister, meanwhile, was blithely floating on down the path, almost out of sight around the bend.

"Isis!" I called after her. My voice cracked. "I think I've got to . . . take a rest . . . just for a little . . ."

She turned back, her forehead furrowed. "Are you okay?"

"I think so." I tried a few steps, and the pain faded in and out. "Yeah, I just . . . I must have done something to my hip. It's not comfortable."

"You want some vitamin I?" Ibuprofen—a bit of hiker slang we had picked up from Maineak on the trip where Isis got her trail name.

"Yeah, I think I'd better."

Three of the extra-strength tabs were enough to get me to the parking lot, where a dayhiker gave us a ride into the town of Rangeley. I leaned against my pack in the back of the pickup, worrying. Every bump on the road sent a fresh jolt of pain through my hip.

We thanked the driver as we unloaded our packs by a pizza place on Main Street.

"No problem," he said. "You guys staying in town?"

We glanced at each other. It was an unwritten rule between us never to tell a stranger our exact plans. He seemed trustworthy, though, and given the lateness of the hour, it was probably pretty obvious that we'd be in Rangeley for the night.

"Yeah," I said.

"There's a good hostel here. Bob, the owner, he's a friend of mine. Here, let me call him on my cell phone."

We thanked him again.

"Silver station wagon. He should be here in a half hour or so."

"Excellent. Take care."

The Gull Pond Lodge was a small two-story cabin at the end of a woods road, right by a lake. "Make yourselves at home," Bob said. A tall, soft-spoken man with a shock of white hair, he reminded me of my grandfather.

We shared the bunkroom with O.D. and Bugbiter. Their gear was spread across every available surface when we came in. Bugbiter looked up with a guilty smile. "Pardon the pack explosion." He hurriedly stuffed clothing and food into his pack, clearing off two of the bunks.

"No problem. How're you guys doing?"

"Good," Bugbiter said. From his bunk, O.D. mumbled something unintelligible. "Dad's not feeling too great, though."

"What's the matter?"

"Some kind of sinus thing," O.D. said, rousing himself. He sounded stuffed-up, and there were dark rings of fatigue under his eyes. "If it doesn't clear up soon, I want to get it checked out."

"Hope you feel better. This is the bunkroom of the walking wounded tonight." I told him about my hip pain.

In the morning, I called the Rangeley medical center. No appointments were available until the next day.

"Guess we've got to take a zero." Bugbiter sat on the couch and picked up the remote.

"Take a zero?"

"You know, like, zero-mile day? I heard some nobos say it."

"Sounds good."

It was wonderful to relax for a day. We took one of Bob's canoes out on the lake with Bugbiter, and looked for moose in the secluded bays and inlets, with no success. Bob took me to the Episcopal church, where I played the piano for hours. It felt as though a part of me that had been missing had returned. Isis shopped for food, and she cooked pizza and apple pie in the evening. Licking the last of the pie from his fingers, O.D. said, "If you cook like this in every town, I'll follow you to Georgia!"

"I have a surprise for you," Isis said, as we sat in the bunkroom packing our resupply. We decanted the rice, macaroni, and crackers from their bulky cardboard boxes into Ziplocs and divided the weight between our two food bags. Isis flashed me a triumphant smile and reached into the last shopping bag. She pulled out a copy of *Time* magazine, featuring the first chapter of *Harry Potter and the Goblet of Fire*. Isis had introduced me to Harry Potter when I was home on winter break from college, and I had devoured the first three books of the series in a week.

"Excellent!"

When we finished packing, she read the chapter aloud. O.D., Bugbiter, and I lay on our bunks, enjoying the spooky tale. It ended with a cliffhanger, of course, and left many intriguing threads of plot unresolved.

"Do you think we can wait six months to read it?" I asked her.

"Oh, it's going to be hard!" She leafed back through the pages of the magazine. "Look, there's a sidebar here with statistics about the book: 734 pages. Two and a half pounds." We fell silent, considering.

"Two and a half pounds . . . that's like, a couple nights of pasta—"

"—or one full water bottle . . ."

"You guys are nuts!" Bugbiter said.

"So, you're hiking the Appalachian Trail?" The doctor made a few notes on his chart. He manipulated my leg in every direction and asked me to walk, stretch, jump. The pain was difficult to pin down, and it seemed to fade in and out. It was never as sharp and unbearable as the day it had happened.

"You have a groin strain," he announced, and showed me some stretches to relieve the tight muscles.

"Can I keep hiking?"

"Well, yes." Relief washed over me. "It would be better if you could rest, but I know it's no use telling that to a hiker. Keep doing those stretches. And you should probably take an anti-inflammatory drug to keep it from bothering you too much."

He wrote out a prescription for 600 mg ibuprofen tablets. "You can take up to three of these in a day. Any more than that and you run a risk of liver and kidney trouble."

I thanked him profusely. He shook his head. "You hikers. I had a guy come in here with a fractured ankle, and he wanted to keep going. Stay healthy out there. Whatever you did to this the first time, don't do it again. Oh, and good luck."

Isis

A light rain was falling when Bob dropped us off at the trailhead, but the air felt warm. Up to that point, jackrabbit and I had put on our rain jackets for everything from thunderstorms to mist, slowing our pace, if necessary, to keep from sweating inside the extra layers of clothing. Hikers who'd been on the Trail longer than we had—Tenbrooks and all the northbounders we'd met—seemed not to mind getting wet. They'd hike through thunderstorms in shorts and t-shirts, then let their body heat dry their clothes when the rain stopped. I suggested that we try this technique. Jackrabbit agreed enthusiastically, saying that the chill of the rain might encourage us to walk even faster than usual.

We were perhaps half a mile into the woods when the drizzle became a downpour. I walked faster and faster, trying to keep warm. Soaked and shivering, barreling along at what must have been three miles per hour, I nearly ran into the first in a long line of dayhikers. I glanced up just long enough to mumble a hello, then returned my attention to the trail. At the rate I was going, it took my full concentration to keep from stepping on sharp rocks or the sawn-off ends of roots. As I hurried past the phalanx of bright blue and yellow rain suits, I heard the whispered rumor keeping pace with me. *Would you look at that, they're barefoot. Barefoot, oh my God!*

One woman, in the center of the line, looked down at my feet and exclaimed, "Barefoot! You're so brave!"

"Thanks," I said, not trusting myself to keep the sarcasm out of my voice for more than one syllable. I had just realized why I couldn't walk fast enough to get warm, even though all the northbounders we'd met seemed to have no problem with hiking in wet clothing. I had neglected to consider the influence of boots, wool socks, and silk sock liners on body heat retention. Being called brave, when I was feeling like a total idiot, made me far more uncomfortable than the cold stream trickling down the back of my neck or the wet shirt flapping against my ribcage.

As soon as we'd left the line of dayhikers behind, I threw down my pack, draped my rain jacket across two low branches, and stripped off all my wet clothing under the makeshift roof, not caring that I was standing two feet from the trail. I changed into dry clothes, then pulled down my jacket and put it on over them. Jackrabbit contented herself with putting on a hat; she looked a bit askance at my strip show.

jackrabbit

Cold rain settled in for several days. The ibuprofen had dulled the pain in my hip enough so that I could keep up with Isis, but I felt pretty miserable. I hated the feeling of pruned hands and feet and the utter lack of traction in places where the trail was only mud. Water dripped down my neck, finding a weak seam in my rain gear. We slipped and slid toward the road to Andover, hoping to find a dry place in town to spend the night.

I rounded a bend in the trail and saw a pile of picked-over white bones lying in the underbrush. They shone dully in the rain. For a moment I feared the worst, but then my mind assembled the skeleton: long shanks, a ribcage like an enormous barrel, a horselike skull. A moose. I burst out laughing.

"Isis, look at this!"

"What?" she turned.

"Remember those nobos at Little Bigelow? They said there was a moose skeleton three days down the trail. I guess this must be it. But we've been walking for, what, nine days? Ten days?"

"Nine, if you don't count our zero," Isis said after a moment. "And we had a short day out of Stratton. But those nobos must have been going twenty or thirty miles every day!"

Twenty miles. It seemed an impossibly large number. I didn't even bother to consider the idea of thirty. Our one seventeen-mile day had been daunting enough, and our typical mileage was more like twelve or thirteen. I wondered if, at our pace, we would ever make it to Georgia.

I had finally bought a watch in Rangeley—it was often impossible to tell the time from the sun on overcast days—and it was all I could do not to glance at the time every thirty seconds on this miserably wet afternoon. In an attempt to make the time pass faster, I tried to put together a silly poem based on the weather. Anglo-Saxon lines seemed to fit best with the oppressive atmosphere. As the day rolled slowly past, an endless stream of dripping trees, the poem took shape:

> Stormward we strode, strong sisters
> barefoot in the brook's bright flowage,
> on forest floor, light leaf-filtered;
> barefoot on the broad granite backs
> of mickle mountains, mist-manacled.
> Stormclouds streaked the stark sky
> and rain rang on rock and log.
> Onward we went, swift-walking,
> seeking our solace silver-roofed.
> Baleful bog bridges, rain-beslickened,
> tried to cast us toward the turds
> of Maine moose, great mounds
> of pellets heaped in our passing-places.
> Still we strode, though the trail streamed,
> and thrice it threw us in the thick mud—
> green Gore-Tex grew brown with grime.
> At last we glimpsed the lean-to's gleaming
> through the thickets, thorn-betangled.
> Northbounders, boasting boldly,

       may call eight miles a morning's mucking.
       We southbounders, seldom slaves to schedule,
       wait out the worst of the weather's fury
       in silver-roofed shelters, sturdy-sided.

It seemed to shorten the interminable gray hours in the woods. In the late afternoon, we came to the South Arm Road, leading into Andover. The town was tiny, hardly more than a crossroads: general store, gas station, church, diner. And three A.T. hostels. We weren't sure where our friends might be staying, so we opted to eat first and ask questions later.

Addie's Place was the only restaurant in town. We left our packs leaning on the porch, secure in their waterproof covers, and put on our camp shoes to enter the restaurant. It was a tiny place, with a counter at one side and tables along the other. And there, in the back, were all the people we'd been looking for: Waterfall, Matt, Tenbrooks, and Blue Skies, sharing a table with a red-haired man I didn't recognize.

"Hi there! Glad y'all made it!" Waterfall was halfway through an enormous burger. "Oh, this is Blade. He's a sobo too."

Blade nodded gravely as we gave our names. His trail name did not seem to fit with his mild appearance. He had a serious, almost scholarly face, with small round glasses and a neatly trimmed reddish beard. "Good to meet you." Traces of a Southern accent lingered in his speech.

We pulled up two chairs from the counter, and the waitress came over. "Our specials today are the roast beef sub and spaghetti with meat sauce. The sub's pretty good, can't say as much for the spaghetti. What can I get you?"

"Do you have anything vegetarian?" Isis asked.

The waitress wrinkled her brow. "Do you eat chicken?" she ventured.

Three plates of French fries and onion rings later, the fiercest rumblings of our bellies abated. We shared jokes and stories with the other sobos, glad that we had caught up with them at last. Blade, seated in the corner, said little until I shared the poem I had written that day.

"I like that," he said. "I studied Anglo-Saxon verse while I was working on my Ph.D. You've done a good job with the form."

"Oh, thanks. What was your doctorate in?"

"English. I studied the battle poetry of Tennyson and the heroic code." His voice seemed to grow larger as he said this, filling the room.

"So are you a professor?"

"No. I'm an adventurer." There was no hint of braggadocio in his voice—it was merely a statement of fact.

"What sorts of adventures?" Isis asked.

"I hiked Denali last fall, and in spring I bicycled across the country with a group. That's where I got my name, actually. One of the guys told me I cut through the air like a knife blade on a bike. And now I'm hiking the A.T."

The waitress came around again. "Anybody for pie? Addie just made blueberry, and I know there's peach. I think we got part of an apple one back there too."

Isis and I both ordered peach. The slices were enormous, each one easily a third of the entire pie. "These are huge!" I said. "Thank you!"

The waitress shrugged. "Addie said the peach had to go, 'cause this afternoon she was all in a flutter and just about dropped another pie on top of it. See, the crust's all smashed-in."

"Oh, it looks fine to me. Looks great, in fact." I couldn't see any damage to the crust.

"Well, she said, 'the peach has gotta go,' and so I told her I'd take care of it." She cleared away the last few plates. "Besides, being vegetarians, you didn't eat hardly anything for supper."

With our bellies full, we decided to resupply—the Trail lingo for buying groceries—and then join our friends at the Pine Ellis Bed and Breakfast. Blade came with us to the general store.

"Five or six days to Gorham, I think," Isis said as we leaned our packs against the front steps. It was still raining; puddles in the parking lot overflowed with rainbows of oil.

Breakfast was easy: a carton of powdered milk and a box of Cracklin' Oat Bran. Lunch proved more difficult. Eight-ounce boxes of crackers cost $3.49. I was beginning to reconsider the wisdom of shopping in every town, rather than sending mail drops; if a lot of places had grocery stores like this, our budget would be shot in no time. While we deliberated, Blade went to the rack of pastries by the checkout counter. He held up a Little Debbie Honey Bun. "My secret weapon." He grinned. "Two ounces, 410 calories. Dollar forty-nine."

"Excellent!" On the Trail, counting calories quickly took on a different meaning. Our bodies craved energy in any form, especially fat and sugar. We were always on the lookout for cheap, packable foods that would provide the most calories for their weight, and health concerns took a backseat.

"Hey Isis! How about these? Ninety-nine cents apiece, three hundred calories!" I carefully avoided reading the long lists of chemical additives as I filled our shopping basket with five days' worth of Honey Buns, Table Talk pies, and Captain Nemo Frosted Banana Bars.

"Okay, what about dinners?"

"There's not much here," Isis said, surveying the shelves. Most of the dinner options were canned or frozen, definitely not packable. We managed to find a family-sized box of instant potatoes and a few packages of Hamburger Helper. Blade stocked up on ramen noodles.

"Why don't you eat ramen?" he asked. "It's the best Trail food—weighs nothing, costs nothing, tastes okay."

"I wish we could," I said. "I'm allergic to MSG. It's in all the seasoning packets."

As we tossed the last few boxes into our basket, Isis surveyed the array of food. "We used to be such health nuts," she said mournfully. "Organic this, organic that, no preservatives, no added anything . . . *now* look at us."

Blade glanced at our basket. "Lo, how the mighty have fallen!"

Over breakfast the next morning at Pine Ellis—huge cheese omelets and a bottomless bowl of home fries—we discovered that most of our friends were farther ahead than we had thought.

"Moody Mountain was really something, wasn't it?" Blue Skies said. "All those metal ladders stuck in the rock—I thought I'd never get down!"

Tenbrooks nodded. "Yeah, I worried about Molly when I saw that big rock face, but she found a better way down than I did."

"I don't even remember all this stuff!" I finally said. "I didn't see any ladders or cliffs. We just slid down Old Blue Mountain in the mud, and there was the road."

Matt put down his fork. "Oh, you came in at the South Arm Road?"

"Yeah. You guys?"

Waterfall looked rueful. "We all came in at the East B Hill Road. It's another ten miles down the Trail."

My spirits fell. After our zero day in Rangeley, we had struggled hard to catch up with the group. Seeing all the familiar faces in Addie's the night before, I thought we had managed to do it.

The manager of the bed-and-breakfast came in with another bowl of potatoes. She was a large woman with short gray hair and a grandmotherly manner. "Does anyone want to slack today?"

"Slack?" I asked. It was a new term for me.

"Slack, you know, slackpack? I'll give you a shuttle to the trailhead, and pick you up at the next road, so you can hike a day without your pack. I've got some daypacks you can borrow for lunch and water."

Isis and I exchanged a glance. Hiking without packs, we would certainly be able to move faster. Maybe it would help to close the gap between us and our friends. "Sounds good," she said, and I nodded.

"So that's two for the South Arm Road. Anybody else?"

Blade spoke up. "I'd like to do that section too. But I will carry my pack."

Blue Skies gave him a puzzled look. "But that kind of defeats the point of slacking."

"I set out to do this trail with my full pack, and I will do it." There was a quiet edge to his words, and his normally mild face glowed with intensity.

"No offense," she said quickly.

"None taken. When I set a challenge for myself, I don't back down."

It was a day of steep climbs and knee-jarring descents, and I was very glad to be carrying a light pack. It gave me an odd feeling at first, like the sensation of taking off ice skates; I felt like I was floating about four inches above the trail.

Blade was in extremely good shape. Encumbered with his heavy pack, he still managed to keep up with us. We told him stories from our trip to Peru, and he related a few of his adventures.

"I want to hear about Denali," I said.

"Oh, that was quite a trek. I was probably the least experienced person in the group . . ."

"Did you summit? What was it like up there?"

"Yes, and it was splendid beyond words. We started our summit push at three in the morning, when the moon was just setting. It was so clear and still. The mountain seemed to glow kind of bluish against the sky with all those stars. We were hiking with headlamps for a long time. Snow squeaks when it's that cold. It made little sounds like Styrofoam under our boots.

"We were under a mile from the summit when the wind picked up. It sounded like a freight train coming at us. The woman behind me on the rope just lost it when that wind hit. She started screaming, you know, 'we're all going to die out here!' She went back to camp with one of the guides. The rest of us made it to the summit. Later I found out she had been up the mountain three times and never reached the summit."

His face grew stern and his voice louder. "Mountaineering is about conquering fear and defeating pain. You must have strength and conviction to persevere."

Isis frowned. "It's about judgment, too, isn't it? What if she knew something you didn't about the wind patterns up there?"

Blade looked severe. "The rest of us finished. We reached the goal of our quest. *She* did not."

"There's more to life than finishing quests," Isis said.

Blade shook his head. "I believe that the Quest is the most important thing life holds." His voice now rung out like a trumpet blast, filling the damp forest around us. "I have decided to live my life according to the Heroic Code."

"The heroic code?" I asked.

Blade smiled. "All my life, I have searched for a meaningful way to live. I found it while I was researching for my thesis; I follow the principles that the Knights of the Round Table held. Life's goal is to pursue the Quest and do heroic deeds."

"But what is the quest *for*? I mean, the Knights of the Round Table were after the Holy Grail. Is that . . ."

Blade's eyes twinkled. "Aha. There's the conundrum. What is the Quest for? The Quest itself is the goal! 'To seek, to strive, to find, and not to yield!'"

Isis

At Baldpate Lean-to, the chattering of squirrels woke me in the predawn. This wasn't the first place we'd had to chase squirrels away from our food; in fact, by the last twenty miles of Maine, we'd come to expect the aggravation of tame squirrels, chipmunks, and mice at A.T. shelters. The squirrels at Baldpate were the most insistent I'd seen yet, though. Two of them were clinging to the outside of our food bags, trying to get enough purchase to bite through the slippery nylon. I waved my arms at them and stage-whispered "Shoo!" They didn't budge. I dragged myself up, sleeping bag and all, and flopped toward the edge of the sleeping platform. When I was within an arm's length of them, they jumped down and scampered away to the forest, where they sat in the trees, chattering at me. By the time I'd snuggled back down on my sleeping mat, the squirrels were in the shelter again, jumping from the eaves of the roof to the food bags. I chased them away, then gathered a pile of sticks and pebbles to toss in their general direction whenever they came too close to the shelter. I glanced at jackrabbit's watch: 4:37. It was going to be a long morning.

At 6:30, jackrabbit woke up. As she stretched and rubbed the sleep from her eyes, I poured out the story of my two hour standoff with the squirrels. Even though everyone in the campsite was waking up, the fearless rodents still scampered around in front of the shelter, chattering at us and each other and pouncing on any food bags left unattended.

Jackrabbit listened to my complaints, shrugged her shoulders, and picked up one of the pebbles I'd gathered. The squirrel was twenty feet away, running, but she must have hit it in the head. It keeled over and lay stunned for a minute, before staggering off sideways into the underbrush. A group of northbounders cheered. A couple who'd told us they were just out for the weekend stared at each other in open-mouthed shock.

"The poor little thing," I heard the woman whisper. "Did you see what that horrid girl did to it? Someone should throw a rock at her head and see how she likes it!"

A section hiker who'd camped across from the shelter called out, "That's some aim you got, kid. Ever think about joining the army?"

"No, I'm a pacifist," jackrabbit answered. "At least when it comes to people."

"Great shot," I said. "Next time I have rodent trouble, I'll just wake you up and let you deal with it."

She stifled a laugh. "D'you think I could repeat that? I didn't even mean to hit it."

We hiked only seven miles that day, setting ourselves up to face the infamous Mahoosuc Notch the next morning instead of trying to tackle it at the end of a long day. Northbounders had regaled us with stories of the Notch, a mile-long jungle gym of house-sized boulders. The three-thousand-foot climb up Old Speck Mountain, our longest ascent since Katahdin, took up nearly half the day's hike. Most of the trail was wooded, but every once in a while we'd come out on a granite ledge, where a vista of rolling mountains would open before us. Framed below by the dark pink starbursts of sheep laurel blossoms, these mountains curved softly as waves in a calm sea, seen from a cottage with flowers in its window boxes.

Unlike Saddleback and the Bigelows, Old Speck Mountain had a wooded summit. Our map indicated an "observation platform" down a side trail to our left. Just as we reached the platform, Blade came out of the woods. We shouted to catch his attention, then pretended to defend the tower against him, drawing our arms back and showering him with volleys of imaginary arrows. He held up his pack cover as a shield and charged. When he joined us on the platform, we played at being knights and ladies surveying our dominion. I pointed down at Speck Pond, barely visible through the fringe of trees.

"See ye not yon fair tarn? There shall I make my dwelling, in a pavilion of purple silk."

Jackrabbit laughed; we had often joked about how incongruous our purple tent looked against the greens and browns of the summer forest. She lifted her arm, gesturing dramatically toward the horizon, where a dark smudge of smoke from the Cog Railway hovered over Mount Washington.

"Behold yon foul vapor! Steel your hearts, my lord and my lady, for there be dragons."

"Then let us forge onward, and vanquish them, and all other perils that stand in the path of our quest!" cried Blade, raising his fist and waving it toward New Hampshire.

That night, as we set up our purple pavilion by the lean-to at Speck Pond, a fly fisherman came up from the water's edge with three live trout in a bucket.

"Anyone want these?" he asked the crowd of assembled hikers.

"Sure," said about fifteen voices at once.

I eyed the trout. Three of them, fifteen of us. It looked liked the instant potatoes, which had been one of two dinner options in the Andover store, were still going to be my main course. Then inspiration struck.

"How about a potluck?" I said to the other hikers. "We'll all share the trout, plus each of us can cook one dinner meal, and we'll share them all around."

To my surprise, everyone seemed delighted by the idea. The fisherman filleted the trout for us, and a man who was section hiking with his ten-year-old son built a wood fire and fried them in his pot lid. While the fish was cooking, all the hikers searched through their food bags for their best meals: angel hair with pesto, homemade dehydrated chili, curried vegetables, and couscous. One of the nobos mixed up instant hummus and spread it on triangles of pita bread for an appetizer. Inspired by the general enthusiasm, I announced that I was going to make a salad.

"Salad?" The northbounders stared at me as if I'd just told them that I was going to pull a wedding cake out of thin air.

"Well," I admitted, "I don't have any dressing, but I can get greens."

Someone handed me a bottle of olive oil, and someone else gave me a few restaurant packets of salt and pepper. The man with the angel hair pasta offered me a bit of his pesto. While jackrabbit cooked our potatoes, I gathered a Ziploc bag full of wood sorrel, and mixed up what turned out to be a very passable dressing for the delicate, lemony leaves.

Perhaps it was the novelty of having a more-than-one-course supper, perhaps the festive atmosphere—and I'm sure my hiker appetite enhanced the flavors of every dish—but that potluck compares in my memory to any Thanksgiving. For dessert, I requisitioned packages of instant oatmeal from all those who could spare them, and mixed them with cocoa, brown sugar, and water to make chocolate-oatmeal pudding, a recipe Tenbrooks had taught me. We sat in a circle around the fire, sharing dessert. Somebody sang a song, someone else told a story, and I felt that, in the brief hours we'd spent together, the band of hikers who happened to be at Speck Pond that night had made ourselves into a family.

jackrabbit

"So this is Mahoosuc Notch." Isis peered at the trail ahead. "The hardest mile on the Trail, they say." The bottom of the steep-sided valley was a jumble of boulders, some the size of Volkswagens. We could see white blazes spattered haphazardly over the rocks, marking a way through the maze.

I kept quiet and concentrated on my footing. At that moment, I couldn't imagine anything harder than what we had just come down: Mahoosuc Arm, a 1,600-foot drop in less than a mile and a half. The trail had been a scramble of open rock faces, and in many places we had lowered ourselves down by grabbing spruce roots. The Nestuntabunt Five-wheel Drive, the Bodfish Squat, and the Piscataquis Pirouette made frequent appearances. It would have been almost fun, but for the pain in my hip. The bone-jarring descent had reawakened the ache, and even the extra-strength "vitamin I" did little to relieve it.

In the Notch, we crawled over, under, and around the tilted boulders, swinging from tree roots and tiny handholds. It was less like hiking than like bouldering—except for the forty-pound weight on my back. I was glad to be barefoot. My feet curled around the edges of stones, forming themselves to the sheer surfaces, gripping the rock better than any pair of boots.

The pain in my hip lessened, and gradually I was able to focus on the beauty of the place. Huge rocks overhung the trail, some covered in ferns and moss, and some so steep no plant could gain a foothold. On either side, the forested walls of the notch closed in, showing only a narrow strip of the overcast sky. In places, a far-off sound of water came from below, and deep crevices between the rocks exhaled a chilly wind.

"This is kind of spooky," Isis said, in a fern-shaded space between rocks where our breath made smoke in the suddenly cold air.

"It's the Icy Breath of Doom." I made a scary face. "If you stop for too long, it will reach up from the depths and claim you!"

"One of those guys at Speck Pond said there's still snow down here, under the darkest rocks. It doesn't melt until August."

"Excellent! I wonder if we'll see it!"

We came around a bend in the trail, gingerly lowered ourselves down a rock face, and looked for the next blaze. Instead of the usual rectangle of paint, there was a white arrow. It pointed straight toward a cave in the rock, angled downward into the pile of boulders, which looked barely wide enough for my shoulders.

"We're supposed to go in there?" My throat tightened involuntarily. I've never been fond of small, dark, enclosed spaces. A wisp of cold air floated out of the entrance.

Isis was already heading for the cave. She took her pack off and leaned it against the rock. "Here, pass this to me when I get through."

"Be careful. You don't know how far down it goes."

In a moment I heard her voice come back. "Okay. Pass it through."

I heaved her pack as far as I could into the dark opening, and she grabbed it from the other side. "Now yours."

"I think I can fit through with my pack on." The cave looked wider than it had at first.

"Suit yourself."

I ducked under the low entrance, and into the chilly air of the cave. It had a scent of old stone, moss and water. The walls were damp. It was only a short ways, I saw now—another few feet and I would be standing in the light of day again. And then I saw the ice.

"Oh, Isis, it's here! There really is snow in here! Old snow; it's almost all granulated and turned to ice . . ." It glinted blue from the base of the cave wall. Snow in July. It seemed a minor miracle. I leaned down lower, trying to reach it, and my pack caught on something on the cave ceiling. When I tried to straighten up, it threw me off balance and I landed on the cold stones, the full weight of the pack on top of me. I wriggled like a hooked fish, and my pack caught in another place. Cold water from the cave wall dripped onto my head, feeling like icy fingers running through my hair. Panic welled up in me.

"Isis, I can't get out. I'm stuck!" I unbuckled my hip belt and struggled against my pack, frantically trying to get my arms out of their straps, but I couldn't get free. "Help me! Help me!" I was almost screaming.

Isis leaned down into the cave. "Icy Breath of Doom got you?" She assessed the situation. "It might help if you unbuckle your chest strap."

Of course. How many weeks had I worn this pack now? How many times had I taken it off? There were two steps to the process: undo the hip belt, and unfasten the little chest strap that held the shoulder straps together. Then it was easy to slip it off. How could I forget something so elementary? I had to laugh as I crawled out of the hole, brushing the mud off my wet clothes and dragging my pack behind me. *This is why I spell my name with a lowercase j*, I thought.

The trail led up into the Mahoosuc Range, in southwestern Maine, a line of imposing 3,500-foot peaks and ridges. It was glorious to be there on these cool, sunny days; not even the prospect of Little Debbie snacks for every lunch could dim our enthusiasm (though I doubt that either of us will ever voluntarily ingest another Captain Nemo Frosted Banana Bar). As we hiked up the broad granite slopes, full-sized spruce and fir gave way to stunted krummholz, tiny clumps of trees battered by the wind. Along the ridge tops, depressions in the pale granite held heath bogs, full of tiny colorful plants: mountain cranberry, cotton grass, heather, cloudberry.

In one patch of woods, a low saddle between the open summits, we found a plywood sign tacked to a tree. It bore a crude outline of the state of New Hampshire painted in red on a white background, and the words *Your in NH Now*. We stared at it for a while.

"Well." Isis said. "Our first state line."

"Is it just me, or is there something a little ominous about that sign? Not 'Welcome to New Hampshire.' Not even grammatically correct! I have to say, after 281 miles, this is a bit of an anticlimax."

"What did you expect, a bunch of angels to start singing all around you?" My sister shrugged. "Here we go." And we walked into woods just like the ones we had left.

That night we stayed at Gentian Pond Lean-to, a large shelter with one of the best views yet. Through a gap in the trees, we could see the Presidential Range looming across the valley, its gray-blue shapes filling half the overcast sky.

"Beautiful mountains," Isis said.

"But scary-looking. Hulking. Man, I hope we get good weather going across there."

"Me, too. I've heard the views are absolutely awesome."

I collected twigs for the Zip stove and went to the pond to fill our cooking pot. By the time I had boiled the water and stirred in the instant potato flakes, clouds covered the entire Presidential Range in a swirling blanket of white.

CHAPTER 3

The White Mountains

jackrabbit

A beat-up green Dodge ground to a halt on the gravel beside us, and the driver rolled down the window and shouted over to us, "thru-hikers?" We smiled and nodded. "Hop in!"

We loaded two packs into the trunk. Isis and Blade clambered into the backseat with the third. The powerful reek of week-old sweat filled up the hot interior of the car, but the driver seemed not to mind.

"I hiked northbound in '88," he said. As we sped down the two-lane road to Gorham, New Hampshire, we exchanged names and hiking stories. He stopped in the driveway of a large B&B at the edge of town. The gray building just ahead of us, an old hay barn, had an A.T. sign by the door, and a crowd of familiar people lounged on the strip of lawn beside the driveway.

"Welcome to The Barn," the driver said. A look of nostalgia stole over his face, a bemused mixture of joy and regret that we would see on the faces of many ex-hikers when they talked about the Trail. "Make the most of your hike. It doesn't last forever."

We thanked him, and the battered station wagon pulled out of the drive and was lost in the stream of traffic.

Inside the Barn, the accommodations were fairly basic: a common room downstairs with a TV and VCR, board games, magazines, and fuzzy plaid-upholstered armchairs that had seen better days. Someone pointed out the side door, where we could enter the back of the house for showers, laundry, and a bathroom. Up a rickety wooden staircase in back, we came to the bunkroom. The old hayloft floor was covered with mattresses. Clothing, gear, packs, groceries, and food bags filled the interstices.

Blade took one look around and headed across the street to the Alpine Tourist Home. "I like my privacy," he said. We did convince him to join us for supper at Mr. Pizza that night.

As Isis and I unpacked our dirty laundry in the quiet shade of the bunkroom, Waterfall and Matt came up to talk. O.D. and Bugbiter had gone on, they said, and Blue Skies and Tenbrooks were leaving that afternoon.

"I'll probably leave in a couple hours, too," Matt said, glancing out the window to the bright blue sky.

"So soon?"

"I already took a zero!"

My heart sank as I realized how far we were behind everyone else. Ever since our zero day in Rangeley, we'd been struggling to stay with them, and now at last we would fall behind for good. There was no way we could take showers, do our laundry, resupply, and be back on the Trail before dark. Even if we somehow managed to keep up this time, we'd never be able to in the next town. I thought of all the nights we'd spent together, laughing, singing, telling stories. "I guess this is it, then."

"Yeah, I guess so." Matt's thin, freckled face didn't betray much emotion. "It's all about flow, jackrabbit. People come, people go. Things change. You ride the river. You can't get too attached to the way things are. Attach yourself to change, because *that* is the only constant in the universe." A wry smile played about his lips.

"Do you really believe that?"

"I try."

He left, heading downstairs. Waterfall remained behind, seated on the edge of an old pink mattress. "I'm gonna stay with y'all," she said. "I've been thinkin' about it, and I just don't want to be by myself through the Whites, with all I've heard about the weather up there. Y'all are some of the best friends I've found on the Trail . . ."

I got up and hugged her.

"Thanks, Waterfall," Isis said. "I'll hug you, too—after I've had a shower!"

At a bookstore just down the street from the hostel, we shelled out the money for a copy of *Harry Potter and the Goblet of Fire*. Hardcover. We had debated endlessly with ourselves and each other: is it worth the weight? In the end, the prospect of truly entertaining trail reading had won out.

I hefted the tome as we walked back to the Barn. "Is this really just two and a half pounds?"

"That's what *Time* magazine said. Besides, I'm going to carry it."

Matt, Blue Skies, and Tenbrooks caught a shuttle out of town in the early afternoon. The rest of us, a motley crew of southbounders and a few northbounders, convened at Mr. Pizza at 6:30. The waitress pulled three tables together and distributed menus.

"This looks interesting," said one of the northbounders, pointing at the bottom of the menu. "The Stomper," he read aloud. "One hundred and ninety-two square inches of our famous Sicilian-crust pizza. A feast for the whole family! Plain cheese, $14.95, add a topping for $1 ... Has anybody ever eaten a whole Stomper by himself?" he asked the waitress.

"Gee, I don't know," she said, looking faintly alarmed. "I don't think so. It's, like, a whole lotta pizza."

"What would you do if I did?"

"We'd probably, I don't know, put your picture up in the restaurant or something. But it's, like, really huge . . ."

"Cool! I'll have a Stomper."

"Plain cheese?"

"Plain cheese."

We all made our orders, and the food had begun arriving when Blade appeared in the doorway, his hair freshly combed and his beard trimmed neatly. He sat down at the end of the table, next to the guy with the Stomper.

"That's an enormous amount of pizza," he said.

"Yeah, it's called a Stomper. The waitress said nobody'd ever eaten a whole one before . . ." The nobo needn't have said anything more. I looked over at Isis and Waterfall and shared a rueful smile. We could see it coming—the light of the Quest was gleaming in Blade's eyes.

He signaled to the waitress. "Bring me a Stomper. With sausage."

Isis and I finished our large veggie pizza, onion rings, and salad and turned our attention to the drama taking place at the end of the table. With an effort, the nobo raised the last piece of his Stomper and folded it in half. The cheese had cooled and hardened; a coating of yellow grease clung to the thick crust. Bite by bite, it vanished. He held the empty pan over his head, and the waitress came by, shaking her head, looking both impressed and appalled. She snapped a Polaroid while the rest of the hikers at the table cheered and hooted. All but one.

Blade sat at the end of the table, glowering, two pieces of pizza left on his tray. He waited until the noise had died down, and solemnly intoned, "uneasy is the head that wears the crown."

He made a sandwich out of the two slices and munched it down as we all watched. Then he wiped his hands on a napkin and sat back from the table. "And *my* Stomper," he announced in a severe tone, "had a topping."

We left Gorham late in the afternoon of the following day, burdened down with nearly a week's worth of food. We had shipped a box ahead to ourselves at Crawford Notch, fifty miles away. That night, we stayed at Rattle River Shelter, a grungy brown Forest Service lean-to a few miles from the road.

"It's the last free shelter for eighty miles," Waterfall said. "Better enjoy it while we can." The Appalachian Mountain Club (AMC) runs a series of pay campsites and full-service huts—practically motels—in the White Mountains. The trouble for thru-hikers, besides the price, is that you need reservations far in advance. We scarcely knew where we would be a week from now, let alone a few months ahead. Northbounders had told us that the huts let a few hikers work in exchange for lodging, and spaces opened up occasionally in the shelters and tent sites. Given the number of thru-hikers passing through the Whites right now, though, we knew we couldn't count on any lodging between Gorham and Glencliff.

The next day, we climbed more than three thousand feet, heading into the Carter-Moriah range. As we struggled up the trail, we watched the vegetation change around us; the lowland forest of maples and birch gave way to evergreens, spruce, and fir like the forests of northern Maine. The air cooled noticeably. It was a clear, cloudless day, and from the highest peaks we could look across to the crags and ledges of Mount Washington. The forests on its lower flanks diminished to small patches of green on the upper slopes. Near the summit, it seemed that nothing grew. The observatory building cut into the skyline, and the auto road was a zigzag scar on the mountain's flank. Cars were visible only as occasional glitters traversing the surface. As we watched, a puff of black, greasy smoke from the Cog Railway rose from behind the mountain.

In midafternoon, we went down to Imp Campsite for water. The first AMC campsite, it was larger than most A.T. campsites we had seen, with many spaces for tents and a two-level shelter. I relaxed on the cool wooden floor of the first level, reading the register, while Isis and Waterfall filtered water from the stream nearby. Matt, O.D., and Bugbiter were a day ahead now. I smiled to myself as I read their entries:

Our sources tell us, Matt wrote, *that G. W. Bush is planning to announce his candidacy from the peak of Mount Washington this weekend! Be on the lookout for Secret Service agents.* I could barely decipher Bugbiter's untidy scrawl: *I saw two guys yesterday hiking in suits and carrying briefcases instead of packs. What gives?*

As we headed back to the trail, a woman in her mid-twenties came up the path. "Hi, I'm the caretaker," she said in a breezy voice. "Are you staying here tonight?"

"Well, actually . . ." Isis said.

"You're going to camp at Zeta Pass, aren't you? We discourage people from doing that."

"Why? Is it an ecologically sensitive area?"

"Not really. You actually can stay there, as long as you're two hundred feet from the trail and the water source. We just don't like people to camp right by the trail." She surveyed us for a moment, taking in our sweat-stained clothing and grimy packs. "It doesn't look good."

We camped that night at Zeta Pass, in a clearing well under two hundred feet from the trail. It was almost dusk when we arrived, and all of us were sore and tired. My hip throbbed from the relentless steep uphills and downhills. Nobody felt like tramping off in the darkening spruce woods, full of fallen limbs and thick brush, to look for an approved campsite.

I was a little discouraged when we looked at the map. Traveling from shortly after dawn to the edge of twilight, we had hiked just over ten miles. On the Maine maps, with their larger scale, this would have corresponded to a respectable eight inches. On the New Hampshire map, it covered barely four. The rest of the map stretched out, miles upon miles of punishing terrain. Every few inches, the elevation profile dipped down into a U-shaped valley with almost vertical sides: a notch. Each inch on the map would mean hours and hours of hard hiking, I reminded myself. We had been on the Trail for more than a month, hiking every day but one, and I felt like I was in good shape. But was I in good enough shape for this?

Isis was still fuming about the Imp caretaker. "It doesn't *look* good," she grumbled. "What are we, L.L. Bean models?"

"I think they prob'ly don't want people gettin' the idea they can camp just anywhere," Waterfall said.

"Why, so they can charge them more money?"

"No," I said. "I think it's . . . well, thru-hikers tend to be responsible with our, you know, waste. They just don't want inexperienced campers fouling the water source."

Isis was not convinced. "Hmph. But two hundred feet off the trail? It's not like we take a crap right where we pitch the tent anyway! I still think it's all about appearances. Thru-hikers just don't *look* good. We don't come up to the mountains for a weekend in our SUVs, with our hair and makeup perfect, wearing the latest in outdoor styles . . ."

"Maybe we need to change the public perception of thru-hikers," I said. "Sure, we don't look good by AMC standards. Maybe instead of trying to blend in with other humans, we should style ourselves after the wildlife. What we need is an informational sign, here at Zeta Pass, about thru-hikers. It could have, you know, our feeding habits, our migratory path, how to spot us in the wild . . ."

"Right!" Waterfall joined in. "With one of those seventies-style line drawings, like a park brochure, with people in ratty tank-tops settin' up tents, filterin' water . . ."

I put on my best David Attenborough voice. "The southbound thru-hiker, somewhat less common than the northbound subtype, can be spotted in the White Mountains in July and August. Look for their distinctive bug bite scars . . ."

Isis took out her flashlight and read a chapter of *Harry Potter* while I stirred our pot of polenta and beans. The contrast between wizards and muggles seemed to mirror our situation on the Trail—we thru-hikers were a cadre with secret esoteric knowledge: how to stealth camp without leaving a trace, how to hike for hours without tiring, how to subsist for days at a time on ramen and Little Debbie snacks. The rest of the world, just outside this corridor of woods, had no inkling of our ways and traditions and probably would be frightened to find out about them. I felt my spirits lifting as the story swept me away. Already the book had proved worth its weight.

A fiery sunset lit up the gaps between the trees. As it faded, wisps of high clouds along the western horizon caught the failing light and a few stars appeared between the shaggy branches overhead.

At noon the next day, we came down the steep, boulder-strewn side of Carter Notch. It was as bad as it had looked on the map. My hip ached constantly on the way down. I tried to focus on the trail in front of me and ignore the fact that beyond Carter Notch, with its 1,500-foot drop, we would have to climb up the other side, and then descend into Pinkham Notch, more than 2,000 feet deep. I was beginning to dread the word "notch" on the map, even more than I had dreaded the word "bog" in the Hundred Mile Wilderness.

At last we reached the bottom of the valley. I had to admit that the view was splendid, no matter how sadistic the approach had seemed. The wall of the notch loomed over us. Looking back, we could see a jumble of huge white boulders dotting the hillside, dwarfing the spruce trees around them. A small tarn in the bottom of the notch reflected the steep walls on either side. Isis stopped to take a picture of water lilies by the shore.

Just then the sun went behind clouds. "You guys go ahead," Isis said. "I'll meet you at the hut for lunch. I just want to wait for the sun to come back out so I can get a good picture."

The hut, a squat brown wooden building nestled among trees, was perhaps a five-minute walk from the pond. It was practically deserted at midday. A few people sat at the picnic tables inside. Waterfall and I sat on the steps of the porch. I tried to ration out my share of the crackers, waiting for Isis.

She caught up in about twenty minutes, looking grumpy. "The sun didn't come back," she said. "I waited there forever, and it didn't come out." We looked up. The sky, which had been blue with tiny wisps of cloud when we entered the notch, was now a mass of swirling gray. The clouds descended rapidly as we watched, and soon the mountains towering above us were hidden in fog.

"I've got a bad feeling about this," Isis said.

The trail over Wildcat Mountain was a series of steep ups and downs, and the thick, clammy mist that gathered around us obscured everything but a narrow strip of trees on either side. Isis went ahead, Waterfall in the middle, and I took up the rear, as we painstakingly maneuvered up and down small cliff faces.

Waterfall leaned heavily on her trekking poles. "What peak is this?"

Isis said, "I think it's Peak C."

"No, I'm sure this is the fourth one. It's got to be Peak D."

"Whoever thought of namin' peaks after the letters of the alphabet, anyway?" Waterfall said. "'Cause what if there's an extra one, like between Third Mountain and Fourth Mountain in the Wilderness? You just can't have a peak called B-and-a-half Kickin'-ass!"

We entertained each other with stories and jokes, trying to ignore the wet weather, until we came to the edge of Pinkham Notch. The clouds swirled and cleared below us for a moment, revealing the road at the bottom. Cars were small as beetles, whizzing past. Then the clouds closed in again. We looked at each other. I knew my face mirrored the worry and exhaustion I saw in Isis and Waterfall's eyes. The wind was rising, moaning in the trees around us.

We took the descent slowly, sometimes turning around to scramble backwards over a particularly steep section. Waiting for Isis and Waterfall to get down the tough pitches, I shivered inside my Gore-Tex and jumped from foot to foot to stay warm. My knees hurt from the long downhill grade. Little drops of water built up like silver beads on my hair.

Everything went well until the last set of rock steps. My attention wavered for an instant, just as a gust of wind threw me off balance. I slipped, sliding perhaps three feet down the mountain and landing hard on a small rock ledge below. I took almost all the impact on the ball of my right foot. Even with the huge doses of ibuprofen I was taking for my hip, I could tell I had done some damage. I cursed vehemently and leaned back against the rock to examine my foot. I wasn't bleeding, and nothing seemed to be broken—gingerly poking the foot, I couldn't find any spots of excruciating pain. But a dark bruise was blossoming as I watched.

"Jackrabbit, are you okay?" Waterfall and Isis were clambering back up the trail toward me.

"Yeah—shit!—I just slipped, but I'm okay." I found I was able to walk. I edged back to the trail along the ledge, trying not to look down. I put my right foot down carefully, balancing most of the weight on my heel and the outer edge of the foot. It was painful when a stone poked directly into the bruise, but I was skillful enough at walking barefoot that this seldom happened. I popped another ibuprofen and we kept walking—scrambling, really—downward into the darkening mist.

Inwardly, I was cursing myself for that moment of inattention. I didn't want anyone to know how badly my foot hurt, not even Isis. When we had started hiking barefoot, I had never meant to prove anything. As the miles went by, though, people's incredulous reactions had fueled my desire to stay barefoot. In the back of my mind, I remembered all the people who had called us crazy, or dismissed us as some kind of freaks, or told us we would never make it through the Whites. Like a Greek chorus, their images had stayed with me, commenting on the action. Sometimes I pictured their surprise and chagrin as I skillfully navigated a rough section of trail or clambered up bare rock. Every step I took was a victory over their disbelief. Now I felt them gathering close, leaning in to inspect the damage, and pronouncing their collective smug, self-satisfied "I told you so."

Isis

We had planned to get through the Whites by stealth camping, or "stealthing," hiker slang for tenting in an unofficial spot. The White Mountains in New Hampshire are one of the few places on the Trail where stealthing is prohibited, presumably due to overuse and erosion. (After our run-in with the Imp caretaker, I felt rather cynical about this rationale.) In any case, I was confident that Waterfall, jackrabbit, and I had enough outdoor experience to camp in relatively non-sensitive areas and leave no trace of our tent sites in the morning. Nerve-wracking at first, the uncertainty about where we'd sleep and find water became a challenge for us, a shared trial that cemented our friendship and bolstered our confidence as hikers.

On the way up Mount Madison, though, our plans for stealth and self-sufficiency fell apart. Near treeline, Waterfall started feeling ill. We considered turning around and hiking the few miles back to Osgood Tentsite, one of the few official campsites in the Presidentials, but Madison Hut was much closer. I wanted to get Waterfall to a place where she could rest as soon as possible.

A bitter wind drove cold mist over the ridges; by the time we reached the hut, Waterfall was wet and shivering as well as nauseated. She and jackrabbit and I crowded through the hut's doorway, pulled the door shut behind us, and looked around in astonishment. Only moments before, in the howling wind and drizzle, we'd been stumbling down slick rocks, fighting hypothermia, struggling to get Waterfall to safety. Now, inside the hut, we huddled in the corner of a bright room, ignored by the clean, well-dressed people who stood around sipping mugs of tea or playing card games at the varnished pine tables along the walls. I was used to crowding into an eight-person shelter with nine other hikers or sleeping shoulder-to-shoulder with jackrabbit in our tent. This room seemed far too calm, spacious, and well-lit to exist on the top of a mountain.

We were trying to dry Waterfall's hair with our tiny pack towel when a member of the hut crew came bustling over. She glanced at our stained, ragged clothing, and our pack covers patched with duct tape.

"Do you have reservations?" she asked.

"We're thru-hikers," I answered. "We were hoping to work for stay."

"There are three of you," she said. "We only take two thru-hikers per night."

"Our friend is sick . . ."

"I'll get the Hut Master," the worker said. "Maybe she can help you out."

The Hut Master was friendly but brusque. No, she was sorry, she couldn't possibly let an extra thru-hiker spend the night; they were overbooked with paying guests already. That said, we were welcome to stay long enough to dry ourselves off, and she'd have someone bring a cup of tea for Waterfall.

I looked around the room in which we stood. It was as big as six shelters. Two doors at the back of it led to bunkrooms; surely, none of the paying guests would be spending the night in the dining room. Outside, the drizzle had turned to rain, which lashed against the windows violently as the wind rose higher.

"Please," I said. "We could sleep under the tables; we don't take up much space."

"You can't do that unless you're in the work-for-stay program. Like I said, there are too many of you."

As she walked away, a man who was standing nearby turned toward us. "I couldn't help overhearing your conversation," he said. "I have a spare bunk; I reserved it for a friend of mine, who wasn't able to join me . . ."

Thank goodness, I thought, *a trail angel.*

". . . so, you could buy it from me," he finished.

We weren't in any position to bargain, and he knew it. We pulled out the plastic bags we used as wallets and scraped together enough cash to pay him. With one of us taken care of, the Hut Master agreed to let the other two work for stay. Jackrabbit and I made sure that Waterfall was comfortable, then asked if there was some work we could do.

"No," said the Hut Master, "not at the moment. You can help us serve the guests' supper, and you can wash dishes afterwards, but most of the work you'll be doing is in the morning."

I explained that we hiked very slowly, and asked if there was anything we could do that evening, so that we wouldn't get too late a start the next day.

"Oh, don't worry about that," she said. "If you're up at six, you can be out of here by nine. You just have to help us serve breakfast and clean the hut afterwards."

Jackrabbit, Waterfall, and I were up promptly at six, but no one else was. Waterfall felt much better after a good night's sleep; she was sure she could hike the thirteen miles we needed to cover that day, as long as we got an early enough start. We packed our gear quietly, then stepped outside to see if the weather had improved since the previous day.

I'd thought the white sky I saw through the windows was overcast, but when I stepped through the door, I realized that it was the eggshell color of predawn. Already a rosy glow illumined the east. When I looked in that direction, I caught my breath; an ocean of clouds filled the valley, its slow surf swirling and eddying around the cliffs of Mount Madison. A lower mountain range, cloaked in dark spruce forest, formed a series of islands in the milky sea. As the sun rose, its beams glazed the cloud-crests red, then bathed the whole valley in a radiant gold light in which the clouds dissolved. The morning sky stretched from east to west, a solid canopy of dazzling blue. Perhaps the White Mountains would be good to us after all.

Around seven, we heard the hut crew stirring, so we went back inside. I told the Hut Master about the sea of clouds, but she didn't seem too impressed.

"Yeah, we get that a lot up here," she told me.

"What can we do to help y'all?" Waterfall asked.

"Um . . . you could serve the food when it's ready," the Hut Master offered. "All the cooking chores are assigned to the crew."

I got out our Harry Potter book and read aloud to pass the time. Things weren't going very well for our hero. "Harry's spirits descended several notches," I read.

Jackrabbit and Waterfall groaned at this image, then we all started to laugh. Two days before, as we lowered ourselves down the steep ledges of our second notch, our knees aching, we had decided that the term "notch" deserved to be used as an expletive.

Breakfast was served around 8:15, and we had another long wait while the paying guests ate. After we helped the crew clear the tables, they ate, then offered us their leftovers: half a serving bowl of congealed oatmeal and two pancakes. It was well past nine, and we were getting frustrated with all the delays.

"Notch this!" exclaimed jackrabbit. "They told you we could leave by nine, didn't they? Let's just go. They can't stop us."

"We've hardly done any work yet," I answered. "I feel like I should fulfill my part of this bargain, even if I didn't know what I was in for."

"I'll help y'all," said Waterfall. "With all of us workin', it won't take long to clean this place up!"

It was almost 10:30 by the time we left. In spite of the clear dawn, the day was rapidly degenerating into a repeat of the past few days' weather. By the time we reached the slopes of Mount Washington, clouds scudded over the ridges, opening every once in a while to reveal a hundred-foot drop-off beside the trail, then coalescing again, obscuring everything more than ten feet away. Suddenly, a long, screechy hoot sounded in the fog beside us.

"The Cog!" cried jackrabbit. "Ladies, it's now or never!"

"They won't see us through this fog," said Waterfall.

"Then we'll have to get closer. Follow me!"

A northbounder in Gorham had told us that mooning the Cog Railway was a thru-hiker tradition. The trains, he told us, use one ton of coal for each ascent of the mountain. Mooning them was a way for hikers, who'd gotten up the mountain with the strength of their own legs, to protest such a waste of resources. He warned us that the conductor would throw coal at us—this was, apparently, the conductors' way of demonstrating their power to waste as much coal as they wanted to.

We'd been debating whether to do it for the past few days. Jackrabbit was all for it. I had some serious reservations. I'd never mooned strangers before, and I wasn't entirely convinced by the nobo's story. What if he'd been playing a practical joke on us? Why hadn't anyone else told us about this "tradition"? Waterfall, who had never mooned anyone, tended to side with me, though she did say, "If y'all decide to do it, I guess I will."

When push came to shove, we were both caught up in jackrabbit's enthusiasm. The clouds parted at just the right moment; we all turned around and dropped trou as the train went past. If there was any aspect of protest in our performance, it was lost on the passengers; they leaned out the windows cheering and snapping photos. ("I'm sure my ass is somewhere on the Internet—www.mycogexperience.com," jackrabbit later commented.) The conductor played his role in the drama with more zeal than we'd anticipated, and we had to scramble up a talus slope, away from the tracks, amid a veritable hail of coal chunks. One of them hit Waterfall's hand hard enough to give her a bruise. On the whole, however, we agreed that our raid on the tracks had been a success. Skipping along the trail, congratulating each other on our membership in "the other AMC—the Association of Mooners of the Cog," we felt more lighthearted than we had since entering the Whites. Even the weather seemed to respond to our cheer; the clouds drew back, exposing a dramatic granite ridgeline, edged with cliffs and rockslides. Far below us, in a wooded valley, a tiny patch of sun gilded the treetops.

We were halfway around the mountain before any of us noticed what was wrong. Waterfall paused and pulled out her map. She frowned at the paper. "Y'all, aren't we supposed to go *over* this mountain, not around it?"

I looked up and down the trail: no white blazes in sight. We hiked back the way we'd come; sure enough, at the Cog tracks, we'd been in such a hurry to escape the conductor's coal that we'd gone in the wrong direction. As soon as we started toward the peak, the clouds closed over us. The higher we climbed, the darker they grew. Soon a thin, driving rain began to fall.

"No matter what the map says, I'm not so sure we should go over this mountain. It doesn't seem to like us," I said.

Jackrabbit grimaced. "Yeah, I get the same feeling."

"It's me," said Waterfall glumly. "This happens every time I go campin' or get to a mountain peak. Y'all remember that hailstorm in the Bigelows? I was on West Peak when it started. On my prep hike for the A.T., I nearly drowned in a flash flood. And one time, when there was a drought in Georgia, a friend of mine who lives down there asked me to camp in her backyard. It worked; there was a storm that night and the drought ended. That's one of the reasons for my name. I make water fall from the sky. I'm sorry, y'all. I shouldn't have come with you."

She looked terribly despondent, with rain dripping off the ends of her blond pigtails. I cast about for anything I might say to cheer her.

"It's not you," I said. "The weather in the Whites is notoriously bad. You can't take the blame for it. It's controlled by—by Murphy, the guy who made up Murphy's Law. You know, 'anything that can go wrong, will go wrong.'"

"Yeah," said jackrabbit, catching on. "The Evil Poltergeist Murphy. He was the only poltergeist in history clever enough to get himself elected to Congress. But he blew it when he wrote that law. Too controversial."

"So how'd he end up controllin' the weather in a beautiful place like this?" Waterfall gestured toward the few feet of rockslide that were all we had for a view at that moment.

We were a hundred yards from the peak when the sky turned to water. I've never seen anything like it, even in Southern thunderstorms where the pent-up heat of August afternoons crackles through the clouds, loosing a deluge. It felt as though someone had turned on an enormous faucet over my head; I could scarcely breathe. On either side of me, I saw Waterfall and jackrabbit struggling through the same wall of water. After what seemed like hours, we reached the observatory at the peak and flung ourselves under a corner of the roof.

"You were right," gasped Waterfall. "That wasn't me. I've brought on some pretty bad weather in my life, but I don't have the keys to Niagara."

"Notch Murphy!" said jackrabbit.

After losing so much time at Madison Hut, we avoided doing any more work-for-stays in the Whites, but we couldn't escape Murphy. Drizzle and cold fog soaked our clothes and wrinkled the skin of our hands and feet as if we'd spent too long in the bathtub. The hordes of dayhikers who crowded the peaks began to plague us also. All they ever wanted to talk about was our feet, and they all asked the same four or five questions. Nine out of ten began the conversation by exclaiming, "Barefoot! Are you crazy?" The other one out of ten, thinking himself very clever, asked sarcastically, "Have you forgotten something?" Some wanted to poke the soles of our feet, others wanted to take pictures. Most of them ignored Waterfall outright, but a few snidely asked her why she was wearing boots.

"Probably for the same reason you are," she'd quip with her habitual good humor, but I could see that her smile didn't reach her eyes.

On the day we hiked down from Mount Washington, we must have crossed paths with fifty or sixty dayhikers: five "Have you forgotten something?"'s, and so many people skeptical about our sanity that we lost count. Early in the day, a man had asked to take a photo of us, and then, when we all posed with our arms around each other's shoulders, he'd peered suspiciously over his camera and asked Waterfall what she was doing in the picture. Jackrabbit and I stood there with our mouths hanging open, too shocked to tell him off. He must've gotten a picture in which we looked as stupid as all the dayhikers seemed to think we were.

By the late afternoon, jackrabbit and I sighed aloud each time a human form appeared in the fog ahead of us, and even Waterfall had stopped trying to get in a "Hi, how are you?" before the questions about our feet started. We had just reached treeline, and we were looking forward to finding ourselves a stealth site soon, when we ran into a family of four: father, mother, and two sullen-looking teens, all dressed as if they'd stepped out of the pages of an outdoor apparel catalog. The father, in the lead, assailed us with the usual questions.

"Barefoot! Are you crazy? Doesn't it hurt? Why are you doing that to yourselves? Are you some kind of religious martyrs or something?"

We gave him the usual answers.

"We do this because it's comfortable for us. I stub my toes every once in a while, but that hurts for a few minutes and heals in a few days. I've seen hikers with boots whose blisters lasted for weeks. I guess there is something religious about walking barefoot—being in touch with the earth—but not martyrdom, kind of the opposite. And yes, we are crazy."

With this last pronouncement, jackrabbit gave him a grin that must have more than satisfied his curiosity on that point. "Er, well, okay," he muttered and walked off down the trail. His family followed, and as the second teenager shoved past us, she carelessly kicked the hiking stick on which Waterfall was balancing most of her weight. The girl didn't even stop to apologize.

Jackrabbit helped Waterfall to her feet, and we all sat down on a nearby ledge.

"Y'all know I have trouble with my balance," Waterfall said as she got to her feet. "I fall down all the time anyway. But when a person *makes* me fall . . ." Her voice trailed off. Tears were streaming down her cheeks.

I leaned over and gave her a one-armed hug, then reached into the top of my pack and pulled out the extra-dark bar of French chocolate that my mom had sent us in Gorham. Mustering all the poise and authority I could, I announced, "This is a situation that calls for chocolate."

The chocolate, a cozy stealth site, and a few chapters of *Harry Potter* put us all in better humor; still, my faith in human kindness was at a pretty low ebb when we stopped to check the register at Mizpah Hut the next morning. We were flipping through the heavy, leather-bound tome, hoping to find some message from our friends ahead, when a shadow fell across the page. I looked up to see a smiling young man in an AMC apron, holding out a tray with three enormous slices of carrot cake.

"Would you like some cake?" he asked.

"I'm sorry, I don't have any money," I told him.

His eyes widened a little behind his glasses. "I'm not selling it. I'm giving it to you. You don't need money."

He put the tray down and backed away a few steps, as though offering food to a shy and potentially dangerous animal.

"Thank you, this is a real treat," said Waterfall, reaching for a slice.

"Thanks," I mumbled, through a mouthful of cake.

"Yeah, thanks," said jackrabbit, "this is awesome!"

The words of gratitude seemed to encourage the young man; he stepped forward again, then sat down on the bench across from us.

"Say, are you the sisters I heard about, the ones who hike barefoot?" he asked.

"Yeah, that's us," said jackrabbit, tipping her head toward me.

"Wow. How does it feel?"

"Great," she answered. "Every stretch of trail has a different texture; spruce needles feel soft and a little springy, like a carpet, moss is even softer, like walking on feathers, and the granite backs of mountains—when the sun warms them, it feels like you're walking on the scales of sleeping dragons."

"That sounds wonderful. Maybe I should try it." He turned toward Waterfall. "Are you thru-hiking too? Southbound? Cool. I've heard that people who go southbound tend to be the more experienced hikers—you have to know what you're doing if you start with the Hundred Mile Wilderness. Did anything on the trail surprise you?"

"I've been plannin' this hike for ten years," she answered, "collectin' the gear I needed, readin' people's trail journals on the Internet, goin' on short backpackin' trips on my weeks off from work. Every day when I wake up I'm surprised to be here, doin' what I've always dreamed of."

jackrabbit

As we descended into Crawford Notch, we traded stories to keep our spirits up. The fog and rain continued, and it was chilly on the high slopes. My foot still hurt. The insistent pain of the first day had given way to a dull ache that occupied a distant corner of my brain. My knees worried me more—they were beginning to feel as though they contained tiny grains of sand. I tried not to think about what kind of damage these nonstop notches were doing. My hip was painful, too. I stretched every morning before leaving the tent, and it seemed to help for a while.

"Did y'all ever watch *Gilligan's Island*?" Waterfall asked.

"No, we never had TV growing up," Isis said.

I grabbed a spruce tree and lowered myself down to the next ledge of crumbly brown rock in a modified Piscataquis Pirouette. "Explains why we're not fit for muggle society."

"Y'all missed out!" She giggled. "I used to have a thing for Gilligan. When I was about five, I was convinced I'd marry him when I grew up!"

"I used to have a thing for Captain Kirk," Isis said, a bit sheepishly. "Our Aunt Nancy has a whole bunch of Star Trek tapes, and she used to let us watch them when we visited. The old Star Trek, you know, the classic series."

"Oh, that was such a great show!" Waterfall sat down on a rock momentarily, doing a Nesuntabunt Five-wheel Drive.

"I think my favorite thing about it was the sets." Isis turned around to scramble backwards down a steep pitch of rock. "You could tell that everything was made of paper mâché and tinfoil. It was so . . . so campy."

"Yeah, and you always kind of knew what was going to happen," I said. "Like, Captain Kirk falls in love with a beautiful woman, and you just know she'll be dead before the episode is over. Or if one of the crew people, what do you call them . . ."

"Redshirts."

"Thanks, Isis. If a redshirt beams down to a planet without any of the main characters, you know something bad is going to happen."

Our talking made the steep, knee-grinding descent go by faster. My legs shook from effort, and my hip hurt, but I was still so glad to be on the Trail. The air felt warmer down in the valley. Just before the final descent the clouds lifted a little, giving us a view of a deciduous forest in high summer green and the bottom of a cliff face across the way. The clouds still cut off the walls of the notch above us; it was impossible to tell how far we had come down or how far we would have to ascend the next day. It was strange to see the bright green of the leaves—on the ridges everything had been gray with mist, subdued and colorless. It had been so cold up there I had half expected to descend into autumn, although it was just the end of July.

Where the trail crossed the Saco River, we saw a young hiker filtering water. He had a kind-looking heart-shaped face and close-cropped blond hair, and he wore a red shirt the exact color of the old Star Trek crew uniforms. My first thought was this: *A redshirt beamed down! We're about to be blasted into smithereens!* I controlled my impulse to run and managed to call a greeting without laughing out loud.

"Hi. I'm Solid," he said. He had a sweet lopsided smile. I thought up a quick mnemonic device to remember his name: *He's filtering water. Liquid, Solid.*

We gave our names.

"Southbound?" Isis asked. From the general grubbiness of his pack and clothing and the sculptured muscles of his legs, it was evident that he was thru-hiking.

He nodded.

"When did you start?" I asked, as I slung my pack off. *I could use a rest*, I thought, *and what better way to spend it than talking to a cute guy? A southbound cute guy.*

"Fourth of July," he said. My spirits sank a little as I calculated exactly how fast he was hiking. Sure, he was cute, but at that pace he wasn't going to stick around for long.

"Man, you're flying!" I said. "You must have been in pretty good shape starting the Trail."

He nodded. "Yeah. I just graduated from West Point."

Waterfall frowned. "I thought you had to go right into the service from West Point. How'd you get time to hike?"

Solid looked pensive for a moment, a shadow of regret in his hazel eyes. "Medical discharge. I can't serve in the Army—I have diabetes."

"When did you find out?" Isis asked.

"Senior year, just before graduation."

"That must have been tough," Waterfall said.

"Yeah." He shrugged. "I'd always planned on being a career officer."

Isis made appropriate sounds of commiseration.

"And now, well, I'm trying to find some other path in life. I like the Trail. I have a lot of time to think out here."

"How do you manage with diabetes on the Trail? I thought insulin had to be refrigerated." Inwardly, I kicked myself for asking a question like that: *Tech Sergeant jackrabbit steers the conversation back to the mundane physical plane.*

"I'm not actually taking insulin," he said. "If I get enough exercise and eat well, I can manage my blood sugar levels pretty well without it."

"Cool." I fell silent, reflecting on how much "enough exercise" would have to be. Isis and I had been hiking for almost six weeks, while Solid had hiked for only four. He would have to be averaging almost fifteen miles a day. I couldn't imagine keeping up that pace even for a day in this kind of terrain. I wanted to spend more time with him, though, and I could tell that Isis and Waterfall did too.

"We have to pick up a mail drop at the hostel here," I said. "D'you want to join us there for the evening?"

"No, thanks." He screwed the lid onto his water bottle and put the filter away. "I like to stay out of towns when I can."

"I'd rather be in the woods myself," I said with real regret. "Take care, and good luck, Solid."

"You guys take care, too. It was good to meet you."

At the road, we stood for a long time in the gritty spray of passing cars, thumbing. Most of the traffic seemed to be SUVs and expensive minivans, and no one stopped. Through the tinted windows, we could just see the drivers' expressions of disdain.

"Notch!" I swore. "Maybe we should just walk to the notchin' hostel."

Waterfall consulted her *Data Book.* "It's four miles down," she said. "But there's a state park about a mile from here. We might have better luck hitchin' there."

We started walking, and in a few minutes we heard the gravel crunch behind us. It was an old silver Chevy pickup, emblazoned with bumper stickers. The laden gun rack behind the driver made me nervous, but I relaxed a bit when I recognized the A.T. symbol plastered in the cab window.

"Going to the hostel?" the driver called. He was in his late fifties, with thinning gray hair and ice-blue eyes.

"Yeah, thanks!"

"I gotta warn you, place is more expensive than it oughta be. Hikers been telling me."

"We have to pick up a mail drop there," Isis said.

"Huh. Climb in, then."

In the back of the truck, we hunkered down behind the cab and held a shouted conversation over the sound of wind and the rush of tires on the wet road.

"How expensive do you think it'll be?" I yelled over to Waterfall. She carried the *Thru-Hikers' Companion*, a book with detailed information on lodging and services in towns, so she was our main source for this sort of information.

"The *Companion* said $16 a night," she shouted back. This seemed reasonable—most of the hostels we had visited had charged $12 to $15.

"Not bad for a bunk and a shower," Isis called. "And we don't have much of a choice. It's too late to just pick up our mail drop and hike out."

Half her words were drowned out in the roar of passing trucks, but we understood and nodded. I felt hopeless, powerless, drained of energy. The constant wet and grayness was dragging me down. My knees ached, my hip sent a spark of pain through me whenever the truck hit a bump. I reached down to touch my bruised foot. It felt hot and tender under my fingers. *My body's falling apart, I thought. Can my will and spirit be far behind?*

The pickup stopped outside a squat white building with vinyl siding. Two smaller white cabins stood nearby in the half-dead lawn, with the edge of the spruce forest beyond them just visible through the fog. We jumped out of the truck and thanked the driver. He sped off in a cloud of exhaust fumes.

When I saw the sign proclaiming "Crawford Notch Hostel," I had to laugh. I felt almost embarrassed to read it; I realized that "notch" had become a four-letter word in my vocabulary, and it was as though the sign said "Crawford Shit Hostel." Inside, there was a sparsely furnished common room with framed pictures of jagged mountains and a doorway leading into a kitchen/dining room area. Across from the entrance, a thin dark-haired man sat behind a desk covered with tourist pamphlets.

"Welcome to Crawford Notch," he said. (It was all I could do not to laugh out loud at the word "notch.") "What can I do for you?"

"We have to pick up a mail drop," Isis said.

"Very well. Name?"

We gave our real names. They sounded strange and false to my ears. For an instant, I imagined what it would be like to leave the Trail, to go back to the world where I was Susan, not jackrabbit. I thought of warm, dry rooms out of the rain, of pianos and books and fresh food. The pain of my injuries gnawed at me, but at the thought of leaving the Trail, a larger pain welled up: the threat of failure. I had set out to hike the A.T., and I planned to do my utmost to finish it. The image of Blade flashed across my mind. *Is this heroic? Am I doing a great deed just by staying out here in the cold rain, beating myself up? Or is this just like eating a Stomper: a neat trick, but rather gross and meaningless?*

"Will you be staying the night?" the man asked.

"Yeah."

"You're in luck! There are three spaces left in Cabin Two. That's $20 apiece. Do you want showers?"

My brain didn't register the price at first. I focused on the word "shower," thinking of the layers of grime built up under my rain gear, and nodded enthusiastically.

"Showers are a dollar. You can rent a towel for another dollar."

Then the financial considerations made their way through my skull. I exchanged outraged glances with Isis and Waterfall.

"Excuse us for a minute," Waterfall said. Of the three of us, she was the best at summoning tact in this sort of situation. We went back onto the porch for a furious whispered conversation. It was growing dark outside, and tendrils of mist curled out of the woods.

"Twenty dollars!" I was incensed. "And two more for a shower and a dry towel. Notch this place! Notch this whole notching state! New Hampshire is one big notching notch after another!"

"Well, what can we do?" Isis said. The damp grayness pressed in around us. The thought of hot showers and dry bunks was tantalizing, even if they did cost more than we had expected.

"It's getting too dark to hitch," Waterfall said, and she was right. "We might as well stay here. The *Companion's* outdated on prices, sometimes . . ."

"We could get a *hotel* room for that much!"

"—if there *were* any hotels around here . . ."

"It's going to be, like, seventy dollars! I wonder how many people they cram into those cabins, anyway . . ."

In the end, we decided to stay. We shared the cabin with nine other people, packed in like sardines. It was dank and chilly in the airless room, and the sound of traffic on the road kept me awake for a long time, wondering. I curled up on my left side to lessen the pain in my hip. We had another fifty miles of White Mountains to traverse, and if they ended up being as bad as the first half, I didn't think I would make it. I pictured an endless elevation profile map stretching out to the horizon, punctuated by bone-jarring notches and huge climbs with no views but wet, gray mist. *Notch,* I thought, feeling my aching hip, my poor pulverized knees, my bruised foot. *Notch, notch, notch.*

Isis

Somewhere on the ridge of Garfield Mountain, the white blazes we'd been following for three hundred miles disappeared. We checked our maps. It didn't look like we could have taken a wrong turn; all the other trails in the vicinity led downhill, off the ridge. We hiked on, up small cliffs and through tangled mazes of roots. As the miles dragged by and still no blazes appeared, we began to worry.

"Y'all? How long has it been since we saw a blaze?" Waterfall asked. "What if we got turned around in this fog and went out on that other mountain that we should've passed four miles ago?"

"Maybe we did," I said, peering at the map. "According to the elevation profile, this ridge should be almost flat, but we've climbed up and down a half dozen two-hundred-foot lumps in the last hour."

"According to the elevation profile, the trail should be flat?" Jackrabbit let out a snort of derisive laughter. "Isn't that kind of like saying, 'according to my horoscope, I shouldn't get the flu this winter?'"

"A fair analogy. But what else have we got to go by?"

"Our instincts. Mine's telling me that I have no interest in hiking back two miles the way we came. Especially if we have to go over all those lumps again."

We decided to go on. A quarter mile farther we came upon a young man in the khaki uniform of the Forest Service, vigorously stacking brush beside the trail.

"This may be a stupid question," I said, "but are we on the Appalachian Trail?"

He nodded.

"Any idea why this section is unblazed?"

"Well, it goes along the ridge top. I guess they figured there was nothing else you could mistake it for."

As he spoke, I noticed that he was building his brush pile on a patch of smooth ground about eight feet in diameter, which looked as if it would have made a lovely stealth site, minus the branches.

"Know what I'm doing?" he asked. I thought I could make a pretty good guess, but I stayed silent. "I'm piling brush on this spot for the third time this week. People keep taking it off. It must be a lot of work, taking it off. Who would do something like that? Who could possibly want a tent site that badly? I just don't get it."

The Forest Service man must have done a good job with his brush piling; we couldn't find any clear, flat ground near the trail that night. We ended up paying our $6 apiece to stay at the AMC's Garfield Ridge Campsite. We found the shelter and campsite full of thru-hikers: ten or twelve nobos and four southbounders whom we hadn't met yet. Waterfall introduced us to Compañero, a tall, slender man whose deeply lined face wore a contemplative smile. We set up our tent, then brought our stove over to the shelter so we could trade stories with the other hikers while we cooked. We told them about Murphy and the meaning of "notch," eliciting a great deal of laughter and a few suggestions.

"Does the converse of Murphy's Law hold?" asked Compañero. "If you're prepared for something bad, it won't happen? For instance, if you put on your pack cover when it's not raining, can you prevent a storm from starting?"

"Wow, that opens up a whole new field of study," I said. "Practical Applications of Murphy's Law. If by some miracle it isn't raining in the morning, I'll put on my pack cover anyway and test your hypothesis."

Another sobo, Orren, said, "Notch ought to have some kind of a symbol—how 'bout this?" He held up his hand in a sort of a truncated version of a peace sign, his first two fingers raised but bent over at the knuckles. "Notch," he snarled, shaking his notch-sign fist at the drizzle blowing past the shelter.

After we all finished supper, we got down to business, trading information with the nobos in the shelter. Jackrabbit and I discussed the relative merits of Mizpah and Madison, encouraged everyone present to moon the Cog, and warned them about the long unblazed stretch of ridge on Garfield Mountain.

"Even if you don't like work-for-stay, you've gotta stop at Lonesome Lake," a northbounder told us when we'd finished talking. In the faint light of someone's candle lantern, I saw most of the other nobos nod their agreement.

"You can swim in the lake; there's a dock and everything. And the hut crew is awesome!"

"They don't get many thru-hikers who want to stay there, 'cause there are some primo stealth sites a quarter mile before the hut—a quarter mile past it, for you guys—but they're real nice to the hikers who do stay."

I thanked the nobos for the tip and headed back to my tent. *The Madison crew might have seemed perfectly nice, too*, I thought, *if only our health and safety hadn't depended on their judgment*.

I awoke in pitch darkness. It felt like only minutes had passed since I'd fallen asleep, but without stars, I had no way of knowing what time of night it was. I lay still, listening for what might have woken me. No sound but the wind in the treetops. And then I heard it: a thin, baleful voice howling in the distance. Was it a wildcat? I listened again. This time, I heard it clearly. It was a human voice, crying "help." I grabbed my flashlight and shone it into my pack to find my first aid kit.

"Whuzzah?" jackrabbit muttered, turning away from the light.

"Someone's calling for help," I told her. "I'm going to find out what's going on."

I found Compañero, Orren, and five northbounders already gathered in front of the shelter.

"Did you hear that?"

"A voice, calling for help . . ."

"It sounded like it was coming from the east, where the trail comes over the mountain."

"Yeah, that way."

"Then let's go! We'll take the trail as close as we can get and hope the person keeps on shouting."

The whole line of us scrambled down the campsite trail, toward its junction with the A.T. As we passed the campsite caretaker's tent, he stuck his head out and shouted, "Wait a minute!"

We stopped to wait for him, figuring that the rescue operation would be safer if we all went together. But instead of grabbing a jacket and joining us, he kept talking.

"I've radioed to headquarters to tell them that there's a person out here calling for help . . ."

I nodded; it seemed like a good idea to tell someone other than a half-asleep jackrabbit where we were going.

". . . and now I'm waiting for them to authorize a rescue."

"You're calling to *authorize* a rescue? Notch authorization!" Although the caretaker couldn't understand him, Orren spoke for the rest of us; we all turned and hurried down the path.

The voice grew stronger as we approached, and soon it sounded more irritated than desperate. After about five minutes' steep uphill climb, I bounded around a corner to find a tall, pale young woman in a rain jacket, standing in the middle of the trail with one arm thrown over her eyes to block the glare of our flashlights.

"Are you hurt?" I asked her.

"No," she said, "I just forgot my flashlight. I'm in the hut crew at Green-leaf, and I was hiking over to visit a friend at Galehead. I didn't realize how late in the day it was."

She peered over my shoulder, noticing the other hikers for the first time. "Who're those people? All of you came looking for me? Oh fuck, this is so embarrassing."

The caretaker, who had apparently received his authorization, arrived just in time to spare her the further embarrassment of being escorted back to the campsite by her would-be rescuers.

"Emmy," he greeted her, "great to see you! How're things going at Greenleaf?" He turned to us. "You can go back to your tents now. Everything's under control."

"I don't know about the AMC's priorities," said jackrabbit. "Have you seen the lawn here?"

She and Waterfall and I were sitting at a picnic bench on the shore of Lonesome Lake, and I had just repeated the story of the baleful voice of Garfield Ridge at her request.

"The lawn?" I asked.

"They're trying to reseed some of the grass, and they've got these cute little signs all over it that say 'Revegetation Project: Please Keep Off.' I wanted to ask them if they were restoring the native prairie ecosystem."

We all laughed at the image of a prairie covering the White Mountains. Suddenly, Waterfall put both her hands to her lips and fell silent. I followed her gaze out over the lake. A man who'd been swimming had just stood up, revealing a torso that Michelangelo could have used as a model for his David. His softly curling hair and strong, handsome profile contributed to my impression that the famous statue had come to life and arisen from Lonesome Lake before our eyes.

"He can't be a hiker," jackrabbit sighed. "No one on the Trail has that much upper-body strength. Not even Solid."

He started to walk toward shore, moving with the jolting, stiff-muscled gait of someone who's been carrying a pack all day.

"He *is* a hiker," whispered Waterfall.

Much to our delight, this vision of loveliness strode over to our bench and introduced himself as soon as he got out of the water. I'm not very good at remembering names under the best of circumstances, and I must admit that his slipped out of my mind the moment I heard it. I was concentrating on his pecs, not his words. However, this didn't prevent me from holding him in conversation for a good ten minutes, with the help of Waterfall and jackrabbit. I listened just enough to gather that he was a northbounder (hiking away from us, alas!) and that he was doing work-for-stay at the hut that evening.

When he had walked up to the hut to help prepare supper, we had a serious two-minute discussion of the possibility of doing work-for-stay again.

"The nobos said they're real nice here."

"Even if they are nice, I don't like the feeling of my time being someone else's to play with."

"Yeah, let's stealth. But first, ladies, our adieux. We can't let that young god vanish from our lives forever without bidding him a fond farewell."

We took turns going into the hut to fill our water bottles. Mr. Statue of David was busy washing dishes, right next to our friend Solid. If the lovely stranger had been alone, I might have left without speaking to him, but seeing Solid there gave me a good excuse to stroll over to the dish basins.

"Bye, Solid," I said, then turned to the nobo. As I met his eyes, I remembered that I had no idea what his name was, even though he'd told it to me only fifteen minutes before. I racked my brains, all the while gazing deep into his warm brown eyes. After a minute or so, realizing that it was too late to salvage any dignity by coming up with his name, I smiled and said "bye" in a voice so low with confusion that it came out sounding like a bad attempt at sultry whisper. Then I spun around and made for the door, as fast as I could go without actually running.

"How'd it go?" asked Waterfall. "Did the prince ask for your hand in marriage?"

"No, I think he wants someone a bit more mature and experienced."

"Then I'm just the woman for him." She picked up her water bottle, laughing. "But I don't want to get married. I want to be an old maid in a house full of books and cats. So I guess I'll have to break his heart, the poor darlin'."

jackrabbit

The omnipresent mist seemed to be thinning as we climbed up Kinsman Ridge. At first I hardly believed my eyes, but there it was—the pale disk of the sun was just visible behind the layers of gray. It was clearing. Soon I felt the warm rays on my shoulders, and my eyes struggled to adjust to the sudden brightness. The path behind us was still wreathed in clouds, but up ahead the stones and spruce branches glittered with a million tiny rainbows. We gave a ragged cheer.

At the top of the ridge, we saw, for once, the splendid terrain around us. On one side, the sheer face of Franconia Ridge jutted up from the forested valley and disappeared into the cloud bank. On the other side, the flank of Moosilauke, the last of the White Mountains, loomed blue-dark and steep. Its bare summit, shining in the sunlight, looked so close we could almost reach out and touch it. Just ahead, Kinsman Ridge stretched out, with its lumps of pink granite visible between the dark trees. Everything gleamed from the moisture the clouds had left behind.

The clouds closed in again in a short while, and the vision of the mountains around made the thick mist seem even more oppressive. I wondered what stunning views were hidden from us now. The trail through the Kinsmans felt like an exercise in pointlessness; we scrambled up and down steep rock faces, often looping around from one "viewpoint" to another, and the view was always the same: gray.

"I hate the White Mountains, y'all," Waterfall said with perverse glee. "My ex-boyfriend said this was his favorite part of the Trail, so I feel extra justified in hatin' it."

"I hate it, too," I said. "One of those nobos at the Barn told me that the Whites are so beautiful, you get up on top a ridge and you forget all about the pain of hiking up and down the notching notches. But when all you see is fog, there's nothing to distract you."

"Yeah," Isis took a running start up a steep rock, her bare feet easily catching hold of the surface. "They don't call them the White Mountains for nothing."

"I will be *so* glad when we get to Glencliff," I said. "Free shelters, no more notches. None of this sneaking around and stealthing. No more notchin' tourists poking our feet!"

"Oh, I'm looking forward to Hanover," Waterfall said. "It's a college town. They have bookstores there, and coffee shops . . . I used to *live* in a coffee shop in college. I'm gonna take at least one zero, maybe two, and just sit in the coffee shop and write. They have a Thai restaurant there, too . . ."

Thai food suddenly rose to the top on my list of desires, edging out even pizza and dry clothes. *Hanover*, I thought. *We'll get to Hanover and everything will be fine.*

"Where are we, anyway?" I had lost track of our progress along the bumpy spine of Kinsman Ridge. Dusk was beginning to thicken under the spruces.

Isis took out her map. "I don't know. It's hard to say." We had followed a long uphill grade for the last half mile or so, punctuated by short drops. "I think we're coming up on Mount Wolf."

"Mount Wolf? Then we're still five miles from Kinsman Notch!" Waterfall was dismayed. "That puts us fifteen miles from Glencliff. How're we gonna do it, y'all? I have to get there tomorrow night—I don't have enough food to stay out on the Trail again."

We didn't either, but Isis set her face in a tight-lipped smile. "We'll manage somehow."

It was cold on the shoulder of Mount Wolf, where we found a clearing just large enough to set up our tents for the night. A soft wind blew through the high limbs of the spruces. Water condensed on the branches and dripped down everywhere, leaving the ground damp and spongy.

"This is gross, y'all! Look at this—somebody left a disgusting t-shirt here. And there's a bunch of cough drop wrappers and like three pounds of peanut shells!"

"Nasty," I agreed, taking a fallen branch and helping Waterfall sweep out a space for her tent.

"We really should pack it out," Isis said. "At least the t-shirt and the wrappers."

I groaned at the thought of extra, useless weight, but I knew she was right. Trash in the wilderness attracts more trash; if people see candy wrappers and clothing left in the bushes, they're less likely to think twice about leaving their own garbage.

"Y'all, we ought to make a game out of it," Waterfall said, beginning to smile. "We can pretend we're looking for a criminal mastermind, and our only clues are the things we have to pack out of the woods."

"Right!" I picked up the smelly t-shirt and wrung grayish water out of it to lessen the weight a little. "So what kind of culprit left this?"

"Well, we're lookin' for a man without a shirt," Waterfall said. She picked up one of the wrappers. "And he's got a cough. Prob'ly from goin' shirtless in this weather."

"Some criminal mastermind!" I said. "What about the peanuts, though?"

Waterfall thought for a moment. "An elephant!" She exclaimed triumphantly.

"An elephant?"

"They eat lots of peanuts, don't they?"

"Right. So we're looking for a shirtless man, with a cold, riding an elephant. Should be pretty easy to spot."

Our jokes made the evening a little more bearable, but it was still a miserable campsite. Wet branches brushed us from all sides. The temperature dropped until we could see our breath condensing in the clammy air. It was hard to ignore the fact that at least fourteen miles of tough terrain still lay between us and our destination tomorrow.

We squatted on our haunches, warming our hands around our stoves as dinner cooked. Waterfall headed down a side trail into the bushes and came back shortly, looking disgusted. "Y'all, there's toilet paper everywhere back there!"

"That's foul!" Isis said.

"See, this is why they don't like people stealth camping," Waterfall said. "They dump all their trash in the campsites, and don't even know enough to bury their—"

"We need a public education campaign," I said. "And I have a theme song for it already. Isis, do you remember that song we made up on the Machias Lakes trip, when we were digging a privy pit for the campsite?"

"Yeah," she said in a tone of dread.

"Oh, come on, it's not that bad! I mean, it's not really suited for polite company, or anything, but . . ."

"If y'all are callin' me polite company . . ." Waterfall pretended to take offense.

"Not at all, my dear. D'you want to hear it?"

Isis stifled a groan, but Waterfall nodded enthusiastically.

"I've got to tweak the verses a bit, but the chorus goes like this." Isis joined me, singing to the tune of a British march whose title I have forgotten, if I ever knew it:

> Dig a hole, dump your load,
> Dig a hole, dump your load,
> That's what you've gotta do (doo-doo)!

Our boisterous, loud voices filled the clearing and seemed to dispel the gloomy mist for a moment. As we finished dinner, I turned over the words in my head and assembled two verses. I taught Isis, in a whisper, and we sang them for Waterfall before our nightly chapter of *Harry Potter:*

> Well, I love to go a-hiking on the Maine A.T.,
> Miles away from any road,
> Where the trees are all green and the air is pristine,
> And you're never gonna find a commode!

> Dig a hole, dump your load . . .

> And you gotta love New Hampshire with the AMC,
> Where you have to pay so you don't spoil it,

But when stealthing on the ridges, swatting flies and gnats and midges,
You're never gonna find yourself a toilet!

Dig a hole, dump your load . . .

By the end, we were laughing so hard we could barely finish the song. *Maybe I'll write a verse for every state on the Trail*, I thought, and immediately dismissed the idea. *Who would want to hear a fourteen-verse song about shitting in the woods?*

As we descended into Kinsman, our final notch, all of us felt a little bit on edge. We needed to get over Moosilauke before dark. It was almost midday, and we hadn't even reached the base of the mountain.

"How is this notch going to notch us over?" I asked. "Besides the obvious, I mean." I grimaced as we descended a steep section of trail, and my knees creaked ominously.

"You never know," Waterfall said. "Maybe something good will happen here."

"In a notchin' notch? Don't count on it!" Isis said.

The sound of traffic grew louder, an unsteady roar through the trees. The sun showed weakly through the clouds again, and the mist was breaking up over the valley. Between the trees, we could see the huge flank of Moosilauke looming on the far side of the notch, looking almost vertical. Cliffs broke through the blue-green spruce forest here and there, and waterfalls cut pale traceries across the mossy rock. The top wasn't visible. This mountain was beautiful, I had to admit, but my body rebelled at the thought of climbing it.

On the gravel shoulder of the road, we saw a tall woman in a t-shirt and black Spandex. "Waterfall?" she called as we came near. The wind ruffled her short brown hair, and her hazel eyes shone with warmth.

I looked at Waterfall. She frowned for an instant, puzzled, as though trying to place the woman's face in her memory.

"I'm Stitches. We met at the Gathering, remember? I was giving a workshop on lightweight backpacking. Anyway, I come up to the Whites every weekend. I was hoping to find you. Oh, and you must be the Barefoot Sisters! I've read so much about you in people's online journals . . . I didn't know what to believe!"

We introduced ourselves.

"You guys must be starving—I know I was, when I came through here in '99, and I was northbound. I don't know how you sobos do it!" She led us to her car in the Forest Service lot at the base of the mountain and offered us a vast array of junk food: Oreos, chips, candy bars, and soda, as well as home-made brownies.

Between bites, we thanked her heartily. "You're an angel, Stitches!"

"It's no problem," she said. "So many people helped me out on my hike, I figure I might as well give something back. Say, would you guys be interested in slacking Moosilauke?"

Slacking Moosilauke! I could have kissed her. "Definitely!"

Isis nodded as well, grinning, but Waterfall looked a little uncomfortable. "I've never slacked before," she admitted.

"Come on, Waterfall, slacking is awesome!" Isis said. "You go twice as fast, and save your knees . . ."

"We could be over that mountain before dark," I said.

Stitches' eyes twinkled with humor. "Everybody's doing it."

Waterfall sighed. "Okay, peer pressure wins out. I swear, y'all are corruptin' me."

We threw the culprit's t-shirt and cough-drop wrappers into a garbage pail and put our packs in the backseat of Stitches' car. Stitches loaned us a day-pack, which we filled with water bottles, the last of our granola bars, and some warm clothing. She drove off with a smile and a wave.

When we started up the mountain, even Waterfall had to admit how wonderful it was to be slacking. "Y'all were right; this is worth it." We floated up the steep trail, flashing past dayhikers who glanced at us, astounded. We didn't even give them time to ask the obvious questions about our feet.

I had heard some northbounders—and Blade—deride slacking as a way of cheating. At the other end of the spectrum, we had heard about a group of hikers doing the entire Trail with van support, effectively slacking the whole thing. I certainly wouldn't want to do that; I loved the independence that a full pack gave me, the ability to stay in the woods for a long time. But slacking occasionally was a welcome change and a chance to see how strong I had become. Accustomed to carrying another forty pounds, my legs felt like pow-erful pistons driving me effortlessly up the slope.

The four-mile climb to the summit seemed to take no time at all. Above treeline, a brisk wind shook the low grasses. We sat on huge rectangular blocks of granite, the foundations of an old hotel, and looked out across the terrain we had crossed: jagged blue silhouettes of stone stretching back to the far horizon. Checking the map, we followed the Trail's turnings: the Kinsmans, Franconia Ridge, the Twins and Guyot, and far in the back, the Presidentials. A puff of black smoke marked Mount Washington. The A.T. ran along each ridge, dropped into the intervening notch and doubled back, winding through the toughest parts of the forbidding territory.

"Cruel and unusual," I said. "They just had to hit all the high points and all the notchin' notches in between."

"Yeah," Waterfall said, but there was something wistful in her voice. "I wish we could have seen it. It must be so beautiful . . . Maybe I'll come back here some day and hope for better weather."

"Not me, man," I said. "I've seen enough of the Whites to last me a lifetime. Good riddance, I say."

Southwards, the terrain looked rolling and smooth, deliciously easy compared to the knife-edged ridges we had crossed. The highest mountains we could see ahead rose perhaps 1,500 feet out of the lake-studded lowlands. Suddenly, I could tell how far south we had come—evergreen trees appeared only on the highest slopes of the mountains; the lower regions were covered in the lighter green of oaks, birches, and maples. And somewhere out there in the valley of sunlit branches, the fabled town of Hanover waited.

"We don't hit another 4,000-footer until we're halfway through Virginia," Waterfall said. I smiled—perhaps the worst was over.

Going downhill should have been easy, with our light loads and our joyful spirits, but my hip ached and my foot began to throb in counterpoint. Ironically, the flatter and smoother the trail became, the more my foot hurt. In the rocky sections, I was able to balance most of my weight on the heel and the outside edge of the foot, protecting the tender bruise. On the level, soft trails on the south side of Moosilauke, I couldn't help slapping the ball of my foot down with each step. I set my teeth and tried to ignore the pain.

The trail led us past open fields—how long had it been since I had seen a farm field full of cows? A golden light filled the valley and everything looked peaceful. It was hard to believe that just yesterday I had been clinging to the rocks, fighting my way against the wind-driven clouds.

Just at dusk we reached the road. A van roared past us, then braked and backed up to where we stood. Stitches stuck her head out the window. "Pizza run," she said. "Care to join us?"

We spent the night at the Hikers Welcome Hostel in Glencliff, perhaps a quarter mile down the road from the trailhead. It was an unprepossessing building, an old barn with mattresses in the loft and an outside laundry room and shower covered with tarps. The kindness of the proprietors, Big John and his wife Ria, made up for the basic accommodations, and the price was right.

"We just opened up a month ago," Big John explained. "Things are improving as we go along." He was a wiry, thin man, balding, with a short-trimmed beard and kind brown eyes. "We've got a freezer full of Ben and Jerry's, though . . ."

"Excellent!" Isis and I picked out two pints of ice cream and headed for the fire circle. Half-built stone benches surrounded a sizeable bonfire. The flickering light revealed a crowd of northbounders talking and laughing. Big John brought out a guitar, and someone started singing country ballads.

"Y'all should sing your song." Waterfall came up behind us with a pint of Cherry Garcia in her hands.

"Which song?"

"That one you sang last night, you know, about digging a hole . . ."

"You really think we should?"

"I'll sing with y'all."

Big John introduced us with much fanfare. "Ladies and gentlemen!" (This was greeted with loud laughter—any pretense of being ladies and gentlemen fades after about a hundred miles on the Trail, we had found, and most of the people at the fire circle had covered more than 1,700 miles.) "I want to intro-duce the Barefoot Sisters! They have a song for us tonight."

I was nervous, and a little embarrassed, but the audience was so apprecia-tive that I forgot my shyness and belted the song with gusto. By the last cho-rus, half the nobos were singing along.

"That was awesome, y'all!" a young man called from the far side of the firepit. He was slight and bearded, with his reddish hair pulled back in a pony-tail. "Y'all got to do that for the talent show at Trail Days."

"Trail Days? What's that?" Isis asked.

"Man, these girls haven't heard of Trail Days? Come on." This was a rail-thin, dark-haired man barely out of his teens. "Best party on the Trail, man. Chicks like you ought to know about it." He winked and attempted a leer.

I could sense my sister's ire rising, and I casually deflected the conversation away from us and back to the topic at hand. "So where is Trail Days? And when?"

"Aw, y'all missed it this year," the red-bearded nobo said. "It's the end of May in Damascus. Little town in Virginia. Awesome place. Everybody gets together for, like, five days, and there's slide shows, and talks, and all that—"

"Nobody goes to Trail Days for the freakin' slide shows," the skinny one said. "It's all about par-tay, all week long."

"There's a talent show, too," the first nobo continued earnestly. "Y'all ought to go and sing that song. I bet y'all would win somethin'."

Someone else picked up the guitar, and we sat on one of the stone benches finishing our ice cream. A few nobos came over to ask the usual questions about barefoot hiking: *Why do you do it? Doesn't it hurt?* I let Isis do most of the talking. I was tired of explanations, and right then, it did hurt for me. Isis let a few people poke and prod her leathery soles, but I kept my feet on the ground; I didn't want anyone discovering that damn bruise. After almost 400 miles, it had become a point of pride that we could safely walk barefoot on almost any surface. I didn't want to show any evidence to the contrary.

The young red-haired nobo had hung around the edges of the group for a while, silently observing. When he came close to us, he shook his head with an appreciative smile. "Barefoot. I'd *marry* y'all!"

Isis

After Glencliff, the terrain seemed so gentle and easy that it became the subject of jokes between us. On the peak of 2,200-foot Mount Mist, Waterfall asked, "Do they call this Mount Missed because it's so small that most hikers walk over it without realizin' it's supposed to be a mountain?"

Later that day, as we strolled along a level stream bank, I joked, "If the Trail goes on like this, I'll have to put shoes on, just to make it a bit more challenging."

A balding, gray-haired man with a tiny pack came striding toward us. "More of you barefoot people!" he exclaimed. "I've been hiking with a kid, about your age, who walks barefoot half the time. Keep an eye out for him— long, black hair, usually hikes with no shirt on. He wears boots when he's in a hurry, so you won't necessarily recognize him by his feet. Calls himself Anonymous Badger. Real nice kid."

When we met Anonymous Badger, he was wearing boots, but his smooth, waist-length black hair and his bare bronze chest certainly caught our attention. Waterfall and I later admitted to each other that we'd started talking to him just so that we could keep him there to look at, but we'd quickly become engrossed in the conversation. This was his second northbound thru-hike. He offered us a brief inventory of Trail secrets, places we should be sure to visit: the Cookie Lady's blueberry farm in Massachusetts; the 501 shelter in

Pennsylvania, where you could order pizza and get it delivered; the Mount Cammerer Firewarden's Tower in the Smokies, an octagonal stone tower on the end of a ridge that boasted a 360-degree view of the surrounding mountains. In spite of all we'd encountered on the Trail, these distant places seemed fantastical, the stuff of Narnian wardrobes and Roald Dahl's chocolate factory.

Even with the smooth ground and good weather, jackrabbit's mood grew more and more somber over the following days. It was all Waterfall and I could do to make her crack a smile. She'd told me that the 600 mg ibuprofen she was taking didn't always suffice to numb the pain in her hip; I assumed this was the problem. She'd also mentioned that she'd bruised her foot on Wildcat, but since she hadn't said anything about it since the day it happened, I thought that injury had healed.

A day and a half before we'd planned to reach Hanover, we were hiking through a marshy section of trail where slippery, rotten bog bridges made for treacherous footing. I heard jackrabbit fall; a moment later, I heard her scream "fuck" at the top of her lungs. I turned to find her lying across the trail, one leg bent under her at such a strange angle that I thought it was broken. Her face looked ghostly pale beneath her freckles.

"What is it?" I asked, dropping to one knee beside her.

"It's my foot," she answered. "The bruise. I just hit it again in the same place. I think it's really bad this time—maybe broken."

"There's a shelter in just a few miles," I told her. "Do you think you can make it that far?"

"No," she answered. "No, I won't go to the shelter. This is going to get worse. Swell up. If I stop somewhere to sleep, I don't think I'll be able to put weight on my foot in the morning. We have to make it to Hanover tonight."

"We've got twelve miles to go," I told her, "and it's almost noon already."

"We have to get there," she repeated. "Tonight."

She couldn't stand to have anything touch the bruise—a dark purple lump the diameter of a quarter that seemed to swell even as I looked at it—so I wrapped all the gauze, duct tape, and spare handkerchiefs I had on either side of it, trying to build up a cushion that would keep it from hitting the ground. Then we walked. Jackrabbit moved faster than I'd ever seen anyone limp; so fast that I had trouble keeping up with her. We reached Hanover by five o'clock, and as we staggered up the main street, she finally slowed down. I offered her my arm, but she shook it off—with one foot bare and the other swathed in an inch of bandages, her chin up and her fists clenched, she limped forward on her own, amid the stares and whispers of passersby.

jackrabbit

Waterfall left a few days after we reached Hanover. She had a schedule to keep, a job to go back to after her thru-hike. As much as we enjoyed her company, we knew she couldn't stay. The town, which had seemed like a promised land when we spoke of it in the cloud-wrapped White Mountains, quickly took on the dimensions of a prison. A few Dartmouth frat houses offered lodging to hikers. We divided our time between the dingy basement of Panarchy and the rec room of Alpha Theta. When one frat threw a party and kicked the hikers out, we would move to the other. Isis cleaned their kitchens in exchange for our stay; she washed counters full of months-old dishes, wiped suspicious-looking stains from the floors and walls, and tackled the fuzzy leftovers in the backs of refrigerators. I think the frat houses got the better end of the deal.

As for me, I tried to rest. The bruise on my foot had swelled up and turned ugly colors. I could barely walk. When we moved between frat houses, less than three blocks apart, Isis ferried both our packs over, and I followed behind, limping. On the fourth day, I caught a shuttle out to the Dartmouth Medical Center. The X-rays revealed that the bones were intact, and the elderly, somewhat condescending podiatrist called for rest, ice, elevation. "Maybe after a few weeks you can walk on. I hope you'll see reason and wear some shoes!" I felt miserable, defeated. I knew I was holding my sister back.

Droves of northbounders moved through town, all confident, slim, tanned, and muscular. They seemed to glow with health and good fortune, and I envied them all. One of the nobos, a lanky dark-haired man who introduced himself as Around the Bend, stayed in town for a few days. He tried to teach us to play pool on the battered table in the back room at Panarchy.

"Your turn, jackrabbit. Are you guys going to the Gathering?"

I hopped around the table on my good leg and lined up my shot. "What's the Gathering?"

Around the Bend chuckled as the ball flew wide and caromed around the table. "You shoot like a girl."

"Yeah, well, look who taught me!"

He shrugged and smiled. "What can I say? The Gathering's a big hiker get-together in West Virginia, Columbus Day weekend. They've got slide shows and talks and stuff, but mostly it's just a chance to meet other hikers. Your shot, Isis . . . nice one!"

"Thanks." She allowed herself a small smile of triumph as the red ball slipped into a corner pocket. "The Gathering sounds like fun. Waterfall told me she might be there. But I don't think we'll be anywhere near West Virginia in October unless jackrabbit's foot heals up."

Around the Bend pursed his lips, considering something. "I'm going to buy a car in Maine when I finish my hike, and I'll be driving down to the Gathering. Maybe I could pick you guys up somewhere." He tore the label from a beer bottle on the windowsill and scribbled something down. "Here's my e-mail. Stay in touch. It'll be fun."

I spent most of my time in the Panarchy library. The room had an ambience of opulent squalor. Floor-to-ceiling bookshelves bore rows of ancient leather-bound books, their gilded titles reflecting the dim light from a high window. More recent volumes, mainly paperbacks, occupied the lowest shelves, and a stack of *High Times* magazines spilled over a corner of the ruined Persian carpet. I sat on the green crushed-velvet sofa, gingerly positioning myself between unidentifiable stains, with my foot elevated on the coffee table (it was some dark tropical wood, inlaid with mother-of-pearl and marred with countless circular stains from beer mugs). The big orange plastic bottle of ibuprofen, now half-full, was propped on the table next to my notebook. I wrote a few letters and made a stab at reading *Anna Karenina*.

One evening, Isis came in with a visitor. He was a man in his sixties, small and wiry, with long white hair and a beard down to the middle of his chest. His eyes sparkled with an inner light.

"I'm Nimblewill Nomad," he said. "It's such a pleasure to meet you, jackrabbit. Your sister told me a lot about you."

"Good to meet you," I said, leaning forward from the couch to shake his hand. "Are you thru-hiking, Nomad?"

He took a seat in a damaged velvet armchair across the room. When he smiled, his eyes gleamed even brighter. "I'm hiking the Eastern Continental Trail, from Cape Gaspé in Quebec down to Key West."

I whistled. "Quite a trek."

"I hiked it northbound a few years ago."

"Oh, Waterfall told us about you! It's a real honor to meet you!" I remembered now—Waterfall had mentioned him several times. He had been a doctor until his retirement a few years ago. Then, with almost no backpacking experience, he had decided to hike from Florida to Canada. Overcoming numerous setbacks and injuries, he had completed his trek and become something of a hero in the Trail world.

"The Trail made a new man of me." Nimblewill Nomad leaned forward in the chair, his eyes closed. His voice had the spellbinding intensity of a storyteller's. "I used to be a very different person from the one you see before you now. I was jealous, and petty, and small-minded. Every step on that hike, I left all that behind me. I became a wanderer, a Nomad." He spoke about the freedom of the Trail and the open road, occasionally pausing to recite his poetry, written in the style of Robert Service. His slightly archaic speech and his formidable appearance made him seem like a character from a legend. Isis and I listened closely to his stories.

"But enough of my adventures!" he finally said. "Tell me about yours, my friends!"

Stories were a kind of currency out here, I realized again. The Trail community, always in motion, was held together by the thin fabric of stories. In the library that evening, I felt the tenuous connection linking us to Waterfall, now miles ahead, and to the rest of the Trail world. I felt such gratitude.

We told a few stories: the day we met Starman; the night of Tenbrooks's birthday party, when he divided the "cake" for everyone in the shelter; the moose skeleton the nobos had told us about. I recounted my adventure in Mahoosuc Notch, getting stuck under a boulder, and recited the poem I had written in the rain outside Andover.

"Wonderful, wonderful!" Nimblewill Nomad beamed. "We are of the same tribe, you and I. You will go far."

I sighed. "Not with my foot like this."

His forehead wrinkled with concern. "Your sister told me about that, jackrabbit. I'm so sorry." He was silent a moment. "Things happen for a reason. Sometimes it may be hard to see the reason. Maybe there's something else you need to do right now."

I sighed. "I can't imagine getting off, after we've come four hundred miles."

"It's not getting any better," Isis said quietly, and I had to admit it was true. Almost two weeks had passed, and the swelling had hardly gone down. I could walk now, hobbling along, but it was still difficult to bear any weight.

"You can always come back to the Trail," Nomad said. He looked straight at me, his eyes shining and intense. "The Trail will be here. You have to consider what's best for you . . . But let me tell you another story: did you hear about the Tuba Man?" It was a welcome distraction. I didn't want to think about my foot anymore, or what I would do if I left the Trail now.

"Tuba Man?" Isis said. "I just heard rumors. Weird stuff. Is he real?"

"Oh, yes," Nomad said with a sparkling grin. "I saw him in town just this afternoon. He carries a tuba in his pack."

"A full-sized tuba?" I couldn't believe it. He nodded. "Those things must weigh, like, twenty pounds!"

"Actually thirty-five, he told me, counting the mouthpiece and the music he carries."

"What does he do with his other gear?" Isis asked.

"Oh, it was stuffed in and around the tuba. He had his sleeping bag and a jar of peanut butter in the bell."

"Does he play it?" I asked.

"I didn't get to hear it, but they say he plays quite well." Nimblewill Nomad chuckled. "I hope so, if he's going to lug the thing all the way to Georgia."

"He's THRU-hiking?" I was incredulous. "Thru-hiking with a TUBA? I thought he must be a section hiker or something. This guy must be totally nuts!" Privately, I hoped I would get to meet him.

Nomad smiled. "People say the same thing about you two."

A few days later, as afternoon shadows lengthened on the grimy wood floors of Panarchy, I sat in the library reading. Most of the people who came through the door were kind, offering sympathy or an amusing conversation. Still, sometimes I wished I could just disappear. A few people seemed to be there just to gawk, or worse, to gloat over the downfall of the Barefoot Sisters.

I was reaching down to adjust my ice pack when one of these characters came in. He was a prototypical northbounder, slim, bearded, dressed in a ratty tank top and shorts.

"So, you're one of the Barefoot Sisters."

"Jackrabbit," I said, extending a hand.

He didn't give his name or bother to shake my hand. "I heard you hurt your ankle. That's so unfortunate, isn't it? But given, I mean, the way you hiked and all . . ." He let his words drift off with a self-congratulatory smile.

"It's not my ankle. And really, I don't think being barefoot had much to do with it. I've seen people in boots get worse—"

"Well, if you got an ankle injury, what you want to do is take lots of ibuprofen—"

"It's not my ankle." I indicated the large ibuprofen bottle sitting next to my foot, but he seemed to be on a roll.

"Take lots of ibuprofen, and get some ice on it—" here I pointed wordlessly at the ice pack on my foot—"and make sure to get some rest. Yeah, rest and ice and vitamin I. That's so unfortunate . . ."

I was sick of his smug voice and useless advice, and I shot him a look of pure poison. Finally, something reached him. "Well, listen, um, Barefoot Sister, it's been really nice to meet you." I kept the glare going while he backed toward the door. "Well, I, um, hope that ankle gets better soon . . . remember what I said, rest, ice, vitamin I . . ."

I opened *Anna Karenina*, which I was beginning to hate, and in my mind Vronsky took on the features of the smug northbounder. *What the hell does she want with a man like that*, I thought. *It's not worth it, Anna; get out of it while you still can* . . . but the book moved on its inexorable course toward tragedy, and the day waned outside, and my foot still wouldn't bear much weight.

As the sun set, I leaned on Isis's arm and hobbled down to the edge of town, where the concrete highway bridge stretched across the Connecticut River. The fierce sky, orange and red and black, glimmered inverted in the water. The bridge had three concrete pylons with balls of stone set on their tops. In the harsh light, they looked like the monuments of a lost empire. We walked out to the central post. I laid my hand on the polished square of granite set in the cement and let my fingers trace the letters: *VT / NH*. The last state line I would cross on the A.T. for a long time. I took one step to the other side, for ceremony, and then we turned around and I limped back to town, my sister supporting half my weight. It was the twelfth of August. On the sixteenth, our mother drove out to Hanover and took me home to the coast of Maine.

CHAPTER 4

Isis Alone

Isis

The preparations for jackrabbit's departure didn't leave me much time to worry about what I'd be doing after she went home. I sorted through our belongings, making sure that the water filter, stove, and cooking pot went into my pack. I transferred some money from my savings account and bought myself a solo tent at the Dartmouth outfitter's store. I also bought a candle lantern, for light and comfort in the long nights of the coming fall. I shopped for my resupply and packed it into Ziplocs, a task that was reassuring, now, in its familiarity. In midafternoon our mom showed up, bringing wine and cheese for a farewell picnic and a tin of homemade cookies to top off my bulging food bag.

It wasn't until the car pulled out of Panarchy's driveway, carrying away my hiking partner of six weeks and our two-person tent, that I realized just what I had gotten myself into. I was going to be hiking alone. Outside of a few nervous moments at the beginning of our hike, when I'd worried that my more athletic sister would leave me in the dust, I had never considered the possibility. From the first time we talked about hiking the A.T., in a camp in the Andes with Maineak, I'd thought of the trip as something we'd do together, as sisters and as friends.

Jackrabbit was my reason for being on the Trail. Walking through rain and sleet, eating food I'd gotten sick of weeks before, and falling behind our other companions seemed much easier to bear when I had a hiking partner who could spin our tribulations into verses of mock-epic poetry. Besides, jackrabbit was my protector. To all the friends from home who worried about two girls going into the woods alone, who asked if we were bringing guns and whistles and cans of pepper spray, I had explained, "My sister's a black belt in Tae Kwon Do." Even when she was injured and grouchy, her presence gave me the comfort of feeling useful; caring for her kept my mind off my own fears.

I packed slowly, pausing every few minutes to make myself a cup of tea, eat another snack, walk out on the porch to check the weather. *Those clouds over the river look pretty dark. Maybe they're thunderclouds. Maybe I should stay here one more night.* But I'd long since worn out my welcome at the frat houses, explaining jackrabbit's injury to an endless series of Dartmouth students, whose reactions ranged from mild concern to boredom to disdain as I begged them to let us stay beyond the usual two-night limit. With jackrabbit gone, I didn't have an excuse to trespass on their hospitality any longer.

Resisting the urge to dump my new tent out on the floor one more time and make sure that all its components were accounted for, I wedged it into the left corner of my backpack. My food bag went in next to it, followed by my sweater and rain gear. I hefted my pack; it felt surprisingly light. I glanced around the basement one more time: sweaty stone walls, red lightbulbs dangling over the built-in bar, a few copies of *High Times* scattered among the sunken mattresses on the floor. Nothing of mine left there.

Waterfall's hiking solo, I reminded myself as I started up the stairs. *And she's doing fine.* In her last e-mail, she'd told us that she was hiking with a couple named Firebreather and Fall Girl, who routinely hiked twenty- and even twenty-five-mile days. "I've finally hit my stride!" she'd written. *Now I'll never catch up with her*, I thought bitterly.

Outside, the clouds had thickened, covering all but the westernmost edge of the sky. I headed down the road that I'd walked so often before, going to the student union to listen to jackrabbit jam with Waterfall on the piano, or, later, lugging our gear back and forth between Alpha Theta and Panarchy. Two short blocks, a left turn, and I was on the Trail again. White blazes painted on telephone poles marked the path to the river, to the next state. And beyond that—all the way to Georgia, if I followed it that far. A flicker of excitement broke through my fear. What mountains waited for me? What lakes and rivers farther south? What new friends would I meet along the way?

Beyond the bridge, the trail followed a four-lane highway—not an auspicious start to the new state. All my dawdling at Panarchy had put me in Vermont just in time for evening rush hour. Cars moved past hardly faster than I was walking, filling the air with noise and exhaust fumes. The cab of a van pulled abreast of me, and a woman's voice hollered out the window.

"Hey, hiker, want some bread?"

Probably a tourist on her way home from vacation, trying to get rid of a stale half-loaf of Wonder Bread, I thought. But the politeness my mother had drilled into me, combined with a new hiker instinct to eat anything I could lay my hands on, compelled me to accept. I turned and smiled at her.

"Sure, I'd love some."

I caught a brief glimpse of a young woman with a light brown ponytail giving me the thumbs-up, before the truck moved ahead of me. As it passed, I noticed the logo stenciled on its side. Red Hen Baking Company—the local bakery that jackrabbit and I had decided was our favorite, after two weeks of sampling every kind of bread the Hanover Co-op had to offer. A hundred yards down the road, the woman pulled over, set a paper bag on the sidewalk, then hopped into the truck and drove off, before I had a chance to catch up and thank her.

At the top of a long steep hill behind the village of Norfolk, Vermont, the trail finally left the pavement. I walked a mile or so into the woods before stopping in a stand of white pines to eat my bread. A doe walked past upslope of me. The sky had begun clearing; her coat blazed red-gold in a patch of sunlight. She glanced in my direction, flicked her tail back and forth, then bent her neck to nibble a few shoots of grass from the forest floor. I wished jackrabbit could have been there—but even as the thought crossed my mind, I realized that the deer would never have come so close to the two of us together. We would have been practicing the poems we'd memorized, joking about the way the weather had changed for the better as soon as we got out of New Hampshire—we might not have noticed the deer, even if she had walked by. I smiled to myself. Companionship on the Trail had its pleasures—but so did solitude.

At Happy Hill Shelter, four miles past Norwich, I found the register full of messages from our friends ahead. Waterfall had invented a new Extreme Hiking Maneuver. "Today, Murphy helped me to perfect my form in the challenging Roundtop Root-ski," she wrote. "It's when you slide down a root and land on a body part other than your feet!" Nor'easter and Creen had left us a few lines of verse:

> . . . Onward we pushed, as is our habit,
> Hoping to meet again with Isis and jackrabbit
> (We hope you're feeling better and moving on south
> We'd say "break a leg" but that'd be putting our foots in our
> mouth!)

In the cartoon sketched beneath the rhyme, Nor'easter was holding a sign that read, "JACKRABBIT: We hope you are feeling back 100%!" I copied their drawing as best I could, so I could send it to my sister.

The light was fading, and I was just about to go set up my tent, when I heard the tramp of boots coming down the shelter trail. A tall hiker with a bushy beard strode into the clearing.

"Hey, you must be one of the barefoot girls! I'm Woodsman," he greeted me. "I met a bunch of sobos that told me to keep an eye out for you. Is your sister okay, the one that broke her ankle in the Whites?"

"She didn't break anything. She just got a bruise, but it's bad enough that she had to get off the Trail for a while."

"Where'd she get off?" he asked.

"In Hanover. Today."

"Man, that sucks. You must really miss her."

Two more grungy, bearded men walked out of the woods, the reek of sweat and well-used gear drifting ahead of them. Woodsman looked up and waved.

"Hey, guys!" he called out. "There's one of the Barefoot Sisters here, and her sister just got off the Trail, so we have to cheer her up!"

The men dropped their packs, grinning.

"I can stand on my head and whistle the theme from 'Cheers,'" one of them offered.

"Don't know how I can top that," said the other, shaking his head. "Let's see, um . . . I can balance a spoon on my nose!"

I stood up to greet them, laughing. If anyone had asked me, earlier in the day, what scared me most about the prospect of hiking solo, I probably would have answered, strange men in the woods at night. Here I was, four hours later, preparing to camp next to three men I had never met before. And I didn't feel remotely threatened by the situation. Of course I didn't—they were hikers, part of my tribe.

Later that night, I spread out my sleeping bag in my narrow, angular solo tent and lay back, watching a few stars flicker through the clear plastic window in its fly. *I love this tent*, I thought. *I love this trail. Bread, wildlife, friendly nobos, a message from Waterfall. Stars between the branches overhead.* Best of all, though, was the feeling of strength and confidence I'd gained in my first day alone. I had faced my fears, and they had vanished. I could hardly wait to see what the next day brought. Even if I was walking toward quagmires and scree slopes, I felt eager to test myself against them. For the first time, I realized that

I wanted to continue the Trail—to finish the Trail—no matter what lay between me and Springer. Even if I hiked it all alone.

I woke to dark clouds hanging over the treetops.

"You're about to find out why we call this state Vermud," Woodsman told me at breakfast. The other two nobos, who were sitting at the front of the shelter lacing up their boots, nodded and scowled.

"We've had nothing but rain for the past two weeks, all the way through Mosquitochusetts and Vermud," Woodsman continued. "God, I'm so glad I'll be in New Hampshire today. One of the prettiest states on the Trail, from what I've heard."

I decided not to debunk the myths he'd heard about New Hampshire. Anyway, there was always a chance that he'd have good weather there. "Mud's kinda fun when you're hiking barefoot," I told him, wiggling my toes.

"Yeah, I guess it would be." He laughed.

"The state you're gonna hate is Pennsylvania," said the guy who could balance a spoon on his nose. "Tore my boots all to hell."

His companion winced, eyeing my feet. "Holy crap. Pennsylvania barefoot. Let's not even go there."

"There's no way in hell I'd go back to Pennsylvania, barefoot or not," Woodsman said. He leapt to his feet and hefted his small pack. "Race you guys to Hanover," he challenged his friends. "Cold beer and frat houses, here we come!"

"Ben and Jerry's!"

"White Mountains!"

"Woo-hoo!" The other two picked up their packs and bounded after Woodsman, laughing and shouting. As their voices faded in the distance, a wave of loneliness washed over me. Would the rest of my Trail friendships be this brief? All the sobos I knew—and all the other sobos of 2000, if they had any fear of winter—were at least ten days ahead of me. From now on, the only fellow hikers I could hope to encounter were nobos, who I'd talk with for an evening at most, before we went our opposite ways.

By the time I finished eating and packed up my gear, a fine drizzle was falling, darkening the trunks of oaks and hemlocks. I sang out loud as I walked, trying to cheer myself up. The songs sounded hollow, though, without their harmony parts; my lone voice seemed too thin to fill the space between the trees.

A few miles into the morning, I reached West Hartford, Vermont: cracked asphalt streets meandering down to an iron-gray river, small clapboard houses with goats fenced in the yards, and a highway with no exit ramps sweeping around the outskirts of the town. Out in the open, I felt the drizzle soaking into my clothing, so I stopped in the shelter of a crumbling cement wall to get out my Gore-Tex jacket. When I stood up again, I saw a group of nobos, three men and a woman, walking up the hill toward me.

"That looks like one of the Barefoot Sisters!" exclaimed the woman.

"Check out her feet! They're for real!" said the gray-haired man to her right.

"What, you didn't believe Waterfall? Of course they're for real," said a man with black curls and round rosy cheeks, who was standing at the front of the group. "I'm Gilligan," he told me.

I'd never seen the show his name came from, but the man certainly fit Waterfall's descriptions of the sitcom character she'd had a crush on as a teenager. Short, dark, and cute. I struggled to hold back laughter. "Hi, I'm Isis," I said. "You guys know Waterfall?"

"*Know* her?" said Gilligan. "I proposed to her two weeks ago."

"Wow. How long had you known each other?" I asked.

"About thirty seconds. I introduced myself, and she said, 'Gilligan, my darling! We meet at last! I've loved you since I was, oh, about twelve years old!' Well, it sounded to me like we were destined for each other, so I dropped down on one knee in the trail. I asked her to marry me and hike northbound and change her trail name to Mary Ann."

"What did she say?"

He hung his head, sighing. "She didn't want to change her name. So much for destiny."

Before we parted, I asked them what the Trail was like ahead and whether they had any recommendations about places to stay in Vermont.

"Go to Dan Quinn's, on Vermont 12," said Gilligan. "That guy rocks. We stopped in around noon yesterday, just to see if there was a register in the barn, and next thing we knew, Dan was ordering us pizza for lunch."

I remembered that Waterfall had mentioned Dan Quinn—she'd heard from friends that he had a piano. Before we split up, she and jackrabbit had looked forward to playing it together.

"You should definitely stop for breakfast at the West Hartford General Store," said the woman, who'd introduced herself as Candy Lady. "It's right on the Trail, just a few blocks farther."

"A breakfast place right on the Trail?" I asked. "Sounds great. Any more advice you guys can offer?

"Just one thing," said Doc, the older man. "Are you carrying any shoes? Good. You'll have to put them on when you reach Pennsylvania."

In the maple woods a mile or so past West Hartford, the rain began in earnest. *Ick. I'm going to get wet*, I thought, as the first fat drops slapped down on the leaves overhead. I pulled the hood of my rain jacket tighter, laughing at myself. "*Ick. Oh bother. Dear, dear, dear.*" *Why am I so prim, even when I'm talking to myself? Jackrabbit would shout "Fuck the rain!" and glower as though her frown could turn the clouds back.*

I tried it, but I couldn't muster enough anger to sound convincing. I was still comfortably sated with the home fries, eggs, and milkshake I'd had for my second breakfast and cheered by the messages friends had left us in the General Store's register. Besides, I kind of liked the rustle of raindrops hitting the leaves. The air smelled clean, sharp with tannins. A bluish mist hovered under the trees, and rose in ragged spires from the valleys. Birches at the edge of a field tossed their contorted white limbs in the air like dancers. *I wonder why I ever disliked rain*, I thought as I waded through the waist-high grass. *Was I just taking jackrabbit's feelings for my own?*

In spite of my discovery that I didn't mind rain, I was reluctant to set up my tent in it. I stopped early for the night at Thistle Hill Shelter. When I got to the shelter, at four in the afternoon, it was almost empty. As the evening wore on, though, more and more grumpy, bedraggled nobos crowded in. It had been a long time since I'd noticed the reek of other hikers, but the damp, close air seemed to concentrate the odors of unwashed bodies and rotting boots. I ended up in the corner next to a scrawny eighteen-year-old boy, who spent the evening courting me with much more enthusiasm than wit. By morning, I was glad to see that the sky had cleared.

I hiked another short day to VT 12, stopping every few hours to graze on the blackberries that clustered along fence lines and overran untended fields. Late in the afternoon, I gathered a Nalgene-full and brought it with me to Dan Quinn's. I hoped he would let me use his kitchen, along with enough flour, butter, and sugar to bake a pie.

As I walked up to the three-story clapboard farmhouse, with beds of white lilies at the edge of its neatly mown lawn, I reassessed my chances of using the kitchen. Here was someone who seemed to be pretty well-to-do, who probably thought of hikers as a favorite charity project. The fact that he gave us pizza and let us sleep in his barn didn't necessarily mean that he wanted a smelly stranger inside his house. I thought of the bored, super-cilious students who had shuffled us back and forth between their frat houses in Hanover. To the people along the Trail who offered hikers free or inexpensive lodging, we must seem like an endless river of wants and needs. *A ride to town? A ride to the hospital? A shower? A piano? May I use your kitchen, please?*

In the vegetable garden beside the barn, a stocky, darkly tanned man with curly brown hair pulled weeds, pausing every once in a while to wipe his forehead with a dusty bandana.

"Hi," I said to him. "Is this Dan Quinn's place?"

"It sure is." He leaned over the split-rail fence, holding out a large, calloused hand. "Welcome. I'm Dan."

"I'm Isis. I, um, I brought some blackberries, and I hoped I could make you a pie." I held out the Nalgene by way of explanation.

He raised his eyebrows. "You want to cook for me?"

"Um, well . . . yes."

"I've been taking in hikers for five years," he said slowly, "and no one's ever offered to cook for me. Now, don't get me wrong, hikers have done a lot of great things for me. They helped me dig this garden and convert the old woodshed into a studio for my girlfriend. Just a few days ago, a hiker mowed the lawn for me. But nobody's ever offered to bake me a pie." He leaned his shovel against the barn and walked around the end of the fence. "Come on over to the house. You probably want to get cleaned up, and then I'll show you the kitchen."

I washed my hair in the outdoor shower that Dan had set up for hikers, a wooden platform under his deck screened from the yard by a couple of scraps of tarp. Sunlight streamed through the deck's wooden slats, making the hot water sparkle. After I dried off and put on my cleanest clothes, Dan gave me a tour of the house, starting with the kitchen and ending with the guest rooms and studies on the second floor. He was a carpenter, he told me, and he'd made a specialty of restoring old buildings. He was still working on his own house; the kitchen, gleaming with hardwood, copper, and slate, had been his latest project. Down the hall was the den, followed by a living room nearly filled with an enormous grand piano. I thought how delighted jackrabbit would have been to see it; I could picture the rare smile, unselfconscious as a child's, that would have lighted her eyes. I felt a pang of some sharp emotion—guilt, pity, or perhaps simply longing for the music she would have played. *What am I doing here?* I asked myself. *Why am I here, and she isn't?*

Upstairs, Dan led me through the library, the study, and two guest bed-rooms.

"Take your pick of the guest rooms," he said as we finished the tour.

"I don't want to put you to any trouble," I told him. "I'll be fine staying in the barn."

"In the barn? You can't stay in the barn. If you're going to cook for me, that makes you family. Please treat my house as your own."

"All this for one pie that I haven't even made yet?" I asked. "I wish I had the time and ingredients to cook you a meal, at least."

"Take a zero tomorrow. We can go shopping in the morning, and I'll buy whatever you need."

I started to explain that I couldn't afford a zero; I was already weeks behind the southbound crowd.

"How far do you hike in a day?" Dan asked me.

"I've been going really slowly," I admitted. "Nine or ten miles."

"So . . . take tomorrow off, and I'll slack you a twenty the day after that. You won't lose any time."

I thought for a moment. The longest day I'd hiked was a seventeen. In the gentle, rolling hills of Vermont, though, a twenty shouldn't be too hard. Espe-cially without a pack.

"It actually looks more like twenty-one," Dan said, glancing down the map I was studying. "But you've got plenty of time. Even if you go only two and a half miles an hour, you'll be back at the house by six-thirty. I'll have din-ner waiting for you."

It was ten in the morning when Dan dropped me off at the Inn at Long Trail. After a quiet day of bread-baking, working in the garden, and writing, I felt more than ready to slack my first twenty-one. I'd packed one of my favorite picnic lunches: peanut butter, banana, and honey sandwiches on chal-lah. My weather karma from the Whites seemed to be paying off; the sky was cloudless and the morning cool still lingered under the trees. Except for a steep thousand-foot rise in the fourth mile, the elevation profile looked pain-less: four or five small hills, followed by a long level stretch, and a gradual five-mile descent to VT 12.

To complete my good fortune, I had a hiking partner for the day: a fellow southbounder named Scout. She had arrived at Dan's farm the previous after-noon after hiking a twenty-two from Hanover. Dan, who felt sorry for me when he heard how I'd lost jackrabbit, had put Scout up in his other guest room and encouraged the two of us to hike together. The slack from the Inn to VT 12 would be a short day by her standards, but she agreed to keep me company for at least that long.

For the first few miles, we chatted as we walked. Scout told me there were still a few sobos behind me. She'd tried to hike with a couple of them, but they were all too slow.

"There was one guy I would have liked to stay with—for a day or two, anyway. A real gentle, philosophical man, thin as a rail, with a beautiful singing voice. But he was creeping along—twelve, fifteen miles a day. You can't change your pace that much, just to stay with someone. It's like changing your whole personality to try to make a relationship work. You end up resenting the person for holding you back, even though it was your choice to stay."

Scout shook her head, her thick, honey-colored braid bobbing back and forth between her shoulder blades. The gesture reminded me of jackrabbit, and I felt a twinge of guilt. In the past few days, I'd discovered the joys of hiking solo. I could take a zero guilt-free, I had time to read all the registers, and I'd found that my mood wasn't ruled by the weather. I wondered what jackrabbit would have done differently, if she'd hiked alone. Perhaps she would have gone ultralight and kept up with the other sobos. Perhaps she would have worn shoes. How much had the plans and choices we'd made together held her back?

Scout's voice broke through my musings. "This must be that steep section we were looking at on the elevation profile."

I looked up. Scout was only a few paces ahead of me, but already, the backs of her knees were at eye level.

"Reminds me of Moody Mountain back in Maine," I answered, starting up the incline behind her.

"Moody? Oh yeah, Moody. Right before Andover. I came down it in a thunderstorm. Felt like I was water-skiing, only downhill. It was great!"

We both fell silent, struggling to keep our footing on the slick, dusty trail. It grew steeper and steeper as we climbed, until I could imagine the top of the mountain curving over us like the crest of a breaking wave. Unlike the steep granite cliffs in Maine and the Whites, this slope offered no handholds. I envied Scout her hiking poles; once she got used to the dust, she charged uphill almost as fast as she'd been walking on level ground. I clenched my hands into fists and swung my arms in time to my steps, pushing myself forward with imaginary poles. *Breathe in, breathe out. Only a little farther . . . and a little farther after that.* Ignoring the stitch in my side, I managed to keep up.

None of the other hills were quite so steep, but that ascent was only the first in a series of small mountains and deep, narrow valleys that resembled the elevation profile about as closely as a grizzly resembles a teddy bear. In some places, the trail plunged straight down a mountainside; in others, it was so heavily switch-backed that I felt as if we were running a treadmill, turning and turning and going nowhere. We stopped for lunch at Stony Brook Shelter, only eight miles from our starting point, according to the map. Scout checked her watch.

"It's almost two o'clock, Isis. I can't believe we've been going only two miles an hour."

"Jackrabbit and I usually make two with packs on, and you've been walking a lot faster than I'm used to," I answered. "There must be something wrong with the map."

"I wish I'd checked my *Data Book* this morning," Scout said, dropping her fanny pack on the shelter floor and flopping down beside it. "I've hiked thirties where I was less tired out at lunch."

We ate quickly and set out again, trying to walk even faster than before. Sunset caught us near Winturi Shelter, still five miles from VT 12. Five smooth, downhill miles, according to the elevation profile. It wasn't much more accurate than it had been earlier in day, but the trail's wild undulations did seem to subside a little in this final stretch. Scout and I flew. Our paces lengthened into a kind of lope, quiet and purposeful as the stride of coyotes tracking down a deer. I spared a thought for my bare feet, pale blurs gliding over the hard-packed earth. If there were thorns or sharp rocks in my path, I wouldn't see them or feel them in time to lessen the impact—my hike would be over in an instant and I'd be home with my sister, figuring out something less crazy to do in the next four months. I didn't feel crazy, though, running barefoot into the dusk. I felt like it was the most natural thing in the world: my taut, dry soles pushing off from the ground, my leg muscles aching but obedient, the darkness slowly seeping through the trees.

The first stars were coming out by the time we reached the meadow above Dan's house. The orange squares of lit windows in the valley beckoned us.

"Eight o'clock." Scout's eyes sparkled in the light of her watch. "We made it from Winturi Shelter in just over an hour."

"That's, what—four miles an hour?" I asked.

"Five, if your map's right."

"In that case, it was probably seven or eight." I held up my hand for a high five. "Congratulations. Let's go see what Dan's made for supper."

The next morning, Dan dropped us off at the Inn again, this time with all of our gear. After hugs goodbye, Scout set out at a pace that seemed undiminished by the full pack she carried. I was still trying to pull the awkward weight of my own pack into balance, tugging at one after another of its umpteen straps, when she turned a corner of the trail and vanished from sight. Cinching my waist belt as tight as it would go, I followed her into the woods at my usual amble. No hurry. No point in pretending I could catch up with her. The muscles in my legs and feet felt stiff from the previous day's marathon; even without my pack, I would have been hard pressed to hike another twenty.

Plodding up the trail, slowly working the tension out of my calves, I felt lonelier than I had since Hanover. Though we'd talked about the difficulty of hiking with partners, Scout's company had reminded me of the good things about it—the shared victories, the games and conversations weaving through the miles, and even the ways in which we tested each other's strength. At the moment, the hundred daily compromises jackrabbit and I had made and the way our moods had swung around each other like tether balls seemed little enough to suffer for the comfort of seeing a familiar face every morning.

A few miles beyond the Inn, I found myself in a young hardwood forest with an understory of moose maple. Here and there, fallen trees fanned their slender, straight limbs across the forest floor. Bending down to remove a branch from the trail, I noticed that it was the perfect size to make a hiking staff. I cut off the ends with my pocketknife saw and tried walking with it for a while. It seemed to help; I could move a little faster, swinging the staff along beside me, and it took some of the pressure off my tired legs. Leaning on it threw me off balance, though. My pack lurched dangerously, loosening its web of straps. I decided I needed a pole for my left hand, too.

Finding a second, matching staff proved a good deal more challenging than cutting the first had been. I checked a dozen dead maples before I found a limb that was neither green nor rotting, with a straight section five feet long and an inch in diameter. Once I had chosen a second branch, I sat down on a rock and carved the tops of them into snakes' heads—symbols of transformation, of shedding my old skin. The project pushed my loneliness to the back of my mind, replacing it with the slightly guilty pleasure of doing things my own way. I knew that jackrabbit, counting our miles against the onset of winter, would never have agreed to spend two hours carving in the middle of the day.

Beyond the valley of moose maples, the trail curved along the western slope of Killington Mountain, through fir woods carpeted with moss and stands of white birches surrounded by waist-high ferns. At first I watched my feet, trying to keep them out of the way of my new hiking sticks. As soon as I settled into the rhythm, though, I found it hard to believe that I'd hiked so far on legs alone. My stride seemed to double in length; the gentle uphill felt like level ground. *See,* I told an imaginary jackrabbit, *I spent two hours getting hiking sticks, and it was worth it.* I could almost hear her answering, *Well, you didn't have to carve them.*

I camped by myself on a tent platform that night, near the top of Killington Peak. From the sound of voices, I guessed that there were four or five late nobos sharing the converted stone cabin that served as a shelter, but the cloud of pot smoke pouring out the door discouraged me from socializing. *It's just as well,* I told myself. *I'm in no mood to be regaled with horror stories about Pennsylvania.*

I slept badly, and the morning cold, at an altitude of almost four thousand feet, made it hard for me to drag myself out of my sleeping bag. At the privy, I discovered that I'd gotten my period, never an easy thing to deal with on the Trail. This time, it had arrived a week early, and I wasn't carrying pads. I dug a handkerchief out of my pack, folded it into a small rectangle, and pinned it to my underwear. *Good for two or three hours, but what then?* The next major road crossing, at Clarendon Gorge, was twelve miles away. I stuffed my tent into its sack and sat down to breakfast, thoroughly out of sorts.

"Good morning! My name's Willin'." A ruddy-faced nobo in his midthirties had just stepped into the clearing. He smiled, eyes sparkling and white teeth flashing from behind his trimmed black beard.

"Isis," I answered, reaching up to shake his hand. I hoped that the terseness of my reply would encourage him to hike on. In my current mood, I didn't think I could stomach his cheerfulness for long.

He let go of my hand but held my gaze, his face still lit with a friendly, open smile. "Isis. Pleased to meet you. How are you doing this fine morning?"

Head bent, he waited for me to answer. With a great effort of will, I resisted describing my predicament to him in gory detail. He'd hike on soon enough; I didn't need to waste my breath being rude to a stranger.

"I'm doing okay," I replied.

He waited for me to continue. His patience, his willingness to listen, disarmed me.

"I just discovered, this morning, that I'm out of some supplies. Something I need soon. I mean, now." I could feel my face flushing. "I'm not fast enough to hike to Clarendon by nightfall. So, I'm not in a very good mood. I'm sorry."

Willin' didn't seem the least bit discomposed or even surprised by my outburst.

"Why don't you come with me?" he asked. "I've run out of a couple things myself, and I was planning to take the gondola down to Killington."

"The gondola?"

"It runs down the east side of the mountain, from the new ski lodge. I heard they let hikers ride for free."

"That sounds great, but I don't want to keep you waiting. I'm not quite finished with breakfast."

"No hurry. We've got all day."

Half an hour later, the two of us floated high over the valley in a purple upholstered car, admiring the cloud-speckled hills and meadows below. At the foot of the mountain, though, the gondola disgorged us into a disconcerting wilderness of pavement, perfume boutiques, and high-rise hotels.

"Is this Killington?" I asked.

"No, this is the ski resort. The village is a mile or so down the road," Willin' replied. "I'm not sure which direction, though. We'd better ask."

He headed for the nearest hotel, a tower of whitewashed adobe and plate glass. In the velvet-draped lobby, I skulked by the fireplace, hoping no one would notice my hiker smell. Willin' walked right up to the counter.

"Good morning, ma'am," he said to the receptionist, a heavyset woman in her fifties. With her starched collar and octagonal bifocals, she reminded me of my tenth-grade math teacher—not someone I would have accosted lightly.

She looked up from her books.

"How are you doing?" Willin' asked her.

A smile that reflected Willin's spread across her powdered face. "Not bad. And yourself?"

"Very well, thank you. I was hoping you could tell me the way to town."

"Killington Village? It's just a mile or so down the hill. You want to go back out to the road and head north. Don't blink or you'll miss it, though. It's only a couple of stores and a shopping mall."

"Thank you very much, ma'am. Have a good day."

"You too, sir," she answered. She beamed at me. "And you, miss. I hope you enjoy the village."

"How did you do that?" I asked Willin', as we walked down the road toward town. "I would never have gotten up my nerve to go in there smelling like a hiker and ask for directions."

"It doesn't matter what you smell like or how fancy a building looks," Willin' said slowly. "It's the human interaction. Saying hello to a person before you ask for anything. Asking how somebody is and actually waiting for their answer. I grew up in Jamaica. Down there, it's just common courtesy. In the States, I think there's this tendency for people to treat other people like machines. If you do that, it's no wonder if they don't want to help you."

We spent the whole morning in Killington, first stopping at the Killington Market for Ben and Jerry's and our sundry resupply items, then heading to the bakery for coffee and donuts, sandwiches, and a whole apple pie. Willin' greeted everyone with a smile, asked them how they were doing, and listened to their answers as if nothing could interest him more. Everyone we met, from the dour shopkeeper to the man out walking his bulldog, smiled back. And more—the man with the bulldog directed us to the bakery; the baker came out of the kitchen and told us stories from his hike on the Pacific Crest Trail. Two old ladies offered to buy us the pie. At the end of his shift, the baker drove us up to the ski resort. By the time we got back on the gondola, helped aboard by an impeccably dressed attendant, I felt like a princess, or some beloved celebrity—someone who could make a stranger's day just by smiling at him.

Over the next few days, I saw more wildlife than human life on the Trail. Sparrows and warblers lighted in the branches around me, cheeping their one-note warning. Little red squirrels and fat gray ones joined in with their scolding trills. In the midday warmth, garter snakes uncoiled from stone ledges and flickered away into the underbrush. Once, picnicking at a place called White Rocks, I watched two goshawks fighting, swooping and screaming and tumbling claw to claw until they nearly hit the trees above my head.

I met only two hikers: an ultralight southbounder who was guzzling water straight out of a stream and a fanatical old nobo who admonished me on the evils of my heathen trail name. One afternoon, I passed a team of maintainers digging trenches to divert the fall rains. They stared at my dusty feet and offered me a handful of candy bars. For the most part, though, I had the trail to myself. In place of conversation, I read the registers cover to cover, practiced the poems that jackrabbit and I had memorized, and made up songs, sometimes singing them out loud while I walked. Inspired by a visit to the Whistle Stop Café, a quarter mile off the trail at Clarendon Gorge, I came up with a Vermont verse for "Dig a Hole":

Oh, I love to hike the switchbacks of Vermont's A.T.
Seeing how much pie I can consume;
There's a café at every road,
But when you gotta dump your load,
You've hiked a half a mile from the restroom!

(Later, when jackrabbit and I performed the song for nobo audiences, the third line of the Vermont verse would invariably raise a few eyebrows. To hikers coming from New York and New Jersey, the Green Mountain State seemed remarkable for its dearth of Trailside delis. For me, though, places like the West Hartford General Store, the Inn at Long Trail, and the Whistle Stop Café provided a pleasant contrast to Maine and New Hampshire's weeklong stretches between resupply stops.)

The first night I tented alone, next to an empty shelter, reminded me of my first stealth-camping experience on Little Boardman Mountain in the Wilderness. Every sound in the darkness woke me. I lay motionless, listening for the next footstep, the growling of bears drawn to the smell of my menstrual blood. Instead I heard a deer snorting, a heron croaking from a nearby swamp, a mouse scuttering among the leaves: the silence of the forest, made up of thousands of soft rustles and swift heartbeats.

Reaching Big Branch Shelter on September first, I found it packed with nobos. After being alone for so long, I felt shy of people, unsettled by their loud voices and the chemical reek of their stoves. After talking with the crowd of nobos for a few minutes, I walked upstream and found myself a tent site beside a deep amber pool. I cooked on the riverbank, listening to the night waking around me. Owls hooted back and forth over the sound of rushing water. A late frog chirped in the reeds. The sounds seemed comforting, now: nature going about her business, unperturbed by the intruder with the big green cocoon and the cupful of fire. In the morning, I rose before dawn and skinny-dipped in the pool, feeling every cell of my skin awaken and dance with cold.

Unfortunately, I couldn't stay in the woods forever. I was running low on food, so I hitched into Manchester with a nobo whom I met in the trailhead parking lot. We caught a ride to the post office, where the nobo had to pick up a mail drop. While he sat on a bench outside the post office, transferring Ziplocs full of noodles and rice into his food bag, I walked into town to buy my own resupply.

Following the directions I'd gotten from the postmistress, I came to what must have been the center of Manchester. A row of storefronts painted in glossy dark purples and greens lined the broad boulevard. Behind them, vast parking lots shimmered in the heat. Families of tourists wandered past me, the daughters in matching floral-print dresses and the sons in miniature suits. I looked around for an outfitter store, a grocery store, somewhere to have lunch, but none of the boutiques were selling anything I could use. Their display windows held little black dresses, clunky handbags emblazoned with faux graffiti, and diamond-studded watchbands. I glanced at the price tag on a dress and recoiled, thinking, *I could live on the Trail for two months on that much money!* Finally, I passed a young woman in jeans and a t-shirt, who looked like she might be a local. I asked her if she knew where I could find the outfitter store.

"The Urban Outfitter?" she answered. "I don't think they have one here. There's, like, Gap, and Old Navy, and Abercrombie . . ."

Half an hour later, on the outskirts of the couture district, I stumbled across a strip mall with an EMS outlet and a supermarket. At the other end of the mall, a pink neon sign flashed *PIZZA*. I'd found the hiker quarter of town. Paying for my flashlight batteries, I asked the cashier at EMS whether there was a hostel nearby.

"Nope. The hostel closed a couple years ago," he told me.

"Is there anywhere for hikers to stay?"

"Well, I've heard there's a guy who gives people bunk space and breakfast for thirty-five bucks. He lives a ways out of town, though. You have to call him."

I ate a pizza and debated with myself. Breakfast sounded tempting— breakfasts were always my favorite town meals, with their fruit juices and fresh baked goods and eggs—but $35 was more than jackrabbit and I together had ever paid for a night's lodging on the Trail, aside from the fiasco of the Crawford Notch Hostel. Was there any reason, beyond promise of a good breakfast, for me to stay around town? I'd just rinsed off in a stream, so I didn't need a shower quite as badly as usual. I had meant to call jackrabbit, to see how she was doing, but I could always try from the next town.

Deciding to leave Manchester proved to be much easier than actually finding my way out. The man who'd brought me and the nobo into town had made a few more turns than I could follow, coming off the highway. After he dropped us off, I'd wandered around for a good forty-five minutes looking for the outfitter. I knew I was about ten miles west of the A.T. and a long ways downhill, but even if I got up my nerve to hitchhike alone, I had no idea where to start.

I hoisted my pack, heavy with cheese, bagels, and, to make up for the lack of breakfast, a single orange. From the center of the parking lot, I could see the dip in the eastern mountains where the highway snaked through, a bit to the north of town. I took my bearings, then started walking north and east, city block by block. Twenty minutes later, following the sidewalk along endless rows of pastel clapboard houses, I had to admit I was lost. I was getting pretty thirsty, too—I hadn't carried any water into the city. Although it was early September, the temperature must have been in the high eighties; heat mirages hovered over the pavement. My head ached, and I could feel the skin on my shoulders starting to burn.

If I'd been in a business section of town, I could have put Willin's lessons to good use. Smile. Care about the person you're talking to. Most people want to help you, if you treat them like human beings. But I hadn't passed a store since I left the parking lot. Only houses, getting smaller as I headed toward the outskirts of town. I had a hard time imagining even Willin' walking up to a stranger's *house* to ask for directions.

A small wooden sign hung from a post in front of a light blue ranch house: *Tutoring Center*. Once I'd gotten close enough to read it, I noticed the gravel path curving around the back of the building. It didn't look terribly public, but by that time, I didn't care. I followed the path around to the back door and knocked. A minute passed. No one home. Suddenly, tears of exhaustion spilled down my cheeks. I sat on the ramp in front of the door and rested my forehead against my hiking sticks.

The door slid open. A strikingly handsome, silver-haired man stared out at me, his eyes on a level with mine. When I stood up, I realized that he was sitting in a wheelchair.

"Come in," he told me. "You look like you could use a drink of water."

I tried to stammer out thanks, but his kind voice seemed to have broken a dam inside me—my tears had turned to sobs.

"No need to talk," he said. "Sit down, rest a little, and then you can tell me what's wrong."

After five paper cups of water and a few Girl Scout cookies, I told him how I'd gotten lost, trying to find my way back to the Trail.

"Appalachian Trail, eh?" His blue eyes sparked. "One of my students hiked it just last year. What a wonderful adventure."

I smiled. "Yeah, it is. Thanks for reminding me."

"You're welcome. Now, to get you back to the highway . . ."

It turned out that I was only three blocks away. Following the tutor's directions, I headed out of town along the shoulder. I doubted that I could walk all the way by nightfall, and I was reluctant to hitch alone. For once, though, my lack of plans didn't worry me. The words of the crippled tutor kept running through my mind: *what a wonderful adventure.* If I could have planned my hike in perfect detail, and prepared for every contingency, it wouldn't have been an adventure. Not knowing where I would sleep that night or how I would get there seemed like a positive thing now—an element of chance that opened my life to things I couldn't have planned.

I'd barely walked a quarter mile when a dilapidated sedan crunched the gravel beside me.

"Need a ride somewhere?" asked a rough voice.

I leaned down and looked through the window. The speaker, a heavily tattooed man with the build of a professional weight lifter, was busy scraping old soda cans and magazines off the passenger seat. Chalky dust coated his arm. With his shaved head and sleeveless t-shirt, he looked like the sort of man I might have crossed the street to avoid if I'd met him under any other circumstances.

"I'm headed to the Appalachian Trail," I told him.

"Where's that?" he asked, glancing up at me. With a start, I realized that he was younger than I was, perhaps only nineteen or twenty. His voice sounded like it belonged to a chain-smoking fifty-year old.

"Ten miles up the highway, where it cuts through the mountains," I answered.

"I can take you there. Throw your stuff in back."

Against my better judgment—against any judgment, really—I put my pack in the backseat and climbed in beside him.

"Pull your door hard and lock it," he instructed me. "It flies open sometimes."

I obeyed, and he gunned the engine, pulling back into traffic.

"You smoke up?" he asked.

"I—uh—no thank you."

"Sorry. Just thought I'd ask. I do, sometimes. Just to have something to cut through the boredom. You know, same fucking job every day."

"What do you do?" I asked him.

"I'm a stonecutter. Industrial."

"Is that where the white dust comes from?"

"Yeah," he answered. "Shot my voice, breathing it. We're supposed to wear masks, but I was young when I started. Young and dumb." He paused, then asked, "What do you do?"

"Well, last year I worked in a bakery and went to school part time. Right now I'm hiking for six months."

"You must really like to walk."

"Yeah," I answered, "I guess I do. But it's not just the walking. You're up in the mountains, hiking along, and all of a sudden this gorgeous view opens out in front of you, you see lakes sparkling in the distance or lightning along the horizon. Or you wake up at sunrise and watch the first light catch in the treetops. Stuff like that happens every day—you're in the right place at the right time, to see something amazingly beautiful. Plus there's a great community of people out there, people from all walks of life—you sit around the fire and tell stories at night, and you make friends with people you never would've met—" I broke off, embarrassed that I'd been bragging about my good fortune to someone who sounded like he'd had so few breaks in his life.

"Sounds pretty cool," he said. "How much dough do you need for a hike like that?"

"Three or four thousand dollars," I answered.

"That's it? Hell, I could save that much in five months if I wanted to. Maybe I'll hike this trail of yours next year. Quit my fuckin' job."

The road curved up into the mountains, longer than I remembered. There were hardly any other cars this late in the afternoon. No other roads branching off of it, either. Finally I spotted the trailhead parking sign.

"That's it. On your left," I told the stonecutter. He swung into the empty lot. I thanked him for the ride and tried to open my door.

"You gotta unlock it first," he reminded me.

When I'd finally unloaded myself and all my gear, he waved goodbye and sped out of the parking lot, heading back down the mountain the way we'd come. I realized that he must have driven at least eight miles out of his way to drop me off.

I spent the night at Spruce Peak Shelter, just a mile past the road. The next morning was warmer than the past week's middays had been; I ate breakfast in my tank top, sitting on a cliff that overlooked Manchester. Not a breeze stirred; a smoggy haze obscured the mountains to the west. By the time I started hiking, the heat of the pavement seemed to have risen out of the valley and thrown its stranglehold around the hills. Just breathing was a challenge; hiking uphill seemed a Herculean feat. Sweat poured down my arms and legs, making my skin prickle. I began to regret my decision to leave town without a shower, though I wasn't sure where I would have found one in that maze of malls and parking lots.

In the early afternoon, I reached the shore of Stratton Pond, seven miles from Spruce Peak Shelter. I hadn't planned to stay there—it was one of the few places where the Vermont trail maintaining organization, the Green Mountain Club, charged a fee for shelter use. A good long break seemed to be in order, though. First a swim, then lunch. I was just about to wade in for my second swim, when a short, burly man with a wild beard appeared at the edge of the clearing.

"I'm Beavis," he said, trotting over to me. "I'm the caretaker here. Are you staying at the shelter tonight?"

"I'll probably hike on," I told him. "It's only midafternoon."

"That's too bad. The northbounders are really thinning out, and I haven't had much company lately." He looked down, and suddenly his face broke into a grin. "Say, are you barefoot because you're about to go swimming, or are you—are you—"

"Yeah, I'm one of the Barefoot Sisters. Isis." I held out my hand.

"Wow! You're my hero!" Beavis cried, practically jumping up and down. "Can I kiss your feet?"

"They're dirty," I answered, laughing. "In case you hadn't noticed."

"Okay. Fair enough. Is there anything I can do for you, though? I mean, it's great to finally meet one of you; I've heard about you for so long."

"Well, actually, there is something you could help me with, if it isn't too much trouble. Do you have a bucket I could borrow, to carry water up from the pond and wash my hair?"

"A bucket? That's easy. Hey, I even have a gray-water pit with curtains around it, if you want to take more of a shower."

Beavis helped me carry full buckets up to his "shower" and gave me a quart yogurt container to dip the water out with. Leaning over the foot-deep pit, I washed my hair, my body, and finally the clothes I'd been wearing. I wrung them out, used them to dry myself off, then wrung them out again and got dressed. In the sweltering afternoon heat, wearing damp clothes felt almost as comfortable as swimming.

I began to reconsider my plan to hike any farther that day. Storm clouds were building to the north and west; already I could hear thunder rattling around that corner of the sky. Beavis had gone to make the rounds of the campsites, so I sat down on the shore with my feet in the water and started writing a letter to jackrabbit.

"Pardon me, Lady of the Lake," a voice asked from behind me. "Is this the water source or is there a spring around?" I looked up into a pair of laughing dark eyes, set in a face the color of polished oak.

"The lake's it. I'll hold the intake valve of your filter between my toes," I told him. I poked one of my feet out of the water and wiggled it. "Just kidding. The spring's over there." I pointed to a trail Beavis had shown me earlier.

Ten minutes later, the hiker returned. He sat down on a rock at the lake's edge and took a long swig from his water bottle, closing his eyes. He was young, perhaps my sister's age, with a slight build and fine, prominent bones. Longish, cinnamon-colored hair framed his aquiline face. Instead of a beard he wore a neatly trimmed goatee.

He met my eyes, a roguish smile playing about the corner of his lips. He knew I'd been watching him.

"Hello," he said. "My name's Big Guy. I suppose yours is something other than Lady of the Lake?"

"I'm Isis," I answered, trying not to laugh. "Where on earth did you get the name 'Big Guy'?"

He shrugged. "I have a friend we call Little Guy. He's six five. How did you get your trail name?"

"That's a longer story."

"That's fine. I've only got seven more miles to go this afternoon."

My heart sank. Northbound, with a Go-lite pack. Of course he wouldn't be stopping for the day at four in the afternoon.

"My first backpacking trip was in the Andes, in Peru," I began. By the time I finished my story, raindrops were spattering down on the lake's surface, and treetops bent in a sudden wind.

Big Guy glanced up at the sky. "Maybe I'll stay here after all."

The two of us spent the rest of the day sitting at a picnic table in the front of the spacious, multi-level shelter, sharing stories and pots of tea. I found out that Big Guy was recovering from Lyme disease. He'd been off the Trail for almost three weeks.

"Before I got sick, I was always thinking ahead to the next mountain, how fast I could get there, how fast I could put it behind me. Now I don't care whether I finish. It's the journey that matters."

"Yeah, that's how I've felt all along," I told him. "I tend to stop and smell every flower in my path. The only trouble is, at the rate I'm going, I'll probably be out here till January."

"Well, that'll be something to tell your grandkids about."

We slept in the shelter's loft, with another nobo and a couple of section hikers. The lower part of the shelter was packed with college freshmen on an orientation trip. ("I hope you guys don't mind," Beavis had told us as he ushered the dripping students inside. "Groups usually stay in the tent sites, but I just couldn't leave them there on a night like this.")

Big Guy fell asleep much more quickly than I did. He lay curled on his side, facing away from me. I sat beside him and brushed my hair, watching the lightning throw his left cheekbone into relief. I felt a painful, almost maternal tenderness toward him; I wanted to pull up his sleeping bag to cover his shoulder and kiss him gently on the forehead good night. *He'll be gone tomorrow*, I reminded myself. *You'll never see him again.* I turned away from him, pulled up my own sleeping bag, and closed my eyes.

The next day, I passed more nobos than I'd seen all week. Many of them stopped for a few minutes to chat or offer advice about the Trail ahead.

"Pennsylvania's gonna suck big time," warned a young man who I met on my way up Stratton Mountain. "See all this duct tape I got on the toes of my boots? Pennsylvania."

A young couple told me to be sure to stay at a hostel called Kincora when I got to Tennessee.

"We were about to get off the Trail when we stopped there," the woman told me. "It had been raining for a week. The bottoms of my feet were solid blister. Bob, the guy who runs the Kincora, set me up on the couch with a cup of cocoa and told me Trail stories for a couple hours. By the end of the day, I couldn't believe I'd thought about quitting."

"Bob's got the greatest attitude," the man added. "It's like he is the spirit of the Trail. I know that sounds kind of whacky, but you'll get what I mean when you meet him."

A nephew and uncle team recommended a place to stay that was closer at hand, Upper Goose Pond Cabin in Massachusetts. It sounded idyllic—a little red cabin perched on a lake shore, with a kitchen and bookshelves and a canoe that hikers could borrow—until the uncle mentioned that it was run by the AMC.

"How much does it cost to stay there?" I asked suspiciously.

"I think it was three bucks a night, suggested donation."

"Wow. Thanks for the recommendation." *Trail magic from the AMC, I thought to myself. I'll believe that when I see it.*

I sat down to lunch with two more nobos, an Iowa farm boy called Optimist and a movie stuntman named Hollywood. Optimist shared around a package of Archway hermits, and told us how the cookies he carried had almost brought him romance.

"One night near the beginning of the Trail, I shared a shelter with a gorgeous woman. After supper, I got out a package of Archway cookies and offered her one. 'Archway cookies!' she said. 'My favorite! If those are hermits, I'll marry you.'" His face fell. "I was carrying lemon cookies at the time. Now I always carry hermits, but she got ahead of me and I haven't seen her since."

"Alas! I can sympathize all too well." I sighed melodramatically. "I met a charming young man just yesterday, but fate tore us asunder. He was northbound, you see."

"So, you're a sobo." Hollywood squinted at me, sizing me up. "No wonder we haven't run into you before. You're really not bad, for a southbounder."

"Excuse me?"

"You don't strike me as a self-absorbed pot-head," explained Hollywood.

"Not *all* of the sobos we met were obnoxious," Optimist added hurriedly. "It's just that the first ones gave us a pretty bad impression. They came into the shelter at five AM and woke everybody up asking for a joint. They said they'd hiked twenty-five miles that night and they really needed a smoke."

"The early northbounders weren't exactly paragons, either," I said. I told them about Patagonia, the guy we met at Little Bigelow, who'd laughed at our measly seventeen-mile day and told us that he'd just hiked a twenty-seven. "I used to think you guys were all braggarts and mile slaves."

"Mile slaves? Hardly." Optimist laughed. "If I put as much time into hiking as I put into picnicking, I would have caught up with my true love and offered her a hermit by now."

I camped that night at Story Spring Shelter along with a few more nobos, a couple who were hiking the Long Trail, and another college orientation group. While I was eating supper, a nobo with a long gray beard started a fire. I walked over and sat in front of it, watching the flames. Slowly, the other hikers gathered around.

"Anyone have a good ghost story?" someone asked. The college orientation kids, sitting along the front of the shelter, leaned forward to listen.

"I've got a good one for hikers," answered the woman who was doing the Long Trail. "Have you heard the tale of the scratch marks on the privy door?"

When she finished, one of the college students told a story about a Ouija board, and another followed with an account of a Halloween prank gone dangerously awry.

After an hour or so, the old man who had started the fire turned to me. "You southbound?" he asked. I nodded. "You ever heard about the folks who disappeared? Right in the area you're hiking through tomorrow. Into those woods."

I shook my head. I hadn't heard any such thing; I wondered if he had just come up with it on the spot.

"First one was a local guy, about a hundred years ago," the man continued. "Hunter, trapper. Folks said he knew these woods like the back of his hand. But one day he went out to check his trap line and never came back." He paused and looked over his audience with narrowed, glittering eyes, as if gauging our abilities to take on his fabled ghosts.

"In the seventies," he continued, "a Bennington College student got lost on her orientation trip. Search parties looked for her for two weeks, with dogs and everything. They never found so much as a scrap of her clothing." He glanced up at the kids in the shelter.

"We heard about that," one of them offered, her voice trembling a little. "We're from Bennington."

"Hmph. Well. You might want to stick close together, if you're headed south tomorrow."

"We're not. We hiked from Goddard Shelter yesterday," answered another woman, one of the trip's leaders. She smiled at the younger students. "I'm pretty sure we're all accounted for."

I slept well that night, but in the morning, hiking south alone, I couldn't help thinking of the old man's words. The weather had been cool and overcast since the thunderstorm. That day, the clouds had descended even farther; mist swirled among the tree trunks. Narrow waterfalls cascaded down mossy cliffs beside the trail. No birds called; no sound broke the stillness except for the steady drip and murmur of water. Perhaps it was the mist, perhaps the moss coating the trees and stones like a botanical form of fur—the forest seemed to have an energy of its own, a quiet, listening presence. I allowed myself a shiver. Here was a place where the line between life and story grew fine.

It didn't feel threatening. Inviting was more like it. I imagined I could hear the call of this forest in the hypnotic drip of water from the trees. *Leave the path. You will never have to walk on pavement again, never lose yourself in a crowd. Here are caves for your shelter, streams to bathe in, blackberries for food. Walk in the water so the dogs won't find your tracks. I can make you immortal, like the hunter who came here at the turn of the century. One hundred years, and still he's the talk of campfires.*

The sky cleared at dusk, just as I reached Goddard Shelter. A heavy band of gray hung across the horizon, followed by orange, yellow, and a blue as sharp as the lower edge of a flame. The wind began rising at sunset; by dark it howled straight into the shelter's open side. I wrapped myself up in my sleeping bag while I cooked. When I walked back to the grove of spruce trees where I'd set up my tent, even the stars seemed to be tossing and swaying among the treetops.

In the morning, the grass crackled with frost under foot. I hurried about my chores and ate breakfast pacing, jogging in place, trying to keep myself warm. I would have welcomed a steep uphill to start the day, but the trail curved steadily down along a ridge. In the hard morning light, the trees looked like ranks of gray soldiers standing at attention. No more mystery, no voice of water tempting me to stay. Already, before a single leaf had turned, the first frost of the winter was nipping at my heels. I had to go south, and quickly.

I didn't stop until I reached Melville Nauheim Shelter, eight miles from Goddard, in the early afternoon. The sun fell straight down through the branches, forming a small island of warmth in the shelter's clearing. Someone had left a few chapters of Edward Abbey's *The Monkey Wrench Gang* in the register box; after lunch, I curled up in the sun to read them. What luxury to be both still and warm. Even when I'd finished reading, I lay there with my eyes closed, half dreaming, until the light moved away among the trees. Then I strapped on my pack, picked up my hiking sticks, and walked another six miles to Congdon Shelter.

A white husky, tied to a tree outside the shelter, announced my arrival with a soft growl.

"What is it, girl?" A young man in fatigues stepped around the corner of the building. Seeing me, he raised a hand in greeting. "Don't mind my dog," he said, and then, after a pause, "but don't get too close to her, either."

I crossed the stream and walked a ways into the woods to set up my tent. After that greeting, I thought I'd steer clear of the man as well as the dog. When I went back to filter water, though, I found a woman about my age filling her cooking pot. It was almost dark, and neither of us wore a headlamp— I was standing right across from her before I realized that she was there. I hesitated, not wanting to startle her. She bent forward, and her straight, dark hair brushed the surface of the water. When she flipped it back over her shoulder, she spotted me standing on the far bank. She didn't seem the least bit surprised.

"Hi. I'm Morgan. Are you staying here?" Her voice sounded warm and confident in the darkness.

"I'm Isis," I told her. "I'm tenting over on this side of the stream."

"Well, I hope you'll come up to the shelter to cook your meal. There's four of us there, and all the others are men. Not that I have anything against men, but, you know—the energy can get a little strange when you're outnumbered three to one."

"Yeah, I can sympathize," I told her. "I'll be over in a minute."

I picked up my stove, my food bag, and a handful of twigs for fuel, then joined Morgan in the shelter. She had donned a long black fleece robe over her shorts and tank top, and she was sitting cross-legged behind her Whisperlite, stirring a pot of soup. For the moment, none of the guys seemed to be focusing their energy on her. A tall young man with a lion's mane of blond hair was rolling out his sleeping bag in one corner, while the dog's owner conversed with a slim, neatly dressed older man on the other side of the shelter.

"So, you're planning to be career Army," the older man was saying. "A fine choice. God will bless you for it. I served in the Korean War, myself, and I've worked as a recruiter ever since."

"That robe looks comfortable," I said to Morgan.

"Thanks," she answered. "It really is. I designed it especially for fall camping trips. I had this idea of what I wanted to keep me warm in the evenings, but I couldn't find it anywhere. I think when I get home, I'm going to make some more and sell them online."

"I'd buy one," said a deep, lilting voice. The lion-maned man sat down on the other side of Morgan. I could picture him wearing such a garment; stretched across his shoulders, it would look like a bearskin cloak.

"I'm Lew." He held out his hand.

"Short for Lewis?" I asked him.

"No, Lugh, L–U–G–H. It's the name of an ancient Celtic god. It's my real name, not just a trail name. My family's all Druids, see."

"You're a Druid?" Morgan asked. "That's great! I'm a witch."

The two soldiers in the corner had fallen silent. I glanced over at them and met the older one's eye.

"A witch and a Druid, eh?" he said. "Maybe the rest of us better find someplace safer to sleep." He sounded as if he was only half joking.

I gave him an apologetic smile. "Actually, I'm a witch, too," I admitted.

"I thought you might be," Morgan said. "The way you just sort of appeared across the water."

"You're—you guys aren't going to curse us, are you?" The dog's owner sounded genuinely worried. "I mean, we're, um, Christians."

Morgan threw back her head, laughing. "Of course we won't curse you. As long as you don't try to burn us at the stake." She looked him straight in the eye, a smile still playing around the corners of her mouth. "Deal?"

"Sounds okay to me," he answered, his voice a little steadier than before. "I guess the things I've heard about witches might be a little—well, exaggerated. What do you guys believe in, anyway?"

"Modern Wicca borrows from a lot of pre-Christian traditions," Morgan told him, "so it's pretty open to personal interpretation. Probably no two witches believe the exact same thing. There are a few traditions most of us share, though—correct me if I'm wrong." She glanced at me, then continued. "We celebrate the changes of the season and the phases of the moon. Our major holidays are the solstices and equinoxes and the four cross-quarters, the days that fall halfway between. Most of us are polytheistic. We practice magic, of course."

The two soldiers exchanged a startled glance, but Morgan smiled sweetly at them and went on. "Magic, the way I like to think of it, is a way of using your energy and willpower to change things in the world. It's kind of like praying, except you're not asking God to do something for you, you're using the divine energy within yourself to make it happen. We don't have a written manual, like the Bible, but there are a few rules we follow. 'Do what you will, and ye harm none' is the most important. It means that you should figure out what your will is, and then follow through with it, as long as you're not harming anyone on your way. The 'harm none' part of it is kind of like your biblical commandment 'thou shalt not kill.' You can interpret it really strictly and be a vegan who wears non-leather shoes, or you can just do your best not to hurt people." She gave the soldiers another smile, then caught my eye, laughing. "I'm pretty sure even the most liberal interpretation forbids us to go around cursing strangers."

"You don't seem terribly dangerous," the recruiter said, cautiously returning Morgan's smile. "Maybe I'll stay here tonight after all."

"Glad to hear it," she answered. "I'd hate to think of you struggling through the mountains all night on my account."

Morgan turned to Lugh. "I've got a ton of questions to ask you. I've never met a Druid before, so I'm really excited to hear about your traditions."

"Unfortunately, I can't tell you much," he answered. "The Druids in my village suffered so much persecution over the centuries that they started swearing initiates to secrecy. Suffice it to say, we're one of the main religions you borrowed from. There are a lot of similarities."

"And you? What do you believe?" the younger soldier asked me.

"Basically, I worship the Earth Mother," I told him. "Though I call her by many different names."

"So you're monotheistic," the recruiter mused. "Like us."

"More . . . pantheistic, I guess. God in nature, in everyone."

"A lot of early Christians were pantheists," he answered. "Until the Catholic Church codified its belief system during the reign of Constantine."

I looked at him, surprised.

"I studied theology when I was younger," he explained. "Before I joined the army, I thought about being a minister." He stood up to hang his food bag, then sat down closer to us. The young soldier moved over, too.

By the time we finished supper, the five of us were sitting in a circle, joking and arguing as if we'd known each other for years. Morgan brewed a big pot of lemon balm tea, and the young soldier offered everyone Oreos. We talked long past my usual hiker bedtime, our conversation ranging from Medieval history to Internet commerce. The one topic we avoided, by an unvoiced consensus, was politics; getting past our religious differences seemed like enough of a challenge for one night.

I hiked another fourteen miles the next day. By late afternoon, my concentration wavered; I stubbed two toes within half a mile. I hadn't stubbed my toes at all since the Whites, and I'd almost forgotten the risk. The second time it happened, just after the Massachusetts/Vermont state line, I sat down on a stump and cried. It was a pretty big break in the skin; I'd have to keep it bandaged for five or six days. For nearly a week, I'd look like an idiot or a martyr to everyone I met. It had been easier when jackrabbit was with me. She hardly ever stubbed her toes; her healthy feet beside my bandaged ones made our endeavor look a little less quixotic.

You've got three miles to hike, and it's almost sunset, I told myself. *Pull yourself together.* I picked up my hiking sticks and limped down the trail, still blowing my nose every few minutes. To cheer myself up, I started singing to a country tune:

> Ask me have I gone insane (yeah!)
> Threaten me with Pennsylvania,
> But I've walked this far from Maine, yeah,
> Barefoot all the way.

That could be the chorus. Now, let's see—verses. I had already picked up my pace and stopped limping.

> I was slackin' down Katahdin
> When a sleet-storm I got caught in;
> Walked five miles completely sodden,
> But at least I wasn't shod in
> wet boots all that day.

I sang as I hiked over the white marble ledges at the end of the ridge. I made up a few more verses, challenging myself to come up with rhymes for the names of mountains and towns along the Trail, before ending the song with a brief apologia:

> I'm slow but I don't take many zeros,
> I'll put on boots when I hit the deep snow;
> I ain't a nutcase nor a hero
> Any more than the other folks out here, oh . . .
> I just like to hike this way.

On my way down the mountain, I stopped to pick highbush black blue-berries in the last light of the coppery sun. I reached Sherman Brook Camp-site half an hour later, with plenty of light left in the sky to set up camp.

In the morning I hiked down to Mass. 2, where I had a choice between two resupply points, each of which appeared to be about two miles from the Trail. North Adams, to the east, didn't show up on my map, but the strip malls and apartment buildings on its outskirts looked dingy and industrial. I headed west toward Williamstown instead. *As a college town, it ought to have at least one good bakery*, I reasoned. *Maybe even a health food store.*

I was right on both counts; I passed a health food store along the highway and found a wonderful bakery in the middle of town. There was no laundro-mat, though, nor any sign of a hostel. It was eleven days since I'd had a real shower, and the situation was getting rather urgent. *Oh well. I can worry about that after I eat*, I thought. I bought myself a first round of bread and ice cream and sat down on a park bench to finish my letter to jackrabbit.

By the time I put down my pen, I was hungry again. I checked my watch—two o'clock already. I had walked all the way into town, a distance of four or five miles, rather than the two miles I'd initially estimated. I planned to walk all the way back. On the way, I had to buy and pack my resupply.

I mailed the letter, bought more bread, and hurried back to the highway. At the health food store, I stocked up on vegetarian protein sources: instant black beans, seitan jerky, and a little container of hummus to eat with my bread that night. I bought the rest of my resupply at the supermarket across the street and sat down on the curb to repackage it. As I stuffed the last Ziploc of crackers into my food bag, I remembered that I had to call home. It had been over two weeks since I left Hanover; jackrabbit might be well by now and eager to return to the Trail. I found a pay phone at the end of the mall, but no one was home. Not prepared to talk to the answering machine, I left a brief, garbled message.

"I'm in Williamstown right now. Actually, I'm leaving Williamstown. I don't know when I'll get to the next place, and I'm not sure what it's called, either, because I'm not looking at my map. Anyway, I'll try to call when I get there. I love you guys. Bye."

It was 5:30 by the time I got back to the Trail. From the map's elevation profile, I knew there was a shelter only three miles from the road, but it was a steep uphill almost all the way. My shins were bruised from walking on pavement, and the toes I had stubbed the day before throbbed beneath layers of white tape. If there'd been a likely stealth spot at the base of the mountain, I would have taken it, but the ground was swampy, thick with jewelweed. Besides, the evenly spaced tall spruces here had the eerie, majestic symmetry of a Van Allsburg drawing—not a place where I'd be comfortable spending the night. I headed up the mountain as fast as I could, pushing myself along with my hiking sticks.

As the chill of evening deepened, I walked into a narrow clifftop meadow where last rays of the sun glowed through the tips of the grass blades. In the west, fine bands of pink and gold streaked the sky above the mountains. To the east, a waxing moon hung in the branches of a gnarled oak tree. I looked around for the Trail. It made a sharp turn and plunged back into the woods at the eastern edge of the clearing—if the map was accurate, I was within a quarter-mile of the shelter. I didn't feel like going on, though. Under the trees, where the trail led, darkness had already fallen. I couldn't bring myself to turn away from the sun. I sat down at the top of the cliff and rebandaged my toes. In spite of the ache, they seemed to be healing faster than I could have hoped. While the sky burned orange above the western mountains, I ate my hummus sandwiches and the apple I'd brought for dessert. I lay on my back watching until the first stars came out, then pitched my tent in the meadow's plush grass.

Around the middle of the next day, I reached Mount Greylock, one of the few peaks on the A.T. accessible by road. The Massachusetts War Memorial, a three- or four-story granite tower topped with a sphere of faceted glass, dominated the grassy area at the mountain's summit. The tower door was locked, but a few hardy families of tourists wandered around its base or sat on the lawn in front of it eating ice cream sandwiches despite the chill. Across the road from the memorial stood a gracious old hotel called Bascom Lodge, which I soon discovered to be the source of the ice cream sandwiches. I also found out that it was run by the AMC. This caused me only a moment's hesitation. Luckily, my old grudges against the organization were no match for my hiker appetite. Inside the lodge, I found a dining room that served spinach lasagna, Caesar salad, and pumpkin pie, priced so reasonably that my whole lunch cost less than the two loaves of bread I'd bought in Williamstown.

"Are you on the A.T.?" asked the young woman who took my order. When I nodded, she continued. "Do you want to do work-for-stay? We don't get many tourists this time of year, so the work's pretty easy. Just a few dishes, and you get all your meals for free."

"I was planning to hike a little farther this afternoon," I told her. "But thanks for the offer."

"Well, if there's anything you need before you leave—shower, laundry— just ask the guy at the gift shop. He usually gives hikers a pretty good deal."

I thanked her and sat down at one of the varnished pine tables. While I was eating, a tall, wiry man whose black beard had a few streaks of gray walked over to my table.

"Hi, I'm Ellis," he said. "I'm the ridge runner for the Greylock area. Are you a thru-hiker?"

"Yeah, I'm hiking southbound," I told him. "My trail name's Isis."

"Isis? You're not—are you? One of the Barefoot Sisters?"

"Guilty as charged."

"Wow. How do you do it? What does the ground feel like? Is your sister here, too? I don't mean to interrupt your meal, but I'd love to hear about your hike."

"Sure. Pull up a chair," I told him.

After lunch, Ellis offered to watch my laundry while I took a shower. We were both planning to spend the night at Mark Noepal Lean-to, so we decided to hike together for the afternoon. In the gift shop, I bought a few postcards and asked the young man behind the counter how much the showers cost.

"Um, a dollar, I guess."

"Is that for five minutes, or seven?" I asked him. "I've got to wash my hair, so I'll probably need more than one token."

"We don't use tokens," he answered. "You can take as long as you want."

He led me up a narrow staircase, pausing to pull a couple of fluffy cream-colored towels out of a linen closet. *This is a different AMC from the one that runs Crawford Notch Hostel*, I reflected. *Very different. Maybe Upper Goose Pond Cabin will live up to the nobos' description after all.*

"The women's showers are right in here." He swung open a heavy oak door and handed me the stack of towels. "I hope you don't mind that I charged you a dollar. Normally, we let hikers shower for free. But there was that ranger guy hanging around, and I wasn't sure he'd approve."

"That's okay," I said, holding back laughter. *That ranger guy* had been Ellis. He didn't seem like the sort of person who'd enforce shower-charging policies.

On the way down the mountain, an hour or so later, I asked Ellis about his job as a ridge runner.

"It mostly consists of keeping people from camping in places they shouldn't," he said.

I kept silent. He was walking behind me, and I hoped he hadn't noticed the back of my neck turning pink.

"I just don't understand it," he continued. "There are five shelters in the area I patrol, two of them on the A.T. But people still feel the need to stealth camp."

"Maybe they like the solitude," I offered. "Or maybe they want to stay someplace with a view. As long as they leave no trace, is it really a problem?"

There was a pause before he answered. "In the Greylock State Reservation, it's illegal. And it's my job to enforce that law."

"So, um, what else does a ridge runner do?" I asked him.

"I'm on duty four days a week," he told me. "I hike all the trails around here, clearing blowdowns. I make sure the shelters are all in good repair. I helped build the one we're staying in tonight, Mark Noepal. Named in honor of a volunteer trail maintainer, a really great guy, who died young of a heart attack. Sawing the logs for the shelter was one of the last things he did."

"A lot of shelters are named for people, and I always wonder who they are," I told him. "It's good to know some of the history behind the place where I'm staying."

"Don't you carry the *Companion*?" he asked. "It tells the stories behind a lot of shelter names."

"No, I've just got the maps." Waterfall had carried the *Thru-Hikers' Companion*, a book that described the services available in Trail towns. Except for the time we spent hiking with her, jackrabbit and I had relied on nobos for that kind of information. Now, I realized, I wouldn't be passing many more northbounders.

"I'll give you my copy of the *Companion*," Ellis told me. "My ridge running job's almost over for the summer. I'll have to buy the new edition next year anyway."

Along with the book, Ellis gave me a few tips he'd gathered from nobos during the summer.

"In Dalton—that's about fourteen miles from here—there's a guy named Tom who lets hikers tent on his lawn. After Dalton, you'll probably want to camp at the Cookie Lady's place, just a quarter mile east of the Trail on the Pittsfield Road. She bakes cookies for hikers, and she'll let you camp in her field if you ask. Try to avoid October Mountain Shelter; a problem bear's been hanging out there all summer, stealing hikers' food."

"Do you have a lot of trouble with bears around here?" I asked, doing my best to sound nonchalant.

Ellis laughed. "No; I've never even seen one in the Reserve. We do have a problem with porcupines, though."

I'd noticed that few of the shelters outside of Maine had porcupine traps; I'd assumed that the creatures were less common in populous states like Massachusetts.

"They're always trying to get into the shelters to gnaw on the floorboards," Ellis continued. "They're not at all shy of humans. One night I was lying on my back in the shelter, and I woke up with a heavy weight on my chest. I had raised my hand to push it off when I realized that I wasn't home, so it couldn't be my cat. When my eyes adjusted to the moonlight, I saw its quills."

"What did you do?" I asked.

"Oh, I just held still. After a few minutes it waddled off."

The spacious, recently built Mark Noepal Shelter had several layers of bunks. I chose a top one, just to be on the safe side. As I drifted off, I listened for legions of porcupines scrabbling up the walls, but the only sound was Ellis's soft, rhythmic snore. Tempting fate, he'd laid out his mat on the floor.

The day dawned overcast. By the time I reached the town of Cheshire, four miles from the shelter, the morning's drizzle had turned to a deluge. Rain slashed against my bare legs and poured down the sleeves of my jacket each time I lifted my hiking poles. *Okay, I like rain, but not quite this much of it*, I complained to the weather gods. *So calm down, will you?* On the other side of town, the woods seemed dark as twilight, all the leaves streaming and glimmering in the downpour. Pausing to tighten my pack straps, I saw the fur—a few long, black strands clinging to a branch beside the trail. *Someone's got a black dog*, I told myself. *A big black dog, and they walk it here.* It made sense—more sense than my initial image of a big black bear roving the outskirts of town. Still, I breathed a sigh of relief when the woods thinned out at the ridge top, and I could see farther than ten feet ahead of me. I ate lunch under a hemlock, with a boulder at my back and a cliff not far in front of me.

A few miles before the town of Dalton, I crossed a power line cut. After the relative brightness of the clearing, it took my eyes a moment to adjust to the forest again—so I heard the creature before I saw it. Crashing, plunging through the underbrush, a blur of dark fur and gathered muscle. As soon as my eyes focused, I realized that it was a relatively small bear, probably not much heavier than I was, and—more to the point—running away as fast as it could go. This gave me courage; I waved my arms over my head, hiking sticks and all, and shouted, "Shoo, bear! Go away!" at the rapidly dwindling creature. As it vanished among the trees, I felt a rush of elation. I, Isis, had scared off a bear. Not the Tae Kwon Do sister. Not the sister who was six feet tall, whose aura of quiet power made men step out of her way in dark streets. Me, Isis. Alone. It didn't matter that the bear had been running before I saw it; I felt as valiant as if I'd wrestled the creature and won.

Nonetheless, I wasn't terribly eager to encounter the bear again. For the rest of the afternoon, I recited poetry, sang at the top of my lungs, and chanted "Bear, bear, go away!" as I strode through the dripping woods. That night, I was grateful for the streetlit haven of Tom's suburban lawn.

In Dalton, I finally reached jackrabbit on a pay phone outside the general store.

"I'm so glad you called," she said. "I'm hoping to meet you in six days." She told me that some friends of hers were driving down to Western Massachusetts for a relative's memorial service. They'd offered to drop her off anywhere within an hour's drive. I checked my maps. At the rate I'd been going, five days would bring me to Great Barrington, where I was planning to stop for my next resupply. Five days and a zero. I could move faster—I knew that I was capable of hiking at least fourteen miles a day—but I wanted to enjoy this last week on my own. Six days seemed like very little time.

"I'll be in Great Barrington," I told jackrabbit.

I hiked an easy nine miles to the Cookie Lady's house the next day. She was away at work when I arrived, but her husband Roy, a genial, silver-haired blueberry farmer, greeted me with a basket full of homemade cookies. For what was left of the afternoon, I helped him prune diseased limbs off his berry bushes. All around us, the hazy golden light of a day after rain saturated the fields with spring-like green. Snipping away the dead wood, enveloped by the scent of ripe fruit, I felt a sense of security that I'd been missing since I woke to frost at Goddard Shelter. At last, I was doing something useful to prepare for winter, instead of struggling futilely to outrun it. For a rural New England girl whose mother kept a quarter-acre garden, fall was the time to harvest and can vegetables, to mulch the berry bushes and fill the back hall with paper bags of potatoes. Time to gather food and firewood and prepare to hibernate. Not the time to head south through the mountains with a change of clothes, a sleeping bag, and one week's worth of food.

My hibernation instincts really kicked in when I reached Upper Goose Pond Cabin the following afternoon. So much about it reminded me of home—the sputtering gas stove, the tea and crackers and canned goods filling the kitchen cupboards, and the shelf full of books in the living room. The cheery, red-painted walls had no insulation, but at least there were four of them—much safer than a shelter in a winter storm.

I took my zero there, skinny-dipping in the pond at midday when I had the place to myself. I wrote one of my new songs in the register, surrounding the words with color pencil sketches. I searched the woods for a pair of long, straight branches, which I carved into hiking sticks for jackrabbit. In the evenings, I sipped tea and chatted with Sarah, the volunteer caretaker.

"This is my first time caretaking here, and you're the first thru-hiker I've met," she told me. "So I hope you don't mind if I ask a lot of questions. What do you eat? What kind of gear do you carry? I don't mean to be rude, but how often do you get to shower? Have you seen any bears?"

These are probably the questions other thru-hikers get sick of answering, I reflected. For me, though, it was a treat to talk with someone who wasn't just interested in my feet. I described the process of resupplying and told her about the hostels and outfitter stores in Trail towns. I recounted my run-in with the bear outside of Dalton.

"Are you hiking by yourself?" she asked, her eyes wide.

"Only for a little while," I answered. "I'll be meeting my sister in Great Barrington in three days."

"I live right near Great Barrington," Sarah told me. "If you need a place to stay while you're there, please give me a call. There's a new caretaker coming in tomorrow; after that, I'll be free in the evenings."

The second night at Upper Goose Pond, we were joined by Kokopelli and Yahtzee, a young couple on the last leg of a flip-flop. They'd started northbound in February, so they'd hiked through a few weeks of winter in the south.

"It wasn't bad at all," Yahtzee reassured me. "Everyone told us February was the worst month, colder than December and icier than January. We only had one snowstorm, though, up in the Smokies."

"Actually, that was my favorite day on the Trail," Kokopelli chimed in. "We woke up to four inches on the ground, like a layer of powdered sugar. Everything glittered. By noon it had melted, and the mountains were steaming with blue mist, just like their name."

In spite of this encouraging news, I had a hard time tearing myself away from the cabin. I made pancakes and dawdled in the living room, reading a magazine. It wasn't just the dark clouds gathering over the pond or the more distant threat of winter. When I left, I knew I would be walking toward the end of my solo hike, the end of my nine-mile days with plenty of time to read registers, pick berries, and swim. The rest of our journey would be a series of compromises, choices that neither jackrabbit nor I might have made alone. *That's how it was for the first few months*, I reminded myself. *And it wasn't so bad. Was it?* The answers swarmed unbidden through my mind. *No, it wasn't bad. But then, I didn't know the difference. I didn't even realize I was capable of hiking alone. I'm stronger, now—stronger than I ever thought I could be. What if that makes me less willing to compromise?*

CHAPTER 5

The Gathering

jackrabbit

"Thanks so much, Sarah," Isis said, as we pulled into the trailhead parking lot on U.S. 7, a small country road between fields. We had met up the day before in a coffee shop in Great Barrington, and Sarah, the caretaker from Upper Goose Pond, had taken us home for the night.

"You're welcome," Sarah answered. "It was good to meet you."

"If you ever need a place to stay in Maine, give us a call."

Isis reached into the back of Sarah's car and drew out a bundle of long sticks. She handed me two stout poles made of maple. "These are for you. Hiking sticks. I picked mine up in Vermont, and they really do help."

We waved to Sarah and headed out across the fields. My feet were still tender; I could feel each separate stalk of grass under my soles. At first, the hiking sticks felt clumsy in my hands. I didn't know quite where to plant them, or how much weight I could lean on them. Soon I settled into the rhythm of walking, swinging the sticks in time to my stride, and they did seem to help take the pressure off my knees. It was hard to keep up with my sister, though. On patches of gravel, my progress was slow and painstaking. I tried to have patience with myself.

My first night back on the Trail, we stayed at Hemlock Lean-to. I lay awake for a long time, listening to the night noises. A light wind smelling of pine and leaf mold sighed in the trees around the shelter, and water murmured far away. *Am I ready for this?* I wondered. *Can we do it alone, just the two of us, without the friends who are months ahead now?* And the largest question, the one I had been avoiding for the whole trip back to the Trail: *Why am I back here at all? What's the point, if not to do a thru-hike?*

In the morning we ate a quick breakfast of granola and hit the trail early. We had gone less than a quarter mile when we heard voices behind us. Turning to look back, we saw two men with packs coming up the trail with the easy grace of thru-hikers. As they came closer, we recognized them both.

"Highlander! Compañero!"

"The Barefoot Sisters!"

We laid our hiking poles aside and hugged our friends. I was overjoyed to see familiar faces, just when I had reconciled myself to a lonely hike. And it was especially great to see these two again. I remembered Highlander's songs and poems in Maine and Compañero's quiet, steady companionship in the Whites. Compañero looked just as I remembered, all lean muscle and sinew, with a kind, clean-shaven face. Highlander had changed, though; his formerly skinny frame had filled out with muscle, his hair had grown longer, and he sported a shaggy beard.

I blurted out the first thing that came to mind. "Look at you! You look like a real hiker!" A moment after the words left my lips, I realized how offensive they might sound. Anyone who had made it this far *was* a real hiker, no matter how he looked. And I, having skipped two hundred miles, hardly qualified as one to pass judgment. But one look at Highlander showed that he was amused and not offended. His brown eyes glinted with a well-remembered spark of laughter.

"It took a while, but yes, I would say I qualify now." The note of quiet confidence in his voice was even more telling than the physical changes.

"And you! I thought you'd be in Pennsylvania by now," Isis told Compañero.

"I hiked the Long Trail." He smiled. "It sure is good to see you two again. I thought everybody would be far ahead by now."

"What are your plans for the next few days?" Isis asked.

Compañero took his *Data Book* out from the side pouch of his pack. "I thought we'd get over into Connecticut tonight. There's a campsite about fourteen from here, and then I'm meeting some relatives in Salisbury tomorrow."

Isis unfolded the map and we looked at the profile. The trail would take us over several peaks in Massachusetts, including one by the name of Mount Everett, and down into the steep-sided Sage's Ravine at the state border. On the Connecticut side, we would climb up into another series of peaks. It looked like a long day. Isis glanced at me, uncertainty showing in her eyes: would I be ready for this on my second day out? I shot back a confident grin.

"Excellent."

"Very well," Highlander said, in a tone of high formality. "We shall be the 2000 Mount Everett Expedition."

I got in on the fun. "Fourteen grueling miles over perilous terrain, including the very summit of the lofty Mount Everett!"

"Many have perished in the attempt," Highlander added. "But to those who return victorious, belongs the glory of the ages!"

Compañero raised one of his gnarled wooden hiking sticks like the honor marshal of a parade. "Onward!"

We did hike the lofty Mount Everett, and others besides: Race Mountain, Bear Mountain, a row of barebacked granite mountains that reminded me uncannily of the granite summits we had crossed in Maine. We ate the last of the blueberries, sun-dried and intensely sweet, that grew on red-leaved bushes beside the trail. It was a splendid September day, with an utterly blue sky and a crisp feeling in the air, and a light wind. Toward evening, the shadows lengthened in the lowlands and horizontal orange light gilded the granite as we hiked over Lion's Head and began the descent into the valley.

My feet were beginning to feel the constant impact on the gravelly trail. My soles felt warm and achy, and sharp little pebbles sent jolts of pain up my legs when I was too tired to shift my weight fast enough. I was glad to see the sign at last: *Plateau Campsite, 0.1.*

I was less glad when I saw, almost simultaneously, the privy and the water source. The latter was a fetid pool about three feet downhill from the former. Isis and I cast each other a glance of disgust.

"I think we have enough water still in our bottles to cook tonight. We can stop at a spring in the morning; there's one about a mile beyond the road, I think."

"Sounds like a plan."

Highlander and Compañero were low on water, so we shared out our remaining supply. The Liptons would be on the dry side tonight, but no one would have to drink privy water.

We set up our tents on the flattest place we could find—the whole tent site seemed to have a ten-degree tilt—and drove our stakes into the gravel. As evening fell, the air filled with the harsh sound of stridulating insects: *neh-neh-neh . . . neh-neh-neh.* They seemed to be everywhere; the sound was dense and almost overpowering.

"What *are* those things?" I asked Compañero.

"I think they're katydids."

"Wow. I somehow thought katydids had a pleasant, soothing kind of sound. These are almost sinister."

"It sounds like they're saying something . . ." Isis cocked her head to listen. "Yes, I can make it out . . ." she imitated their raspy tone: "dig-a-hole . . . dump-your-load . . ." When we stopped laughing, we sang the song for Highlander and Compañero.

"Very nice." Compañero gave a broad smile and shook his head. "You guys are something else. Have you heard about the talent show at Trail Days?"

I slept well that night—nothing, not even the dig-a-hole bugs, could overcome the fatigue I felt after fourteen miles. As I was drifting off, I heard Isis shriek: "Nightcrawlers! Everywhere!" I wasn't sure if I had dreamed it. In the morning, she told me why she had screamed.

"I went to pick up my food bag, and there were four or five huge earthworms under it. Like, eight inches long." She held up her hands with an expression of disgust and horror. "They didn't wiggle around like normal ones, either. They *thrashed*. By headlamp light, they looked dark and slimy, like . . . like . . . leeches." She shuddered. "I *hate* leeches. There were nightcrawlers under every single piece of gear I picked up, and then I turned my headlamp on the forest floor, and there were *thousands* of them. I was so freaked out that I couldn't sleep. I kept hearing acorns fall, all night. I thought it was animals going after our food bags. I wanted to go check, but then I thought of all those nightcrawlers . . . Ick."

We packed up quickly and hit the trail before the sun had burned off the early morning mist, glad to be leaving Plateau Campsite.

Isis

Compañero left the Trail for a few days to visit his relatives near Salisbury, and jackrabbit and I hiked on with Highlander. I could tell that we were hiking shorter days than he wanted to, as jackrabbit readjusted to the Trail, but he stayed with us and lent his formidable wit to the task of easing jackrabbit's transition. He joked about the slow, muddy river that the Trail crosses four or five times as it winds through Connecticut, and which we crossed even more often, taking short road walks to convenience stores to buy ourselves fruit or ice cream. Each time we reached a bridge, he'd strike a mock-heroic pose, shading his eyes with one hand and gesturing with the other, and intone, "The Mighty Housatonic!"

One night, we set up camp at a place called Belter's Bump, a small patch of pine woods in the middle of a poison ivy swamp. Highlander had already gotten into his tent, and jackrabbit and I were hurrying to get our food bags hung before the impending thunderstorm struck. As I rushed past High-lander's tent, my candle lantern held aloft, I heard him call out in alarm.

"Did you see that—headlights! A car just drove past my tent!"

"Don't worry," I called back over the growl of thunder. "That was just my candle lantern."

"You can't fool me," he answered. "That was way too bright and steady for a candle's flame. What I just saw was the Phantom Car of Belter's Bump!"

The next morning, jackrabbit found the rusted-out skeleton of an ancient station wagon half-hidden in a tangle of poison ivy behind the privy.

"What did I tell you?" laughed Highlander. For the rest of the morning, we took turns coming up with verses about the fate of a hapless city couple, out on a weekend hike, who made the mistake of camping at Belter's Bump.

> They did not know the etiquette for camping in Connecticut,
> And so they were completely unprepared
> To face the Phantom Car that lurked within the forest's gloom
> and murk
> With doors agape and hubcap talons bared . . .

Even on days when he was miles ahead of us, Highlander found ways to lift our spirits. One damp, gray afternoon, jackrabbit and I came across an old spruce tree with lollipops hung like Christmas lights from its lower branches. Beneath the tree, twigs laid end-to-end spelled out the words, "A.T. candy tree."

In our turn, we revived some of the jokes that had entertained jackrabbit and Waterfall and me through the Whites. When we found a soggy newspa-per, an old sock, and a few beer cans in the firepit of a shelter, we told High-lander about the game in which pieces of garbage we had to pack out became clues to a mystery.

"Let's see," I said, stuffing the newspaper into a plastic bag. "This was open to the business section. Clearly, the culprit is a drunk stockbroker wearing only one sock."

The next day, when jackrabbit and I caught up with Highlander at the shelter where we planned to eat lunch, he showed us the culprit's latest leav-ing; it appeared to be the torn-off corner of a garbage bag with a scrap of duct tape clinging to it.

"I found some more culpritude," he announced proudly. "Our suspect appears to be carrying a black plastic bag and some duct tape. This should make him really easy to identify!" We both doubled over laughing. Most long-distance hikers we'd met lined their packs with garbage bags, and many used them as pack covers also. As for duct tape, everyone carried some, wrapped around water bottles or hiking poles. I'd seen it used for everything from boot repair to bandages.

Highlander finished lunch before we did, and he set out to hike the six or seven miles to the campsite where we planned to spend the night. Twenty minutes later, when we picked up our packs to hike out, jackrabbit discovered that she was too weak and exhausted to go on. I left my pack at the shelter and ran down the trail, hoping to catch Highlander and tell him what had happened, so he wouldn't worry about us that night. When I finally caught up with him, after two miles and a steep thousand-foot drop in elevation, he insisted on turning around and walking back to the shelter with me.

"Oh, Highlander, you shouldn't have," jackrabbit exclaimed when she saw him. Tears welled up in her eyes. "I'm really glad to see you, but . . . you know that expression the nobos use, 'Hike your own hike?' Don't let me hold you back."

"This *is* my own hike," Highlander replied, giving her a quick hug. "What does it matter which direction I go in? An afternoon of walking through the forest and an evening in good company. This is exactly what I came to the Trail for."

A few evenings later, we celebrated the autumnal equinox together in a dingy, brown-painted shelter on the banks of the Mighty Housatonic. I brought out some packages of instant hot cider I'd been saving for the occasion. The three of us took turns reciting poetry by the light of my candle lantern, and jackrabbit read aloud highlights from the register. One northbounder wrote that there was a wonderful restaurant in Kent, a little beyond your average hiker's budget, but well worth the price. He proceeded to describe in excruciating detail the warm pear and stilton salad, trout amandine, and pineapple tart he'd eaten there.

"There should be a law against writing stuff like this in a register," jackrabbit groaned. "We just ate the best meal we were carrying, and now I'm hungry all over again."

Highlander sighed. "I used to work as a chef. I hadn't realized how much I miss good food."

I did a quick calculation. Working for two years after college, I'd managed to save more money than I needed for the Trail. "Guys," I said, "we're going to that restaurant. My treat." Highlander started to protest, but I continued. "It's almost my birthday. This is how I want to celebrate it—an evening of good food and good company."

The Connecticut A.T. traverses one of the wealthiest regions in the state, and Kent typified the quaint clapboard villages we'd hiked past, full of upscale boutiques and coffee shops. I wasn't sure we'd be welcome there, with our smelly packs and ragged clothing. As we strode up the main street, a slender blond woman stepped out of a shop door in front of me and walked toward us. Not a strand of her pale hair was out of place; her gray silk suit gleamed with the subtle luster of haute couture. She moved with a grace and dignity that would have made her look regal even if she'd been wearing rags. I stepped aside to let her pass, mentally preparing myself for the disgust I expected her to evince as soon as she got within smelling distance of us. Instead, she met my eye, smiled, and asked, "Are you hiking the Trail?"

I told her we were.

"Welcome to Kent," she said, still smiling.

The memory of this encounter gave me courage when we arrived at the restaurant that evening, to find a notice on the door that said, "Formal attire requested." Jackrabbit and I had had time to shower and change, but Highlander, who'd been busy dealing with gear problems at the outfitter's store, was still dressed in the same clothes he'd been hiking in. They had suffered quite a bit since the day we'd met him in the Wilderness, when he'd looked too clean to be a hiker. He glanced nervously at the sign.

"I'm not sure they'll let me in," he said.

"I'm not sure they'll let *any* of us in," said jackrabbit, fingering the frayed hem of her one clean tank top.

"Of course they will, it's my birthday," I retorted, with more confidence than I felt. I pretended to myself that my black Gore-Tex rain pants were made of satin and my Coolmax tank some drapey knit silk. I lifted my chin and breezed into the restaurant, gesturing for jackrabbit and Highlander to follow.

"A table for three, please," I said to the maître d'. He led us into the dining room without a backward glance.

As we opened our menus, jackrabbit leaned over and asked me, "How did you do that? You looked like you were dressed in silk."

"Something I learned from the lady in gray," I answered. "The one who welcomed us to Kent."

jackrabbit

On an overcast day, we stopped for lunch at the Ten Mile River Shelter. It was a beautiful new shelter, open and spacious, still smelling of the pine logs it was made from, and it opened out onto a meadow. The river gurgled nearby behind a fringe of trees.

Isis was enchanted. "A meadow," she breathed. "This whole trail, I've been waiting for a shelter with a meadow. Oh, it's so perfect! There's even a river here. We could swim if the sun comes out." This didn't look likely—the sky was a uniform gray and had been darkening steadily all afternoon. "Let's stay here!"

"No," I said flatly. I knew Compañero was close behind us, and I wanted to spend more time with him. I didn't think he would be willing to stop so early in the day, even for such a beautiful place. I was also eager to cross from Connecticut into New York, putting another state line behind us.

"Why not? You never want to stop and enjoy anything. All that matters to you is your damn mileage, and you can't even—" Isis stopped as the sound of many voices came up the trail. In a moment, a scout troop filled the space in front of the shelter. The boys caught sight of us and fell silent, too.

"Hi," I said. "Where are you guys from?"

One of the older scouts stepped forward. "We're from Wingdale, in New York."

"Troop 421!" one of the younger kids shouted.

This seemed to break the ice. While the scoutmasters stood off to the side, looking bemused, the scouts quizzed us on every aspect of our hike. "Where do you sleep? What do you eat? Do you carry a gun? A knife? Have you seen a bear? What's the most beautiful place on the Trail?"

We tried to field the questions graciously. One of the smallest scouts edged forward through the crowd but stopped when he got within a certain distance. He wrinkled his nose. "Do you ever take a bath?"

After the scouts left, I convinced Isis to go on. "If it makes you happy," she said with a certain edge to her words. And it didn't make me happy to walk on under the overcast sky; I hadn't been happy for a while. The sense of failure and defeat that had caught up with me in my time off the Trail still clung to me like an invisible cloud. It was September already. I knew that no matter how fast I hiked we wouldn't stay ahead of winter. And no matter how long I stayed on the Trail, I wouldn't be a real thru-hiker, given the section I'd missed. *Why am I here?* I thought, and the question weighed on me like a stone at the bottom of my pack.

Wiley Shelter was only four miles away, but it took all afternoon to reach it. We forced our way through brush that looked like it hadn't been cleared in several years. Webs of grapevines and thorny rose stems crisscrossed the trail. The blazing for southbounders was poor; several times, we had to look over our shoulders for northbound blazes to make sure we were on the right path. The air grew colder and it began to drizzle. I took a perverse pleasure in the dismal weather and the difficulty of the trail—it matched my mood.

The shelter was nothing like the spacious, lovely one we had left. A small enclosure built of particle board and brown-painted planks, it was set on a hill in a welter of vines and dark thickets, close to the road. There were stacks of newspapers and magazines along one edge of the sleeping platform, obviously intended for entertainment, but so mildewed they qualified as culpritude in my book. The rain picked up, drumming on the fiberglass roof, as we laid out our sleeping bags.

Compañero appeared as dusk fell, humming to himself as he came up the trail. "Oh, hi, jackrabbit, Isis. Good to see you. You know, I almost didn't come here tonight. That last shelter was so beautiful."

Some large rodent, perhaps a porcupine, gnawed on the particle board under my head all night long, and I hardly got any sleep.

We camped with Compañero for a few days. I loved to watch him hike; his lean frame moved with such grace and precision that he seemed to float effortlessly over the trail. He had a quiet, reassuring presence, and when he spoke he considered the weight of his words. True to his name, he was a good companion.

One evening, we tented together on the shore of a suspect place called Nuclear Lake. There were wide green meadows along the shore, but the water was dark and brackish-looking, reeking of rotten fish. It looked as though a dam had recently gone out. Mudflats with half-dead vegetation extended out into the water. Luckily, the wind blew offshore from where we tented and the stench was not overpowering.

"I wonder how it got that name," Isis said, eyeing the murky water.

"The *Companion* says there used to be a nuclear research station here," Compañero said. "They cleaned it up in the seventies."

Isis looked skeptical. "Do you think it's safe to camp here?" I hoped it would be—the trail here ran along a gravel road, and my feet felt sore from walking on it. I needed a rest. These fields were the nicest tent site I'd seen all day.

"Should be safe as long as we don't drink the water." Compañero reached into his pack and took out a spare bottle full of water. "This ought to tide us over for tonight."

"Thanks so much!"

He grinned wryly. "You saved me from drinking privy water at Plateau. Figured I should return the favor."

I excavated a small firepit in the gravel road while Isis and Compañero gathered dead branches in the woods. Clouds wrapped the sun as it fell, and the chill of evening came down. After supper, we took the last of the extra water and made a pot of tea from the wild bee-balm in the field.

Compañero took a tentative sip and then smiled. "You'll have to show me which plant this is. It's really good."

"Thanks." Isis threw another branch on the fire. "I started making tea every night when I was solo. I like the ritual of it. It gives me time to reflect."

I watched her as I sipped my tea. She was staring into the coals of the fire, and I wondered what she was thinking. She hadn't told me much about her time on the Trail without me. I felt jealous, almost resentful, for an instant: why had she been able to stay on the Trail while I was forced to leave?

"I feel like a hobo, stealth camping and building a fire right in the middle of the Trail," Compañero said.

I grinned. "I know. Isn't it great?"

As the coals died down, we sang all the songs we knew and parts of some we didn't. The wind changed, bringing the rank stench of the lake onshore, and we turned in for the night.

In the morning, a steady cold rain was falling. I could hear it hitting the tent and see the trails it made on the fabric, each drop sliding down in the cold, diffuse light. I cursed under my breath; the tent had to be stowed in the bottom of my pack. How would I keep the rest of my gear dry while I packed up? For a moment I was tempted to roll over and go back to sleep. The undertow of depression tugged at me. But Isis was awake, rubbing her eyes, rolling out of her sleeping bag and pulling on her rain gear. She nudged me. "Looks like another beautiful day. Rise and shine."

I fought back the inertia and hopelessness and put my energy into solving the problem at hand. I packed up all the gear inside the tent, stuffing our sleeping bags into their sacks and rolling up our mattress pads, while Isis took our food bags down from the tree where we had hung them the night before. I threw our gear into a spare garbage bag, and then, still muttering curses, I took down the tent and squeezed some of the water out of it. The purple nylon bundle in its stuff sack, still dark and slick with water, filled the bottom of my pack. Isis returned with the dripping food bags. We brushed some of the water off, wrapped them in plastic, and transferred the rest of our gear out of the garbage bag, working fast in the cold rain. Perhaps this strategy kept things drier than they would have been, but my pack still felt like a ton of rocks when I hefted it into place and buckled the straps. "Notch this wet tent!"

Compañero's eyes twinkled. "It's been a while since I heard that one!" He was still packing his tent when we left, and we wished him luck. Before we started down the gravel woods road, we scuffed out the traces of the firepit, burying the drowned ashes under the gravel. When we were done, it was impossible to tell where it had been. We ate granola bars for breakfast with the last sips of water, and we only stopped to filter more when we were far from the watershed of Nuclear Lake.

Near midday, we crossed a two-lane road with traffic whizzing through. The skies were clearing, but the cars' wheels still kicked up a gritty spray. Just beyond the road, we found a railroad bed. This was not so unusual—we had crossed many of them before. But this set of tracks had a small platform, with a blue and white sign reading "Appalachian Trail Station."

"This is so surreal," Isis said. "I wonder if trains really stop here."

"We could go into New York City!"

"Right, just hop a train like real hobos."

"Hey, we *are* sobos, after all."

At the platform, we found a schedule posted. Trains did indeed stop there, but only on weekends.

"What day is this, anyway?" Isis asked.

"How should I know? Wednesday, Thursday. It's not a weekend, because the Trail's not mobbed with Boy Scouts."

We ate lunch on the platform, thinking of New York City. I had visited the place a handful of times. The fast-paced bustle of humanity that I remembered from the city seemed the antithesis of the slow, peaceful life we were leading in the woods. It was hard to believe two worlds so different could exist so close together.

Isis spread out the bags of crackers and dried fruit and carefully rationed the last of our cheese. In a few minutes, Compañero arrived, floating over the road with his long graceful strides.

"Hello, ladies."

"Hey, Compañero."

"You know, it's funny we were just talking about hobos last night and here we are by the tracks. I should get a picture."

"Wait for a train to show up." I laughed. "Then we'd really look like hobos." Just then we heard a moaning wail, far off down the tracks.

"Speak of the devil." He shook his head. The headlight of the train was visible now, rocketing down the track. This was no slow-moving freight train—the thing was barreling along at probably sixty miles an hour. We watched it getting larger, alarmingly fast, and after a few seconds I realized that maybe it wasn't such a good idea to be so close to the tracks. I grabbed a few bags of food and scooted to the back of the platform. When I looked up, Compañero was standing right by the tracks, holding his camera. He snapped a picture, and then all hell broke loose. The wind of the train's passing hit us, tossing plastic bags skyward and knocking over Isis's half-full water bottle. The shock of it threw me backwards against the far wall of the platform. *Compañero!* I thought, but when I looked up, he was still standing by the tracks, cool and unperturbed, while the train vanished in the distance.

"Wow. That took some nerve." I said.

He smiled. "Clang."

"What's that?"

"Oh, it's Highlander's expression. 'To have clang.'" He looked a little sheepish. "It's the sound you would make if you had balls of steel."

A few nights later, after a day of cold driving rain, we camped at the RPH Shelter. It was a strange building, right by the road, and much larger than a typical shelter; it almost looked as if someone had cut away one side of a cabin. There were three sturdy walls of cinderblocks, but the front was totally open. It looked out on a concrete patio with a picnic table, and beyond it a wide green lawn down to the road. After the day-long rain, puddles in the grass sent back dull reflections of the last gray light. Out back, an iron well pump stood in a block of cement. Inside the shelter, heavy-duty wooden bunks and a table with magazines and old spiral-bound registers stood against the walls. I could see someone's gear spread across one of the bunks—another sobo?

"A shelter with a patio." Isis looked a little skeptical. "Weird."

Compañero chuckled. "Hardly suitable for hobos."

Highlander came around the corner. "My fellow Mount Everett conquerors! Glad you made it!"

"Highlander! I thought you were hiking fast to get ahead." I knew that had been his plan when we parted ways in Kent.

He made a face. "I was. I have to get off for a few days to go to a wedding. I was trying to put some mileage behind me before I left the Trail, but I just thought, well . . . I wanted to see all of you again."

While we were unpacking, laying out our mattresses and sleeping bags on the sturdy wooden bunks, another hiker came in. He was built like a bear, broad-shouldered and stout-legged. His shaggy blond hair had curled into ringlets in the dampness.

"Hi. I'm Yogi." He had the longest eyelashes I had ever seen and a charming little-boy smile that hardly matched his bulky, muscular body.

We introduced ourselves. "Southbounder?" I asked.

"Yep."

"I didn't think there were any more of us out there. Good to meet you."

Yogi laughed. "Didn't mean to be out this late in the season. I'm still gonna finish by Christmas, though. Got it all worked out." He had a faint Southern accent.

Compañero looked interested. "How much do you have to average to do that?"

"About fifteen."

His plan didn't sound all that good to me. "But that's fifteen miles every day, with no zeros."

"Right. Or you take a zero, then you pull a few twenties." He draped his sopping rain jacket over the end of a bunk. "It's do-able."

"Yeah," Compañero said. "I think I might do that."

I looked at Isis. Fifteen miles was still a long day for us; we had never hiked more than seventeen. Twenty was a number that seemed beyond the realm of possibilities, and we were planning to take quite a few zeros in the next week. In Kent, I had gotten an e-mail from Around the Bend, the nobo we had met in Hanover. We planned to meet him in Greenwood Lake, just over the border in New Jersey, and go to the Gathering down in West Virginia. Considering the travel time, we would probably spend at least five days off the Trail.

While we deliberated, a jovial laugh came from the open front of the shelter. "Oho! Lots of hikers here tonight!" It was a rotund man in a plaid wool jacket. "How goes it? I'm John, the caretaker. Big John, some call me. So, anyone in a mood for pizza this fine evening?"

There was a hearty chorus of assent.

"Well, you're in luck. I like to do something for the people crazy enough to hike on a day like this. There's a pizza place in the next town over that's pretty good. Here's a menu. Let me take your orders."

"Wahoo!" Yogi made a wild sound of joy. "This place is too good to be true!"

Big John returned in half an hour with a carload of pizzas and our change, and we settled in around the picnic table. "You might be wondering why the shelter looks like a cabin with one wall cut off," he said as we opened the boxes and began devouring the hot slices. "Matter of fact, that's kind of what happened. See, this place used to be a regular cabin, but when the Forest Service took it over, they had to make it conform to shelter guidelines. Said it had to be a three-sided structure. My uncle was the caretaker then. He basically just knocked a wall out . . . Oh, I could go on and on about this place. But don't let me keep you from your supper."

We thanked him again for his kindness, and he drove off into the drippy night. I could see my breath in the blue light of Isis's headlamp. The temperature was dropping and the damp chill seemed to seep into my bones. We made a fire, combing the nearby woods for standing dead trees. Compañero and I found a buckthorn snag that was barely dry enough to burn. We coaxed the flames into life with remnants of our pizza boxes—and a smidgen of Highlander's white gas. Compañero volunteered to light the pile. We stepped back. He touched a lighter flame to the wood with a flick of his wrist, and with a *whoomp!* a circle of blue flames appeared, writhing over the cardboard and the wet bark of the buckthorn. He had pulled his hand back fast, but the hair on his fingers was slightly singed.

"Now that's clang," Highlander commented from the shadows, and we all agreed.

We stood around the small fire and sang a few songs. Highlander's clear tenor and Yogi's gruff, smoke-stained bass lifted into the low clouds. Mostly, we were quiet. We didn't talk much about the next day, when we'd all be parting ways, but it came across in the songs we chose: *you'll take the high road, and I'll take the low, and I'll be in Scotland afore ye . . .*

By the light of our headlamps and flashlights, we read a few articles from the old copies of *National Geographic* on the table in the shelter. Highlander was fascinated by an article on "The Gliders of Borneo": mammals, insects, frogs, lizards, and even snakes that have evolved ways to glide through the air like the flying squirrels of our northern forests. "I think that's what heaven is like," he said. "You can do anything you want there, the way I picture it. Even if you're a snake, you can fly though the air. Maybe all the snakes fly in heaven."

Isis

It was a good thing we'd celebrated my birthday with Highlander in Kent, because neither of us felt much like celebrating the day after we parted from him and Compañero. I knew I'd miss our friends, but it was the loss of their company for jackrabbit that really worried me. When we were around other people, she tended to confront setbacks with humor, trying not to discourage our companions—and in doing so, she usually managed to cheer herself up. Alone, I knew I couldn't distract her from her pain and fear of failure.

We hiked up the ridge from RPH in tense, gloomy silence. Jackrabbit walked ahead, her shoulders hunched in the pack straps. After a long, slow climb, we crossed a cedar clearing, open toward the valley beside us. Out of a sea of swirling mist, the far ridge rose like the spine of a distant island, crested with morning sunlight.

"Look, how beautiful," I said, and instantly regretted breaking the silence.

Jackrabbit spoke softly, without turning to face me.

"What am I doing here? Even if I make it to Georgia, I won't have completed the Trail. I should have stayed home—but I felt even more out of place there. We had beautiful weather; we went blackberry picking and harvested all the vegetables from the garden. I haven't been home for the harvest in four years. I missed it so much in college. But all last month, I felt like I was trapped, in limbo, going nowhere. I smiled for our mom's sake and hated it. There was no point to my life. I wanted to die."

"Do you still?"

"Sometimes."

To my eyes, the curve of the far ridge, the clean shadows of cedars stretching toward us, and each backlit blade of grass burned with a sudden, dazzling clarity. My mind raced forward through all the years I might live, until I felt like an old woman at the edge of death, looking back into a world I was leaving. I felt such love for all that I saw, it seemed that my heart would break for the loss of a single leaf. I didn't dare look at my sister.

We stopped to eat lunch at the top of a cliff overlooking a lake. The midday sun glazed the yellow rocks and the leaves of the forest, turning toward autumn, far below us. The morning's chill had given way to dull heat, full of the drone of insects. The light seemed to lie on the surface of things the way sunlight lies in a nightmare, coating everything, illuminating nothing. After we'd eaten, I sat still, unwilling to move forward into such an afternoon. I heard jackrabbit get up and walk around in the bushes at the back of the cliff. After a few minutes, she came up behind me and tapped me on the shoulder.

"I have something for you." She proffered a handful of tiny, shriveled blueberries, dried on the bush. "The last of the season," she said with a tentative smile. "Happy birthday."

jackrabbit

I have struggled against depression for most of my life. It is difficult to write about; all its metaphors have become trite and shopworn. I see depression as an undercurrent in my life, a swift and dark river flowing along beneath my calm surface. The water is cold and deep, the banks slippery, but there is something in its glittering surface and unquiet murmur that invites me closer. To me, depression seems the ultimate form of self-absorption; I become trapped in the refracted rays of my self-awareness. I examine my life in minute detail, and each new detail is a revelation of failure. Losing sight of everything outside my own misery, I begin to wonder how I can justify the existence of something so wretched, so entirely horrible, as myself. Every day I struggle against depression; like a recovering alcoholic or an addict, I can keep my self-destructive urge under control, but I will never be entirely free of its seductive pull.

On the Trail in fall, after Highlander and Compañero left, some stray arm of that dark, subterranean river had lurched out and captured me in its icy current. The world seemed flat around me, two-dimensional and lifeless. I could see the fall colors glowing on the ridges around us, but their brightness seemed muted. Even the warmth of the sunlight falling on my shoulders felt distant. The question that loomed in my mind—*What am I doing here?*—became more and more an indictment of failure. I had lost the ability to judge myself fairly, and, worse, to judge the impact I was having on Isis. She tried everything to lift me out of my depression—kindness, humor, exasperation, and finally companionable silence. My negativity and gloom must have been terrible for her to bear.

Somehow, the presence of other people was the only thing that lifted my spirits. I could smile and act perfectly happy for the people who gave us rides to town or the few other hikers we met along the Trail. I couldn't let a stranger see how miserable I was. Also, there was something in the act of reaching out to another person that allowed me to look beyond my depression. This, more than anything, must have been horrible for my sister: to see that other people had the power to do what she could not and make me happy. Ironically, it was because I loved her, because I trusted her, that I let her know how I felt.

Two days after Isis's birthday, on the last day of September, we found ourselves in one of the strangest sections of the Trail yet: the Bear Mountain Zoo. Throngs of children and their harried-looking parents filled the asphalt walkways. I felt better, momentarily distracted.

"Why do we always hit state parks on the weekend?" Isis muttered under her breath.

"Oh, are you thru-hikers? Jimmie! Diane! Come see the thru-hikers!" This was a young mother with a baby in a sling. A pair of older children materialized out of the crowd and hid behind her legs, watching us with wide-eyed stares. "What's it like out there? Have you seen a bear? Do you carry a weapon?"

A few other families gathered around us as we began answering her questions, and some of the parents fired off questions of their own. "What do you eat? When did you start the Trail? What's in those huge packs?"

We finally managed to extricate ourselves from the group, and we were heading for a museum building when one of the onlookers gave a shout of surprise. "Look, they're barefoot! Barefoot! Are you crazy?"

Isis looked back and gave a manic grin. "Uh-huh."

We ducked inside the darkened interior of the museum before the crowd could catch up with us. I was glad; I was tired of being an exhibit. When my eyes adjusted, I saw case after case of stuffed birds and mammals. "Look at this. These are all the species that used to live around here. I wonder how many are left."

"Look at *this*." Isis pointed at a case with two large gray dovelike birds, looking lifelike on their wooden perches. "Passenger pigeons."

I had never seen anything but illustrations of them before. I stood in front of their case for a long time, thinking of accounts I had read of passenger pigeon flocks so thick they blocked out the sun. It was disturbing to think how easily that remarkable abundance had been reduced to two moldering relics in a museum. I thought about the endless crowds outside: my species, co-opting the world with our extraordinary capacity for destruction.

After the zoo, we headed up Bear Mountain itself. The warm wind carried the odor of dry grasses and oak leaves and the murky green smell of the Hudson, with a hint of iodine this close to the tidewater. The hum of cicadas

filled up the woods. The stream of people was undiminished; every few minutes we passed a cluster of dayhikers, and the auto road up the mountain had a
steady flow of traffic in both directions.

At the summit, we paused for a late lunch near the brick observation
tower. Among the nattily dressed city people out for the day, we stuck out
from the crowd with our grungy clothes and oversized packs. Most of the
dayhikers gave us a wide berth, probably due to our rank odor.

A man in a ranger's uniform came over as we finished our crackers. He
didn't seem to mind our hiker funk. "You guys thru-hikers?"

We nodded, licking the cracker crumbs from our filthy hands.

"Great! I try to talk to every thru-hiker I find. Someday I'm gonna do the
Trail myself. Matter of fact, that's why I took this job." He spoke in a clipped
south Jersey accent. "Couple o' months ago I was workin' construction, and I
saw this job was openin' up, and I says to myself, Mike, that's what you gotta
do. You gotta be out there rangin' parks, 'cause there's no f—" he stopped
himself "—freakin' way you'll learn about hikin' when you're welding I-beams
together in Jersey." I noticed that he was still wearing his steel-toed construction boots. They looked incongruous with his khaki uniform and Smokey the
Bear hat.

He asked us all the typical questions, and then moved on to the specifics
of rain gear, tents vs. tarps, filters vs. iodine, and the best Trail foods.

"Wow. You've done your homework," Isis said.

Mike grinned. "Like I said, I talk to everybody. I heard a lotta crazy stories
about hikers this year. I met a whole family hikin', kids and everything."

"The Family from the North!" Isis said. "I heard about them up in Vermont. I hope we'll get to meet them some day."

"Oh, they're a couple weeks ahead now. Great bunch o' people, though.
Mom, dad, five kids. What else? Oh, there was one guy came through here
with a tuba. I heard that, I said, 'Sh-shucks, I gotta get a picture of that.'"

"Tuba Man! Did you meet him? What's he like?"

Mike's face fell. "I just missed him. I bought one o' those one-time cameras, you know. Had it all ready for when he came through. That day somebody slipped off a ledge on West Mountain, and I had to go do the rescue and
all that sh-stuff, and by the time I came back, the tuba guy was here and gone.
Just left a note in the register." He brightened. "Know what else I heard? They
say there's a couple o' sisters hikin' the trail barefoot. 'Barefoot,' I says. 'I'll
believe that one when I see it.'"

Isis and I exchanged a glance and said nothing. We began packing up our lunch, still chatting with Mike. When we hefted our packs and took up our hiking sticks, still not wearing shoes, Mike made no attempt to restrain his language. "Holy shit! It's you! You're the ones I heard about! Is it really true? How do you do it? What about broken glass and sharp rocks and stuff?" We answered his questions as fast as we could, and he spouted more, obviously fascinated. "Well, shit. I gotta get a picture." Then his face fell again, and he regained a little composure. "You know what? I left the f- freakin' camera in my truck. At the bottom of the mountain."

We camped that night on the shoulder of West Mountain, just as the sun went down. I felt more peaceful than I had in a long time. At last, I began to notice the beauty of things around me. We set up the tent in the loveliest stealth site we had found yet. It was a tiny meadow of low, tawny grasses under a grove of oaks. A few stands of young birches rimmed the campsite, their leaves golden with fall. On a ledge right next to the meadow, we could see a 180-degree vista. Bear Mountain, with its observation tower, stood just across from our camp, and the Hudson flowed through the valley beyond, a wide ribbon of bright silver. The rounded shapes of the mountains across the way looked like sleeping animals. Horizontal light picked out the trees on the far ridges, illuminating the fall colors that touched their leaves. Blue shadows collected in the lowlands. There was a slight chill in the air.

"Check out the firepit," Isis said.

"We can't have a stealth-fire here! The whole valley will see us!"

A slow smile spread across her face. "Not with this firepit, sister."

She pointed to a granite ledge that rose perhaps four feet above the meadow. A circle of blackened stones and a small stack of dry wood lay behind it.

"Excellent! We could have a *bonfire* here and nobody would know!"

As we relaxed by the light of the fire that night, sipping our peppermint tea, I felt myself surfacing from the dark river of my depression. I lay back on the soft grass beside the fire. A wind stirred the birch leaves, sending a few of them drifting toward the ground. I looked up at the stars between the branches. The days were shortening fast and the weather was cooling. All the friends we had known had left us behind or gone elsewhere. My feet were still tender, compared to my sister's, and now I was the one who had trouble keeping up. And yet I knew there would be moments like this all the way down the Trail: lying beside a fire, watching the stars. *Is this worth it?* I asked myself. I knew things would get harder, much harder, but right then, just being there was enough.

In the morning, fog filled the river valley. Mountaintops became islands in a white sea. The early light caught in the dew-covered leaves of the birches, sparkling gold. We ate granola and packed up quickly, watching our breath turn to steam, rubbing our hands together for warmth. *October*, I reminded myself. *It's the first of October. That gives us two and a half days to get to Greenwood Lake to meet our nobo friend for the Gathering.*

Isis started out fast to keep warm in the chilly morning air. I could hardly keep up with her on the gravel trail. My feet were most sensitive in the early morning, and today, with the cold, it seemed like I could feel every sharp corner of the pebbles. I decided to walk on the vegetation beside the trail instead. This was much better; soft grasses and moss and—

"SHIT! Oh shit, oh shit!"

Isis turned around as I sank down on a rock next to the trail, cradling my foot. "Jackrabbit! Are you all right? What happened?"

I fought back tears. "I stepped on something sharp. A cut-off root or something. Right on my heel. How could I be so fucking stupid?" The pain was intense.

"Are you bleeding? Let me see."

It hadn't broken the skin, but a dark bruise the size of a dime was forming on my left heel. I was terrified for a moment—it was happening again. Just when I had decided it was worthwhile to be back on the Trail. "It's just like the first time, Isis. Why does this happen?" Now my tears were flowing freely.

Isis was calm and businesslike. "It happened because you weren't paying attention. But it's not like the first one. That was much worse. Rest here a minute. I'll give you some vitamin I, and we can go on."

"No." I said, managing to control my tears again. "The reason it got so bad the first time was all that damn ibuprofen. I couldn't feel what I was doing to it."

"You need to take something to keep the swelling down. And we need to keep hiking if we want to reach Greenwood Lake in time to get to the Gathering."

I couldn't argue with her logic.

"Maybe . . ." she looked away for a moment, across the mountaintop that glowed golden in the early light. "Maybe you should take some vitamin I and put your camp shoes on."

I started to protest, but she turned to me fiercely. "This hike is about more than just proving something! You don't need to stay barefoot, damn it!" For an instant, resentment welled up in me. *She* would stay barefoot, of course. *She* still had the chance at proving something. I had failed already. Once again, I wondered what I was doing here. I didn't belong here any more. She did. But her face softened, and she said quietly, "Remember what we said to that ranger at Daicey Pond, way back at the beginning of the Trail? 'As long as it's comfortable. As long as it's fun.'"

Wordlessly, I swallowed the two ibuprofen tablets she gave me and untied my ratty old camp sneakers from my pack. With the shoes on, I felt disconnected from the world. Losing contact with the trail was like losing one of my senses; the woods flowed by with a strange unreality, a silent film with no subtitles.

Isis

The evening before we planned to get off the Trail for the Gathering, we set up camp in a clearing near the top of a small mountain. Near sunset, a handsome young man came jogging out of the woods. Without other thru-hikers passing us, either north- or southbound, I had grown wary of strangers. My first thought was *oh no, someone knows where we're going to be camping tonight.* Jackrabbit, delighted to have company, struck up a conversation with him, while I stubbornly continued to collect firewood. As I brought an armload of wood back to camp, I overheard jackrabbit telling the stranger how wonderful the Trail was and how glad she was to have the time to hike it. *Is this the same person,* I wondered, *who told me she was "fucking sick of this whole fucking hike" when she had to put on shoes a few days ago?*

After he left, she came over to help with the fire.

"That was a really neat guy," she said, sounding almost as cheerful as when she'd been talking to him. "You should've stopped working and joined us. He said he grew up around here, and he told me the stories of all those ruins we passed yesterday. You know that old mill canal . . ."

As she spoke, my mind drifted. Normally I would have been fascinated by the stories of ruins, but now, all I could think of was how to find more people to spend time with. If we quit the Trail, we'd be surrounded by people, but then no amount of company would cheer jackrabbit. If we skipped ahead to rejoin the other sobos, we'd soon fall behind them again. I hoped that somehow it would be enough to reconnect with our old friends at the Gathering.

The next day, under a cold, uniformly gray sky, we hiked the last six miles to the town of Greenwood Lake, where we were planning to meet Around the Bend. Jackrabbit, still in shoes, strode faster and faster, until I struggled to keep pace with her. Normally, we warned each other about broken glass in the trail, but that day she walked over glass and sharp stones alike without saying a word to me. I might have realized that, wearing shoes, she just didn't notice the glass—but the pain of walking so fast on rough ground brought the past week's frustration to a head. *She's mad at me for being barefoot when she has to put on shoes,* I told myself. *She wants me to fall behind or beg her to slow down.* The day before, the thought had crossed my mind that I should offer to put my own shoes on when she put on hers. No, not even offer: just put them on. But now I felt only resentment. *Why should I hike her hike?* I gritted my teeth, focused on the gravel of the trail with such fierce concentration that my head ached, and kept up.

jackrabbit

A dilapidated silver station wagon sat in the trailhead parking lot in Greenwood Lake, with a familiar dark-haired man in the driver's seat. He rolled down his window as we came out of the woods. "The Barefoot Bombshells!"

"Around the Bend!"

He made a face. "Please, call me Brian. I'm off the Trail now."

"Okay . . . Brian." I made a mental note. "Tell me, how'd you choose the name Around the Bend, anyway?"

"Oh, some guys I was hiking with gave it to me, 'cause I hiked so fast. I was always disappearing around the bend."

I laughed. "Thought it referred to your mental state."

"My mental state?"

"You know. Nuts, whacko, bats in the belfry, around the bend . . ."

He looked slightly hurt. "I've never heard it used that way before."

Isis and I laughed together. One of Brian's defining features, I remembered from the time we had spent together in Hanover, was that it was almost impossible to tell when he was serious.

"I finally figured out the trail name I really want, the day before I finished my hike, but by then it was too late to change it," he said.

"So what would you call yourself?" I asked.

"Boy Yonder."

"I like it."

"When did you summit?" Isis asked him.

"September 25, baby. Most glorious day a man could hope for: clear, calm, nice and warm. There were about forty thru-hikers on Katahdin and these two Austrian tourists. International relations were good until we started taking our naked summit photos."

We went out for pizza in town before we began the long drive. Isis and I split a plate of onion rings, a Greek salad, and a large veggie pizza, wolfing down the hot grease. Brian contented himself with one slice of cheese pizza. He watched us somewhat mournfully. "I've been off the Trail too long. I've lost my superpowers."

On the long drive, Brian regaled us with stories of his hike, and we related some of our more outrageous experiences. Despite my navigation ("oh, we were supposed to go *west?*") and Brian's driving (twice, he pulled illegal U-turns on four-lane highways), we arrived safely at the Appalachian Folklife Center in Pipestem, West Virginia. We tumbled out the station wagon and staggered around—sitting in a cramped car for two days had not done anything to help our hiker hobble.

The wide field was marked off into parking areas and tent sites. We had arrived early, apparently—there were only a few other cars on the grass and a few tents up in the far corner of the field. At one edge of the open expanse, several modest wooden buildings stood by a small patch of woods. Signs by the doors identified them: *Kitchen, Library, Bathrooms.*

Brian got out and stretched luxuriously, unfolding his lanky frame. "Hey, ladies. Listen, I had a great time driving down with the two of you, but if you can find another ride back, I'd appreciate it. I'm gonna take this hunk of junk down to Tennessee, visit some friends of mine there." He patted the silver car's bumper, and I noticed patches of duct tape holding it together in places. "Don't know if this baby's got it in her to go back up the coast."

I looked around the field. We didn't know anybody else there. The prospect of getting stranded in West Virginia was a little scary. I started to say something, but Isis was nodding. "I'm sure we can find a ride," she said.

As we set up the tent, I asked her where exactly our ride was supposed to come from. She shrugged. "We'll ask around. Somebody's bound to be going back that way." I wished I could have her confidence.

The main events of the Gathering took place at Concorde College, a small Baptist school a few minutes' drive from the Folklife Center. Brian drove us over there in the evening, and we registered at the tables in the glass atrium of the student union, receiving name tags and information packets. It felt a little surreal to be attending a conference in the middle of the Trail. Everyone else there was well-dressed and clean.

We walked into the auditorium next door, where the opening ceremony would be held. The red velvet of the seats and the curtain seemed far too luxurious for our ragged clothes and none-too-clean bodies. As we walked through the crowd, though, a whisper seemed to follow us: *Real hikers! They're actually on the Trail right now!* I stood up straighter and smiled at the people near me. For once, our scruffiness was a mark of honor.

A man in his mid-fifties took the podium at the front, and the crowd quieted after several calls to attention. "Welcome to the 2000 Gathering of the Appalachian Long Distance Hikers Association!" There was a deafening cheer from the audience. "I want to welcome everybody here tonight. How many of you have hiked the Appalachian Trail?" Almost half the audience stood up, and there was another loud whoop. "And how many of you are dreaming of hiking the Trail?" The other half of the crowd rose with an even louder cheer. "Welcome, all of you. This Gathering is for the hikers, but most especially for the dreamers . . . We've got a great program this weekend. If it's your first time here, I urge you to try a lot of different things. Go to a slide show, watch a demonstration, visit our vendors. But whatever you do, make sure you spend some time with your friends. Meet some new friends. That's why we're here. The A.T. has been called 'a pathway for those who seek fellowship in the wilderness.' Well, this is our chance to have some fun and fellowship."

Several people came up to the stage to speak about the importance of hiking in their lives or to tell funny stories from the Trail. A man with thinning white hair sang a song with a verse about every state on the Trail, and perhaps a third of the audience joined in.

The MC took the microphone again, and announced, "Now for the moment we've all been waiting for: class years!" Isis and I exchanged a puzzled glance, but the rest of the audience buzzed with excitement.

"How many of you hiked in '99?" A large contingent in the back of the auditorium stood up, shouting and pumping their fists in the air.

"Ninety-eight!" A smaller, but no less vocal, group. I understood what was happening now. "Ninety-seven!" The MC counted down through the years, and with each passing decade fewer people stood up. There were a number of hikers from various years in the eighties, and a handful from the seventies. In the sixties and fifties, years rolled by and no one stood up.

"Fifty! Forty-nine!" An expectant hush came over the crowd. "Forty-eight," he said with great solemnity. A solitary man in the third row stood up and turned to face the crowd. His face was thin and wasted, but his dark eyes glowed with enormous intensity under shaggy brows. "Earl Shaffer!" the MC said, and the crowd gave him the largest cheer yet.

Even with my utter lack of preparation for the Trail, I recognized the name: he was the first thru-hiker. Before his hike, no one had even thought it would be possible to hike the Trail in one season. It had been designed for weekend outings. But Earl Shaffer returned from the battlefields of the South Pacific with a lot of demons to exorcise and a dream of walking in the mountains. He had finished his hike, and in 1998, fifty years later, he had hiked again at age seventy-nine. In the auditorium of Concord College, the cheering went on and on; here was the person responsible for all of this.

The MC called us to order again. "There are still a few classes I haven't called. A.T. class of 2000!" Another group rose up shouting. I saw Brian down near the front, hugging a thin blond woman and grinning like a maniac.

"Current northbounders!" A few hikers stood up.

"Last but certainly not least. . . . current southbounders!" With a loud whoop, my sister and I rose to our feet. It felt like graduation, or the induction into a secret club; all of a sudden we were a part of something larger than ourselves. I looked around the auditorium. There were perhaps twenty of us standing and only a few I knew. Down in front, I saw Solid with two men I didn't know, a wide smile on his handsome face. We turned around to see who else we might recognize, and there in the back was Waterfall! She jumped up and down when she spotted us, and we ran toward each other through the crowd as soon as the ceremony finished.

"I just knew y'all would come! Oh, I'm so happy!"

"Waterfall!" I threw my arms around her and picked her up off the floor. "There's nobody else quite like you out there."

"There's nobody like y'all, either."

"Oh, we missed you so much!" Isis said. We drew aside to let the rest of the crowd pass. "Who are you hiking with? Where are you on the Trail? You have to tell us all the gossip . . ."

"Well, I'm in Harpers Ferry right now. I'm kinda hikin' with Matt, but . . ." she made a face. "Well, I don't have to get into that right now. Oh, gossip. Let's see . . . well, Blue Skies and Tenbrooks are officially a couple . . ."

Isis laughed. "I should have figured."

"It's so funny how they got together. I think they both kind of liked each other, but neither one wanted to admit it. So one day, I finally asked her if there was anything goin' on between them. She just blushed, and she said, 'Well, he's awfully cute. And we *are* sharin' a tent.'"

I shook my head and smiled. "That counts as 'something going on' in my book! So what else is new? How's Matt?"

Waterfall sighed. "Matt got Lyme disease."

"Oh. Is he still on the Trail?" I didn't know much about the tick-borne disease, except that it could cause chronic pain and arthritis.

She sighed again. "Yes. But I swear, y'all, the first thing Lyme disease does to a person is to make 'em hell to live with. He didn't get it diagnosed for a long time, and before he did he was just so negative and *mean*."

I could picture Matt becoming negative, but mean? I remembered the evenings we'd spent with him around campfires in Maine. I couldn't imagine his placid profundity giving way to meanness.

"I hope it gets better."

"Oh, he's on antibiotics right now. He says he's feelin' better, but it's takin' a while . . . That's one reason I got off for the Gathering," she continued. "Besides seein' y'all, of course. I wanted to take a little time off and get with a different crowd of hikers."

"Who's behind you? Do you know?" It was always easy to tell who was just ahead, because of the registers, but knowing who followed you on the Trail was a matter of rumor and guesswork.

"I'm not sure. I think Blade's a couple days back, and there's a young couple, Firebreather and Fall Girl. I hiked with them in Vermont. Other than them, I don't know. I'll take my chances."

"So Blade's still on the Trail?" I asked. He seldom wrote in registers, and we hadn't seen him since the night of the Stompers in Gorham.

Waterfall laughed. "Can you actually picture him quittin'?"

"What about O.D. and Bugbiter? I haven't seen anything from them in registers for ages," Isis said.

"They got off in Hanover, a couple days before we got there. I thought y'all knew."

"No. That's too bad."

"Yeah." Waterfall said. "From what I heard, Bugbiter wanted to go faster and faster, and O.D. just wasn't up for it."

"So the fellowship is broken, but the Quest continues," I said.
Waterfall nudged me. "You sound just like Blade!"

At lunch the next day in the Concorde College cafeteria, the hikers and
Gathering attendees were easy to pick out from the crowd of well-groomed
students. Isis and Waterfall sat down with Solid and his new friends, and I
went back for drinks. As I filled a glass with grape juice, I heard footsteps
coming up behind me.

"Jackrabbit?" I turned. It was a tall blond man with a scruffy beard and
bright blue eyes. From his ragged clothes and muscular legs, I could tell right
away that he was on the Trail. "It's so good to meet you! I wanted to meet
you in Hanover, but I didn't know where you were staying . . ." There was
something very compelling in his earnest manner, and he was certainly pleas-
ing to the eye. I was flattered that he recognized me.

"Good to meet you," I said, and glanced at his name tag. He had drawn a
goofy smiley-face, and written *support the arts! Tuba players have great lips.* "Tuba
Man!"

He nodded, grinning.

"I've been wanting to meet *you* for a long time. I want to hear all about
your hike. Can you join me for lunch?" I said.

"Looks like our friends are all at the same table," he said. Waterfall, Isis,
and Solid were waving to us from across the room, along with a blond man I
didn't recognize. A grungy magenta pack leaned against the edge of the table,
and sure enough, I could see the golden bell of a tuba protruding from the
top. One side of it was strangely crushed in, as though it had hit the rocks
pretty hard. I wanted to ask about it, but I waited for the introductions first.

"I guess you know Solid. This is Playfoot," Tuba Man said, indicating the
hiker beside Waterfall. He had a round face and wore tiny glasses, and he
looked up with a slightly mischievous grin.

"Playfoot? How'd you get a name like that?" I asked.

He finished chewing and took a sip of water. "Well, when I hiked seven
years ago, I got a stress fracture in my foot." (I was surprised—he hardly
looked old enough to have hiked seven years before.) "When I got back on
the Trail after it healed, I decided to go by Clayfoot, you know, feet of clay.
But somebody misheard it as Playfoot, and I decided that's a better name
anyhow."

Solid gave an impish smile. "What about your other name, Playfoot?"

"Oh, yeah." Playfoot rolled his eyes. "Well, when I hike, I sweat a whole lot. Even when it's cold I have to go shirtless. So these guys, well, they started calling me Streaker." He shrugged with a slightly embarrassed smile.

"Streaker!" Tuba Man shouted, and half the cafeteria looked up in alarm. Tuba Man looked around with an innocent smile, as if trying to figure out who had yelled.

I decided it was time to change the subject. "You're probably sick of telling this story, but I want to know what happened to that tuba of yours."

He seemed eager to tell the story—his eyes glowed. Solid and Playfoot exchanged a glance: *here we go again.*

"Poor Charisma," Tuba Man said.

"Your tuba has a name?" Waterfall asked.

He looked hurt. "Of *course* she's got a name. Charisma's my best buddy." He continued the story. "There's a ridge in Pennsylvania called the Knife Edge. It's a stack of bare rocks about a quarter mile long, all piled up, and they all tip when you step on them. Kind of like the rest of Pennsylvania, actually, except for the drop-off. Solid and I hiked across the Knife Edge in a thunderstorm. We were going as fast as we could. Those rocks were pretty slick, and I took a bad fall."

"He must've fallen twenty feet," Solid said. "I thought he was a goner."

"I could see my life flash before my eyes, you know? And then I heard this *whump!* and a sort of crumpling sound, and I hit the ground. I got some cuts on my hand and a pretty bad one on my leg." He showed us the healing scars, angry purple against his tanned skin. I resisted the urge to reach across and touch his leg. "I was okay, though. I could move, I could walk . . . You know what happened?" He waited.

"The tuba," I said.

"Right! Charisma took the hit. She saved my life." He patted the battered bell of the tuba. "If her bell hadn't been sticking out of my pack, over my head, I would've died right there." He looked around the table with utter seriousness.

"You could argue that he wouldn't have fallen in the first place without that top-heavy seventy-pound load," Solid said dryly.

Tuba Man shook his head. "It could have happened to anyone. I'm just a lucky guy."

"I don't know if I'd call that lucky," I said. "I mean, sure it's lucky that you had the tuba, but that fall doesn't sound like a lucky thing at all."

He considered for a moment. "Accident-prone, but lucky."

"I got down to him as quick as I could," Solid said, "and I bandaged up the cuts and stuff. He was bleeding quite a bit. We managed to walk another six miles off the ridge, and then we tried to hitch to a hospital."

"Nobody would pick us up," Tuba Man said. "Can you imagine? There I am, wrapped in bloody bandages, and Solid's ripped up half his t-shirt to help tie them on. We looked like hell. No wonder nobody stopped."

"So we finally walked into town, like, four miles," Solid said, "and we knocked on doors until we found an old lady who drove us to the hospital. They were really good to us. He got stitched up, and they gave me some sterile syringes for my insulin."

"You're taking insulin now?"

He gave a sad smile. "Yeah. I just couldn't get along without it any more . . . We stayed the night there, and one of the nurses drove us back to the Trail in the morning."

"And guess how far they hiked that day," Playfoot said. He had obviously been waiting to deliver his line in the story. We all shook our heads. "Twenty-seven miles!"

The rest of the Gathering passed way too fast. I was amazed by the kindness of strangers; many trail angels stopped us in the halls of the college and offered their assistance.

"Are you southbound? I'd love to have you visit. Give me a call when you get to Boiling Springs. Here's my card."

"If you need any help between Troutville and Pearisburg, here's our number."

"Y'all have got to come see me in Erwin, Tennessee!"

We spent every spare moment with Waterfall, reminiscing about our time together and telling stories of our recent adventures. One afternoon, we found our way into the band room and played blues on the piano. Tuba Man arrived shortly afterwards. We played some jazz standards and I taught him a few ditties I had written, including "Dig a Hole." I had never really heard the sound of a tuba up close. It was a more mellow and beautiful tone than I had expected; something like a deep, rich, French horn. As the afternoon light from the windows faded, Isis and Waterfall found excuses to disappear. Tuba Man played sweet songs to me and flashed his devastating smile. *Is he flirting with me?* I wondered.

We spent the evenings in the kitchen and common room of the Folklife Center with the other younger hikers. Playfoot, Solid, and Tuba Man cooked up hot chocolate and passed around some homemade cookies from their mail drops. We shared jokes and stories, and flirtatious banter flew around the room. I hadn't realized how much I missed the company of people my age. Anonymous Badger, who we had met in New Hampshire, came in on the second night, and after a long talk about barefoot hiking, dreams, philosophy, and religion, Isis convinced him to come hike with us in January, if we were still on the Trail by then.

We lit a fire in the woodstove and sang songs. One night, a large group of hikers and dreamers gathered in the common room. We ended up singing "Dig a Hole" with tuba accompaniment. The crowd joined in exuberantly on the chorus. We had a few more verses now:

> . . . Oh, I loved Mosquitochusetts, with its hordes of bugs
> Man, I wish those lean-tos came with screens
> When you're camped in a bog, with the bugs thick as fog
> It's awful hard to find the latrines!
>
> Dig a hole, dump your load . . .
>
> And I loved the Housatonic in Connecticut
> Don't know how many times we went across it
> Having lunch off the Trail, but back on, without fail
> Just in time to need the water closet!
>
> Dig a hole, dump your load . . .
>
> And I loved the white-blazed sidewalks of New York's A.T.
> Full of city people on vacation,
> But when you're outta the zoo, where the main exhibit's you
> You're never gonna find a comfort station!
>
> Dig a hole, dump your load . . .

As we sang the last chorus, I noticed an elderly man in a plaid shirt sitting in the back of the crowd, smiling and singing along. His powerful gaze was unmistakable. I felt a surge of pride: *Earl Shaffer likes our song!*

Each day of the Gathering, the weather grew colder. Thick frost coated the grass around our tent in the mornings, and even this far south, the leaves were dropping rapidly from the trees. We bought polar fleece jackets and long underwear from a booth at the hiker fair. On Sunday night, I was very glad we had. We sat around the fire in the common room at the Folklife Center, singing. Someone burst though the door with a rush of cold air. "It's snowing!"

At first I didn't believe it. I stepped outside, and there it was; thick white flakes swirled down in the columns of light streaming from the windows.

"It's the eighth of October!" I said to Isis.

"I know. And we're not even halfway done with the Trail."

There was a bonfire outside on the field that night. Tuba Man wandered over, playing Christmas carols. I followed, feeling like a child captured by the pied piper, and stood in the outskirts of the crowd around the fire, jumping from foot to foot in an effort to stay warm. Tuba Man stood in the firelight with his eyes closed, playing songs I wouldn't have imagined a tuba could handle: everything from "Linus and Lucy" to "Für Elise." The clear sound rang out across the snow-muffled landscape. Little drifts of snowflakes collected in his hair and beard and in the crumpled bell of his tuba. He was the focus of the crowd, and he knew it. *Charisma—that's the word for what he has*, I thought. *He takes it for granted that everyone will love him, and so they do. He wasn't flirting with me. It's just his way of dealing with the world.*

All weekend, I had worried in the back of my mind about finding a ride to the Trail. Brian had taken off on Sunday afternoon, wishing us luck and pulling off the field in his duct-taped silver station wagon. Monday morning rolled around, leaving the campsite under four inches of thick snow, and we still didn't have a ride lined up. I had gathered a few leads, or people who might be able to take us within several hundred miles of our destination, but nothing definite.

As I brushed snow off the tent, wondering what to do next, I heard a familiar voice. "Isis! Jackrabbit!" A tall, slender woman with short brown hair was dashing across the field.

"Stitches! How are you?"

"I'm great! How are you guys doing?"

"Pretty decent." I collapsed the tent, shaking the last snow from the purple nylon, and folded up the poles. "We're still looking for a ride, though."

"Where are you going?"

"Greenwood Lake. New York–New Jersey border."

"Man! You guys are way up there. You're going to hit some serious winter before you see Georgia."

"Tell me about it." I gestured to the field and the tent sites, blanketed in white. "You know anybody driving up that way?"

"Oh, I can take you. I'm going to Boston."

I hugged her. "Stitches, you're an angel! That's two we owe you."

By the time we hit the trail again, the bruise on my heel had disappeared, and we could hike barefoot again. (The snow, apparently, had been a West Virginia phenomenon—the ground in New Jersey was still clear.) I was more cautious in placing my footsteps now than I had been before. I didn't want to risk having to leave the Trail again. It was chilly and the sky was gray, and almost all the leaves had fallen; we were alone and would probably be alone for months now. But I felt a new determination; we were a part of something, a larger community. The Gathering had given me the strength to continue.

CHAPTER 6

The Rocks of Pennsylvania

Isis

Somewhere in New Jersey, shortly after the Gathering, we night-hiked for the first time. The sunset caught us at the end of a road walk, five miles from the nearest shelter at Pochuck Mountain.

"This doesn't look like good stealthing ground," I said, eyeing the thickets on either side of the trail that, in the deepening twilight, looked suspiciously like poison ivy. "I guess we'll have to go on a ways."

"Let's go to the shelter," said jackrabbit. "I've been wanting to night-hike ever since Badger told us about it at the Gathering."

I remembered Anonymous Badger's description of night on the trail: the calls of nighthawks, the stars glinting through gaps in the leaves overhead, deer pausing in the flare of your headlamp. *We don't have headlamps*, I remembered.

"What about light?" I asked jackrabbit.

"We'll use our Photons if we need to," she said, flashing the thin white beam of the dime-sized flashlight, one of the advances in backpacking technology we'd discovered at the Gathering. "But the moonlight might be enough."

She was right. The moon, only a few days from full, brightened as the last glimmers of daylight faded from the horizon, and its milky light was enough to reveal the slight indentation of the trail, striped with tree shadows. For a few miles we walked in silence over the smooth ground, letting our senses adapt to the darkness. A barred owl called in the distance, and its breathy *woo-woo, woo-woooaw* seemed to echo across the still forest—another owl was answering. Close by us, a mouse or vole scurried through the leaves; farther off, I heard the sharp, regular rustle of a deer's hoof pawing the underbrush. As we crossed the edge of a meadow, the rank odor of fox filled our nostrils.

In places where the trail lay in deep shadow, the soles of our feet found the pebbly, dusty path between its borders of dried leaves and moss.

At one point, the trees opened on our left, and we found ourselves on a cliff overlooking a valley. Overhead, the near stars shone dimly through the moonlight. Below us, clusters of lights marked the houses: orange of street-lights, rich yellow of windows, flickering blue of a TV screen.

"It's strange how much light people use," jackrabbit whispered. "It looks like they've shut themselves up in bubbles of daylight."

"You sound like you're describing some foreign culture," I whispered back. It felt natural to lower our voices to the pitch of the forest twilight, the rustling of mice and the distant calls of birds.

"I feel like I belong to a different culture now. An older, nomadic one. I feel like I belong to the woods and stars and not at all to the houses."

A mile or so later, we came to the rocks. A whole jumbled hillside of them, ranging from fist-sized stones to boulders the size of tables with sharp uneven edges that glimmered faintly in the moonlight.

"This could be interesting," I whispered to jackrabbit as I started down.

"Interesting? Notchin' notchy, is what I'd call it." The five days we'd spent off-trail had given her foot time to heal, but I knew how nervous she was about reinjuring it.

In the first few steps, we discovered that most of the rocks were unstable as well as sharp. One would tip ten degrees forward as my weight landed on it; the next one tipped forty-five degrees to the right. I could hear the rocks creaking and thudding as jackrabbit came down behind me. *I'm too tired for this, I thought. We're both too tired. Why didn't we stealth at that overlook? It's going to take all my concentration not to break an ankle.* I crept down the hillside, apply-ing the full force of my concentration to the treacherous rocks. Soon, I found myself going faster, sensing the cant of each stone as my foot touched it and shifting my weight to adjust for the movement. Though it was a struggle to maintain the necessary mental focus, I found myself enjoying the game of bal-ance. To judge from the decreasing frequency of the thuds and expletives coming from behind me, jackrabbit had discovered the same trick.

It wasn't until we reached the shelter that I noticed the scrapes crisscross-ing the tops of my feet and the tender skin of my arches.

"I thought I was doing pretty well out there, but this will take some get-ting used to," I said to jackrabbit. She held her Photon light over my foot while I bandaged a particularly deep scratch. "The nobos say the whole state of Pennsylvania's like that, don't they?"

"If I remember correctly," she answered grimly, "a fair number of nobos told us we'd never make it through PA barefoot."

I grinned at her. "We'll make it. Just as long as we don't try to night-hike the whole way."

Over the next few days, we encountered sporadic patches of the tippy rocks, which jackrabbit jokingly referred to as "asteroid fields." For the most part, though, the trail was smooth, with little elevation gain. We made excellent time, by my standards, hiking twelve- and fourteen-mile days as easily as we had once hiked tens. Jackrabbit aspired to the twenty-mile days that, according to their register entries, most of our sobo friends had hiked through New Jersey, but my lack of ambition and her half-healed injuries still held us back.

One morning, as we hurried through a grassy section of the trail to make up for a late start, my foot brushed against a hornet in the tall grass. A burning red welt blossomed on the top of my big toe. I treated the sting—at my resourceful sister's suggestion—with some of our baking soda toothpaste. The pain went away almost immediately, but I was worried that it might swell and become difficult to walk on, so I took a Benadryl tablet just for good measure.

Fifteen minutes later, when the Benadryl kicked in, I remembered why I wasn't in the habit of taking pills "just for good measure." A dull weariness settled in my limbs; it was hard to pick up my feet high enough to step over small rocks in the trail. Hours seemed to pass while the sun moved only inches up the sky. After lunch, jackrabbit consulted the map.

"I can't believe it. We're getting nowhere," she exclaimed. "If we're going to make a thirteen today, we'll have to pick up our pace."

She set off at a rapid stride. I struggled along behind her, feeling as though I was trying to run through hip-deep water. At last, we stopped at Mashipacong Shelter for our afternoon snack break. I spread my wool shirt on the ground and lay down in a patch of sunlight.

"Don't get too comfortable," jackrabbit warned. "We've still got six miles to go to the campsite."

"I'm not going to the campsite. I'm staying here." My voice seemed thick and distant to my own ears.

"The hell you are. We've only hiked seven miles today. If we hike seven miles a day, we'll be on the Trail till March! Besides, this shelter's less than a quarter-mile off that road we just crossed. It'd be too dangerous."

"I'm not feeling good. I'm kind of sick, actually."

"Oh." She sounded contrite. "Why didn't you tell me that in the first place?"

By evening, the underwater feeling of the Benadryl had nearly worn off. Jackrabbit and I crouched by the stove, taking turns feeding twigs into the fire box. Just at dusk, a hunter in full camouflage stepped out of the darkening forest, with a wicked-looking compound bow slung over his shoulder.

"Are you ladies planning to stay the night here?" he asked.

"Well, uh . . ."

With our tent clearly visible in the light of the near-full moon, any attempt at denial seemed pointless. Still, we knew that *don't tell a stranger where you're spending the night* was one of the cardinal rules of safety for women on the Trail. Of course, we were already breaking the other: *don't camp alone near a road crossing*.

The hunter waited a moment, then continued. "I wouldn't stay here if I was you. There's a minimum security prison 'bout a quarter mile down the road and twenty bears hang out at the dumpsters there every night."

"Thanks for the warning," I said. "Maybe we'll hike on after supper."

"That's what I'd do if I was you. Have a good evening." He vanished into the woods on the other side of the clearing.

Jackrabbit and I considered the situation—convicts, bears, and the proximity of the road, versus the idea of night-hiking another six miles to the campsite. New Jersey's exceptionally high bear population made it dangerous to simply hang food bags in trees at night, as we'd done in other states. Instead of mouse hangers, New Jersey shelters came equipped with metal, safe-like bear boxes where hikers could store their food. The next place with a bear box would probably be the campsite where we'd originally planned to stay. In the end, inertia won out. What if we hit a patch of rocks? The idea of night-hiking another "asteroid field" didn't appeal to jackrabbit either. As luck would have it, our encounter with the bow hunter was the most exciting thing that happened that night.

jackrabbit

The beauty of the New Jersey ridges surprised me. My only prior experience with the state had been the airport in Newark. These open, grassy summits and the views of lakes and farmland in the valleys hardly seemed like they belonged to the same world, let alone the same state.

Early one morning, we climbed toward Sunrise Mountain. Several towns-people had told us this was a great place to watch the raptor migration. I realized it was a weekend; we would probably meet a large number of people today. I sighed and reconciled myself to answering the litany of questions again. Sometimes I wished I could make my bare feet invisible.

We saw the first dayhikers perhaps a half mile from the summit, an elderly couple walking together. They smiled and wished us well. The man carried a stout walking stick.

"You-uns best watch for snakes," he told us. "All kinds of rattlers up there on the rocks." And then his glance caught our bare feet. "Barefoot! Well, bless you, girls, I don't know how you do it . . ."

"Very carefully," I replied. This routine was old hat by now.

The dayhikers laughed. "Where are you bound to?"

"Georgia."

"Well, I'll be! Two girls a-going to Georgia barefoot. Here's one for the books . . . here, would you mind if I took a photo?"

We struck a pose in the trail, our arms around each others' shoulders and two grimy feet in the air.

"You-uns watch for those snakes, alright? You best be double-careful with those feet of yours."

"We sure will. Have a great day."

It was scarcely a minute before the next dayhiker hove into view. He was probably in his late fifties, with a shock of white hair and a lean, hawk-like face.

"Barefoot! Well, as soon as I saw you, I said to myself, there must be some reason for it. I mean, either you're raising money for something, or doing a, a, a, penance, or you're the absolute dumbest pair of lunatics in the U. S. of A!" He hardly paused for breath. "So what's the deal? Why barefoot?"

"Because we like it," Isis said.

"No-no-no. There's gotta be a reason for it. Nobody *likes* going barefoot on rocks!"

"We do."

"But—but . . . why?"

"It feels good." As he stood there, openmouthed, inspiration came to me. "Imagine you lived in a society where you had to wear gloves all the time. Your hands are delicate and fragile, and you might damage them, after all. Imagine one day you take your gloves off."

While he pondered this, we moved on up the trail, walking with as much grace and speed as the sharp, uneven stones allowed.

Isis

Ever since jackrabbit had returned to the Trail, she'd seemed exceedingly preoccupied with time and distance. "We have to make at least fourteen today," she'd announce as we packed up in the morning, and, when we stopped for a snack break, "this is pathetic. It's ten in the morning and we've only gone three miles!" She complained most bitterly when her own weakness slowed us, but she also took issue with my blasé attitude toward pace. At some point, she'd calculated that, in order to cover the 215 miles of Vermont and Massachusetts in the three weeks she was off-trail, I must have averaged less than ten miles a day. When she confronted me with these calculations, I argued that I'd hiked slowly on purpose, so that she wouldn't have too many miles to make up. Still, I had to admit to myself, she had a point; on my own I'd been much more concerned with the view in front of a shelter or its proximity to good blackberry patches than the number of miles I'd hiked to get there.

Our arguments came to a head one day when we stopped for lunch at a register box that perched like a mailbox beside the junction of a side trail. We took turns reading the register as we ate. The notebook had been left by a nobo named Jester. In a lengthy introduction, he wrote that he'd gotten off the Trail because he felt unwelcome in the Trail community, but he was leaving a register in case he still had any friends who wanted to write a parting message to him. It didn't seem like he'd made many friends, after all; instead of the usual banter about gear and the weather, every other entry consisted of invective against the man.

I pieced together the story from the few cautiously friendly entries. Someone wrote that hiking forty- and fifty-mile days really was pretty impressive, and boasting about it wasn't entirely unmerited. Another person suggested that the insults about other people's paces and challenges to "race to Katahdin" that Jester had written in earlier registers could be interpreted as jokes.

I was trying to formulate a tactful way to say *Hike your own hike. Honestly, people. There's no point in doing something just so you can brag about it, but there's even less point in letting somebody else's boasting get to you.* I deliberated for a minute before deciding to go ahead and write what I was thinking—nobody else in that register seemed to have worried much about tact. As I put the pen to the paper, jackrabbit got to her feet and heaved her pack onto her shoulders.

"We have to go," she said. "It's already two o'clock."

"Just a sec, I want to finish with the register."

"We've been sitting here forty-five minutes. You've had plenty of time to read the register. If we don't start moving now, we'll never make another seven miles before dark."

I should have just answered, "go ahead, I'll catch up to you," but I was too angry for words. Who did she think she was, telling me where I should go and when? Didn't she realize that she depended on me, and *not* the other way around? I'd been doing just fine hiking solo—*I still would be solo*, the thought flashed through my mind, *if I had any choice in the matter.* That first bitter thought brought a wave of others—*jackrabbit played her trump card, telling me how miserable she was in the month she spent off-trail. Knowing that, I can't leave her. Not for the rest of the hike, anyway. For the next few hours I damn well can!* I slammed the register into its box and hiked away as fast as I could go. I knew that jackrabbit's feet were still tender from her month off the Trail. There was no way she could keep up with me on the sharp gravel of the New Jersey ridges.

I hiked as fast as I could for the next four miles, fueled by my anger. At one point, I passed a lovely little pond full of fall leaves, and wished briefly that I had a companion to share the view. I snorted. *If jackrabbit were here, she'd be telling me how much time I was wasting looking at the view.* I hurried on, knowing she might catch up with me if I waited there.

By the time I reached Culver fire tower, on the summit of a small ridge, I had expended enough energy to calm myself. I sat down to wait. Five or six hawkwatchers with binoculars stood on the tower's platform, and some families of dayhikers had set out picnics on the grass below. A brother and sister from one of the picnicking families, both in their teens, struck up a conversation with me. The brother reeled off questions like a practiced interviewer; he asked me how much my pack weighed, how long I expected to spend on the Trail, and how much money it would cost me. His sister, a few years younger, stood half-hidden behind him, fidgeting with her watchband and avoiding my eyes, but listening intently to all my answers. When her brother finished talking, she glanced up and asked, in a tone of mingled awe and terror, "Are you hiking by yourself?"

"I know a lot of women who hike solo," I told her. "As long as you're cautious and observant, the Trail's a pretty safe place. But I'm hiking with my sister. She's a little ways behind me now. I stopped here to wait for her."

"Hey, maybe you and me could hike together!" exclaimed the young man, turning toward his sister. "Maybe when we both finish high school!"

"I'd like that," the girl answered. She glanced at me again. "Do you always get along?"

I laughed. "Goodness, no. We argue. In fact, we're in a fight right now. But we'll talk about it, and make up, because we know we'll have to see each other's faces in the morning—and every morning after this, for another three or four months. And every once in a while for the rest of our lives. You can walk out on a marriage, if you get sick of it. But you can't walk out on your own family."

"I'd never want to," exclaimed the girl, throwing her arms around her brother's shoulders. The tips of his ears turned pink, and he attempted to extricate himself.

"Do *you* always get along?" I asked them.

"No way!" she said, releasing him. "Jerry picks on me real bad."

"Kim's got a temper like you wouldn't believe!"

"But when we're not fighting, there's no one more fun in the world."

Just then, jackrabbit limped up to the tower. Her face looked pale and drawn, her body thinner than I remembered. I waved to her and held out the granola bar I'd been saving. She shook her head.

"It's four thirty. We still have three miles to the campsite. We'd better go."

There was no trace of anger in her voice, only weariness, and a note that sounded almost pleading. Pleading? My strong, brave sister, so loath to ask anyone's help or pity that she'd walked sixty miles of the Whites without telling me that the sole of her foot was bruised? Suddenly, I realized why the calculation of miles meant so much to her. It was one thing I wasn't—and most likely never would be—terribly good at. If I were hiking the Trail alone, I'd probably take a year to get from one end to the other. Taking over the logistics of our hike was how jackrabbit could contribute without feeling dependent on me.

I waved goodbye to the kids, picked up my pack, and followed her into the woods.

The next morning we woke to a wet, cold fog blanketing the forest. The maples, at the peak of their fall color, blazed in the damp gray air. Jackrabbit and I chatted more than usual as we walked, pointing out particularly brilliant trees to each other, wondering aloud when we'd see our first New Jersey bear. Jackrabbit avoided harping on how many miles we had left to cover, while I, for my part, tried not to dawdle over views and registers.

Just in time for our lunch break, we came to the shore of Sunfish Pond. Months back, a northbounder had told me to look for this place, the last glacial pond on the Trail. I knew that I would miss the imprints of the most recent ice age when we hiked beyond the range of glaciation: the U-shaped valleys gouged from the rock and the deep, clear tarns that sometimes filled them, so much like the landscape of home. I had looked forward to this final glacial pond, hoping it would grant me a memory worth carrying into the unfamiliar mountains of the South.

The motionless water darkened from blue-gray to black under its curtain of fog. Across an inlet from us, flame-orange blueberry bushes blended their leaves with the red maples above them. Their reflections plunged toward the pond's dark center like the sparks of a bonfire leaping into the night sky. Through the fog, the crowns of birches and maples marked the far shore: blurry spheres of yellow and red hanging in the indeterminate space between water and air.

For a hiker, I didn't pay much attention to my lunch. I gazed out over the water, trying to fix every detail of the scene in my mind. Jackrabbit seemed just as transfixed as I was. "Look at the trees on the far shore," I murmured, and she answered in the same reverent tone, "Look at that red leaf down at the water's edge." As we packed up to leave, I felt a brief, wrenching sense of loss. *However long I live*, I thought, *I will never again stand on the shore of Sunfish Pond in the fog, on the loveliest day of October, having walked hundreds of miles to get here, without even knowing what awaited me.*

"It's hard to leave this place, isn't it?" said jackrabbit. I smiled, comforted by the thought that we would share this memory. Far down the trail, after all the leaves fell, we would be able to sit in a shelter at night, passing words back and forth like a loom's shuttle, until the tapestry of Sunfish Pond clothed the gray walls in vibrant autumn color.

"Youse may've heard some bad things about Pennsylvania, but you've got to agree it's a beautiful state," PA Mule told us. He was a trail angel we'd met at the Gathering, a carpenter from Philadelphia. We shared a booth at the pizza parlor in Delaware Water Gap, the first Trail town in Pennsylvania. A platter of rapidly vanishing garlic twists sat on the red Formica table between us; Mule had arrived early and ordered the twists to tide us over while we waited for our pizza.

"The trail runs along the tops of ridges all through this state," Mule continued, "and this time of year, with the leaves falling, it's nothing but views. You're closer to the sky up there." With his soft, deliberate voice and the lock of dark hair that shadowed his eyes, he'd struck me at first as an intensely shy man. Now, though, he seemed perfectly at ease keeping up the conversation while we attacked the food.

"Sure, there's rocks," he responded to a mumbled interrogative from jackrabbit, "but they're no worse here than they are in Jersey. I don't know about barefoot. Youse are the first people I know who've tried to do it that way. But after coming this far, I don't reckon youse'll be scared off by a few rocks."

Sheltowee, another trail angel we'd met at the Gathering, arrived just as we finished the garlic twists.

"Sorry I'm late!" He grinned, his blue eyes sparkling above round, ruddy cheeks, and he shook a few raindrops from his curly reddish-blond hair. "I had to work overtime."

"You look pretty cheerful for someone who's been working overtime," I remarked. "Don't tell me—you just figured out that you'll have enough vacation time to hike the John Muir Trail next summer." I knew that Sheltowee had hiked the A.T. the year before, and I'd discovered from talking with people at the Gathering that the rate of recidivism among long-distance hikers was pretty high.

"You got the right idea. But what I'm planning is much better than that!"

"You're taking five months off to hike the Continental Divide Trail?" jackrabbit volunteered.

"Close, but no granola bar. Ladies—and gentleman—I am quitting my job. If all goes according to plan, I'll be hiking for the next six years on a path that takes me through all of the lower forty-eight states."

"I didn't know there was a trail through 'em all," PA Mule said.

"Well, there isn't, really. I'm connecting up a lot of different trails. I'll hike all the big ones: the A.T. again, the Continental Divide, the Pacific Crest Trail, and that new one that runs cross-country, the American Discovery Trail. But I'll also hike a lot of smaller trails and do some road walks to connect them up."

"Wow. How'd you decide to do this?"

"Well, I pull down a pretty good salary, working in management. Before I hiked the Trail, my goal was to be a millionaire by the time I turned forty. After the A.T., I started looking at it differently. What was I doing with three houses and four cars, when I was so much happier living out of a tent? I realized that I could *retire* by age forty, if I cut my expenses and lived a bit more simply.

"I'm not promising to do this hike. If I get sick, or hurt, or just plain tired of walking, I might buy a little cottage somewhere in the woods and try my hand at gardening. I might move to Mexico and live on a houseboat. Or I might go back to work. But right now, just thinking about those trails makes me happy. I'm smiling when I get out of bed in the morning and smiling when I work overtime. 'Cause I see it all as a path leading back to the forest. The forest, the cornfields, the desert, the little backroad towns where they never see a stranger unless he's buying gas. I love this country, and I want to see it all."

jackrabbit

In the morning, PA Mule took us into Stroudsburg, the nearest large town, to resupply. We stocked up on the usual Trail staples: noodles, granola, dry milk. At the outfitter's store, Isis finally bought an ultralight headlamp. It would make cooking after dark much easier. After we brought our shopping bags back to the hostel in Delaware Water Gap, Mule drove us out to Fox Gap so we could slack the seven miles back to town.

A steady cold rain streamed from the low clouds. Bright leaves spiraled down from the trees and plastered themselves to the ground, a Persian carpet of cool flames, vivid reds and oranges and yellows. The colors were beautiful, but the leaf-covered rocks made for treacherous footing. With the quick reflexes I had developed from hiking barefoot, it was relatively easy to predict how the rocks would tip, and to shift my weight to protect myself. It was harder to avoid the small rocks, hidden under the leaves, which occasionally jutted up into my insteps. No wonder the northbounders had told horror stories about the Pennsylvania rocks. I could see how hikers in boots, lacking the skills that I'd developed, could easily turn an ankle or worse. Remembering Tuba Man's tale of falling off the ridge, I was suddenly thankful for the awareness and traction that bare feet provided, no matter how much the sharp little rocks could hurt.

Back at the Delaware Water Gap hostel after our slack, dripping wet, we found the common room full of children. The sound of young voices came though the door and lightened the gloom of the day. A black-haired girl of about ten and a younger girl with ash-blond hair lay on their bellies, intent on a picture they were both drawing. A thin woman with round blue eyes and waist-length brown hair sat on the couch, cradling a younger child in her arms.

"Are you Isis and jackrabbit?" she asked with excitement. "We've heard so much about you, and we've wanted to meet you for so long."

Isis smiled and held up a bare foot, pink and wrinkled from the wet day. "I'm Isis . . ."

"Oh, Paul is just gonna flip out! This is so great!" Her wide, ingenuous smile seemed to fill the room with warmth, and we were instantly captivated. "But let me introduce my family—"

"Are you guys the Family from the North?"

She beamed again. "Yeah, that's what they call us . . ."

"Excellent! We've been wanting to meet you for a long time, too."

"Aw, thanks. Well, I'm Mary, and this is Faith." She held up the youngest child, a baby of perhaps two years, who gave us a sleepy-eyed smile. "And that's Joy—" pointing to the girl with dark blond hair, who looked up with a shy grin and went back to her drawing. "And—"

"Hi, I'm Hope! Do you guys really go barefoot all the time? Are you really from Maine?" The oldest girl had vivid green eyes that sparkled with curiosity.

There was the sound of a car pulling up outside.

"Oh, that's probably Paul and the boys. A trail angel took them into town for our resupply."

The door burst open and a man walked in, loaded down with bags of groceries. He had a long black beard and a black braid halfway down his back and the most intense dark eyes I have ever seen. He was small and wiry, projecting an air of quiet competence. Every inch of his body rippled with lean muscle. My first thought was, *here is somebody not to mess with.*

"Go out and help," he barked, and I instinctively moved toward the door, following Hope and Joy.

He put the groceries down. "Oh, I'm sorry," he said, and his face changed instantly from brooding to apologetic, flashing a charming smile toward me. He had the same powerful charisma that Mary had shown. "I was talking to the children."

He came over to shake my hand. "I'm Paul," he said. His grip was like iron. I could see a network of small scars crossing his hand and forearm, the mark of a lifetime of physical labor.

"Jackrabbit," I said.

"This is Joel—" a stocky brown-haired boy in his early teens grunted a greeting from behind a box of groceries "—and John." The younger boy, ten or eleven, had olive skin and a shoulder-length braid of dark hair and delicate elvish features. He nodded solemnly in greeting.

The Family unpacked their groceries with practiced ease, transferring food from boxes to Ziplocs and stowing it in their packs. Most of it went into Paul's, an enormous magenta internal frame that dwarfed mine.

While they worked, I thought back to all the things I had heard about them. A young sobo couple at the Gathering had told us they were homesteaders, with a strict and unbending interpretation of the Bible. An argumentative flip-flopper had characterized them as tax cheats and uneducated bums, "a couple of crazies with way too many kids and no common sense." I hadn't known quite what to expect. As I watched them unpacking the food, the thing that struck me most about the Family was their politeness.

"It's my turn to carry the bagels, John," said Hope, her face taking on an adult seriousness.

"But they're heavy. I'll take 'em again, I don't mind."

There was little squabbling; they all put their heads down and did what needed to be done. I could imagine them running a homestead together, quietly shouldering responsibilities and sharing the burdens.

When the work was done, Paul settled into a well-worn armchair and busied himself with the register, checking back over the old entries. Joy glanced toward us but held back, looking nervous, and Mary picked up a storybook and started reading to her. Joel stayed in the corner, rooting for something in his pack, but Hope and John, the ten-year-olds, came over and said hello. They stood before us uncertainly, shy but brimming with curiosity.

"Are you guys twins?" I asked.

"No," Hope said. "People ask us that a lot. Mary's my mom, but Paul ain't my dad. Him and mom met when I was real little. John and Joel was from Paul's other marriage. Faith and Joy's theirs together."

"Are *you* twins?" John asked, and I laughed.

"Isis is three years older."

With this established, the kids quizzed us about our hike. We gave them a short history of our adventures so far. (Hope made appropriate noises of concern and patted my knee when Isis got to the part where I was injured.) Isis demonstrated how to walk barefoot over rough ground, a skillful roll of the foot from ball to heel. She navigated the maze of gear on the floor with her eyes closed, feeling her way with her feet. The children looked up at us with wide, shining eyes. They drew pictures for us: rainbows and flowers and smiling faces, but also full shelters and mountains with small hordes of figures in packs climbing the sides.

"This is us," John said. "Here's me and Hope, on the top of the mountain, and there's Joy and Dad way out front like they always is, and Joel right behind them. Mary's in the back like usual."

"Where's Faith?" I asked.

Hope gave me a slightly exasperated look, as though I had asked a very dumb question—a glance that I recognized immediately as the mark of an older sister. "Mom carries Faith. She ain't big enough to walk yet." Sure enough, there was a blue Kelty kid-carrier pack leaned against the far wall, with all manner of things—clothing, foam pads, a cooking pot—strapped to the outside. The pack frame alone looked like it must have weighed ten pounds, and I didn't want to imagine how much it would weigh with all that gear and the chubby two-year-old.

"No wonder she walks in the back with all that weight!"

Hope gave me another older-sister kind of look, this one with a tinge of severity. "We all got to carry a lotta weight. Paul's pack weighs seventy. Mine's twenty-five, mostly—"

"—except when she carries the bagels—"

"How much is yours, John?" I asked.

With everyone's attention on him, he became shy, his dark eyes turned down toward the carpet. "Maybe thirty."

"Mine's forty, unless we get extra cream cheese," Joel broke in from the corner where he'd been repacking his clothes. His voice cracked in mid-sentence, and he reddened and turned back to his packing.

I knew adults who carried less than thirty pounds, and my own pack was generally about forty. "Wow. How many miles a day do you guys do?"

"Our biggest day was twenty-one. We usually do fourteen, fifteen. Depends on terrain," Paul spoke up from the armchair. His voice was deep and slow, with an accent that I couldn't quite place; possibly Midwestern.

"That's impressive." A strange mix of feelings flowed through me: amazement, at the strength and endurance these kids must have, and sadness, that they would be ahead of us almost immediately, if we continued at our snail's pace. Some uncharitable corner of my brain felt a good deal of resentment, too, that we were being out-hiked by seven- and ten-year-olds.

There were many questions still churning under the surface of my mind. I wanted to know about their history, this rumor of their religious fervor, and why they were hiking in the first place. I wondered about the stories of their tax evasion, and I worried a little about the kids' seeming lack of education—their grammar wouldn't have held up at any elementary school. But I was still a little nervous about awakening Paul's wrath, and I decided that if we were only going to have a short time with the Family, it would be better spent playing with the kids than arguing about politics.

Later that night the pastor came by, a solidly built woman with gray curls and kind eyes the color of the sky after rain. Her face crinkled into a wide smile as she surveyed the mayhem of the room: empty grocery bags, clothing, and hiking gear, scattered everywhere on the burgundy carpet, and the children lying on their bellies in the midst of the clutter, writing and drawing. We thanked her for the church's hospitality.

"Oh, it goes both ways," she told us. "The hikers have brought a lot to this town. Is there anything else I can do for you?"

This was my chance. "Is there a piano here that I can play?" My fingers itched for a keyboard. It had been weeks since I'd played.

"Well, I can let you into the sanctuary. Please lock up again when you're done. And I'd rather not turn all the lights on up there, if that's all right—the bills, you know . . ."

I took the candle lantern up the narrow stairs and into the main room of the church. Polished dark wood gleamed back faintly from all the corners of the room, and the ceiling arched up beyond the reach of the fragile light. The grand piano stood in the corner.

My fingers felt clumsy at first, as though cobwebs covered my memory. I closed my eyes and let the music flow through me. Gradually it returned—Chopin, Bach Debussy; the pieces I'd worked so hard to polish for my senior recital just six months earlier. It seemed like another lifetime. My memory drifted back to college, all the friends I'd known, the classes and practice sessions, the Tae Kwon Do tournaments, the late-night talks and endless discussions. *And now I walk,* I thought. *Dawn to dusk, I walk, and the thoughts I have are mine alone.* The music flowed on through my hands, moving from memory to improvisation. I tried to fill the echoing space of the church, my loneliness, with rich and unrelenting sound.

When I opened my eyes, Joy was standing beside me. The candlelight glowed golden on her fine hair and her tiny solemn face.

"Did you ever go to church?" Her voice was little more than a whisper, swallowed up in the giant room.

"I never have."

"Paul took us once when I was little. There was a man there that said things, and Paul said they was lies. We never did go again." She was silent for a moment. "You play nice music."

"Thank you, Joy."

I started playing again, a slow lament. She stood watching in the outskirts of the candlelight, with a respectful silence I'd never seen in a child her age. I turned my attention to the keyboard, clutching at the memory of notes to catch them before they faded. When I looked up again Joy was gone.

The Family decided to take a zero day at the hostel. I didn't blame them—it was another day of cold rain. PA Mule took us back to the trailhead at Fox Gap, where we had slacked from the day before, and wished us luck. "Youse want some extra water? I got a couple of liters in the back there. Go ahead. The springs are iffy on this ridge."

"Maybe we'd better. Thanks, Mule." Isis grabbed two Gatorade bottles, full of clean water, from the back of his truck. We stowed them in our packs, made a few last-minute adjustments. Each of us was carrying three liters of water now. I could feel the extra weight dragging against my hips and shoulders. It was only twenty miles from Fox Gap to Palmerton, though, so we weren't carrying much food.

"Oh, one other thing I mention," Mule said. "Up at the other end of this ridge, maybe three, four miles out of Palmerton, that's the Superfund site. There was a zinc smelter in the valley there. Heavy metals just about stripped all the plants off the ridge. Still a wasteland. You'll know it when you see it. Whatever you do, don't drink out of the puddles up there." He winked.

"Thanks for everything, Mule. We really appreciate it. Take it easy," I said. He waved and pulled back onto the road. We headed into the woods. Maples, oaks, and hickory glowed with fiery colors, red, orange, school-bus yellow, intense and bright in the foreground and muted in the distance by rain and fog. Like yesterday, the leaf-covered rocks made for difficult walking.

As the day wore on, the air began to clear and a wind blew the bright leaves swirling down out of the trees, fluttering between the gray trunks like exotic butterflies. It was amazing how fast the leaves fell; the day before, the forest canopy had been bright with color, and by noon today the color was all on the ground. The ridges were narrow, and between the suddenly bare branches, we could see all the way to the valley floor on both sides. Orderly farms and small towns made a patchwork of gold, green, and brown behind the vertical gray stripes of tree trunks. The ridges here had a totally different shape than other mountains I had known; flat-topped, skinny, and sinuous, they stretched across the landscape like wrinkles in a piece of fabric, interrupted only by the gaps where rivers had cut through them.

We stopped for lunch at the Leroy Smith Shelter, a somewhat run-down wooden lean-to in a clearing among oak trees. The sun came through the clouds, and we basked in the warm rays for a long time, savoring our cheese, crackers, and dried pineapple.

"Should we get water here?" I asked.

Isis consulted the map. "The spring's a long ways down. I think we can hold out till we get to the next one."

"Okay." I took a small sip of my water and chewed my last slice of pineapple, watching hawks and vultures soar in the thermals beginning to form above the valley.

"I've got a surprise," Isis said. She reached into her food bag and drew out a pomegranate. Isis knew that the smooth-skinned red fruit, with its hundreds of tiny seeds, was one of my favorites. "I picked it up in Stroudsburg yesterday, while you were getting our dinners."

"Excellent!" Fresh fruit of any kind was a welcome change out here, and my mouth watered at the thought of a pomegranate. But as I peeled back the tough outer skin, I felt a few misgivings. "Isis, you remember the legend of Persephone, don't you? She would have been able to escape the Underworld, except that she ate those six pomegranate seeds. That's why we have six months of winter . . ."

"Of course I remember."

"Well, doesn't it, I mean, don't you worry . . ."

She shrugged and smiled, already digging into her half of the pomegranate. "Maybe we'll just have to spend a few extra months on the Trail."

We had planned to camp that night at Delp's Spring, six miles down the trail from Leroy Smith, but night caught up with us on the ridge. I set the tent up in a tiny stealth site, overhung with branches. We mixed up our instant potato flakes with very little water, trying to save some for breakfast, and as I drifted off to sleep, I thought about Persephone.

In the morning, we found the trail down to Delp's Spring after maybe a quarter mile. A sign nailed to a tree trunk proclaimed the name, and a register box below it held a tiny notebook labeled *Flow Report*. I didn't bother reading it, thinking that after such a rainy summer we would be guaranteed at least a trickle. Our last bottle of water, perhaps three-quarters full, sloshed in Isis's hip holster.

"I'll go down," I said, unshouldering my pack and letting it fall in the dry oak leaves. I took out my fleece against the morning chill, put on my camp shoes, and took off at an easy jog down the trail to the spring with our empty water bottles and the filter. A few leaves still clung to the maples and sassafras, bright yellow in the horizontal early light, but the woods were mostly brown and gray, a monochromatic vista of dead leaves, dead grasses, naked tree trunks. Everything looked dry and dormant. The cool air whipped past as I descended, trotting down switchbacks and leaping over stone steps, down toward the distant valley floor.

Suddenly the trail came to an end. The stone steps ran out in a tangle of brambles and tawny grass. I stopped on the bottom step and waited for my breath to calm down, straining my ears for a hint of water-sound. I stood there listening until my heart rate slowed again, but the only sound was the soft rustle of dead oak leaves. Then I looked around. Under the last stone step there was a small space of gravel. A metal pipe protruded from the hillside above, its spout blocked by cobwebs. I grabbed a stick and dug down among the stones, but the gravel was bone-dry. Only a powdery dust rose out of the old spring.

As I climbed back up the trail, going slowly now to conserve energy and sweat, I considered what I would say to Isis. We were still ten miles out from Palmerton—ten slow and painstaking miles, if the rest of Pennsylvania was anything to go by—with less than half a liter of water between us. The morning air was chilly, but I knew that the temperature would rise with the sun. And somewhere ahead of us on this ridge was the Superfund site. I tried to come up with some heroic turn of phrase to sum up our situation. "We will need our reserves of strength and fortitude to get through this day . . . no, that sounds like a spoof of Blade . . . maybe something more like this: we're facing a big challenge . . ."

Isis was waiting at the top of the trail, her face set in a grim smile. Before I could bring out one of my bon mots, she supplied her own: "We're screwed, aren't we." It wasn't a question. She held out the *Flow Report* notebook. "Pretty entertaining reading. *10/5: this is supposed to be a spring? . . . 9/15: Delp's gravel pit is more like it . . . 8/27: RIP Delp's spring.*" The last record of any water coming out (*a slow drip. Bring a Tolstoy novel for entertainment while you wait*) was in March—of 1999.

She divided our remaining water into two bottles, taking care not to spill a drop, and each of us poured out a little into our cups for breakfast. We mixed up dry milk, dumped in granola from a Ziploc, and ate fast. The sun was higher in the sky now, the air warming rapidly. We licked out our cups and set off, making our way slowly along the leaf-strewn trail.

Around midday the vegetation began to look strange. The trees became stunted, twisted shapes that clung together in groups, and the ground between them was bare except for sparse hummocks of pale grass. The gravel trail felt warm and sharp underfoot. As the forest thinned out on either side, we could see down into the valley below, where clusters of houses and occasional water towers spread out from a snaking roadway. At the far end of the valley the shimmer of a river was just visible, and beside it, the squat gray rectangles of factories and warehouses sprawled over several acres. *Probably the very smelter that did this*, I thought.

Farther along the ridge, the trees gave way to blasted stumps and the rocks took on a blackened cast. The trail, a yellowish-gray gravel, was the only hint of color in the funereal landscape. It curved along the top of the ridge ahead, vanishing into mirages before it touched the horizon. The wind had died, leaving the air still and hot. Thirst clutched at my throat.

Distant pools shimmered in the mirages. As we came closer to one of them, I gave a shout; it truly was a pool of water. It was all I could do not to plunge my hands in and dip it out to drink, but I remembered PA Mule's warning—"whatever you do, don't drink out of the puddles up there." I looked around at the scarred ridge, the gray stumps that were the only remnants of the lost trees. Whatever had done this to the forest, zinc, cadmium, lead, sulfates, nitrates, it was still here in the water. With a great effort, I walked past the poisoned pools. *It's in the ground, too*, I thought, *probably seeping up through the soles of my feet.*

We walked for what seemed like hours through the desolation, stopping twice for a sip of water. The sound of the last few mouthfuls sloshing around in the bottle as I walked was maddening. I could feel hunger coming on as well, gnawing at my belly. I didn't want to stop in the middle of this wasteland, but I knew I had to keep my energy up.

"I've got to eat something," I said, and Isis agreed. We stopped beside a semicircle of dead trees, their trunks snapped off perhaps eight feet above the ground. They offered little shade, with the sun beating down from overhead, but at least there was the illusion of protection. Isis took out some dried fruit and granola bars. Something in the still air above our heads caught her attention, and I followed her gaze. High up on a thermal, but riding lower with each passing moment, five or six vultures hung in the air on their great black wings. Their naked heads pointed toward us, and I imagined their beady eyes gleaming in anticipation.

We scarfed down the rest of the granola bars fast and staggered to our feet. The flock dispersed, but they followed us over the rest of the ridge at a discreet distance, wheeling around us in lazy circles. Lines from "The

Wasteland," half-remembered from lit classes in another age of the world, crept into my mind. I had seen it that morning, *fear in a handful of dust*. A handful of smooth, cold gravel that should have held water. What if something happened to one of us up here, in this wasteland? My mind conjured up images of setting up the tent to ward off vultures, running down to the valley for help. *How long can the body survive without water? Several days*, I thought. *Time enough, surely.* We staggered onward through the miles of scarred and blighted rock.

Looking down into the gap at the far end of the ridge, I saw a jumble of boulders, some the size of my head and some the size of a small car, stacked haphazardly at a steep angle. The trail zigzagged down the slope before vanishing among the broken stones. Thirst was weakening me. Things at the edge of my vision shimmered and wavered as I watched; I felt utter weariness creeping into my legs. I vowed to save my last mouthful of water for the valley floor. I knew I needed strength, but I also needed some incentive to get me down safely. I focused my mind around water, getting down to the valley floor so I could have water. I curled my right foot around the contour of a stone, planted my sticks against another boulder, and started down.

I have little memory of the climb down Lehigh Gap. All I can recall are fragments, images of broken stone and stacked-up boulders, some smooth and some sharp underfoot. In one place we had to lower ourselves down a rock face with our hands, reaching for invisible toeholds below. Sounds of traffic rose up out of the gap. Sometimes we could look straight down on the highway and the gray-green river. The ground seemed to wobble and sway unpredictably. I narrowed my concentration into balance and movement, thinking only of the mouthful of water waiting for me at the bottom of the trail.

At last we stood in the parking lot under a grove of still-yellow sassafras trees, looking up at the wall of crumbling stone. I unscrewed the cap of my water bottle with trembling hands and drank the sweetest water I had ever tasted.

"Here," Isis said. "Drink some of mine."

I refused. "If you're feeling anywhere near as bad as I do right now, you've gotta drink that."

Her forehead wrinkled with concern. "How bad are you feeling?"

I told her about the way the ground had lurched on the way down, and how even now the edges of my vision shimmered and threatened to go dark.

"Good Lord! Drink it all, then."

"You mean you don't feel it, too?"

"Well, I'm not exactly feeling great right now, but I haven't been halluci-
nating or anything. Go on, drink it."

After swallowing her last water and sitting down for a few minutes, I felt
good enough to get up and begin the long walk into town. I was amazed at
my sister's endurance. When we started this hike, I had secretly thought to
myself how well-suited I would be for Trail life. I was an athlete who spent
long hours in the gym, training mind and body to conquer any obstacle. My
sister's main form of exercise was a walk in the woods every few days. And yet
it turned out that she showed up stronger and more resilient at every turn. I
was the one who was forced off the Trail by injuries, I was the one unable to
stop my despair at being constantly left behind, and now I was the one almost
overcome by dehydration. Isis had enormous reserves of strength that she was
just beginning to discover, while I felt that the Trail so far had only served to
show me the limits of my strength.

We stayed in the borough hall that night. It was a stocky yellow brick
building in the center of town, with window boxes of red geraniums half-
wilted from frost. Tuba Man had told us about the place at the Gathering: the
town of Palmerton lets hikers stay for free in the basement, which used to be
the county jail. He said it was a standard hiker joke to call your parents from
Palmerton and tell them you were in jail somewhere in Pennsylvania.

The front door was locked when we got there, but a small sign in the
window read, *Hikers: Please sign in with the Police Department (back of building)*.
The officer on duty, a portly, balding man in his fifties, had us sign our names
in a spiral-bound notebook. He scrutinized our drivers' licenses for a moment
and directed us to the basement side door.

I had expected the place to look more jail-like, but the cells had been torn
out long ago, and now it had the ambience of a typical municipal-hall basement, aside from the rows of bunks along the back wall. The blue-painted
walls and floor exuded a faint odor of sweat and mildew. Old issues of *Reader's
Digest* and *National Geographic* cascaded over a plywood table in the center of
the room. Padlocked storage cupboards in one corner were plastered with
handwritten posters of Cub Scout mottos and badge requirements.

"Evening." The sudden, gravelly voice made me jump. An old man with
glittering blue eyes and a short beard stood in the doorway across the room,
leaning on a broom. He wore a plaid shirt and paint-spattered jeans. I was still
wobbly and disoriented from water loss, and it seemed that he had appeared
out of the woodwork. "I'm Bill, Bill the janitor they call me. And you are . . ."

We offered our trail names and Bill nodded his head, unsmiling, as though weighing the information.

"Is there a water fountain here?" I asked.

"There is," he said solemnly, leading us to the top of the stairs. I filled my water bottle and drained it twice, the cold pulsing through me. Isis did the same. Bill watched without comment.

"Let me show you around the place," Bill said when we put our bottles down at last. He indicated the hallway leading off to the left beside the water fountain. "The gym's down that way, if you want to play some basketball. Showers are off to the left, in the locker rooms. Nicest showers on the Trail, many hikers tell me. Best watch out for the alligators, though." He said all of this in the same quiet, deadpan tone, not smiling even for the alligators, and it was hard to know whether to laugh or not. The floor seemed to sway beneath me; I wondered if Bill was another figment of my imagination.

Bill showed us where the stairs led up to the second floor. I felt a little better as the water coursed into my veins. Bill stayed just as strange. I decided he wasn't a hallucination after all. "Ladies' room is up there, on the left," he said. "And don't worry if you hear funny noises in the conference rooms across the hall. Bunch of ghosts play poker up there every Friday. Don't mind 'em."

He led us back downstairs. "Now, this is the room where the hikers stay, unless you get too noisy. Then we lock you in the cupboards over there," he said matter-of-factly. "Now when George Washington crossed the Delaware and built this place, back when I was a little boy—" he winked, the first outward sign that he was laughing at his own jokes "—he forgot to put a light switch in that outer room there, so the lights always stay on. Should be dark enough to sleep back where the bunks are. Never had any complaints. 'Course, if they did complain I would've locked 'em in the cupboards anyway. Have a nice night now. Bill's got to get back to work."

We thanked him for the tour. As he receded up the stairwell, we heard his gruff voice call out once more: "Watch out for the alligators!"

We decided to stay in Palmerton for a day to recover our strength. It was our first zero in a long time. We ate breakfast at an unapologetically 1950s diner across from the borough hall, washed our already-grimy clothes, ate a leisurely lunch at a pizza place down the street, and resupplied. Isis had heard that the next town, Port Clinton, had almost nothing in the way of groceries, so we shipped a box of food there. We spent the afternoon writing letters in the park, where yellow leaves still clung to the maples and hawthorns. The light gilded the tops of the ridges as it slanted toward evening. We could see the blasted, bare surface of the ridge we had crossed the day before, a black smudge that spread upwards from the buildings of the erstwhile smelting plant. I thought of the bulletin board downstairs in the borough hall, with its faded posters: "Fifty Uses for Zinc, the Miracle Metal!"

Palmerton reminded me of the college town I'd left, in a way: a quiet place stuck a few years in the past, where all the teenagers' main ambition is to leave town. Groups of them drifted through the park, reeking of perfume and cigarettes. Signs on the light poles downtown read NO CRUISING and NO LOITERING. Many storefronts were dark, and FOR SALE signs sprouted on lawns around town like a new kind of toadstool.

When the sun dipped below the ridge and cold shadows began to gather in the park, we heard children's voices echoing down the street.

"The Family's coming!" Isis said, and sure enough we could see their six small silhouettes against the storefronts down the road. The children came running to meet us, putting on a remarkable burst of speed at the end.

"Isis! Jackrabbit!"

We lead the Family to the basement of the borough hall, where there were just enough bunks to go around.

"You're supposed to sign in at the police station just to let them know who's here," I said, and Paul and Mary grew quiet. "Just show them a driver's license or something; I don't think they check it too closely."

"I hope they won't come by here tonight," Mary said softly.

"We don't have any identification," Paul said, his voice tinged with a kind of weary pride.

"None?"

"None."

"Why?"

Paul gave the explanation as though he had answered this question thousands of times, and I was reminded of the litany of questions people asked about our feet. His explanation made no more sense to me than ours had made to the incredulous man on Sunrise Mountain, but I listened, fascinated.

"We do not carry identification because the Bible says, 'thou shalt not bear false witness.' To carry a piece of paper that says 'I was born on December 4, 1965,' is to bear false witness against yourself. You are not conscious on the day you're born."

I started to protest. "But there are other people present. Your mom can vouch for it, certainly, and the doctor, and anybody else who was there—"

"Yes, but you *yourself* have no idea when you were born. And if you say that you do, or carry a document to that effect, you are committing a falsehood and bearing false witness against yourself."

"But if you don't have any ID," I said, "I mean, doesn't that make it hard to . . ."

"We are emancipated people," Paul said. "We pay no taxes, we take no money from the government. I went to Washington myself to resign my Social Security number."

I nodded and fell silent. I was still puzzled by Paul's reasoning, but I had a sense that no amount of discussion would clarify things. *Some people just have a different worldview*, I thought. *As long as it's not harming anybody, I guess I just need to accept it. Agree to disagree.*

The Family went to the grocery store and returned shortly, all laden down with bags of food. Paul took out a loaf of bread and a jar of peanut butter. "Suppertime," he announced, and the kids lined up by the plywood table in the center of the room. He gave each of them two sandwiches, saving the heels for himself and Mary. I was amazed; two sandwiches would be barely a snack for any hiker I knew, and the little ends of the loaf would be nowhere near enough. No wonder Paul and Mary were so thin. Isis looked over at me and we had a wordless conversation.

"Hey, can we take you guys out to dinner?" she said.

"We have our dinner," Paul replied, but Mary was watching him with a pleading look in her eyes. He sighed, proud but reconciled.

Isis and the Family and I took up three tables at the Chinese restaurant across the street. The kids ate and ate, puzzling over the unusual flavors of cashew chicken, sweet and sour pork, egg rolls, and shrimp in lobster sauce. They grew more comfortable with us as the meal progressed. Even Joy, who had seemed shy at first, began telling jokes and stories. The whole restaurant rang with our laughter.

Back at the borough hall, Isis and I were ready to settle in for the night, but the kids were full of energy. They ran up and down the stairs. When Hope and John discovered the gym, they enlisted us for a wild game of tag.

Joel explained the rules while his brothers and sisters waited impatiently. "See, one person is the Moon and runs around tagging people. If you get tagged then you're frozen, and you have to stay there. One person's the Sun and they unfreeze you.

"What happens if the Moon tags the Sun?" Isis asked.

"Then they switch what they are. The Sun turns into the Moon and then—"

"That's not what happens, Joel, remember?" Hope said, indignant. "The last person that the Sun tagged turns into the Sun, and the last person the Moon tagged turns into the Moon!"

Joel shrugged. "We always make it up as we go anyway," he said.

The game of Sun and Moon tag went late into the evening. Isis and I were soon panting and wheezing like old women, but the kids dashed about with their energy undiminished.

"How many miles did you guys hike today, anyway?" I asked when I caught my breath again.

"Oh, about seventeen," John said casually.

"Let's play another game!" Joy shouted, grabbing my hand and jumping up and down.

At long last, the tag game came to a close and we returned to the basement. I sat on my bunk and tried to write a letter home, but I kept thinking of the Family. Everything we had heard from the other hikers was true, at some level. I could certainly believe that they had been homesteaders—the quiet determination and steely strength I saw in all of them was something not tempered by the soft life of suburbia. Their interpretation of the Bible was strict and a little strange. Paul had admitted to being a tax resister. But the most apparent thing about the Family, their strongest characteristic, was their love and respect for each other.

I looked around the room. Hope was sprawled out on the floor, laughing. John brushed his dark hair out of his eyes with one hand, offering the other to Joy to help her up from the ground. Joel was playing catch with Faith, using a crumpled piece of newspaper for a ball. Faith's chubby hands almost closed around it, but it slipped through her grasp time after time and rolled away. Her brother picked it up each time and tossed it gently back to her. And Paul and Mary sat beside each other on one of the bunks, still for once, surveying the scene with a tender, quiet look. Whatever their history, wherever they were going, they were a family.

Isis

The hike out of Lehigh Gap was much easier and more pleasant than the hike into it. The south side of the gap didn't seem to have suffered nearly as much from the pollution; instead of a jumble of bare stone, the trail climbed through high yellow grass and even some patches of forest. And this time, we were carrying plenty of water.

The Family caught up with us a few miles outside of Palmerton. Since we were headed toward the same shelter, we decided to hike together for the afternoon. Hope skipped along beside me, engaged in a cheerful monologue about what kind of horse she wanted and what she might name it. Midnight and Star topped the list, but she liked the sound of Ember. By the way, her favorite color was purple. A black horse would look good with a purple saddle, didn't I think? They should make saddles in more different colors, not just icky brown. If I hadn't known her family's history, I would have thought her a pretty typical ten-year-old girl. All that vanished, however, when we came to a cleared area full of lowbush blueberries.

"Do we have time to pick?" she asked Paul.

"Sure," he answered. "It's only a few more miles to the shelter."

As soon as they had the go-ahead, all four of the ambulatory children dropped their packs and began to forage. I'd always prided myself on being a fast berry picker, but Hope could have rivaled a grizzly bear. By the time I had one handful ready to eat, she'd cleaned five or six bushes and moved on to the next patch. Paul picked just as feverishly as the children, but he gave most of his berries to Mary, who sat under a pine tree, nursing Faith. After half an hour, he called out, "Okay, let's get moving." Without a word, the children hurried back from their corners of the field, donned their packs, and set off down the trail.

For the last two miles, I walked with Mary. I asked about her life before the Trail. Her soft voice grew wistful as she reminisced about her homestead garden, her kitchen, and her books.

"It's not too easy to homeschool the kids out here," she said. "They get some practice at math, calculating how far we've gone every time we reach a signpost. But we're all so tired in the evenings, I'm afraid their writing's suffered. They know their wild berries, though. They can build good fires—even Joy—and they know how to read weather changes in the clouds. They all seem to love it out here."

"Do you like it?" I asked her.

"Hiking's the hardest thing I've ever done. Every day, at the end of the day, I feel glad that I've been strong enough for my family, glad that I've had the courage to go on. Sometimes I stand up straight and look at the views; I feel like I'm finally getting used to it, and then I fall. With Faith in my backpack, I have to fall forward, on my knees. But most of all, I miss the company of women."

As we set up our tent in a clearing behind the shelter on Bake Oven Knob, the four older children stepped out of the darkening woods. They dropped off armloads of firewood in front of the shelter and stood watching us for a minute. Then Hope stepped forward. "We're all done setting up our stuff. What can we do to help you?"

"You ought to rest," said jackrabbit. "Read the register or something. You just hiked eight miles. You deserve a break."

"Eight miles is nothing." Joy sounded indignant. "One time, we hiked a twenty-one."

"We want to help you," said John.

"Okay," I said. "You can help me get wood for our Zip stove. I need sticks about as big around as your first finger."

They scattered among the trees, returning in a few minutes with enough sticks to cook five or six dinners.

"What size should we break them to?" asked Joel.

I showed them, and they sat in a semicircle breaking the twigs and sorting them by diameter into neat piles. Like any other group of hikers encountering an unfamiliar item of gear, they were eager to see how the stove worked. They asked all the pertinent questions: how much it weighed, how long the battery lasted, whether it worked with wet wood.

"It takes longer to boil water than most canister stoves, especially if the wood's wet," I told them. "But it's great not to have to carry fuel. And personally, I love the excuse to build a fire every night."

"I like building fires," said Joel. "Someday, I'm gonna hike this trail solo. Maybe I'll get one of those, when I do."

"Supper's ready," Paul's voice called from the shelter. The children jumped up.

"Just a sec," I said. "Hope, would you take something to your mom for me?" I tore a page from my notebook, folded it in half like a card, and wrote on the inside, "Dear Mary, please join us for tea this evening. Love, the Barefoot Sisters." I scrawled a hasty heart on the front and handed it to Hope.

Mary came over after supper, with Faith on her hip and her camp cup in her hand. She and jackrabbit and I sat in the grass in front of our tent, sipping tea and passing around a pot lid heaped with Pecan Sandies.

"Cookies! This really is a tea party!" exclaimed Mary. "I used to make cookies every Friday in winter; my favorites were oatmeal chocolate chip. You put in just the tiniest bit of flour, so they spread out all thin and lacy."

I, in turn, described my favorite kind of chocolate chip cookies, my mother's recipe including walnuts, sunflower seeds, and whole wheat flour. This led to stories of our mothers and grandmothers, of Ireland and Illinois, the people and the places we came from. Faith nursed for a while, then curled up asleep in Mary's arms. The sight of the two of them made the darkened clearing, with its half-bare trees and tangled hanging vines, seem warm and familiar as a living room.

Long after dark, I heard a rustle from the direction of the shelter. By the dim glow of our Zip stove's coals, I could see Joy standing at the edge of the clearing with her legs apart and her arms crossed. "Is tea over yet?" she asked. "'Cause we built a big fire, and we want you to visit the shelter."

Sitting on rocks and logs around the firepit, we sang, recited poetry, and told each other stories for hours, long past our usual Trail bedtime. When at last we returned to our tent, jackrabbit and I slept so soundly that we didn't even hear the Family leave in the morning.

CHAPTER 7

"As Long as It's Fun"

jackrabbit

I lost track of the days we spent in the mountains of Pennsylvania. It was hard to tell where we were from the maps; aside from the gaps, where the trail dropped down a thousand feet or so to cross a river, we followed the flat, featureless tops of ridges just wide enough for a few trees and the occasional clump of brambles. To either side, the valley floor showed between leafless branches. In places freeways uncoiled at the base of the ridge, cars glinting as they rounded the cloverleaf turns, so distant the sound of their passage hardly reached us. Sometimes we saw red barns and silos standing guard over still-green fields and the occasional herd of cows dotting a pasture.

After the Family from the North got ahead of us, we saw hardly anyone in the woods. Sometimes a family of dayhikers or a scout troop passed us, but days would go by without human contact. The incessant wind, sighing in the bare trees and rustling the heaps of fallen leaves, was our only companion when we stealth-camped in tiny clearings beside the trail. Each morning dawned later and colder. Frost often glittered from the trail as we packed up our camp. The rocks continued, sharp, uneven, treacherous stacks that shifted and clattered underfoot, often hidden under drifts of leaves.

I thought about Tuba Man often. When we came to the Knife Edge, the rock-jumbled ridge where he had fallen, I studied the stack of boulders, trying to imagine where he had slipped. I felt a frisson of fear and pity. I imagined him hiking down the mountain, hurt, and then hitchhiking with Solid. The cars rushing past and no one stopping. *If I had been there*, I thought. *If I had only been there, to bind up his cuts and let him lean on my shoulder all the way down the mountain. Or maybe I could have saved him in the first place, calling out a warning just in time—don't step there!* The thought of Tuba Man became a necessary distraction as the nights lengthened and cold took hold of the land.

213

When the evening star appeared, hung low among the empty branches, I would stare at it and think of him. I was sure that I exaggerated his good looks and kindness in my memory, but it hardly mattered—I was also sure I'd never see him again. I had sent him a casual e-mail from the library in Palmerton, asking him to keep in touch. I doubted that he would even remember me, though, among his many fans.

One day, we came down into the tiny town of Port Clinton, a few houses and two bars sandwiched between the Schuylkill River, a railroad yard, and a four-lane highway. The town was too small to even have a grocery store. The sound of traffic on the freeway reverberated everywhere in the streets. Willows along the riverbank still bore a few yellow leaves, but the grass on the fields in town was nearly all dry and dead.

Isis picked up our mail drop while I sat with our packs on the porch of the post office—the lobby of the small building was too cramped to fit both of us and our gear. A shadow fell across the postcard I was writing, and I looked up to see a frail-looking woman in her seventies, wearing a blue housedress and orthopedic shoes.

"Are you hiking the Trail?" she asked.

"Yeah."

"It runs along those ridges, doesn't it?" She pointed one gnarled finger toward the mountain across the river. The sun was low already, and the highest branches of the bare trees were gilded with its horizontal rays.

"Yeah, we came down right there." I pointed out the trailhead across the railroad yard, and showed her where the A.T. switchbacked down the steep end of the ridge.

She looked off into the trees, wistful. "You know, I've lived here all my life. I was here before the highway went in. I've never been up on those ridges. And now I don't think I ever will. Good luck to you, young one."

"Thank you," I said gravely. She crossed the street and turned between two rows of houses, disappearing from view. I looked back up at the sunlit ridges, and I wanted more than anything to be back there among the trees. I felt trapped, suffocated, here among the high houses, the bars, the cracked asphalt and omnipresent traffic sounds.

Isis came out of the post office with our box of food. It didn't take long to pack it into Ziplocs and divide it between our food bags; we had only sent ourselves three days' worth of meals.

"Where's our next town stop?" I asked.

Isis took out the map. "Duncannon," she said.

I leaned over her shoulder, looking at the elevation profile along the top of the map. "How far?"

She frowned. "It should be right here. I know it's here, at the end of this map. Thirty miles. Three days."

"It's not here, though," I said. "Swatara Gap is not Duncannon. Are we missing a map? . . . wait a second." As the sunlight came through the open map, it illuminated something on the back of the paper. I felt a sinking sensation in my chest. All of the other Pennsylvania maps had been one-sided. It couldn't be . . . but there it was, the missing section, thirty-five miles of flat ridgeline. Thirty-five miles for which we had no food.

It took a while to realize the full extent of the mess we'd gotten into. "There has to be some place to buy food around here," Isis said. The only business open in town, besides the two bars, was a candy store. We spent the last of our cash—they didn't take credit cards—on fudge and chocolate-covered mints, the most caloric-looking things we could find. Thirteen dollars didn't go very far. Isis asked if there was an ATM in town, but the woman at the counter shook her head with a tight-lipped smile.

"We'll think of it as an adventure," Isis said as we headed up the ridge. "We can pretend we're on a quest or something." Over the next few days, she was mostly silent and stoic, bearing her burden. Maybe the quest idea worked for her. As for me, I soon discovered that I would rather hike injured than hike hungry. I became short-tempered and hostile. My powers of concentration failed; I tripped and stumbled constantly, and once the edge of a rock cut the tender skin in the arch of my right foot. The gnawing emptiness in the pit of my stomach was the only thing that occupied my mind for more than a few minutes. A packet of oatmeal in the morning, a handful of crackers at noon, and a meager serving of pasta or potatoes at night hardly touched the surface of my hunger.

On the way out of a gap, somewhere between Port Clinton and Duncannon, we got lost. The A.T. ran along a smooth grassy track with forests on one side and an old field on the other. A hint of midday warmth lingered in the dry grasses, where a few crickets scraped their monotonous, rusty song.

"I haven't seen a blaze in ages," Isis said. She took out the map and frowned at it.

"I think it turns into the woods soon . . . Wait! Are those blazes up there?"

A narrow trail turned off the main track and headed up into the maple and hemlock forest. The trunk of a tall sugar maple bore a few indistinct white marks, just about the right size for A.T. blazes. We followed the trail for perhaps half an hour. It started out as a narrow but worn track, marked with faded blazes. As we proceeded deeper into the woods, it became indistinct, scarcely more than a game trail. The white blazes faded out, and the traces of the trail took a sharp turn uphill. Still, we followed it. The sun had sunk below the next ridge, and the chill seemed to rise out of the lifeless ground.

At last, we came to a small stream. There was no sign of a trail on the far bank. It was more than I could take. "What are we doing here? We're hungry, we're cold, we're lost. Fuck this! Fuck this whole damn trail!" I sat down by the stream bank, sobbing, pounding my fists into the ground. Dimly, at the back of my mind, I was aware that this was not helping our situation.

"You girls okay?" It was a gruff male voice. *Shit*, I thought. *Just what I need. Somebody to watch me hit bottom.* I looked up to see a hunter in full camo gear and a blaze orange vest, carrying a large gun.

"We're fine," Isis assured him. "Do you know if this is the Appalachian Trail?"

"Appalachian Trail." He considered for a moment. "Runs along the next ridge over. Don't know how you ended up here."

"Thanks," Isis said, and the hunter melted back into the woods. I collected myself gradually, still cursing.

Back where the trail had turned into the woods, we examined the blazes closely. The paint was chipped and faded, barely more than a stain on the gray bark. "Look at this, Isis," I said. "It looks like these blazes used to be painted over with a darker color." Sure enough, a few flecks of grayish paint still covered the white in places.

"Notch this!" Isis swore. "This must have been an old relo." We'd seen a few other places where the trail had been relocated, but generally the right direction was much more clearly marked. We stayed on the flat, grassy trail beside the field, hoping that this path, at least, would lead us in the right direction. My stomach rumbled loudly, my limbs felt weak, and my temper was ready to snap at the slightest provocation. We didn't find another blaze for almost half a mile.

One consolation on these cold, hungry days was our pot of tea at night. For a few minutes after my half liter of hot water, I would feel full and content. We always had enough water, often more than enough—we weren't going to make that mistake again. Isis carried a few flavors of herbal tea: peppermint, blackberry, chamomile, Red Zinger. After supper, when the wind rustled the dry leaves along the ridge tops and the lights in the valleys began to emerge from the gloom, I collected another handful of twigs for the Zip stove. Huddled in our fleece jackets and long underwear, we tried to find a place out of the wind to sit and drink our tea.

One night, Isis laughed to herself as she added teabags to the pot.

"What?" I said, slightly annoyed. Everything bothered me: the cold, the endless wind, my grumbling belly. What bothered me most at that moment, though, was seeing Isis happy. It made me feel inferior, diminished. *If I were a better person I would be laughing too, but instead I'm moping*, I thought.

"Oh, I was just thinking about a chapter in *Lord of the Rings*, where Sam and Frodo are heading into Mordor, and Sam thinks to himself, 'it was the hour of the day when civilized people would be having tea.'"

"Civilized people would have eaten more than half a cup of instant potatoes!"

"Yes, but think of it this way; at least we don't have malevolent supernatural forces on our tails."

"The consequences of our own stupid mistakes are bad enough."

She sighed. "Do you have to be so negative?"

"I can't help it! I'm fucking hungry!"

"Please don't use that language with me."

"You sound just like our mother."

"I'll take that as a compliment." She leveled her stare at me for a moment, and then brightened as though remembering a secret. "You know what, though? The 501 Shelter is coming up!"

"Hmph. What's so great about a shelter?"

"Anonymous Badger told me about it at the Gathering. It's a huge shelter, all enclosed like a barn, right by the road. There's a caretaker who lets you use his phone. You can call for pizza and get it delivered!"

"Pizza . . ." I sighed.

"If we are where I think we are, we should get there tomorrow."

The next day the trail underfoot was littered with tiny sharp rocks. The frost, which now lingered well into the morning, made them seem twice as painful. My belly growled insistently, as it had since we left Port Clinton, but now I cheered myself with thoughts of pizza. Mozzarella, juicy tomato sauce, substantial crust, onions, broccoli, olives, mushrooms . . . I held the image in my head and ignored the gnawing hunger and the cold. Tonight, I knew, we'd be in a shelter with four walls, out of the wind, eating a full meal at last.

It must have been a weekend—we saw more people on the Trail that day than we had seen all week. Two middle-aged men stopped to talk to us while we filtered water from a stream. The one in front did most of the talking and his companion held back, watching us.

"You guys thru-hiking?"

"Yeah."

"Oh, I've always dreamed about it!"

"You ought to do it, then," I said. "It's a free country. All you've gotta do is save up some money, get six months off, and walk."

He shook his head and sighed ruefully. "It's the time off that's the problem. Me and my buddy here, we teach high school. I teach English, he does chemistry. We hike as much as we can in the summers, but we can't get more than those three months off."

"You could always hike it in sections, a couple hundred miles at a time. We've met a lot of people doing that."

"It's hard to get away from the wife and kids. Maybe when they're older . . ." He caught sight of our feet. "Are you hiking barefoot? Barefoot, in Pennsylvania?"

We nodded.

"Did you come all the way from Maine? Barefoot?"

We nodded again, and Isis held up one of her splendidly callused feet for inspection.

"Well, my hat's off to you! Boy, this'll be part of my campfire stories for years. I'll tell the grandkids about you. When I have grandkids, that is . . ."

Finally his companion spoke up. "Would you like a beer?"

"That would be awesome. Thanks." The can felt numbingly cold under my fingers, and wisps of steam rose from the metal.

"It might be a little cold." The chemistry teacher grinned gleefully. "I'm packing them on dry ice."

"Wow. We'll save it for tonight, I guess—might be thawed out by then. Thanks again."

As evening drew on, we finally heard traffic: PA 501. We quickened our footsteps and I licked my lips in anticipation: *real food!*

The shelter was a converted studio, built of dark wood, across the lawn from the caretaker's one-story home. We unlatched the door and stepped inside. The final rays of the sun streamed through a hexagonal skylight in the center of the roof. For a shelter with four walls, it was not as cozy as we'd hoped. The ever-present wind worked its way through cracks in the walls and floor, and the persistent chill of a day in the shadows hung in the corners. We looked around: mouse hangers dangling from the ceiling, sturdy wooden bunks, metal trash can, shelves of magazines and ragged old registers, a hiker box picked through to the dregs, a table scattered with candle stubs and the detritus of old feasts. Red and white printed menus, napkins, stray spots of pizza grease reflecting the last sunlight like coins from a lost treasure.

We laid down our packs, hung the food bags, and set out our sleeping bags on the most sheltered bunks. Isis emptied our trash bag into the metal barrel. With the preliminary chores done, we salivated over the menus: pizza, subs, salad, all manner of fried appetizers. It didn't take long to choose. We'd get a pizza primavera for tonight—white pizza with broccoli and onions— plus a Greek salad and onion rings, and two eggplant parmigiana subs for tomorrow. It would be our first full meal in three days.

I rubbed moisturizer on my feet, put my camp shoes on, and went out to look for twigs and water so we could boil a pot of tea with supper. Isis went to the caretaker's house to ask if we could use the phone.

I was drawing a pot of water from the spigot on the side of the shelter when she returned, her face set like stone. "They don't take credit cards at the pizza place, and we don't have any cash left," she said in a small voice.

I wish I could say I reacted in a sympathetic way, but my temper took over and I let loose a string of expletives instead. The visions of a scrumptious, filling dinner vanished as the last slice of the orange sun sank below the horizon. The leafless skeletons of oak trees, silhouetted in the purpling sky, seemed to be mocking us as they tossed their arms in the rising wind.

"Now what?" I growled between my teeth, but the answer was obvious. I slouched off to gather more twigs for the stove as Isis wordlessly unpacked dinner from my food bag. As a consolation prize, she chose the pasta and not the infernal potatoes. Then I remembered the beer that the weekenders had given us—at least we'd have something to drink with supper.

We crouched outside the corner of the shelter to cook, not wanting to risk a spark on the tinder-dry wooden floor. The wind ripped past, stirring the dry leaves on the ground and wicking our body heat away, even through layers of clothing. It took several tries to get the stove going; eventually, a crumpled-up pizza menu with its cargo of grease did the trick. The meager pot of noodles bubbled and steamed as Isis fed the fire. I sat just upwind, breaking the wood into thumb-sized pieces. Neither of us spoke much, lost as we were in dreams of unattainable pizza.

Inside the shelter, Isis scraped the last of our olive oil (now a gelatinous solid) out of its bottle with a debarked twig, and mixed it with the noodles and a half-packet of dry pesto. The scent of basil lifted into the cold air. We lit a few candles. In their flickering light the shelter was transformed. Even though my stomach still growled, and the wind whined like a hungry dog around the eaves, everything seemed warmer and softer. As I sat back in the chair I thought, *yes, we are lucky indeed.* We divided up the pot of pasta, and I opened the beer.

"Damn it!" Half the beer gushed out over the table in a foamy rush, and the other half (mostly water, I guess) sat in the can, still frozen. We drank the little that we could get and savored the few bites of angel hair.

I got up from the table after dinner, and my stomach gave a huge empty rumble. "I can't take this any more!" I shouted. "Why can't we fucking get enough to eat, just for once?" Isis sighed and stared at me for a moment. I waited for another comment about my language. And then, as often happens between us, we had the same thought at the same time. We both glanced toward the hiker box, and our eyes met. We smiled.

In a moment, we were laying out the contents of the box on the pizza-stained table. There were the ubiquitous bags of unidentified white powders, a Ziploc of instant rice with a suspicious ragged hole in the lower corner, sugar-free Kool-Aid, a very postdated tube of Squeeze Parkay, and a nearly-empty jar of Jiff. A mysterious dehydrated substance resembling jerky. Near the bottom, though, there was more promise. A couple baggies of grains, which we tentatively identified as millet and quinoa, and two Instant Breakfasts.

Isis took her headlamp and fetched a pot of water, and I found more firewood by the dim light of the Photon. We huddled outside the door, sheltering the stove from the blasts of wind, but our mood had changed from glum to triumphant. We had faced down adversity together, once again. As we do sometimes to cheer each other up, we began exchanging lines of doggerel:

"It was late one night down at 501, and we were running low on cash—"

"We were glad for four walls around us, and a place to put our trash, but we couldn't order pizza . . ."

". . . so we were feeling blue, till we had the bright idea of making Hiker Box Stew!"

We had a name for our concoction, and the list of ingredients grew more and more outlandish as our rhyming went on. In reality, the stew was a sweet pudding with the grains, Instant Breakfasts, dry milk, sugar, and cinnamon and nutmeg from Isis's stash of spices. We'd managed to salvage a bit of the instant rice from the top of the mouse-chewed bag, checking it carefully for nasties and finding it clean.

Isis tried a tentative spoonful. "It's, well . . . it's like rice pudding, except with not much rice, and no raisins, and no eggs . . ." It was certainly unusual, but our hunger made it delicious. We'd made enough to fill our two-liter pot, and we ate half of it, saving the rest for breakfast. At last, our bellies were full.

In the gleam of the many candle stubs, the feeling of satisfaction returned, and this time nothing marred it. We decided to transcribe our silly poem for the register:

> It was late one night down at 501
> and we were running low on cash
> we were glad for four walls around us
> and a place to put our trash,
> but we couldn't order pizza,
> so we were feeling blue
> till we had the bright idea
> of making Hiker Box Stew!
> We added a box of instant rice,
> perhaps some millet too,
> and something that might have been quinoa
> went into our Hiker Box Stew.
> We added an Instant Breakfast
> to make it nice and sweet,
> and shaved off part of a Snickers bar
> for an extra special treat.
> Then we added a handful of peanuts
> to make it look less like glue,
> and half a packet of Gatorade,
> and a bunch of Skittles too!
> So next time you're feeling hungry
> and you don't know what to do
> think of us here at 501
> eating our Hiker Box Stew.

It took me a long time to get to sleep that night. Even bundled in my fleece jacket, long underwear, hat, and gloves, I was barely warm enough inside my sleeping bag. The cold wind came up through the cracks in the floor and rattled the windows. I felt peaceful, though. With enough food in my stomach, I could finally see things in a more rational light. I realized how incredibly selfish I'd been. At the shelter that evening, I had been angry at Isis for not double-checking the map or stopping by the ATM on the way out of Palmerton, angry at the pizza place for not taking our credit card, angry at the weekenders for packing their beer on dry ice, angry at the caretaker for not taking pity on us and driving us into town. As I hunkered down in my sleeping bag, trying to keep the cold air from coming in the top, I wondered what had possessed me to feel that way. *How could I have blamed the very people who are helping me—my sister, friend and companion, the weekenders who kindly shared their beer, and the caretaker, who provided this shelter for us?*

The world doesn't exist to do my bidding, I thought. *I can't assume that just because I'm a thru-hiker everybody will lay out the red carpet for me.*

Isis

It had been months since we'd hiked with anyone besides the Family, and that encounter, with the gypsy-camp atmosphere of our night of singing and their silent disappearance in the dawn, seemed more like a dream than a memory. I was sure that jackrabbit and I were the last of the southbounders, hiking into winter alone. One afternoon, though, a woman in a colorful knit cap stopped beside the stream where we were filtering water. Her grungy pack, nominally a dark shade of pink, looked far too well-used to belong to a casual weekend hiker.

I jumped to my feet and held out my hand. "Hi, I'm Isis."

"Then you must be jackrabbit," said the woman, glancing at my sister with bright brown eyes, lively as a bird's. "I am Netta. Or Almond Tree, if you prefer. Netta means 'small tree' in my native Hebrew. The blossoming almond is my favorite tree."

"Are you—are you a sobo?" I asked. When she answered that she was, I could barely restrain myself from hugging her.

"So we're not the last?" asked jackrabbit.

"Not at all!" Netta laughed. "There are many of us. Dave, Heald, Sharkbait, Mohawk Joe. And Black Forest. He is from Germany. He is . . . well, you will meet him very soon."

As if on cue, a slender young man with a halo of light blond curls sauntered down the trail. He came to an abrupt halt when he caught sight of us. Up close, I noticed that he was trying to grow a beard without much success.

The sparse facial hair, combined with his fine bone structure and wide blue eyes, gave him the look of a high school kid cultivating Kurt Cobain-esque grunge. He held out his hand and addressed us in a clipped accent that reminded me of Arnold Schwarzenegger.

"You must be the Barefoot Sisters. I am Black Forest. Today is my birthday. At the next road, I will hitch into town to drink beer. Some beautiful women, such as yourselves, would be welcome to join me."

After going to so much trouble to ration our food, hitching into town a day early seemed like a cop-out. The Hiker Box Stew had given us much-needed extra calories. Besides, we hoped that by staying on the Trail an extra day and getting ahead of them in trail miles, we'd be able to keep up with our new friends a bit longer. We left them waiting at the road, promising to see them in town the next day, and hiked up the last ridge.

We came down into Duncannon the next afternoon, crossing the wide brown Susquehanna River on a highway bridge. After securing a room at the truck stop at the edge of town, we walked perhaps a mile to Duncannon's business district to meet our friends at the Doyle Hotel. The *Companion* had described the Doyle as one of the "great Anheuser-Busch Hotels," the height of elegance when it was built in the late 1890s, but never renovated since. That assessment seemed to sum the place up—the room Netta showed us had two ratty mattresses lying on the floor, a bare bulb dangling from the wreckage of an antique brass fixture, and a garden of mildew spreading across the walls. I was glad that jackrabbit and I had opted to stay at the clean, inexpensive truck stop motel.

Unlike the rest of the building, the Doyle's barroom had been lavishly refurbished. Bronze and varnish reflected the subdued light. After our supper at the local pizza place, we returned to share a drink with our new friends. We found Netta and Black Forest sharing a booth with three other hikers. I thought I recognized the round-faced man on Netta's left, but I was surprised to see him so far north on the Trail.

"Playfoot!" jackrabbit greeted him. "I thought you were hiking with Tuba Man!"

"I was, but I got tired of the long miles," Playfoot answered. "Tuba and Solid go twenty, twenty-five miles a day. I was hurting, so I decided to get off for a while. Take a road trip, do a little trail magic."

"Well, it's great to see you again," jackrabbit said.

We set our packs down, and Netta introduced us to the other hikers.

"This is Ox; he is from Britain." A stocky man with a crew cut nodded in greeting.

"This is Cutter." She indicated the tall, white-blond man to her right. "He is getting off the Trail for his cousin's wedding soon; maybe Black Forest will go with him."

Cutter gave Black Forest an encouraging smile. "Come on, man. Free food and beer. How can you refuse?"

Black Forest, who was sitting in the corner with his eyes half-closed, let out a groan. "Do not talk to me about beer. After last night I do not want to drink any more beer, ever."

"There'll be a lot of pretty girls there," Cutter coaxed.

Black Forest's eyes snapped open. "When do we go?"

"So, have you tried Yeungling yet?" Playfoot asked us. "It's Pennsylvania's most popular beer, but hardly anyone knows about it outside of the state. Pity."

"I think we almost might have had some." Jackrabbit told him about the frozen beer the weekenders had given us.

"Man, what a tragedy! Well, you can make up for it tonight. Hey, Amy," he called to the bartender. "Could you bring us a couple pitchers of Yeungling?"

The beer did taste good, light and wheaty, but I switched to water after the first glass. Jackrabbit and I had to cross a four-lane freeway to get back to our hotel; at least one of us had to be clear-headed at the end of the night. Ox wasn't drinking much either, I noticed, and Black Forest was sipping cold coffee out of a foot-high Styrofoam cup. He grimaced and shook his head when the bartender offered him a glass.

"Ox and Black Forest spent one hundred and seventy dollars here last night," Netta explained. "I am not sure how they did this. I had three beers, which cost two dollars and twenty-five cents in total."

"Some of it was for the jukebox," Ox protested. "And we had those shots . . ."

"Does anybody have an aspirin?" Black Forest asked, from his shadowy corner of the booth.

"How're things going?" asked the bartender, setting down another foaming pitcher of beer. "This one's on the house." She beamed at Ox and Black Forest, who answered her with rather sickly smiles.

"Thanks, Amy!" Jackrabbit said from the other side of the table. "Hey, Isis, pass that over here, if you're not having any."

The beer kept coming. Not wanting to miss out on calories, I ate a few orders of onion rings and fries, then sat back, full and contented, while the stories swirled around me. Black Forest was giving Playfoot a morose account of his birthday revelries, and Cutter was trying to talk Ox into joining the hiker delegation at his cousin's wedding. Jackrabbit had checked her e-mail in the library that afternoon; she was telling Netta a funny story she'd heard from Waterfall.

"So our friend is hiking with this guy who keeps hitting on her, and one day he asks her, 'so, if you don't like me, who *do* you like?' She gives him a name, just to shut him up. She says 'Shepherd'—that's this guy we met in Hanover. He uses a shepherd's crook for a hiking stick. He *was* pretty hot, if you ask me. So, anyway, this guy asks our friend why she likes Shepherd; what's so great about him? And our friend's pretty sick of the guy by this point, so she says, 'well, I like Shepherd 'cause he's got the biggest stick on the Trail!'"

"Yeah, that's the ticket," Cutter didn't seem to have heard jackrabbit's story; he was still talking to Ox. He turned to Playfoot. "How 'bout you, man? Want to crash a wedding?"

"Sorry," he said. "You'll have to count me out. I'm heading back down to Virginia tomorrow, to see if I can find Tuba and Solid again." Playfoot shook his head. "I don't know what it is about those guys; they hike like bats out of hell, and all they talk about is beer and women, but I've never had more fun than I had with them." He paused. All the other conversations had stopped, too.

"I know what *I* like about Tuba Man," jackrabbit said, raising her tenth or eleventh glass of beer in a wobbly hand. I reached out a foot, but she was too far away to kick. "He has the biggest instrument on the Trail," she concluded happily.

I caught Playfoot's eye. He looked dumbfounded. *Don't tell*, I mouthed at him across the table, trying to make my expression severe. He gave me a wink and a small nod, as we both broke into laughter.

"Okay. Okay," I gasped, pushing myself to my feet. "It's getting pretty late. I think jackrabbit and I better get back to our hotel."

"Whuz the hurry, Isis?" jackrabbit asked. "There's still half a pitcher of Yeungling here. Can't let it go to waste."

"I thought you were staying here," said Cutter.

"No, we're over at the truck stop," I told him.

"But . . . that's across the highway," Playfoot said. "You can't *walk* there."

"I'm afraid we're going to have to."

"I've got my Jeep here," he answered. "Is anybody sober?"

"I only had one glass," I told him. "But you'd still need someone to drive it back over here."

"I will drive," said a voice from the shadows. Black Forest sat up. "I am the soberest German in the room."

Playfoot led us out to his Jeep, parked behind the Doyle. Jackrabbit and I sat in back, and Playfoot got in the passenger's seat. Black Forest turned the key in the ignition. As we pulled out of the parking lot, he flicked on the turn signal. It came off in his hand. He looked at Playfoot.

"I broke your car," Black Forest said in his usual deadpan tone.

That wasn't the end of our adventures in the Jeep. When we reached the freeway (fortunately not very busy at that time of night), Black Forest missed the on-ramp for the westbound lanes. Instead of going right and looking for a place to turn, he sped up, crossing both eastbound lanes and bouncing over the sidewalk-height divider in the middle of the road.

As jackrabbit and I climbed out of the backseat at the truck stop, he told us, "I am not sure my driver's license is valid in your country. I am only twenty-three."

"I think you're right," Playfoot groaned, his head in his hands. "I think you have to be twenty-five to drive in a foreign country. I've got to say, though, I'd be surprised if *your* license is valid anywhere."

"Playfoot, you should not insult me," Black Forest answered. "I am driving your car."

Two days past Duncannon, we came to the end of the Pennsylvania ridges. We were on our own again—Netta had already passed us, Cutter and crew had taken off for the wedding, and Playfoot had gone south. It was late afternoon; ahead of us stretched the Cumberland Valley, sixteen miles of level farm fields. A web of highways crisscrossed the fields, with clusters of hotels and fast food restaurants sprouting at their intersections. Here and there, a neat fan of suburban tract houses spread out from a loop of road. It didn't look much like hiker territory. I'd read in my *Companion* that the Trail had been relocated through the Valley at great expense, so that it followed the few remaining patches of forest instead of the four-lane roads. Still, the *Companion* warned against drinking any water we found there or trying to find a place to camp in the narrow strips of trees between fields and suburbs.

Unfortunately, sixteen miles was too far for us to hike in one day over Pennsylvania's stony ground. Ishmael, a hiker we'd met at the Gathering, had offered to slack us through the Boiling Springs area, but I hadn't been able to reach him from Duncannon. Nothing for it—we hefted our hiking sticks and headed downhill, toward the perils of civilization.

Two or three miles into the Valley, we found a place to camp beside a stream. It wasn't directly visible from any of the nearby houses, and it was as far as we could get from a road. We ate a cold supper, so as not to attract attention with the light from our stove. At dusk, we pitched our tent.

In the morning, we rose before dawn and packed our gear. We were sitting on our packs eating breakfast when I noticed a black-clad man bounding toward us, followed by a large shaggy dog. I froze, my cereal spoon suspended in midair. He was already abreast of us by the time I noticed that he was wearing a sweat suit, with reflective bands strapped around his ankles. A jogger, not a thief or a murderer fleeing the scene of his crime. He passed us without so much as a nod good morning. The dog, though, turned its head, stuck out its tongue, and slurped the rest of my cereal out of my cup, without so much as breaking its stride.

"Yech," I said to jackrabbit, examining the globs of saliva it had left behind. "It's a good thing we're getting to Boiling Springs today; I'm not carrying enough water to wash this off."

As it turned out, we got to town even sooner than we had hoped. At a bridge over one of the highways, I saw a slender, middle-aged man with dark curly hair climbing up the embankment on the other side of the road. He looked up and waved, grinning.

"Ishmael?" I called out. "What are you doing here?"

"I just got back from a timber framers' conference in Colorado and found your message on my answering machine. I didn't want to miss you, so I came out to the Trail."

"Perfect timing," jackrabbit said.

"Yeah, it worked out pretty well. Here, throw your packs in the back of the truck. I know this great breakfast place a few miles down the road. After we eat, I'll slack you the rest of the way to Boiling Springs."

We spent three days at Ishmael's house, an elegant, spacious log cabin that he'd built at the base of the Blue Ridge. On the first day, we took a zero to celebrate the end of the Pennsylvania rocks—Ishmael told us that the last sixty miles of the state were much smoother than the part we'd hiked. Jackrabbit played Ishmael's grand piano, overjoyed, while I cooked a harvest dinner: tarte à l'oignon, beet salad, carrot salad, and dark rye bread.

The following day, Ishmael had to return to his construction site. He slacked us over a section between Pine Grove Furnace State Park and Whiskey Spring Road, seven miles south of Boiling Springs. As he'd promised, the footing was much easier than it had been in the rest of Pennsylvania. Instead of tippy rocks, the trail was smooth bare earth in many places. We reached the road in midafternoon, with time to sit down for a snack. Ishmael arrived a few minutes later. As we walked to his truck, I noticed a black plastic bag lying in the ditch. There was something large inside it, something made up of smooth lumps and a few jutting projections. *A dead body*, I thought.

"I wonder what's in that bag," said jackrabbit. "The way it's shaped, it's kind of disturbing."

"Should we look, in case . . ." my voice trailed off.

"It's a deer," Ishmael told us. "Poachers get them, cut off the antlers and the best pieces of meat, and leave them by the road."

"Why the plastic bag?" jackrabbit asked.

"I don't know," he answered. "They always do it that way."

The deer was still there when we came back to the road the next morning.

"Want venison for dinner?" Ishmael joked. He had gotten a friend to drop us off so that he could slack the last seven miles back to town with us.

"We could have it for lunch," jackrabbit answered. "It's probably already cooked, from sitting in that black plastic bag in the sun for so long."

"Seriously, though," Ishmael said, "there's something on the side of this road that you've got to taste. Whiskey Spring. It comes straight out of the mountain; you don't have to treat it at all." He led us over to a metal pipe, hidden behind a ledge. A steady stream of water trickled out of the end, and the three of us took turns filling our bottles under it. I took a sip; it was cold, sweet, and somehow smooth-tasting, like the whiskey it was named for.

All through the day, Ishmael told us about the history of that stretch of trail and showed us its secret springs, its viewpoints, and its camping spots. We were on his beat, the section where he worked as the principal volunteer maintainer.

"This place is Center Point Knob," he told us. "It used to be the midpoint of the Trail. There's a famous picture of Earl Shaffer standing in front of that rock."

Later, as we crossed a field on the outskirts of town, he pointed to a patch of trees at the base of the slope. Railroad tracks stretched across the level field beyond. "Over there behind those cedars is the old hobo camp. Sometimes hikers still camp there, but I wouldn't recommend it. There's a crazy guy who wanders around the tracks, muttering stuff under his breath. I've never gotten close enough to hear what he says, but he always sounds angry."

As he spoke, we followed the trail closer to the hobo camp. We were only ten feet away from the cedars when a tall, heavy man lumbered out from behind them. He had a short reddish beard and a mop of light brown hair, which was tousled as if he'd just woken up from a nap. He squinted at us from behind small, oval glasses, with an expression that reminded me of a grizzly bear trying to decide what to do about an intruder. While we waited for him to speak, a large red dog burst out of the trees, baring its teeth and thrashing its body back and forth.

"Is that your dog?" jackrabbit asked the man.

He grunted.

"Is it friendly?"

"She don't bite."

"Hi, doggie," jackrabbit said, holding out a tentative hand. The dog thrashed its way over to her and rubbed its back against her legs. From this close, its strange grimace looked more like a smile than a snarl.

"Her name's Annie," the man said. After a pause, he added, "I'm Heald. Chris Heald."

While jackrabbit, Ishmael and I were introducing ourselves, two more men stepped out of the trees. The younger one was obviously a hiker; he wore shorts, a fleece jacket, and a pair of lightweight hiking boots. He had a handsome, angular face, shadowed by a week's growth of beard.

"Hi, I'm Dave," he said, reaching out to shake Ishmael's hand.

"Mohawk Joe," said the other. He was tall and wiry, with high cheekbones, jet-black hair, and a fantastically lined face. He was dressed in jeans, work boots, and a ratty white t-shirt. If I hadn't been standing downwind of him, I would never have guessed he was a hiker.

"Are these guys friends of yours?" Ishmael asked me uncertainly.

"They are now," I told him. "They're hikers—I think."

Ishmael turned to the men. "Do you guys need to resupply?" he asked. "We were about to head to town for a dinner, and I've got plenty of space in my truck."

Twenty minutes later, I was crammed in the back of the truck between Mohawk Joe and Annie. Dave was up front with Ishmael, jackrabbit sat on the other side of Mohawk Joe, and Heald lounged along the other side of the truck bed.

Heald glanced over at us and gave what sounded like a grunt of satisfaction. "Better company tonight," he said, to no one in particular. "Last night it was just me and this nutcase sleeping by the tracks. He kept muttering about his ex-wife's bad habits, saying she used to wash her silverware in old bathwater and strain her soup broth through a sock. It was kinda interesting, as monologues go, but I had a hard time getting to sleep with all that noise."

jackrabbit

It was hard to leave Ishmael's house. The three days we spent there had been the longest time we stayed in one place since the Gathering, I realized. Still, the Trail was calling. Ishmael told us we were nearly through the infamous Pennsylvania rocks, aside from a few patches that spilled over into Maryland. I was eager to try to put some more barefoot mileage behind us before the snow fell. I knew there were other hikers on the Trail now. Meeting Dave, Heald, and Mohawk Joe, strange as these characters had seemed, had been a boost to my spirits.

Ishmael dropped us off at the road in the late morning. It looked like something had gotten into the bag of deer guts in the ditch, but none of us felt like investigating too closely. The woods were quiet—the insistent wind that had prowled the ridges between Palmerton and Duncannon had finally died down; only a slight breeze rustled the dry oak leaves. We made good time over the trail. There were fewer patches of the infernal Pennsylvania rocks, and the ones we did run into seemed less tippy and treacherous than their more northerly cousins.

In the evening we came to the Ironmasters Youth Hostel. A converted Victorian mansion, it loomed against the sunset, tall and imposing with its ranks of high windows. The wide double doors swung open, and we saw a thin young man in a striped hat, smiling broadly. He had tightly curled brown hair, hazel eyes, and a multitude of freckles. "Welcome to Ironmasters. I'm Shawn, the hostel manager."

We gave our names.

"The Barefoot Sisters! I've heard about you. C'mon in and make yourselves at home. Now, is it true that one of you plays the piano?"

Two points in his favor, I thought. *He didn't ask the litany of questions, and he knows something about us besides our preferred footwear.* I grinned and nodded. He gestured toward the instrument in the corner of the high-ceilinged room. Two pianos in two days—this was almost too good to believe.

"I'd love to hear you play."

"Thanks, Shawn! Let me get cleaned up first."

After we had stowed our packs in the bunkroom and taken showers, we changed into fleece pants and marginally clean t-shirts. I sat down at the piano and lost myself in music. Memories came flooding back with the sounds; I pictured my first piano teacher's house, with its darkened rooms and overgrown backyard where cats stalked under the raspberries. I remembered walking there hand in hand with my mother, every Thursday after kindergarten. Later, the living room of my father's house, after the divorce, when it seemed that the strands of music I drew from the black and white keys were the only meaningful thing in the world. Then the practice rooms in college, with their green carpets and dark wood. Watching the sunlight fade outside the warped glass while I worked on the same passage over and over. Standing on stage after my senior recital while friends passed bouquets of bright flowers up to me. Here on the Trail, there were no flowers, no rounds of applause. The rewards were more subtle, but much deeper: trust and companionship. The light between the branches. The taste of water after a day of thirst.

"Suppertime!" My sister's voice drew me back to the present. It was almost dark outside. Shawn had turned on a few lamps in the common room of the hostel. A rectangle of brighter light projected from the kitchen, where Isis had set a table for four. "Hiker box stew again," she said, and produced a brimming pot of pasta with parmesan cheese and fresh tomatoes. It looked like enough food to serve four or five hungry hikers.

"That must've been some hiker box!" I looked over at Shawn, who was stirring a pot of something on the stove.

He shrugged, grinning. "I work at an organic farm off and on. Last week, when the killing frost came, we had more tomatoes than we knew what to do with. I figured hikers this time of year might like some fresh food."

"Thanks, man! This is quite a treat." I took a plate from the dish drainer and sat down across from Isis. Shawn sat at the head of the table. Isis dished out pasta for all of us. "Who's the other place for?" I asked.

"Dave. He's in the shower. He came in while you were playing."

"Cool." I had been so wrapped up in the music I hadn't even noticed him at the door.

He came to the kitchen in a few minutes, still rubbing his short hair with a towel. "Sounded good, jackrabbit."

"Thanks, Dave."

"Want some hiker box stew?" Isis asked him.

He looked a little doubtful, but when he saw the proffered pasta his blue eyes widened. "Yeah, thanks. Awesome." He grabbed a plate and sat down. After several forkfuls, he gave Isis a puzzled look. "This is great. Why do you call it hiker box stew, anyway?"

I told the story of the night at the 501 shelter and the frozen beer—"definitely a cold one!"—and Dave and Shawn laughed heartily.

Dave told us about his adventures with his hiking companions, from Heald trying to hop a freight car in Port Clinton to Mohawk Joe chasing down a woodchuck for his supper. "Those guys are a little strange," he said, and it seemed like the understatement of the evening.

Shawn related a few of his adventures. He had graduated from college a few years earlier with a degree in studio art and worked on organic farms in France and Italy for a year before returning to the states to run the hostel.

After supper, Isis brewed a pot of peppermint tea for us to share. It was good to have company for tea again. We hadn't shared it with anyone, I reflected, since we had invited Mary to join us on the ridge outside Palmerton. I wondered what had happened to the Family, and I hoped they were okay in the gathering chill of winter. They seldom signed in registers. In the warm, bright kitchen of Ironmasters Hostel, I asked Shawn if he had seen them.

"Oh, yes. They came through here a week, maybe ten days ago." He shook his head and smiled. "I've never seen a family that looked so happy together. Those kids were something else."

"Do you think they'll make it to Georgia?"

"They'll make it as far as they set their minds to go. Every single one of them has more backbone than about five regular people put together."

I nodded. "That's what I thought, too. I wish we could have stayed with them longer."

When we hiked out with Dave the next day, the trail was so smooth and comfortable underfoot that we were able to keep up with him. We stealth-camped together in a clearing among oak trees. Isis had carried out some popcorn from the hiker box as a treat. She wrapped her hand in several layers of handkerchiefs and shook the pot over our campfire for a few minutes. Only a few kernels burned and stuck to the pan; the rest popped up as light and fluffy as if they'd been microwaved. Dave applauded and offered a generous amount of butter from his food bag. We watched the sunset through the gnarled branches. With its infinite, subtle permutations of purple and orange, it was better than any movie.

In the morning, we sat on the logs around the old fireplace eating our breakfast of instant oatmeal, mixed up cold with a little powdered milk. The sky had become sullen and threatening, and the colors of the forest floor seemed to glow brighter against its gray: the dark kelly green of laurel thickets, the chestnut-colored backdrop of fallen oak leaves, and the light speckled gray of tree trunks. All around came the sound of wind stirring the fallen leaves.

As we packed up our camp, we heard a rustle of footsteps and the click of trekking poles. Two hikers, trotting along at probably four miles an hour, in the midst of an animated conversation. *These guys look like sobos*, I thought, *but I'll probably never see them again. They'll reach Springer before I'm halfway through Virginia.* Still, I walked over to the trail to introduce myself.

"Hallo, jackrabbit."

"Black Forest?" It was him, all right. A red knit cap covered his blond curls, and he looked even thinner than he had in Duncannon. But there was no mistaking his deadpan tone and German accent or the sly, mock-innocent look in his enormous blue eyes.

"Ja. How are you?"

"Good, good. Man, it's great to see you again. And who's your companion?"

"Hey, I'm Lash." The other fellow extended a hand. He was probably in his late twenties, tall (about my height), dressed in black Capilene with high gaiters, and wearing a fluorescent orange hat over his dark hair. He had ruddy cheeks and the usual scruffy beard. His pack was probably half the size of mine. The most distinctive thing about him was the color of his eyes, a startlingly beautiful bronze like an ancient coin.

"Pleased to meet you, Lash," I said.

"Dude! Are you one of the Barefoot Sisters?"

Dave and Isis came out of the woods, and we made introductions again. We traded stories as Lash and Black Forest leaned on their hiking poles. Lash had started the first of September and traveled fast enough to keep ahead of the winter, though his water bottles had frozen solid on Moosilauke. He and

Black Forest had teamed up just south of Duncannon, while the German was still recovering from his night of drunken revelry.

I asked about their plans for the immediate future, and Black Forest's eyes lit up. "We are doing the Half-gallon Challenge today and the Maryland Challenge tomorrow. Will you join us?"

"That's nuts. Maryland's more than forty miles! And besides, we're still twenty-five miles from the border."

"Miles do not matter to me. I am a German badass."

"You guys are insane."

"No, listen. This is how it's gonna work." Lash explained the plan. They would stop for lunch at a pizza place on US 30, perhaps six miles away, and do the Half-gallon Challenge. (This disgusting tradition involves eating an entire half gallon of ice cream in one sitting to commemorate the midpoint of the Trail. Some of the northbounders we'd met in Maine and New Hampshire had bragged about it. I thought southbounders were too smart for that kind of stunt, but Lash and Black Forest were quickly undermining my assumptions about my fellow sobos.) So they would consume a lunch of pizza and hideous amounts of ice cream, and thus fortified they would hike to the border. The following day they would get up at the crack of dawn and hike the entire length of the A.T. in Maryland. (This was another feat I had heard bandied about by nobos.) Lash explained the crackbrained plan in a very reasonable voice, which made it seem all the more surreal.

I looked over at Dave. He shook his head with a dumbfounded smile. "The only part of it that sounds any good to me is stopping for pizza."

"Amen to that." Isis, Dave, and I planned to meet the others at the pizza place. They would hike ahead and go down the road to a grocery store to purchase their half gallons.

"I still don't understand why you guys want to do that," I said. "It's so gross. I mean, think how much ice cream that really is. Just the volume of it alone. Why would you do a thing like that?"

Lash fixed me with an inscrutable stare. "Because it's there."

"Suit yourself. But just don't get one of those weird flavors like Moose Tracks or Cookie Dough. I couldn't even bear to watch that."

The sky opened up with drizzle as we neared the road to the pizza place. I heard the sound of traffic getting closer, the rush of wind and the wet slushing of wheels turning on the rain-slick road. We put our camp shoes on at the edge of the tarmac and headed for the distant green and red sign of the pizza parlor.

Inside, the smell of baking bread and fresh pizza was almost overpowering. We put in our order—one large veggie and two sides of onion rings for Isis and me, one large pepperoni for Dave—and took a seat in one of the yellow plastic booths by the window. Lash and Black Forest came in a moment later, grinning and carrying a grocery bag. They held up their ice cream boxes for our perusal: Lash had Moose Tracks; the German had Cookie Dough. I groaned.

We demolished our pizza in a short while and turned our attention to spectator sports. The TV in the corner was tuned to ESPN2, a special on trout fishing in the Housatonic. The commentator's voice sparkled on about the joys of fishing in a natural setting, the excitement of feeling the tug on your line, the beauty and majesty of wild trout. Black Forest was unimpressed. "You Americans," he intoned. "You are so weird. You do not even know how weird you are."

Later the sport changed to women's bowling, which was not nearly so interesting. We began to watch Lash and Black Forest instead. The German slumped on the bench, idly trailing his spoon through the frothy, half-melted ice cream. Occasionally he would turn up a lump of cookie dough and spoon it into his mouth with a look of high disgust. Lash, meanwhile, kept his spoon moving, but just barely. All the color had drained from his red cheeks, and he looked like one of the living dead.

Isis and I, in a moment of mischievousness, went up to the counter and ordered ice cream cones. Lash and Black Forest pointedly looked out the window, where the drizzle had thickened to a steady rain, and continued eating their soupy ice cream. Finally they poured the dregs into their water bottles and drank it through straws. They finished it, though, and held their boxes aloft as proof, with swollen bellies and somewhat nauseated grins.

"Lash, I am feeling not very good. I am feeling like sheet."

"Dude, I'm not gonna be able to move."

We sat in the restaurant for probably another hour, as the rain hammered down outside. Eventually the ice cream eaters could move again, albeit slowly. Some of the color had returned to Lash's cheeks, and Black Forest no longer drooped over the table like a wet noodle. It was late afternoon, though, and Isis and I decided to just head for the next shelter, three miles out.

"It's a double shelter," Dave said, consulting his *Data Book*. "There should be plenty of room for all of us . . ."

"We are not stopping. Tomorrow we do Maryland."

"Yeah, man. Party in Harpers Ferry tomorrow night. See you there, hmm? H.F. is where it's at." Lash held up his hands and made an encouraging face, like a used car salesman trying to get rid of a lemon.

We tried to argue, but it was no use. The half-gallon challengers were intent on challenging Maryland as well, even though they were still nineteen miles from the border, the rain was pouring down, and night was falling fast. *That's the last I'll see of these guys,* I thought once more.

At the shelter that night, we met Sharkbait. He stood under the eaves just inside the dripline, grinning, smoking a cigarette. He wore a dark blue fleece jacket and shorts. It was hard to guess his age—like most younger men on the Trail, he could have been anywhere from nineteen to thirty-five. He was tall and almost skeletally thin, with close-cropped blond hair, wire-rimmed glasses, and a long braided goatee tied with a rubber band. I was about to ask about the trail name when I saw his legs, a bare mass of scar tissue from the knees down. The skin had healed over long ago, but the right calf muscle was completely missing, and the left had an enormous chunk taken out of it. The shins and the remnants of the left calf were rock-hard thru-hiker muscles. I tried not to stare.

After supper, Dave lit a ring of candles. We shared stories in the soft light, speaking loudly over the drumming of the rain on the tin roof.

"So you're probably wondering how I got this way." Sharkbait gestured toward his mangled legs and grinned. "I was down in Baja, year after high school. Got drunk one night; thought it'd be a good idea to swim off the docks. So I was out in the water, way out there. This guy yells, 'shark!' And next thing I know . . ." His speech came in sharp scattershot bursts, and between sentences he paused, looking downward as if lost in his memories. In these moments he looked years younger, and somehow fragile. "I woke up in this hospital with four hundred stitches in my legs." He laughed as if he'd just delivered the punchline.

Isis and I made sounds of sympathy.

"God, that's horrible. I guess you were lucky to get away, though."

"That's awful. It really happened like that?"

He stopped laughing. "No," he said, and then laughed even louder. "I tell that shit to section hikers and Boy Scouts about forty times a day. Thru-hikers, I mostly tell the truth. I got hit by a Volkswagen. A fuckin' van. This friend of mine was driving. I was in a phone booth, talkin' to my girl-friend . . . This guy wants to scare me or something, so he revs the engine, comes up on the booth . . . but he's stoned, and the brakes are bad, and . . .

"My girlfriend, she hears this crash over the phone. I was, like, blacked out. She calls 911. Her mom's a nurse on the ambulance. Later on she told me they were picking up bits of my bones outta the rubble. Pieces this big." He held up a hand, thumb and forefinger maybe three inches apart. "So I spent eight months in the fuckin' hospital with my legs up in the air. They put me back together.

"And the thing of it is that before that, in high school, I used to be a run-ner. Used to win meets and shit, and I had these legs . . . Girls went crazy over my legs . . . But that shit's all in the past. At least I can walk now, you know? At least I didn't buy it in that fuckin' parking lot.

"My momma told me later, she knew it was gonna happen . . . she had this dream where I died. And she prayed every day after that, she said, 'God, please spare my son.' And when they called her from the hospital, she knew what they were gonna say. So sometimes I think . . ." he looked down at the shelter floor and lowered his voice. "I think I'm alive because my momma prayed for me. But most of the time I don't believe in all that shit."

The shelter was quiet for a moment, the words hanging in the rain-laden air. Sharkbait's thin face was frozen in remembrance. All of a sudden he came to life again, his face contorting into a tough-guy smile.

"Can't wait for H.F.," he said. "Gonna get driggity-drunk."

Isis

By morning, the rain had lightened to drizzle. Sharkbait and Dave took off early, planning to hike a twenty to Devil's Racecourse Shelter in Mary-land. Jackrabbit and I entertained the more modest ambition of crossing the Pennsylvania-Maryland border, some fifteen miles away, before nightfall. We expected to be alone for the next few days, but we hoped to catch the guys if they took a zero in Harpers Ferry.

Six and a half miles into our day, we reached the Tumbling Run Shelters, a pair of tiny brown and white buildings set in the middle of a rhododendron thicket.

"It's a little early to stop for lunch," jackrabbit said, glancing at her watch. "Shall we take a look at the register, anyway?"

"Sure." I checked the shelter to the left of the trail, while jackrabbit headed for the one on the right. No register in the left-hand shelter. As I turned around, I noticed jackrabbit waving excitedly from the front of the other building. With her other hand, she held a finger to her lips.

"Isis, there are *people* in here," she whispered. "I think they're asleep."

I hurried over. A yellow bivy sack lay against one wall, and a red sleeping bag against the other, each filled with the unmistakable bulk of a supine body. The bags were cinched tight at the head; only the tip of a pinkish nose showed at the opening of the red one.

"Do you think they're okay?" I asked jackrabbit. "Should we wake them up and see?"

"I don't know." She shook her head slowly. "Who would be sleeping in a shelter on the A.T., in this season, at eleven o'clock in the morning?"

As if in answer to her question, the red sleeping bag emitted a soft groan. The yellow bivy squirmed around a little, and a brown beard emerged from the top end.

"Is it morning already?" asked a feeble voice.

"Lash!" jackrabbit exclaimed. "Is that you? And Black Forest? I thought you guys would be halfway across Maryland by now."

The bivy sack answered with a moan. "It was the fog. Our headlamps died, man. Both of them. We thought we were lost in all those rhododendrons, with the fog swirling up in our faces like a bunch of wet ghosts." Lash pushed himself upright and stuck the rest of his head out of his bivy. "I almost cried," he concluded mournfully.

"Black Forest?" Jackrabbit poked the end of the red sleeping bag. "Are you awake?"

"Is it still raining?" his muffled voice responded.

"Only a little."

"Do not talk to me. If it is raining, I am not awake."

We hiked on in high spirits, joking about Lash and Black Forest's Maryland Challenge attempt and making bets as to when they would catch up with us. About a mile down the trail, we reached Antietam Shelter to find that it, too, was occupied. Heald and Mohawk Joe, the rough-looking guys we had met in Boiling Springs, sat side by side at the front of the sleeping platform. Mohawk Joe had an open beer in each hand, and Heald was swigging the last few mouthfuls from a bourbon bottle. His red dog Annie thrashed her way across the clearing to greet us, grinning her toothy grin.

"Hey, guys! Where's the bar?" jackrabbit asked.

"Righ' here," said Mohawk Joe. "Drop your packs an' join us."

"Joe and me hitched into town last night," Heald explained. In spite of the now-empty bottle in his hand, he looked up at us with a clear and level gaze. "Got ourselves some drink. Here, have a beer." He pulled two cartons of beer out of a shaded corner of the shelter.

Jackrabbit's eyes widened. "That's a lot of beer. Are you guys planning to finish it?"

Heald shook his head. "I'm about ready to hike on, myself. I'm out of bourbon, and I don't drink that other shit. Joe's going to stay here and finish it. Unless you girls want to help him out."

"Help me," Mohawk Joe said. He took a full bottle of brandy out of the corner where the beer had been and waved it in our direction. "You gotta help me. Have summa this. Iss the best."

Jackrabbit shook her head. "Thanks for the offer, but we'd better not. We can't drink and hike barefoot."

"Take some with you," Mohawk Joe offered. "Drink it tonight. I got plenty."

I glanced at jackrabbit. "Sure. That'd be a treat. Thank you."

While Heald hefted his pack and walked away down the trail, Mohawk Joe poured half the brandy into my spare Nalgene.

"I'd like to get to Maryland tonight, but maybe we'd better start looking for a campsite," jackrabbit said.

I agreed. Dusk was falling as we hiked down the last ridge before the state line. I knew I didn't have the energy to hike five or six more miles to Devil's Racecourse Shelter, and I didn't want to end up searching for stealth spots in the dark, either.

"The map showed a stream in the bottom of the valley," I told jackrabbit. "Maybe we can find a spot there."

"Either that or we can fill our water bottles there and camp at the next level place."

When we reached the stream, though, we found an official-looking yellow plastic sign nailed to the bridge. *Contaminated Water*, it read. *Do Not Drink.* There was no note whether the contaminants were bacteria (which our filter could have handled), viruses (which we could have used our emergency chlorine tablets to treat), or heavy metals or hydrocarbons, which we had no way to remove.

"I guess we'll have to go on to the next water source," jackrabbit said. "How far is it?"

"Let's see . . ." I pulled out the map. "Well, there aren't any springs or streams until Devil's Racecourse, but there's this place called Pen Mar Park right on the other side of the state line. It looks like a sort of a city park, with streets and buildings all around it. It's probably got a fountain, or maybe a restroom where we could get water from the sink."

"Or maybe there's a gas station or a restaurant on one of the streets," said jackrabbit, brightening. "We'd better hurry, though; it's almost dark."

We didn't stop to take pictures of each other at the state line, as we usually did, and we hardly spared a glance for the brown wooden sign marking the Mason-Dixon Line. By the time we reached the roads near Pen Mar Park, streetlights were flickering on.

Jackrabbit spotted a drinking fountain behind the park restrooms, but when we pressed the button, no water came out. The restroom doors were bolted. In desperation, we headed across the grass toward a decorative fountain, only to find that it had been drained for the season.

"What about the town?" jackrabbit asked.

All around the park, the bright rectangles of windows glowed in the dusk. I could picture the people inside the houses, turning on their faucets to fill glasses, pots, and bathtubs with fresh, drinkable water. Who cared that it smelled like chlorine, or that it came, perhaps, from the same watershed as the contaminated stream? What mattered was the unlimited supply of it, right there behind every door. Old ladies were pouring it into bowls for their cats; happy young couples were washing their dinner dishes. I imagined knocking on one of the doors, asking for water. Perhaps the kind people who lived there would take pity on us, or maybe even take an interest in our story and ask us to stay the night.

Reality check, Isis. Jackrabbit and I are no longer sweet blue-eyed girls from a good family, with all the unfair advantages of race, class, and beauty recommending us to the goodwill of strangers. If people we meet on the Trail like us and trust us, it's because they're just as grubby as we are, or because they've seen so many hikers that the grime and odor no longer surprise them. I imagined how outlandish we'd look to an ordinary suburban family, stepping out of the darkness with our tall hiking sticks and our mud-stained clothes. We belonged to the woods, the night, and the rain: the very things those house walls had been built to keep out.

"We'd better go on," I told jackrabbit. "It's been raining so much; I'm sure we'll find water somewhere. A puddle at least." We had filtered water out of puddles before, on mountaintops in Maine and New Hampshire. I'd always felt particularly sanguine about the purity of puddle water; instead of passing through a vast unknown watershed, it fell directly from the sky, touching nothing but the stones that contained it.

"Maybe we should walk along the street for a ways," jackrabbit suggested. "There might be a gas station."

I shook my head, remembering my long, dispiriting trek through the streets of Manchester, Vermont, before I found my way to the tutoring center. "I don't want to get lost in a town at night. In the woods, at least, we can find a place to sleep."

Sure enough, the ground beyond the park was nice and level, with plenty of places to pitch a tent under the oaks. Half a mile into the woods, we found our water source: a puddle that stretched across the middle of the trail, two inches deep and filled with dead oak leaves. Nothing pure about this water; Heald's boots and Annie's paws must have splashed through it within the hour. I met jackrabbit's eye and shrugged. Nothing our filter couldn't handle.

Supplied with the two liters I'd filtered from the leafy pool, we made camp at the base of a rockslide a little farther down the trail. The dark water blended well enough with the color of our instant black beans, and we were hungry enough to ignore the slightly bitter flavor. After dinner, we made ourselves cups of cocoa heavily laced with the brandy Mohawk Joe had given us. We went to bed somewhat dehydrated but happy.

In the morning light, it was much harder to face the water I'd filtered the night before. The tannins in the oak leaves had stained it as brown as strong tea. When we mixed it with our granola, the dry milk turned a foul linty gray. Jackrabbit wrinkled her nose.

"Maybe we should have mixed our cereal with brandy instead," she said, holding up the remaining quarter liter of alcohol next to a bottle of puddle water. "It's a slightly lighter shade."

jackrabbit

We camped that night at Pine Knob Shelter in Maryland, with Lash and Black Forest and a troop of Boy Scouts. The scouts had already taken over the shelter when we arrived, covering the floor with packs, sleeping bags, and spare gear. Lash, who wasn't carrying a tarp or a tent, took offense.

"These shelters were built for thru-hikers!" he protested to the scoutmaster.

I thought about telling him off: *The shelters are for anybody, first come first serve, and if you aren't smart enough to bring a tent, you should probably count on sleeping out, dude* . . . But I hadn't known Lash for very long, and I wasn't sure how he would react. Also, I was tired from a long day; finally out of the nasty Pennsylvania rocks, we had hiked seventeen miles, tying our longest day yet. I decided to hold my tongue and let the scoutmaster handle this.

The man looked at Lash blankly. "There aren't any more thru-hikers."

"We are thru-hikers. We are here," Black Forest tried to make his voice sound menacing, but it came out petulant.

"I talked to the ATC last night," the scoutmaster said. "They told me there weren't any more thru-hikers this late in the season, so we'd be free to use the shelter. You're welcome to join us in here; I'm sure we can make space."

Grumbling, Lash and Black Forest scooted into one corner of the shelter while the scouts reorganized their things. Isis and I tented, as we had planned all along. I didn't envy the men; they could probably look forward to a night of fart jokes and twelve-year-olds' ghost stories. I was kind of ashamed of the way they had acted, though, trying to claim the space as their own when the scouts had obviously been there first. I decided they deserved their fate.

Lash and Black Forest came by our tent in the morning before we were fully awake. "Simpsons season premier tonight at seven, ladies," Lash said. "See you in town."

Isis grumbled something unintelligible in reply, but I snapped awake. "What do you think?" I whispered. "Do you think we could hike twenty-three miles in a day?" I remembered her story of slacking with Scout in Vermont. She could do it, but could I?

Isis turned over and stretched. "We could try."

It was still early when we began hiking, with a pale light slanting through the bare trees. We started out with our fleeces on, and it was quite a while before I took mine off. The path was cold underfoot. I could feel the edges of the gravel and the occasional sharp point poking up through the thickness of my calluses, a dull chilly pain. By now, we had developed an almost uncanny sense of balance, knowing if a rock would shift as soon as a foot touched it, and being able to transfer weight from toe to heel and from side to side without thinking about it. This sense didn't help on gravel, though, where the many small points made it impossible to find a comfortable stepping place.

In midmorning, we passed a troop of maybe fifty Boy Scouts, with a few harried-looking scout leaders at either end of the line. As I stepped off the path to make room, the tender arch of my foot came down on a blackberry bramble. I clamped my teeth together to prevent any outburst of language in front of the kids. But as the line of them trooped past, one skinny ten-year-old, safely out of hearing of the adults, took a look at us. "Holy shit! They're fucking barefoot!"

The trail took us past the ruins of an old confederate farmhouse. Across the next road, a stone building of the same vintage had been fixed up as a restaurant. I glanced at the sign as we crossed the road: "Stony Mountain Inn. Fine Dining for All. Sunday Brunch 10:30-1." My watch read 10:28. "How about brunch, Isis?"

We stashed our packs in a corner of the courtyard, made ourselves as presentable as possible, and proceeded to demolish the stacks of eggs, home fries, bread, muffins, pastries, and fresh fruit. An hour and six plates later, I was ready to hit the trail.

On the far side of the road, we found a *Gone with the Wind* postcard left on a stump. Rhett and Scarlett embraced while Atlanta burned in the background. Among the flames was a crude sketch of a bare footprint. On the back, Heald's blocky capitals spelled out *Dear Sistahs, we are in HF at the Cliffside Inn because they take smelly dogs. Come find us. Cross the Shenandoah River Bridge, turn left, walk a ½ mile.* Lash and Black Forest had signed it, too.

Isis laughed. "Those boys."

The sun was higher now, and the cold no longer seeped into my soles from the rocks. The ridges were almost as steep-sided and skinny as those of Pennsylvania, covered with the same reddish-brown carpet of fallen oak leaves, but the patches of tippy, knife-edged rocks were fewer and farther between. Fueled by the plates of brunch we had eaten, we made good time, stopping only to talk to other hikers.

At the high point of one ridge, a Girl Scout troop practiced their rock-climbing skills on an outcropping of dark stone. We paused to talk to one of the leaders, and she called the troop over. They quizzed us about our hike. Somehow, the familiar questions were much more exciting coming from a group of ten-year-olds than they would be from the average middle-aged dayhiker.

"How many of you want to hike the Trail someday?" Isis asked, and an enthusiastic chorus of "me!"s came back. It was heartening; I felt as though what we were doing was actually important, as though it could matter to people besides ourselves. I felt a new lightness in my step as we continued along the trail.

The sun sank low over the distant mountains, painting the treetops on the ridges gold while the rest of the land sank into purple shadow. The trail was hard to see in the gathering gloom, and I could feel my concentration weakening. Already I had hiked more miles today than ever before. Once or twice I nearly kicked my foot into a rock or stepped down onto something sharp, but I managed to recover at the last moment.

We could see lights in the valley below winking on as we reached the end of the ridge and began to descend at last. The trail here was dry dust, powder-smooth and silky underfoot, and I let my concentration relax a little bit. We stopped for water. I hit the Indiglo button on my watch, igniting a brief blue-green flash that suddenly made the night around me several shades darker. "Seven oh-four. The Simpsons is on; I guess the guys will have to tell us how it went."

"We're still a few miles out, I'm guessing. Didn't Heald say the last part of it is on a canal towpath?"

"Something like that. Hope it's not gravel." But it was, two miles of it, and my mind went numb with the effort. The moon rose over the river beside us, gleaming silver through the bare trees and reflecting off the turmoil of the water. The canal on the other side of the path gave off a faint stench of rotting weeds and catfish. It would have been beautiful and peaceful, except for the ceaseless pain of the gravel. Each step brought a new stab of awareness somewhere on the soles of my feet. My calluses had never really recovered from the time I'd spent off the Trail. For probably the last mile, I was leaning heavily on my sticks and cursing through my teeth. Isis, walking ahead, seemed not to mind the gravel at all. Her thicker calluses and wider feet carried her over the sharp little stones with no problems.

At last the trail brought us to a bridge, with the little town of Harpers Ferry nestled on the point beyond at the confluence of two rivers. I remembered the directions on Heald's postcard.

"Is this the Shenandoah River?"

"Hang on a sec." Isis switched on her headlamp, its brilliant blue beam slicing through the darkness, and unfolded the map from her waist pouch. "No, this is the Potomac. We have to cross here, go through town—it's kind of confusing here—and then there's another bridge. We go back out the same direction we came in, but on the other side of the river."

"I didn't see many lights across the river from the towpath . . ."

"I didn't either, but that's where Heald said to go."

"Okay, let's do it."

The trail led to a historic park at the head of the island, a small space of grass surrounded by half-ruined stone walls. It was slightly eerie in the moonlight, with the low murmur of rivers gurgling past and the distant whistle of a freight train. A light mist was coming off the water.

"Now what?" I said, whispering despite myself.

"I don't know. The Trail's supposed to go through town somewhere in that direction—" she pointed toward a row of silent antebellum houses set on a hill, "—but I don't see any blazes."

"Lemme see the map." I took out my Photon light, on a string around my neck, and created a circle of blue-white light. "If we follow this road up and take the third left, that gets us to the bridge. We can walk the white blazes tomorrow before we leave town."

We sat down on the curb to lace up our camp shoes for the road walk.

When we reached the Shenandoah River, the moon had retreated behind a low bank of clouds. It was hard to see clearly in the gloom, but there seemed to be two bridges. One was narrow and shabby-looking. A steady stream of cars flowed over it, very close to the edges, and I couldn't see any space for pedestrians. The new bridge was a four-lane concrete affair with a walkway on the near side. Although the traffic wasn't routed over it yet, it looked complete.

"Solid said something about this at the Gathering, remember? He said there was a new bridge under construction, and the Trail was hard to find here."

"It'll be easier to find in the morning. Look, are you sure you want to do this, jackrabbit? There's a Comfort Inn right over there . . ." Sure enough, I could see the glowing yellow and orange sign just down the road.

"Yes," I said. "After all the miles we've hiked today, what's another point-five?" And here was the heart of the matter: "And after all the effort we've put into catching up to these boys, can't we at least spend one more evening with them before they get ahead of us for good?"

She sighed. "If you want to. But all I can say is this Cliffside place better be good."

"It will be."

We chose the new bridge, with its walkway, because even at this hour the traffic was still roaring past on the other bridge. The moon flashed in and out of the clouds. Its light revealed the pale span of the new bridge stretching out

ahead of us, with shoulder-high railings on our left. Through the spaces
between railings, we could see the pearly waters swirling at the rivers' confluence, the solid black outlines of the high cliffs on either side. Over us, the
indigo sky hung with wisps of silver cloud and a few stars. The moonlight
dimmed as a cloud came over.

About halfway across the bridge, the railings ended. There was only a single cable, knotted to posts every six feet or so, between us and the dizzying
sweep of the river far below. And then the cable ended.

We made our way gingerly along the shelf of the walkway, hugging the
inside. Isis turned on her headlamp, and I hung back, trying to keep my eyes
adjusted to the darkness and feeling my way slowly along. After a few feet, Isis
came to a halt. There was a waist-high block of concrete set in the pathway,
with maybe a foot of room on the outside. I held all of our hiking sticks while
she inched around it, and then passed the bundle of wood to her. As I stepped
around the outside of the block, my hands on the bumpy concrete for balance,
something on my pack hung up and nearly threw me off balance. I lurched
back just in time, acutely aware of the river sounds behind me, the gurgle and
roar of rapids.

On the other side of the block, I paused. "This is insane! What are we
doing in a fucking construction site? That block was probably there to keep
people from doing what we just did. What if the walkway dead-ends? What if
there's a hole in the fucking thing?"

Just then the moon reemerged from the clouds, revealing the rest of
the bridge. We were getting close to the far shore. There were only three
more blocks in the pathway, and all of them seemed to be set in a way
that would give us more room. I took another deep breath and we started
walking.

The rest of the bridge wasn't as bad. There was plenty of space around the
blocks, and (though I constantly tapped with my sticks like a blind person to
be sure) the walkway was solid all the way across. On the other side, a set of
steps led down and around, under the highway.

"I wonder if this is the Trail."

"I don't see any blazes." I had a nagging feeling that something was
wrong. I didn't recall seeing anything that looked like a motel from across the
water. This didn't really look like the kind of road you would find a motel on,
anyway—a roaring four-lane highway, with hardly any shoulder. The cliffs rose
up right beside it, and on the other side it dropped off steeply to the river.
There were no signs, no buildings, just the silence of the woods and the
scream of traffic.

"Well, it's called the Cliffside, isn't it? There are definitely cliffs here. 'Cross the Shenandoah River, turn left, walk half a mile.' We should be there in ten minutes." I wished I could feel as confident as I sounded.

Ten minutes went by, fifteen. The shoulder narrowed until there were only a few feet of space between us and the cars whizzing past. Isis stopped. "This is crazy. There *is* no Cliffside Inn, and if we don't get the hell out of here we are going to be roadkill."

We turned around. I was numb with exhaustion, anger, defeat, and I let my sister's rage explode around me. "You wanted to see the boys again. *You* would risk our lives just to see a bunch of assholes who don't give a *shit* about us! They were probably laughing when they wrote those *fucking* directions." (I knew she was truly angry—I hardly ever heard her swear.) "If I *ever* let you do something like this again . . . Listen, you got us into this mess. *I'm* going to get us out. I'm not going back over that bridge."

I was too tired to argue. Isis took out the map. The sudden glare of her headlamp reflecting on the paper made the night grow blacker around us.

"The road we saw coming down the cliff back there is the Chestnut Hill Road. About a mile up, it intersects the A.T. If we follow the Trail down we'll find the safe crossing."

We came to the base of the road in a few minutes. By the light of my sister's headlamp and the passing cars, I could see the road angling steeply up the cliff. My legs felt weak and shaky, and my stomach growled. It had been almost nine hours since my last meal, I realized. The plates of brunch had certainly been substantial, but so had today's mileage. Twenty-three miles of barefoot hiking on the Trail, another mile or so on the road, and at least two more to go. "I need something to eat," I said woodenly.

Without a word, Isis reached into the top of her pack for a granola bar. She handed it to me, her eyes still flashing with anger, and we began the long uphill grade.

That night at the Comfort Inn, we discovered it was too late to order pizza. We dumped out our food bags on the carpet, wolfing down the last of our crackers, cookies, and dried fruit. It was not nearly enough to quell the rumblings in my stomach, but I was too tired to look for other food. I was too exhausted to even shower before I slept. I said a silent apology to the maids as I crawled between the clean sheets, hungry, sore, and stinking to high heaven. Behind my closed eyelids, as I fell asleep, I saw my feet following the trail down from the Chestnut Hill Road in the moonlight. Step after step, blue shadow and silver light and the sound of rapids.

Isis

The morning after our disastrous attempt to rejoin them, we found Heald, Lash, Black Forest, and Sharkbait at the outfitter's store. In the seconds before they noticed us, I considered turning around and walking out the door. The misanthropic corner of my mind, where memories from junior high ranged themselves beside history lessons like the files of a prosecutor's most incontrovertible case, had almost succeeded in convincing me that the postcard's false directions were intended as a brutal practical joke.

Lash was the first to notice us; he walked across the store, cheerfully calling out, "I was afraid I wouldn't see you ladies again! Did you just get into town?"

I looked away, pretending to examine a shelf of water filters on the wall beside me. I was afraid of what I might say if I tried to answer.

"We got in last night," said jackrabbit. "No thanks to you guys." Her voice sounded bantering, scolding, as though she knew it was all a joke, and was just waiting to hear the punchline. "Tell me, boys, what the *fuck* are these directions supposed to mean?" She held out the *Gone With the Wind* postcard.

Heald took it, and examined the directions he'd written. After a minute he glanced at jackrabbit, who stood with her hands on her hips. "Well shit. You didn't do what this says, did you? These are the directions for north-bounders, before the new bridge got built. Don't know what I was thinking."

"What happened?" Sharkbait asked. "Are you okay?" All the tough-guy swagger was gone from his voice; he sounded like a child whose playmate has just fallen off the jungle gym.

Jackrabbit recounted our journey over the half-built bridge and along the freeway's shoulder.

"Dude, I'm so sorry," murmured Lash. "I shouldn't have pressured you guys to get here last night."

"It's my fault," Heald said. "Shit. I gave you the wrong directions."

Black Forest looked away from us, shifting from one foot to the other, and said, "I did not write that card. I do not know these people who wrote it. It is not my fault." Part of me wanted to shove the card in his face and ask if he didn't recognize his own signature; part of me wanted to laugh and forget the whole quarrel.

"It's all of our faults," said Sharkbait. "Anything we can do to make up for it?"

"Sure," said jackrabbit, grinning. "You can take a zero and go out for pizza with us tonight. After all we went through to catch up with you, you had better give us a day of your company before you hike on."

I found myself agreeing. These guys were our friends, even if we hadn't known any of them for more than a week. Even though they'd written those directions. It would be good to spend a day with them before we all hiked on at our separate paces.

Late that afternoon, as the walls of mountains on either side of town blocked the sunlight from the gorge, we walked over to the headquarters of the Appalachian Trail Conference. For an organization in charge of several thousand miles of trail and all the associated lands, the ATC had a very unprepossessing national office. The white clapboard-sided building, on a side street near the center of town, housed a small gift shop selling maps and t-shirts on the ground floor.

The woman at the counter looked up as we came in. "Hikers!" she said. "Welcome to Harpers Ferry. Are you southbound?"

Heald, at the head of our group, grunted an affirmative.

"Excellent! I need to get pictures of you guys for the books," the woman said, taking out a Polaroid camera. "It's a tradition," she explained. "We take photos of all the hikers who come through here every year." She pointed out the thick stacks of leather-bound photo albums on a back table in the shop.

After our Polaroids were slipped into their plastic sleeves, we leafed through the most recent album. On the early pages came droves of northbounders and a few early southbounders whose names we recognized from their register entries. Then I spotted Solid and Playfoot standing beside their packs and Tuba Man with his tuba held aloft, grinning like a maniac. Here were the southbound friends we had hiked through the Wilderness with: Matt, freckle-faced and now skeletally thin. Blue Skies and Tenbrooks, arm in arm, laughing. Waterfall grinning at the camera, her hair in two pigtails. Then Blade with his chin up, looking severe. Pages of section hikers and strangers. The Family from the North, huddled together in their warmest clothes. All the children had the same expression: a fierce, almost defiant smile. They were almost three weeks ahead of us now. I wondered whether we would ever see them again.

I set the book down on the table, suddenly astonished at the weight of it, the multitude of stories those pages of photos contained.

After pizza that night, jackrabbit and I checked in at the Cliffside (which turned out to exist after all, albeit on the near side of the river and much more than half a mile out of town). We took our second showers in as many days— ah, luxury!—then joined the boys in their room for bourbon and ice cream. We all sat cross-legged on the two beds, holding our spoons and passing around the cartons and the bottle.

"I saw Mohawk Joe in town this afternoon," said Heald. "He asked me if there were any bars open. I told him yup, Armory Pub, right down the street. I ain't seen him since. Typical. Guy seems like he fell off a barstool and onto the Trail."

"Did I ever tell you about the first time I met Heald and Mohawk Joe?" Lash asked me. I shook my head.

"Well, it was a little ways outside of Boiling Springs. Black Forest and I had just started hiking together. Just met each other the day before. So we were night-hiking along and we came to a road, and there was this plastic garbage bag in the ditch with something big and kinda lumpy inside. The bag was ripped open in one place. I couldn't see what was inside it, but there was this blackish stuff that looked a lot like blood oozing out. I asked Black Forest if he thought it was a body in there. He poked it with his hiking pole, and he said it was only a deer. Still, I hiked out of there pretty fast. About a mile down the trail, we started having this really trippy conversation. Black Forest was like, 'What would we do if we found a dead body in the woods, and it was still warm? Would we stay together, or would we split up?' I was like, 'Dude, we'd stay together. Safety in numbers.' And Black Forest went, 'Wrong. We would split up. That way one of us would survive.'

"So I was still thinking about that conversation when we got to the shelter. The first thing I saw, in the beam of my headlamp, was this plastic shopping bag hanging from a tree branch. It looked like it was dripping blood. Then I looked around the clearing, and I saw this skinny guy with huge biceps wearing jeans, steel-toed boots, and a white t-shirt with the sleeves torn off and the front all smeared with blood. When I turned my headlamp toward him, he got this look on his face like I'd just trespassed on his private property. Right behind him in the shelter was a big bear of a guy in a bloodstained flannel shirt, giving me that same kind of look. And then *that dog*—" he pointed to Annie, who was sprawled between the beds, snoring. "That dog came around the corner of the shelter, baring her teeth and thrashing around like she was having a seizure." Lash paused and gazed at me and jackrabbit, his huge golden-brown eyes brimming with remembered suffering. "I almost *fainted*."

"Where did all the blood come from?" I asked.

"Me and Mohawk Joe found that dead deer in the bag," said Heald. "It didn't hiss much when Joe poked his knife in the stomach, so we figured the meat was okay. Most of the good cuts were gone. We took the heart and the liver. Grilled 'em up that night. You shoulda had some, Lash. It was real good."

"Dude, I'm a vegetarian."

"Huh. You never tried fresh deer liver?"

Lash looked as though any prolonged description of deer organs might put him in danger of fainting again, so I decided to change the subject.

"Anyone want a back rub?"

Black Forest jumped off the other bed, gleefully exclaiming, "Do I have an ass?!"

"Black Forest! That's *not* what I was talking about!" I scolded.

"It is an expression. You do not know this expression? It is a way to say 'yes, certainly.'"

"Kind of like 'does a bear shit in the woods?'" asked jackrabbit.

"Does a bear sheet . . . you Americans, you have some good expressions. Also you have some beautiful women, even in the woods. I would stay in your country, if you would put less water in your beer."

"Have a swig of this," said Sharkbait, passing him the bourbon bottle. "Not much water in this baby."

Black Forest took the bottle, sniffed at it, and wrinkled his nose. "This is not beer. I will have a back rub instead." He threw himself down on the bed beside me.

I gave Black Forest his back rub, then Lash, then Sharkbait. As I lifted my hands from Sharkbait's shoulders, he asked, "Isis? Would you do me a big favor?" He didn't meet my eyes as he spoke, and his voice had a hesitancy to it, as if he feared that he was asking something shameful, something too personal for our brief acquaintance. My mind skipped through the frightening possibilities. And then I remembered his voice that morning, when he'd asked if we were okay. Sharkbait was a person I could trust.

"Yes," I said.

"Stand up."

I stood at the foot of the bed, facing him.

"Back away two steps. Okay. Turn around."

I turned.

"Stand on your tippy-toes."

I lifted my heels from the floor, feeling the muscles of my calves tighten. I held the pose for about thirty seconds, before he spoke again.

"That's all. Thank you." He sighed, then said very softly, as if to himself, "I always had a bit of a calf fetish, even before the accident."

jackrabbit

The first night out of Harpers Ferry, we stayed at the David Lesser Memorial Shelter, a tall, spacious open-fronted building, newly constructed and still smelling of fresh wood. Frost hung around in the shadows; the temperature hadn't climbed much above freezing all day. Lash and Sharkbait huddled in the back of the shelter cooking dinner when we arrived.

Sharkbait was moaning about the cold. He was bundled inside his sleeping bag, a wool hat pulled down low over his ears, and his voice was muffled by a scarf that covered most of his face. "Two hundred fuckin' miles. Two-oh-one point six, that is. That's all I got left of this fuckin' trail. Weather keeps up like this, I might just say fuck it and hitch out at the next road."

"Come on, dude," Lash said. He was wrapped in his sleeping bag, too, and his fluorescent orange fleece hat came down to his eyebrows. "You can't quit, just like that. Think about all the miles you've put behind you already. You can't throw that away."

Sharkbait lit a cigarette and stared at the floorboards, brooding.

Black Forest came up the hill behind the shelter, carrying a few full water bottles. "Cold does not scare me. I am a German badass. Sharkbait, you are a badass, too." He noticed us. "The Barefoot Sisters." A small smile glimmered in his eyes. "They are the most badass of all."

"Thanks, Black Forest," I said with a grin.

Sharkbait peered out at us from the slit between his scarf and his hat. He shuddered. "Holy shit. You're standing in a patch of fuckin' frost." I looked down—it was true. Ice sparkled on the ground around my bare feet. The calluses on my soles were not as substantial as my sister's, but they were still thick enough to withstand the cold of the ground. "How in hell do you *do* that?"

Isis shrugged. "Practice, I guess. You get used to it."

Sharkbait fell silent. We didn't hear another word of complaint from him that night.

I made the long trek down to the spring, three tenths of a mile off the ridgeline. A leaf-filled pool of water, rimmed with fingers of ice, stood at the base of a jumbled rockslide. The filter was slow and cranky in the cold; I wondered how much longer we would be able to use it. I brought back four liters of clean water for the next day's hike and two unfiltered liters for cooking and tea. My hands were numb where the water had splashed them; I rubbed them together inside their gloves as I jogged back up the trail to the shelter.

Isis made extra tea that night so we could share with the men. "Wild cherry-blackberry," she said. The aroma of summer fruit filled the shelter, incongruous but sweetly welcome against the backdrop of odors: new wood, sweat, a lingering whiff of Lipton dinners, dry leaves, rock, the nose-tingling scent of frost.

Sharkbait smiled, slightly bemused, as Isis filled his cup. "This smells really good. It smells kind of . . . purple. Everything else around us smells brown, and this is purple. Thanks, Isis."

We watched the stars come out through the trees, glittering like gemstones in the evening sky. When I saw the first one, as usual, I thought of Tuba Man: *I wonder where you are. I hope you're okay, hope you're warm enough on a night like this. I wonder if you ever think about me. And I hope that someday, somehow, I'll see you again.* Even as these thoughts crossed my mind, I was aware how ridiculous they were. *Wishing on a star. That's so seventh-grade.*

Winter clamped down that night. I was glad we had picked up our cold-weather sleeping bags—our mother had sent them to us in Boiling Springs—and bought warmer liners. Early in the morning, I awoke with a strange sensation on my face. Tiny prickles of cold touched my skin momentarily and disappeared. It was still dark. I found my Photon light and switched it on, shielding the beam with my hands so it wouldn't disturb the sleepers on either side. Snowflakes danced in the faint blue light.

In the morning, a few thin strands of wind-blown snow wove themselves wraith-like across the floor of the shelter, but the sky was clear. Dawn came up golden and pink between the bare branches. Lash, sleeping on my left in his yellow bivy sack, groaned and turned over. In a few minutes he sat up and emerged from the top of his mummy bag, pushing the folds of his bright orange hat up out of his eyes.

"Dude, I had the craziest dream last night . . ." he blinked and stared at the snow that had collected in the corner of the shelter, surprise and wonder in his eyes. "Oh, man. Maybe I wasn't dreaming."

Black Forest sat up too. His rumpled blond curls stuck out in all directions from under his red hat. His blue eyes were red-rimmed, and he looked grumpy. "Isis, why did you give us tea last night? Three times I got up to piss!"

"Hey, it was only a cup of water!" she protested.

"Learn some bladder control, man," I said.

Lash had a rather smug grin on his face. He took a bottle of something out of his sleeping bag and oonched forward to dump it over the edge of the sleeping platform. "Oh, I was dehydrated!" he murmured to himself.

"Lash, was that what I think it was?" I asked him, preparing to be scandalized.

He shrugged, and his sleeping bag amplified the gesture. "Hey, it beats getting up in the middle of the night."

"That's gross! You sleep with a bottle of . . ."

"Your urine is sterile to you," he said, sounding hurt, but with a glint of amusement in his eyes.

All day, little wisps of snow flickered across the trail, moving before the wind. Winter had arrived, and we were still barefoot. The woods looked dead all around, empty skeleton limbs above us and brown crackling leaves underfoot. The trail had frozen into uneven ridges of soil, and ice patches remained in the shadows of rocks and trees. As long as I kept moving, though, the cold didn't really bother me.

Toward evening, Isis and I came to Bear's Den Rocks. It was a jumble of boulders, set among jack pines. On one side the ridge fell away sharply, leaving a view of the valley floor below. Winter had reached the low elevations, too. In Pennsylvania we had seen green fields and the occasional leafy tree in the lowlands, but here the fields in the valleys were dry and yellow, and the forests wore the same uniform grayish brown all the way down to the lowest elevations. In a short time, I knew, it would all be pale with snow. We stood at the overlook and watched the sun sink lower over the far ridge.

"The side trail to Bear's Den Hostel should be around here somewhere," Isis said. I remembered Anonymous Badger's descriptions of the place: an old stone mansion that had been converted to a youth hostel. He said it was one of the most beautiful buildings along the trail. "Oh, here we go." The side trail was marked with blue blazes, as usual, but instead of the customary rectangle, they were shaped like bear tracks. The hostel was an immense building of dark stone, set in a wide lawn that still held improbable vestiges of green. The light of sunset caught in the tall windows and the tops of the trees. We hurried for the door, amid the gathering chill of the shadows.

Sharkbait sat on the porch smoking a cigarette. Bundled in all of his spare clothing, he looked a little like a scarecrow. "Hey, ladies. Where did Lash and Black Forest go?"

"Hey, Sharky. The others decided to go on," I said.

Sharkbait grinned. "Their loss. I met a trail angel here, guy named Fanny Pack. He's gonna slack me a twenty-three tomorrow. You in?"

The prospect of slacking and returning to the hostel for another warm night sounded wonderful. I knew we could slack a twenty-three—we had hiked that distance and more into Harpers Ferry, with our full packs. "Definitely!" I said.

Sharkbait ground out the last of his cigarette and dropped it in the ashtray, and we headed inside.

"Welcome to Bear's Den." This was a compact, vivacious woman with sparkling blue eyes and short gray hair. "I'm Melody. Patti and I are the caretakers here. Let me show you around. You can leave your packs here for now." She gave us a quick tour, pointing out the kitchen, the dining room, the bunkrooms, laundry machines, and a freezer full of Ben and Jerry's. The common room caught my interest above anything else, even the ice cream; in one corner of the burnished wood floor, behind a row of comfortable couches, stood a piano.

"May I play it?" I asked breathlessly.

"Of course," Melody said with a smile. "The only rule is no 'Chopsticks' and no 'Heart and Soul.'"

"Got it. Thanks." For the next few hours, there was nothing but the black and white keys, and the sound, and I was happy.

Isis cooked dinner from the hiker box: rice and beans with fresh onion and slightly stale bread toasted with butter. Afterward, we each bought a pint of ice cream and moved into the common room with Sharkbait.

"Apple Crumble," I said. "Hmmm. I think I'll go back to Cherry Garcia in the next town."

Melody joined us on the couches and introduced her partner Patti. She was a tall, slender woman with long dark hair and deep brown eyes. We shared stories from our hike, and Melody reminisced about her own hiking days—she had finished the A.T. in 1999. Patti, who had hiked only a few sections of the Trail, was quiet at first, but as the evening went on she spoke more often. Her words revealed a sharp sense of humor.

As the moon rose outside the windows, Sharkbait told the story of his trail name—the real story.

"Tough break," Patti said, her forehead wrinkling with sympathy.

"Yeah, well, you play the cards you're dealt." He dug into his ice cream. "I don't get it. This is my second pint tonight. I eat like this in every town, and I still can't keep the weight on."

Patti's eyes sparkled with amusement. "That's because men are expendable."

"What?" Sharkbait looked up at the four women around him, slightly alarmed.

"Oh, it's true," Patti said. "Biologically speaking, men are a dime a dozen. It doesn't take much sperm to keep the population going. Women, on the other hand, are built to last. Childbearing is pretty important. That's why men lose so much weight on the Trail, and women just keep plugging along." She gave a beatific smile. "It's just biology. Don't take it personally."

Melody shook her head. "There you go again." She turned to Sharkbait. "That's how *she* got her trail name."

"Which is . . ."

"Fembah." Patti smiled again, looking sweet and saintly. "It's short for Feminist Bitch from Hell."

In the morning, we woke before dawn and ate our usual quick breakfast, instant oatmeal mixed up cold with a little dry milk. Sharkbait gnawed on a hunk of bread from the hiker box, bleary-eyed, saying little; he was not a morning person. We heard wheels crunch on the gravel outside, and we bolted the last few bites.

The sky in the east was crimson, a bright bloodstain between the bare trees. To the west, stars still hung behind the branches on a curtain of indigo. A little wind sent the dry leaves scuttering across the ground. We shivered in our fleeces and Gore-Tex pants.

"Hi there! You must be the Barefoot Sisters. I've been wanting to meet you!" Fanny Pack shook our hands enthusiastically. He was a heavyset man in his fifties, with sparse gray hair and a wide, animated face. His silver minivan was emblazoned with A.T. stickers. A banner taped to the rear window read, "not all those who wander are lost."

As we drove out to the trailhead, Fanny Pack regaled us with stories from his '99 hike. "Best six months of my life. I'm saving up right now to do the PCT." At the Gathering, I had seen slideshows of the Pacific Crest Trail traversing sharp-crested western mountains. I knew many A.T. hikers who'd gone on to hike the PCT, and I could imagine why.

"I've got to get back in shape first, though," Fanny Pack continued. "Working with computers, I don't get out as much as I'd like to."

As we drove, the light in the sky changed from red to orange to gold. The sun's blinding rays came through the trees on the ridge at last. "Tell you what," Fanny Pack said. "I could slack you guys all the way through Shenandoah. I'm due for a few vacation days anyway."

"Are you sure?" Isis asked him. "I mean, it would be awesome for us . . ." We had been wondering how we would carry enough food for the national park. In summer, we knew, concession stands and convenience stores kept hikers well-fed. In this season, it would be 107 miles of trail with no amenities but the shelters and a few pay campsites, and without easy access to towns—hitching was forbidden on the parkway.

"Oh, for sure," Fanny Pack said. "That way, I could come and park at road crossings and hike in to meet you guys, and then hike back out . . . I'd get some exercise, that'd be good. Then I could take you guys down to a hotel in town at night. You wouldn't have to sleep out in this cold."

As he spoke, he became more and more excited. I did, too. I had been a little worried about Shenandoah; even though I knew the trail in the park was supposed to be well-graded and smooth, and even though we were in much better shape than we had been at the start of the Trail, I didn't relish the thought of another Hundred Mile Wilderness. Especially not in this season. Fanny Pack was offering us an easy way out, and we jumped at the chance.

"I have to work tomorrow," he said, "but I can drop you guys off at the trailhead in the early morning, like today, and then I'll meet you the day after, in the park. How's that sound?"

"Sounds perfect. You're an angel."

"Great. Oh, here's the trailhead." He pulled into a gravel parking lot by the side of the road. We jumped out of the vehicle with our hiking sticks and the daypacks that Melody had lent us the night before. "You guys take care. I'll see you tomorrow!" Fanny Pack sped off with a cheery wave.

Sharkbait zoomed down the trail. Even with his flat-footed stride, he was one of the fastest hikers I had ever seen. In no time, he rounded a bend and disappeared. Isis and I moved faster than we had with our packs, but still not exactly fast. The chill of morning made my feet sensitive, and half the trail here was gravel. I leaned heavily on my sticks.

The trail started out flat, but toward afternoon we hit the Roller Coaster. It was maddening; the trail went up and down over steep-edged spurs that extended down from a ridge. We struggled upwards maybe 500 feet, then dropped down in a knee-jarring descent, over and over. I lost track after ten of these mindless hills. The most exasperating thing was that we could see easier potential trail routes all around us. At every vista, we saw the long, flat-topped ridge extending above us on the right side. Below, the valley floor was smooth and level. The trail seemed to be routed in the hardest possible place.

The slack took us all day and into the night. The wind picked up, chilly and fierce, as darkness cloaked the ridges. Luckily I had a headlamp now; I had decided to buy one in Harpers Ferry after our epic night-hike. The days were only getting shorter. It was the lightest headlamp I could find, made from the same LED technology as our Photons. It would run for nearly a hundred hours on two double-A batteries. The glow it cast was cool, though, bluish-tinted and faint. When I glanced down, my feet looked pale and corpselike. For once, I longed for an old-fashioned flashlight, with its comforting yellow glow.

My left knee began to hurt on the downhills. It was an old injury; I had torn my ACL in high school track. Usually it would begin to ache when a storm was coming, and given the red sky that morning, I tried to dismiss the pain as the usual weather warning. But this time it was more insistent, and it began to slow me down as the dark miles went by.

At last we came back to the hostel, tumbling into the common room and shutting the door quickly behind us to keep the cold wind out.

Sharkbait wore a look of concern. "I was about ready to come lookin' for you two."

"What time is it?"

"Six thirty."

"That's not so late. What time did you get in?"

He looked a little sheepish. "Four."

Fanny Pack picked us up before the crack of dawn again. The sky was overcast; instead of the brilliant colors of yesterday morning, we saw a blanket of oppressive gray. Fanny Pack was as cheerful as ever. "Ran into some friends of yours yesterday!"

"Who? Where?" Isis asked.

"Oh, a couple of young guys, hiking fast. One of them had a bright orange hat—"

"Lash and Black Forest!" I cried, delighted.

"Right. Those were their names. And a girl, too. Curly hair. Name started with N . . ."

"Netta!" I was glad to hear she was still on the Trail and so close ahead. She hiked fast and hardly ever signed in registers.

"Yeah, that was it. And a guy with a dog. Heald. Well, I saw them at a road crossing yesterday. I told them about slacking you guys through the park, and they wanted in on it too. So here's the new plan: I'm going to meet you guys tomorrow morning in Front Royal. Place called the Pilgrim's Court Motel. We can all slack from there."

"Sounds great," Isis said. "Thanks so much, Fanny Pack."

"Hey, it's no problem. I got my trail name 'cause I slacked so much on my hike. I like to pass on the favor. What goes around comes around, you know . . . well, here we are again." He pulled into the parking lot. The sky was lightening gradually, almost imperceptibly. "See you tomorrow!"

It was a short hike, slightly more than half yesterday's mileage, but by the end of it I was exhausted. My knee felt a little swollen and hot to the touch, and it ached on long downhills. I was ready for a night in a motel and a few more days of slacking.

The sun was just above the ridgeline when we reached the highway into Front Royal. Traffic sped past us without slowing down. We waited, and the sun sank under the rim of trees. Shadows thickened along the spines of the ridges. I was cold, tired, hungry. Still the cars raced past on the highway, a ceaseless stream.

"I'm going to try something," I said, taking my hat off.

"What, let your hair down?"

"Yup." I started loosening my braid.

"Jackrabbit, I don't know if that's such a good idea. I mean, I know it worked for Waterfall a couple times, but we might just get a ride we don't really want . . ." The last word trailed off as an oversized pickup that had just flashed past us hit the brakes, swerved into the breakdown lane, and began backing up. We glanced at each other, then at the driver. I saw a cowboy hat, a puff of blond hair, a kind face decorated with an abundance of blue eye shadow and shocking pink lipstick.

"Y'all hop in," she called through the open window. "Go on and toss your bags in the back there. At first I wasn't gonna stop, but then I saw y'all was ladies."

She dropped us off at the Pilgrim's Court motel as dusk thickened. We checked in at the office, with the mouthwatering aroma of a Pakistani dinner wafting in from the room next door. The owner, a tiny wizened woman with dark eyes, told us that our friends were expecting us in room twelve. She indicated the one-story complex across the parking lot. When I asked about ice for my knee, she ducked into the room next door and brought out a bag of ice cubes from her own freezer. Isis asked about restaurants in Front Royal.

The woman wrinkled her nose. "Not any good restaurants in this town. McDonald's, Burger King, steakhouse, pizza, Mexican, Chinese food. Have nothing good."

Isis thanked her. We took our stinking packs over to the room, where Netta met us at the door. We tossed our packs down and hugged her.

"It is very good to see you," she said. "I miss talking to women. The boys are in room sixteen. They watch television." She made a face. "They ask me to watch with them, but I am tired of men. You know what I mean."

While Netta was in the shower, Isis and I did pay a visit to the boys' room. We had been hiking by ourselves for so long that we weren't tired of their company yet. The guys were watching "The 100 Greatest Artists of Hard Rock" on VH1. Black Forest bounced on the bed in time to an Iron Maiden tune.

"Any thoughts on dinner?" I asked him over the electric scream of guitars.

"We are going to the steakhouse. We are men. We are meat-eaters." A gleeful smile lit up his round face.

"Lash, I thought you were a vegetarian," I said.

Lash was lying on the bed, braiding Isis's waist-length hair. He looked up with a slightly dreamy smile. "Whatever, dude."

Heald and Annie curled in a corner of the floor, exuding a stench of wet dog and unwashed human. "I want steak," Heald said simply and went back to waxing his boots. Sharkbait said nothing. He was busy addressing his first six-pack of the night.

I made an argument for Chinese food, but there were no takers. The odor of humanity in the close-packed room and the noise of the television were beginning to grate on my nerves. "I'm going back to the girls' room," I said. "I've gotta ice my knee. Maybe Netta will have some better ideas about dinner."

Isis and I left for the sanctuary of our room, with its plaid curtains and paisley bedspreads in shades left over from the 1970s. Netta sat on the bed, combing out her wet hair and softly singing a Hebrew song. After icing my knee, I began the town chores, which were now so automatic I barely thought about them: washing and filling water bottles, sorting through my food bag to separate trash from reusable Ziplocs, hanging the tent and the ground cloth over the bathroom door to dry out. Isis stepped into the shower. In a few minutes the phone rang. I picked it up.

"Black Forest says he has a compromise," came the dry voice of Sharkbait. "He says we can go to Burger King, and he'll give you his tomato." There was a pause and then a burst of laughter in the background. "He says he'd like to give you his pickle, too!"

Over the next few days, we slacked the smooth trails of Shenandoah National Park and stayed in cheap motels in town. The cold of winter deepened; once an inch of water left in one of my bottles froze solid. The trail was rough gravel underfoot. But we always had enough to eat now, and we slept in a warm place each night in the company of friends. Compared to the preceding month on the Trail, when we had suffered from loneliness, hunger, dehydration, and cold, this was a life of total luxury.

One night, we went to the Mexican restaurant. The place was packed. The waitress found a few extra chairs, and we just barely managed to cram all seven of us into a booth made for four. When all our food arrived, the little table creaked ominously. There was no conversation for a while, as we addressed the quesadillas, enchiladas, and heaping plates of nachos.

"This has been the best year of my life," Lash said, wiping the salsa from his beard and sitting back from the table with a satisfied smile.

I agreed. "Yeah. Finishing college, and now hiking the Trail. It's been pretty sweet."

Black Forest made a face. "I do not think so."

"What was the best year of your life, then?" I asked.

"The year I was fourteen." We all laughed, but he protested. "No, this is true. I had no worries. I would like to be fourteen for the rest of my life."

"I don't know," Isis said. "I'm a lot happier at twenty-five than I was at fourteen. Trail life is pretty worry-free, too. The biggest concern I've had in the last couple days is trying to find gloves that fit—my hands are so big . . ."

Lash held his up for comparison. Her hands were almost the same size as his. "Wow. They are pretty big, for a woman's."

Black Forest, crammed in next to Lash, immediately put his hand up against my sister's. His fine-boned, almost delicate fingers were easily half an inch below the tips of hers. He looked incensed. Just as the crowd around us reached a lull in conversation, he shouted out loudly, "you should not judge my manliness by the size of my—" He stopped, noticing the silence around him and the looks of shock on the restaurant patrons' faces. "—hands," he finished in a tiny voice.

That night, while Isis was in the shower, I sat next to Black Forest on the bed in the girls' room, watching the Simpsons. His hand gravitated toward mine, and eventually our bodies leaned together as well. We ended up lying there, side by side. He put his arm around me, and I reached out to embrace his shoulders. It felt strangely innocent and necessary, as though holding him could somehow make up for the pain, the cold, the loneliness of the last few months. Netta watched with a sad and knowing smile.

Black Forest kissed my forehead. "You are a beautiful woman."

"Don't flatter me. I won't fall for it."

A sly, calculating look came into his eyes. "Everybody has a price. What's yours?"

Coming from anybody else, that remark would have elicited a swift slap in the face. I couldn't hit Black Forest, though. I thought about what he had said in the restaurant: *fourteen was the best year of my life*. I knew he was twenty-three, a year older than I was, but he looked about fourteen then, with his wide blue eyes and eager face. The thought of sleeping with him was laughable. "What's my price? Well, more Snickers bars than *you* could carry!"

He sighed. "Jackrabbit, you are killing me."

I glanced at my watch. It was ten already. On the Trail we usually went to bed soon after sunset, 8:30 at the latest. "Time for bed," I said, yawning.

Black Forest looked hopeful.

"Your *own* bed," I said firmly and rolled away from him. He slouched off the bed with a sigh and went out the door, moping.

A few minutes later the phone rang. It was Lash. "*What* did you do to the German?" He sounded outraged.

"Nothing. Why?"

He gave an exaggerated sigh. "Black Forest is bouncing up and down on the bed, singing 'Sex Machine.'"

"Oh." I thought fast. The A.T. slogan, which we had heard at the Gathering and seen on Trail signs all along the way, popped into my head. "We weren't doing anything," I said with all the innocence I could muster. "We were just 'seeking fellowship in the wilderness.'"

Over the next few days, Lash and Black Forest took every opportunity to present us with Snickers bars. They would hike fast to get ahead and ambush us at a bend in the trail, candy bars in hand. The exchange rate was pretty poor—after perhaps ten Snickers, I gave each of them a peck on the cheek.

Isis

Around Thanksgiving, jackrabbit and I got off the Trail to visit our father's relatives in central Virginia. We both knew that, without Fanny Pack's help slacking, we stood no chance of keeping up with our companions. It seemed fairer to all of us to leave the Trail for a celebration, knowing that they would be far ahead when we returned, than to tag along behind them indefinitely trying to keep up. Netta joined us for Thanksgiving, on the clear understanding that she would be hiking twenty-fives to catch the guys as soon as we got back to the Trail.

Our Aunt Nancy picked us up at Thornton Gap and took us to her farm high on the Blue Ridge, where we spent a few days reading, writing letters, eating delicious homegrown food, and helping to store food from the garden. It felt good to exercise the muscles that I didn't use for walking; even shelling dry beans, usually one of my least favorite harvest chores, seemed to loosen the cramps my fingers got from grasping hiking sticks all day.

The day before Thanksgiving, jackrabbit, Netta, and I went down to our Aunt Katie's house in Lexington. When she found out that we were planning to spend Christmas on the Trail, she made our visit into a double holiday, stacking foil-wrapped boxes of cookies and chocolates at our places at the table. To Netta, both Christmas and Thanksgiving were foreign holidays; watching her unwrap her presents and taste the unfamiliar dishes of the feast brought back some of my earliest memories, from years when each celebration came as a surprise.

The warm welcome we received from relatives we hadn't seen in years made it even harder to leave their bright, cozy homes for the winter trail. Jackrabbit and I knew that we would be alone for weeks at a time, quite possibly for the rest of our hike. Before we left town, we stocked up on bread from a local bakery and cheese from a gourmet food store to supplement the cookies Aunt Katie had given us, hoping that a luxurious resupply would help to keep our spirits up.

On a cold, windy afternoon, with patches of sun and shadow racing over the mountainsides, our Uncle Pete dropped us off at the trailhead. Netta walked with us the first three miles, up to an outcropping of boulders called Mary's Rock. A recent forest fire had burned through the undergrowth on this side of the gap; great swaths of blackened ground looked like scabs on the forest floor, and the scorched leaves of mountain laurel rattled in the wind. At the junction of a side trail, a charred concrete signpost, standing in a pile of ashes, proclaimed "No Fires" in blocky white letters. I felt as though I had wandered into a Magritte painting; the sign's confident proclamation seemed to countermand the desolate and neatly sketched reality.

On steep northern slopes, where the trail lay in day-long shadow, an inch or so of snow covered the ground. My toes tingled as I walked through it, but it felt wonderful, like cool feathers, to my soles. As we traversed a small patch of snow near the top of the ridge, we met a family of dayhikers on their way down. By this time, jackrabbit and I had perfected the trick of greeting day-hikers as soon as we saw them and making eye contact to keep them from noticing our feet. On the smooth, broad trails of Shenandoah, it had worked like a charm.

"Lovely day for a hike," I called to the mom, who was first in line.

"It certainly is," she answered.

"Great views up top. Enjoy!" said the dad, stepping past us.

Their son, a child of perhaps eight, paused as he came abreast of us and looked straight down at our feet. Children's reactions to our lack of footwear tended to be more original than those of adults, so we stood still, waiting to see if he had any questions.

After a few seconds, he looked up and asked, "How do you *do* that?"

Jackrabbit winked at him. "By magic."

His eyes lit up and he grinned from ear to ear.

At Mary's Rock, we shared a final meal with Netta: open-faced sandwiches of rye bread and chèvre, sprinkled with salt and caraway seeds.

"This is delicious," Netta sighed. "If only we had sliced tomatoes, it would be just like a luncheon in Israel." She looked down at the foothills and valleys, where the bare branches of deciduous forests interlocked in a gray mesh, tinged bluish purple in the distance. "I have to go on," she said suddenly. "I have to hike fast, to stop myself from thinking about the trees. At home, trees never lose their leaves. I cannot stop thinking that the forest here is dead."

She packed up her food bag, gave each of us a hug, and strode away at a pace I would have been hard-put to match even if I'd been wearing shoes.

Jackrabbit and I packed slowly, then followed Netta's tracks southward through the patchy snow. We waited until we had gotten out of the burned forest to look for a stealth site; a few stars glimmered between blowing clouds by the time we set up our tent.

In the morning, low, dark clouds filled the sky and a raw wind chased crumpled oak leaves over the forest floor. We huddled in a small hollow in the ground, trying to keep out of the wind while we ate breakfast. We'd slept with our water bottles inside the tent to keep them from freezing; still, the milk I mixed up for my granola was so cold it made the backs of my teeth ache. As we often did on chilly mornings, we left camp still bundled in our wool shirts, sweaters, and rain gear, but this time, neither of us stopped to take off any layers once we got going. The clouds descended lower and lower, until an icy mist beaded our sleeves and hair. At the same time, the sharp gravel under our feet turned slippery, as if we were trying to walk over marbles coated with oil.

"Ice storm," said jackrabbit.

"Are you sure?" I asked. The pebbles in the trail looked dark with rain, but I couldn't see any ice on them. I reached down and picked one up; it burned in my palm. I brushed the thumb of my other hand over it. Slippery, painfully cold. The third time I touched it, a thin sheath of ice cracked and slid into my palm.

"I read an article in the newspaper about a couple of ice storms in the peach orchards in Georgia last March," I said. "The story made it sound like ice storms were unusual that far south."

"We're not in Georgia yet, sister."

"I know, but it's only November. Even at home, we don't really get snow and ice till mid-December. I'm worried about how much winter we're going to see before we're through."

"I'm worried about how we're going to hike more than four or five miles *today*," jackrabbit responded. "I think the body heat in our soles is melting the top layer of ice and making the layer beneath it even more slippery. Kind of like ice skating, only heat instead of pressure. I think we could walk faster if we . . ."

"Let's try to make it to the shelter, before we decide," I said quickly.

"Good idea," said jackrabbit. "That way we'll know exactly where we stopped, in case we want to calculate the miles."

Maybe the sun will come out before we get there, I thought, *and all the ice will melt*. Instead, the mist thickened until small branches beside the trail were encased in thick translucent rinds, and the beads on our sleeves grew into a heavy, brittle armor that crackled as we moved. After four miles and nearly as many hours, we staggered up to the shelter. Five college guys on a weekend trip had holed up there to wait out the storm.

"Look at that, they're barefoot!" one of them exclaimed. "Are you crazy?"

"Yeah, I guess we are," sighed jackrabbit, unbuckling her pack.

"How far have you hiked that way?" asked another guy.

"Thirteen hundred miles, if you want to believe it," I told him. "But it's over. If we're going to walk any farther in this ice storm, we'll to have to put on shoes."

"Well, that's the only intelligent thing I've heard you say yet," said the first guy.

Jackrabbit and I sat down on the edge of the sleeping platform, clasped hands, and looked each other in the eye. "As long as it's comfortable," I said.

"As long as it's fun," jackrabbit answered.

We untied our camp sneakers from our packs, slipped them on, and walked back into the storm.

CHAPTER 8

Boots and Snowshoes

jackrabbit

The coating of ice thickened all afternoon. It was almost impossible to make progress, even in shoes. My knee felt better after the Thanksgiving break, but I was acutely aware that one misstep could damage it again. Rocks, trees, fallen leaves, all glittered with a quarter-inch glaze. As dusk fell, we came to the Big Meadows campground. The buildings looked abandoned and dark. On the open ground of the tent sites, blades of grass had a spun-sugar coating of ice. We followed the curving asphalt drive, shuffling along on the slick surface. My canvas sneakers had soaked through long ago, and I tried to ignore the protests of my cold, wet feet.

"I think this is the ranger station," Isis said. The building was locked up tight and deserted. We stood under the small overhang of the roof and discussed our options.

"Aren't the campsites supposed to be open?" I asked.

"Yeah. Tomorrow's supposed to be the last day. I imagine the parkway's closed in this weather, though."

"What should we do? I mean, we could tent, but with the ice . . ."

"No," Isis said. "I don't know if the tent would even stay up with a load of ice on it." This was true, I reflected—our tent was lightweight and good for summer camping, but it wasn't designed for conditions like this. "It's too risky. We've got to find a building somewhere, or a bigger overhang, at least . . ."

Inspiration struck. "Isis, back in H.F., Heald told me a story about an obnoxious nobo . . . no, this is good, trust me. When Heald hiked in '96, there was a guy who everyone detested. One of those ones, you know, who would race to town and sit there drinking beer as everybody came in, and then tell them how slow they were. So one night, up in Maine, he came to a packed shelter after dark. It was raining and cold. This guy said, 'You have to make room for me! I don't have a tent!' but nobody would move. So guess what he did?" Isis shook her head, and I grinned. "He slept in the privy!"

"You mean we should sleep in the *bathrooms* here?"

"You got a better idea?"

"Well, I guess it's better than tenting in this stuff." She gestured toward the line of semisolid drips falling from the eaves, inches away.

We skated across the slick surface of the parking lot and found the bathrooms and laundry room miraculously unlocked. Even better, the lights and heat were still on. From the sloppy, frozen, windy twilight, we stepped into warm, bright, calm air with the faint hum of electricity. The frenetic tapping sound against the roof was the only reminder of the maelstrom we had left. We cracked the ice off our pack covers and sodden rain gear and hung them up over the doors of the dryers. I put the ground cloth down on the slightly grimy red tile floor in front of the washing machines, and we set up our sleeping bags there.

"What'll we do for dinner?" I said. We were already presuming enough on the Park's hospitality, and I didn't think it would be exactly appropriate to light a fire inside the building. Besides, neither of us wanted to venture back out to gather Zip stove wood.

Isis grinned. "I have a plan." She went into the bathroom side of the building next door, and I heard the shower running. She returned in a moment with a pot of steaming water. "It's not exactly boiling, but it'll do . . ." She mixed in the instant potato flakes, half a packet of dry milk and a few tablespoons of olive oil. "Voila."

The whole situation seemed surreal to me. "When we started the Trail, I never thought I'd end up stealth camping in a laundry room," I said, shaking my head. "Or cooking dinner with water from a freakin' shower. You know, I used to be respectable . . ."

Isis grinned. "The Trail has changed us, no doubt about it. I imagine we'll do a lot more things we never thought we would before this hike is over."

As evening wore on, the ominous tapping on the roof outside continued and intensified. Isis rinsed out the pot in the sink and mixed up hot chocolate.

"I wish there was a register here," I said. I missed reading about the adventures of our friends, far ahead. I wondered where Netta had gotten to, and where Lash and Heald and Black Forest were hunkering down in the storm. At the thought of Black Forest, I felt a touch of—what? Regret? Amusement?

"What we need now is a trashy novel," I said. "It would be perfect on a night like this."

"We could write one! The A.T.'s a great setting, don't you think?"

"Excellent! What should we call it?"

"It has to be something Trail-related . . . like *Lust in the Lean-tos* or *Peaks of Desire* . . ."

"I've got it!" I said. "*Passion's Stealth-fire!*"

"Perfect! Our main characters are a sobo and a nobo who meet and fall madly in love."

"MEGA Maid," I said, using the abbreviation for Maine to Georgia that southbounders often appended to their names in registers.

"And the nobo can be GAME Boy!"—the northbounders' acronym.

We entertained ourselves for a few hours with the adventures of our protagonists, writing in a miniscule hand on the few sheets of stationery that I carried. We wrote a new verse for "Dig a Hole," too.

"It ought to be something about the bears," Isis said. "Aren't there supposed to be more bears in this park than anywhere else on the Trail?"

"I think so. Good thing they're all hibernating right now."

"Yeah," she said. "It wouldn't be such a bad life, being a bear here . . ." Then her eyes gleamed. "I've got it!"

"Let's sing the other verses, and then you can do the new one. Don't forget to change the chorus for Pennsylvania . . ."

We sang through our verses for New England and New York, and then the most recent states on our journey:

> And I love to hike New Jersey, it's the Garden State
> poison ivy forms the understory;
> like the bear and the deer, my understanding is clear:
> all of nature is my lavatory!
>
> Dig a hole . . .
>
> And I love to hike the ridges of P.A.'s A.T.,
> where the famous rocks are always rollin'
> well, despite some folks' predictions, they caused us no
>   afflictions,
> but it's hard to find some dirt to dig your hole in!

Move a rock, dump your load . . .

And I loved the state of Maryland, it's short but sweet,
never even had to change my skivvies.
I went through in two days—I'm a wimp, but, well, hey!
I never dumped my load inside a privy!

Dig a hole . . .

And I hiked through West Virginia in an hour or two,
one look at the state and then you're gone,
but it's really rather paining, in those few miles of maintaining,
they never even built us a john!

Dig a hole . . .

I stopped and Isis sang her new verse:

Oh, I wish I was a bear in Shenandoah Park
I'd sneak right up behind you and I'd scare ya
then I'd open your pack, and I'd have me a snack,
and the whole A.T. would be my privy area!

When 8:30 rolled around, we fell asleep in the back of the room by the washing machines.

I slept uneasily, plagued by strange dreams. In one, Lash had become an evil renegade ninja whom I was trying to defeat. We had our showdown in an abandoned movie theater. His bronze-colored eyes flashed a challenge from his dark mask as he leapt over the rows of musty folding seats. He attacked relentlessly, and I dodged, blocked, waited for my moment to counterattack. I woke up before the end of the fight. The sleet had changed to rain outside, a calmer sound on the roof.

I sank back into another dream; a tour bus pulled up outside the laundry room where we lay, and a group of blue-haired old ladies got off, carrying bags of dirty clothes. Seeing us through the windows, they dropped their laundry and waved their arms in consternation. I distinctly heard one of them, a matronly woman in a green dress, yelling, "Call the authorities!" I woke up again. The window was empty—no old ladies after all—but a thin washed-out light was leaching into the sky. Isis stirred beside me.

We ate our granola and packed up quickly, not wanting to risk discovery if the parkway had reopened. Outside, the temperature had risen enough to melt most of the ice. Mist rose up from the ground. A herd of maybe thirty deer grazed in the empty campground, backlit, their elongated shadows stretching through the mist.

Wearing shoes gave me a strange feeling of dissociation from the trail. The last time I had worn my shoes on the A.T., in New York, the feeling had been one of loss, disorientation, but now I welcomed the separation. I was tired of stepping carefully over gravel and sharp rocks. Without the strict concentration that barefoot hiking required, my mind wandered freely. I noticed the subtle colors of the woods, a thousand shades of brown and gray, and the shapes of clouds framed by the bare branches.

As long as it's comfortable. As long as it's fun. Barefoot hiking hadn't been comfortable for a while now, as the temperature dropped and the trail became more and more gravelly. As for fun, there were times when I loved the sensation of floating over rocks, knowing exactly how my feet would land and form themselves to the surfaces. For the most part, though, it felt like a job. It wasn't a question of fun; it was what I did. By the time that ice storm hit, I was ready to stop doing it.

Wearing shoes, we could travel much faster than we had barefoot, especially on gravel. I was eager to see exactly how fast we could go—maybe we could even catch up to Lash and Black Forest and the rest of the crowd. Isis was not as sanguine about the prospect, but she agreed to try it. On our first day out, we covered more than twenty miles of the smooth gravel trail.

We came down the side trail to Hightop Hut, a large wooden shelter set in a grove of oak trees, just as the sun dipped below the treetops. I glanced at my watch: 4:59. Considering the time we left in the morning, and the lunch break we had taken, we had sustained a 2.5-miles-per-hour pace all day long. Barefoot, we had barely made two miles an hour. "We're all that and a bag of chips!" I said as I threw my pack down on the sleeping platform of the shelter.

Isis gave me a puzzled glance. "Did you just say, 'We are Black Forest's badass chicks'?"

Since Shenandoah was a national park, we passed more dayhikers than we had seen in a long time. At first I expected everyone we met to comment on our feet, and then I realized that we were wearing shoes just like the rest of them. We discovered that even shod thru-hikers face the same questions over and over, though: *Where do you sleep? What do you eat? Do you carry a gun? What possessed you to do this?* Even without our bare feet, we were still a curiosity, a strange fringe element of American culture.

On the side of a steep scree slope, where a few trees had managed to get a foothold in the jumble of rocks, we met a man out for the weekend. He carried a pack easily twice the size of mine. All his gear looked brand new: unscuffed leather boots, spotless nylon pack cover, the latest in high-tech breathable fibers in his pants and jacket.

"Thru-hikers," he said in a somewhat accusatory tone. "I shared a shelter with thru-hikers once. It had been raining all day. The thru-hikers came in and hung their wet gear all across the entrance of the shelter!"

"Hmm," I said, wondering what else he thought they should have done.

"I mean, they didn't even leave any *air space*! The smell was terrible." He leaned forward conspiratorially, and then caught a whiff of us and stepped back. "I almost *expired*," he announced.

At an overlook where the trail crossed the parkway, we met another man, a heavyset executive type in his forties, who stepped out of his car to take a picture of the view.

"Where does that trail go?" he asked as we emerged from the woods.

"Maine," I said.

He looked at us blankly. "Any good views?"

We covered more than sixty miles in our first three days as shod hikers and discovered the kinds of problems we had avoided by going barefoot. At lunch the second day, Isis took her shoes off and examined her toes. "I think my feet must have grown, because these shoes are way too small. Look at this." There were ugly dark bruises under both her big toenails.

"Oh, that's bad!" I said. "The only time I ever had something like that was when I dropped a piece of firewood on my foot a couple winters ago. Lost the toenail."

"I'll probably lose them, too." She grimaced. "I've got to get some better shoes. In the meantime, I'm going to hike barefoot again."

I started to protest. "Rockfish Gap is thirty miles from here! If we want to get there tomorrow, there's no way . . ."

Her face was set. "I can do it."

I didn't doubt it. I knew her feet were tougher than mine. I resented it, though; she was implying that I was the reason we had gone so slowly, even though she walked ahead of me as often as not.

"Fine." After lunch I set off even faster than before. She did keep up, with a visible effort of will; every time I looked back she was right behind me, her head down, scowling.

On the third day, the problems of hiking in shoes caught up with me, too. My left heel burned like fire. Seven miles from Rockfish Gap, as the sun began to swing toward afternoon, I had to stop. I took off the shoe and gingerly peeled back the sock. An ugly blister the size of a dime stood out on the back of my heel. I dealt with it as best I could, cushioning it with moleskin and covering it with duct tape. It still hurt.

As we continued down the trail, Isis and I exchanged a glance. "How do people *do* this in shoes?" I said.

Isis

From Rockfish Gap we caught a ride into the town of Waynesboro. The *Companion* didn't list any hostels here, so we decided to splurge on a night in the Comfort Inn. We unpacked our cleanest clothes, took quick preliminary showers to remove the first layer of grime, and headed toward the neon pizza sign that beckoned from a mall across the street. As if my body took its release from the pack's weight as a signal to collapse, I found myself hobbling down the corridors of the hotel, the muscles in my legs threatening to cramp at every step. Walking downhill was even harder; on the gentle incline of the wheelchair access ramp my feet thumped down hard and flat, sending jolts of pain up my legs to my spine. Halfway across the lawn, I found the way blocked by a short, steep descent.

"My knees aren't going to take this," moaned jackrabbit, who had stopped beside me. "I'll probably end up *rolling* down."

"Good idea," I said, lying on my side at the top of the hill.

"You're not really going to—"

"Better than trying to walk." I pushed off.

A moment later, I heard jackrabbit's laughter ring out as she rolled down the hill behind me.

We ordered two large pizzas and split a few greasy appetizers while we waited for them to arrive. As we left the restaurant after our meal, jackrabbit said, "I don't know about you, but I'm not nearly full enough." I agreed. We bought a half gallon of cherry vanilla at the grocery store across the plaza and limped back to our room with it.

As we worked our way through the ice cream, lying back against the overstuffed pillows on the hotel bed, jackrabbit examined the hotel's pay-per-view movie menu. "Ick. Yuck. Gross. Is there anything rated R or under? Oh, other side. Hmph. A selection of last year's blockbusters," she said in a perky announcer's voice, "with emphasis on gratuitous violence and formulaic plots. Shall we try the TV?"

"I guess so. Maybe we can find some interesting nature program." Jackrabbit and I had grown up without a television. From the programs I'd seen while visiting friends or babysitting, I didn't think we'd missed much.

"There's always The Simpsons," said jackrabbit.

She found the last fifteen minutes of a Simpsons episode, after which we flipped through the channels with little success, until—

"Hold on. Back one. What on earth is he doing?"

"He appears to be holding a very angry snake by the tail."

We had found the Crocodile Hunter. In the months that followed, as blizzards replaced the ice storms and each week on the Trail brought a host of new challenges and dangers, we tried to schedule our town stops for Wednesday nights, when *Crocodile Hunter* was on. As jackrabbit put it, "it's reassuring to see that there's someone out there who's crazier than we are—and he's still alive."

We found other ways to entertain each other as we hiked into winter on our own. Way back in Maine, somewhere in the Barren-Chairback Range, the words of a song I'd been trying to write for years had suddenly fallen into place. Jackrabbit had woven a harmony for my simple melody line, and "The Nightbirds," as we called it, had become the serious theme of our hike, as "Dig A Hole" was the comic theme. Now we sang almost every night, between tea and sleeping—our own songs, folk songs, bluegrass, jazz standards, and spirituals. The spirituals inspired me to write a winter song, a hymn of loss and longing for home: *east of the sunset, and west of the moon, there stands a bright island; I'm going home soon.*

With all our friends ahead of us, we counted more than ever on the registers to cheer us. Sometimes, we'd find an entry in Waterfall's fine, bubbly script, and we'd pore over her descriptions of the lovely fall scenery she was hiking through. She'd sign off with the words, "Life is good!" and draw a smiley face with pigtails next to her name. Other times, jackrabbit amused me by deciphering the entries of an early sobo named Porkchop. His handwriting looked like it belonged to a hyperactive preschooler, but, once decoded, his entries displayed a marvelous offbeat sense of humor, applied to the most random subject matter. In my all-time favorite Porkchop entry, he ranted for

a full page about the relative merits of five or six off-brand versions of
Dr. Pepper.

The best registers of all were those that contained entries from Pilgrim
and Gollum, a father-son hiking team who'd started in Maine only a few
weeks ahead of us. They were both fast hikers; the dates of their entries indicated that they had probably reached Springer before Thanksgiving. Although
we'd given up hope of meeting them long ago, we'd followed their progress in
the registers so closely that it felt as if we knew them. In Maine, Gollum had
earned his trail name by leaving a series of clever, original riddles for the hikers behind him to puzzle over. His later entries reminded me of conversations
with college friends in the early hours of the morning: meandering essays on
topics ranging from "Why do flying grasshoppers bump into people?" to
"What if Monty Python hiked the Trail?" Pilgrim, his father, wrote contemplative passages on the changing of the seasons and the sweetness of a spring's
water. Once, he filled two pages of a register with his graceful retelling of a
Hasidic folk tale in which a man travels to a distant city in search of a treasure
he has dreamed of, only to find it under his doorstep when he returns home.
Pilgrim's gentle, thought-provoking words always lifted my spirits.

Besides these glimpses into the lives of distant friends and strangers, the
registers provided a final link to the people we'd been hiking with just before
Thanksgiving. Netta wrote mainly Hebrew, but we could tell that she'd caught
up with the guys when she scrawled #%$!* Black Forest! at the bottom of one
entry. Underneath it, Black Forest had written I am sorry I stole Netta's granola
bar. I thought it belonged to Heald. Now the only beautiful woman in this shelter is
angry with me. Sharkbait offered to beat up Black Forest if Netta wanted him
to, complained about the cold, and counted the days to Catawba. Heald poked
fun at everyone with his dry New England sense of humor.

Often, Lash and Black Forest collaborated on goofy messages to us, in
which they threatened to hijack Snickers trucks and park them at road crossings. At Paul C. Wolfe shelter, just outside of Waynesboro, they duct-taped a
couple of Snickers bars to a mouse hanger, with a little note reading some
Thanksgiving leftovers for the barefoot girls.

I have lost my motivation, Lash wrote in the register there. Dear motivation,
where did you go? We were hiking so well together . . .

Jackrabbit's eyes lit up as she read. "If he's lost his motivation, maybe we'll
catch up to him!"

"I wouldn't count on it," I said. "He'd probably get it back the day before
we caught him and pull a thirty."

"Then we'll have to keep his motivation from getting to him before we do," said jackrabbit. Her eyes twinkled. "Let me see. If he lost it at this shelter, it's probably still somewhere around here. Motivations don't travel very fast without a host. We'll find it and hold it hostage until we see him again."

I got into the game. "Look, it's right there. Lash's motivation!" I said, leaning over and pointing to the word *motivation* on the register page.

"But how can we capture it?" jackrabbit asked. "We can't tear it out of the register."

"Easy. Watch this." I took the notebook and carefully traced Lash's signature from the bottom of the page. I added an apostrophe and an S, then traced the word "motivation."

"See? Lash's motivation. Put it somewhere safe." I handed the scrap of paper to jackrabbit.

She laughed. "My sister the voodoo artist. Can you slow down Black Forest too? I was rather fond of my German badass."

"Sorry. I can't help you there—unless he's foolish enough to leave *his* motivation lying around in a shelter somewhere."

The next day, to our great surprise, we came within a few hours of catching Lash and company. Some northbounders I'd met in Vermont had told me to be sure to visit Rusty, a homesteader who let passing hikers stay the night at his farm. Jackrabbit and I left the Trail at a parking lot and followed the road southwest, as the nobos had instructed me. It looked as if few cars traveled that way; the previous night's snow covered the asphalt, undisturbed except for footprints. Footprints—five pairs of hiking boots, plus one large dog. Annie? Two of the boot tracks were flanked by the marks of hiking poles: Lash and Black Forest. The tracks led away from Rusty's, toward the trailhead.

"We're within a day of them!" jackrabbit exclaimed. "Shall we go back to the trail?"

"It's only an hour till dusk," I answered. "I don't think we'll catch them tonight, and besides, I really want to meet Rusty."

After a few miles of road walking, we came to a driveway that seemed to fit the nobos' description and started down it. Soon, we found an iron gate barring the driveway with a small enamel sign nailed to a tree beside it. "This gate stays closed!" said the sign. Farther down the driveway, I could see an orange rectangle against the trunk of another tree. Was it a "No Trespassing" sign? Had we come to the wrong place?

"The footprints seem to come from here," said jackrabbit, behind me. "This *must* be it." She didn't sound very certain, though.

The orange rectangle on the tree was another sign, but it didn't say "No Trespassing." Instead, it said "If you don't like the Trail, get the hell off it!" Across the driveway, two more signs proclaimed "There is no such thing as a free lunch," and "Hike your own hike—don't tell anyone else how to hike his!" More signs hung in the trees farther down the driveway. "Pick up your trash!" "I didn't ask you to come here; don't make me ask you to leave." Several signs warned "beware of dog!" The house, when we reached it, looked like a mosaic of brightly colored enamel. "This is my house! You are my guest! Act like it!" said a sign on the peak of the roof. A board nailed over the lintel read "Closed for the winter," but a sign beside the door stated "Rusty's Hard Time Hollow is open 365 days a year, 7 days a week, 24 hours a day—or until the Lord returns!" I was trying to decide which to believe, when a tall, gray-bearded man in a plaid flannel shirt flung open the door.

"Y'all must be the Barefoot Sisters," he rumbled. "Heard all about you from your friends. Come on in, and welcome. Don't mind the signs; they're just there to weed out the riff-raff. Y'all hungry? I've got some sloppy joes on the stove." He led us through a screened porch, where dozens more signs flashed at us from the shadows, to a kitchen with smoke-darkened walls, lit by a single gas light and warmed by a blazing wood stove. A little orange dog made its appearance, wagging its tail enthusiastically and leaning its head against our knees.

I wondered aloud if this was the dog we were supposed to "beware of."

"Punkin?" Rusty sounded affronted. "Punkin wouldn't hurt a mouse. Had him ever since he was a puppy. He's real smart, he can do all sorts of tricks. Only reason it says beware of him, is he can tell a good person from a bad. He starts growling at someone, I tell 'em to get the hell out." He flashed us a glare from beneath his shaggy eyebrows, but immediately smiled again. "He likes y'all, though."

When we told Rusty that we were vegetarians, he insisted on making grilled cheese sandwiches. As we sat around eating supper in his living room, he passed us a photo album labeled A.T. 2000. In the early pages, we found Polaroid snapshots of some of the nobos we'd met. Around the Bend was there; a few pages later was the hunk who'd arisen from Lonesome Lake, and there was the young couple who'd given me directions to the Hollow, smiling and waving at the camera. Rusty pointed to a picture at the bottom of the page, in which a man in his late twenties, with a thin face and bright red hair, held what looked like a gold-painted circle of metal behind his head.

"My first sobo this year. Porkchop, I think his name was. I have sobos wear the halo for their photos, so I can tell 'em apart from the northbounders."

In the following pages, we found a lot of our old friends. Jackrabbit lingered over a picture of Tuba Man serenading Rusty's goats. ("Now there was an odd character," Rusty commented. "Touched in the head if you ask me, luggin' that thing all the way to Georgia.") On the next page, Blade's eyes shone brightly as if he had just heard the word "challenge," and he held the sobo halo aloft like a crown. Beside him, Waterfall squinted in the pale, wintry sunlight, the corners of her eyes crinkled and her lips pursed as if she was trying to hold back laughter. Matt was there, too, so thin that he looked even taller than I remembered him.

At the end of the book, we found photos of the friends just ahead of us: Lash grinning from under his fluorescent orange hat, Sharkbait pulling his elbows in close to his chest as if he was shivering, Heald staring at the camera from under his brows as though he was posing for a mug shot. Beside him, Annie wore much the same expression. Black Forest held the sobo halo tipped to one side, and his eyes sparkled mischievously. Netta looked past the camera, her lips smiling but her brow contracted with worry.

"Y'all missed 'em by just a few hours," Rusty told us. "They were here for days. I think they were waitin' for y'all."

We set out early the next morning, fortified by the pancake breakfast Rusty had made for us and encouraged by the news that our friends were close ahead. In the shelter register at Maupin Field, a couple miles down the trail, Lash and Black Forest announced their plans; to make up for the time they'd lost waiting around at Rusty's, they were going to night-hike thirteen miles, ending with the three-thousand-foot ascent of a mountain called the Priest. Heald wrote that he, Sharkbait, and Netta planned to blue-blaze—hiker slang for taking a side trail rather than the white-blazed A.T.—going up the Mau-Har Trail to cut six miles from their night-hike and meeting the boys on top of the Priest.

Jackrabbit and I looked at each other in dismay. If they'd followed this schedule, we were already a day behind them.

"Lash must have borrowed some of Black Forest's motivation," said jackrabbit. "I'm tempted to take this Mau-Har Trail to try to catch them. It looks almost level, and it's a lot shorter than the Three Ridges Trail, where the A.T. runs."

"Do you really think they went through with their plan? Don't forget the Maryland Challenge."

We both laughed at the image of Lash and Black Forest blinking at us from their sleeping bags at eleven o'clock in the morning, whining about the rain.

Jackrabbit laughed. "Yeah, we'll probably find them still asleep in the shelter right before the Priest, what's it called, Harper's Creek?"

Sharp gravel and patches of ice on Three Ridges Trail slowed me down. I hadn't found any boots in Waynesboro wide enough for my feet, so I was still barefoot. I did have my town shoes—a pair of sandals—and some neoprene socks I had picked up from the sale rack at the outfitter's store in Harpers Ferry. Kayakers used them to keep warm, I knew, and they would keep out dampness better than wool. I wanted to save the footwear until I really needed it, in case the sandals gave me blisters. Jackrabbit was having a hard time, too, despite her shoes; her blister from the Shenandoahs still hurt, and some steep climbs among boulders had brought back the old twinge in her hip.

"I wish we'd taken the Mau-Har Trail," she said, as we picked our way down what looked like a frozen mudslide.

"Next time," I answered vaguely, trying to step on frost fingers in such a way that the crystals wouldn't scratch my arches.

We found Harper's Creek Shelter empty, but we were so tired that we decided to stay the night there anyway. While I cooked our instant rice and beans, jackrabbit read aloud from the register.

My noble companion Black Forest and I now set off toward the dangerous and cursèd "Priest," to conquer it as we have conquered so many others. Scared? Aye. Intimidated? Aye. Brave? Aye. Double aye. Because kicking ass is what it's all about.

Peace out, Lash.

P.S. Ladies, we left two boxes of Snickers bars on the picnic table. We won't be needing them where we're going.

Stand up, Lash, tonight we hike. Today is the day the myth of the Priest will die.
Black Forest

Jackrabbit and I hiked the Priest the next morning, in the teeth of our first blizzard. The steady uphill kept me warm, though the light, dry flakes sliding over the tops of my feet threatened to numb my toes. When we paused to catch our breath, I cleared the snow from a rock and danced back and forth on top of it.

"Why don't you put on your sandals?" asked jackrabbit.

"I will at the top of the mountain."

"Your feet are cold."

"I want a finishing place. I think this is the last time I'll be barefoot this winter, and I want to put my shoes on because I've gotten somewhere, not because I've given up."

"You're too damn stubborn. Way too fucking stubborn."

When I rubbed my feet dry in the shelter at the top of the mountain, they burned and tingled, as they used to when I came back from long evenings of ice skating on the town pond behind our dad's house. I felt a twinge of regret, not for the fact that I'd waited so long to put my shoes on, but for the sense of touch that I was losing. The soft brush of snowflakes, the ribbed boards of the shelter floor, even the burning that subsided as I pulled on my neoprene socks, seemed to be keeping me aware, awake to the world in a way I didn't want to give up.

jackrabbit

When I woke up at Seeley Woodworth Shelter, on the ridge south of the Priest, frost fingers nearly covered the small breathing hole I had left in the top of my mummy bag. The air coming in felt like spikes of ice impaling my lungs. I rummaged around in the bottom of my sleeping bag and located my gloves. It was too cold to put my contacts in—they had frozen solid in their case overnight. I sighed and took my glasses out of the top of my pack.

Isis was sitting up already, with her head out of her sleeping bag. Her cheeks were very pink, and her breath was a cloud of steam. She was reading the register, laughing at the entries the boys had left a few days earlier. "Look, Lash wrote a song for us: 'Oh, the weather outside is frightful, and the girls without shoes so delightful. What the German and I want to know, is where'd they go, where'd they go, where'd they go?'"

"Silly boys," I said. "If they had waited another few hours at Rusty's—"

"—and not night-hiked the Priest—"

"—maybe we could have caught up with them!" I shook my head. It was strange, I reflected, that the loneliness did not hit me with the same desperate intensity it had in New York, when we had lost Highlander and Compañero. Although we were by ourselves now, and the chances of anyone catching up to us were pretty slim, I didn't really feel alone. Maybe we would still be able to catch up to our friends ahead. Even if we didn't, I knew that we were still part of a community. I thought back to the Gathering—so many people had shown us such goodwill and respect, just because we happened to be on the Trail. I could picture the invisible strands of kinship binding us to the larger world, and it gave me hope.

"Ooh, it's nasty this morning," Isis said, clapping her gloved hands together. "Where's the water for breakfast, jackrabbit?"

"In my pack, right side pocket."

She was closer to the packs, so she oonched over in her sleeping bag and took out the water bottle. She frowned and tossed it over to me. "Ice." And it was. The half liter of water left in the bottle was frozen solid. "I think we're going to have to sleep with our water from now on, to keep it warm." Her voice was remarkably calm, considering the circumstances.

"You're probably right. What should we do in the meantime?" But the answer was clear. I got out of my sleeping bag—the air sent a jolt of cold through me—and quickly put on all my warm clothes, forced my feet into my frozen sneakers, and went to the spring for a pot of water. On the way back, I gathered a handful of twigs for the stove. Isis boiled the water while I sat in the corner packing up our gear, wearing my sleeping bag as a shawl. It would be the last thing to go into my pack.

When the water reached a boil, Isis poured half of it onto the ice in my bottle. "Good thing about Nalgenes; they won't crack with temperature changes," she said. I was grateful that we weren't arguing. The boiling water dissolved the edges of the ice, and the rest of it bobbed up and down, a pale cylinder. The water in the bottle was lukewarm. We poured out enough to mix up our instant oatmeal, and Isis made tea with the remaining hot water. By the time we drank it, it was tepid.

We had a few days of bitter, unrelenting cold. The trail wound among water-carved ridges here, the last vestiges of a mountain range that once rivaled the Himalayas. The light snow on the ground revealed the folds and contours of the mountains, their silhouettes softened by a fringe of trees. Most of the world looked like a black-and-white photograph: bare branches, vertical slashes of dark trunks, the white backdrop of snow. Far ridges blended into gray.

One afternoon, we came out of the forest into a high meadow, a saddle of grassland between two wooded peaks. It was still, and in places the sun had melted through the thin layer of snow to reveal the warm yellow of fallen grasses.

"I guess this is what they call a bald," Isis said.

"A what?"

"Bald. Anonymous Badger told me about them at the Gathering. It's a high grassland on top of a ridge. Nobody really knows how they got here. Maybe they were ceremonial sites for Native Americans, maybe they were the sites of old forest fires. There are supposed to be quite a few of them along the Trail."

"It's beautiful," I said. We could see in all directions: the rumpled ridges in the distance, with a clear snow line halfway up; the rectangular golden fields and irregular wooded patches of the valley floor shining in the midday light. The sky was suddenly open all around us, no longer hemmed in with skeletal branches, and it was cloudless and limitless blue.

The cold continued. We boiled drinking water every night (the hot water bottles in our sleeping bags were a comfort), and wore the bottles under our jackets all day to keep them from freezing. After lunch every day, my hands and feet went numb as the blood flowed to my stomach. It took perhaps half an hour of hiking before the blood came back with an excruciating pins-and-needles feeling.

I soon learned to tell the temperature by how tightly the rhododendron leaves curled. When they were partway open, usually at midday in a sheltered spot, it was warm enough to stop and eat a granola bar without my hands and feet losing their warmth. When the leaves curled into cigar shapes as thick as my thumb, I knew it was warm enough to hike in my wool shirt, Gore-Tex jacket, and wind pants. On the mornings when the rhododendron leaves were tight as pencils, I wore my long underwear, fleece jacket, and hat under my outer layers, and I knew I would have to hike for a long time before I could feel my feet.

One night, darkness caught up with us before we reached the shelter. It had been a long day—almost eighteen miles over rough terrain. We had dropped down to the James River in the morning, a wide, placid stream with patches of ice in the slow eddies, and then climbed back more than three thousand feet into the mountains. The trail hadn't been smooth in the afternoon, either; we had followed the high points of the ridge from the amusingly named High Cock Knob to Thunder Hill and dropped down precipitously into the gaps between them.

Shadows pooled in the valleys on either side and thickened behind the tall maples and hickory. The first stars glimmered between the tree limbs as the light around us faded. Rhododendron thickets by the trail, leaves curled tight against the cold, captured the almost-full moon in their maze of branches. The white blazes that marked the trail seemed to glow on the trees, and the surface of the snow held a pale sheen. There was a somber stillness in the woods, broken only by the sound of our footsteps crunching the snow and our quiet, steady breath. I watched the moon through the rhododendrons and imagined I could feel the faint touch of its light on my face. I thought of the millions of miles the light traveled through utter emptiness, reflected back and traveled again. Words began to shape themselves in my head, distilling into a haiku:

> Winter moon, tangled
> branches—now not even dreams
> return him to me.

And who was "he"? Black Forest, Lash, Tuba Man, someone, anyone. I watched the orb of the moon until it swam at the edges like a reflection and threatened to brim over. I touched my cheek. Wetness soaked through my glove, and I realized I was crying.

We reached the shelter late. The spring was frozen. I gathered extra twigs for the Zip stove, and we spent perhaps an hour tending the fire, melting snow so we could drink and eat.

The next day, the cold broke. Clouds came over, making a gray backdrop to the black-and-white woods, and the temperature hovered around freezing. In the afternoon we stopped for water at a creek in the valley—it was just warm enough for the filter to work. We carried extra water up the ridge to Cove Mountain Shelter, since the map showed no spring there.

I awoke in the morning to a strange sound on the shelter roof. It wasn't rain, and it wasn't quite snow, and it plopped and glooped and plinked against the fiberglass. The light was still gray outside, and without my glasses, the trees were composed of impressionistic vertical brushstrokes, glinting strangely.

"Ice storm," Isis said. I rolled over and grabbed my glasses case, where I'd left it beside my impromptu pillow of fleece and Gore-Tex. The world resolved itself into gray forest covered in ice: the thin rain and mist had coated all the branches, the trunks, and the ground perhaps a quarter inch thick, with more accumulating all the time. Chunks fell from the trees in a slow but steady progression, making the sounds that had woken me.

I swore. "No twenty for us today. Why don't we just stay here?"

"There's no water."

I swore again. She was right, of course. Water was falling from the sky all around us, but not in a very accessible form. Rain would have dripped off the eaves, at least, and if there had been snow, we could have melted it for water. Besides, neither rain nor snow would have prevented us from hiking the twenty we had planned.

I looked out at the icy trail. I'd seen the profile map yesterday, and as I reached full wakefulness, the details came back to me. We would have to hike about six miles, up and over Cove Mountain, to reach the next shelter with a water source.

Isis untied the food bags from the mouse hangers, and we ate a quick breakfast of granola as the light grew paler outside. We packed up our gear, speaking little, and stepped into our half-frozen shoes.

We made slow progress down the slippery trail, leaning on our sticks. I quickly remembered the lessons of the first ice storm, the one that had forced us to sleep in the laundry room at Big Meadows: step on leaves, never rocks. Always be prepared to slide. If you fall—*when* you fall—catch the brunt of it on your pack. It was slow and exhausting work.

After a few miles, the trail crossed the Blue Ridge Parkway. Explanatory signs named the mountains usually visible from the overlook. Our vista that day was dreary ice fog and stark trees close by, and the signs were so coated in ice that it was impossible to read them anyway. We skated along the road for a while, taking refuge under a stone overpass to eat a quick snack. By now, icicles were forming on the hoods and sleeves of our jackets. We cracked the thin coating of ice off our pack covers.

We reached Bobblet's Gap Shelter at about three in the afternoon, sore and tired. My nerves were on edge from treading so carefully for seven hours.

"Where's the register?" I asked, reaching the shelter just after Isis.

"There isn't one," she said.

"This is what, like, the fourth shelter without one?"

"Third."

"How will we know where anybody is? And how will we entertain ourselves for the rest of the day?"

"We'll manage. There's always *Passion's Stealth-fire.*"

Isis hung our food bags while I went to the spring and filtered water. Luckily, it was right in front of the shelter: a concrete box half full of dead leaves and mud, with a slow upwelling of water from one end. I rigged a few twigs to keep the filter intake out of the grime, tied a mostly clean handkerchief over the end, and pumped four liters of drinking water. I used my cup to scoop some marginally particulate-free water into our pot for tea.

There were a few dry sticks and scraps of wood under the shelter, enough to get a smoky fire lit in our Zip stove. I gathered handfuls of fallen twigs from the nearby woods, breaking off the ice. Isis made a pot of blackberry tea. Its rich sweet scent filled the damp shelter. I smiled to myself, thinking of Sharkbait. I wondered where he was and wished again for a register. We got out our last few bags of crackers, a few chunks of dried papaya, some Archway cookies, and ate lunch at last.

We spent the afternoon writing scenes in our silly novel, drinking tea, and staring out into the glistening gray landscape. Icicles lengthened on the eaves of the shelter. Toward evening, the woods took on an unearthly look, full of mist and double-outlined, with vertical bars of light and shadow.

I filled the pot with water again, gathered more twigs for the stove, and Isis cooked some macaroni. After dinner, I lay on my foam pad, worrying about the next day's hike. Our food would last another day, two if we stretched it. Would the weather clear by morning? Would I be able to hike another day of slipping and sliding over an uncertain trail? My right hip was throbbing; my left knee felt weak and watery again. I curled up on my left side to spare my hip and fell asleep.

Isis

Most of the ice had melted by morning, though the weather didn't seem to be any warmer. We hiked through a uniformly gray world: sky, trail, and tree trunks blended into each other in a chill mist. Luckily, the trail was easy, and the cold encouraged us to make good time. We took a very short lunch break at a shelter with no register. ("Damn, I wish I had a notebook I could leave," jackrabbit said.) We had set our sights on a shelter only five miles out of Troutville, a drab little cinderblock building that we reached about an hour before dusk. I had set down my pack and taken out the water filter, when jackrabbit, who'd been searching around the shelter, threw up her hands in exasperation.

"There's no register here either! That does it! Let's go to town."

Going on would mean hiking a twenty-three, equal to our longest day so far. I didn't feel inclined to argue about pace, though. *Cold gray shelter? Last of our food? And who knows, maybe another ice storm tomorrow—or pizza, showers, and a clean bed. Hmm, let's see . . . I think I've got a few more miles in me.*

We reached Troutville just as its impressive maze of street lamps and neon signs began lighting up for the night. This was no Trail town, but an interstate town: a tangle of intersecting freeways, around which truck-stop motels and fast-food joints rose from a sea of asphalt. Nothing except the gray-on-gray of cinderblock and concrete recalled the shades of the winter woods, though this industrial version was much less nuanced. The maze of pavement contained no crosswalks or sidewalks; apparently this town belonged to a world in which no one walked. In the last of the daylight, jackrabbit and I scampered from freeway island to freeway island until we reached the supermarket plaza. After securing our resupply and a pizza, we didn't venture out of our hotel room even for ice cream. We took turns showering, then watched the Crocodile Hunter as we packed our resupply into Ziplocs.

"He reminds me of Tuba Man," jackrabbit sighed. "He's cute and blond and so enthusiastic about his own eccentricities that everyone loves him for it."

"You're still mooning over the Amazing Tuba Man? I thought your pet German had helped you forget him."

"It's winter. I need someone to moon over, to keep my mind off this damn cold."

"Sounds like a good idea. Who should I set my heart on? Solid? That guy from Lonesome Lake? Anonymous Badger?"

"Not Anonymous Badger. He said he might come out and hike with us in January. If you moon over someone you're actually going to see again, it could get embarrassing."

"Maybe I should go for my high school standby. Percy Bysshe Shelly. A safe couple of centuries away."

On our second morning out of Troutville, we hiked up to Tinker Cliffs. Below us, a broad farm valley, its meadows dark gold in the weak sunlight, wound between wooded ridgelines. The early morning light cast the crinkled flanks of the ridges, carved by the paths of hundreds of streams, into sharp relief. The same rains that had shaped the ridges had gouged and scoured the yellow limestone of Tinker Cliffs into a series of sculptural promontories. Spotted with small black curls of lichen in a pattern that resembled leopard skin, they overlooked the valley like a row of abstract sphinxes.

"If this is Tinker Cliffs, I can't wait for McAfee Knob," said jackrabbit. "That's it, see? At the end of this ridge. A bunch of nobos told me it's got the best view on the Trail."

We hurried on along the ridgeline. By the time we reached McAfee Knob, though, the sky had clouded over completely. Perhaps it was my overactive imagination, but I thought that the raw, damp wind from the valley smelled like an approaching ice storm. We hurried over the exposed top of the knob, unimpressed by the pitted, lichenless gray cliffs.

Out of the wind, we paused for a snack. Jackrabbit took a sip from her water bottle and shivered.

"This water's very close to solid," she complained.

I sighed dramatically. "I wish *I* could be like that water!"

"What, almost frozen?"

"No, very close to Solid."

Jackrabbit laughed. "What about poor Shelly?" she asked. "I thought you were planning to stick with him."

"It's too hard to imagine the perfumed zephyrs of the Mediterranean on a day like this. It's like trying to see color when you're night-hiking. I have to dream about someone closer to real."

jackrabbit

In late afternoon, we stopped at an overlook to eat a snack. The bitter damp wind across the valley intensified. Isis passed me a rock-hard frozen granola bar. With the first bite, I felt a disturbing crunch inside my mouth: something besides the granola bar had broken. I spat the bite of food into my gloved hand. "I think I just broke a tooth on that granola bar!"

"Oh, come on. They're not that hard."

"No, seriously. I really did." I couldn't see any fragments of enamel in my hand, but running my tongue across my teeth, I felt a small divot taken out of my left front incisor.

Isis's forehead wrinkled with concern. "How bad is it?"

"Well, it doesn't hurt, but the edge is pretty sharp . . . ow! I think I just cut my lip."

My sister frowned. "Maybe we should get off at the next road and try to find a dentist." We hadn't been planning to stop in the next town, Catawba— we had just left Troutville, carrying enough food for the ninety-mile stretch to Pearisburg.

"Is there anywhere to stay in Catawba?" I asked.

"The *Companion* said there are a couple bed-and-breakfasts."

"Can we afford to stay there?"

She sighed. "Can we afford *not* to?"

By the time we reached the road, drops of not quite rain pattered down out of the sky, sticking to every surface. We paused only long enough to glance at the trailhead register.

"Hey, Sharkbait finished!" I told Isis.

"What has he got to say?"

I read his scrawled message. "*Heald, Lash, Black Forest, Netta, Barefoot Sisters—nice knowin ya. I am so out of here.* December ninth. Looks like he finished just in time, right before that nasty ice storm that caught us at Cove Mountain."

"Speaking of ice, we'd better get going."

"Yeah."

We slid and skated down the road to the Crosstrails Bed and Breakfast, a short ways off the Trail, only to find a board reading "closed for the season" hung beneath the sign in front of the tall white building. While we stood there deliberating, a dark-haired woman opened the front door. "Hi there! Y'all must be freezing in this weather. Come on in."

With my grubby pack and sweaty clothes, I felt entirely out of place in the spotless white-carpeted living room. Hand-crocheted doilies were draped over the antique wooden end tables by the brocaded sofa. In the corner stood a twelve-foot spruce, decorated with red and white bows—suddenly I remembered that Christmas was less than two weeks away.

"We're not actually taking guests right now," the owner told us. "But I know a couple in town who just opened a B and B. Let me give them a call. Would y'all like some tea or anything while you wait?"

"Thank you so much." Even after so many months on the Trail, I was continually amazed by people's generosity. There we were, reeking, dressed in ratty clothing, and she treated us with as much consideration as if we had arrived in a chauffeured limousine. I hoped that someday, on the Trail or beyond it, I would have a chance to repay the kindness that so many people had shown.

Dave, the owner of the Down Home Bed and Breakfast, arrived in his pickup a few minutes later. He was a tall round-faced man with short gray hair. "Good thing y'all came in when you did! A few more minutes and these roads would be iced over."

Dave and his wife Lucy welcomed us like family, even sharing their dinner with us. We ate bowl after bowl of broccoli soup and told stories about our hike as the ice built up outside. I tried to imagine where we would be if we had stayed on the Trail. The next shelter was more than seven miles from the road; we would have had to night-hike in the freezing rain or set up our tent and hope it held. The sharp edge of my broken tooth was disconcerting when I ran my tongue over it, and the inside of my lip was cut in several places. When I considered where we would be right now if it hadn't happened, though, I was almost glad I had chipped a tooth. Dave called his dentist and set up an appointment for me at noon the next day.

In the morning, a dazzling coat of ice transformed the tree limbs to crystal chandeliers. When the roads were clear enough, Dave took us into Christiansburg, the nearest large town. We picked up some extra groceries, in case we got caught by another ice storm between here and Pearisburg, and Isis bought a pair of real hiking boots. I held off; my sneakers had worked well so far, and I didn't feel like spending anything more than I had to in this town. I worried about the cost of the dentist appointment. The last time I had any dental work done, it had cost me hundreds of dollars. Even routine cleanings were $80 or $90 where I had lived before the Trail. As it turned out, I shouldn't have worried; the dentist ground the sharp edge off my tooth in less than five minutes and handed me a bill for $35.

By the time we left Catawba, the ice had melted almost completely in the warm, bright afternoon sun. The A.T. led along steep ledges of gray stone, with an almost vertical drop-off on one side, up to the abrupt scarp of rock known as Dragon's Tooth. *This would have been totally impassible in an ice storm, in the dark*, I realized, and I shivered at the thought. I ran my tongue over my front teeth. I could still feel the chip, though the edges were no longer sharp.

Isis

On the ridges beyond the Dragon's Tooth, the sun flashed in and out of ragged, bruise-colored clouds. The bare trunks of oaks and the dark green crowns of pines caught the light and stood out in sharp relief against the glowering sky.

My new boots felt wonderful compared with the neoprene socks and sandals I'd been wearing for the past week. Inside the neoprene, my feet had sweat constantly. By the end of a day they'd become wrinkled and clammy; by the end of the week they had started to smell bad. Cocooned in wool socks and boots, my feet felt warm and dry. The inch of boot sole between them and the trail gave me a curious but pleasant sense of levitation. Only an occasional twinge where the boot tongues pressed against the front of my ankles reminded me that I was breaking in new footwear.

At Pickle Branch Shelter that night, jackrabbit studied the maps while I gathered firewood. When I sat down to light the stove, she leaned over, her eyes gleaming, and pointed to the altitude profile of the stretch of trail we'd covered that afternoon.

"Look at this! We hiked twelve miles today, starting at two o'clock. If we can do that, we should have no trouble hiking this . . ." she pulled the next map forward, and her finger skimmed along the profile. ". . .twenty-three!"

she finished, triumphantly, her fingertip resting above the words *Laurel Creek Shelter.*

"Twenty-three? That's the most we've ever done in a day."

"I know! Now that you've got boots, we can start moving fast."

"It might be easier to wait until I've broken them in a little."

She frowned. "Are they giving you blisters?"

"Well, no . . ."

Her voice took on a note of mild exasperation. "Look, we've got two choices tomorrow. We pull the twenty-three to Laurel Creek, or . . ." her finger moved to the words *Sarver's Cabin.* "Or we hike a measly sixteen miles and stay in a ruined cabin half a mile off the trail, downhill, which is supposed to be mouse-infested *and* haunted."

"Haunted? That could be fun. Okay, okay. I was just kidding. Twenty-three it is."

We packed our gear by the light of our headlamps in the morning and left in the blue-gray murk of half-light. Shadows crouched under the pines like large nocturnal animals retreating from the sunrise. As we reached the top of the ridge, the sun lit the pine trunks with a brief orange flare, then vanished into the belly of a low cloud. We hiked down the last mile of that ridge and up the next. Under the heavy cloud, the forest around me seemed drained of all but its most somber hues. I ran through all the poems I'd memorized, letting my mind dwell on the lines that evoked color. *Blood-red were his spurs in the golden noon; wine-red was his velvet coat,* I repeated to myself, trying to picture the dramatic end of "The Highwayman." But it seemed that color had faded from my imagination as it had vanished from the landscape; the scene I called to mind had the flickering, dusty quality of a badly preserved film.

Near the top of the third ridge, Sinking Creek Mountain, we huddled behind a pile of boulders and ate a hurried lunch. A scrawny brown-and-black striped hound, fitted with a radio collar, came trotting out of the woods as we packed up to leave. When she spotted us, she put her tail between her legs, backed away a pace, and started baying.

"Oh, hush. We're not bears, even if we do smell like them," I told her. "Go on, go back to your people. Shoo."

She did hush, but she refused to go away. When we started to hike, the hound tagged along behind us. Every once in a while, jackrabbit would turn around and try to chase her off. The dog cowered, staying well out of reach, but as soon as we started walking again, she stood up and followed. After a while, she trotted past us and started to lead us down the trail, looking over her shoulder every few minutes to check that we were still there.

The first drifts of mist caught in tree branches high over our heads. It wasn't until we came to a stretch of bare ledges that we realized another ice storm had started. The dog found footing in small cracks and tufts of grass, but jackrabbit and I could scarcely keep our balance on the slanted stone. Our pace slowed to a crawl. The sky was darkening with night as well as storm by the time we reached the Sarver's Cabin side trail. We paused in the shelter of an enormous fallen log.

"What do you want to do?" asked jackrabbit.

"We have to get this dog somewhere. We don't have any food for her, and she looks like she's starving. Let's go on."

"Good. That's just what I was thinking." She consulted the map. "Looks like there's a road in the next valley. Maybe we'll find a farmhouse or something."

Down in the valley, the ice-mist changed to a light rain, but a series of farm fields fenced with barbed wire posed us a new problem. The stiles, set up to help hikers get over the fences, offered no footholds for the dog; jackrabbit had to lure her close with a handful of goldfish crackers, then pick her up and pass her over the fence to me. The dog wasn't very happy about this procedure; after the second fence, she followed a good distance behind us, and when we reached the third stile, she turned and ran away. We waited, but she didn't return. We were almost ten miles from the place where she'd started following us, and as far as we knew, she was trapped inside the fenced field.

"Here, dog! Please come back, dog," I called into the night.

"The road's close," jackrabbit said. "Maybe we can find a house and tell the people there's a lost dog in this field."

"I guess so." I sighed. "I wanted to get her to some place where she could get some rest and food."

"We've got to get *us* to some place where we can rest and eat," said jackrabbit. "We still have three miles to go before the shelter, and I'm pretty tired."

As soon as I thought about it, I realized that I, too, was exhausted. My shoulders ached, and my feet felt bruised and swollen, especially in the places beneath the boot tongues. I turned and headed slowly down the trail. Five minutes later, the dog rejoined us, her sleek coat covered with mud; she must have found a gap under the fence to wriggle through. I lured her over with the rest of the goldfish and some water poured into my camp cup. While she ate, I tied a length of string to her collar. She accepted the makeshift leash with resignation and trotted along beside me, her head hanging.

In fifteen minutes, we came to the road. Luck was with us; just around a corner, the bright, warm lights of a house glowed through the drizzle. It turned out to be a tiny building, set in a yard full of rusting cars. Strips of peeling paint dangled from the walls, and a few mossy shingles looked like they were about to fall off the roof, but Christmas lights blazed from two small bushes beside the door. I stood in the road for a minute, just looking, letting my eyes drink in the dazzling colors.

Jackrabbit waited in the driveway, holding the dog, while I went up and knocked. A small, muscular woman opened the door a crack, stared at me for a moment, then opened it a bit farther. Over her shoulder, I caught a glimpse of twelve or fifteen people, ranging in age from two to eighty, clustered around a television set. One of the young girls held a lap dog. *Good*, I thought, *they have dog food.*

"Well?" asked the woman at the door.

"My sister and I found a lost bear hound. We're hiking the Appalachian Trail, so . . ."

"It ain't mine. All my huntin' dogs are in the backyard."

"We were wondering if you could help us return it to the owner?"

"Has it got a collar?" I nodded. The woman opened the door the rest of the way and motioned to jackrabbit. "Bring it here."

She inspected the tag on its collar, and her voice softened, as though finding the address there had finally convinced her that we weren't trying to play some nasty trick on her. "Oh, sure. Jim Somers. I know him. Lives just the next gap over. I'll get this dog back to him."

"Could you—if you have any dog food—feed her something? I think she's really hungry."

"'Course I'll feed her." She turned and hollered back into the room. "Bobby! Get some dog food, and get this hound out to the pen." Then she looked back at me, her eyes narrowed with suspicion as they had been when she first opened the door. "Anything else?"

"No, thank you, ma'am," I answered and retreated to the driveway. As jackrabbit and I turned the corner of the road, I glanced over my shoulder and saw her still standing behind the half-open door, her arms crossed, watching us.

"That was strange," I said. "She kept looking at me as though she thought I was some kind of burglar."

Jackrabbit stopped under a streetlight and looked me up and down. "Well," she said, "you can't see yourself, so you'll have to use me as your mirror."

I looked at her. Mud streaked her skin and clothing, and strands of wet hair, escaped from her braid, clung to the sides of her face. Her eyes caught the flash of my headlamp, bright in the murky shadows beneath the brim of her hat. A long stripe of dried blood ran down her right forearm; she must have scratched it on one of the barbed wire fences. Framed between her heavy hiking sticks, she looked even taller than her six-two, and the thick sleeves of her wool shirt, pushed back to the elbows, made her biceps look as powerful as her hiker calves.

"Wow," I said. "You look dangerous."

"Thanks," she answered. "So do you."

I may have looked tough, but I didn't feel it. Without the dog to worry about, my mind settled, with a vengeance, on my ankles. Only the task of finding our path through the dark fields distracted me from the pain of breaking in my new boots. In some places, finding the trail wasn't easy. The posts with white blazes on them were set much farther apart than the beams of our headlamps could reach; in pastures, I had to distinguish the A.T. from dozens of crisscrossing cow paths. At the edge of one hayfield, I followed a beaten trail up a steep embankment, only to find that it fanned out into a half dozen faint animal tracks that disappeared into the underbrush.

"Are we lost?" jackrabbit asked, scowling.

"We're off the Trail. I must have lost it at the foot of the hill."

Sure enough, the A.T. made a sharp, right-angle turn at the base of the hill. As soon as we found it again, jackrabbit took the lead. I limped along behind her, my ankles throbbing as though I'd been walking in iron shackles instead of boots. My shoulders, too, burned under the pack straps, and every muscle in my arms and legs ached. I tried to drag scraps of poetry and bright days from my memory, but every thought turned ugly under the influence of pain; the smoke of a campfire changed to clouds of burning ash, leeches swarmed under the surface of a pond, someone's arms hugging me became binding ropes. Dimly, I could see jackrabbit striding up the trail in front of me, the top of her hat just showing above her pack cover, but at the same time, I walked in a nightmare forest, where the tree branches scratching my legs turned into clawed arms reaching out to trip me. How far did we have to go? Four miles? Six? It felt as though we'd hiked tens of miles, from one night into the next, since we'd passed the road and the house with Christmas lights.

Just when my conviction that Laurel Creek Shelter did not exist had grown to a certainty, we arrived. Jackrabbit threw down her pack and checked her watch.

"We done good, sister," she said. "It's only nine-thirty."

We woke to a cold, steady rain.

"Brrr! Nasty weather," jackrabbit muttered, jumping back into her sleeping bag after a visit to the privy. "Five hundred feet up, I bet this is one hell of an ice storm."

I pulled out the map and checked our elevation on the altitude profile. Only 2,700 feet here at the shelter, but the next mile of hiking would take us to 3,700 feet. "It looks like we're stuck here," I said, trying not to betray how cheerful the prospect made me. I knew jackrabbit would chafe at the delay, but for myself, a full day of rest for my ankles, with unlimited hot tea, singing, and reading out loud, sounded like heaven.

We spent the day in our sleeping bags, venturing out only to gather firewood or get water from the stream. Foreseeing the possibility of getting stuck in ice storms, we had picked up *The Monkey Wrench Gang* at a used book store in Christiansburg. All morning, we took turns reading aloud. Our imaginations wandered the golden canyons of the southwest, where grubby, inarticulate, and spectacularly resourceful George Hayduke waged war on the corporate interests of four states with his rag-tag band of comrades. After lunch, too hoarse to read, we brewed ourselves a pot of tea and added a chapter to *Passion's Stealth-fire*. A mouse showed up in midafternoon and spent hours performing increasingly dramatic stunts in an attempt to reach our food bags. After we watched him make a daring leap onto the mouse hanger nearest the wall, setting it swinging like a trapeze toward the one where our food bags hung, jackrabbit dubbed him Hayduke.

By the next morning, the ice storm had descended to our altitude. Black ice glazed the rocks around the shelter; just getting a pot of water to make tea became an adventure. Sitting still felt much less comfortable than it had the day before, partly because our muscles had stiffened painfully from the forced inactivity, and partly because the air was so cold that we didn't want to take our arms outside of the sleeping bags to read. We settled for watching the antics of Hayduke the mouse, telling stories, and brewing tea to keep our minds off our hunger. We were almost forty Trail miles from the town of Pearisburg, with a scant two days worth of food left. I remembered an ice storm in Maine that had lasted a week. I wondered what we'd do if this one settled in for that long. Slide and stumble back down to the road and beg the woman who'd taken the dog to help us again? Eat tree bark?

For once, jackrabbit seemed to feel more confidence that I did. "The air's warming up," she said as we packed our food bags after supper. "We should get an early start tomorrow to make up for the time we've lost."

"Okay," I said, humoring her. "What time should I set my internal alarm for?"

"Let's see. It's eight now. Five-thirty would be good."

Sometime in the middle of the night, I awoke to the rumble of thunder. Lightning flashed close overhead, illuminating huge, downy snowflakes that drifted silently through the clearing. Without the rattle of rain on the shelter roof, it seemed that we were caught in the ghost of a thunderstorm, just as the bare tree limbs, outlined in snow against the stormy sky, looked like the ghosts of a forest. As the storm drifted away to the west, I fell back asleep, into a dream of color. I was standing in a sunlit meadow, full of enormous flowers. Sky-blue dahlias the size of dinner plates nodded on stems as high as my shoulders; spikes of gold and crimson gladiolas rose above my head. I made my way to the edge of the meadow, pushing through the tangle of flower stems and stepping around the tilted slabs of slate that lay hidden among them. Beyond the flowers, perhaps a quarter-mile distant, a sleepy village of thatch-roofed cottages lay still in the midday sun. All around it, fields of ripe grain glowed against a backdrop of rolling green hills, but no figures, either human or animal, moved through the verdant landscape. On my left, not a hundred yards distant, I could see the white walls and spire of a country church, bright against the cloudless sky. Suddenly, I realized that I was standing in the church-yard; the slabs of slate were gravestones, and all that profusion of glorious color rose from the bodies of the dead.

That discovery shocked me awake. Darkness filled the shelter; only the faintest pallor, like a hovering wisp of fog, marked the snowy clearing beyond the edge of the sleeping platform. I reached for my headlamp and checked jackrabbit's watch. Five twenty-three. Outside, the snow was still falling. Small quick flakes drifted across the front of the shelter like static on a TV screen. I dressed quickly, pulled on my boots, and tested the ground. Stable footing. The snow had stuck to the surface of the ice, leaving a surface we could walk on. I crawled back into the shelter and woke jackrabbit.

For the first mile, we climbed steadily uphill. On either side of the Trail, the tightly curled leaves of rhododendrons looked black in my headlamp light, like thousands of frozen bats hanging from the branches. The sky lightened slowly without changing color. Our two days' rest had healed the bruises around my ankles, but I felt as though my will to continue had vanished in the churchyard full of flowers. I wanted to stop jackrabbit, to say, *it's over. We're in the wrong place, at the wrong time; can't you see that we couldn't outrun winter? We gave it our best try, and now I want to go home.* In the gray hour of gloom before dawn, it seemed so obvious that our hike had failed. I felt certain that jackrabbit would offer no opposition to my plan. Working out the logistics of getting home, though, seemed even more difficult than putting one foot in front of the other. I would wait until Pearisburg; perhaps we could find a bus from there or convince some kind soul to drive us to the nearest airport.

Just as we reached the top of Kelly Knob, a creamy yellow light suffused the thin band of horizon between gray earth and gray cloud. As I watched, stacked bands of lavender, blue, and pink lit up the western rim of the sky, while the eastern horizon deepened to the color of an egg yolk. The sun blazed momentarily through the gap beneath the cloud bank, tinting the snowy branches reddish orange. In another minute, it had risen into the clouds, returning us to the drab winter landscape. But that one moment of sunlight was enough to break the dream's spell. *Of course we can go on,* I told myself. *We've made it this far. We'll finish.*

jackrabbit

We came to Bailey Gap Shelter as the light faded between the trees. I was so accustomed to camping alone that it was a shock to find another hiker there: a skinny young man with long blond hair and ragged clothes, sitting at the edge of the sleeping platform. He was definitely a hiker, but his pack was nowhere in sight.

"Hey, what's up?" he called as we came into the clearing. "They call me the Kid."

"Good to meet you," I said, and we gave our names. "Where's your pack?" I asked him.

He grinned. "A pair of trail angels're slacking me. They should be here any minute now."

"Are you southbound?" I asked him.

"Just filling in a section I missed. I hiked northbound this year. I had to get off for a week in summer with really bad pack sores, and then I skipped ahead to be with the crowd. These great trail angels I met in the Smokies—Jill and Bill—they're slacking me back to Catawba. That'll be the end of my thru-hike."

"You're close, then. Congratulations," I said.

A petite woman with short white hair came into the clearing, carrying two packs. "Kid? Oh, there you are! I've got your pack here." She had a gentle Southern accent. "Sorry we're late; took us a while to find the place." She noticed us. "Hi there. I'm Jill. I didn't expect to see any other hikers out this time of year!"

We introduced ourselves. Jill looked surprised. "Are y'all the Barefoot Sisters? I heard rumors y'all got off the Trail! It sure is good to see y'all out here."

"We got off for Thanksgiving," Isis said, "but only for a few days."

Jill shook her head. "It's amazing, isn't it, how rumor travels?"

"We're not really barefoot anymore, either," I said, indicating Isis's brand-new boots and my own sneakers.

"When did you put shoes on?" the Kid asked.

"The end of November," I said. "The first ice storm hit us in Shenandoah, and we had to call it quits."

The Kid whistled. "It's a wonder you kept it up that long. Pennsylvania and everything?"

"Yeah, even Pennsylvania. It was fun while it lasted," Isis told him.

It was almost dark now; the first few stars shone between the bare branches. I heard footsteps coming up the path.

"That'll be my husband Bill," Jill said. "We call him Whispering Bill, 'cause he can't talk very loud." He was a tall man, slender almost to the point of gauntness, with thinning brown hair pulled into a ponytail.

"Hi there," he said in a broken voice that was barely above a whisper. "It's good to see all these hikers out on a night like this."

As we cooked supper, Isis and I told a few of the better stories from our hike so far. The Kid talked about life as a northbounder—throngs of hikers, hot weather and terrific thunderstorms, trail magic cookouts by the side of the road. His descriptions of the Trail in summer were so different from the scenery we had passed in the last few months that I could hardly reconcile the two.

Jill and Bill told us about their dreams of hiking the Trail. "We've hiked a lot of sections," Jill said, "but we really want to do a thru-hike. It's been our plan ever since we got married."

"And that's a long time," Bill wheezed.

"Right," Jill said. "I've been thirty-nine for so many years I've lost count!" She laughed brightly. "But the year after next, we're hiking for sure. The kids'll all be through with school, the house'll finally be paid for." Her voice grew quiet. "I think we've got to hike soon, 'cause Bill's not getting any better."

"Not any worse, either," he protested.

"You said you were having trouble with your hands again, honey."

"What happened?" I ventured.

"Bill used to work for the state of Tennessee, in the waste disposal department," Jill explained. "He was out at a dump site one time, and he got into some kind of chemical. It burned his lungs pretty bad. Now he's starting to have trouble with his circulation, too. When his hands get cold, it takes 'em forever to warm up again."

"I'm still healthy enough to hike," he said.

"Best of luck," I said. "This Trail is an awesome experience."

"It sure has given us some fun times over the years," Jill said. "I think the hikers are what keep us young. Like this fella here." She patted the Kid on his shoulder and beamed. "Wasn't for him, we'd be home gettin' fat in front of the TV. Listen, Isis and jackrabbit. Y'all have got to come visit us when you come through the Smokies."

"Definitely," I said.

She took a scrap of paper from the top of her pack and wrote her phone number. "It'd be great to see y'all again."

When they saw our meager pot of instant potato flakes, Jill and Bill shared their food with us: home-dehydrated vegetable stew, with peppers, tomatoes, and zucchini from their own garden. It was the best thing I had eaten in days. We stayed up far into the night, talking, singing, laughing, appreciating the company of other hikers.

The sun was well below the horizon when we packed up and left in the morning. Jill, Bill, and the Kid were asleep; we shielded the beams of our headlamps and spoke in whispers so we wouldn't wake them. We had planned a long day, another twenty-three miles.

Four inches of new snow clung to the ground, and more was falling, swirling down in the light of our headlamps. My feet were sopping wet inside my cloth sneakers before the sun rose. By midday I could no longer feel my toes. The shoes gave no traction on the steep, snowy hills; I slid constantly.

Coming down off the ridge into Pearisburg as darkness closed in again, I felt exhausted and miserable. A factory at the edge of town, a huge network of pipes and smokestacks, tanks and flashing lights, gave off a low persistent hum that grew stronger as we came down the ridge. The air filled with its vile reek:

vinegar, brimstone, bile. I was hungry from the last few days of short rations, but the thought of food turned my stomach, with the nauseating smell in the air. As we crossed the bridge over the New River, I sloshed through puddles of salty brown road-water, no longer caring where I put my feet. Passing cars sprayed a slurry of ice, salt, and gravel all over us, and a piercingly cold, damp wind ripped across the bridge.

We walked up the shoulder of the road to a grocery store at the edge of town. Under the washed-out light from the store windows, I could see snowflakes whipping past. I took my pack off and slumped against the wall of the store, one hand over my face to keep the biting wind off my cheeks. The last few days of hiking had worn me out more than I wanted to admit.

"Are you okay?" I looked up. A tall, thin man was getting out of a pickup truck. His forehead wrinkled with concern.

I tried to sit up straighter. "Yeah, we're okay. It's just been a long day. Couple of long days."

"Are you hiking the Trail? In this weather?"

Isis grinned, a slightly maniacal expression that I recognized all too well. "Southbound."

The man shook his head and smiled. "Well, I wouldn't have imagined, not in this season . . . I've lived here fourteen years, and this is the worst winter I've seen yet."

I chuckled grimly. "Just our luck."

"Do you guys need a ride anywhere?"

I looked at Isis. We needed to buy groceries, but we also needed to find a place to stay before night fell. Our chances of hitching after dark would drop precipitously, we knew. Pearisburg was a town built for automobiles, not walkers, and it was several miles of sloppy, shoulderless highway to the center of town where the motels were.

"That would be awesome," Isis said.

We stowed our packs and poles in the back of the pickup, and both of us piled into the front seat. As the warm blast of the heater hit me, I felt a profound weariness overtaking me. My hands and feet began to tingle painfully as the blood returned to the chilled tissue.

"I'm Larry," our benefactor said, and we introduced ourselves. My real name felt strange on my tongue. We gave the usual statistics—how long we had been on the Trail (almost six months), our planned finishing date (now mid-February), our daily mileage.

"What about you, Larry?" I asked. "What do you do?"

"I'm an electrician. I work at the Celanese factory. You probably saw it on your way into town."

And smelled it, too, I thought. "What exactly does the factory produce?"

"Well, we make acetate fibers. Cigarette filters, mainly, but we also make industrial filters. The factory's the biggest employer in this part of the county. It's pretty steady work, too. Our business actually seems to go up in a recession—I guess people smoke more when they're out of work, or something. Like I said, I've been here fourteen years. They've hardly ever had to lay anybody off."

"Where are you from originally?" I asked. He had a slight Southern accent, with an undertone of something I couldn't quite place.

"I'm from New Jersey, actually. What about you guys?"

"We're from Maine."

"Really! My wife's from Maine. I bet she'd love to meet the two of you. She's always going on about how tough Maine women are." Larry shook his head. "I don't doubt it . . . well, here's the motel. Listen, I'd like to take you guys out to dinner. Give me an hour to pick up my wife, let you guys get cleaned up and all that, and we'll swing by here at—" he glanced at his watch, "—quarter after seven. How's that sound?"

"That sounds great. Thanks so much." I felt a new strength as I unloaded my gear from the back of the truck and headed for the neon sign that marked the motel office.

Later that night, feeling contented after many plates of Southern Country Buffet and a good conversation with Larry and his wife, we lay back on the beds in our hotel room, planning for the next week of hiking.

Isis unfolded a few maps. "It's about ninety miles to Atkins. Six days of food, plus an extra in case we get trapped somewhere again."

"Sounds about right." I yawned, feeling lazy and luxuriating in the warmth of the room. But something was bothering me. I knew there was something else I needed to do before we returned to the Trail. I glanced around the room. My pack cover, draped over my hiking sticks to dry out; my almost-empty food bag sitting on the floor; my sleeping bag airing out beside the bed; the deflated carcass of my pack, containing only the tent. And then my eyes caught on the ratty, sopping wet cotton sneakers by the door. I didn't think my feet would survive another day of damp cold inside of them. "Isis! I have to get boots before we leave town."

She yawned. "We'll find a place. Call the front desk; they probably know where to find an outfitter's store."

I dialed, and a sleepy woman's voice answered. "Hello?"

"Um, hi. I'm wondering if you could tell me where I might find an out-fitter's store in town."

"You mean, like, clothing?"

"No, I mean camping gear, hiking boots, that sort of thing."

"Oh. We don't have no stores like that in Pearisburg. Closest one's in Blacksburg."

"How far is that?"

There was a pause. "'Bout thirty miles, I'd say."

"Okay. Thanks." I hung up the phone and told Isis. "It's too far to hitch. But I don't think I can make it to Atkins in those shoes, not without doing some damage to my feet."

"Wait a minute," she said. "We met somebody at the Gathering . . . a cou-ple, I think . . . they said if we needed any help between Troutville and Pearis-burg . . ."

"Walrus and Roots!" I exclaimed. I could picture them clearly. Walrus was a dark-haired, middle-aged man with horn-rimmed glasses and a mustache that gave him a passing resemblance to his namesake. Roots was tall and slen-der, with short gray hair and bright blue eyes. We'd had a brief conversation with them after a workshop at the Gathering. I remembered their thoughtful comments and their wacky senses of humor.

"I'm sure they could help us out," Isis said.

"I've got their number here somewhere . . ." I leafed through the back pages of the notebook I used as a journal. "Here we go."

The phone rang a few times and a man's voice answered.

"Hello. Walrus?" I said, fervently hoping I had the right number. There was a moment of silence. "Uh, Walrus, this is jackrabbit. We met at the Gathering . . ."

"Jackrabbit of the Barefoot Sisters? How are you? *Where* are you?"

I gave a quiet sigh of relief and explained my predicament to him.

"Well, you called at a good time, jackrabbit. Karen—Roots—is working the night shift right now, but then she's got three days off. I just finished up a painting job, so I'll be free for the next couple of days, too. I can pick you guys up in the morning to resupply and get those boots. If you want to take a zero tomorrow, you're welcome to stay with us. It's good to hear from you again. We've been wondering about you guys."

"Thanks so much. You're a true angel, Walrus. It'll be great to see you and Roots again." I gave him the location of our motel. "See you tomorrow, then. Bye."

After I hung up the phone, I found myself smiling so broadly my cheeks hurt. "People are so *good* to us out here," I said to Isis. "Those trail angels sharing their food. A total stranger taking us out to dinner. People we met for five minutes inviting us into their home."

"I think people are usually good, if you give them half a chance. I think our basic instinct is to help each other out."

"I guess so. I wouldn't have believed it before the Trail, but now I'm starting to."

Walrus came to the motel early in the morning, and we stowed our packs and hiking sticks in the back of his truck among paint cans and drop cloths. We went to breakfast at Gillie's, a vegetarian restaurant in Blacksburg. Over huge plates of scrambled eggs, home fries, salsa, and biscuits, we told Walrus about the last few months of our hike.

"I'd love to see the northern part of the Trail," he said. "When Karen and I hiked, we only got as far as Harpers Ferry. It took us six months to get there from Georgia."

"You must have seen a lot along the way," Isis said.

"Yeah, we had a great time out there. Karen's got back problems, though, and we couldn't go more than seven, eight miles a day. I had a hard time with it at first, because I had such a desire to finish the Trail. But I decided, you know, this is the woman I love, the woman I want to spend the rest of my life with. I can't let a little thing like pace get in our way."

Isis and I nodded. Our biggest disagreements on the Trail had been about pace; she wanted to slow down and enjoy the views, and I wanted to go faster to finish the Trail. We always reached a compromise, because we both knew that our bond as sisters was more important and lasting than any argument.

"We got up to Harpers Ferry," Walrus continued, "and winter was coming on. We decided to get off, and this area was about the nicest place we'd seen to settle down. I got a job as a contractor and Karen went back to nursing. We've been here ever since."

"When did you hike?" I asked.

"Ninety-six."

"Do you ever think about going back out there?"

"Oh, I'd love to. I know we will. We've got to put the kids through college first, though."

"Best of luck."

We settled the tab at Gillie's and headed for the outfitter's store. I bought boots, finally, real leather boots that came up over my ankles. They were Garmonts, the same brand Isis had bought, and the only kind that actually fit my broad, exceptionally high-arched feet. We also invested in knee-high gaiters to keep the snow out of our boots. The salesman was a guy in his mid-twenties who had thru-hiked northbound in '99. He listened to our stories of Trail life with a wistful expression on his freckled face.

"I miss the Trail," he said. "Every day I miss it. Sometimes when I'm walking in town somewhere, I'll catch myself looking up, scanning the buildings and telephone poles, and I realize I'm looking for a blaze . . ." He looked pensive for a moment and then laughed and returned to a more salesman-like demeanor. "Is there anything else I can get for you?"

"Actually, we were wondering about snowshoes," Isis said. There was a display of them on the wall beside the boots. These snowshoes were nothing like the wood-and-rawhide ones I'd used as a child; made from polished aluminum and brightly colored plastic, they looked streamlined and modern. Isis and I had talked about buying them a few times—considering the weather we'd had so far, we knew we might need them before the end of winter. This store had the best selection we'd seen yet.

The salesman considered for a moment. "The place where you'll probably run into the most snow is the Grayson Highlands, north of Damascus. That, and the Roan Highlands in Tennessee. Smokies, too, depending on when you get there. I've done some winter hiking in all those areas. It can get pretty rough. Snowshoes might be a good idea."

I had a sudden memory of summer in Maine, everything green and humming with life, my bare feet in the mud. There had been a time when I had imagined doing the whole Trail barefoot. Here I was, buying not only boots but snowshoes. "What kind would you recommend?"

"Well, the best ones we have for backpacking are actually out of stock right now. Those ones on the wall are all metal-frame, and they're six, eight, ten pounds a pair. If you're carrying a lot of weight, you want something lighter on your feet. Something like . . ." he picked up a catalog from the counter and leafed through it. "Like these." He indicated a pair of snowshoes made from molded red plastic, with small ridges of steel along the edges for traction and crampons under the feet. "MSR Denali model. The pair weighs about four pounds. I use these myself. They've got awesome traction. They're kind of expensive . . . I might be able to wrangle you some kind of discount, though."

"Can you ship them to us on the Trail?" I asked.

"Where are your mail drops?" He seemed thrilled to be using hiker terminology again.

"We'll be in Atkins in six days, Damascus a week after that."

"Hmm. They usually arrive in about ten days. I can send 'em to Damascus. You'll have to go through Grayson without 'em, but you'll have 'em for Roan and the Smokies."

"I guess that's what we'd better do." We arranged for the snowshoes to be shipped, and we left the store poorer but better prepared to face the onslaught of winter. It was strange to walk in boots. On the thick, cushioned soles, I felt like I was floating a little ways above the slushy sidewalks of Blacksburg.

Walrus took us to the grocery store for our resupply, and he and Roots cooked a feast for us that night: pasta with fresh tomato sauce and a big green salad. Isis made French bread and brought out a wheel of Brie she had bought at the market. We sat around the table late into the night, telling stories and reminiscing. More snow fell, white and thick and silent, leaving the landscape outside the windows soft-edged. I felt safe and content, for once, and that evening prepared me to go back out and face winter.

We spent the morning gathering a few last-minute items: lithium batteries for Isis's headlamp, and some cheese and fresh bread for the first few days. It was noon by the time we started hiking. The sun barely skimmed above the trees; our shadows were long and blue across the new snow.

"It's winter solstice," Isis said. "Shortest day of the year."

"That's right. First day of winter. Man, it's felt like winter ever since we left Harpers Ferry. How much worse can it get?"

"You say that every time we leave town, and every time it gets worse."

"But we go on anyway. We've been snowed on, sleeted on, iced into a shelter for two days. Every week we get into town, and we say to ourselves, 'that was nasty, but we've come this far; maybe we can make it a little farther.' Then we eat a bunch of town food, and we take showers and dry out in a warm room, maybe watch *Crocodile Hunter*, and we say, 'well, it's really not so bad.' Then we go back out." I laughed. "Are we crazy or what?"

"Of course we're crazy. We're the Barefoot Sisters."

The trail turned sharply uphill. I remembered the profile map: a steady, steep two-mile climb. "Isis, I'm going to take a few layers off. This hill keeps going for a ways." I stopped by the side of the trail and unshouldered my pack.

A mischievous glint came into my sister's eyes. "You know the thru-hiker tradition for *summer* solstice, don't you?"

"It's way too cold to hike naked!" Several northbounders had told me about the custom of hiking *au naturale* on June 21. I'd never thought it would apply to December 21 as well.

"Well, we couldn't go totally naked. But maybe on the uphill we could hike topless . . ."

"What if somebody comes along?"

"Do *you* see any footprints on this trail?"

"Well, no, but . . ."

"C'mon, it'll be fun."

"Okay . . ." And that was how we found ourselves hiking out of Pearisburg clad in nothing but wind pants, boots, and gaiters. It was an odd sensation. The effort of climbing kept me just barely warm. Cold air brushed against my ribcage, rushing down my back between my pack straps with every step. It did feel liberating, but I knew I would be mortified if anyone came along. *Being caught naked in a temperate season is a bit embarrassing*, I thought to myself. *Being caught naked in this weather is risking a trip to the loony bin*. But the trail was empty; the only footprints were the ones we left behind us. We climbed steadily toward the ridge top, where the level terrain and the cold wind made us put our upper layers back on in short order. By that time I was glad to be wearing a shirt again—my breasts felt like twin lumps of ice. I was doubly glad we had reclothed ourselves when, a few minutes later, we came around a bend in the trail and met a family bundled in winter coats. The youngest child looked to be about seven.

The father carried a large rifle. "Y'all seen any bears?" he asked by way of greeting.

"Nope, sorry." I could tell Isis was trying hard to keep a straight face: *none but us*.

We spent the night at Doc's Knob Shelter, a small wooden lean-to at the end of the ridge above Pearisburg. The spring was one of the most beautiful I had seen yet; water welled up in a crevice between dark boulders under a hemlock tree. The water seemed to be lit from within, filled with golden sparks, as it caught the last sunlight. *Solstice*, I thought as I filtered our drinking water. *The light is coming back. Spring is somewhere under the earth, waiting*.

At my mother's house, we had celebrated the return of the sun every year by burning a brush pile in the backyard—an appropriately Pagan way to mark the Northern Hemisphere's most ancient holiday. We would invite friends and neighbors to drink mulled cider and dance around the bonfire with drums, welcoming back the light.

Isis and I tried to make a bonfire that night at Doc's Knob, but all the wood we could find was coated with layers of ice and wet, sticky snow. It was all we could do to light the Zip stove, even though its fan blew air onto the coals. We managed to keep the stove burning long enough to cook supper and make our tea. Our attempted bonfire smoldered out the minute my back was turned. The fire sputtered up from the wrinkled scraps of paper we used as tinder, refusing to take hold of the kindling. At twilight I went to look for drier wood, perhaps a standing dead tree or a fallen branch that had stayed above the snow layer. When I returned, not even a hint of smoke rose from the half-charred wood in the firepit. It was the first time in six months, I realized, that we had tried to build a fire and failed.

I lay awake, bundled in my sleeping bag, for a long time. I wondered what this season would bring, and I worried. *The worst winter in fourteen years*, I remembered Larry saying. And that was before it had officially started.

CHAPTER 9

The Scales

Isis

We reached Helvey's Mill Shelter at dusk, after nineteen miles of bumpy ridgeline. We'd planned the long day to set us up for an easy fourteen the next day, which would be Christmas Eve. Jackrabbit usually got our water while I cooked, but that night her knee hurt so badly that I offered to make the steep trek down the stream trail. I set off in the gathering dusk with all six of our water bottles in my arms and our filter tucked into an inner pocket of my jacket. Lately, water had become almost as difficult to find as it had been on the dry Pennsylvania ridges. Half of the springs and streams marked on our map were frozen over, or dry, or buried under snow. A few times, we'd even had to melt snow for cooking and drinking. Our water filter became clogged with ice when the temperature dropped too far below freezing. On particularly cold days, jackrabbit and I had taken to carrying the filter under our shirts, between the hip belt and the chest straps of our packs. At night, we took turns sleeping with it to keep it warm, for which I nicknamed it "Don Juan."

I had high hopes for the Helvey's Mill water source. It looked like it would be a half-mile hike downhill from the shelter, but the distance hardly mattered given the prospect of open water. On the map, the thin blue line indicating the stream flowed down a mile of valley before the trail from the shelter intersected it. The curve of ridge looked like enough of a watershed to form a deep, strong-flowing stream, one that wouldn't be likely to have frozen over entirely.

In the time it took me to negotiate the stream trail's half dozen switchbacks, the sky changed from deep blue, with a single evening star hanging among the pines, to pitch black. The trail ended at a steep rocky bank. To either side of me, an arched tunnel of rhododendron branches curved away into the darkness, floored with jumbled, snow-covered stones. *This must be the streambed*, I thought, *but where's the stream?* I searched up and down the banks, but there was no sign of a continuing trail and no sign of water. Finally, I turned off my headlamp, closed my eyes, and held my hands up behind my ears to catch the slightest sound. I turned my head upstream—nothing. Downstream, it was hard to tell whether I heard the faint trickle of water over stone, or whether my wishful mind had invented the sound.

I started downhill, stumbling among the slippery rocks. After a few hundred yards, I put my hands to the backs of my ears again. This time I was certain. I found the pool beneath an overhang of the bank. A semicircular opening in a crust of ice, perhaps two feet in diameter, revealed a ledge of stone covered in a thin sheet of flowing water, half an inch at its deepest point. At the edge of the pool, the water trickled over a seven- or eight-inch drop and disappeared beneath another sheet of ice. I could tell it wasn't deep enough to submerge Don Juan's intake valve; we'd have to purify it by boiling. I tried to dip a water bottle in the pool, but it was too shallow to get the rim beneath the surface. I stomped on the ice, both above and below the opening, hoping to break it and find deeper water underneath, but I only succeeded in stirring up mud. Once the mud settled, I held a bottle to the edge of the rock. Only a few scant drops trickled into it. In exasperation, I grabbed one of the other bottles and scraped it across the ledge, pushing a wave of water into the open bottle. It worked, though slowly. Most of the water missed the bottle and splashed over my ungloved hand; I had to stop every five minutes and stick my hand in my armpit to thaw my aching fingers. When I staggered up to the shelter, laden with the six full bottles, I found jackrabbit tying our first aid kit to her belt. She looked up, her face ghostly white in the light of my headlamp.

"Are you okay? I was about to go looking for you."

I set down the bottles and flopped on my back on the shelter floor. "I'm okay. But this is the last time I'm trading chores with you!"

For the first few miles of the next day, we played with verses of popular Christmas carols, making them applicable to the Trail.

> We a pair of white-blazers are
> Bearing packs, we've traversed afar

sang jackrabbit, and I answered,

Field and fountain, lots of mountains,
Always by foot, not car. Oh, oh . . .

When I paused, she sang back the rest of the verse.

Yellow-blazing sure looks good;
Brings us fast to yummy food.
Food, warmth, laundry: here's the quandary—
Why are we in the woods?

(Yellow-blazing was a hiker euphemism for skipping part of the Trail by hitchhiking, following the yellow "blazes" of the road.)

I thought for a few minutes and decided to tackle a new song:

Silent night-hike, oh-so-cold night-hike,
My food is gone, except things I dislike.
My once-burgeoning food bag's now thin
Only Pop Tarts and ramen therein,
So I'm going to to-own, so-o I'm going to town.

On the steeper uphills, when singing took too much of our wind, we talked about what we would do to celebrate Christmas. I'd kept one pair of socks clean so that we could use them as stockings. I'd bought two oranges and a couple packages of fancy chocolates when jackrabbit wasn't looking. By way of gifts, we'd written each other spoofs of some of the long poems we had memorized. Jackrabbit had been working on a hiker version of Poe's "The Raven" since New York, and I'd started writing a take-off on Alfred Noyes's "The Highwayman," starring jackrabbit and Tuba Man, just after the Gathering. It had been quite a challenge to keep them secret for so long. Every time I came up with a clever verse, I wanted to recite it to her, and every time I heard her giggling over her notebook, I was tempted to ask what she'd written. Now, she announced that she'd finished her poem and was coming up with a new one, a spoof of "The Night Before Christmas."

"Think about the lines '. . . and what to my wondering eyes should appear but a miniature sleigh and eight tiny reindeer,'" she said. "Isn't that a bizarre image?"

She laughed to herself and wouldn't tell me anything more.

After lunch, we didn't talk much. Jackrabbit walked ahead of me, seemingly lost in thought; as the afternoon wore on she moved more and more slowly. I wondered if she was too busy coming up with her new poem to pay attention to our pace—something she usually cared about a lot more than I did. I hesitated to interrupt her versifying, but I wanted to get to the shelter early enough to decorate it for the holiday.

"Hey, jackrabbit," I called.

She answered with the slightest shrug of her shoulders.

"Could we go a little faster? I want to . . ."

She rounded on me, her face contorted with fury. "I'm walking as fast as I can! My fucking knee is fucking killing me. If you want to go faster, go ahead."

"I'm sorry," I answered. "I didn't know you were in pain, I thought you were just walking slowly because . . ."

"The only reason I *ever* walk slowly is because I'm in pain. Go ahead. Go *away!*"

I strode past her, gripping my hiking sticks so hard my knuckles ached. I didn't know why she'd snapped at me, and for the moment I was too angry to care. Even though I was choking back tears, I stormed up the hillside at a pace that was almost a run. As I neared the top of the hill, a fierce surge of pride broke through my anger. Here I was, running uphill while crying . . . as far back as I could remember, I'd been brought to tears easily, and crying usually incapacitated me. This time, it wasn't even slowing me down. I thought of the day we'd started south from Katahdin, when I'd sat down in the middle of the trail, crying, and jackrabbit had to spend ten minutes comforting me before we could go on. For weeks afterward, I'd been so afraid of getting left behind that I'd begged jackrabbit to let me walk ahead of her all the time. She hadn't been entirely happy, staring at my heels all day, but this was, after all, something we'd both anticipated. I was the weak one; some accommodations would have to be made.

Suddenly, I understood why she had lost her temper when I'd asked if she could go faster. Contrary to both our expectations, I had grown strong on the Trail. My body adapted to whatever I asked of it—notches, cold rain, hunger, consecutive twenties—with a minimum of complaint. The most pain I'd experienced had been while breaking in my boots, and that had only lasted for one evening. I remembered the feeling of walking in a nightmare I couldn't wake from; the memory alone made me shiver. How often had jackrabbit walked in the shadow of such pain? I knew that the same challenges that had strengthened me had injured her, over and over again.

By the time I got to Jenkins Shelter, my indignation had faded, giving way to worry. I shouldn't have left her, even if she told me to. What if she fell and got injured? I was carrying the first aid kit. I had all the snack food, too, and an extra bottle of water. To stave off my fears, I gathered some pine and hemlock branches and twisted them into a wreath. I hung it under the shelter sign, and then, as an afterthought, tore a strip from the bottom of my red handkerchief and made a bow. Just as I finished, jackrabbit limped into camp.

"That looks nice." She attempted a smile, but it ended up more like a grimace. I noticed heavy blue shadows under her eyes. "Listen, I'm sorry I jumped on you."

"I'll forgive you, just this once," I said, giving her a hug. "It's Christmas Eve."

As I stepped back, I saw her eyes light up with a hint of their old sparkle. "That reminds me!" she said. "Where's the register? I've finished my Santa poem. I want to write it down before I forget it."

I searched the back corners of the shelter and unearthed a green spiral-bound notebook from a pile of Mormon and Jehovah's Witness proselytizing pamphlets. As I handed it to jackrabbit, I caught sight of the names and address on the back cover.

"Pilgrim and Gollum! It's a Pilgrim and Gollum register!"

This time jackrabbit gave me a real smile. "Excellent!"

In most places along the Trail, shelter registers were replaced by hikers. Many carried spare notebooks on spec; if you were lucky enough to find a shelter with a full register, you could replace it with your own. You would then carry the full register to the next town and mail it to the hiker whose address appeared on the back. If your notebook stood up to a season's worth of weather, grime, and rodents, the tattered chronicle of a few hundred hikers' jokes and complaints would eventually arrive in your mailbox.

Pilgrim and Gollum had been entertaining us for months; finding a register that belonged to them was the only way that we could return the favor. Also, I noticed as jackrabbit flipped through the pages, both of them had written long introductory entries in the front of the notebook: something to look forward to reading that night. It was the perfect Christmas gift.

"Maybe we should give that Jehovah's Witness pamphlet another look," jackrabbit joked. "Miracles happen."

"'Tis the season," I answered. "Return of the light, by whatever name you call it."

While jackrabbit wrote, I went looking for water. To my delight, I found a deep, open stream not fifty yards from the shelter. A few late golden sunbeams slanted through the snowy hemlocks on its banks. The evening air, above freezing for the first time in a week, felt surprisingly warm. I stripped to the waist and rinsed quickly—not that the icy water would take off much of the accumulated sweat and wood smoke, but the rush of blood to my skin as the water evaporated felt as renewing as a hot shower.

When I returned to the shelter, jackrabbit was busy making a swag of hemlock boughs, decorated with bows of the blaze-orange survey tape we'd worn on our hiking poles in hunting season. She hung the branches along the back wall of the shelter, while I tied my clean socks to two separate mouse hangers, labeling them "I" and "J" with strips of duct tape. Jackrabbit helped me gather firewood. Together, we cooked the meal we'd saved for the occasion: polenta mixed with instant refried beans, dried tomatoes, and parmesan cheese. As we sat in our sleeping bags drinking cocoa after supper, jackrabbit read aloud from the register, first Gollum and Pilgrim's entries, then Waterfall's, Heald's, Black Forest's, and finally her own.

> 'Twas the night before Christmas, and all through the shelter
> the rodents were running about, helter-skelter.
> Our food bags were hung from mouse hangers with care
> in hopes that the buggers could not get up there,
> and Isis and I in our polypro caps
> had just settled our brains for a long winter's nap,
> when up on the roof there arose such a clatter
> I jumped from my bag to see what was the matter.
> And what to my wondering eyes should appear,
> but a miniature sleigh and eight tiny reindeer,
> and Santa was there, too, just four inches tall!
> "Good gracious!" I blurted. "How'd you get so small?"
> St. Nick shed a tear—it was sad to behold—
> and gathered his courage, and solemnly told
> how a bunch of mad scientists, early that day
> had caught him and his reindeer in their Shrinking Ray.
> "So now," Santa moaned with an audible sniff,
> "it's obvious I can't deliver my gifts,
> unless someone helps me out, me and my deer.
> And now you know, jackrabbit, that's why I'm here.
> I've heard hikers are an ingenious lot,
> who jury-rig pack frames, and straps, and what-not . . ."

"Don't fret, Santa!" I said. "It happens that I
have a science degree too. I'll give it a try."
And I used all the cells in my brain to devise
some method to bring Santa Claus back to size . . .
"Eureka!" I cried, and I built a machine
the likes of which on earth has never been seen:
some pieces of foil in Ziplocs (well-sealed)
I used to correct for the magnetic field.
The neutron-colliding reactor I strove
to assemble with Shoe-goo and parts from my stove.
My trusty white Photon provided the beam
that would re-enlarge Santa and his reindeer team . . .
KAZAM! The Enlarging Ray worked like a charm
and Santa and team were restored without harm.
"A miracle! How can I thank you?" he said.
"You could slack me to Springer on that reindeer sled!"
So if you see reindeer aloft in the sky
weeks after Christmas, well, now you know why!
And thus ends my rhyme, which I hope people like.
Merry Christmas to all, and to all a good hike!

jackrabbit

We woke in the predawn darkness, as usual. Stars glimmered between the branches, swimming into focus as I put on my glasses. The metal of the earpieces burned with cold. I put on all my upper layers—Capilene shirt, wool shirt, sweater, fleece, Gore-Tex jacket—while keeping my legs warm in my sleeping bag. Then I slipped my hands into liner gloves, braided my hair, tied on my fleece hat, and pulled on my outer gloves. The process took perhaps a minute; I had learned to dress quickly in the weeks of cold.

"Merry Christmas," Isis whispered. She turned on her headlamp and shone the pale blue beam on the mouse hangers dangling from the rafters. The green socks we had hung up empty the night before now bulged with mysterious lumps. "Looks like Santa came."

I had forgotten what day it was. Sitting in my sleeping bag in the dark shelter, I thought of the Christmas mornings of my childhood: breakfast with the whole family, a warm fire in the wood stove, a tree laden with mismatched ornaments, and the presents piled beneath it in their bright paper. I remembered lying awake in the early morning, wide-eyed with excitement, waiting for my sisters to get up so we could open our stockings. Even after our parents divorced, when we spent half the day at our mother's house and half at our dad's, Christmas had been a family celebration. Now it was just the two of us, in a shelter miles from the nearest road. I reached over and hugged my sister, feeling stiff and clumsy inside many layers of clothing.

"Well, aren't you going to open your stocking?"

I took the socks down from the mouse hangers. "This one has a J on it; I guess it's for me." I extracted the loot: an orange, a few chocolate coins, some dried fruit, and a Snickers bar. "Why is Santa sending us Snickers bars? You don't suppose *he* wants to get in on the action . . ."

"You never know," Isis said as she bit into a chocolate half-dollar. "It gets pretty cold and lonely up there at the North Pole."

"Sicko!" I tossed an orange peel at her.

She laughed. "The oranges might be a little frozen." They were, but they tasted wonderful.

By the light of our headlamps, we ate our Christmas breakfast. It was nothing like the feasts of citron buns, scrambled eggs, tempeh bacon, fruit salad, and orange juice that I remembered from Christmases past, but in its own way it was just as good. In our last mail drop, our dad had sent home-made granola. We ate it with powdered milk and our mom's dehydrated cran-berries. I felt close to our whole family, even though they were more than a thousand miles away. Even our half sister Claire was there in spirit; I had hung my socks to dry over the ends of my hiking sticks the night before, and the way they had frozen reminded me of her long, graceful feet propped up on the end of a couch. I could easily picture Claire's stunning freckled face, her eyebrows delicately arched with humor or genteel disdain. Our younger half sister was a hedonist who didn't suffer fools gladly. *Would she think we're foolish to be here?* I wondered. *Are we?* We ate quickly in the cold. The last of the milk froze to the cup, and I chipped it out with my spoon.

The leaves of the rhododendrons near the shelter were curled tight as pencils, so I left my long underwear on beneath my Gore-Tex pants and only took off a few of my top layers. Then I pulled my frozen boots over my feet and buckled my high gaiters. It was still dark when we started down the trail, with stars caught in the branches, though a thin spiderwebbing of blue light crept between the trees on the eastern horizon.

Dawn came slowly to the ridges, a gradual, barely perceptible brighten-ing. For the first time in quite a while, we began to see traces of footprints on the trail ahead of us. There were many pairs, large and small, making the passage easier as we struggled along the snow-covered ridgeline of Garden Mountain.

"I wonder whose tracks these are," Isis said.

"Probably another family out bear-hunting," I said. But the tracks continued all day, following the white blazes along the bumpy top of the ridge. Though it had looked almost level on the elevation profile, in reality the ridge top consisted of countless ups and downs of maybe fifty feet, sometimes steep and difficult in the snow. In places where new drifts covered the footprints, I thought longingly of the snowshoes we had ordered in Pearisburg: *another week, and we'll be able to float over trails like this.*

Down through the bare trees, we could see the valleys on either side. To the left, the long, sinuous ridge of Walker Mountain rose up parallel to the ridge we followed, and the low land between them was a patchwork of fields and houses, a small grid of roads. Half-frozen creeks sent back glints of reflected light, startlingly bright. On the right-hand side was the neat circular depression of Burke's Garden, hemmed in on all sides by mountains. A few red barns and silos, small and perfect as toys, stood in the snow-covered fields far below.

In early afternoon, we came to a steep climb up the end of a narrow ridge to Chestnut Knob. A chill, steady wind blew out of Burke's Garden. The right side of my face felt numb after a few minutes of climbing. The snow dragged at my feet, and I could feel my tired thigh muscles protesting against the long uphill. *I've gotten lazy,* I thought to myself. *I can't handle a climb without switchbacks any more. This is only a mile. One measly mile, one thousand piddling feet of elevation gain. How hard can it be?* We trudged onward, upward, in the knee-deep snow. Only the footprints made the climb bearable. *Somebody else has done this recently. A bunch of small somebodies, it looks like.* I wondered again who it might be. We had followed the tracks for ten miles now—a pretty long ways for a family dayhike—and we were still five miles from the nearest road.

At last we came out onto the bald summit of Chestnut Knob. The horizon opened out around us, a panoply of long ridges gleaming in the sun. The snow between the trees highlighted the forms of the mountains, the endless self-similar contours of ridge and spur, gap and hollow and valley. The wide sky arced above us, with tiny wisps of cloud moving westward overhead.

A shelter stood in the middle of the bald, a small building of mortared stones. Inside, the chill of shadows hung in the corners. The wind somehow found its way through the cracks, rustling the mouse nests of shredded paper in the corners of the rafters.

"I think it's warmer outside," Isis said, and I had to agree. We ate our lunch on the downwind side of the building, sitting on our packs above the snowdrifts.

Isis looked over at me. "Jackrabbit, is your face okay?"

"Last time I checked. What, am I growing a third eyeball or something?"

"No, but you have this white patch on your cheek . . . Your ear doesn't look so good, either."

I took off a glove and touched my right cheek. It was numb and felt like ice under my fingers. Not good. My ear was cold, too, and along the outer rim I couldn't even feel the touch of my fingers. "You're right. I think I got a bit of frostnip. Man, I didn't realize it was *that* cold."

"We've got to be more careful from now on," Isis said, in her older-sister-takes-charge voice. For an instant I was tempted to fire back an angry retort, but there wasn't anything I could say to defend myself. It was my own fault I hadn't noticed the cold and put a hat on, or pulled a handkerchief over my face. Besides, it was Christmas. I didn't want to start an argument.

The bright sun bouncing off the wall of the shelter and the snow all around felt almost warm. I leaned back against the stone wall, savoring the warmth of the sun. A small consolation; with the relative heat of our lunch spot, perhaps my hands and feet wouldn't get that pins-and-needles feeling in the afternoon. Though my ear and cheek began throbbing painfully as they thawed, the rest of me appreciated the respite from the cold.

"We'd better get going," Isis said, almost apologetically. "We've got to cover another nine miles."

"Yeah." I yawned and stretched, and rose to my feet, feeling the persistent creak of hiker hobble settling into my joints. I had been sitting still for too long. "Wait a sec, though. There's something I want to do before we go." I went back into the shelter, and Isis followed. "I bet this place has great acoustics." In the echoing stone interior, we sang our favorite Christmas songs.

Our Christmas day ended as it had begun, under the stars. Darkness overtook us on the trail several miles short of the shelter. By the pale light of our headlamps, we followed the blazes over a few more small, bumpy ridges and up into the rhododendron thickets of Knot Maul Branch. With snow covering the branches and sticking to the tree trunks, it was much harder to find our way after dark—white blazes blended into the white background. The steady line of footsteps that had led us over the ridges continued, though, all the way to the shelter.

The spring was frozen over, lost under deep drifts. I gathered extra wood for the stove, and Isis melted snow for dinner and the next day's water while I read the register aloud for entertainment. I was gratified to find out that Lash and Black Forest, though now almost a week ahead of us, had done exactly the same mileage on the day they arrived here.

The Deathmarch to Springer continues, Black Forest had written in his slanted, almost illegible hand. *Our heroes are almost frozen. They are brokenhearted of missing the company of barefoot women, yet they continue. Isis and jackrabbit—you have my heart. If you will catch up I will give you my liver also.*

Isis laughed. "Those boys!"

"The Deathmarch to Springer seems to be going better than the Maryland Challenge," I said. I remembered the day we'd found them at Tumbling Run Shelter, still in their sleeping bags, on the morning after their Half-gallon Challenge. I wished for an instant that we would find them again, lying in a shelter somewhere, waiting for us. *They're a week ahead now,* I told myself, and put the thought out of my mind. I decided to focus on Tuba Man instead. *It's probably better in the long run to hope for the unattainable than the unlikely. If I know from the beginning that it's impossible, I won't be disappointed.*

The next day's hike was exasperating. Instead of following the ridge tops, as the trail had almost all the way through Virginia, it crossed a series of low ridges that reminded me of the Roller Coaster south of Bear's Den Hostel. I lost count of the ups and downs fairly quickly. The most annoying thing, though, was that we seemed to climb straight up the back of every lump, without a switchback in sight, while the downhills were gradual and winding. The deep snow had drifted overnight, obscuring the line of footsteps we had followed.

Although today was a short day—only fourteen miles, compared to yesterday's nineteen—it seemed to take longer. Shadows were already collecting in the hollows when we stopped for an afternoon snack at the Davis Path Shelter, two and a half miles from the road into Atkins.

"Is it just me, or was that trail route gratuitously lumpy?" Isis asked as she threw down her pack.

"It's better than saying we're getting soft."

She lobbed a snowball in my direction. "Who says we're getting soft? We're still on the Trail, aren't we?"

I dropped my pack and thumbed through the register. "Hey, Tuba Man signed in here!" He didn't always leave messages in the registers; when he did, it seemed like a small gift. I immediately recognized his sprawling, untidy handwriting, decorated with smiley faces. "Listen to this, Isis! 'Hey, what's with this trail? The last twelve miles of this felt like twenty-five in Pennsylvania . . .' Even *Tuba Man* had a hard time here. I guess I don't feel so bad."

Isis laughed. "You and your Tuba fixation. It's going to get you into trouble one of these days."

Evening shadows filled the valley by the time we reached the road into Atkins. Cars sped past, spattering us with road grime and slush, their headlights blindingly bright. I didn't mind too much; soon we would be in a warm hotel room. We'd take showers, order pizza. Maybe the Crocodile Hunter would be on. In the morning, we'd hitch to the market for our resupply and start the whole crazy cycle again. I decided not to think about the following week. I would just focus on tonight: *Warm room. Pizza. Shower.*

We checked in at the motel lobby, where the scent of potpourri was thick and cloying in the air. I'm sure our own scent was just as thick, but in the time we had spent on the Trail—more than six months now—I had ceased to notice the hiker funk we exuded. As the desk clerk handed the key to Isis, I heard a wild shriek of excitement behind us. Several half-size, fleece-clad figures were rushing across the room.

"Isis! Jackrabbit!"

"Hope! Joy! John! Joel!" We knelt down to hug them, and soon we were buried in a pile of children. They all looked healthy and strong, and taller than I remembered. "How *are* you guys? We never thought we'd catch up with you!"

Joy stuck out her chin and grinned proudly. "We're doing really good. We hiked all the way from Knot Maul yesterday—"

"And today we're takin' a zero day with our friend Dachs," Hope said, her green eyes bright. "Oh, I'm so glad you guys came!"

"Dachs is a trail angel," John said with the seriousness I remembered. Then he jumped in the air and twirled around, shouting, "Isis and jackrabbit are back! Isis and jackrabbit are back!"

"Isis and jackrabbit?" came a soft voice from the doorway. I glanced up. Mary looked like a ghost of her former self. She'd been skinny in Pennsylvania; now she was positively skeletal. The blue veins in her face and hands stood out under the pale skin.

"Mary! Are you okay?" Isis asked her.

"Oh, yeah, I'm fine. Around Harpers Ferry I felt a little weak 'cause I'd lost some weight, but we've been going slowly ever since then. I'm feeling much better." Her smile was as charming and frank as I remembered.

If she was feeling better now, I hated to think what she had looked like at her worst. "I'm so glad we caught up with you guys!" I said, smiling back.

"Me, too. I missed you."

We heard tiny footsteps pattering down the hall. "Mommy, gack-a-wab-bit? Isis?" Faith toddled up to us. "Isis! Isis! Gack-a-wabbit!" She made a chant out of our names and danced in time to it.

"Look who else missed you," Mary leaned down and picked up her youngest daughter.

"She's getting so big!" I said. "And walking around, too. The last time we saw you guys, she was just a baby."

Mary gave a wan smile. "A lot can happen in two months."

She invited us back to the Family's room. Barely a square inch of the brown carpet showed between the heaps of scattered clothing, equipment, and food. The beds, too, were stacked high with packs and gear.

Paul nodded as we came in. "Good to see you two again. I was wondering when you'd catch up." He looked thinner, too, his cheeks hollow and the wiry muscles like cords under his tanned skin. His dark eyes had the same forceful gaze that had struck me when we first met. His smile, though, was genuine and full of warmth.

"It's great to see you," I said.

We made plans to stay together for the next week. In the snow, the Family was hiking eight or ten miles a day, about half the mileage that Isis and I had been doing. I was ready to slow down for a while, though. We had little chance of catching Lash and Black Forest. There was no longer any point in hiking fast to stay ahead of winter—the winter had caught up with us long ago. We stayed up late that night, laughing and singing and telling stories with the children. It was wonderful to be part of a group again.

After a filling breakfast at the hotel restaurant in the morning, Isis and I met the trail angel Dachs. He was a thin man with graying short hair and a contemplative manner. We gladly accepted his offer of a ride to the grocery store.

"So you've been helping the Family out?" I asked as we sped down the road. White fields and gray forests whizzed past.

"They've helped me, too," Dachs answered. "I met them for the first time when I was section hiking up in Vermont. I spent the night with them at a shelter, and I just thought, this is what a family is supposed to be. They all get along, they're kind to each other, they work together. I thought, if I could be like that with my kids . . . At that point, my eldest son hadn't spoken to me for two years. Seeing the Family from the North, I realized what I was missing. I called him up that night. I wouldn't say we're exactly best friends now, but he talks to me. Last week *he* actually called *me*. . . It was this family that set it all in motion. I've bought them some gear, and food, but compared to what they've given me, it's nothing." He was quiet for a moment. The snowy Virginia landscape rolled by outside the window, bare trees and empty fields, houses and hedgerows.

"Here's the grocery store." He pulled into the parking lot.

"Thanks for your help, Dachs," I said. "And thanks for everything you've done for the Family. I know they appreciate it."

He smiled. "I know they'd be out here whether or not I helped them. They're all pretty extraordinary people. And like I said, what I've given them pales in comparison to what I've learned from them. I give them material things, boots and packs and a stove; they gave me my son back."

Isis

We had two reasons to look forward to Partnership Shelter. First of all, we'd be meeting the Family there. The prospect of another evening in their company made even the clumps of wet snow that slid off the rhododendron leaves and down the backs of our necks seem bearable. Second, Partnership, a two-story timber frame building behind the headquarters of the Mount Rogers National Recreation Area, was famed as one of the few shelters on the Trail from which one could order pizza and get it delivered.

Hope, Joy, and John ran out to meet us in front of the shelter, accompanied by a familiar orange dog who was baring her teeth gleefully and thrashing her whole body back and forth in greeting.

"Annie?" said jackrabbit.

"Yup. That's her," came a gruff voice from under the shelter eaves. We looked up to see Heald and, right behind him, Netta.

The group of us ordered six large pizzas and a few subs from the pay phone behind the park headquarters (this time, I'd made sure to bring cash), and I sat down to chat with Netta while we waited for the food to arrive. She told me that Lash had gotten off the Trail for Christmas. He planned to return the next day, right here at Partnership, so he'd be close behind us. Black Forest had hiked on ahead, fast and alone. In Atkins, he'd received a letter from his grandparents, who were planning to spend a few weeks in Hawaii at the end of January. They invited him to join them, if he could finish the Trail by January 21.

"He decided to try." Netta shook her head, her dark curls bouncing. "He will have to average twenties . . . that means four twenty-fives if he ever takes a day off . . . and he will be all alone." She and Heald, Netta told me, had gotten so tired of being alone that they'd hiked four- and six-mile days for the past week, hoping we'd catch them.

The next morning, Mary and Paul set out early, followed by the children. Heald wanted to stay around the shelter for a few hours in case Lash showed up, so Netta, jackrabbit, and I hiked out together. The children had left us messages, scratched in snowbanks: our names framed in hearts, their own names beside sketches of stick figures with packs. This inspired us to leave notes to the people behind. *Happy Trails, Heald,* I wrote, and made a quick sketch of Annie beside the words. Jackrabbit, feeling more flirtatious, wrote *See you tonight, Lash,* with a heart.

"Poor Lashy-Lash," said Netta. "You are teasing him."

"'Lashy-Lash?' I like it," said jackrabbit, and she added an "y-Lash" to her snow message.

A few miles later, the Trail turned sharply up a steep embankment next to a tangle of snow-covered rhododendrons. In the relatively warm afternoon, the dark leaves had uncurled a little beneath their blanket of white. On cloudy winter days they looked black, but today, the sun shone on their glossy evergreen surfaces. Jackrabbit stopped, pointing to some more words beside the trail; Mary's neat blocky capitals spelled out *STOP. LOOK. LISTEN.*

All three of us stood still, looking out at the patch of rhododendrons. As the sound of our breathing grew quieter, a new sound reached my ears; beneath the snow and the leaves, a hidden brook laughed in its stony bed. We would never have noticed it over the noise of our own footsteps—even our breathing might have drowned it out. *Running water!* After all the dry springs and frozen streams, the sound alone filled me with delight.

We stayed at Raccoon Branch Shelter that night. Lash never showed up, but the rest of us had a wonderful evening. We all worked together to find wood. In about fifteen minutes we had a pile big enough for a bonfire. Some of the smallest people brought back the largest bundles of wood; at one point, I saw John dragging an entire fallen tree perhaps twenty feet long. Paul built the fire while Mary strung up a clothesline, and soon we were all sitting around the firepit, prodding the coals beneath our cooking pots, under three tiers of drying socks. After supper and a few songs, jackrabbit and I had tea with Mary and Netta. Our mom had sent us a tin of Christmas cookies in our Atkins mail drop; luckily, there were enough to share with everyone. I fell asleep feeling more peaceful and content than I'd felt in months. Jackrabbit and I were no longer alone. We had found our tribe.

jackrabbit

As we walked up toward the Grayson Highlands, the air grew colder and the snowdrifts deepened. We could see the trees on Iron Mountain, where we were headed, silvered with ice rime above about 3,500 feet.

We clambered over a stile, the bottom third of it buried in snow, and the Trail came out into a pasture. An abandoned school bus lay in the strip of woods between this field and the next, up to its rusted hubcaps in snow.

"See ya later," said Heald. "Me and Annie are gonna quit hiking and move in right here."

Joy laughed. "Heald's gonna live in a bus!"

"Beats walkin' in this weather." Heald reverted to his usual silence, but after a few footsteps he spoke again, a slow sarcastic grin coming over his face. "You know, if you hike in the winter, and your feet never touch the Trail 'cause of the snow, can you really say you've hiked the whole thing?"

I had an answer for that one. "If you hike in boots and never actually have skin contact with the Trail, can you say you've done it then?"

I heard Heald's rare chuckle over the sound of our boots crunching the snow. "You got a point there."

Isis

Later that afternoon, Hope and John walked with me and jackrabbit, while Netta and Mary brought up the rear. Hope was busy trying to decide where she wanted to live when she grew up (the Bahamas topped the list, but she also quizzed me and jackrabbit about Peru), when we came to a fallen tree maybe four inches in diameter, lying at waist height across the trail. Hope ducked under easily, followed by John, but they stopped on the other side and turned around.

"This is gonna be real hard for Mary," Hope said, frowning. "She can't bend down with Faithie on her back."

Both Hope and John seized hold of the tree and tugged it toward the side of the trail. Even when jackrabbit and I joined in, we got nowhere; there were too many small branches tangling the blowdown with the living trees around it. Finally I thought of the saw on my pocketknife. We all took turns sawing with a blade no longer than the trunk was wide, until we had cut it in two places and pushed the pieces off the trail.

"Mary's not the only one benefiting from that bit of trail maintenance," jackrabbit told the children. "It's really going to help my knees, not to have to duck under that tree. Wish I had you guys around all the time."

John looked up at her with his solemn green eyes. "We want to keep hiking with you, too," he said.

Late in the afternoon, Hope and I dropped back to hike with Mary.

"Did you notice a tree that was sawed through?" Hope asked, skipping alongside her mom.

"No," Mary said.

"Oh." Hope stopped skipping and kicked at a lump of snow beside the trail. "We sawed through that tree, 'cause it was right in your way, and it was real big."

"Well, you must have done a good job getting it out of the way, if I didn't even notice it."

Hope threw back her shoulders and beamed.

"I'm going ahead now," she announced. "I'm going to make sure there aren't any more trees in the way!"

She dashed up the trail. Mary shook her head, smiling. "If I had a tenth the energy those kids do . . ."

A quarter mile later, we caught up to Hope. I could see the dark curve of a well-traveled road cutting through the snow. On the other side, several cars were parked in a trailhead lot. Hope took Mary's hand to cross, looking, for a moment, much younger than her ten years. Just as we reached the parking lot, a family of four, parents and two grown children, jumped out of one of the cars. They hurried over to us, exclaiming, "are you the Family from the North? We've heard so much about you! We're just out for the day; don't know how you do it in this cold! Can we take your picture?"

My first reaction was relief to find that I wasn't the center of attention. My second reaction was astonishment at the incongruity of the scene. Here we were, struggling to survive and help each other through the winter. Gather wood, find water, walk. Carry enough food to share. Watch each other for signs of hypothermia. Push tree trunks out of the trail. And suddenly, someone was pointing a camera at Mary, as if she were a spectacle to entertain him, not a tired woman with three miles left to hike and dusk swiftly descending.

Hope preened, obviously delighted with the attention, but Mary's smile looked forced as she posed beside the trail sign. They took three photos, then peppered Mary with questions. "Where's the rest of the family? We missed them? Oh, no! Here, if we give you our address, will you send us a picture of the whole family? How long have you been on the Trail?"

Mary leaned against the sign, her face pale. I caught her eye and glanced past her to the trail, then back to her again. She nodded. I stepped to her side and faced the dayhikers, smiling.

"I'm not a part of the Family," I said, "but I've been hiking with them for a while. Maybe I can answer some of your questions."

I told the wife that the Family had been on the Trail since July, that they had been homesteading before they started hiking, and yes, they did home-school the children. Hope got their address from the dad, promising to send him a photo of the rest of the family "if we ever get a camera again."

With a sigh of relief, Mary slipped away and headed up the trail.

jackrabbit

We camped at Old Orchard Shelter, packing into the small wooden building. A ratty camouflage tarp strung across the entrance had kept the snow from drifting in. Heald set up his bivy sack on the ground just in front of the shelter, under the tarp. Netta, Isis, the Family, and I occupied the sleeping platform. Hope and Joy, with a minimum of bickering, set up their mats end-to-end across the bottom edge of the shelter floor.

Joy bounded out of the shelter when her camp chores were done, still full of energy. She scooped up a handful of the powdery snow and ran toward Heald, who was returning from the spring with a pot of water. "I'm gonna getcha! I'm gonna hit ya with a snowball, Heald!"

He jumped out of the way with surprising speed for someone of his size and set the pot down on the picnic table. "No you ain't. No girl's gonna hit me with a snowball." He tried to look fierce, but he was grinning. Joy came closer. Heald reached forward and batted the snow out of her hands.

Joy was indignant. "That's not fair, Heald. You're not s'posed to do that. It's against the rules!"

As we cooked supper, we saw a hiker coming up the trail in the gloom. The loping stride, somewhat shortened by the foot-deep snow, looked familiar . . . and the bright orange hat was unmistakable.

"Lash!" The kids took up the cry. "Lash is here! Lash is here!" Mary had told me that the Family had camped with Lash a few days after Thanksgiving.

The kids looked as excited as I was to see him again. I thought of the first time I had met him, when he and Black Forest hiked past our campsite in Pennsylvania. At the time, and so many times since then, I had thought I would never see him again. But here he was, dropping his pack and fending off John and Joel's attacks, picking up Hope and Joy and swinging them around by their arms.

Faith tottered up to the edge of the sleeping platform. "Lath? Lath, Mumma?"

"That's right, sweetie," Mary said with a weak smile.

The kids finally tired of climbing on Lash and returned to the warmth of their sleeping bags. He put on all his extra layers of clothing, and sat down on the edge of the platform to cook supper.

"Hi, Lash."

"Hey, jackrabbit. What's new?"

"Not much. Same old same old, you know? I walk, I sleep, I eat. Missed you. Do you still pee in a bottle?"

He sighed theatrically, looking wounded. "Jackrabbit, there's more to me than my bathroom habits!"

"Did you see our messages in the snow?" Isis asked him.

"Yes. 'See you tonight, Lash,' and all that?" He gave her a sidelong smile. "That's why I hiked a twenty-five today. Wanted to catch up with you."

"Lash, I've got something for you," I said, opening the Ziploc where I kept my journal. "Here you go." It was the little scrap of paper where Isis and I had traced "Lash's motivation" at the shelter south of Waynesboro. "I thought you might want this back. You seem to be having a bit of trouble without it."

He looked at the paper and laughed. "So it's you guys that stole it! I should have known."

I handed it to him. "Now that you've had to catch up with us for a change, I figured you should have it back."

In the early morning hours I felt the snow begin, tiny pinpricks of cold that stung my cheeks. I pulled the hood of my mummy bag tighter over my head and tried to ignore it. The shelter was still in the predawn blackness, but far from silent. Mice scrabbled somewhere in the rafters, and off to my left I heard the tandem snores of Heald and Annie. One of the children murmured something in a dream. I tried to go back to sleep, but my hips and knees were aching and my brain was wide awake, fretting about the future. Heald had mentioned something about balds ahead on the Grayson Highlands. I wondered how we would find our way across the open space if the snow kept up.

Eventually the others stirred and began to stretch. I lay in my sleeping bag, relishing the last few moments of warmth, before I sat up and pulled on my polypro gloves. My hair crackled with tiny sparks of static as I combed and braided it. I heard the roar and hiss as Paul started the stove and the clink of pots and pans. Paul had offered to share the Family's hot breakfast with us, as long as we carried some extra cereal. It seemed like a good trade. The children got their cups out and Isis fetched oatmeal packets from our food bags for Hope and Joy. Paul poured hot water into the oats and stirred instant grits into the pot for the rest of us. In a few minutes he dished out the thick white gruel. We ate quickly before it could freeze to the sides of the cups.

Lash and Heald were still closed up tight in their mummy bags, lying on the ground at the foot of the shelter. The big camouflage tarp across the entrance had kept out some of the snow, but handfuls of flakes had swirled in around the edges. The foot of Lash's yellow bivy sack was almost lost in a pile of white.

"Look at Lash," Hope said, her voice full of concern. "He looks like a snowdrift!"

"A yellow snowdrift," I said.

Joel giggled. "Don't eat the yellow snow!"

The rest of the children took up the cry, laughing and pointing. Lash stirred and peeked out, his amber eyes just visible between the yellow edge of his bivy sack and the brim of his day-glo orange hat.

"I hike twenty-five miles in the snow to catch up with you, and this is the welcome I get," he said petulantly.

"Yellow snow, yellow snow!"

Lash gave a dramatic sigh and rolled over, shedding his personal snowdrift.

After breakfast, we packed up quickly, stamping our feet to keep warm. Joel checked the thermometer Dachs had given him. "Thirteen degrees," he announced triumphantly.

Heald grunted. "It can get nasty out there on the Highlands. I'm gonna take the horse trail." He stared moodily out at the gray sky and the thickening snow. "Come on, ya smelly dog," he told Annie. He fastened on her filthy green pack and they headed into the woods.

Isis, Paul, and I held a quick conference. "We've followed the white blazes this far," Paul said, "at least, for as much of the Trail as we've done. Might as well stay with the proper trail."

Isis got out the map. "The horse trail is shorter, but who knows if it's as well-marked. If we follow the A.T., there's a shelter six miles out and another at eleven. We can hole up at the first one if it gets really bad."

I remembered something Heald had said when we met up at Partnership Shelter. "That second shelter, Thomas Knob, has an attic. Heald said it's like Partnership. If the snow keeps up, at least we'll have four walls around us there."

It was calm and eerily still in the woods near Old Orchard Shelter. The snow had drifted knee-deep in places, but it was light enough to push through without too much difficulty. More was falling, brushing against our faces like tiny cold fingers. It clung to the branches of the trees in powder-soft piles, stacked six inches high and growing. The soft, gray light, diffused in the snowy sky, seemed to come from everywhere.

Isis and I went out ahead of the group, breaking trail. The path led steadily upward, through a forest that changed from bare-limbed hardwoods to spruce and fir. As we hiked higher, the wind picked up, dislodging puffs of snow from the branches and sending them down, soundless white explosions against the white background. The temperature seemed to be dropping, too. I had started the day wearing my Gore-Tex rain gear, fleece jacket, hat, and gloves. On a warmer day, I would have taken the fleece off after a few minutes of hiking, but as it was, we'd been climbing uphill for several miles and I was still almost too cold.

The light between the tree trunks ahead strengthened, and soon we came to the edge of an open space. I couldn't see the other side between the wraiths of blowing snow.

"We don't go out there, do we?" I asked, but Isis was already making her way through the V-gate and into the field. I tightened the hood of my jacket and followed.

"Hey, there are ponies here!"

Sure enough, a cluster of shaggy brown and white animals stood in the snowbanks under the overhang of the woods. One of them came over and stood on the trail in front of us, watching us with its wild brown eyes. We shared some crackers with the pony. It was wary but eventually accepted them from our gloved hands. Its delicate lips revealed gnarled orange teeth; ice from its breath had condensed on the whiskers of its muzzle. It was comforting, in a strange way, to know that other animals were surviving the winter outside.

As we walked out into the open, it became clear that the bald extended farther than we had thought. We walked for ten minutes, fighting the rising wind, and the trees on the other side were nowhere in sight. The Family caught up with us, moving with their usual speed even through the deep snow. We let them go ahead.

Away from the edge of the woods, the wind picked up. My right cheek, still tender from the frostnip on Chestnut Knob, burned from the force of the wind-driven snow. My pack caught in the stronger gusts like a sail. Several times, the knee-deep snow was the only thing that prevented me from being blown off course. Ahead of me, I could see Mary's huge pack swaying as she struggled to stay upright, and just ahead of her Hope and Joy strained against the wind and the snowdrifts, which came nearly to their waists.

The trail turned and the wind was at our backs, but still it was a relentless force ripping at us, whipping our hair into our eyes and eddying snow around us until it was almost impossible to see the posts that marked the trail. Mary dropped back to the end of the line, her thin face pale with exhaustion, and Isis stayed with her. In between gusts, I saw Joy floundering in a snowbank. I ran up to help her. Her shoulders shook with rage and frustration.

"This stupid, dumb, piece-a-junk wind and snow! I hate it!" she roared over the sound of the wind. She was up to her waist in the snowbank, blown off the path. I remembered how she had run up to the front of the line with her father in fall, when the ground was clear. She was one of the strongest hikers in the Family, but not in this weather. I helped her up, back onto the path that Paul and her brothers had packed down.

"C'mon. If I walk just upwind of you, you won't get blown around as much. That way, when we get to the shelter, you'll still have all the energy you need to throw snowballs at Heald."

Slowly the anger left her frame, and she smiled, a wide fierce grin. "I'm gonna get 'im with lotsa snowballs this time!"

We walked for what seemed like hours. It was impossible to tell how far we had come, or where we were, in the blinding horizontal blizzard. Several times I had to grab the strap on top of Joy's grubby pink pack to hold her upright when a strong gust of wind came. Frost clung to my eyelashes. I could tell I was getting too cold. I wanted to put more clothes on, but I knew I couldn't stop until we found shelter. If I opened my pack in this maelstrom, I might lose all my warm clothes to the wind.

Finally we saw woods again, scattered glimpses through the driven snow. Under the branches, shielded a little from the wind, we stopped for a rest and a snack beside a large boulder. I put on my Capilene long underwear and wool shirt. I had no scarf, so I tied a cotton bandana across my face to keep the cold wind off my cheeks. It would be better than nothing.

Mary leaned against the rock, breathing heavily. The veins in her temples pounded under her pale skin. "That's the hardest thing I've ever done in my life," she said. "Thank God it's over." Hope and Joy moved silently to her side, putting their arms around her waist. The wisps of hair that had escaped from their hoods were blown sideways and coated in thick solid ice rime. Faith was buried so deeply inside the down sleeping bag in Mary's pack that her face didn't show.

We ate our frozen granola bars in silence, reflecting and conserving our strength. (I chewed carefully—I had never been laissez-faire about frozen granola bars since my experience above Catawba.) Isis tried to locate us on the map, but there was no marker for the edge of the woods. The only landmark was the end of a Forest Service road, which we hadn't seen in the snow, and the word "Scales." *We have been weighed by the Scales,* I thought, *and found wanting in common sense.*

Toward midday the clouds lifted and the sun came out briefly. The glare on the snow made it difficult to see. We stopped for lunch at Wise Shelter, a small plywood and cinderblock building, with the opening facing directly into the wind. Snow had drifted two feet deep in the back of it. Paul and the boys had arrived just ahead of us, and Lash and Netta caught up soon afterward.

Netta was wrapped in all her layers of clothing, her face barely visible between cap and scarf. "I have not ever seen weather like this."

"Dude, this is insane." Lash turned to Joel. "What's that thermometer say now, bro?"

Joel picked up the little plastic rectangle, frowned, shook it, frowned again. "It says zero."

"Crazy, man . . . Whoa, look out!" John had picked up one of Mary's hiking poles and was charging toward Lash with the pole held like a fencing foil, grinning gleefully. Lash slung his pack off in one smooth motion, lifting his own pole to counter John's attack. Joel soon joined the fray, and poles were forgotten as it became a wrestling free-for-all.

I took out my food bag and Isis made tortilla wraps out of cream cheese and dates and honey (the latter so thick she had to open the container and spread it with her knife). I scanned the register. It was mostly weekend outing groups in the last month—almost all the southbounders we knew had already reached Georgia.

"Water source frozen . . . have fun melting snow . . . freezing my nuts off, just for the hell of it. Doesn't sound promising." While I read the highlights of the register to Isis, I kept one eye on the boys wrestling outside. I loved watching

Lash. He had a certain fluid grace and economy of movement that made me miss the Tae Kwon Do classes I'd taken for years. I thought of the dream I'd had at Big Meadows, with Lash as an evil ninja, and I smiled.

"Alright, guys, I gotta eat lunch," Lash said, shaking the boys off him and climbing to his feet with feigned weariness.

Isis handed me a sandwich and a few extra dates. "Go ask Lash if he wants one," she said, her eyes sparkling.

I put on a sweet, seductive tone. "Lashy-Lash, do you want a date?"

"Lashy-Lash!" he rolled his eyes and then glared at Netta. She shrugged with an impish grin. "But yes, I would like a date." He took the sticky fruit in his gloved hand and smiled at me, and in spite of myself I felt my cheeks grow warm behind the cotton bandana I wore as a scarf.

After lunch the clouds closed in again, the sky resuming its steel-gray opacity. Lash and Joel ran ahead to search for the A.T. The shelter was set in an open space with thickets of rhododendron, and the trail seemed to have vanished somewhere at the edge of it. Pony trails wound in and out among the bushes. If there were any blazes, they must have been painted on rocks under the knee-deep snow. It was a full twenty minutes before Paul spotted the first blaze, on a stunted tree across the clearing, and a few more minutes before we all assembled on the trail. I thought—I imagine we all thought—that the worst was over, and I began to relax, enjoying the rhythm of walking, getting warm at last under the shelter of the trees. And then the trees ended.

As we headed out into the open again, I realized that the Scales had been nothing compared to the bald we were about to face. The trail turned and the wind had shifted slightly, so that now we were walking directly into its onslaught. The snowdrifts were higher here, too. The blazes on the Scales had been on posts, mostly visible above the snow, but here they were painted on rocks. Except where the wind had blown the snow from the taller rocks, we could only find the trail from where it passed through the occasional rhododendron thicket. The wind picked up as the afternoon wore on, and the snow returned, thickening the air with white.

Ice rime stood out four inches deep on the twigs of small bushes and stunted trees. The wisps of snow whipping past on the wind had an eerie beauty, tracing out half-seen figures against the gunmetal sky, vanishing in a heartbeat. Snow formed a rainbow halo around the dim and distant sun. In one place, Paul and I carved a path through drifts that were as high as my chest, passing the younger children hand over hand to Netta and Isis and Lash.

In places where the snow had blown clear, I held onto Joy's pack again, and Isis took charge of Hope, to make sure they didn't blow off the trail. I had no concept of time and distance—there was only the screaming wind, the cold, the bare necessity of moving forward.

As dusk drew on, I was breaking trail. I found myself following an unsteady line of footsteps, half drifted-in with new snow. I hadn't seen a blaze for a long time. I wondered if this path would lead to shelter—or to someone's frozen corpse. I was acutely aware of the fragile lives behind me: Lash, Netta, the Family, my sister. I thought of the children and forced the doubt from my mind. My strength was failing in the deep drifts. It was so tempting just to sit for a moment, just to rest . . . but I willed myself forward, mentally forcing my cold, exhausted muscles to keep up the fight.

The line of ragged footsteps vanished in a high drift. I was ready to fall down and cry—but I looked up, and there was a fence. A gap in the fence. A rough wooden building: Thomas Knob Shelter. I staggered toward it, too exhausted to even feel relief.

A party of camouflage-clad men, out for the weekend, had already set up their sleeping bags in the loft, and Heald had arrived several hours before us, having taken the horse trail. "I was about ready to come lookin' for ya," he said. Worry was etched in his face. "Where are those kids?"

Lash and Netta stumbled out of the snowdrifts with Hope a moment later, and then Isis emerged from the blizzard, carrying Joy. Paul and Mary stumbled into the clearing a few minutes later with the boys. The other campers seemed shocked to see so many people, and especially the children, but they were kind and made space for us in the loft. The wind around the eaves made an unearthly moaning sound, and snow drifted in through holes in the corners of the roof.

I was nearing the end of my strength, but I still felt energized by a sort of manic thrill. Isis went in search of water, while I struggled out into the wind again looking for Zip stove wood. Generally I was glad we didn't have to carry our fuel, but tonight I would have given anything for a canister stove. I managed to fight my way over to the evergreen woods in front of the shelter. I found a half-dead tree and tore the lower limbs off, apologizing to the spirit of the tree. I had never taken wood from a living tree before, but this was an emergency. The roiling gray sky was darkening visibly; cold was setting into my bones. I could feel my muscles cramping and my tongue sticking to the roof of my mouth as dehydration sapped my strength; I'd had one liter of water all day.

"There's no water," Isis reported, back at the shelter. "The spring's waist-deep in snow."

"We'll melt snow, then. We can take turns." The adrenaline in my veins still gave me the illusion of energy.

"Okay," she said, taking out the pot and the stove. She handed me a book of matches and a few scraps of paper to start the fire. I squatted in a corner of the shelter's ground floor to cook. Isis clambered up the ladder to the loft, where I could hear her helping the children unpack in the tiny crowded room. "Why don't you put your foam pad here, Joy? There's space on this end, Joel . . ."

I scooped up a potful of snow and tried to pack it down, but the powdery flakes didn't compress. The pot was still filthy from the night before, with a thin frozen scum of pasta bits and tomato sauce. *Soup for the first course*, I thought. I took my water bottle out from beneath my shirt and added the last sip of liquid water so the snow would melt and not sublimate.

With my numb and fumbling hands, it took four matches to get the fire going. I don't know how long I sat there, knocking ice rime from the broken spruce branches, breaking up the twigs, and feeding them into the smoking belly of the stove. It seemed to be generating no heat; the snow in the pot was not even steaming.

Isis came down to check on dinner. She found me sitting in the corner, rocking back and forth, my hat and gloves off.

"Jackrabbit, your lips are blue! Get in your sleeping bag! Now!"

I was too numb to protest. My hands refused to hold onto the ladder up to the loft; I had to pull myself up by hooking my bent elbows over the rungs. I stumbled across the small room, slow and uncoordinated. The floor was littered with packs, sleeping bags, gear, and hikers, covered in wisps of snow, details that barely registered in my cold brain. I crawled into my sleeping bag, still wearing all my clothes, and faced the wall. Silent tears stung my cheeks. I had failed in even the most superficial task of heating water. I was weak, I was a burden, once again incapable and slow. My shoulders shook with the effort of holding in my sobs. I didn't want the children to see my strength fail. Mary was right next to me, though, and she could feel me shaking.

"What's wrong, jackrabbit?"

"I'm no good—I've failed—I can't do this any more—"

"Shhh . . ." she put an arm over my shoulders. "You found the shelter. You led us here. We're safe now. We're okay."

Her calm voice led me back out of the abyss. I lay still, and in twenty minutes I was warm enough to start shivering.

Isis came up the ladder after nearly an hour had passed. She carried a pot of lukewarm snowmelt the color of dishwater, flavored with wood smoke and the diluted remnants of the tomatoey pasta dish we had eaten the night before. "The stove just doesn't work in this weather. I had to empty out the ashes and rebuild the fire before the snow even started melting."

I drank my share in small sips, trying not to retch. I knew I needed the water badly, but I felt sick and my throat rebelled each time I tried to swallow. I was able to force down perhaps half a liter of the acrid soup before I turned out my headlamp and tried to sleep.

Sleep was impossible, though. The wind moaned and rattled around the roof eaves, forcing snow through the cracks. Wrapped in my sleeping bag and all my warm clothes, I no longer felt the bone-chilling, soul-sapping cold that had threatened to consume me, but I never got warm. The painful pins-and-needles sensation of blood returning to my hands and feet never came. I kept shivering. So I stayed alert and wakeful, knowing that if I drifted off I might never come back.

After an eternity of darkness, a stark blue light crept into the little room. The air was still bitter cold, hitting the back of my throat like a strong drink when I undid the hood of my mummy bag and looked around. A knot of fear settled in my chest. How would we face another day out in this weather? None of us had come prepared for something like this. I didn't know if there were any more balds, or how long they might be, or how they would be blazed. I didn't know if we would be able to find water, and I wouldn't be able to keep my strength up much longer without it.

I remembered a nobo's description of winter in the South, long ago. "It'll snow one night, four inches maybe, and it's absolutely gorgeous. Generally it'll melt by noon." At the time, we'd considered the possibility of finishing the Trail barefoot. But the nobos had been describing the mountains of Georgia in early March, and we were caught instead in the Virginia highlands in December.

The weekenders began stirring, throwing off their thick down bags. By the dark circles under their eyes, it was evident they hadn't slept either. One of them, a heavyset blond man probably in his fifties, turned to Paul. "I been coming here seventeen years, and I never seen weather like this. I can't believe y'all came through that with all those younguns. Y'all have got to get outta here. Listen, I got a phone in my car down at Elk Garden, 'bout four miles down. I got friends in town who'd be more'n happy to pick y'all up."

I could see the independent, rebellious spirit flashing in Paul's eyes, but before he could respond, Mary said, "You are an angel!"

So we arranged it; we would stay at the shelter for another three hours, giving the men time to get to the road and arrange the rescue.

"May God bless you and keep you," Mary said softly as they left.

When we emerged from the dark womb of the attic, it took a long time for our eyes to adjust to the brilliance of the refracted sun. All of the branches were sheathed in crystalline white rime six inches thick, and the snow everywhere threw back tiny rainbow-colored specks of light. It was one of the most beautiful landscapes I had ever seen. *Beautiful*, I thought, *in the same way as a great white shark: gorgeous and deadly, with the two attributes so intertwined as to be indivisible.*

We reached the road after four hours of pushing through the waist-deep snow. The clouds closed in again as we hiked, turning the sky a pearly gray. Twice we lost the trail and had to backtrack. When I saw the fence, the plowed road, and the parking lot, at first I thought it was a mirage. Between the wisps of blowing snow, I thought I could see trucks and the figures of people, but I had seen many things in the snow that morning, phantoms brought on by dehydration and sleeplessness. Joy, walking downwind of me as she had the day before, gave a great shout and started running so fast I couldn't keep up, and that was when I understood the trucks must be real.

A group of men, bundled up in thick winter gear, met us at the road. They had brought enough vehicles to carry us all to town, and they offered us coffee and hot chocolate. They gave their names, but my sluggish brain could not remember them. As we drove down the mountain, my stomach lurching at the sharp turns, a strange feeling of unreality overtook me. The warm interior of the truck, and the kind, quiet voice of the man behind the wheel, seemed to belong to another universe. Part of me was sitting there, watching the snowy trees flash by outside the window and listening to my rescuer talk about the landmarks we passed. Part of me was safe. The rest of me was still out there, struggling against the wind and the chest-high drifts, the life-sucking cold. Distantly, I felt pins and needles finally creep into my hands and feet as the blood flowed back into the tissue, but a different kind of cold took up residence inside my ribcage. The realization settled like a hard seed of ice: *We could have died out there. Easily we could have died.*

Isis

On the steep, winding drive down the mountain, I held a paper cup while Hope, carsick, threw up all the hot chocolate she'd just drunk. Once we got to town, I called around and found out what lodgings were available. One bed-and-breakfast, the Lazy Fox Inn, was open this time of year, and there was also a half-built hostel we were welcome to stay in, but it had no heat. I called the owner of the Lazy Fox, a woman named Ginny who spoke in a lovely Southern drawl. She found a way to get all of us into the B&B (except Heald, who wanted to stay in the hostel so that Annie could sleep next to him, as she was accustomed to doing).

After our reservations were made, we all hung around Mount Rogers Outfitters. Damascus Dave, the owner of the store, had been part of the team that came to rescue us at Elk Garden. He was a soft-spoken, white-bearded man with many years of experience in the mountains. Though it was a holiday, he kept the store open for us.

"Whenever there are hikers in town, the doors are open," he told us.

Mount Rogers Outfitters had the best selection of hiking gear I'd seen anywhere since the Dartmouth Co-op in Hanover. We perused the selection of tarps, sleeping bag liners, down vests, and thermal undershirts, trying to decide what we wanted to add to our already bulging packs. The shelves of new gear held my attention for a few minutes, before the wave of exhaustion I'd been holding at bay for the past day and a half washed over me. I sat down on a bench and closed my eyes.

The image of relentless snow swirled across the backs of my eyelids. I saw Hope clinging to my hand, looking up at me with heartbreaking confidence as we stumbled along what was perhaps the trail, perhaps the track of a pony lost from the herd. I could feel the wind burning my face, then numbing it, but I couldn't reach up to tighten my hood. If I did, I'd have to let go of either my hiking sticks or Hope's hand. Beside me, jackrabbit tried to shelter Joy from the wind. Ten feet in front of us, the dim outline of Joel pushed through a snowdrift as high as his shoulders, then reached back to help John. Netta and Lash, breaking trail, had vanished into the white blur up ahead. Paul and Mary, with Faith, were somewhere far behind us; I hadn't seen them for hours.

The snow piled deeper and deeper, filling in Lash and Netta's tracks until we had only the faint edges of footprints to follow. We had to walk single file now; I let Hope walk behind me, out of the wind, but I glanced back every few seconds to make sure she was still there. Jackrabbit went ahead to help Joel break the trail. Joy tried to catch up to her, plowing doggedly through the fine snow, which rose to her knees even where jackrabbit had trampled it down. Perhaps half an hour after jackrabbit disappeared into the blizzard, Joy stumbled and went down on her knees. She got to her feet slowly and turned to face me. The tears froze to her skin as they fell; I could barely hear her howl above the wind. Instinctively, I reached out my arms to her, dropping my hiking sticks. I picked her up, pack and all. *I don't know how much strength I've got left*, I thought, as her small arms tightened around the back of my neck. *Half a mile's worth? Five hundred yards? Please let it be enough.*

Netta was shaking my shoulder. "Are you okay?" she asked.

I was sitting on a bench in the back of the outfitter's store, sobbing and shivering.

"We're all okay, aren't we?" I asked her, between sobs. "I mean, we made it. I don't know why I'm so frightened now. Now that it's over."

"You need some rest. Come on, let's go to the bed-and-breakfast." She helped me to my feet, and I tottered the two blocks to the inn, leaning on her arm.

By that evening, I had recovered enough to help figure out what to do about supper. It was New Year's Eve, so all the restaurants in town were closed, as were all the markets except the tiny convenience store by the gas station. I borrowed Ginny's phone book and started calling pizza delivery places in the nearest city, Abingdon, thirteen miles away.

"Hi, I'd like to order some pizzas, and I was wondering if you could deliver as far as Damascus?"

"Damascus? We only deliver within a three-mile radius." Click.

By the time I dialed the seventh and last number, I was starting to contemplate a supper of chips and granola bars.

"Hi . . . um, I know this sounds crazy, but is there any possible way that you could deliver six pizzas to Damascus?"

"Let me ask the manager."

This was further than I'd gotten with any of the other places. I held my breath. A minute later, I was handing the phone to Ginny so she could give directions to the driver.

While we waited for the pizza, jackrabbit went on a foray to the gas station to see if they had any champagne.

"Get the most expensive thing they have," I told her. "I want to celebrate."

She returned with a bottle of Black Dog Merlot. "Seven ninety-nine!" she announced proudly. "The other wine there was four bucks a bottle."

The grown-ups among us stayed up late, finishing off the pizza, sipping our Black Dog, and watching reruns of *Crocodile Hunter*. Finally, afraid that I'd fall asleep on Ginny's sofa, I got up, stretched, and headed for the stairs. At the bottom step, I turned around to say good night to Paul and Mary.

"Good night," Mary answered.

Paul looked up at me. "Good night," he said, and then asked, "are you going to stay on the Trail?"

"I haven't started thinking about that yet. Are you?"

"I don't know," he said, sounding hesitant for the first time since I'd known him. He glanced at Mary, who sat rigid, intent on his words. "I'd like to, but maybe it's the wrong thing to do, with the children so young. I guess we'll decide tomorrow."

jackrabbit

The night we came into town, the sense of unreality that I had felt in the rescuer's truck continued. I felt as though I was slightly outside of my body, watching myself, as I ate pizza in the beautifully appointed dining room of the Lazy Fox, where gold-rimmed china plates glinted from glass-fronted cases in the corners. I went with Lash to the only grocery open in town, to buy a bottle of wine to celebrate—it was, after all, New Year's Eve. I watched myself talking, laughing, walking in the empty streets of the small town. Part of my mind was still in the mountains, lost in the snow and struggling to find the traces of a trail.

Back at the inn, I went into the bathroom to take a shower. A small framed painting on the wall showed a scene of sand dunes at the edge of the ocean. When my eyes passed over it, the white sand turned into heaps of glittering snow, shifting, moving as I watched. I could hear the roar of the wind, eddying down out of the picture and flooding into the room. I hugged myself, wrapping my arms around my ribcage, and turned the picture to face the wall. Undressing, I found gray patches of frostnip on my upper thighs. Several toes had turned an ugly purple. From the swollen, tender feeling of my ears and cheeks, I knew they must have been damaged, too. The warm water of the shower fell on me but did not touch the cold inside me.

Later that night, when the lamps in the wooden hallways were turned down low and almost everyone slept, Lash and I stayed up in the living room. We sat on the brocaded couch, finishing the wine.

"We ought to celebrate," Lash said. "Come on; Ginny said we could put some music on. Quietly, I mean, 'cause everybody's sleeping . . ."

We looked through the stack of CDs on the table beside the stereo. "This," I said.

Lash looked doubtful. "The Tallis Scholars? I've never even heard of them. What are they, some kind of punk band?"

"Just listen."

He started to protest, but the music came on. One voice, and then a choir, the rich harmonic tapestry of Gregorio Allegri's *Miserere*. The sounds hung in the dark air, glorious and unrelenting, four centuries old. I closed my eyes. I could feel the threads of music reaching down through time, weaving into each other, weaving me back into the world. I followed that music out of the mountains; out of the cold and endless night, out of paralyzing fear, I followed the river of sound and it brought me back to myself.

We didn't speak until the music ended. "You were right," Lash said quietly.

Then my tears started, silent, melting the last of the ice inside me. A clock struck somewhere. We counted the twelve booming chimes.

"Hey, it's 2001," Lash said. "Happy New Year."

CHAPTER 10

The Last of the Sobos

Isis

Iwoke to sunlight streaming through lacy curtains, and the most wonderful blend of scents wafting up the stairs: coffee brewing, bacon frying, apples baking. I lay still for a few minutes, relishing the warmth of the blankets and the softness of clean sheets against my skin. Mercifully, I could not remember any dreams.

In the dining room, I found Ginny setting a pan full of apple dumplings in the last free space on the table. Platters of scrambled eggs, bacon, sausage, sliced fruit, banana bread and fresh biscuits, vats of gravy, apricot compote, and cheese grits (the real thing, a far cry from the flavorless gruel we'd been eating on the Trail), tiny glass dishes of apple butter and preserves, and pitchers full of orange juice, milk, and coffee covered every inch of the hardwood dining table. Mary sat near one end of the laden table, sipping a steaming cup of coffee, her thin face transfigured by a beatific smile. Faith, still half asleep, snuggled in the curve of her arm, cooing "Mum-ma . . . Mum-ma." As I sank into a chair across from Mary, Paul led the other children into the room. Hope came in skipping. She grabbed the back of the chair next to me and bounced up and down on her tiptoes, staring at the food.

"Gosh, is this for *us*?"

Joy, in equally high spirits, grabbed a bleary-eyed jackrabbit, who had just come downstairs, pulling her over to the table and wrestling the chair beside her away from John. "I'm sittin' with jackrabbit, 'cause she's my favorite hiker in the world!"

After a few hours, the children tired of eating and went into the living room to watch a movie. Paul, Mary, Netta, Lash, jackrabbit and I sat around the table until noon, gradually emptying the platters of the feast. As I worked my way through the last apple dumpling, Paul repeated the question he'd asked the night before.

"So, are you going to stay on the Trail?"

I felt jackrabbit shiver beside me. "Maybe," she said. "After that . . ." she didn't finish her sentence.

"I think I will go home," said Netta. "I do not like this winter hiking enough to spend all my money on gear for it."

Lash looked at her as if hurt and a little surprised. Then he glanced at me and jackrabbit, Mary and Paul. "Whatever you guys do, man. We should stick together."

"We don't need to decide yet," I said. "We could buy some new gear— enough to keep us from freezing at night—and ask Damascus Dave for a shuttle back to Elk Garden. It's two days into town from there. One night in the woods. We could decide whether to keep hiking once we got back to town."

"I guess so," said jackrabbit.

Paul looked at Mary. "Faith and I are staying here," she told him. Paul's eyes flashed. I held my breath, waiting. Mary continued, her voice calm and gentle as ever. "I need to gain some weight. But when you get back from Elk Garden, if you still want to go on, I'll go with you."

Jackrabbit and I checked the post office for our snowshoes, but they hadn't arrived yet. We had better luck at Mount Rogers Outfitters, where we and our companions spent most of the afternoon sorting through shelves of zero-degree sleeping bags, four-season tents, and ultralight down jackets, trying to decide what we could afford, and what we could live without. Lash and jackrabbit both bought compasses, and I got a tarp that we could tie over the entrances of shelters to keep the snow out. Instead of new sleeping bags, we bought warmer liners and an extra layer of silk long underwear. Jackrabbit and I also bought a canister stove. Our Zip stove became dangerously inefficient at low temperatures; the night we'd spent at Thomas Knob, I had stayed up for two hours, trying to melt some snow for us to drink the next morning. By the time I had half a liter of water, I was so hypothermic that I'd decided that it would be a good idea to fill the other half of the bottle with snow, take it to bed with me, and let my body heat melt it overnight. (As it turned out, I didn't even have enough body heat to warm it—in the morning, the bottle had still been full of icy slush.)

Paul bought a few new pairs of socks for Mary and some warm, light-weight sleeping bag liners for the children. That evening, we sat in a circle on

Ginny's living room floor, helping Mary cut an extra-long liner in half and sew it into two small liners for Faith and Joy. Ginny brought us mugs of cocoa, and Ben passed around a bowl of Christmas candies. The snowflakes drifting past the windows looked as harmless and pretty as the glitter on a holiday card. Sitting in the warm, lamplit room, it was easy to forget the blizzard we'd come through to get there, and the five-foot-high snow drifts, dry or frozen springs, and subzero temperatures we were preparing to face again.

After another sumptuous breakfast at the Lazy Fox, Damascus Dave and his friends Jeff and Steve drove us back to Elk Garden. As I stepped out of Jeff's pickup, a cold wind stung the raw patches where frost-damaged skin had peeled off my cheeks. I fought the urge to jump back into the truck and stay there until I was safe in Damascus again. Instead, I pulled on my new balaclava and knelt down to help Joy, who was having trouble tightening her pack straps. Hope came over and watched me for a moment.

"Mom usually does that," she said, in a subdued voice.

We headed into the woods, Paul and jackrabbit breaking trail in the knee-deep snow. Netta, who had decided to hike the Elk Garden to Damascus section with us before leaving the Trail, brought up the rear along with me, Hope, and Joy. (Heald, along with Mary and Faith, had opted to stay in town.) Lash hiked just behind Paul, with Joel and John trotting along in his wake. Scraps of their conversation drifted back to me; it sounded as though Lash was instructing the boys in the fine art of flirtation.

"When a girl starts laughing at everything you say, even if it isn't a joke, that's when you know she's into you."

"I guess Hope likes *you*, then," came John's high voice.

"Yeah, man. It's a bummer. I'm hikin' with all these pretty girls, and the only one who likes me is ten years old!"

"I wish there was a girl my age on the Trail," I heard Joel say, just before they got out of earshot.

I expected Hope to react to Lash and John's comments with indignation, but she said nothing. She was walking just ahead of me, and I noticed her thin shoulders shaking in her pack straps.

"Hope, what's wrong?" I asked.

She turned around, her eyes streaming. "I miss my mom," she sobbed. I knelt down in the snow. Hope buried her face in my shoulder. Netta stood beside her, patting her arm and murmuring something soothing in Hebrew. Joy walked a few paces up the trail, then turned to face us, hands on her hips and her eyes narrowed with frustration. Her expression reminded me of my own little sister, Susan-now-jackrabbit, at times in our childhood when she'd had to wait for me to get through a fit of tears. After a minute, Hope lifted her head and spoke.

"Mary and me, we never been apart for this long since I was four. That's when I lived with my dad for a month, but his wife didn't feed me nothin', so Mary came and took me away again." She paused, as sobs overcame her again. "I shouldn'ta come. I knew I'd miss Mary. When I was going to leave, she told me that she'd be with me in my heart, even if she was still in town. But she can't do that, can she? Be two places at one time? She's in town with Faithie. She ain't here."

"Close your eyes," I told her. "Can you picture your mom?" She nodded, the beginnings of a smile curving the corners of her mouth, though tears still trickled out from under her eyelids. "What would she say, if she were here now?"

"She'd say I gotta be a big girl and help the others," Hope said, opening her eyes. "She'd say we oughta start hiking now, so we can get to the shelter before dark." She stepped back, squaring her shoulders. "Let's go."

A mile or so later, we caught up with the others in an orchard on the side of Whitetop Mountain. Though sunlight gleamed on the polished white surfaces, a brisk wind blew swirling clouds of snow through the gnarled apple branches. As I stepped out of the shelter of the woods, a haze of snow engulfed me, and my limbs prickled with adrenaline. *Where is the trail? I can't see the others. Snow is filling their footsteps, faster than I can walk.* My knees buckled; I fought back a wave of nausea. Then the snow blew past, and once more a sparkling field stretched before me under a placid blue sky. Not twenty yards away, Lash and jackrabbit pushed their way through a five-foot-deep snowdrift, while Paul waited to help the small children through it.

We plowed through another mile of deep drifts, Netta and I taking our turns with the others breaking trail, then slogged steadily downhill for four miles to Lost Mountain Shelter. The snow grew shallower as we descended; only half a foot of it covered the ground around the shelter. Jackrabbit had gotten there before us; as I walked into the clearing, she and Lash came up the spring trail, empty water bottles clattering at their belts.

"Frozen?" I asked. Jackrabbit nodded.

I slipped out of my pack and stood up. It felt as though the snowdrifts on Whitetop had barely put a dent in the energy I'd accumulated during our zero in Damascus. *If we decide to quit the Trail, what will I do for exercise?* I thought. *Get a job as a construction worker and spend all my free time at a gym?*

"There was an open stream by the road about a mile back," I said. "Anyone want to join me for an expedition?"

Jackrabbit wrinkled her nose. "I wouldn't drink from that stream. It's probably full of road runoff."

"Good point. Let's see what there is in the other direction."

I took out the map. "Looks like the trail crosses another stream in about half a mile. Shall we look for it?"

Jackrabbit, Lash, and I collected water bottles from everyone and set out to look for the stream. We jogged through the monochromatic forest, around curve after curve of the ridge. We passed several dry streambeds before we found one that contained a thin trickle, frozen solid.

"Notch this," muttered jackrabbit, poking at the ice with a stick. "I guess we'll find out how well our new stove melts snow."

Paul had already started melting snow by the time we got back. As soon as we had put on our sweaters and jackets, he offered us cups of hot water mixed with powdered milk. Jackrabbit and I set up our new canister stove as we drank, and Paul gave us some water to put in the bottom of the pan. The stove worked even faster than I'd hoped. In fifteen minutes, we were pouring the first pot of boiling water into Hope and Joy's Nalgenes, and in less than an hour, we'd filled our own hot water bottles, cooked supper, and made tea for everyone. As I snuggled into my warm sleeping bag, wedged between Joy and jackrabbit, I found myself hoping that we would stay on the Trail. Just as I had become accustomed to the constant exercise the A.T. provided, I had grown used to the winter rituals of survival—putting on all our outer layers as soon as we reached the shelter, so that our arms stuck out like the limbs of overstuffed dolls; looking for water and melting snow when we didn't find any; comforting each other at night with tea and songs. A little technology in the form of a new stove was useful, but I wouldn't know what to do with my evenings if I could get hot water out of a tap whenever I wanted it. Most of all, I would miss the way our simple, vital work bound us as a community, how deeply we depended on each other and how carefully all of us—in spite of our diverse backgrounds and profound religious differences—upheld that trust.

The weather held clear, and in spite of a series of short, rough climbs, the sixteen miles into Damascus felt like easy hiking. After the first few miles, we stripped down to our wool shirts and shorts; by afternoon, red-brown leaves showed through the snow on the southern slopes of hills. From the top of one small mountain, we could look back to see the wrinkled white balds of the Grayson Highlands shining against the sky.

"God, it's beautiful," whispered jackrabbit, coming to a halt beside me.

"When it's not trying to kill us," I said.

"No," she said. "It was beautiful even then."

"So you want to go on?"

"That's not what I meant. But yes, I do want to stay on the Trail."

"Good," I said with a fierce grin. "So do I."

When we got back to the Lazy Fox, we were greeted by two familiar but unexpected faces: Playfoot and Anonymous Badger. Both of them had been following jackrabbit's e-mail updates, so they knew where to find us. Playfoot, who lived a couple hours' drive away, had just read jackrabbit's account of our harrowing day on Grayson. Deciding that we needed some support and encouragement, he'd gotten in his Jeep after work and driven straight to Damascus. Anonymous Badger hadn't read the Grayson e-mail yet. He had just quit a job in Pennsylvania, and he wanted to spend a month hiking with us before his new job started. He'd never been winter camping before.

"That's okay," jackrabbit told him. "Isis and I had only done three days of winter camping before the A.T."

With a start, I realized that she was right.

jackrabbit

We left Damascus in midmorning, with the sun glaring bright on the half-melted snow in the valley: me and Isis, the Family, Lash, and Anonymous Badger. Netta waved from the window of the outfitter's as we passed. I had the parting gift she had given me, a Hebrew blessing copied onto an index card, stowed in the top of my pack. I would carry it for the rest of my hike.

Perhaps a mile out of town, a set of wooden steps marked the beginning of the A.T.'s ascent out of the valley. Six inches of snow clung to the ground, disturbed only by the footprints of Heald and Annie—they had left town several hours earlier. Rhododendrons grew thick around the trail, and their lower leaves, in shadow, were half-curled against the cold. Anonymous Badger ran ahead, moving lightly over the snow. Lash and Joel followed him, soon lost to sight. John and I walked together, followed by Paul and Joy, and Isis brought up the rear with Mary.

The snow was deeper on top the ridge. In places the drifts beside the trail came to my knees, but the footsteps of the people ahead had packed down the treadway. It was only on the northern slopes, where the snow was still powdery, that the effort of plowing through it was a problem. The snowshoes we had bought in Blacksburg had arrived at the Damascus post office the day before we left, and mine were strapped to the outside of my pack. I thought about wearing them several times. I wanted to hike with John, though, and I didn't think he could keep up if I did.

Three miles out of town, on the ridge top, we came to a small wooden sign tacked to a tree. "Welcome to Tennessee," it read. An outline of the state had been burned into the wood, with a sunburst in one corner. We stared at it for several seconds and broke into cheers.

"The state line! The state line! We made it through Virginia!"

After eight weeks and 546 miles, more than a quarter of the A.T., we had finally reached the next state. I thought back to crossing the West Virginia line, coming into Harpers Ferry at night. At the time, I couldn't have imagined anything harder than that twenty-six-mile hike, ending up lost among shoulderless freeways and half-built bridges, hungry, in the dark. The danger we had faced on the Grayson Highlands made the memory almost comical.

John hugged my waist. "We did it!"

I hugged him back, and then I put my gloved hand up against the sign and lowered my head, silently thanking whatever power in the universe had helped us through that nightmare blizzard.

John and I walked together all afternoon. With the hood of his green fleece pulled up around his pointed face, he looked like a woodland elf. He was surprisingly quiet for a child of his age. Occasionally he stopped to point out interesting things along the trail: vines twisted into a corkscrew pattern; the wing marks and drops of blood in the snow where an owl had caught a mouse.

We stopped for a drink at the top of a small rise, brushing the snow from a fallen tree trunk so we could sit down. The sun was sliding toward evening, a filigree of slate-blue shadows lengthening on the snow.

"What do you want to do when you grow up, John?" I asked him.

He considered for a moment, chewing on his lower lip. "I want to be free. What do you want to do, jackrabbit?"

"I wish I knew."

"Are you a grown-up?"

"Yes. No. I'm kind of at an age where everyone expects me to be a grown-up, but I don't feel like one, really."

"Why not?"

"Well, I used to think that when you became a grown-up, all of a sudden everything would make sense. You'd have some idea of what you were doing with your life, some plan."

"Why do you wanna have a plan? I wanna be like Paul." His voice was strong with conviction, and his eyes looked just like his father's for an instant. "He doesn't have no plans, or nobody telling him what to do. He just does things." John stood up and brushed the snow off his pants. "I think we oughta hike some more now."

It was almost dark by the time we reached Abingdon Gap Shelter, a tiny, dingy building with cinderblock walls, a plywood sleeping platform, and a corrugated tin roof. Lash and Joel sat at the picnic table in front of the shelter. By the pattern of footsteps in the snow on the blue-blazed trail to the water source, I knew that Heald and Badger must still be at the spring.

"Hey, guys. Where's the privy?" I said.

Lash gave an enigmatic smile and pointed wordlessly to a shovel leaning against the outside wall of the shelter.

"You've got to be kidding me."

He shrugged. "Welcome to Tennessee."

I took my pack off and quickly emptied the essentials (food bag, warm clothing, sleeping bag, and foam pad) onto the platform. As I crawled to the back of the shelter, rolling out my sleeping bag, a placard on the wall caught my eye:

ABINGDON GAP
This shelter, built in 1952 by the Forest Service and
maintained by the Tennessee Eastman Hiking Club,
will accommodate five people.

I made a quick mental count: the Family, me and Isis, Lash, Badger, and Heald. Twelve of us, plus a dog. Isis and I had shipped our tent home a few towns back, after we realized it was practically useless for winter camping. (The last time we had tented, the water in our breath had condensed on the nylon walls, and flakes of ice had drifted down on us all night.) I knew none of the others carried tents, either, so I consolidated my gear into the smallest possible space.

Heald came up from the spring trail just as Joy tramped into the clearing. Seeing him, she scooped up a handful of fresh snow. It wouldn't quite pack into a ball, but she tossed it at him anyway. It hit his legs in a soft puff of powder.

"I hit Heald with a snowball! I got Heald!" She danced around in front of the shelter. If she was tired from a day of hiking through snow up to her waist, it didn't show.

"I'm gonna getcha," Heald said, grinning. He held up his hands like claws and roared, looking more bearlike than ever.

Joy gave a shriek and dove behind the shelter. She reappeared a moment later, peering cautiously around the corner. "Heald, what's on your face?"

"My beard and my glasses, that's what."

"No, you got somethin' in your beard. Looks like icicles." Sure enough, Heald's breath had condensed on his reddish mustache as he hiked, leaving a fringe of ice around his upper lip.

Heald wiped his face. "Snotsicles is more like it." He picked up a double handful of snow and lunged toward Joy's side of the shelter, grinning again. "You're gonna have somethin' on your face in a minute!"

Joy gave a screech that ended in a giggle, and she quickly ducked inside the shelter and tossed her pack down. "I'm safe in here, Heald," she told him fiercely. "Jackrabbit won't let anything happen to me."

I picked her up and set her on the sleeping platform, trying to ignore the lump in my throat. She was right; I would do anything to protect her if she was in danger. I loved her; I loved all of the Family. But I knew we wouldn't hike with them forever, and I wondered if I would ever see her after the Trail. Most of our other friends had fixed addresses. The Family didn't even have a last name.

We did manage to fit all of us into the shelter, with the children sleeping end-to-end and the adults occupying spaces perhaps eighteen inches wide, just big enough to lie on one side. Foam pads and sleeping bags covered every inch of the shelter floor. The mouse hangers dangling from the rafters bulged with brightly colored food bags, like inverted bunches of balloons for a child's birthday. It was impossible to move without bumping into someone. Tempers began to flare.

"I'm not sharing this stupid foam pad with my stupid dumb sister!" Joy announced, crossing her arms.

Hope glared back at her. "Oh yeah? Well, I don't even wanna *sit* next to you!"

"Hey, you guys got it easy," Joel said. "I'm twice the size of you, and I still have to share mine with stinky John!" He cuffed his brother hard on the shoulder. John said nothing, but his eyes narrowed.

"Hey, guys, that's enough." Mary spoke up wearily from the back of the shelter. "We all have to share our space. You don't hear Isis and jackrabbit complaining."

It was a lot easier to behave well, I reflected, when I knew I was being used as an example for someone. I thought back to the crises Isis and I had faced alone: our short-supplied week in the Pennsylvania mountains, our night-hike into Harpers Ferry. *I probably would have complained a lot less and helped a lot more if it hadn't been just the two of us*, I thought, and I felt a little ashamed.

"Hey, who wants to play Hangman?" I said. I knew the kids liked the game, and it was a good way to help them practice their spelling—as well as keep them from squabbling. I picked up the ratty spiral-bound register and opened it to the back page. Mary gave me a grateful smile.

"I want to play!" Hope scooted her sleeping bag to the back of the shelter beside me.

"Me too, me too!" Joy snuggled in on my other side. The boys settled at the foot of my sleeping bag.

"Who wants to start?" I asked the children.

"Me," Joy said instantly. Then she looked uncertain. "Jackrabbit, will you spell a word for me?"

"Okay, but I can't guess letters if I do."

"All right." She leaned close and whispered, "How do you spell 'snot-sicles'?"

In the morning, I was eager to leave the crowded shelter. I wanted some time alone to reflect. I ate a granola bar for breakfast, packed up quickly, and strapped on my snowshoes. The rest of the hikers were stirring now, rolling over and wiping the sleep from their eyes. I left the shelter clearing just in time to hear Lash's outraged yelp.

"A mouse chewed a hole in my jacket! Little bastard! What am I gonna do? It's not even mine—I borrowed it from my brother!"

Other sounds drifted from the shelter as I began striding along the trail. "Mary, Joy kicked me all night! I didn't sleep at all!"

"Ow! Stop it, Joel!"

I picked up my pace, and soon all I could hear was the soft shuffle of my snowshoes and my steady breathing. It was barely dawn. A rose-colored light came through the branches, draping itself over the tree trunks and the snowy ground.

I had been hoping that solitude would give me time to think, but I couldn't seem to focus my mind on anything in particular. Thoughts slipped through my head, drifting past like the wisps of snow that blew over the ground: recipes, song lyrics, Tae Kwon Do movements, Spanish verb conjugations, parts of the periodic table. Memories from the Trail, from college, from my childhood. Back in Maine, at the beginning of our hike, I had imagined that the A.T. would give me time to reflect and consider what I wanted to do with my life. I had started college intent on getting a biology degree, going straight on to graduate school, and becoming a professor before I reached the age of thirty. Somewhere in there, I'd gotten sidetracked. I had graduated with a double major in biology and music, much less certain of my path. And now I was on the Trail. I was dimly aware, even at that point, that the A.T. was a stand-in for my larger life goals; if I could work toward a goal just by putting one foot in front of the other, I wouldn't have to think about the rest of it. We had planned to finish the Trail in December. Now it looked like we wouldn't reach Georgia until February—and even then, I would not have completed a thru-hike, given the section I'd missed. *Why am I out here?* I asked myself for the umpteen millionth time.

The air warmed up as the sun climbed above the ridges, and I stopped to take off my jacket. The snow around threw back tiny rainbow sparks of light. I took a sip of cold water and put the bottle back under my shirt. *Why am I out here? Because I have no idea what else I'd be doing.*

I heard footsteps behind me. It was Anonymous Badger. His long, blue-black hair cascaded over his shoulder, and his dark eyes sparkled beneath the brim of his wool hat. "Isn't this a beautiful morning? I'm so glad I came out to hike with you guys. I wouldn't miss this for the world."

I looked around at the snowy ridge top: black trees, glittering snow; distant ridges visible between the branches, their outlines framed by woods. Up ahead, a white blaze beckoned from the broad trunk of a maple. I had seen similar scenes every day since the first snowfall, several hundred miles north of here, but now I saw it with new eyes. "Yeah, you're right. This is pretty awesome."

Badger stepped past me, and his slim form soon disappeared around a bend in the trail. I smiled.

A few nights later, we stayed at Vandeventer Shelter. It was a typical Tennessee shelter, built of plywood and cinderblocks, perched on the end of a long ridge. Once again, there was no privy, only a rusty, disreputable-looking shovel leaned against the outer wall. I found Lash behind the shelter, sitting on a rock, staring down through the trees at the valley 1,500 feet below. In the bottomlands, the slate-gray surface of Watauga Lake shivered with little breezes. The air had warmed slightly over the afternoon; a damp, chilly wind came up from the water. Heald was nowhere to be seen, and I realized that I hadn't seen Annie's tracks since the last road.

I sat down next to Lash. "Hey, man. Where's Heald?"

He looked up. "Oh, hey, jackrabbit. Heald hitched out on the last road. You know why?"

"Looked like the snow was getting pretty deep for Annie again." I sat down next to him on the rock.

Lash shook his head with a mysterious smile. "This shelter's haunted."

"What do you mean?"

"Dude, that's what he said. He told me there was a guy, a local, whose girlfriend was cheating on him. He brought her out here one night in the middle of winter and he killed her."

"That's horrible." I knew that several murders had taken place along the Trail in its seventy-five-year history, but I had never heard about this one. I shivered a little, looking around the clearing and out over the lake.

"Yeah. Heald said ever since then, weird shit has happened here. People hear a woman's voice coming down the trail, but when they go look, there's nobody there. And—" he leaned close, lowering his voice "—there's a bird with bright red eyes that lands in the firepit at midnight."

I shrugged and tried to put some confidence back into my voice. "With any luck, we'll be asleep by then."

"I don't know, jackrabbit." Lash shuddered. "I don't know if I *can* sleep, with ghosts around . . ."

"Lash, you're too jumpy."

The clearing filled up with voices as the rest of our party arrived. Mary sat down on the edge of the shelter platform and helped Faith climb out of her pack. Badger, Paul, and the children tossed their packs down and ran off to look for firewood. Isis took Hope and John on an expedition for water. The spring here was half a mile straight downhill, and my sister knew I was having trouble with my hip again. As they disappeared from sight, I heard Hope's eager voice: "What if there's a big fortress there? What if there's dragons guarding it?"

I smiled. Trust Isis to make a routine trip for water into a quest. The nervous chill that had settled over me dissipated as I went to work on the normal camp chores, hanging food bags, stringing a tarp over the entrance in case of rain, laying out our sleeping bags and mattresses, and collecting firewood. I knew it was too cold for the filter to work, and we didn't have enough fuel for cooking and water purification. All of us, even the Family, would need to boil the next day's drinking water over a fire.

The firepit, a square of cement with a recessed center, sat directly under the dripline of the roof. Chunks of wet snow slid into it as I watched.

"Anybody seen any good rocks for a fire ring?" I said. With the official firepit out of commission, we would need some other way to balance our cooking pots above the flames. Paul, Joy, Badger, Lash, and I kicked aside the snow, looking for good-sized stones. Aside from the boulder where Lash and I had sat, though, the stones around the campsite were no larger than pebbles. I had a flicker of nostalgia for something I'd thought I would never miss: the rock fields of Pennsylvania.

There had to be a way . . . Then my eyes fell on a maple log in the stack of firewood, perhaps as thick as my ankle. From the bark, I could tell it hadn't been dead for very long. *Maybe this will work*, I thought. I took Isis's pocketknife from the outside pouch of her pack and used the little saw to cut two foot-long sections of the log.

Lash looked doubtful. "What are you going to do with that? It's so green it won't burn anyway, even if we do get a fire going."

"That's the idea," I said. "Watch."

I used another branch like an adze, digging into the frozen ground across the clearing from the shelter. Soon I had excavated a pit perhaps a foot square. I sunk the green maple logs into the ground on either side of the pit, lengthwise, so a pot could rest on them. In the middle, I stacked small twigs and bits of dry inner bark around a scrap of waxed paper, part of a cereal bag I had saved from our last resupply.

Lash shook his head. "Man. You Mainers know a thing or two."

"Thanks." I stepped back, grinning. "You want to do the honors?"

Lash took his lighter and touched the flame to the edge of the paper, just as Isis and the kids returned with the water.

After supper, we held our usual discussion to plan the next day's mileage.

"Hopefully, we can put a good number of miles behind us tomorrow," Paul spoke up from the shadows. "It looks like it's almost all downhill to the Dennis Cove Road. Damascus Dave told me there's a great hostel there. Kincora."

"How far is that?" Mary asked.

"It's eighteen from here. If we get an early start, we could do it."

"I guess so. I got some rest in Damascus. I guess I'm up for a long day."

"Kincora's wonderful," Anonymous Badger said. "I spent a lot of time there on my first thru-hike. Bob—the owner—is a pretty amazing guy."

Late that night, a strange sound woke me. It was coming from somewhere in the woods. *A woman's voice, I thought sleepily. Somebody talking to herself on the trail* . . . My eyes snapped open and adrenaline flooded through my body. I could feel my heartbeat pounding against the floorboards. I sat upright and stared out into the clearing in front of the shelter. I couldn't see much without my glasses: attenuated silver moonlight on the trees, patches of shadow dancing on the ground as the bare branches scraped together. I strained my ears, listening . . . the sound of mice scrabbling in the rafters, wind in the trees. Then it came again, closer: *who-who* . . . *who-who*, coming through the moonlit woods. *An owl*, I thought, and took a deep breath, relaxing onto my foam pad. As I lay back, I saw a flicker of motion at the edge of the clearing. With a soundless rush of feathers, the bird landed on a low branch. Then it came closer, landing right in front of the shelter. Right in the old firepit.

I suppressed a shriek and pulled my mummy bag over my head, curling up tight. I didn't wait to see if the bird had red eyes. I lay there for a long time, shaking. Eventually I fell back asleep. By morning light, it seemed a little silly. Had I dreamed it? I surreptitiously checked the snow around the firepit for wing marks and found nothing.

As we packed up, a light rain began falling. No, it wasn't rain, I saw. It stuck to the twigs, the rhododendron branches, the ground, forming a hard casing of ice on every surface.

"Freezing rain," Isis said with resignation.

Paul finished cinching the top compartment of his pack and came to take a look. He sighed, looking suddenly older. "You're right. Guess we can't make it to Kincora tonight."

We took out the maps and had a short conference. "Watauga Lake Shelter's six and a half miles," Mary said. "I know we can make it that far."

"There's a road a couple miles beyond it. I'm gonna go there and hitch out to Kincora," Lash said.

Badger nodded. "I think I'll do that, too. I'm getting pretty bad blisters. Maybe we can get Bob to come meet you guys at the road tomorrow morning and slack you over to the hostel. He's always doing things like that for hikers." Badger shouldered his pack and started to walk away.

Hope was the first one to notice something strange. "Badger, why aren't you wearing your boots?" she asked in a tone of older-sisterly alarm. I took a closer look; sure enough, his boots were tied to the outside of his pack. He wasn't exactly barefoot, but his thin pair of neoprene socks gave his feet very little protection from the cold.

He shrugged. "I'm more comfortable without them. To each his own. Surely, after hiking with these fair ladies, you understand."

I almost protested—*we never walked barefoot with six inches of snow on the ground!*—but I remembered all the people who had called us crazy for hiking barefoot at all. Though Badger was taking it to an extreme that I would not have chosen, I had to trust that his approach would work for him. A saying that we had heard from many nobos came to mind: *hike your own hike.*

Joel stood up and fastened his pack. "Hey, can I go with you guys to Kincora? Can I?" He looked more eager than I had seen him in a long time. Paul and Mary exchanged a glance, and Paul nodded. Joel drew himself up straighter and swaggered a little as he headed down the trail. Lash looked a bit discomfited but said nothing.

It took us most of the day, slipping and stumbling down the icy trail, to reach the valley. We followed Badger's almost-bare footprints through the snow and mud. True rain fell at the lowest elevations, a hard stinging rain that bounced off the asphalt of the road across Watauga Dam. Cliffs rose up behind and before us. On the right side, the concrete apron of the dam dropped off into the valley, the foot of it barely visible between sheets of rain. On the left side, the gray-green water stretched out, tossing in the wind and pockmarked with raindrops. It was strange, almost unsettling, to see so much open water among these mountains. Squinting at the flat expanse of it, I could imagine that it was a far-flung arm of the ocean. The smell was wrong, though; instead of the iodine tang of the sea, this lake had a raw scent of decaying leaves and dead fish.

We didn't stay very long by the water. The cold rain drove us back into the woods, where the trail meandered up and down small hills. Sodden brown vegetation poked up through the remaining patches of snow. The dead lake made a gray backdrop for the lifeless scene. *I have never seen a landscape so utterly devoid of charm*, I thought.

The rain was changing back to ice when we reached the shelter. Badger had left a half-full fuel bottle and several packets of Jell-O. The register was open to an otherwise empty page, with a note in his precise handwriting: *This is hypothermia weather. Get in your bags and make some hot Jell-O to warm up! See you tomorrow.* He had signed it, as usual, with his initials and a sketch of a badger.

Paul fired up the stove as John and I trekked back to the lake for water. We returned to find Paul presiding over a pot of steaming red Jell-O. Isis, Mary, and the rest of the children gathered around the pot with looks of horror on their faces. John and I exchanged a glance and elbowed our way through the crowd to get a better look.

There was something absolutely foul floating in the red liquid: a pink, mottled mass that resembled some kind of organ, perhaps a lung or a stomach.

John jumped back. "Eaugh! What *is* that?"

Paul looked almost apologetic. "Well, I thought to make it more nutritious, I might add some dry milk . . ." He reached in with his spoon and prodded the mass. It seemed to contract. He sliced off part of it with his spoon and raised it to his lips.

"Oh, I can't watch!" Hope pretended to swoon backwards, and Isis caught her.

Paul chewed for a long time, his expression impossible to read. "I don't think that was such a good idea," he finally conceded.

Isis

Two level miles from Watauga Lake Shelter, Lash and Anonymous Badger met us at a road crossing. I gave each of them a hug, then turned around to find myself facing a small, wiry man in a baseball cap. With his merry brown eyes, red cheeks, and bushy gray mustache, he reminded me of a leprechaun.

"You must be Isis. I'm Bob Peoples. I run Kincora Hostel, over on the Dennis Cove Road." He grabbed my hand in both of his and gave it a hearty shake. Then he turned to the semicircle of hikers gathered around him. "I'd be glad to slack you over Pond Mountain, if you'll do me a favor."

I caught myself speculating about the sort of task a leprechaun might want us to do in return for his assistance. *Spin straw into gold? Build a city in a day? Wear out nine pairs of iron shoes?*

"Sounds great," said jackrabbit. "What can we do for you?"

"I maintain the next section of trail," Bob said. "I'd be obliged if you'd make note of any blowdowns you see, so that I can take my saw in tomorrow and clear them." He glanced around the circle. "Good. I'll see you tonight."

Paul and Lash both said that their packs felt light enough with only one day's worth of food in them, but the rest of us joyfully loaded our heavy gear into the back of Bob's truck, then headed across the road toward Pond Mountain. The prospect of sheltered bunks and readily available water put us all in a festive mood. Hope, Joy, John, and Joel scampered up the switchbacks, pausing in rhododendron thickets to ambush each other with snowballs. Jackrabbit, Lash, and I joined the children in a few skirmishes, and Mary sang verses of "Dig a Hole" to Faith as she walked. "Dig hole, Mama! Dig hole!" I heard Faith call out every time Mary stopped to catch her breath.

Pond Flats, as the map designated the mile-and-a half stretch of ridge at the top of the mountain, wasn't at all flat. As far as I could see, it didn't have any ponds, either. Like the rest of the nine miles we slacked, though, it was exceptionally well maintained. In the past few months, finding our way over, under, or around the blowdowns that littered the trail had become part of our daily routine. The ice and snow storms of this harsh winter had brought down many trees, both dead and living, and few trail maintainers had braved the bad weather to remove them. *No one expects hikers to be passing through in this season*, I had to remind myself. *Why shouldn't the maintainers wait until spring to clear the trail?* But in Bob's section, fresh sawdust above the recent snow showed where he had been working in the past few days. Neatly cut arches through the rhododendron brakes, high enough that the tops of our hiking sticks didn't bump them and knock snow down our backs, provided further evidence of his industry.

Along with the delightfully obstacle-free trail, the day brought splendid scenery. Snow and ice on the trees made distant mountains glitter like pyramids of sugar where the sun touched them. Strips of blue sky peeked out between cottonball clouds. By the time we reached the Flats, the air had grown so warm—perhaps forty degrees—that I stripped down to my wool shirt, shorts, and gaiters for the first time in a month. Drops of water sparkled in the tassels of pines, and the cracks in the bark glowed a soft grayish red under trickles of meltwater.

As the last rays of the sun painted the eastern mountains orange, we shuffled up the icy driveway of Kincora. We found Bob's truck parked beside two rough-hewn log cabins connected by a covered porch. Wood smoke poured from the chimneys of both cabins. A low, wobbly baying, punctuated by a few even deeper barks, heralded our arrival. As we reached the porch steps, a chubby coonhound trotted up to a fence beside the buildings, her ears flapping. Close behind her strode an Irish wolfhound almost as tall as Joel, who gazed at us from dark, intelligent eyes. We all turned as the door of the left-hand building banged open. Bob stood on the porch, smiling and waving us forward.

"This is the hostel. Come on in. I've brought your gear in already. Paul, Mary, I've given you the private room—right across from the woodstove. The rest of you are upstairs. There's a friend of yours staying in the bunkroom behind the kitchen. Guy named Heald. He was hoping you'd catch up to him, but . . ." He looked at Hope and Joy, who were bouncing up and down with excitement. ". . . I'd recommend that you greet him quietly. He's recovering from a bad bout of flu."

As he talked, Bob ushered us into a lamp-lit living room full of cushy, worn armchairs. Hundreds of photos covered the walls. Many showed north-bounders standing behind the sign on Katahdin, in snow or rain or sunlight, their arms flung wide in a gesture of triumph. Others showed southbounders grinning as they posed beside a metal plaque on the wooded summit of Springer. A few showed hikers standing at other places along the Trail with the same grin and the same gesture of triumph: flip-floppers and section hikers who had reached their finishing points.

"That's my Wall of Heroes," said Bob, noticing the direction of my gaze. "I'll be expecting a copy of your summit photo to add to the Wall when you finish."

Finish. It had been months since I'd allowed myself to think about finishing the Trail. Each week, I thought only as far as the next resupply point. Even in Damascus, when we'd seen exactly how bad it could get and we had seriously considered quitting, I had thought of the argument in terms of staying on the Trail or getting off it, not in terms of reaching Springer Mountain. I tried to picture myself posing beside the plaque, reaching down to touch the last white blaze. And then—shopping for a used car, driving home. I imagined sitting by the fireplace with jackrabbit, taking turns recounting our adventure on the Grayson Highlands to a rapt audience of friends and neighbors. From that perspective, the blizzard seemed like a legend, something that had happened to someone else a long time ago. I shook myself out of my reverie. *Four hundred miles to go, and it's still January*, I reminded myself. *And our trek across the Grayson Highlands is no fairy tale. It's the reality we'll be walking back into tomorrow, or the day after.*

We decided to take a zero the next day, in spite of the warm weather. After Damascus, even the most ambitious hikers in our group agreed that we should take every chance we got to rest, re-waterproof our boots, and gain back the few pounds of fat and water weight that we lost in each week's hiking. Hurrying down the trail, "making miles," seemed pointless now that we had lost all hope of outrunning winter. Bob drove us down the hairpin turns of the Dennis Cove Road into Elizabethton, the nearest large town in the valley. Mary and I picked up a whole cartload of fresh food, including ten pounds of fruit, seven loaves of bread, and four gallons of ice cream.

We rose early in the morning to prepare our best approximation of one of Ginny's epic breakfasts: eggs, toast, pancakes with whipped cream and ice cream, cinnamon rolls, hot chocolate, and fruit salad. Bob came by just as we were finishing our third platefuls and getting out the lettuce, cheese, and tomatoes for the transition into lunch. He introduced us to his wife Pat, a gracious, soft-spoken woman with short blond hair and a wide smile. She took off her jacket in the warm room; underneath it, she wore a t-shirt that said *Horses are like candy; you can't have just one.* Hope's eyes lit up, and soon she had engaged Pat in an animated conversation about the horses that lived down the road from the Family's homestead in Maine.

"Isis and jackrabbit are gonna visit us when we get back, 'cause they live in Maine, too." I overheard her saying. "I'm gonna show them the horses, and our swimming hole, and our favorite tree."

Anonymous Badger kept the woodstove burning all day, chopping and carrying wood from the pile behind the cabin. Lash, Paul, and jackrabbit helped Bob chop the ice out of his driveway, while Mary and I packed our resupplies. The children practiced reading out of the pocket Bible they carried and the *National Geographics* we found in a basket beside the couch. Every once in a while, the energy they usually spent in hiking would erupt, and they'd drop their books and race up and down the stairs in a spontaneous game of tag, until Mary reminded them to be quiet so that Heald could sleep. (He had yet to emerge from the back room of the hostel. When I went to check on him, he groaned and turned away from the light of the doorway.) We all took turns sitting by the stove, re-waterproofing our boots: rubbing beeswax into the leather, heating it up so that the wax would sink in, then adding another coat. In the afternoon Mary baked cookies, her special oatmeal recipe that she'd described to me way back in Pennsylvania.

I sat on the end of the couch, trying to write a letter home. *How could I describe the Grayson Highlands?* Sooner or later, we'd have to tell our parents the whole story, but I didn't want to worry them while we were still so far from finished with our hike. So far from home. Beside me, Anonymous Badger was trying to teach Hope how to play cat's cradle. I watched his long, graceful fingers arrange the threads in her hands: a crown, a nest, a spider's web. He leaned forward, intent on a slipped strand, and his long black hair caught the light from the window behind him. I reached up, wanting to stroke his hair as I would a cat's, then drew my hand back quickly and returned to my letter. *We miss you. The weather's been terrible, but we are okay—we bought lots of new winter gear in Damascus.* Pretty obvious that something went wrong. I scribbled out "lots of" and wrote "some" above it, but I couldn't come up with anything else to say. *The lack of detail alone will tell them that I'm hiding something,* I thought. *I'm transparent.* I set the letter down.

Hope had lost her patience with the intricacies of Badger's string patterns; she was trying to engage him in a wrestling match.

"You ought to pick on somebody your own size," he laughed, flicking his wrist out of her grip and spinning her in a circle without moving from his place on the couch. "Then maybe your enthusiasm would make up for your lack of technique."

Hope's eyes glinted. She balled up her fists and rained down a series of quick punches, which Badger easily deflected. "Mind if I turn my back?" he asked her. "I could use a massage."

"I'll give you a backrub," I offered, in the most ingenuous tone I could muster.

"Okay," he said, his dark eyes full of laughter. He glanced at Hope, who was trying to tie his right arm to the table with the cat's cradle thread. "Shall we go upstairs, where it's quieter?" he asked me.

The smell of Mary's cookies baking, sugar and nutmeg and cinnamon, filled the dark bedroom. I sat behind Badger, on an upper bunk, working the knots out of his shoulder muscles. We didn't speak. I leaned forward and let my cheek rest against his sleek hair. He turned in my arms and kissed me.

After a minute he leaned back. "It's not that simple," he said. "I love someone else."

"Someone you're dating?" I asked.

"No. A friend who I've had a crush on for eight years. She isn't interested. But no one I've been with, in all those years, has taken her place in my mind."

"I won't even try," I told him. "I just want a little comfort."

"I suppose that's possible." He laughed, gave me another quick kiss, then slid off the bunk and walked downstairs without looking back.

Some time in the night, I woke from a nightmare of falling. The planks of my bunk lay solid beneath me, but my head pounded, and cold sweat made my arms and legs stick to my sleeping bag liner. A sudden wave of nausea sent me scrambling out of my damp sleeping bag. I didn't have time to dig out my headlamp; I felt my way downstairs to the toilet in the dark. Long after I had emptied my stomach of all that remained of supper, I huddled on the rough plank floor, retching. The sound of water dripping on the roof—was the snow still melting, or was rain falling?—seemed inordinately loud; each drop echoed inside my skull like the tick of an enormous clock. Eventually the nausea subsided, and I dragged myself back up the stairs to bed.

For the next day and a half, I left my bunk only to creep downstairs to the bathroom. Mary brought me cup after cup of tea, but I could only keep down a mouthful every few hours. The children's footsteps on the stairs sounded like the charge of a cavalry regiment, and even the thin gray daylight from the bunkroom's single window hurt my eyes. I drifted in and out of fevered sleep, uncertain of the edges between dreams and reality. Anonymous Badger leaned over me, washing my forehead with a damp cloth. I reached up to touch his face, but the skin changed to wood beneath my fingers—I woke with my hand pressed against the bedpost.

By the time my fever lifted, Heald had gone to visit some friends in town, and Lash had left the Trail—whether permanently or only until his hiking companions were no longer contagious, he would not say. The rest of us stayed at Kincora for nine days while the flu ran its course. Those of us who were healthy tended the sick, fed the fire, and ate constantly, trying to gain as much weight as possible before heading back into winter. Bob encouraged us to stay as long as we needed; every day, he and Pat came over, bringing us extra blankets, books, and medicine.

Mary took advantage of the hiatus to catch up on homeschooling, drilling the children on spelling and addition. Jackrabbit and I took over the lessons during the three days that Mary and Faith were ill. We tried to make the math component more fun by teaching it in the form of algebra. Even seven-year-old Joy understood the concept—a number disguised as a letter, and a set of tricks you could use to unmask it—but none of the children took our lessons seriously. To them, algebra was an elaborate game, like building snowmen or sketching in the margins of registers, a pastime unworthy of the grave attention they gave to waxing their boots or gathering kindling.

In the evenings, I read aloud from a copy of *The Hobbit* that Bob had found for me at a used book store. In contrast to the algebra lessons, this story of danger and adventure on a mountain path seemed perfectly relevant to our own lifestyle. Joy spent whole days pretending to be Bilbo Baggins; she wrapped my green jacket around her shoulders as a cloak and led expeditions out to the woodpile. Hope and John drew maps on which the Roans and the Smokies intersected with the Misty Mountains of Middle-Earth.

For me, the familiar words came to new life as I watched the play of expressions on my listeners' faces. John drew in his breath at the mention of Smaug the Dragon, and Joy shivered, nestling closer under my collarbone. A few paragraphs later, though, the children laughed when the phrase "a journey from which some of us . . . may never return" caused the book's diminutive hero to collapse in a fit of nerves. Across the room, Mary tried to darn a sock while Faith nursed, but she kept undoing the stitches she had just sewn, her attention caught by the story. When I closed the book after the first night's reading, she sighed, a rueful smile flickering over her face.

"I never read that book before, but I feel just like that hobbit. One day I was canning blueberries for the winter, and the next, I was walking to Georgia with a bedroll tied to my shoulders, trying to keep up with all these tough hikers." She waved a hand toward her husband and children, smiling wryly. "I left twenty pints of blueberries in the cupboard and a garden full of zucchini and scarlet runner beans. A sunny kitchen with a shelf of books. The bed Paul made us out of the trees we cleared for the corn field. I don't know who's living in our house now. I don't think we'll ever go back. But I'd like . . ." She glanced at Paul, and her voice trailed away.

Paul looked up from the magazine he'd been reading. "Do you want to go back?" he asked.

"Not to Maine. But I do want a home someday. A place where we can shut the doors on winter."

Nights at Kincora, after everyone else had gone to bed, Badger and jackrabbit and I sat around the coffee table, eating cookies and playing Scrabble. One evening I made the molasses-oatmeal bread that my mother used to bake for our family once a week. By then, half of our group had fallen ill— even Paul, who claimed that this was the first time he'd been sick in ten years. Mary and Faith seemed to be recovering, and John had slept peacefully since three that afternoon, but Joy mumbled and cried out in her fever. When I checked on her, she didn't recognize me. Once she called me her mother; an hour later, she thought I was a character out of *The Hobbit*. The thermometer read a hundred and two degrees, then a hundred and three. I wondered if I should pound on Bob's door, wake him and ask him to take her to the hospital. Sleet rattled against the windows; there would be ice on the ten miles of steep curving roads that lay between us and the nearest town. I waited, played Scrabble. Joy's temperature held for an hour, then fell half a degree.

I baked bread as a ritual, to bring something wholesome into that house full of sickness. I baked bread to invoke my mother, a woman who would have known what to do, between an ice storm and a child's fever. I followed her recipe from memory: honey and molasses, hot water, salt, oats. The rhythm of kneading calmed me, and the smell of the bread rising cleared the sour stench of our fevers from the air. I started late; jackrabbit had gone to bed by the time I brushed milk over the tops of the loaves and turned the oven on. The air seemed to brighten as I worked; I turned around to find that Badger had lit candles in every corner of the room. I lay down beside him while the bread baked, and he kissed the tips of my fingers one by one.

jackrabbit

After nine days, the sickness had run its course for all of us. I packed up quickly that morning, more than ready to be moving again. I'd been ready to go two days ago, before the sledgehammer of the flu came down on me, so it was a simple matter of stowing everything in my pack. For the Family, though, it was hard to get everyone's gear taken care of.

"Where's my hairbrush?" Hope shouted down the stairs. The other children joined the refrain.

"Now where are my boot laces?"

"I can't find my stupid gaiters!"

"Mary, what'd you do with Faith's dolly?" Mary groaned. Dolly had been carefully hidden in the hopes that Faith would forget her, giving Mary a few less ounces to haul around. Paul, unfortunately, hadn't been apprised of the plan.

Faith looked up at the mention of the old rag doll. "Mama, dowwy! Where dowwy?"

Bob came in about noon. "Rain's gonna start soon," he said. "You might wanna think about staying tonight." Outside, the air had a weight and dampness to it, and I could tell he was right. But more than anything, I wanted to hike. I think we all did—too many days of being cooped up, tied down. Our boots were waterproofed, packs ready. Even the children, who usually perked up at the thought of a zero day, looked at their feet and made small noises of dissent.

"Whatever you want," Bob said. "Just thought I'd let you know you're welcome for another night." He smiled at the kids like a proud grandfather and headed back to his house across the breezeway. I wish I'd said something to thank him. He had opened his hostel for us in the middle of winter, given us shelter, wood for heating; he'd fixed the plumbing for us and tended us through our sickness. He'd put up with us in our lowest moments, carefully sidestepping all the arguments and bickering. We could never repay him for all he'd done, not in money or in deeds, and as I had many times before, I vowed to pass on the kindness when I had the opportunity.

As it was, that was the last I saw of Bob for a long time. We left in the early afternoon for the 5.8 miles to Moreland Gap Shelter. Just as Bob had predicted, the rain began shortly after we left, a steady cold rain halfway between drizzle and downpour. Strangely, I found I didn't mind it. I was so happy to be hiking again, even though the weight of my pack dug painfully into my shoulders and hips, and the cold water soon soaked through my hat and began trickling through my hair. I looked around at the newly visible ground—leaf litter in a thousand rich shades of brown, dark green ferns, the mottled gray stones the color of tree bark. It was the first time in more than a month that I'd seen bare ground, without snow. Everything looked bright and new. I thought back to the summer, hiking in the Whites with Waterfall and her indomitable optimism.

"I love the rain, don't y'all?" she'd asked as we worked our way down another precipitous mountainside in the cold August drizzle. "It makes all the colors look brighter somehow. Like the plants are all happier bein' wet."

As my mind wandered back to summer, I heard a shout from Joel up ahead.

"Hey, check this out!" He pointed out a tiny red eft beside the path. The bright red-orange salamander moved at a glacial pace in the cold rain, but it was alive. It was the first sign of spring we'd seen; like a tiny, bright beacon, it signaled hope.

As the afternoon wore on, though, my capacity for optimism was severely strained. After the first few miles, the weight of my pack became more and more intolerable. Eight days' worth of food had been forced into my food bag, threatening to split the seams, and I was also hauling all my winter clothing, spare fuel, and three liters of water (to save the fuel we'd use to purify it). The snowshoes, suddenly superfluous, hung on the outside of my pack, clanking and shifting with every step. Isis later told me that her pack, leaving

Kincora, weighed seventy-two pounds. Mine was certainly less than that, since she carried much of our joint gear now, but it still weighed more than I ever want to carry again.

The trail turned sharply up the hill. The twinge in my right hip returned, like a needle driven into the joint. I fell behind the Family. The sounds of the children's happy laughter receding into the woods only served to deepen my despondency. At the top of the first hill, I paused to set my pack down and stretch, hoping to ease the pain in my hip.

Anonymous Badger came over the crest of the hill, thin and wiry, golden-skinned, with the rain in his hair. "Hello, Miss Jackrabbit." His voice was soft with concern.

"Hello, Mr. Badger."

"Are you okay?"

"I—yes—no."

"Miss Rabbit, why are you crying?"

Because I'm afraid—we walked the razor's edge on the Grayson Highlands, and Lord knows what we'll find on Roan. Because I feel more and more like deadweight on this expedition, unable to take the physical strain, cut out of the decision-making. Because I'm lonely. Because my sister chose you first, and I could never get in the way of that.

Instead I said, "This fucking hip. It's killing me."

The next day the cold returned. A light snow fell, streaking the sky with white again, but only a few inches stuck to the ground—not enough for the snowshoes. My pack must have still weighed upwards of sixty-five pounds. The dinner of instant potato flakes we had eaten the night before had hardly lightened my load. I was in a foul mood. Every little dip and rise in the trail—and there seemed to be an inordinate number of them—loomed like a New Hampshire notch.

A low-grade sense of dread weighed on me more than my overloaded pack. At Kincora, Bob had warned us about this section of the trail. "Now, I don't want to frighten ya, but I gotta say, when you go through Campbell Hollow, it's best to stay on the trail and keep your eyes open. The park service took that land by eminent domain, and the Campbell family didn't take kindly to that. Years ago, just after the government took the land, some hikers found fishhooks strung up above the trail, right at eye level. That didn't happen again, but there's been stories of people setting their dogs on hikers . . . We used to have a shelter in the middle of that stretch. Burned to the ground—twice. Like I said, it's been a few years since anything's happened back in there, but I always tell sobos to keep their eyes open, just in case."

For the first few hours of hiking, I stayed alert and nervous. There were signs of humanity everywhere. The edges of all the gravel roads we crossed were festooned with garbage. Once or twice I caught sight of houses between the trees or heard the buzz of a chainsaw in the distance. One hillside had been used as a dump; fifty years' worth of old refrigerators, rusty cans, and auto parts cascaded down from the road, scattered among snowy underbrush.

After a few hours, I let my vigilance relax. The weight of my pack, the pain in my hips and knees, and the necessity of following the white blazes occupied the bulk of my attention. One corner of my mind noticed the spare beauty of the woods in the new snow.

I came to a sapling that had fallen across the path at knee height. I tried to lift one foot over it, straining my muscles and leaning hard on my hiking sticks, but the leg simply refused to obey. My clumsy boot kept catching on the top of the log. I threw my sticks down and cursed vehemently.

I heard footsteps crunching the snow behind me. I whirled around, my paranoia returning in a rush, but it was only John.

"Hi, John," I said with a quiet sigh of relief. Belatedly, I realized he had heard me swearing. "Man, I'm sorry I said that in front of you. You really didn't need to hear that."

"That's okay. It's not like I ain't heard those words before." He lowered his voice as though confessing a secret. "Paul says 'em all the time. We ain't supposed to, though."

"It's not a good habit to get into. I curse more than I ought to. Sometimes it makes me feel better, when nothing else works."

John nodded. "Want to know what I say?"

"Yeah."

"RATS!" His eyes flashed. "Rats, rats, stupid, dumb, piece-a-junk, rats! It means the same thing, but Paul and Mary can't get mad at me for it." He gave a satisfied grin. Then he noticed the fallen tree. It was almost up to his waist. "I hate blowdowns. Joy showed me a trick for 'em, though." He sat down on the log and swung his legs over it easily.

I followed suit, a little less gracefully. My heavy pack threatened to throw me off balance. I had to admit, though, that this was easier than trying to step over the log. "Thanks for showing me that move, John. I'm glad you came along."

"Maybe we oughta hike together today. Badger said there was some big open fields coming up. Like balds. A horse pasture and a cow pasture, he said. I bet there ain't horses out now!"

The snow had picked up by the time we reached the first field. Thick white flakes filled the air, obscuring the trees at the far edge. I thought I could see the rough outline of pine trees, half a mile away, but I wasn't sure.

John reached up and took a firm grip on my hand. "I don't like this."

The two pastures were poorly blazed, and the snow thickened to a full blizzard. We followed the half-drifted footsteps of Joel and Anonymous Badger, who had gone ahead. I carried my hiking sticks in one hand, holding John's hand with the other. I repeated to myself, *this is only a pasture. This will end soon. This is only a pasture . . .* It was difficult to fight down the images of the Grayson Highlands that came into my head.

Both of us breathed a sigh of relief at the other side. John finally let go of my hand. "Thanks, jackrabbit," he said quietly.

After a few miles, we heard the sound of fast traffic coming through the trees. "Route 19E," I said. "The shelter's just a half mile on the other side."

"Yippee!" John raced down the last steep downhill, sliding in the new snow.

"Hey, wait for me!" I ran after him, ignoring the protests of my aching hips and knees. With the extra pack weight, each footstep slammed down heavily on the frozen earth.

The trail followed the slushy shoulder of the road for a short ways, with white blazes marked on the telephone poles. *Another half mile, and we'll be able to eat and rest.* After the stress and worry of the day, my brain felt numb. I heard the hum of a car approaching and glanced up.

"John! Look out!" I grabbed him by the top of his pack and jumped into the ditch, just in time to avoid the pickup truck that was barreling straight toward us. It swerved at the last minute, the tire tracks slicing through the road-side snow just inches from where our tracks jumped aside. I caught a glimpse of the driver as he passed; there was pure malice in his steely blue eyes.

John looked up, dazed. "He wouldn't have hit us, would he?"

I realized I was shaking. "No, of course not," I said with more conviction than I felt.

"Jackrabbit, why did he do that?"

"I don't know, John." I got to my feet slowly, feeling my body aching. The weight of my pack seemed to double as the adrenaline receded from my limbs. "He probably did it because the government took his land away so people like us could use it."

John was quiet for a few moments. I helped him brush the snow off his jacket. "The government took our land away, too," he said. "Paul wouldn't pay no taxes. That's why we're hiking. We had to leave. I still don't see why that guy was gonna run us over."

"He probably hates us. He must have been really angry when the park service took his land. Every time he sees a hiker, he probably thinks, 'that guy wouldn't be here if this land was still mine.'"

John considered for a moment. "I was real mad, too, when the guys came out to our homestead and said we couldn't live there no more. But I wouldn't ever hurt nobody because of that, especially somebody who wasn't there in the first place. That's just stupid."

We climbed back out of the ditch and followed the road to where the trail turned into the woods. When a screen of trees came between us and the asphalt, I finally felt safe.

Isis

A few ridges after Campbell Hollow Road, twelve miles into our fifteen-mile day, Faith began to cry. I was hiking with Mary. With more first aid training than any of the other members of our group, a relatively high resistance to hypothermia, and a tendency to carry a lot of extra snacks, I felt most useful bringing up the rear. I enjoyed the company of the other slow hikers: Mary daydreaming aloud about the subtropical island where she had first met Paul, Faith cooing and singing to herself in the backpack, and occasionally Hope, John, or Joy skipping down the trail to meet us, out of breath, glowing, bringing news from the others ahead.

Today, though, no one spoke or sang as we slogged through the new wet snow. I could see the muscles in Mary's curved shoulder straining against the pack strap. She took each step slowly, deliberately, as though the snow clinging to her gaiters weighed twenty pounds instead of two. Joy, unable to move as fast as she liked to in the heavy wet snow, had dropped back to hike with us, where the path had been beaten down a little. She slumped along with her head bent, kicking at clumps of snow and fallen branches. I tried to think of a story I could tell to distract her, but the act of imagining anything beyond the swirling snow and dark mesh of branches seemed as difficult as trying to pull open a window in the air and step back through it to Maine in the summertime. My mind pounded out the phrase "once upon a time . . . upon a time . . ." over and over, in time with my heavy steps, the words sounding more and more nonsensical.

The wind rose, and the thin, eerie shriek of two trees scraping against each other came closer as we climbed. Faith began to fret: "Num-num, Mommy. Num-num."

"I can't nurse you now, honey," Mary sighed. "We'll get too cold if we stop."

Faith's voice rose to a sob, and then a wail. Mary offered her a piece of a cracker, some dried fruit, the end of an energy bar. Each offer met with a more indignant scream: "Noooo! Nuuuum-num!" The words blurred into sobs, and the sobs became screams, cut off with a choking sound—but a moment later, the screaming began again, louder than ever, drowning out the wind in the trees.

I had thought I was exhausted before, but the sound of a child's voice crying, endlessly and without comfort, seemed to drain my resolve as easily as the wind sucked the warmth from my body. I could hardly imagine what Mary must be feeling. When she finally stopped on a narrow, windswept ridge and unbuckled her pack, I hadn't the heart to argue with her. I knew the hazards of standing in the wind, our clothes damp from sweat and snow. Several of the books I'd read in preparation for our hike had mentioned that the greatest risk of hypothermia occurred at temperatures on the edge of freezing, with cold rain or wet snow falling. Jackrabbit and I had joked about this information when I first discovered it ("Yeah, that's because there are a lot more idiots in the woods when it's thirty than when it's thirty below!"), but by now I'd had enough experience with borderline temperatures to take the books' warnings seriously. In case I needed any reminder, my teeth began to chatter before Mary's pack hit the ground.

Mary knew we were in danger, too. "You go ahead," she told me and Joy. "No point in you guys waiting around and freezing." Her shoulders shook as she unzipped the front of her jacket and leaned over Faith.

"No," I said. "I'll stay with you."

Joy shrugged her thin shoulders up around her ears and stood still, her back to the wind. Snowflakes clung to her fleece jacket, then piled up, making a drift between her pack and the back of her neck. The thought crossed my mind that I should reach out and brush the snow off so it wouldn't melt and get her hood wet, but before I could lift my arm, another, far more persuasive thought supplanted the impulse. *Why bother? More snow will fall as soon as I brush that off.* I hunched my own shoulders and faced away from the storm.

Holding still produced an agreeable sense of calm, a sort of suspension of discomfort. The wet sleeves of my wool shirt no longer slapped against the undersides of my arms. After a few minutes, I couldn't feel my feet, which had been aching all afternoon. The prickles of cold, where snowflakes melted on the exposed skin of my face, changed to a curious tingling sensation like the taste of mint.

A sharp howl broke through my daze; Mary had tried to take her breast away and Faith was sobbing again. Mary sighed and leaned back over the opening in her pack.

"You guys go on. Really. I don't know how long this is going to take."

I knew I was too cold, but so was Mary. I couldn't leave her. But Joy . . . there was no reason Joy should have to stand in the snow, shivering. "I'll wait," I told Mary. "But maybe Joy should keep moving."

"Yeah, maybe so." Mary glanced at Joy. "Go on ahead, honey. We'll catch up."

My feet and hands had just returned to life, burning, when we came to the edge of the bald. In a warmer season, it might have been no more than a small pasture, but the blizzard hid the woods on the other side of it and blurred the footprints of our friends ahead. Mary turned and looked at me, her face white as the field beyond her. In my mind's eye, I saw the same image she must have been seeing: Joy crossing the bald alone, perhaps hypothermic, struggling through snowdrifts that would have been up to her thighs in some places. We hurried up the ridge, silent, scanning the blank field for any tracks that wandered off the trail. Near the hill's top, we had a hard time finding blazes. One path led upwards, into a cluster of trees; the other took a sharp right turn, crossed a stile, and descended through another pasture. Tracks of churned snow marked where many people had walked, recently, in both directions. Which was the Trail, and, more importantly, which way had Joy gone?

I bent over the paths, studying the shapes of the waves and indentations. The ones going uphill seemed a little less clear, a little older. I looked more closely at ones on the other side of the stile; did that narrow, semicircular dip mark a child's heel print? Perhaps, but farther down the field, the track blended with the rest of the footprints and seemed to be covered by other, larger prints.

A few paces behind me, Mary stopped at the crossroads. She peered up the hill, and then down the pasture, as if, by staring hard enough, she might see through the snow. She dropped her hiking poles and clutched the top step of the stile. She shouted Joy's name three times, the drawn-out "o" divorcing the word from its meaning, making it sound like the wind's wail. She turned and looked at me, her staring blue eyes the only points of color in her face. "God help us. Isis, where is she?"

I closed my eyes for a second and saw Joy walking along a wide, smooth path, hand in hand with Paul. Wishful thinking—no help in that.

"Down this way," I said, trying to sound confident.

A hundred yards into the lower pasture, we found a white blaze on the back of a tree trunk, but it wasn't until we reached Route 19E, two miles later, that we could be certain that Joy had taken the right trail. Three pairs of tracks crossed the bike lane side by side, so recent that hardly any snow had collected in them. I recognized the prints of Paul's boots in the middle, flanked by Hope's and Joy's. That night, at Apple House Shelter, Paul told us that he had heard Faith crying, and he and Hope had turned around to see if we needed help. Joy had met them only a few minutes after she left us.

jackrabbit

John and I reached Apple House Shelter a little before dusk. He ran out into the woods to help Joel, who was already gathering firewood. I dropped my pack at the edge of the shelter. It landed with a resounding thump, and suddenly I noticed how exhausted I was. My back and shoulders ached worse than ever; my legs trembled; the soles of my feet felt as though they had been pummeled.

"Quite a day, wasn't it?" Anonymous Badger leaned against the back wall, wrapped in his sleeping bag.

"Yeah, that was nasty. I've never seen so many PUDs in one stretch of trail." I had heard many northbounders use the term, an abbreviation for "pointless ups and downs." Aside from the Roller Coaster in Virginia, it had never seemed quite as appropriate as it did that day.

He gave me an enigmatic smile. "The worst and the best of the Trail, back to back. Tomorrow we go up into the Roans. The most gorgeous balds on the A.T."

Balds. I shivered involuntarily.

"I wish you could see it in spring, though, when the grass is green," Badger said.

"So do I." I looked out at the trees across from the shelter, a darkening collage of white on white. The snow was diminishing in the uncertain light.

Huge soft clumps of flakes spiraled down through the air. I tried to picture spring, a profusion of new leaves and wildflowers rippling out of the snow-bound woods, and I found I could not.

"Jackrabbit, are you afraid?"

"I try not to be." Badger's directness was unsettling sometimes. I didn't want to admit my fear to anyone, especially not to him.

"We could hitch out at the road back there and wait for the weather to clear," he said.

"I'm not going to hitch on that road." I told him what had happened to me and John.

His forehead wrinkled with concern. "Wow. I never had anything like that happen on either of my hikes. Of course, I've never hitched on 19E."

"Maybe the snow will stop. Maybe the weather will be better tomorrow." I crossed my fingers and made a wish.

Paul came to the shelter a few minutes later with Hope and Joy. They stowed their gear in the shelter and cleared the snow out of the firepit. Isis and Mary came in as dusk settled, their indistinct silhouettes traveling up the dark trail. I could hear them singing quietly:

> I know dark clouds will gather 'round me,
> I know my way is rough and steep,
> but beauteous fields lie just above me,
> where souls redeemed their vigils keep.

Mary set her pack down gently and picked Faith up. "Sing more, Mumma? Sing?" the toddler asked.

"Not now; Mumma's tired," Mary murmured, and sat down heavily on the edge of the shelter. Joy came running out of the forest across the path, where she'd been gathering firewood. Mary hugged her with one arm, ruffling her honey-colored hair. "Oh, my sweet, sweet girl. How could I have let you run off like that?" She was shaking.

"I was only on my own for a couple minutes. I didn't get scared on that nasty bald, 'cause I knew God was watchin' me. Remember what you always used to say?" Joy's face grew serious as she recited. "'The Lord is my shepherd; I shall not want . . .'"

We all unpacked our gear and filled the shelter floor with sleeping bags and foam pads. Even with Lash off the Trail and Heald hiking ahead of us, it was a tight fit. The wind shifted, and snow blew into the front of the shelter.

Isis and Badger rigged a tarp to block the doorway and we settled back to cook dinner. Paul built a fire outside—the Family didn't have enough fuel to use their stove every night. The children tumbled out of the shelter, wearing their warmest gear, to look for more firewood. Anonymous Badger lay back and tucked his head into his mummy bag. "Good night, ladies."

"Good night, Badger . . . What'll we have for dinner tonight?" Isis asked me.

"Something heavy," I said. "How about this pasta and beans thing?" It was a dinner we hadn't tried before, bowtie noodles and black beans with basil.

"Sure." She set up the canister stove on the small area of bare floor at the foot of our foam pads. I ducked under the tarp to fetch a pot of water from the creek behind the shelter. I was grateful for the warm weather and rain of the previous few days; though a few ice fingers had reformed in the slow eddies, the stream was running strong. The surface glittered in the light of my headlamp.

Isis poured some water into our two-liter pot and began cooking dinner. "This stuff smells kind of funny." She wrinkled her nose. The steaming pot balanced on the tiny three-pronged stove did have a strange and not entirely agreeable odor, but I was too hungry to care. "And it's thickening up really fast. Is pasta supposed to do that? . . . Oh shit."

It seemed to happen in slow motion. I watched helplessly as the viscous, half-cooked dinner slopped toward one side of the pot, unbalancing the stove, and spilled out across the grimy shelter floor. *Day two of an eight-day resupply*, I thought miserably.

Isis and I exchanged a look of despair. She shut the stove down. We scooped as much of the dinner as we could back into the pot. Then, without looking at each other, we scraped the rest off the shelter floor and ate it, spoon by spoon.

I thought back to what Isis had said the day we put our shoes on, when an ice storm forced us to sleep in the laundry room at Big Meadows. *The Trail has changed us, no doubt about it. I imagine we'll do a lot more things we never thought we would, before this hike is through.* This was yet another thing I had never imagined myself doing, and it was a good deal less pleasant than bedding down next to a washing machine. The food tasted musty and stale, as though it had been sitting on a supermarket shelf for years. We ate carefully, spitting out the grit, but the flavor of the shelter floor came through, a rank essence of accumulated sweat and grime. By the time we had recovered as much as we could from the floor, the stuff in the pot had begun to freeze around the edges.

"I think we've got enough fuel to heat this up," Isis said.

"I hope so."

"Why don't you read the register to me?" She lit the stove again and put the pot back on, keeping a firm hold on it as she stirred.

"Sure." With Badger asleep and the Family outside around their fire, it was a little like the weeks we had spent by ourselves in the early winter, when the registers had been our main form of entertainment. I leafed through the tattered spiral-bound notebook. "Hey, here's an entry from Waterfall!"

At the sight of her loopy handwriting, I could clearly picture her smiling face, framed by braided pigtails. She had a way of finding the bright side of everything. I wondered what she would have said about eating off the shelter floor. As I read her entry, though, I began to frown. *I hate to say it, but this weather is getting me down. Today I hiked all the way up to Hump Mountain, at the edge of the balds, and I had to turn around and come back here. That wind was too much for me. If it doesn't stop by tomorrow, I think I'll hitch out and call Bob. On a brighter note, all this snow makes the woods look lovely. Y'all hike safe. Life is good— Waterfall.*

"All the way to the balds?" Isis said. "But that's five miles from here! For her to have gone all the way up there, and then turn around and come back . . ."

"There isn't another entry from her. I guess she must have gone on the next day."

I barely slept that night. Mice scrabbled around in the rafters, and the tarp across the entrance flapped unsteadily in the wind. My body ached. I worried about the coming day: *Will the snow continue? Will the wind die down? Will I be strong enough?*

By some miracle, the morning dawned clear and calm. The new, powdery snow clung to the trees and rhododendron branches, dazzlingly bright under a cloudless sky. It was thick enough for snowshoes. I left the shelter ahead of everyone else, my footsteps the first marks on the sparkling white surface. As the sun climbed higher, a small wind came up, dislodging puffs of snow from the trees. The falling powder flashed golden as the sun caught it. In protected hollows, the layers of overlapping snow-covered branches almost blocked out the indigo sky.

Anonymous Badger caught up to me in a few minutes and passed. His line of delicate footprints were the only sign of human presence in the white woods. I kept climbing, struggling uphill against the weight of my pack. My hips and knees began to throb, and I focused on my breath, trying to ignore the pain and keep going.

Abruptly the vista opened out ahead of me. The trail came to a wide meadow, drifted in with knee-deep snow. Down in the valley, I could just see roads snaking between the snow-covered fields, patches of trees, and clusters of houses. Badger's neat handwriting, in the snow at the edge of the bald, spelled out *Welcome to the Highlands of Roan*.

I shivered as all the worst-case scenarios ran through my head: *What if the wind comes up? What if the snow comes back? What if we all get separated out there?* In my first few steps into the bald, I walked cautiously, half-expecting the weather to break without warning. But the air stayed calm and almost warm. No clouds marred the blue sweep of sky that encircled me. These balds were like an antidote to the Grayson Highlands. The smooth, grassy flanks of Hump Mountain and Little Hump lay quiet under sparkling snow. The mountains in the distance had an austere beauty, sparse and geometric: long ridges and undulating spurs stacked up, layer after layer fading toward the horizon, black and white under snow. Each step brought a new twist of the mountains into view. I forgot the pain in my hips and knees as I crossed the open fields.

Toward evening, weariness crept into my limbs. My arms hurt from lifting my hiking sticks out of the knee-deep snow; my legs hurt from the added weight of the snowshoes on my feet. As the sun sank to a few degrees above the horizon, gilding the snow and deepening the shadows, I sat down on a rock beside the trail to rest, holding back tears with difficulty. I felt overwhelmed and exhausted, and I didn't know whether I had the strength to make it to the shelter.

I heard soft footsteps on the trail behind me. It was John. "Hey, little buddy."

He gave me a look of disdain. "I'm nobody's little buddy. I am Super John!" He spread his arms and gave an exaggerated bow.

I smiled and tried to stand up. "Can your superpowers get me to the shelter?"

"No. But yours can! You've got superpowers too. Come on. Hey, I bet we can see the shelter from the next ridge!"

I staggered to my feet and followed him. *That's two I owe you*, I thought. Sure enough, from the top of the ridge, we spotted the shelter roof reflecting the low sunlight.

Overmountain Shelter was an old tobacco barn, with cracks between the diagonal wallboards to allow the air to flow through. Narrow beams of light came through the slats in the loft, where we set up our sleeping bags. There was space for probably forty hikers there. Isis and Badger came up after supper to sing songs in the fragile light of the candle lantern, but they retired to the lower level of the shelter for the night. I felt loneliness settle over me, a familiar blanket.

A wind came up overnight, rattling the walls, and in the early morning the strips of sky visible between the boards were streaked with a thin web of clouds. I stowed my gear quickly, thinking of the miles of balds still ahead of us. Paul and the kids packed quickly too, but Mary lay in her sleeping bag, not moving.

"Are you okay?" I asked her.

She groaned. "I feel horrible. It's like the flu all over again."

Paul put his pack down and sat next to her. "Can you hike?" he asked gently.

"I don't think so." She was crying softly. "You guys go on. Take the kids over the balds before the weather changes."

"We can't do that," I said. "What about Faith?"

"You guys should go, at least, you and Isis and Badger," she said. "Go on while you have the chance."

"No." Isis had come up to the loft while we were talking, and her voice was forceful when she joined the discussion. "We stay together. Safety in numbers."

"You don't need to do this for me," Mary said.

"No. We need to do it for all of us," Isis answered.

The air warmed up that day, melting the patches of snow in front of the shelter and leaving mud puddles. The children became cheerfully grubby. Joel and I gathered wood for a fire. Badger wrestled with the boys in the field in front of the shelter. Paul helped Mary move to the lower level, where she could get some fresh air. She threw up twice and felt a little better, but still weak.

I tried to relax and take in the beauty of the place, with its view of a sharply cut valley and distant mountains under snow. All day, though, wisps of cloud collected in the sky, twining and thickening into bands along the eastern horizon. Worries gathered in the same way at the edges of my mind; I knew the weather wouldn't hold.

For once, thankfully, the warning in the clouds was wrong. The snow held off as we crossed Round Bald and Jane Bald, broad open summits with rhododendron tangles on their lower slopes, and the dark fir forests of Roan Mountain itself. It was strange to stand among fir trees again. The forest looked like my father's backyard in Maine, with the same scent of crushed evergreen needles and snow, the scent of winter. But here it was an island of trees, a tiny remnant floating above the gray seas of deciduous forests. I tried to imagine the time when fir trees covered the valleys, too, perhaps fourteen thousand years ago, when the glaciers last rolled down over the continent: an eyeblink in geologic time, but longer than the entire written history of our species.

Isis

The ten of us packed like sardines into tiny Clyde Smith Shelter—not the first time we'd fit so many hikers onto such a small sleeping platform, nor even the most crowded we'd been, but the closeness was wearing on everybody's nerves. Hope and Joy complained stridently about having to sleep end-to-end, Mary snapped at them, and Faith began to fuss.

"Let's hike out. Night-hike," Badger said to me and jackrabbit, as I carefully stirred our pot of beans and polenta. "That way everyone will have enough room."

"Hike to where?" I asked. "The next shelter's nine miles from here. That's as far as we hike in a day now."

"Yeah, it is, and I'm sick of it," jackrabbit said quietly. "Nine miles. Fuck! There was a time when we could hike twice that in a day. Barefoot."

Badger studied his *Data Book*. "I think I'll hike in to Erwin tomorrow. Want to come with me?"

"How far is that?" I asked.

"Twenty-four. Or maybe I'll just hike the twenty to Curly Maple Gap Shelter."

"I'm up for the twenty, at least." Jackrabbit's voice had an edge to it; she was challenging me to offer any resistance to the plan.

"Are there balds?" I asked Badger.

"One. A wonderful one, Beauty Spot. You can see the whole ridge of the Roans from it. When I crossed it in spring, there were blackberries blooming at its edges and white wood anemones coming up through the grass." He noticed my worried expression. "It's low altitude, and the trail's well blazed. Even if it's snowing, they'll be safe."

"Okay," I said. "As long as we wait for the Family once we get to town. I want to stay together through the Smokies. We're the last of the sobos. We have to look out for each other."

I didn't add how much I'd miss the Family's company—the sound of the children's voices singing in the night, and the way they raised both fists and shouted the third verse of "Wade in the Water": *who are all those children dressed in blue? . . . Must be the people gonna make it through!* Sharing our tea and cookies with Mary made it seem like a party every evening, instead of just another excuse to add calories to our diet. And sharing difficult decisions with Paul— the only member of our group who resisted hypothermia better than I did— eased the burden of added responsibility I had felt since the onset of winter.

The cold took a much greater toll on jackrabbit than it did on me. Her weight dropped rapidly between town stops, the skin of her face drawing tighter over her cheekbones, so white it looked translucent beneath the faint dusting of freckles. She lost the feeling in her hands and feet every day after our lunch break, for half an hour if the weather was relatively mild, and for hours at a time if the temperature was in the single digits. A few nights back, when we reached Overmountain, I'd stepped into the shelter to find her crouching against the wall, shivering, still dressed in the thin sweaty clothes she'd been hiking in. She looked up, not at me, but somewhere over my shoulder. "Oh . . . I was supposed to get water, wasn't I?" Perhaps out of fear, or perhaps because I was in the first stage of hypothermia myself, I answered sharply. "Forget it. I'll do it. Just get in your sleeping bag, okay? And put your hat back on, while you're at it!" Alone at the spring, I wept. It terrified me to see my sister so helpless. And myself—I'd always thought of myself as a gentle person. What would become of us, if we went on alone?

If we got ahead of the Family, it seemed likely that we would be alone for the rest of our hike. Badger's month with us was almost over. Lash had called Harpers Ferry at Christmas, and found out that seven southbounders had come through since we'd been there—Dave, Cutter, and two couples and one other man we didn't know. By the time we left Kincora, though, separate rumors had reached us that each of these people had gotten off the Trail. We hadn't heard anything from Lash in a week and a half; it seemed that he, too, must have quit. Heald had told us that he was planning to skip the Smokies; dogs weren't allowed in the park. Also, he'd gotten caught there in a winter storm during his first A.T. hike and run out of food and dry clothing. In desperation, he had recorded a last message to his family on the video camera he was carrying, before an unexpected break in the weather had allowed him to hike out. If he'd already hitched to the southern end of the Smokies, he would be two hundred miles ahead of us—not much chance that we'd catch up to him again. As for Black Forest, his brief, profane register messages indicated that he was over a month ahead of us, on target to catch his plane to Hawaii. *Americans: I do not like your winter. It is fucking cold. Germany is much better.*

That night at Clyde Smith, I dreamed that we hiked to the top of a mountain and found Black Forest standing at an overlook, frozen solid, one arm raised and pointing to the south. In the bitter predawn, as we huddled in our sleeping bags eating granola, I told jackrabbit about my dream. She picked up the register, wrote a quick message, then handed it to me with a wink. *January 23, 2001. The last of the sobos slept here*, I read. *Many are cold but few are frozen.*

"There are two things you won't like about this stretch," Badger told us. "Little Bald Knob, which is neither bald nor little. Straight up, turn ninety degrees, and back down almost the same way. After that there's Unaka. It's even higher, and, like Little Bald, the summit's wooded. Other than that, it's a pretty easy twenty—the last four miles are almost level."

He was right about Little Bald Knob: a steep uphill without switchbacks, made even more grueling by the deep snowdrifts that lingered on the north slopes of the mountain. The unpleasant little climb did nothing to dampen our spirits, though. Seven miles behind us, and the sun still in the east! I had forgotten how good it felt to use the full length of my stride. When the trail, which had been so straight on the uphill, wandered back and forth across the level ground at the summit, I joked that we were the famous archeologists Georgia and Carolina Jones, discovering the Lost Switchback Burial Ground.

"Yeah, and for our next adventure, we should search for the Tomb of the Tennessee Privies!" jackrabbit responded. Suddenly she burst into song:

> Oh, I love to hike in winter down in Tennessee
> Where the snowflakes whirl and dance about us;
> Every shelter's got a shovel, but you're gonna be in trouble,
> If you go a-lookin' for an outhouse!

Laughing, breathless, and ridiculously out of tune, I joined her on the modified chorus: "Shovel snow, dump your load . . ."

By the time we reached Unaka, I felt a bit less enthusiastic about our plan to hike a twenty. Hiking fast used different muscles, and some of mine were really beginning to ache. Badger had gone on ahead of us. I didn't know when we'd see him again; he'd mentioned that he might hike all the way to town if he reached the shelter early. While I thought I had a twenty in me, I knew I wouldn't make it twenty-four, especially if another, even larger version of Little Bald Knob stood in front of me. Jackrabbit and I were running low on water. I was kicking myself for not boiling more the night before. Badger had told us of a spring on the north side of Unaka, but we hadn't found it yet. I should have known better than to trust a spring in winter; we'd probably passed it already, buried under ice.

The trail wound slowly upwards, among thickets of rhododendron with their leaves barely curled in the still, bright air. I started reciting "The Lady of Shallot" in my head to make the time pass:

> Only reapers, reaping early,
> Hear a song that echoes cheerly,
> From the river winding clearly
> Down to towered Camelot.

Suddenly, I realized that the song of running water wasn't only in my imagination. Around the next bend, the spring gushed out of a metal pipe and splashed across the trail, before disappearing under a thick sheet of ice. I filled my bottle, drank, filled it again, and drank another liter, feeling my knotted muscles become supple as the water seeped into them. We took all that we could carry, in our bodies and our packs: eight or ten pounds each.

A mile later, we reached the summit of Unaka. Black-barked spruce trees grew close together, their trunks rising like pillars into the sun-flecked canopy. Their sharp, clean perfume filled the chilly air. Here and there, a golden birch splayed its limbs across the backdrop of spruce boughs like a dancer caught in mid-twirl. As we started down the southern slope of the mountain, we crossed a small meadow where clumps of fine yellow grass showed through the melting snow. Off to our right, in another open space, I thought I saw an ancient, gnarled apple tree, its bark stippled with woodpecker holes. I could almost smell salt in the wind that had begun to rise; this Southern mountain was so similar to the islands of Maine's coast. I turned to say something to jackrabbit, but found that I couldn't speak around the lump in my throat. She looked up at me, her own eyes bright with tears.

"It's just like home, isn't it?" she said.

Five minutes later, we were back in the drab southern winter: mile upon mile of leafless beech trees standing in the snow. Through the thin web of their branches, ahead of us and to either side, we could see ridges the same shade of gray. Even the sky had clouded over, quickly, as it often did in the mountains.

We caught up with Anonymous Badger at the edge of Beauty Spot. He stood still as a wild animal, waiting between the trees. Only his long black hair, flickering in the wind, allowed me to spot him at a distance. A few snowflakes swirled down from the darkening clouds, and we hurried across the bald, with the blue crest of the Roans towering over us like a wave about to break. For the rest of the afternoon, the three of us walked in silence, as fast as our aching legs would carry us, our heads bent to watch the trail. We crossed a burned forest, where blackened rhododendrons shook their dead, leather-colored leaves with a sound like chattering teeth, climbed a small ridge, and came down into a wide gap between the folds of the ridgeline. Four miles to go; the trail stretched smooth and even ahead of us, skimming the edge of a wide west-facing valley. Then the sun shone out below the clouds, flaming on red-brown fallen leaves where the snow had melted and shining in the lacy branches of a young hemlock. For a moment, the whole forest turned the color of autumn; I felt as if I could warm my hands in that light. I stopped to take a picture, and Badger vanished up the trail ahead of us.

That night at the shelter, he found the husk of an enormous, burned-out candle, at least a pound of paraffin. He broke chunks of it into an empty tuna can, added strips of cardboard from a cracker box and white gas from his fuel bottle, and touched his lighter to the edge of it. A foot and a half of flame leapt from the small container. It kept burning high and bright through the evening as he added more scraps of cardboard and candle wax. Late in the night, when I had curled up between him and jackrabbit, ready to sleep, he still sat staring into the flames. I wanted to catch his attention—he would be leaving us in a few days, and I loved him a little, hard as I had tried to keep my emotions at bay. I lifted my head from my folded fleece jacket and whispered his name. He didn't seem to hear me. The fire mesmerized him, and in its shifting light, he looked like a traveler from another age, a thousand years distant. Not foreign, but ancestral: a memory encrypted in the blood. Those eyebrows, that began glossy and even as a single paintbrush stroke, then thinned to a delicate herringbone pattern at the outer edge, were the same eyebrows I had seen on the frozen faces of Inca mummies, gifts to the lightning god, in a *National Geographic* article at Kincora. His golden skin, smooth as glazed pottery, and his half-shut eyes, full of reflected sparks, brought to mind the colors of cave paintings in Southern France. I could place him everywhere, in history and in space, except here, beside me, within reach.

I remembered when he had taken his shoes off, leaving Vandeventer Shelter. I'd followed his bare footprints in the snow, pretending I was tracking him—but by the time I reached the next shelter, he and Lash had already hiked to town. When I least expected to find him, he'd be waiting at the edge of a bald, his hair streaming out like a banner, but wherever I looked for him, he eluded me, walking ahead, turning his eyes toward the fire. I thought that I might shout his name, if I had the strength to do so, and still he wouldn't hear me. I closed my eyes and fell asleep instantly. When I woke the next morning, he was gone.

jackrabbit

We came into the town of Erwin early in the day. A light snow fell, softening the edges of the mountains that framed the town. Traffic sped past on a four-lane highway across the river. In the distance, we could see the glowing signs of hotels and gas stations at an exit. Anonymous Badger wrinkled his nose in distaste as we came out of the woods onto the road.

"I don't like this town much. Everything's made for cars, so spread out it takes you an hour to walk anywhere. The only good thing in Erwin is Miss Janet."

"Oh, yeah. I think we met her at the Gathering."

"She's a trail angel. The sweetest woman you could ever meet. I hurt my ankle just outside of town here in '99, and she invited me home for five days while it healed. We've got to give her a call."

We found a room at the Holiday Inn at the edge of town, near the highway. The sound of traffic came through the window, even with the curtains drawn, an incessant rush and hum. I took a shower, then washed our dirty clothes and sleeping bag liners in the hotel laundry room.

Miss Janet met us that evening at a pizza place a quarter mile from the hotel. I recognized her instantly when she came through the door, a rotund woman with reddish-tinted hair and a wide, friendly smile.

"Isis! Jackrabbit! So good to see y'all! And is this Anonymous Badger?" Badger nodded. "Indeed."

"Hi there. It's been way too long!" She settled into a seat across from us. "I want to hear all about y'all's adventures out there."

We recounted our experiences in the last few months, from night-hiking into Harpers Ferry to crossing the Grayson Highlands. When we mentioned catching up with the Family, Miss Janet's eyes lit up.

"Do y'all know where the Family is now? I've been dying to meet all of 'em."

"They're a day behind us. They'll probably be in town tomorrow. We're planning to stick around and hike out with them," Isis said.

"No! They're coming here? Tomorrow?" She pursed her lips. "I'm leaving town for the weekend. There's a hiker gathering up in Pennsylvania that I go to every year. I just can't miss it. It's called the Ruck."

"Ruck?" Isis asked.

Miss Janet smiled. "It's supposed to be an Old English word. It means, 'a gathering of disreputable people.'"

"Sounds like my kind of place," I said.

Miss Janet pursed her lips, thinking. "I've wanted to meet the Family for so long, but I just can't miss the Ruck . . ." Then a mischievous gleam came to her eyes. "There's only one way around it. Y'all have got to come with me!"

"Come with you to Pennsylvania?" I asked. "How?"

While the Family took showers and washed their clothes the next day, I spent the morning at the hotel desk with Miss Janet, calling all the rental car companies in the county. Finally we found a van big enough for the twelve of us—Badger, Isis and I, the Family, Miss Janet, and her youngest daughter, Kaitlin. We left most of our gear at Miss Janet's house and strapped into the back of the monster vehicle. At about 3 A.M., after driving all night, we found ourselves in the parking lot of a familiar tall mansion—the Ironmasters Youth Hostel.

All the bunks were full, so I slept under the piano. I awoke too early to the sound of footsteps on the hardwood floor just beside my head. Dawn light was threading through the windows. It took me a moment to realize where I was; I caught myself automatically scanning the area for rhododendron leaves to judge how much clothing I should wear, before I realized that I was indoors. Right in front of me, I saw a pair of well-worn hiking boots. A familiar face peered down at me from a great height.

"Good morning, jackrabbit! I should have thought you guys would be here . . . Did you sleep well?"

"Stitches! How are you?" Feeling groggy, I blinked the sleep from my eyes, scooted out from under the piano, and sat up.

"Good, good! Come and get some breakfast, and tell me about your hike." She ushered me into the kitchen, where a crowd was beginning to form around the tall silver coffee urn. The counter in the center of the room was piled high with donuts, muffins, bread, fruit. "Jackrabbit, have you met all these folks? This is Mother Hen, and Wyoming Skateboarder, and Ready . . . Wood Elf . . . Sandpiper . . ."

The crowd in the kitchen had the easy, relaxed feeling of a group of hikers at a shelter; it seemed like everyone there had known each other for years.

"Jackrabbit, of the Barefoot Sisters?" Ready asked. She was a tiny blond woman with a cherubic face.

"Yeah. We're not barefoot any more, though."

"Are you still on the Trail?" This was Wyoming Skateboarder, a thin, gray-bearded man with a droopy hat and coke-bottle glasses.

"Yep."

A sort of sigh went through the group, and people's faces assumed bitter-sweet expressions of nostalgia.

"So where exactly are you guys on the Trail? And how did you get *here*?" Stitches asked, pouring coffee into a travel mug.

"We're in Erwin . . ."

"Miss Janet," Stitches shook her head, smiling. "I should have known."

"Mornin', y'all," came a playful voice from the doorway.

Stitches laughed. "Speak of the devil."

"That's 'angel,' if you please," Miss Janet said, her eyes sparkling.

"I don't know how you do it, Miss Janet," I said. "It's seven o'clock in the morning, and you've got your hair and makeup perfect already."

"I don't know how *y'all* do it," she said. "If I was out on the Trail this mornin', I'd have to fetch water and boil it up myself before I could have my coffee. Somebody pass me a mug, if you would . . . Thank you! And I honestly don't know how I'd ever get along without my makeup."

"Makeup can be dangerous on the Trail," Wyoming Skateboarder said earnestly. Everyone laughed, but he protested. "No! Really! On my '98 hike, I knew a guy who wore cherry-flavored lip gloss . . ."

"That's not makeup!" Miss Janet said through the renewed laughter.

"No, but seriously. It was winter when we started, February, you know, and this guy had a real problem with chapped lips. So he picked up some lip gloss at Fontana Dam. The only kind they had there was this cherry-flavored stuff. The next night, up in the Smokies . . ." he let his voice grow quiet, and we leaned in to listen. "I was right next to him in the shelter. I woke up in the middle of the night to this blood-curdling shriek! I turned on my headlamp and looked at him . . . the guy had a mouse hanging from his lip!"

"Eaugh!" I could picture it all too clearly. "I thought it was going to be a bear attracted to the scent. But a mouse, getting bitten by a mouse . . . oh, that's gross. I don't even want to think about that."

Miss Janet laughed, a warm booming sound that filled up the kitchen. "I'm glad it's y'all out there and not me."

"Yeah, the mice can be pretty bad," Ready said. "In '99, I hiked with a guy who was really scared of them. He didn't let people know it, though, 'cause he didn't want anybody to think he was a coward. One night, down in Georgia, there were a bunch of us packed into a shelter. Just as we all lay down to sleep, a mouse dropped out of the rafters and started running everywhere in the middle of people's stuff. This guy just kind of pulled his sleeping bag over his head and curled up in a ball. Then all of a sudden he jumped straight up into the air—the mouse had run right into his sleeping bag!"

When the laughter died down a bit, Ready winked conspiratorially across the circle. "Oh, but the best part of it was, when he jumped out of his bag, he was completely naked!"

"Hmm," Miss Janet said. "Maybe thru-hikin' wouldn't be so bad after all."

After breakfast, I found a quiet place to sit down and collect my thoughts. I still didn't feel entirely awake. In the foyer beside the bunkroom, a table under the window held stacks of photo albums from past years' hikers. I leafed through them, rubbing the sleep from my eyes and sipping the fourth helping of strong coffee from my camping cup. Book after book of similar photographs—strong, thin, tanned men and women grinning for the camera at overlooks, views of distant lakes and mountains. I saw stark granite mountains I didn't recognize, sandwiched between photos of the familiar soft shapes of the Appalachian range. *This must be what the Whites look like, when you can actually see them*, I realized.

I drew another album toward me and opened it at random. It was a page of closeups of spring wildflowers. Reddish-brown trilliums, tiny yellow-and-purple violets, and the exotic creamy white blossoms of mayapples. In the lower right corner was a photograph of dwarf irises, looking soft and ephemeral. In that moment, I could not imagine a more powerful expression of hope than those delicate purple petals with the light coming through them. Somewhere underneath the snow, down on the slopes of the Southern mountains, even now these flowers were waiting. *Maybe I'll hike till I see a dwarf iris*, I thought. *Maybe then I'll be able to turn around and go home.* I stared at the picture for a long time, imagining all the cold hillsides opening out with life.

A man sat down at the far end of the table. I glanced up at him and smiled, noting his lined face and serious gray-blue eyes. "These pictures are awesome," I said. "Do you know who took them?"

He smiled, though his eyes didn't lose their grave expression. "I did."

"Wow. Very impressive. I'm jackrabbit, by the way."

"Spur." We shook hands.

"When did you hike?"

"Ninety-nine and this past summer. I'm hoping to get out there next year, too, with my wife. You might have met her—Ready."

"Yeah, I met her this morning. Sweet woman."

"She's wonderful," he said with a sudden shyness.

"Hiking three years in a row, that's dedication."

He laughed softly. "Hiking through the winter, like you guys, *that's* dedication."

"Or pigheadedness, depending on your point of view."

Miss Janet's daughter Kaitlin came running up to the table, pink in the face and looking flustered. Her pale blond hair stuck out in all directions. "Jackrabbit, where's Isis?"

"I don't know, Kaitlin. I have no idea where she ended up last night. The last thing I remember is dragging myself under the piano there. What's going on?"

"Hope and Joy are lookin' everywhere for her." Kaitlin lowered her voice and gave me a mischievous look that reminded me of her mother. "Wherever Isis is, Badger is too. We've got to create a distraction. Come on!"

I gave Spur a sheepish smile and excused myself. Kaitlin intercepted Hope and Joy at the bottom of the stairs, before they could search the upstairs rooms. "Hey, guys! I think she's in the bunkroom!"

"She's still got her sleeping bag pulled over her head, though," I said. "She must be tired! Let's not wake her up." There was a blue sleeping bag on one of the bunks that looked a little like hers; I hoped it would be enough to convince the kids.

Hope and Joy paused at the foot of the stairs and peered into the semi-darkness of the bunkroom. "Are you sure that's Isis?" Hope said. "Well, where's Anonymous Badger, then?"

Kaitlin and I exchanged a rueful glance: so much for Hope not realizing what they were up to.

"Hey, guys, I've got an idea," I said. "It's perfect weather for a snowball fight. Let's go outside!"

It was a bright, clear morning, just below freezing. The snow packed well. We hid behind trees and lurked around the corners of the building, lobbing snowballs at each other. Hope and Joy raced across the lawn, shouting. John and Joel came running outside to join the fray. It seemed that most of Joel's snowballs were intended for Kaitlin, and when she turned around to chase him, he blushed scarlet.

"I'm tired of fightin'," Joy said, leaning on the picnic table and brushing the snow off her jacket. "Let's make snow people."

We all rolled the wet snow into balls. I helped Joel and Kaitlin stack them. "Hey, let's make a family!" John said. "Let's make us!"

"Good idea!" Joy stopped rolling the ball she was working on, a lopsided one about half the size of the others, and dropped it near the largest snowman. "This can be Faith."

We decorated the snow people with chips of bark, small rocks, grass and fallen tree branches. Snow-Paul got a bristling beard of spruce twigs, and Snow-Faith had flyaway blond hair made of grass and gray pebble eyes.

"We've got to make Isis and jackrabbit, too," Hope said. I braided tufts of grass for our hair, and John found some pieces of bark that looked like my old brown hat.

The real Isis came outside as I was shaping mounds of snow into bare feet at the base of her snow effigy.

"Isis, where have you been?" Hope said, with a note of older-sisterly exasperation in her voice. "We couldn't find you anywhere!"

Isis gave a broad smile. "No need to worry. I was . . . sleeping in."

The Ruck passed far too fast. We reminisced with many other hikers, telling our stories again and again. In the evening, we sang "Dig a Hole" for the assembled crowd. The Family joined in; all the children marched in place and swung their arms in rhythm. The hikers cheered loudly when we finished.

"Bravo! Bravo!" Spur called from the front row. "You've got to sing that at Trail Days!"

"We just might," Isis said, and I nodded, grinning.

I had to laugh, thinking of how the Trail had changed me. Seven months ago I had marched across a stage in cap and gown to pick up my college diploma. At that point, if someone had told me that I'd be singing about privies in front of anyone, I would have thought he was nuts. And now we were contemplating singing the song for an audience of hundreds. *I'll never be able to run for office*, I thought, *but that's probably a good thing. This is a lot more fun than politics.*

We drove back to Erwin late on Sunday night. Miss Janet dropped off Anonymous Badger at a truck stop in Virginia. He planned to meet some friends there and stay with them for a while to look for a job. Half-awake, I watched him take his pack from under the seat and sling it over his shoulder with an easy grace.

"Until we meet again," he said. Isis took his hand for a moment and held it, hard.

"Safe travels," I whispered sleepily.

He turned and vanished into the empty parking lot, and we pulled back onto the highway. I looked over at Isis, half-expecting to see her crying, but her eyes were dry. "It's okay," she said. "I wasn't in love with him."

"If you weren't in love, what was that?"

I could just see her smile in the light from the passing cars. "'Seeking fellowship in the wilderness,'" she said.

Back in Erwin, Miss Janet invited us to her home for the day while we sorted out our gear and prepared to leave town. She lived in a small one-story ranch house at the edge of town, with a slightly overgrown hedge of roses and brambles. A huge trampoline took up most of the lawn. The children headed straight for it as soon as we had unpacked the van. It was warm in the valley; the snow had melted over the weekend and the dry grass of the lawn was bare.

Isis, Paul, and I went with Miss Janet to the car wash, where we scrubbed and vacuumed the rented van before returning it. At the agency, we climbed into her battered gray Toyota minibus. The rear seats had been torn out, and the back of it was covered in thick shag carpet. Piles of cushions were stacked against the wheel wells. Trail maps and photographs of hikers plastered the ceiling. Strings of Mardi Gras beads hung in all the windows, and a large sign reading *this van brakes for hikers* was taped to the rear windshield.

"Welcome aboard the Shaggin' Wagon," Miss Janet said cheerfully. "We almost could've fit all of us in here, but I didn't want to take those kids around without seatbelts. Besides—" she patted the steering wheel "—I don't know how many more miles this old girl has got in her."

Miss Janet ferried us across town to resupply. When she picked us up at the market an hour later, her eyes were sparkling. "I've got a big surprise for y'all. Just wait till you see . . ." We pressed her for details as we loaded bag after bag of groceries into the back of the van, but she wouldn't say a thing.

Back at the house, we found a crowd of unfamiliar people sitting by the trampoline in the backyard. By their well-worn clothing and slim figures, I could tell right away—they were hikers! I jumped out of the van almost before it stopped moving, eager to meet them. Was it possible that other people had hiked through this crazy winter? For weeks now, I had been convinced that we were entirely alone.

"Are you guys sobos?" I asked, hardly daring to believe it.

"Yeah! I'm Tiny Tim," said a tall young man with a bushy blond beard. "Wait a sec! You're one of the Barefoot Sisters, aren't you? You remember Dave, the guy you hiked with at the Pennsylvania border?"

"Yeah, you know him? What's he up to? Where is he?"

"I don't know what he's doing now, but we hiked together for a couple of weeks in Virginia." Tiny Tim gave a wicked smile, dimples showing through his beard. "You guys had us running trail to catch up with you, with everything you wrote in the registers . . ."

"Oh boy," I said ruefully, thinking back to the messages we had written just after Lash and Black Forest got ahead of us near Rusty's. "We didn't think anyone was actually behind us to read that stuff. Sorry . . ."

"Oh, are you jackrabbit?" asked a wiry man with a short-trimmed blond beard and intense hazel eyes. "'Last of the sobos,' eh?"

"'The few, the proud,'" said a slim red-haired woman across the circle.

"'Many are cold, but few are frozen,'" Tiny Tim chortled. "Man, we've been trying to catch you guys for months!"

"I had no idea . . ."

"Evidently!" the hazel-eyed man said. "But we should introduce ourselves. I'm Big Ring. This is my girlfriend, Granny Gear." He put his arm over the red-haired woman's shoulders, and she smiled and gave a little wave. Both of them were extremely thin, I noticed; Big Ring looked like a stick figure inside his hiking clothes, and all the bones in Granny Gear's hands were visible even from a distance.

Isis came up with an armload of groceries and introduced herself. I watched Tim's eyes measuring her.

"I'm Spike," said a petite woman with horn-rimmed glasses and close-cropped dark hair.

"And I'm Caveman," said a tall, clean-shaven man with dark brown eyes.

"You don't look much like a caveman," Isis told him.

Spike gave a gloriously melodious laugh, and Caveman turned to look at Isis. "I like caves," he said in a carefully measured tone that was equal parts righteous indignation and bafflement. Somehow, it was hilarious. Tiny Tim began to laugh, and soon we all joined in. "I am very fond of spelunking," Caveman continued in the same tone, but his composure began to crack. In a moment he was laughing along with everyone else.

"Hey, come on, the Barefoot Sisters are here!" John's voice came from inside the door. He ran out, followed by a hiker who looked strangely familiar; he was tall but stocky, with curly dark blond hair that fell across his broad shoulders. When he smiled, his blue eyes flashed behind thick lashes.

"Hey, I'm Yogi."

"I remember you! I haven't seen you since New York. It was at the RPH Shelter . . ." I fell silent for a moment, remembering the day that Highlander and Compañero had left. "I thought you'd be far ahead of us by now."

Isis put the groceries down and crossed her arms. "You know, Yogi, we were kind of mad at you for a while, after Compañero ran off ahead to hike with you."

Yogi shook his head. "We didn't hike together long. That dude, after he got going, he just didn't stop." He gave a rueful little smile. "I couldn't keep up with him."

"So where have you been all this time? How on earth did we pass you?" I asked.

"Well, I got off in Blacksburg to spend Christmas with my fiancée, Tina. Then I got the flu real bad, and before I knew it, six weeks had passed. I almost didn't get back on the Trail. But I . . . I had to, you know? Even with the snow and everything. I had to come back out here."

I nodded, understanding completely. Even when I knew I wouldn't be able to complete a thru-hike, given the two hundred miles I had missed in Vermont and Massachusetts, I'd felt the same compulsion to return to the Trail.

"Yogi!" Hope came tumbling out of the house and launched herself at him. In one smooth motion, he hoisted her up to sit on his shoulders.

"Long time no see. How are you, little lady?"

Miss Janet stood on the porch with her hands on her hips, surveying the crowd as if she were the matriarch of our motley band. She had produced a case of beer from somewhere, and she handed out cans. "Y'all enjoying the party?"

"This is the best surprise we could have hoped for," Isis said. "Is there anything we can do to help you out in return?"

"Seeing all of y'all happy is enough reward for me," Miss Janet said, beaming. "There is something y'all could do, though. That hedge of roses at the edge of my yard has got all kinds of brambles in it. The girls and I just can't seem to get 'em out. I think there's some leather gloves in the shed over there . . ."

"Say no more!" Tiny Tim sprang into action. He found a few pairs of ragged gloves, and soon Isis, Tim, Yogi, and I were pulling blackberry vines from between the thorny red branches. We uprooted the plants and untangled the stems with ferocious energy, laughing. The air smelled of dry grass and sun. In that moment, it seemed that everything that had happened to bring me to this point had been worthwhile: the days of hunger and pain and cold, my despair at being left behind time after time. I was here, with the sun resting warm on my shoulder blades, surrounded by friends old and new. I was here, and it was enough. I couldn't imagine leaving the Trail.

A little boy on a bicycle wobbled past in the lane. "Hey, hiker trash!" he called out cheerfully.

"Hiker trash!" Tim cackled. "Hiker trash, that's us!"

A thought had been growing in my mind for a long time now. *What if we didn't leave the Trail in Georgia? What if we just turned around and headed back to Maine?*

"Hiker trash has too much fun," I said to Isis. "Let's yo-yo."

CHAPTER 11

"Bye, Never See You Again"

jackrabbit

The air was still warm the day we left Erwin. Paul had fallen sick, and the Family decided to stay in town for another day. The rest of the sobos were leaving, though. Isis and I hiked out with them. We would wait for the Family in Hot Springs, the next Trail town.

The first night out, we stayed at Bald Mountain Shelter, in a grove of twisted beech trees at the end of a long ridge. Big Ring and Granny Gear had already reached the shelter. They sat in the back, wrapped in their thick sleeping bags. Their packs, I noticed, were enormous, almost the size of Paul's. Big Ring had a pair of heavy aluminum-frame snowshoes strapped to the outside of his pack, although there hadn't been enough snow to use them for quite some time.

"Hey, guys," Granny Gear said. She was so bundled in her mummy bag that her red hair barely showed around her thin face.

"Hey, Granny Gear." I still couldn't get over the *non sequitir* of her name. I tossed down my pack and sat beside her. "Tell me, how did you guys get your trail names? I mean, Big Ring has no rings of any kind, and you're definitely no granny."

She laughed and started to answer, but Big Ring took over. "It was in Andover, at Addie's place," he said. "The town was full of bikers, and there wasn't room in the restaurant for everybody. We crammed into a table with six or seven of them, and believe me, these were big guys. At first they were making all kinds of snide comments about hikers, and you know, I couldn't take on the whole gang, so I just kept quiet. And then Juliet—Granny Gear—and I ordered our food. We ate about as much as the rest of the table put together." He chuckled and shook his head. "Then they gave us a little more respect. They started asking us all kinds of questions about the Trail. We told them about trail names. They decided to give us biker names. Apparently two of the gears on a bike are called Big Ring and Granny Gear, so that's what we became."

"Cool."

Yogi returned to the shelter with an armload of firewood. "We oughta have a fire tonight."

"It's not that cold," Isis said.

"That's just it." Yogi smiled. "It's warm enough to actually sit around the fire, instead of huddling up in our bags."

"Good point." I followed him into the forest to collect more wood. As I left, I heard Big Ring and Tim arguing about the temperature.

"You think it's warm enough to sit around outside your bag?" Big Ring said. "Man, that's crazy! This weather . . ."

The sound of Spike's unmistakable laughter came through the trees a few minutes later, and I knew she and Caveman must have arrived. She had a laugh like a wild bird, a high, trilling whoop that echoed through the forest.

I tossed my load of fallen branches down beside the fire ring and rejoined the crowd at the shelter. Tim was in the middle of a story.

"So there I was, sitting on a rock and eating my lunch. I'd never met the guy before. He just came and sat down beside me, without a word of introduction. He looked at my lunch, which was Betty Crocker frosting spread on crackers—"

Spike's warbling laugh filled the shelter. "Betty Crocker frosting?"

"Hey, it's tasty," Tim said with an air of wounded pride. "So he looked at me, and he looked at the frosting, and he said—" Tim gave a fair imitation of a well-remembered deadpan German accent "—he said, 'Peanut butter has more fat.'"

When the laughter had died away, I asked, "Black Forest?"

"Black Forest," Tim confirmed with a growl. "You know what else he did? A couple days later, a bunch of us were all camped at a shelter together. There was another shelter at fifteen, and the next one was at thirty-something, so it was pretty clear where we'd all end up the next night. So Black Forest got up super early and hiked ahead of us all day. And then he stood there by the shelter as we all came in, and he said to everybody as they arrived—" once again Tim imitated the German's tone "—'I win. You lose.'"

"Black Forest," I mused. "Really, he wasn't so bad, once you got to know him."

Isis threw me a meaningful glance across the shelter. I hoped it had passed too quickly for Tim to pick up on it, but he saw. He nodded his head, smirking a little bit as the facts fell into place. "So you and Black Forest . . ."

"We didn't really do anything," I said. "We were just 'seeking fellowship in the wilderness.'"

"Oh, I like that!" Caveman said, laughing. "'Seeking fellowship . . .'"

"Yeah, I like it too," Spike said, snuggling closer to him.

"Did you guys meet on the Trail?" I asked.

Spike gave her marvelous laugh. "Not at all. I'd never really been backpacking before Jim—Caveman—asked me to join him on the Trail."

"This is our third date, actually," Caveman said in his well-modulated voice.

"Your third date?" I said, incredulous.

"Well, our whole relationship has been kind of interesting," Spike said. "On our first date I was mugged—"

"And our second date was a court appearance—"

"And our third date started in September, when he called me from the Trail in Hanover. He said he wanted to finish his hike, but he couldn't imagine spending another four months without me." She squeezed his shoulder. "Isn't it wonderful?"

"So wait a second," I said. "On your first date, Spike, you were mugged?"

"Yeah. Well, we went out to dinner at a nice little place Jim knew in the Village. He was walking me to the subway afterwards, and this guy just jumped out of an alley and said, 'give me all your money!'"

"He was high on something," Caveman said. "The guy was not in his right mind. He didn't even have a weapon."

"So Jim did some kind of move. I don't know what it was. But all of a sudden he had the guy's arm twisted behind him. I took out my cell phone and called the cops." She smiled at Caveman. "He saved me on our very first date."

"Saved your wallet, anyway," he said. "Possibly. I think the guy was too strung out to know what he was doing."

"Then our next date was the guy's court appearance. We had to testify against him, and then we figured we might as well go to lunch together."

"This was two weeks before I left for the Trail," Caveman said. "All the time I was hiking, from Maine down to Hanover, I thought about her. I decided I couldn't spend any more time away from her. So I called her up to see if she wanted to hike the rest of the Trail with me."

"And here we are." Spike laughed again. "Crazy, huh?"

"We actually knew each other for a while before we started dating," Caveman said. "We were in the same graduate program at NYU."

"Drama therapy," Spike said, and he nodded.

"Drama therapy?" I asked.

"It's kind of like art therapy," Caveman said, "but instead of drawing or painting you use role-playing exercises. I work with abuse victims, mostly teenagers."

"I work with mentally disturbed children," Spike said.

I whistled. "That must be exhausting."

Caveman considered for a moment. "I guess it's like any medical profession. You develop a degree of separation from your work pretty fast."

"It's definitely tough sometimes," Spike said. "Especially the little kids with schizophrenia. Because when it develops at that young an age, you just know it's going to be with them all their lives. I had a little girl I used to work with, and one day she told me, 'Miss Dana, if you don't come in on Thursday, I'll feed you to Satan.' A ten year old."

Caveman nodded. "It can be really hard. The Trail is a good place for us right now. Things . . . *flow* here. I feel a lot more centered than I ever did in Manhattan."

"A lot colder, too, I bet," Big Ring grunted.

Caveman gave him a quizzical look. "It's not so bad tonight. It might even be above freezing."

"I thought we went over this," Tim said. "I saw *puddles* today. Liquid water. I was a chem major, okay? Unless something really screwy has happened to the atmospheric pressure, the temperature *has* to be above freezing."

"Yeah, but *I'm* freezing," Big Ring said. "Hon, is supper ready?"

"Just about." Granny Gear's voice was muffled by the hood of her mummy bag. She reached out with one thin arm to stir the pot of noodles on the stove beside her. "Where's the butter?"

Big Ring oonched his sleeping bag to the mouse hanger where his food bag dangled and took out a stick of butter. I expected Granny Gear to slice off a few tablespoons, but she unwrapped it and put the whole thing in the pot.

"Do you guys always eat that much butter?" Isis asked. The two of us had eaten a fair amount of butter in winter too, but never by the stick.

"Yep," Big Ring said. "We usually have some with breakfast too."

"And they *still* don't have enough body fat to stay warm in this weather," Tim said. "I keep telling them, if they cut their pack weights down, they won't have to worry." He gestured toward his own ultralight pack, barely a third the size of Big Ring's, and then patted his own midriff. Unlike the run-of-the-mill emaciated hiker, Tim had a small protruding belly. "Still got my love handles, baby." He leered at Isis, and she made a face.

Big Ring sighed. I could tell that the pack weight debate was territory they had covered many times. "We like to be prepared," he said. "What would you do if it snowed three feet tomorrow? Besides," a glint came into his eyes, "*we* still have our toothbrushes."

Isis looked over at Tim. "You don't carry a toothbrush? That's disgusting!"

Tim gave a slightly guilty chuckle. "It was extra weight—I didn't use it much when the weather got cold, so I got rid of it."

Yogi looked up from the fire ring, where he had just lit a good-sized blaze, and shook his head. "Weather's warm now, man."

Tim grinned. (I tried not to look at his teeth.) "Yeah, and now I've gotten lazy."

Over the next few days, the warm weather continued, melting the snow even on the highest ridges. Through the thin haze of gray branches the contours of the land showed clearly; mountain chains extended like giant serpents, twisting and writhing across to the horizon. The world was no longer black and white. Brown and gold and the blue of the sky had crept back into the spectrum. I missed green. I could feel the nearness of spring in my bones; for the first time since fall, we could take leisurely lunch breaks, and our hands would not grow stiff and cold. The horrible pins-and-needles feeling of thawing out was gone.

Isis and I walked with Yogi much of the time, matching our stride to his, and we talked about what we would do after the Trail. *After the Trail.* It seemed like such a distant concept. The A.T. was life.

"I'm planning to marry Tina, but I just don't know," Yogi said. "I like my freedom. I'm a wanderin' boy, you know?" Dimples appeared when he smiled, and his impossibly long eyelashes brushed his cheeks. He had a roguish, charming look. I worried a little for Tina's sake.

"How long have you been together?" I asked.

"Almost two years. Since my first hike."

"Do you love her?"

"I do, but we're so different. She doesn't hike. She doesn't even like the outdoors. She'd never even gone backpacking before we met. I bought her a pack and a good pair of boots, and I took her out once. After a day and a half we had to come back because she was freaking out being away from her kids."

"Kids?" Isis asked.

"Two. Ages three and five, from her first marriage."

"Do you get along with them?" I asked him.

"Yeah, they're good kids. They're okay."

I fell silent, trying to get my mind around the thought of Yogi as a dad. We stopped for a drink of water at a place where the trail was narrow, and a view of the valley opened on one side. The fields down below had suddenly taken on a softened aspect, not green but almost green. The sun had melted the frost along one edge of the trail and dark brown mud showed, the first mud I had seen in a long time. The scent of the ground was richer, more complex, as though the odors locked in by frost had been released.

"I'm jonesing bad for a cigarette," Yogi said.

"Thought you gave it up."

"I did. No more cigs. Tina and me, we promised each other." He paused, staring into the valley. His solid, stocky frame cast a thick shadow. "That doesn't make it any easier, when she's a thousand miles away. Listen, you guys, when we go into Hot Springs, you gotta help me. You gotta stop me from going into the store first thing and buying a pack of cigs."

"I'll try to help you out," I said.

"Me, too," Isis told him. "But I think it's something you've got to really want for yourself. It's not like anybody else can motivate you to quit."

"I hate it so much," he said quietly. "It's like, I know it's bad for me. I know it's these big corporations trying to keep me hooked so they can take my money before they kill me. I know all that shit . . . and I still can't help it."

"Try this," I said. "Picture Tina and the kids. Think about all the years you could spend with them. You know how many years smoking takes off your life expectancy? Think about that before you light up again."

I looked over at him, but he didn't seem to be happy thinking about it. There was a trapped look in his eyes for a fleeting second. He stared out over the valley, deep in thought, and then shook his head and turned back to the trail. "I'll find a way."

The trail wound in and out of gaps, dipping steeply down and climbing just as steeply up. Dead leaves in shades of brown and gray crackled underfoot. My feet, inside their boots, ached to feel the new earth. Frost lingered in the shadows, though, and I knew it was still too cold to walk barefoot. In fall, I had walked over patches of frost and snow without a second thought. This spring was different. A winter in wet boots and the intense cold of the Grayson Highlands had left half my toes numb and tingling, with an acute sensitivity to cold. It would be a while before I could walk barefoot again.

As we came down into one of the gaps, Yogi paused and sniffed the air. "Devil's Fork Gap," he said. "In springtime, this whole valley's full of trout lilies, spring beauties, all kinds of little wildflowers. So many flowers you could hardly even see the green of their leaves. I remember coming into this valley on my northbound hike. There was a wind that blew the smell of flowers up the slope. Sweetest thing you'd ever hope to smell."

His words awakened the memories of other springs, and we stood for a moment surrounded by the ghosts of flowers. We paused and sniffed, too, but there was only the scent of dry leaves, bark, and a faintly chill wind between the trees. And then, far off, came the sound of running water.

A day out from Hot Springs, the weather shifted back to winter. We hiked the last eleven miles into town under a dark gray sky with occasional sleet and snow. Isis and I kept pace with Yogi until the last descent, down a razor-backed ridge with sleet blowing in off the river to our left.

"I'll see you guys in town," he called, and lengthened his stride until he vanished in the gray woods ahead.

I thought of reminding him of his promise to Tina, and our promise to him, but it was too late. When we came to the edge of town, we found him standing under the eaves of the general store, smoking. A fresh pack of Marlboros bulged in his front pocket.

He looked at us with guilty eyes. "You gotta understand, it's just this once."

I shrugged. "It's your choice."

Isis and I bought hot chocolate at the general store and walked on, looking for the hostel that Bob at Kincora had described. The town of Hot Springs was almost deserted, battened down against the storm. The sleet changed to wet snow as we walked through the center of town, passing a gas station, a few restaurants, and another store.

"Hey, guys!" Tiny Tim hailed us from across the street, where he stood on the steps in front of the squat brick post office. He gave a gloating smile and put on his best German accent. "'You lose.'"

"Hey, Tim! What's happening?" I called as we crossed the empty street. I tried to ignore his smirk.

"Nothing much. Always a pleasure to see such lovely ladies. Yogi." He nodded at our companion. "We got rooms reserved for you guys at Elmer's. You've got to see the place to believe it. Best hostel I've seen yet . . . Is the Family with you?"

"No, they're about a day back," Yogi said. "Hey, who's the letter from?"

I noticed the small white envelope in Tim's hand.

"Oh . . . a friend." His smile failed for a moment. I caught a glimpse of a Damascus postmark before he tucked it into his jacket pocket. "I'll meet you guys at Elmer's. A couple blocks up on the left—big Victorian house with a porch out front."

"Come on, Tim," I said. "Who's the letter from?"

He looked at his toes. "I guess I know your 'seeking fellowship in the wilderness' story. You might as well know mine." He took out the envelope. On the back was a drawing of an airplane and unfamiliar cramped handwriting that spelled out, *I am going home now. I will miss you. By-by.*

"Who was it?"

"Well, I guess maybe you wouldn't recognize the handwriting. After she got ahead of me, she hardly ever signed in registers . . ."

"Netta?" Isis asked, incredulous.

Tim nodded. "Uh-huh."

I remembered Netta's sad and knowing smile as she watched me with Black Forest, months ago in Front Royal. It made sense now.

"So she's leaving?" I asked Tim.

"Yeah. She stayed in Damascus for a while, thinking that if she felt stronger, or the weather got better, she might come back out . . ." The bantering laughter was gone from his voice, for once, and he sounded almost sad. Then he caught himself. "Hmph. There's other fish in the sea. Ladies," he saluted and winked, and turned to walk away.

At the post office, Isis gave our ID cards to the clerk. I hadn't expected any mail, but he returned with a large cardboard box. Above the address, our mother's graceful cursive spelled out *Happy Birthday Susan!* It was strange to see my real name. Even stranger, I realized I had forgotten my birthday entirely. Every day was so similar out on the Trail, a struggle to stay warm, find water and a safe place to sleep, and get enough to eat. It was as though the calendar, the entire outside world, had no bearing on us.

"What day is it?" I asked the clerk.

He gave me a strange look. "It's Monday. The fifth of February."

"Thanks."

As we walked to the hostel, Isis balanced the box on her head while I managed our four hiking sticks. I was silent, thinking. Some time around two o'clock this morning, I had turned twenty-three. I hadn't even realized.

The main entrance to the hostel seemed to be around back, where the porch was heaped high with mail drop boxes. Isis set our package down on top of the stack and rapped on the door.

"Hello?" A tall, slightly heavy man with graying curls and dark, bushy eyebrows opened the door. He wore a cotton apron over his plaid shirt and jeans. He looked distracted. Over his shoulder, I could see a small kitchen. Well-used pots and pans hung from a rack above the counter, and a giant black cookstove dominated the far wall. Tantalizing aromas drifted out of the room. "You must be the Barefoot Sisters," he said. "Leave your sticks and boots outside, if you would. It's hard enough to keep this place clean as it is . . . Bob! Give that soup a stir and check on the rice!"

I noticed a young man with blond dreadlocks standing by the stove. "Yeah, I'm on it," he said.

"I'm Elmer, by the way," the man who had opened the door told us. He smiled, and there was genuine warmth in his expression. "Welcome to my place. Make yourselves at home." Elmer gave us a guestbook to sign ourselves in, and he bustled off into another room to check on something.

"Don't mind him," the man at the stove said. "Elmer's always a little bit touchy when he's cooking. He's an awesome dude, but he can get grouchy. Are you guys really the Barefoot Sisters?"

"Yeah. I'm jackrabbit."

"I'm Isis."

"Wow! Far out. Pleased to meet you, I really am. I'm Bob." He wiped his hand on his apron and held it out.

I noticed his tiny round glasses, goatee, and bleach-blond dreadlocks. "You just don't look like a Bob to me," I said as we shook hands. "No offense, but the name Bob always makes me picture a middle-aged insurance salesman."

"Hey, there's some cool Bobs," he said, turning back to stir the soup.

"Such as?"

"Well, there's Bob at Kincora. And Bob Marley."

"Any others?"

He shrugged, conceding defeat. "I like to think of it as a challenge," he said. "Maybe if I'm cool enough, you know, I can change the way people think about Bob-ness. Bob-hood. Bob-itude."

Isis and I took our packs up to the bedroom Elmer had prepared for us. Lamps in wall sconces, turned down low, illuminated the spacious, high-ceilinged room. Dark wooden furniture contrasted with the cream-colored wallpaper. Behind gauzy curtains, a broad window with panes of wavy antique glass gave a view through treetops of the street below. Cars slopped past, the hazy cones of their headlights reflecting from the snow in the gathering dusk, but otherwise it was a space that belonged to a previous century. I set my pack down in a corner, suddenly aware of my ragged clothes and filthy, sweaty self.

After a shower and a change into my least dirty clothes, I felt better. Bob gave us a tour of the old mansion, ending with a room that made me feel as though I had stepped into heaven.

"This is the music room." He flicked a light switch, and the room materialized around us. Three guitars and a banjo leaned against the pink satin settee; African drums, beaded gourds, tambourines, and castanets occupied corners of the slightly threadbare oriental carpet. Various shelves and tables held flutes from around the world. And in the corner, a piano. It had been months, but my fingers still remembered the patterns. I lost myself in Bach, Schubert, Beethoven, Chopin.

My reverie was interrupted in the middle of Chopin's D flat major nocturne. Bob appeared in the doorway in his apron. "Suppertime!" he said with a flourish and pointed me toward the dining room. Most of the hikers were already assembled. The long table groaned under tureens of soup, bread baskets, dishes full of rice and spicy stewed vegetables, and two enormous salads. The salads were the most tantalizing sight: bowls piled high with mixed greens and sprouts, decorated with sunbursts of cherry tomatoes, pepper strips, feta cheese, and raisins. After the iceberg lettuce and pallid tomatoes of most Southern Trail towns, these salads were an ambrosial vision.

"Welcome, everyone," Elmer said from the head of the table. Now that all the guests were present and the feast was ready, his deep voice sounded considerably calmer. "We have a tradition here called the dinner question. We go around clockwise, and you can start eating as soon as you've answered. Tonight's question: if you could be any kind of animal, what would you choose, and why?"

Bob, at Elmer's left hand, said, "I'd be a lemur. It would be pretty excellent to have a striped tail that I could hang from trees with."

"I think I'd be a kangaroo," Spike said. "I read somewhere that their muscles are like springs. They store up the energy from their landing and use it to propel their next bounce, so they don't get tired. I'd like that."

"Hmmm." Caveman rested his chin on his hand for a moment, thinking. "A squid."

"A *squid*?" Spike said through a mouthful of bread.

"They live in the sea. They have tentacles. Some of them glow in the dark. Does there have to be a reason?"

Isis

A brief heat wave melted all the snow from the ground during our stay in Hot Springs. The temperature reached sixty-five for three days in a row;

even at night, it stayed so warm that we were able to bathe in the town's famous springs by starlight. During the day, we congregated on the lawn of a seasonal hotel near the center of town, reading, writing letters home, or conversing in small groups under the bare maple trees. Jackrabbit found out that Caveman and Big Ring were also black belts, each in a different martial art; the three of them spent hours sparring and demonstrating their forms for each other.

One afternoon, Spike told me the story of her relationship with Caveman. "It really is our third date," she said. "Pretty unbelievable, but there it is." She laughed her marvelous laugh, wild and deep as a stream in spring rush, her head thrown back and the sun glinting in her short dark curls. Across the lawn, Caveman paused in the midst of a sparring match to glance our way, failed to block jackrabbit's round kick, and ended up flat on his back on the grass, laughing also. Jackrabbit leaned over to offer him a hand up.

Granny Gear told a different story. Before the Trail, she and Big Ring had been involved in a long-term, long-distance relationship. A few weeks of hiking together had proven to both of them that the romance was over. Still, their paces matched pretty well, and they both wanted to finish the Trail. They'd decided to stay together as hiking partners, posing as a couple to avoid awkward explanations.

She looked out over the rooftops, toward the mountains we'd hiked down from two days before. "If I had it to do over, I'd hike alone. Carry a light pack and walk faster. As it is, he makes all our decisions, from what to eat for breakfast to whether to stay with a group of friends or leave them. I argue and give in. For instance—I weigh ninety-eight pounds, and my pack weighs sixty, because he's decided that we need a lot of gear. It's not my pack weight that bothers me, though; it's the . . . the slow erosion of sympathy. Every day I ask myself what I loved in this person, and every day it gets harder to remember."

At night, we stayed at the Sunnybank Inn, fondly known in the hiking community as "Elmer's." Like Kincora, Elmer's is a Trail legend; as early as Massachusetts, northbounders had told me about a hostel in a Victorian mansion, run by a famous vegetarian chef. Of course I hadn't believed them. At that point, I hadn't been on the A.T. long enough to know that Trail rumors, however outlandish and wonderful, tend to arise from realities more extraordinary than a five-minute conversation between sobo and nobo can convey.

No rumor could have prepared me for Elmer's. For the usual hostel price of $15, we slept in a high-ceilinged room decorated with what appeared to be the original Victorian wallpaper, formal armchairs and end tables, and heavy mirrors with ornate gilded frames, in which I was always surprised to see myself dressed in tattered shorts instead of a ball gown. Bookshelves filled the corridors: geography and poetry, ancient history and Zen Buddhism; books in French, Latin, and Japanese. The kitchen, where the orange-and-yellow light from a stained-glass window filtered through racks of spices and columns of fragrant steam. And the dining room, where we ate four-course meals every evening by candlelight.

When he wasn't busy cooking, Elmer was a fascinating conversationalist. He had a wealth of knowledge in areas ranging from Chinese architecture to organic gardening. With his thoughtful, measured arguments, punctuated by brusque, dramatic gestures that betrayed his enthusiasm, he reminded me of a favorite professor.

For most of our stay in Hot Springs, I felt like I was back in college. Sitting in the sun, writing or chatting with the other young adults of our group, reminded me of the long weekend at the end of spring term, when the warm, clear days and the sense of freedom so near at hand tended to outweigh my worries about the upcoming finals. In this case, our final exam would be the Smokies in February, and neither worry nor study could prepare us for it. This strange thaw, too early to herald spring, might melt the heavy snow from the ridges, but it could also be the calm before a winter storm as ferocious as the one that had caught us on Grayson.

By the dictates of logic, we should have hiked as far and as fast as we could while the warm weather lasted, but Hot Springs held us in a strange spell. Between the antique splendor of our lodgings and the springlike temperatures, it seemed that we'd stepped out of time, out of the Trail's relentless progression of miles and seasons and storms. I imagined that winter was waiting for us, just outside of town, and I wasn't in any hurry to walk back into it. Even jackrabbit, usually so eager to cover ground, raised no argument about staying in Hot Springs.

"Every time I want to hike out, I close my eyes, and I see this vision of Elmer's salad," she sighed. "Lettuce, olives, cherry tomatoes, sprouts, carrots, cucumbers, feta cheese . . . and that incredible tahini dressing. I could stay here for the rest of my life!"

We took one zero, then a second and a third. On the first day, the Family caught up with us, and the children joined us on the hotel lawn for an energetic, hour-long game of tag. On the second day, Miss Janet visited, bringing some photographs that I'd left in Erwin to be developed. Although we'd planned to meet Miss Janet somewhere down the Trail, her sudden appearance in Hot Springs added to the town's mystique; along with gourmet vegetarian cuisine and its own weather pattern, this small Southern town seemed to have the power to gather friends from other times and places on the Trail.

jackrabbit

On our third morning in Hot Springs, it was so warm that Elmer threw open the windows to let the fresh air wash through the old house. After a breakfast of granola, biscuits, scrambled eggs, fruit, and orange juice that satisfied even my winter hiker appetite, I came to the music room again. I don't know how long I had been there, playing, when I felt a tap on my shoulder. At first I was annoyed at the interruption. When I saw who it was, though, I was overjoyed.

"Lash! How are you, man? Hey, it's great to see you!"

"Hey, how's it going, jackrabbit?" He gave me a lazy smile. He was fresh off the Trail, still sweaty and dressed in his rank Capilene, but I hugged him anyway.

"When did you get back on Trail?"

"Like a week ago. Kincora." He shrugged.

I did a quick mental calculation. Traveling with the Family, we'd gone slowly and taken a lot of stops along the way. The 120 miles or so between Kincora and Hot Springs had taken us nearly a month, and he'd done it in a week. "You must have been flying."

"Yeah, well, I kind of missed you guys. It's not as much fun out there alone."

"I'm glad you came back." I tried to say it lightly, but I felt the color rising in my cheeks. For some reason, I remembered the dream I'd had in the laundry room at Big Meadows, with Lash as an evil ninja, his eyes flashing behind the mask.

"I kind of liked going fast, though," he said. "Me and Tim were thinking about hiking together, finishing the Trail by the end of the month, you know? I feel like we've been out here way too long already."

"Come on, Lashy-Lash. Don't leave us, we'd miss you too much."

He rolled his eyes. "Enough of this 'Lashy-Lash' business! But I guess I'd miss you guys, too." He looked around the room. "Dude! There's guitars here. Sweet!"

"You play?"

"Yeah, a little. I gotta take a shower, get cleaned up."

As it turned out, Lash played beautifully. He sang in a smoky voice that was strangely different from his speaking voice. He'd written some lovely songs, mostly bittersweet ballads. I listened, spellbound.

After a while I noticed Isis standing in the doorway. Her hair was unbraided, a dark blond cascade down to her waist, and she wore a clean white tank top and the red miniskirt she had sewn from handkerchiefs. She didn't look like a hiker any more. I felt eclipsed.

Lash stopped in the middle of a song, the chord hanging unresolved. "Hey, Isis," he said, almost shy. "It's good to see you."

"Yeah, good to see you, too. Lash, would you do me a favor?" There was a glint in her eyes.

"Sure, Isis. What is it?" he said, a little too eagerly.

"It was my sister's birthday a couple days ago. Take her to the pub tonight to celebrate."

"Oh." He looked at me. "Yeah. Sure."

The Paddler's Pub was bright and loud and empty. Lash and I took a seat in an orange Formica booth near the door and ordered a pitcher of the local dark brew. On the table, a red fighting fish circled in its glass bowl.

"I've had a good time hiking with you, Lash. It's really been fun."

"Yeah, I've had a good time with you guys." He stared into his glass. His last word hung in the air.

"It's weird; the first time I met you, I thought I'd never see you again. You were hiking so fast."

He laughed. "It is weird, isn't it? I thought I'd be done with the Trail by now. Thought I'd be done in, like, December. And it's weird, too, how . . . *different* it feels. Winter hiking. Dude, it's not hiking, it's *survival*." He took a long swig of his beer. "My brother hiked in '99, northbound, in a normal season. When he got done with the Trail, it was like it had been this grand adventure, and then he just went back into his ordinary life. And for me, even just going into towns now is strange. I look at all these people, and I think, none of them know what I've been through. Nobody else knows what it's like out there. I mean, I think about the Grayson Highlands, and that place where the drifts were over the kids' heads, and we just had to pick them up and pass them to each other . . . And how do you go from that back to working in a bank or whatever?"

"It's going to be hard, leaving the Trail."

"There's some things I won't miss. Lipton dinners. Mice, the bastards." He fingered the hole in his jacket pocket, scowling. "I'm just gonna miss . . . the way things *are* out here. It's all so intense. It's like life in the 'real world' is all sleep-walking, and out here we're the only ones awake. You know what I mean."

I nodded. "Lash, I just want to say . . . I mean, I know you want to hike faster than Isis and me and the Family. And that's cool, you know, hike your own hike and all that . . . but I wanted to say, I'll miss you."

"Yeah, I'll miss you, too, jackrabbit. Take good care of your sister for me . . . Hey-hey! Tim, my man!"

Tim came in and sat down next to me. Soon he and Lash were deep in conversation, planning how fast they could get through the Smokies. I sat in the corner and drank down the last of my beer and poured another one from the pitcher, feeling stifled and conflicted. There was so much I wanted to say and couldn't. Instead, I sat there drinking, steadily emptying the pitcher.

After a while I excused myself. Tim and Lash looked up vaguely as I left the pub, as though they had forgotten I was even there. "Hey, take it easy," Lash called as I stumbled toward the door, and then he turned back to Tim.

It was late, and the streets were almost empty as I walked back to Elmer's. The full moon cast thick shadows everywhere, even in the orange pools of streetlights. The air still felt warm. The loud music of the pub faded until my footsteps were the only sound. I took a deep breath of the night air, smelling the catfish rankness of the river at the edge of town, and looked up at the heavy moon. With the alcohol coursing through my veins, the night seemed freighted with possibilities, and I felt powerless in the face of them all.

In Elmer's driveway, I found Miss Janet and Yogi and another hiker gathered around a bottle of wine.

"Jackrabbit, come have a drink with us!" Miss Janet said.

"I think I'm drunk already," I answered, hearing my own voice slur the words.

"Nonsense. This is just muscatel, anyway; ain't no harm in it. Jackrabbit, have you met Yurt Man?"

The unfamiliar hiker stepped forward to shake my hand. In the moonlight, I could just see his dark curly hair and clean-shaven face. I thought his eyes were blue, but I wasn't certain.

"I've heard quite a few stories about you and your sister," he said. "It's a pleasure."

"Well, thanks. Good to meet you. I'm going to bed."

"Jackrabbit," Yogi said thickly. "You can' do that. You're in the South now. You gotta come with us, have a drink. You Yankees don' know how ta have a good time."

"Come with you? Where?"

"We're going up to the balds around Max Patch," Yurt Man said. "Build a little fire, drink a little whiskey, have a good time. You coming?"

"No thanks, man. I'm tired. I got to sleep."

Yogi leaned forward. "Jackrabbit. You don' unnerstan'," he said, stabbing at the air with his index finger. "There are things, you know, things in your life . . . if you don' do them, y' always gotta wonder." He stumbled sideways and leaned against Miss Janet's van for support.

"Yeah, that's the truth, Yogi." *And there are things that you do, and regret, and it's impossible to tell beforehand which is which.* But I took the cup of perfume-sweet muscatel from Miss Janet's hand, and I climbed into the back of the van as she settled herself unsteadily into the driver's seat.

"Don't y'all worry one bit," she said cheerfully. "I been driving drunk since I was sixteen, and I never once had an accident."

The ride to the balds was short and uneventful, punctuated only by Yogi's wild Rebel yells. "Wahoo!" He shouted as we careened down the gravel road. "We're gon' show you how South'ners have a good time!"

The moonlight on the balds shone so bright I could see colors—the yellow stubble of grasses and the rainbow stripes of Yurt Man's sweater. He and I gathered firewood from the edge of the forest, where the moonlight painted the ground in bands of black and blue and silver.

"You hiking this year, Yurt Man?"

"Just a section. I was living in a yurt outside Asheville this winter. It got so cold there I just said, I've got to keep moving. So I came back out on the Trail. I started hiking in '95, I guess, and I keep coming back to it." He grabbed another fallen branch and added it to his load. "The Lord leads my steps in mysterious ways sometimes. I don't question it."

He lit the fire in an old blackened ring of stones in the middle of the field, and we sat watching the flames, saying nothing. Somebody brought out a whiskey bottle and we passed it around. The moon danced in the air, distorted by smoke and heat, and I had the sense that I could feel the earth turning underneath us.

"So, Yogi, are you having a good time?" I asked.

He didn't answer. I looked over and saw him slumped next to the fire, heavy and inert, passed out.

Isis

On the morning of our fourth day in Hot Springs, Elmer, who must have been tired of working long hours in his off season, announced that he wouldn't be cooking supper that night. Jackrabbit and I took this as the sign we'd been waiting for: time to hike out. Big Ring and Granny Gear wanted to stay another day and eat a little more town food, even if it wasn't Elmer's cooking. Caveman's mail drop hadn't arrived yet, but Spike wanted to get back on the trail. She decided to hike with us and wait for Caveman at Roaring Fork Shelter, fifteen miles out.

We left in the late morning, after a final breakfast at Elmer's. The sixty-five degree heat, so comfortable in town, seemed stifling in the forest. I remembered what Lash had told us: slack-packing this section the day before, he had decided to hike naked.

"Dude, it's not like I was going to run into anyone," he had responded, when jackrabbit and I pretended to be scandalized.

The three of us weren't likely to run into anyone, either. We decided to take a layer off. In unison, we slung down our packs and stripped off our tank tops. Although our shorts, bras, boots, and packs covered a lot more skin than most bathing suits would have, there was something vaguely illicit about going shirtless on a public trail that made us almost giddy with delight. First one, then another of us burst into laughter; the sound swirled around us like a flock of sparrows. The humid air, which had seemed so oppressive, now felt like a caress. I found myself delighting in the minute variations in temperature between weak sun and rhododendron shadow, dry meadow and streambank.

A mile up the trail, though, as we climbed steadily out of the valley, I realized that I was still soaked in sweat. We stopped at a stream crossing, and jackrabbit looked at me.

"Are you thinking what I'm thinking?"

I nodded. We both bent down and began to unlace our boots. Wading through meltwater streams that cascaded over the trail at regular intervals, and rediscovering the textures of leaf and stone, I felt my feet come back to life after their long confinement. The strange, delightful tingle in the soles that I had often felt in the first five minutes of hiking barefoot lasted a full half hour.

Three miles out of town, we stopped for lunch at Deer Park Mountain Shelter. Lash had left a register there. *Slackin' naked in February,* he wrote. *Is the weather way too hot, or is it just me? Tell me about your naked hiking adventures. With illustrations please.* At the bottom of the page, he'd drawn a quick sketch of himself wearing nothing but boots, a pack, and his orange hat, holding the register notebook in a strategic location with one hand and making a peace sign with the other. I drew a picture of myself and jackrabbit hiking naked, from the back: two pack covers, like enormous blue potatoes, with our legs from the knees down, our arms from the elbows out, and the tops of our heads just showing at the edges.

In midafternoon the wind changed and blew cold from the northeast. The morning's haze thickened into clouds. We stopped on an uphill to put on a few layers and eat a quick snack. Spike ate only half her granola bar, then sat with her arms around her knees, staring out across the valley. When jackrabbit and I stood up to put our packs back on, she didn't move.

"You go ahead. I want to sit here for a few more minutes." Her voice sounded shaky.

"Are you okay?" I asked.

"I'm fine. Just tired." She pulled her knees closer to her chest and bent her neck so that her forehead rested on them. Her shoulder muscles stood out, tense beneath her jacket.

Jackrabbit's eyes met mine. Hypothermia? I knew it could set in quickly, but the air didn't feel that cold. Even with the wind change, the temperature must have been still in the fifties.

"We'll wait for you," I said. I did a few stretches, then bounced up and down on the balls of my feet to keep warm. Spike sighed, uncurled her arms from her knees, and stood up slowly. For the next few miles, jackrabbit and I moved at a snail's pace, waiting for Spike at every turn of the trail. At the top of a ridge, in a clearing surrounded by small pine trees, she unstrapped her pack and lowered it to the ground.

"You guys go ahead. Please."

She hurried toward the nearest pine. Jackrabbit and I walked a few hundred yards down the trail, then stopped. Spike caught up with us ten minutes later, her pale face shiny with sweat. She wore her pack on her shoulders only; the waist and chest straps dangled unbuckled at her sides.

"Flu?" I asked.

"I guess so."

"Did you throw up? Do you feel any better?"

"Yeah. A little."

I made a quick calculation; Spike's pack, with a four-day resupply, must weigh about thirty-five pounds. Mine weighed forty-five or fifty, so little, compared to the seventy-plus pounds I had carried into the Roans, that I hardly felt the pressure on my hips. Struggling up White Rocks Mountain behind Kincora, with the rain seeping through my duct-taped pack cover and mud sticking to the soles of my boots, I'd felt certain that I'd reached the limits of my body's strength. I was ready to test those limits again.

"Here, let me take your pack," I said to Spike. With jackrabbit's help, I bound it crosswise to the top of mine. I stuck my arms back into the straps

and clasped the buckles. Getting to my feet was the hardest part; I rolled my
legs around so that I was kneeling, then used my hiking sticks to pry myself up
from the ground. Jackrabbit pushed on the packs from behind. Suddenly I was
underway again, lurching awkwardly down the hill. Spike's pack stuck out on
either side of my head, like the back of an enormous armchair. It bumped into
the embankment on my left, and I ricocheted over to the other side of the
trail, where the pack bounced off a tree. Behind me, I heard Spike and
jackrabbit's raised voices.

"Stop! Please, don't hurt yourself!"

"Look out for that branch!"

I imagined how I must look, stumbling back and forth under the billowing, amorphous pile of pack covers. *Woman Devoured by Monster Amoeba.* In
spite of the ache in my ribs, which seemed to be grinding against each other
with the weight, I felt a burst of laughter welling up inside of me. Spike and
jackrabbit's voices paused, and then they started laughing, too. By the time I
caught my breath, I had found my gait: rolling, bowlegged and hunchbacked,
but I knew it would carry me the three miles to Roaring Fork.

We caught up with the Family at the shelter. They had hiked out a day
ahead of us. After a week and a half on our own, I found the hubbub disconcerting. Hope and Joy argued over who got the shorter sleeping mat. Joel and
John argued over who had to sleep next to "the sick person." Mary read out
loud to Faith from a tiny picture book she'd picked up in Damascus. *You can't
be cats, said the mother cat. You don't know how to meow. So the three ducklings went
to the mother horse. We want to be horses, the three ducklings said. You can't be horses,
said the mother horse . . .* I'd found the story depressingly inane the first time I
heard it, and by now, its repetitive phrases lurked in the back of my mind like
the lyrics of a bad pop song, waiting to ambush me when I was too tired to
think of anything else.

Paul poked at something in the firepit, and a cloud of rank smoke drifted
into the shelter. I had argued with him about burning trash before. He had
explained that back in Maine, the Family had farmed organically, sewn their
own clothes, and wasted nothing. In their first four months on the Trail, they'd
used cloth diapers for Faith, rinsing them in a basin that Mary kept for the
purpose and hanging them on the backs of their packs to dry. When the
weather turned cold, though, it got hard to find water for washing. At the
same time, it became more and more difficult to carry enough food to replace
the calories they expended in hiking. They had gotten rid of their extra med
kit, traded their flashlights for Photons, and cut their summer pace by half.

Still, it was a delicate balance. Joel carried thirty-five to forty pounds, as much as most adult thru-hikers. Joy, at seven years old, sometimes left town with twenty pounds on her back. Mary, whose body weight hovered between 105 and 115 pounds, carried a sixty-five pound pack. Paul took as much of Mary's gear as he could, plus food for the whole family; his pack weighed about eighty pounds in winter. If he had to pack out all of Faith's used diapers, he'd be carrying an extra five pounds by the end of the week. And carrying them to a dump, where they'd either be buried or burned anyway.

I had thought about offering to help the Family pack their trash out, but I knew that jackrabbit and I were reaching the limits of what we could carry, too. Since the beginning of winter, I'd put more and more of our communal gear in my pack in an attempt to ease the strain on jackrabbit's old injuries. Every pound of garbage that I took from Mary would be one less pound that I could take from my sister's burden, one less chance that the Barefoot Sisters would make it to Springer together.

Paul and I had reached a tacit agreement on the subject. Paul burned as little trash as he could, and he tried not to burn it in front of us. When he did, I didn't complain. The Family had its own ways of surviving, established long before we started hiking with them. If I couldn't help, I shouldn't try to judge.

That night at Roaring Fork, though, I found the smell intolerable. There I was, trying to enjoy a beautiful, natural place while choking on the fumes of somebody's garbage. I felt indignant on Spike's behalf, too; noxious smoke wasn't likely to alleviate her nausea.

"Could you, maybe, burn that in the morning, after we've left?" I asked Paul.

"We have to get an early start, too."

I let out a loud, ungracious sigh. Paul looked up at me, his eyes narrowed. I remembered how formidable he had seemed when jackrabbit and I had first met the Family, back in Delaware Water Gap. When he spoke, though, his voice sounded more weary than angry.

"Listen, Isis. I know how you feel about this. When we finish the Trail, we'll try to find a place where we can live like we did in Maine. Buy food that don't come wrapped in half a dozen layers of plastic. Throw out less in a year than most people do in a day. But right now, we can't afford your fancy ethics. I have only so much strength. I can carry my wife's sleeping bag, or I can carry my daughter's shit."

Spike woke up feeling much better. She decided to wait for Caveman at the shelter, as she had planned. Mary gave her a packet of Gatorade mix, and

John and Joel gathered a big pile of firewood to leave with her. Faith tottered over to her and gave her a hug before clambering into Mary's backpack.

Early in the day, jackrabbit and I hiked with Hope, John, and Joy, telling them stories in which they were the main characters; the steep stream gorges and lovely hemlock forest we were hiking through served as a setting.

"Once upon a time, three bold adventurers decided to attempt the trek to Max Patch, a bald of fabled beauty."

"I was a princess, okay?" Hope piped up. "With a winter dress made of velvet, and four noble lords to carry my food and jewels."

"And I was a hobbit!" cried Joy, jumping over a root.

"What were you, John?" asked jackrabbit.

"I was an Indian. 'Cause Indians really lived here, and they didn't need no trails nor packs nor hostels. If I was an Indian, I'd be the leader, 'cause I'd know how to keep us safe even better than Paul does."

We had to hurry over Max Patch when we finally reached it; a steady, biting wind blew clouds of ice fog across the open space. It was a far cry from the golden field surrounded by waves of soft hills blushing with maple blossoms that Badger had described to us. Instead, the bald had a fierce, unearthly beauty that made me feel as if I was trespassing in an environment too harsh for my kind—a pass in the Himalayas, or rural Norway in a Bergman film. Half of the bald, ending at the path, had been burned recently. On our left, a plain of short yellow grass, the tips of the blades silvered with frost, vanished into the fog. On our right, charred blackberry canes rose out of the black ground like Precambrian water weeds, a fan of ice an inch wide clinging to each stem. Ice rime coated the posts that marked the trail, too; patterns of overlapping crystals, like the breast feathers of gulls, covered the white blazes that we knew must be painted there.

Yogi and Yurt Man caught up with us at Groundhog Creek Shelter that evening. Yogi had picked up a local pop station on his pocket radio, and Faith, instead of crying for "num–num" or "story," started stomping back and forth to the beat as soon as Mary lifted her out of the backpack.

Yogi grinned. "You know, most people, if they were just out for a weekend or whatever, they wouldn't wanna hear pop music. They'd listen to the wind in the trees and the sounds of nature and all that. But when you're out here six, seven months, sometimes you need a little music." He set the pocket radio on the edge of the shelter and danced around with Faith.

Jackrabbit, Yurt Man, and I had time for a quick game of hide and seek with the older children before night fell. Jackrabbit counted. Joy grabbed my hand, tugging me toward a large tree.

"I'm gonna hide with you, Isis!"

John disappeared without a trace, his light green fleece becoming part of the pattern of moss on the forest floor. Joel ducked into a thicket of saplings, his blue jacket blending into the darkening air. Hope's silvery laughter drifted back to me as she raced away uphill. I watched the peaked hoods of their fleeces fade into the twilit forest, where frost rimmed each hemlock needle in glittering white, feeling that I had stumbled into a realm of fairies.

Later that night, we sat in the shelter waiting for our suppers to cook. Yurt Man was using an alcohol hobo stove, even slower at low temperatures than our Zip stove had been. He'd lit it ten minutes before I fired up our propane canister, and his water wasn't even steaming yet.

Hope bounded over to check on his progress. "Your stove is so slow, Yurt Man! How can you wait that long for your dinner?" she asked.

"I have patience." He glanced up at her, his dark eyes sparkling. "And options."

"Options?"

He reached into his food bag and pulled out a package of granola. He took a handful, then offered the bag to Hope. "Options. Want some?"

jackrabbit

Down in Davenport Gap, at the north end of the Smokies, Isis and I found a van parked by the side of the road, waiting for us. A petite, white-haired woman leaned out the window and called to us, "Barefoot Sisters!"

It took a moment for me to place the memory. "Jill?" I asked. "Where's Whispering Bill?"

"Oh, he's right here. Y'all remember us!"

"Who could forget?" Isis said. "You guys helped us out north of Pearis-burg, after we were icebound at Laurel Creek. You were the first people we met for weeks. It's so good to see you again!"

"Good to see y'all." She got out of the van, and Whispering Bill stepped down from the passenger's side. He was as tall and gaunt as I remembered, with his thinning brown hair in a ponytail.

"I'm so happy we found y'all," he said in his barely audible voice, grinning from ear to ear.

"Miss Janet called us up and said y'all were headed this way," Jill added. "She said y'all were hiking with the Family from the North. Are they still—"

Just then, John and Joy came out of the woods, arguing. They stopped short, suddenly shy, when they saw Bill and Jill.

"Hi, guys," I said. "These are some friends of ours. Trail angels. They want to hike the Trail too, maybe next year."

In a few minutes the children were chatting excitedly with Jill about what they would find in the next section of the Trail. Joel and Hope came out of the woods, followed shortly by Paul and Mary. Faith peeked out of Mary's pack. "Mumma, who dat?" There was a new round of introductions.

"Great to meet y'all, after all the stories I've heard," Jill said. "Listen, would y'all like to come down to town? We've got plenty of space for you, and plenty of food."

"I could use a rest," Mary said.

"A down day, a town day!" Hope and John chanted, dancing around.

I was torn—it was a beautiful warm day, clear and perfect for hiking. I hated to leave the trail. I wanted to spend more time with Jill and Bill, though, and Isis and I had planned to stay with the Family at least until we got through the Smokies.

"Jackrabbit," Bill whispered. "Didn't you say you play the piano? We've got one in the living room. I'd love to hear you play."

I was the first one in the van.

Bill drove us back to the trail in the early morning. It was overcast and slightly chilly, with wisps of fog drifting through the forest. I felt energized and ready to hike, though. Music, food, friendship, and a good night's sleep on a soft mattress had renewed me. Once again, I marveled at the generosity of people who had been strangers such a short time ago.

At the edge of the Smokies, a fire had recently blackened the hillside. The ground was scorched bare; not even fallen leaves or pine needles remained. The rhododendrons and laurels, usually green, were reduced to charred branches. Mist thickened around us. The whole landscape looked dead, and the damp wind smelled sooty.

John, hiking just ahead of me, stopped in the middle of the burned area and looked around. He spoke in a quiet voice, full of dread. "Are there still dragons in the world?"

Though I tried to reassure him that dragons were imaginary, I noticed that he looked around nervously as he hiked and stayed closer to the group than he usually did.

The pathway rose steeply out of Davenport Gap. I remembered the elevation profile clearly—six miles of steady uphill. I readjusted my pack straps, shifting the load for the long haul, and started walking. The thick trunks of maples and tulip poplars, with their corrugated tawny bark, gave way to huge hemlocks and spruces. The mist beaded up on their needles and began to drip. Rhododendron thickets closed in on either side of the path, dark green and slick-leaved.

Yellow tufts of grass and olive-green mosses lined the edges of the trail. The snow had melted entirely now, except for occasional patches of ice in the path.

Isis and I hiked fast, going ahead of the Family, enjoying the quiet of the woods. Yogi stayed back with the children. I heard him laughing and talking with Joel as I walked on. We had made plans to meet them that night at a fire tower that Anonymous Badger had told us about, up on Mount Cammerer. *It's one of the prettiest places on the Trail,* he had said. *There's room up there to sleep about twenty people.*

I wondered where the other sobos were. Spike and Caveman were still behind us. The rest of them were somewhere up ahead, as far as I knew; I hadn't seen a register for a few days. I hoped we would all meet up again, but there was so little Trail mileage left. My thoughts kept straying to Lash and all the things I had wanted to say to him that night at the Paddler's Pub.

"Isis, what do you think of Lash?" I asked.

She laughed. "What do I think of Lash? He's cute, he's charming, but he's not my type. All he wants is some woman to treat him like dirt and dump him so he can write another sad song about it."

"Yeah, you're probably right."

We walked on in silence for a while, and the sound of our footsteps on the gravel path blended with the sound of water dripping everywhere.

"Jackrabbit, you know what you said in Erwin, about yo-yoing the Trail? Were you serious?"

I thought hard. "Yes."

"It's another six months. Another eight, if we go as slow northbound."

"We won't. It'll be summer."

She smiled. "You know, when I was solo in Vermont, I thought about it. I thought maybe I'd yo-yo by myself, if you didn't want to. We still have that money we were planning to spend on a car so we could drive back after the Trail. Why not walk? Neither of us really has anywhere to go next fall—"

"I was planning to apply to grad school, but I don't really need to start until October—"

"And it'll be spring by the time we reach Georgia. All the nobos will be starting. The weather will get better; we won't have to carry as much."

"And we'll see flowers." I thought of the pictures I had seen at the Ruck, and especially of the dwarf iris in Spur's photo album. I looked at the bare ground between the trees, strewn with fallen leaves, and I imagined tiny wildflowers pushing their way through the brown husks. Just under the surface, they were waiting.

"You really mean it? You want to yo-yo?"

"Yes."

The fire tower perched on a spur of gray granite that jutted out from the end of the ridge. We caught sight of it through the rhododendron thickets when the mist blew back; an octagonal one-room building of wood and stone with windows on all sides, it reminded me of a lighthouse. A weathered wooden balcony rimmed the structure. From the map, we knew that the land dropped away steeply on three sides, but the fog was so thick that it was impossible to tell.

Badger had been right about the size. The building looked small from the outside, but from the inside, I could see that the single room would fit all of us and our gear with room to spare. Miraculously, all the glass windows were intact. Some of the damp chill crept through the walls, but I knew that when everyone arrived, our body heat would dry the place quickly.

"This is awesome," I said, and my voice echoed, amplified in the small space.

"And great acoustics, too!" Isis exclaimed.

"Let's sing something." I took off my wet boots and set them by the door, then hung my dripping rain gear and pack cover over a rafter by the far wall.

"Oh, I'd love to. But let's wait until everybody's here. You know how the kids like singing."

"Okay."

In a few minutes the Family's front-runners jumped across the gray rocks: John and Joy, racing each other. At the last second John held back a little, and Joy scooted through the doorway half a second before her brother.

"I win! Nyah-nyah!" she shouted, sticking out her tongue.

John slumped against the doorway, feigning exhaustion. "I was real close, but you was faster," he said in a mournful tone, but he smiled at me and Isis behind his sister's back.

The rest of the Family, Yurt Man, and Yogi came in a few minutes later. Packs and wet gear lined one wall and festooned the rafters above it, and the rest of the room filled up with foam pads, sleeping bags, and hikers. The open space vanished as everyone claimed a patch of the floor. The inevitable arguments broke out, turning into wrestling matches that threatened more than once to overturn people's cookstoves. Paul and Mary shouted at the children several times, but after brief periods of calm the conflicts escalated again. I thought about the other sobos, wondering where they were, envying the peace and quiet they must be enjoying.

After supper, we lay back in our sleeping bags. The mist had turned to rain, a steady thin drumming on the roof. Isis lit the candle lantern and set it on the floor. Its flickering orange light gilded our faces.

"Let's sing something," she said. "How about 'Wayfaring Stranger'?"

"Naw," Mary said. "That's so gloomy."

"'Wade in the Water'?"

Mary sighed. "Let's sing something new. We've been singing all these old songs for months. Yogi, do you know any songs?"

He shifted his bulk in his sleeping bag. "Yeah, I guess I know a couple. Let's see . . ." He sang a few folk songs that no one else knew, and half a verse of "Imagine." Mary wracked her memory for the rest of the words.

I sat back and reflected, watching the little flame in the lantern. I remembered a conversation I'd had in Damascus with Isis, Mary, and Paul. It was late; the children had gone to bed and the streets of Damascus were deserted. We sat in the living room at the Lazy Fox, with the lamps turned down low. We were still shaken by the memory of the blizzard on the Grayson Highlands.

"We'll stay with you guys," Isis had said. "We don't mind slowing down."

"At least through the Smokies," I added. "That's the last place where we might get really bad weather in an exposed spot."

"Are you sure?" Mary said. "I love having you guys around. I know the kids can get to be a bit much, sometimes."

Paul sat back, a thoughtful look in his deep-set eyes. "We appreciate all you done for us out there. Don't feel like you got to stay, though." The message was clear: *we can take care of ourselves.*

"It's not a matter of feeling like we have to," I said. "I've had a lot of fun hiking with you guys. And besides, there's safety in numbers."

Isis spoke quietly. "*I* feel like we have to stay together." Paul sat forward and started to say something, but fell silent as she continued. "It's not for you that we have to. It's for us. There were a couple times out on that bald when I was just about ready to give up. I might have just stopped out there and sat down in the snow. But I thought about the kids. I thought, *I have to do this for the children.* I'm not sure we would have survived without you guys. We need you."

Us. We. I thought, but I didn't say anything.

"Safety in numbers," Paul said solemnly. "We'll stay together, at least until the Smokies."

"Maybe we'll finish the Trail together," Mary said. "The Family from the North and the Barefoot Sisters. Wouldn't that be great?"

In the fire tower on Mount Cammerer, Yogi gave up on the Neil Young song he had tried to piece together. It was quiet. I looked around the room, watching the light reflect off the faces I knew and loved, and I felt an immense sadness. Our time with the Family was coming to an end. Isis reached forward and snuffed out the candle lantern.

In the morning, the fog had cleared around us. As I sat up, distant blue mountains came into view, rimming the horizon, wreathed in thin scarves of cloud.

"Y'all have got to see this," Yogi called from the doorway. A breath of chilly, damp air came in with his voice. I pulled on my wind pants and fleece and headed outside.

The view from the balcony was something straight out of a Chinese scroll painting. Under our feet, the end of the ridge dropped precipitously into a blanket of thick fog from the Pigeon River. Little wraiths of mist rose as we watched, vanishing into the overcast sky. In all directions, a sea of mountains rose around us, grayish pink in the foreground with the twigs of beech and maple, fading to blue-green with distance. All the hints of cities, technology, other people, were hidden under the cloud layer; we could have been the last people on earth.

Yogi stared across the mountains. "The last time I came through here, I didn't see nothing but fog for six days," he said.

I grinned. "That's kind of what we had in the Whites. No wonder you didn't like the Smokies too much."

By now, Isis and the Family had roused themselves and joined us on the balcony. The kids leaned over the rails, exclaiming breathlessly.

"Oh, I feel like a fairy-tale princess!" Hope said. "This is my castle!"

"We came all the way from over there," Joy announced proudly, pointing to the range of mountains across the cloud-filled valley.

"And a whole lot farther," Joel added.

Mary came out last, with Faith in tow. "This is so beautiful! It's like a real wilderness."

Only Paul was frowning. "It's beautiful except for that," he said.

"What?" I looked where he was pointing, down at the far end of the valley. It was a moment before I realized what he meant—the thick reddish-brown haze that settled just above the cloud layer, obscuring the distant mountains in places.

"That's probably Gatlinburg, over there," Yurt Man said. "The smog just sticks around."

"Smaug? Like the dragon in *The Hobbit?*" John asked with a bit of his earlier trepidation. I hadn't quite been able to convince him that dragons lived only in storybooks.

"Smog," I said, and tried to explain what it was and where it came from.

John was quiet for a few seconds. "Huh. I bet if more people walked places, like us, there wouldn't be none of that."

The trail led up into the islands of spruce and Frazier fir on the highest ridges. The clouds closed in again, bringing chilly rain. In places, the trail was so narrow it looked like a suspension bridge, dropping off on either side, lined by huge trees like pylons. The way ahead vanished in the blowing mist. We began to see the ravages of acid rain. Every other tree, it seemed, was dead or dying; the gray, weathered poles of standing deadwood dotted the forest around us, the color of the clouds, stark against the green of their living neighbors. Blowdowns crisscrossed the trail.

In an ecology course in college, I had studied the effects of air pollution on the Southern fir forests. The trees, weakened by acid rain and ozone damage, were falling victim to an introduced insect species, the balsam woolly adelgid. It was one thing to read about it, though, in dispassionate scientific journals in a library two thousand miles away, and quite another thing to see it firsthand. I felt as though I was walking through a forest of ghosts.

Tri-Corner Knob Shelter, where we stayed that night, was a low-slung stone building roofed with corrugated tin. Like the other Smokies shelters, it was much larger than a typical A.T. lean-to—there was space for probably twenty hikers. A chain-link fence closed off the front of the shelter to protect the occupants from bears. Inside, the rain made a steady din. As my eyes adjusted to the gloom, I could see two levels of bunk platforms, with barely enough space to sit up, built into the back wall. A smoke-blackened fireplace took up most of one side wall, with a few large logs scattered near it as seats. The floor in front of the bunks was three inches deep with mud. Looking back through the fence, I could see an expanse of gravel runneled with small streams and a grassy hillside sloping back to the dark evergreen woods. The rain gave fuzzy edges to the scene, blurring the background as dusk settled under the trees.

Isis and I slung off our wet packs and hung them from nails on the rafters, where they wouldn't drip on the bunks. The air inside felt clammy, as though cold was oozing out of the stone walls.

"This'd be a good night for a fire," I said, rubbing my hands together.

"Hey, ladies!" Tim and Lash came through the gate in the bear fence.

"Hi, guys! Where have you been? I thought you'd be miles ahead by now. Take a load off." I indicated the nails for hanging packs, but Tim made a face.

"We weren't planning on staying here," he said. "Just stopping for a snack."

I looked over at Lash. He shrugged. "Still light out there, man. Got to get some more miles behind us."

"Come on, you guys," I said. "The next shelter's, like, six miles, if you count the side trail. Do you really want to get there in the dark?"

"Trail's well-marked," Tim said.

I shifted my argument. "But really, what's six miles? Wouldn't it be better to do it in the morning, when it'll be light? Maybe by then the rain will stop." *If I can get them to stay tonight, maybe I'll have the courage to say the things I couldn't say in Hot Springs,* I thought. *I have to try.* "Besides, you've got to tell us where you've been all this time. I thought for sure you were ahead of us."

Lash laughed. "Dude, we got hooked up big time. We were hiking with Big Ring and Granny Gear. They have family that owns a restaurant in some little town near here. Granny's Chicken Palace. They invited all of us—me and Tim, plus Spike and Caveman, too—for this all-you-can-eat buffet. It was outrageous. There was more food on that table than I've seen in the past three months. We ate it all, and then, well, you know that feeling you get when you eat way too much? Like if you move, you're gonna puke? We were all like that. Way past full. So the owner of the restaurant comes out, and she says, 'y'all can just sleep in the back room if you want.' She was awesome."

"So you slept at Granny's Chicken Shack?"

Lash gave me a severe look. "Chicken *Palace*. They fed us breakfast, too. Then they dropped us off, and we staggered on down the trail."

"The others are back there somewhere," Tim said through the last mouthful of his granola bar. "Come on, man, we've got to hit the trail."

"It's getting dark," I said. "Dark and rainy. Muddy."

"We've got headlamps," Tim said, but I could tell he was beginning to give in.

"Hey, if you guys stay here, we can collect wood and have a fire going by the time the Family gets here."

"Six miles; we'll be there in two hours, tops," Tim said to Lash. (This seemed like an incredibly optimistic estimate to me.)

I played my last card. "I might have a Snickers bar in my pack somewhere." In Erwin, we had told the rest of the sobos about the secret significance of Snickers bars.

Tim looked at me for a long moment. "You drive a hard bargain, jackrabbit." He slung his pack off and hung it on a nail. Lash sighed and followed suit. In a few minutes, we were out under the darkening trees, looking for firewood.

It was a busy evening in the shelter. Yogi, Yurt Man, and the Family came as full dark settled, and Spike and Caveman joined us a few minutes later. Isis started a fire. The building, which had seemed so gloomy when we arrived, soon filled up with light and voices. Multicolored raingear was draped over the bear fence, decorating its utilitarian chain-links. Packs hung from every hook in the rafters. We found plenty of space on the bunks, though the lower level had very little headroom.

Lash and I sat up by the fire late that night, after everyone had gone to bed. The drumming of rain on the roof blended with the small sounds the children made in their sleep. The flames popped and crackled on the wet wood, and smoke blew down the chimney into the shelter when the wind shifted. We didn't speak for a long time.

"There's something about a fire," he finally said. "You just can't stop watching it. It's like a river or something, you know, how it's always changing." He spread his hands in front of the coals to warm them. "Jackrabbit, do you ever think about the purpose of life? Like, why are we here? What does it all mean?"

I almost laughed—it was like a badly written scene in a movie. I could picture the directions in the script: *Interior. Night. Brooding young intellectuals stare into the flames.* But something in Lash's voice called for a serious reply.

"Yeah, I think about it a lot out here," I said. "I wish I had an answer. Sometimes I think there's some great, far-reaching explanation for all of it. Usually I think it's just a big crapshoot. There is no why." I took a stick and stirred the fire. The coals were beginning to die down, glowing a richer red. "But I think maybe that *believing* there's some mystery behind it, *hoping* there's a reason for the way things happen—maybe that's what makes us human."

Lash looked over at me. In the fading firelight, his eyes shone the color of dark amber. I thought I saw a wellspring of sadness in them, an echo of depression, that flood I have struggled against so many times. He said nothing, and after a moment he turned back to watch the embers.

I'm not in love with him, I thought. *I'm in love with the idea that someone could fill up this emptiness in my life. No one will. No one can. This sadness is something that no one outside me can touch.* Strangely, this thought brought a kind of peace. *Until I can learn to manage it on my own, I'll stay alone. I don't need to drag anyone else down with me.*

A mouse rustled something in the rafters. The rain continued, a steady din on the metal roof. I yawned. "Got to get an early start tomorrow. Good night, Lash."

The mist cleared a little bit the next day. Occasionally we could see giant cliffs and scarps of dark rock, breathtakingly steep, that swooped toward the valley floor and vanished in a lower layer of clouds. The evergreen forest, with its ranks of dead and dying trees, cloaked the gentler slopes.

At a curve in the path under some giant hemlocks, Isis turned to face me. "So many people think we're crazy to stay out here. If they could just be here for one second, on this path, in our strong young bodies—they'd understand."

We came to Icewater Springs Shelter late in the day. The wind had picked up, blowing shreds of fog across the clearing in front of the shelter, and the temperature was dropping. Spike and Caveman had rigged a tarp across the entrance, trying to keep the wind out. They lay inside in their sleeping bags.

"Hello, ladies," Caveman said. "Happy Valentine's Day!"

"Oh, I'd forgotten," Isis said. "It is, isn't it?"

"Fourteenth of February."

"Wow. We ought to celebrate. I'm all out of candy, but maybe I have some cookies left."

We unshouldered our packs and changed into warmer clothes against the clinging damp and cold. Isis found half a bag of crumbled Pecan Sandies in her food bag, which we passed around. Spike broke a Hershey bar into pieces. Caveman reached into his food bag and came up with a packet of ramen noodles.

"The greatest delicacy on the Trail!" he said, making a tragic face when no one wanted any. We all laughed. "I think there might be something else, though . . ." He took out a bag of candy hearts inscribed with messages: *U R sweet, foxy lady, no way, outta sight, be mine.* "I know they taste like toothpaste, but it just wouldn't be Valentine's Day without them."

"Aw," Spike said. She turned to us. "Isn't he great? You should read what he wrote in the register. It's so sweet it gave me the warm fuzzies."

She passed the battered spiral-bound notebook to me. *Happy Valentine's Day! Here at Icewater Springs it is chilly and damp. My feet are wet and I smell like something the cat dragged in. But there is nowhere on earth I would rather be, because the love of my life is here. Dearest Dana, thank you for hiking the Trail with me. Thank you for sharing your life with me. Thanks for everything. Love, Jim.*

"That is really dear," I said, and to my surprise I was blinking back tears.

Tim and Lash came to the shelter a few minutes later. Lash, with a grin, handed out mini Snickers bars. "Here you go, ladies."

I punched him on the arm. "*Mini* Snickers? Is that all we're worth now?"

"Hey, it's the thought that counts, right?" He gave a lascivious smile that looked just like Tim's.

I raised an eyebrow. "And what precisely did you have in mind?" It was somehow easier to flirt with him, now that I had decided nothing would come of it.

"Well, we could act out a few scenes from your novel," Lash said.

Tim perked up. "What novel is this?"

"Dude! You mean they didn't tell you about the book they're writing? *Passion's Stealth-fire?*"

"*Passion's Stealth-fire?*" Tim said carefully, as though testing out the words. There was a gleam in his eye.

"It's a romance novel," Isis said, a little sheepishly. "Set on the A.T."

"Oh, this sounds good," Tim said. "Tell me more."

"Well, it's about a sobo and a nobo who meet and, you know . . ." Isis said.

"We started writing it when we were icebound in Virginia."

"Yeah, jackrabbit was lonely for Black Forest," Isis said, and I elbowed her in the ribs. "Hey! Anyway, we decided to kind of bend the genders, 'cause romance novels are usually so stupid. We made the heroine big and tough, and the hero kind of delicate. She's a sobo. MEGA Maid. She meets this skinny little nobo, GAME Boy." There was general laughter at the names. "And, well, one thing leads to another . . ."

"You've got to read us an excerpt," Tim said.

"Oh, it's really bad," Isis told him.

"Come on! It's Valentine's Day! Just a few paragraphs?" He grinned. "I'll do my Elmer Fudd Sings Wagner act." He spread his arms wide. "Oh, Bwoon-hilda!" he sang in a ridiculous falsetto, batting his eyelashes. "Bwoon-hilda, I wuv you!"

"All right. Just for that," I said, when I finished laughing and caught my breath. I reached into the top of my pack for the grimy sheets of stationery covered in tiny writing.

"Let's see . . . oh, this is where they meet for the first time: *It was late in the afternoon when the scrawniest, scraggliest nobo she had ever seen staggered up to the shelter. Perhaps the drenching rain, which plastered his thin shirt to his chest and thighs, contributed to his drowned-rat appearance, but MEGA Maid could tell at a glance that the boy was carrying too little food—and had been carrying too little food for months. She could also tell from the lingering redness in those large, soft eyes that he was hiking off a hangover—not an unusual state for a nobo. But there was something unusual about this one. Was it that satiny dark hair that shone in the rain, or those deep brown eyes into which she had been staring far longer than she had intended?*

"'Excuse my lack of manners,' she said, rising from her Thermarest with the languid grace of a lion. 'I've been in the woods too long. My name's MEGA Maid.' She extended a large, tanned hand.

"'GAME Boy,' the nobo grunted, placing his small hand in hers. She marveled at the delicateness of that hand—she could feel every bone of his fingers, feel the slight tremor that ran through them. She glanced down and saw that his whole body was trembling. Was it only the chill of his wet garments, or did some ill-disguised emotion hold him in its grasp? MEGA Maid had had this effect on men before, and she had taken many of them into her sleeping bag, from the innocent farm boys whose hearts she had callously broken and tossed aside, to the tawdry but talented Trail bums who sold their services for the price of a Snickers bar . . .

Lash looked down and mumbled something into his beard. Everyone laughed and he began to blush.

"But this time it felt different. The lad's trembling awakened in her not the instincts of a predator, but a new, gentler emotion. Something akin to pity softened her steely eyes as she told him, 'Go put some dry clothes on, kid. I don't want to take the blame when you freeze to death.'

"'I'm warm enough,' GAME Boy protested hotly, not letting go of her hand, 'And anyway, I don't carry a change of clothing.'

"'Strip!' she ordered, and continued (ignoring his shocked expression), 'I'll lend you something.'" I put the paper down.

"And?" Tim said eagerly.

"And nothing," I said. "That's all there is. The ice storm ended; we packed up."

Spike and Caveman applauded, laughing. "You ought to give Harlequin a call," Spike said.

Tim looked sorely disappointed. "You mean that's as far as they got?" Then he grinned wolfishly. "If you ever want any help with your novel, you know, any ideas about what comes next, I'd be glad to show you a thing or two." He winked.

Isis looked taken aback, but I laughed. "You'd better start stocking up on Snickers bars, then."

Lash gave a wicked grin and passed out the last of his mini Snickers. Then he closed his food bag, stuffed it in the top of his pack, and took up his hiking poles. Tim packed up as well.

"Are you guys leaving?" I asked.

"Yeah," Lash said. "This shelter's probably not big enough for all of us." It was true; the shelter was not quite as large as the others in the Smokies. We probably could have made room, but it would have been a tight fit.

"I guess this is one of those 'bye, never see you again' moments," Tim said.

"What?" I asked.

Caveman explained. "When we were hiking with Tim back in Vermont, he liked to move a lot faster, but he also took more time off. We lost track of how many times we said goodbye to him, thinking it would be the last time. After a while, that became our standard thing to say, even when somebody just went to the privy: 'Bye; never see you again.'"

"Okay. Bye; never see you again," I said to Tim and Lash as they headed out.

"Never see you again," they called back over their shoulders as they hiked into the gathering dusk, and I wondered if this time it was true.

It was a crowded night in the shelter, even without Tim and Lash. The Family, Yogi, and Yurt Man packed into the interstices. Packs and food bags hung from every available peg. Yogi added his tarp to the one Spike and Caveman had strung across the entrance. The blue-green light filtering through the fabric gave the interior of the shelter a strange underwater glow before the day faded.

I slept poorly; the wind moaning around the eaves and flapping the tarps woke me up each time I drifted off. Some time in the middle of the night, I heard Yogi yelp with fright, perhaps in a dream. Hope whispered, "Miss Janet?" and someone shushed her. I heard footsteps in the shelter, and I wondered if I was dreaming too.

As the gray light of dawn came up, I saw that I hadn't dreamed after all. Miss Janet sat on the end of the sleeping platform, watching us all with a motherly smile.

Yogi rolled over and sat up. "My God! It is you! You know, you just about gave me a heart attack last night."

She chuckled. "Sorry 'bout that. I didn't mean for anyone to notice me when I came in."

Yogi looked a little sheepish. "Well, I'd just gotten up to take a leak, and I headed back to bed. I turned around and there you were, not two feet away from me. You'd've been startled too!"

The children were beginning to stir. "I knew it was true!" Hope said. "Look, she *is* here!" Soon everyone was awake and talking at once. Miss Janet handed out candy and Valentine cards.

Joy looked puzzled. "How'd you get here? Where's your pack?"

"Oh, I just hiked in from the parking lot at Newfound Gap. It's only three miles or so. Alls I had to bring was a daypack."

"Thanks for coming out here," Isis said. "It's great to see you again."

"Oh, I wouldn't miss it. It's so good to see y'all." Her face turned serious. "Besides, there's a storm front moving this way. It's gonna hit tomorrow sometime. Ice, lightning, high winds. I came to see if y'all want to go down to the valley. I talked to Jill and Bill; they'd be glad to have y'all back. Spike and Caveman, y'all are invited, too," she added, almost as an afterthought.

They conferred for a while. "Thanks, but I think we'll stay out here," Spike finally said.

"If it gets really bad, we can hole up in a shelter," Caveman added. "We've got plenty of food to get to Fontana. I don't really feel like going back into town just yet. Thanks, though."

I felt exactly the same way. The woods were so mysterious in the fog, and the occasional glimpses of cliffs when the clouds opened were like windows onto a different world. More than anything, I wanted to stay out here among the mountains. To return to civilization now would be to break the spell. The Family wanted to go to town, though, and Isis would follow them, I knew. Wherever she went, I would have to go. We hiked to the parking lot in pouring rain.

Isis

"Whoa! Check it out!"

"Direct hit!"

We had just settled into Jill and Bill's tiny house, piling our packs and jackets into the spare bedroom until they covered all the floor space. Jackrabbit, Yurt Man, and I were helping Jill chop vegetables for tacos, while Miss Janet, Yogi, and the Family clustered around the television with Bill. To judge from their gasps and exclamations, they were watching either an action movie or some exceptionally dangerous and well-played sport.

"Isis, jackrabbit, c'mere! You've gotta see this!"

I stepped around the counter into the living room, fighting back a twinge of annoyance. I knew the children hadn't seen much television in their lives; it was still a novelty to them. But what sporting event could be more important than dinner?

On the left side of the screen, a calm, neatly dressed woman waved a long pointer. I couldn't hear her voice above the children's rustle and chatter, but to judge from her sparkling eyes and unruffled brow, she seemed to be sharing some trivial yet delicious piece of gossip, meant for our ears alone. I turned my attention to the green wall beside her. It was a weather map; Tennessee on one side and North Carolina on the other. A few white patches flickered across its upper right-hand corner. As I watched, they coalesced into an elliptical mass and advanced down the wall like an enormous fuzzy caterpillar, right along the jagged line labeled "Great Smoky Mountains." The woman poked the white ellipse with her baton, and it began to spout symbols: cute little clouds with raindrops, snowflakes, and lightning bolts protruding from their bellies.

"Shh . . . shhh . . . Turn up the volume!"

The announcer's sultry voice rose. ". . . a *severe* winter storm warning. Around noon tomorrow, arctic air from Canada will clash with this *warm* front . . ." She indicated what looked like a string of red Mardi-Gras beads advancing across the left side of the map. ". . . producing *ice storms* and *thunderstorms* with winds of up to *sixty* miles per hour."

I tore myself away from the television, stepped over Hope and John, and slipped back into the kitchen.

"Was that the weather forecast?" asked jackrabbit, who was still chopping onions.

"Yup. It looks like we'll have to take a zero."

"Take a zero?" She spoke in a voice so low that only I could hear her, but her eyes blazed. "We took three zeros in Hot Springs, less than a week ago. If we let every winter storm keep us penned up indoors, we won't get to Springer till June. Fuck the weather. I'm hiking tomorrow. I want to finish this fucking Trail."

"What about our plan to yo-yo?"

"That's exactly what I mean. We won't have time to yo-yo, if we finish the Trail too late. People are already starting northbound, and I want to be with them."

"We've got plenty of time."

"You mean *you've* got plenty of time. You can dawdle all the way to Georgia, and as long as you get there before the summer solstice, you'll have completed a thru-hike. I'll still be missing two hundred miles. I want a thru-hike. It's what I came out here for. And unless I catch a bus back to Massachusetts as soon as we reach Georgia, it looks like northbound is my only chance."

"I guess so," I answered.

I preferred the "hiker trash has too much fun" rationale, I thought to myself.

Dark clouds obscured the mountains to the east, but in the valley the air felt soft and springlike. Jill showed me and Mary where the thin, bright leaves of crocuses and the pale shoots of hyacinths were beginning to break through the leaf mold in her garden. Mary sighed as she brushed a clump of dried moss off a hyacinth. I knew what she was thinking; in the mountains, where we lived, spring would not come for at least another month.

Jackrabbit spent the morning checking the weather on the Internet at ten-minute intervals. When she wasn't seated in front of the computer, she paced up and down the hall, three steps in each direction. It wasn't until she called the local weather station, confirming that a massive thunderstorm was due to strike Clingman's Dome in a few hours, that she resigned herself to the idea of a zero.

"As long as we get an early start tomorrow," she said, throwing herself into an armchair and opening the Smokies map.

We didn't get an early start the next day, after all. Jill and Bill fixed us an enormous breakfast, and it was past ten by the time we had eaten, helped wash dishes, located everyone's gear and packed it all into the back of Miss Janet's van. We stopped for lunch on the way through Gatlinburg, then went to the outfitter's to replace someone's ripped gaiters. At last, we headed toward Newfound Gap, only to find ourselves caught in a traffic jam. Hundreds of tourists were taking advantage of the clear weather to go for a drive in the mountains, and very few of them, it seemed, had any experience with icy roads. Near the Gap, we had to stop three or four times to help people push their cars out of the ditches. In between car-pushing expeditions, jackrabbit chatted with John in the back seat, braided Hope's hair, and traded tourist jokes with Yogi. I could sense her impatience, though—in the way she held her shoulders, as if trying not to touch the people on either side of her, and in the way she fixed her attention on the mountains each time we stepped out of the car—not just her gaze but her whole body, tense as a drawn bow.

We reached the Gap at three in the afternoon. The low sun flickered through the fir trees, and a bitter wind whipped across the parking lot.

"Let's go," said jackrabbit, slinging her pack onto one shoulder.

"Wait, Miss Janet's taking a picture."

I should get a picture too, I thought. *This is probably one of the last times we'll all be together.* I started to dig out my camera, but thought better of it; my hands felt too cold.

"Where are you going tonight?" I asked Paul, as we lined up by the van for the photo.

"Mount Collins Shelter, I guess. It's five miles from here, and that's about all the daylight we have left. Where are you going?"

"I don't know. Maybe Mount Collins."

Miss Janet put away her camera and bent down to hug Hope goodbye. Mary tucked Faith into her pack. Suddenly, I realized that jackrabbit had reached the other side of the parking lot already. She was about to disappear into the woods. I snapped my pack straps closed, seized my hiking sticks, and sprinted after her. Halfway to the trailhead, I paused for a moment, looking back. Mary was hugging Miss Janet. Paul was helping John adjust his pack. Hope and Joy danced around, trying to keep warm, and Joel nodded, grinning, in response to something Yogi had said. I waved; only Faith stuck her mittened hand out of Mary's backpack and waved back.

"See you. Maybe. Goodbye," I shouted, wondering if anyone would hear me over the wind. Mary looked up and waved, smiling. I turned away and plunged into the forest, following my sister.

CHAPTER 12

Sobos on the Wrong Side of the Tracks

Isis

Jackrabbit and I paused at the side trail to Mount Collins Shelter to leave messages in the snow for the Family. *FFTN, we love you*, I wrote, while jackrabbit spelled out their names, one by one, with the tip of her hiking stick. As I wrote, I let my mind wander down the shelter path. We could turn now and find water before the sun set. We could start a fire, cook supper early, and listen for the children's laughter ringing through the twilit woods. We could sing together once more, as the stars came out, and sleep shoulder to shoulder, sharing our warmth. We could say our goodbyes properly, when the time came.

I looked up from my writing. The sun seemed no lower than it had been when we left Newfound Gap. Partly a trick of perspective, I knew—we had climbed about a thousand feet in the past five miles—but it felt as though we were flying. The trail stretched ahead of us, a bright blank ribbon of snow. On either side of it, the beech and birch trees held their glittering crowns aloft, the thin branches glazed with ice shining like torches in the evening light. We could outrun the sunset, or stop and let it catch us in a high place, then walk all night under the stars. *Jackrabbit was right*, I realized. *It is time, past time, for us to strike out on our own.* Even the sharp air, burning the back of my throat, felt cleansing.

We reached Clingman's Dome, the highest point on the A.T. at 6,643 feet, just as the sun touched the tips of the evergreen trees on the ridge ahead of us. Dropping our packs, we sprinted for the observation tower. Long beams of amber light pierced the fir forest and caught in the corners of our eyes. Ice coated everything: the ramp, the hand rail, the maps at the top of the tower that were supposed to tell us which mountains we could see. I had left my own map in my backpack, so we looked at a landscape without names: thin scalloped ridges, glowing gold, the skeletons of old fir trees thick with ice rime, the wind blowing curtains of snow or mist like orange scarves across the sun. A round hill rose in front of us, its fir-covered peak vanishing under the orange mist, then reappearing like the shore of some fairy country, shining for a moment through its veils.

Night fell swiftly as we hiked down from Clingman's Dome. The wind quickened and the stars shone out between the branches. Still, the unbroken snow held its soft gleam long after twilight; we only turned on our headlamps in the last half hour so we wouldn't miss the shelter trail.

As it turned out, we needn't have worried. Double Spring Gap Shelter sat right beside the A.T., a hulking brown building with a mesh of chain-link across the front. We let ourselves in through the bear gate and set to work, changing into our warm clothes and rolling out our foam pads in the middle of the wide sleeping platform. Jackrabbit gathered up our empty Nalgenes and went looking for the spring trail while I unpacked our food bags. I had just found the couscous, and was still looking for the butter, when the gate creaked, and jackrabbit strode back in, smiling and humming "Wade in the Water" to herself. She set four full bottles down in front of me; in spite of the freezing weather, Double Spring had lived up to the promise of water in its name.

It surprised me how quickly my body returned to the rhythm of hiking alone. I woke an hour and a half before dawn and brushed my hair in the darkness: a cold silky river washing over my hands, with blue sparks of static snapping at the edge of it. I pinned it in a tight braid around my head, pulled on my hat and gloves, and had water hot for cocoa by the time I woke jackrabbit. We left the shelter before the first streaks of color touched the eastern sky.

As we walked, a pale blue light suffused the landscape, changing the fir boughs from black to a green-tinged indigo. Downward and downward we strode, through fields where snowdrifts looked like waves on the sea. Near sunrise, the ridge we followed narrowed to a slender catwalk of stone, arching out over the valleys like a buttress to Clingman's Dome. Range upon serried range of mountains, all weathered in the same pattern of sharp peaks and furrowed edges, spread out below us. Small clouds clung in the valleys, blazing white when the first rays of sun struck them, and a fine blue mist rose off the ridges.

The air grew warmer as the day progressed; by midafternoon, patches of meltwater glistened on the trail. Around two o'clock, we came to a shelter with a Pilgrim and Gollum register. Pilgrim's graceful cursive began the book; he wrote out a traveler's blessing similar to the one Netta had given us. On the next page, Gollum waxed rhapsodic on the virtues of duct tape. Further on, we found an entry from Waterfall, who sounded cheerful in spite of the cold weather she'd encountered in the Smokies. *Less than two hundred miles to Springer! Go sobos! Life is good.* We unpacked some dried fruit and chocolate for our afternoon snack and sat in the sun for a full forty-five minutes, coming up with messages worth leaving for the register's owners, as well as for our friends behind. After much deliberation, I wrote a riddle for the children.

> I drag at your feet when you're weary;
> When you're lost I am no friend,
> But I'm water you don't have to carry,
> Paper you write on without a pen.

"Way too easy," jackrabbit laughed. "The answer's all around us."

"If it stays this warm, the snow will have melted by the time they get here," I said. "Then they'll have to think a bit."

"I hope it stays warm for them." Jackrabbit squinted up the trail to the north, her lips pursed and her brows drawn together. "It's supposed to, isn't it?" Then she looked back at me, and the lines of worry vanished from her face. "Well, sister. The Trail beckons. Shall we?"

The sky clouded over briefly, around dusk, as we hiked down a ridge covered in beech trees. The sun went down between the branches in vivid bands of yellow and pink. The clouds vanished again as night fell, and familiar stars swung slowly overhead. The miles, which had seemed so short by day, uncoiled themselves slowly in the darkness, stretching across icy ridges and muddy stream valleys and countless hundreds of footsteps. My legs felt stiff and heavy as if they were made of wood. My sweaty socks chafed at my feet; one spot, on the side of my left big toe, felt like it was beginning to blister. I tightened my grip on my hiking sticks, glanced up at Orion, and hurried on.

"Twenty-three miles, and it's only quarter of nine!" jackrabbit announced, as we dropped our packs and slumped down on the sleeping platform of Birch Spring Shelter. "If we keep this up, we'll catch Lash and Tim in a week!"

I felt as though we'd walked half the night, and I wasn't too optimistic about the prospect of "keeping it up." I didn't want to be a spoilsport, though. Jackrabbit sounded more cheerful than she'd been in months.

"Lash and Tim will be happy men, if they stocked up on Snickers bars in Fontana. After a week at this pace, I'll be desperate for extra calories," I answered, as I peeled off my wet sock and began to doctor the blister.

jackrabbit

From Birch Spring Shelter, it was an easy four miles downhill to Fontana Dam. The snow diminished as we descended, from ankle-deep to a tiny dusting, and then bare ground appeared. The lake, dark blue and shimmering in the thin sunlight, began to show between the trees on our left-hand side as we followed the muddy switchbacks. The water stretched off toward the horizon, following the curves of the valleys, winking in and out behind the far hills. A stripe of reddish rocks and clay outlined the lake, a hard boundary between the rippled surface and the gray-green leafless trees. On the far side of the lake, the water-contoured, irregular shapes of the Nantahala Mountains rose jagged into the hazy blue sky.

The dam itself was a monstrous wall of concrete plunging down out of sight into the gorge below us. Strange gurgles and hums came from inside the structure as we crossed the walkway at the top. I tried to imagine the force of the water that it was holding back, hundreds of thousands of tons of pressure. The dam seemed as solid as the mountains around it, but I found I was glad when I stood on the other side.

By the empty parking lot, a vast plain of cracked gray asphalt, we found a tattered poster stuck up above the pay phone advertising cheap lodging for hikers. We called the number, and in a few minutes a blue pickup pulled into the lot.

We spent the rest of the day in our hotel room, sorting through a mail drop our mother had sent to Fontana Village. It was still warm outside, though the hazy clouds were gathering. I felt a little guilty for taking a half day off. We were both tired from our twenty-three the day before, though. And as much as I had hoped to catch up with Tim and Lash, it didn't seem likely—in the Birch Spring register, they were already three days ahead of us.

Toward evening, the phone rang and I picked it up.

"Hello?"

"Jackrabbit?" said a male voice on the other end of the line.

"The same. And who do I have the pleasure of addressing?"

"You mean you didn't recognize my voice?"

Suddenly I did: *Tiny Tim!* Where was he? Why was he calling us here? I decided to play it cool. "Why should I? There are so many men in my life."

"Jackrabbit, you've hurt me. You've cut me to the quick."

"Where are you, Tim?"

"We're in a hotel down in Robbinsville."

Robbinsville—the only big town in the area, just down the road from Fontana. Which might mean . . . "Who's this 'we,' anyway, and where are you on the Trail?"

"Me and Lash. We're at the Dam."

"No way! Slackers."

"We missed you too much to go on," he said in a pained voice.

"Right."

"Actually, we got some serious trail magic. This friend of my sister's, who I hardly know—well, have you heard of Mayfield Dairies?" I had seen the brand often in Southern grocery stores. "This woman, the Mayfield heiress, came out to meet us in Fontana. She heard I was hiking and wanted to check it out or something. Anyway, she met us at the dam in this pimped-out car. There was, like, a full bar in the back of it. And cigars. She gave us cigars. She was like, 'make yourselves at home, boys; we're going for a ride.' So she took us out on the town and—" he gave a startled exclamation. "Lash! Dude! Don't do it, man! Oh, I can't watch!"

"What's he doing?" I asked in alarm.

"Oh, it's horrible!" Tim regained some of his composure. "He shaved a *stripe* in his beard," he said in a voice thick with indignation.

"A stripe?"

"Right down the middle. Like an inch wide. Looks hideous."

"Why'd he do it?"

There was a muffled conversation. "He says, 'chicks dig it,'" Tim relayed.

"I guess that remains to be seen. You guys hiking out tomorrow?"

"Yeah. We're going to Brown Fork Gap. Easy day; like fourteen."

"Sounds good. Maybe we'll see you there." I hung up the phone and turned to Isis. "The boys are back in town."

The air was warm the next day, probably in the fifties. We walked barefoot for the second time since fall. My feet felt wondrously alive, awake to every pebble or patch of smooth mud in the trail. The skin on my soles was still tender, but I quickly adjusted back to the rhythm of hiking barefoot, test-

ing each step and shifting my weight minutely to compensate for the rough-
ness of the trail. Without the accustomed weight of boots, my legs felt
stronger than ever. The fourteen miles sped past. Although we had started at
almost noon, after a leisurely town breakfast, we reached Brown Fork Gap
well before sunset.

The shelter there gave me a powerful feeling of nostalgia; it was built like
the ones in Maine, hewn of rough logs, with a corrugated tin roof. It even had
a porcupine trap. I expected to see Lash and Tim there waiting for us, but
instead we found a small group of northbounders. A gray-haired man probably
in his seventies leaned against the back wall of the shelter reading the register,
his face drawn and pale with exhaustion. A young couple in matching blue
rain suits, looking and smelling entirely unlike long-distance hikers, were
cooking dinner on the picnic table in front of the shelter.

The woman looked up and smiled as we came in. "We hiked eleven miles
today!" she said, full of pride.

My first instinct was to laugh. We'd hiked fourteen in an easy half day.
Then I remembered the northbounder we had met at Little Bigelow Lean-to
in Maine, so many months ago, on the day we'd hiked our first seventeen. I
had vowed that no matter how long we stayed on the Trail, I wouldn't
become like him.

"That's great," I said. "The trails around here are pretty steep. Lots of little
ups and downs. When you get up in the Smokies, it's smooth sailing for a
couple days."

"You don't get really flat trails until Pennsylvania, though," Isis said, laying
down her hiking sticks and unbuckling her pack.

The northbound woman's expression changed to awe. "Are you guys
southbounders?" she breathed.

We nodded.

"Did you go through the whole winter? Wasn't there ice and snow? Greg,
they're southbounders! Real thru-hikers!"

"You guys will be real thru-hikers, too, with a little luck and a lot of per-
sistence," I told her.

Then she noticed our bare feet. "No way. Are you guys the Barefoot
Sisters?"

"That's what they call us." It was alarming how far our notoriety had
spread.

"Wow. I didn't even think you even existed. This trail gets weirder every
day. It's awesome."

"It's true; the A.T. is one of the craziest places on the face of the earth. All the rumors turn out to be true. By the time you get to Maine, nothing will faze you."

I went to the shelter and dropped my pack. As I laid out my sleeping bag and foam pad, Tim and Lash marched into the clearing.

"Hey, boys," I called. Lash looked over at me. He had indeed shaved a stripe down the middle of his thick brown beard. It made his face appear puffy-cheeked, twice as wide as it actually was.

"Lashy-Lash!" I said. "What did you do to yourself? You look like a chipmunk!"

He gave me a wounded look. "Chicks dig it."

"Not this chick, man."

He turned to Isis, a pleading look in his eyes.

"Sorry, not this chick either."

We wished the nobos well in the morning and hiked another short day, sixteen miles, still barefoot in the warm weather. Toward evening, the sun came out from the clouds and slanted between tall pines on the ridge, filling the hillside with orange light. The valley bottom was already in shadow, and the Nolichucky River wound through the gray bottomlands like a thread of spilled milk. As we got closer, the sound of the rapids rose above the thin whisper of wind in the leafless branches.

"There's supposed to be a good outfitter's store down there," Isis said. "It's some kind of outdoor adventure camp in the summer."

"Yeah, those nobos said they've got Ben and Jerry's. And our mom said she might send a mail drop there, if she gets time. Store probably closes at five, though."

"We can make it."

"You think?"

We raced down the path, which became slick with red mud on the lower slopes. Through the trees, we glimpsed a few squat buildings and a wide expanse of gravel. A sign proclaimed "Welcome to the Nantahala Outdoor Center." At the near edge of the parking lot, ranks of bright blue buses and vans stood ready, awaiting rafting trips in a warmer season. The sound of the river strengthened as we drew near. I glanced at my watch: a few minutes before the hour. We put on our camp shoes at the edge of the lot—our feet were not nearly tough enough, after a winter in boots, to brave that much gravel.

The white blazes led past restaurants, information kiosks, and equipment rental centers, all deserted in the chill of early spring. We crossed the river on a wide wooden footbridge. Tim and Lash were sitting on a bench by the door of the outfitter's store, halfway through their pints of ice cream.

"Hey, ladies," Lash called. "Wondering when you'd get here."

"We've been lonely," Tim said with a lascivious smile.

In the few minutes before the store closed, Isis and I arranged to rent a room in the bunkhouse. The off-season rates were very hiker-friendly. We bought a couple pints of Ben and Jerry's and picked up our mail drop. It was a package from our mother, containing our Zip stove and a huge amount of food—cookies, chocolate, dried fruit; boxes of pasta, polenta, beans, freeze-dried tofu; gourmet backpacking dinners.

"Look at all this!" Isis exclaimed as she dug into her ice cream. "We could get to Springer on all this food."

"If we could carry it," I said through a bite of Cherry Garcia.

"We just need to have a feast tonight," Isis said decisively. "Boys, can you join us?"

Tim and Lash deliberated.

"We were gonna hike out to the next shelter," Tim said.

Lash frowned and squinted at the sun. "We could still hike after dark, maybe."

"Come on, you guys," I said. "How often do beautiful women ask you to dinner?"

That settled it. We dropped off our gear at the bunk house and headed over to the kitchen, in a building next door. Lash ducked out the door, muttering something about a proper dinner. We didn't see him for a while.

The kitchen, designed for feeding crowds of kayakers and rafters, had two gas stoves and a large empty refrigerator. A well-stocked hiker box, left over from the previous season, stood on the counter by the windows. Isis found some olive oil in the bottom of the hiker box and started preparing fried polenta with sun-dried tomatoes. Pasta boiled on a back burner. Tim and I offered to help, but Isis, as usual in the kitchen, had everything under control. Darkness gathered outside; the view of the river became blue-tinted, indistinct.

Lash came back just as the meal was ready. He carried a shopping bag, from which he drew a bottle of red wine, two bags of salad greens, and some dressing.

"Lashy-Lash! Did you go all the way into town for this?" Isis asked.

He shrugged. "Easy hitch."

She kissed him on the cheek. "You're an angel."

He blushed scarlet. Then he gave Tim a smug glance. "I didn't even need a Snickers bar for that one," he said.

"Salad greens are even more precious than Snickers, out here," Isis said. She eyed Lash reflectively. "You might have better luck if you got rid of that stripe in your beard, though."

He protested. "Dude, chicks dig it."

"Lash, you really oughta shave the rest of it off," I said. "I'm not kidding. It makes you look like some kind of rodent."

"Hmph." He tried again, flashing Isis a sultry smile. "It's a highway to heaven, baby."

"You've been spending too much time with Mr. Innuendo there," Isis said, shooting a glance at Tim.

"Ha! Me? Who started the whole Snickers bars thing?"

"Black Forest!" I retorted.

The banter was cut short when an older hiker walked in the door. He was tall and gaunt, with a grizzled beard and long thinning gray hair. He said nothing to the four of us, but instead walked over to the hiker box and began rifling through it. "Hiker boxes ain't what they used to be," he grumbled to himself, as Isis began dishing out huge plates of pasta, polenta, and salad.

"Would you like some food? We've got plenty to go around," she told him.

With almost superhuman quickness, he grabbed a plate and sat down at the table. "Oh, much obliged." Then he noticed the bottle of wine, which Lash had just uncorked. "And wine, too? Don't mind if I do." He produced an empty Gatorade bottle from somewhere and poured off a generous amount of it. "I'm Charlemagne, by the way. Pleased, very pleased, to meet all of you. Great food."

The heaps of food vanished in a short time, and we sat back, bellies swollen. I savored the last sips of wine from my camping cup. Only Charlemagne, it seemed, was not sated; he went back to rummaging the hiker box, exclaiming sadly over the contents.

Isis took pity on him. "We might have some extra food in our mail drop," she said. At once he left the hiker box and began sorting through ours, which we had just begun to unpack. He set aside a few of the boxed dinners, the Clif Bars, and the Pepperidge Farm cookies. I wanted to say something as he lifted the box of cookies—they were Mint Milanos, my favorites, and a rare enough commodity in Trail towns. But the unwritten code of hiker ethics stopped me. If someone needs something you have (food, water, shelter space, duct tape), you give it freely, because you never know when you'll be on the other end of the equation. I noted with some annoyance, though, that most hikers who needed food would at least ask about the items they took.

Charlemagne lifted a newspaper-wrapped bundle out of the bottom of the box. "What's this, eh?"

Isis took it from him. "It's our Zip stove." She carefully unwrapped the metal canister, set it up on the table, and flicked the switch to test the fan battery. A satisfied smile crossed her face as the fan whirred to life. She explained to Charlemagne how the stove burns twigs and pine cones, eliminating the need to carry fuel.

"Interesting gadget." He cocked his head and stared at it. "I've hiked this trail three times, and I never heard of it."

"Yeah, it's great for warm-weather hiking," Isis said. "In winter, though, we couldn't empty the ashes fast enough to heat anything. I asked our mom to send it back when I called home from Hot Springs. I think it's finally warm enough."

"Warm enough for our tent, too," I said. "Maybe we should have asked her to send that back. Wonder what we'll do when the nobos start filling up the shelters . . ."

Charlemagne's ears perked up. "A tent, you say? I've got a tent I'm looking to sell. Got to buy my resupply, you know? Can't eat a tent." He had a fit of wheezing laughter that ended in a strained cough.

"What kind of tent?" Isis asked.

"Clip Flashlight. Two-man. Nice and cozy; here, I'll get it for you." He went into the next room and came back with a blue nylon stuff sack and a collection of poles, which he quickly assembled. Tim and Lash held the tent upright—without its stakes sunk into the ground, it wasn't free-standing—while Isis and I circled it, examining the blue fabric. The tent was almost as spacious as the one we had sent home from Atkins, with one distinct advantage; the fly covered the whole foot of the tent body, so rain would drain off it. The fly of our old tent had left a few inches exposed, getting our feet wet each time it rained. We crawled inside. The colored nylon softened the fluorescent lights, filling the interior with a pale swimming-pool blue glow. There was just enough space for the two of us, lying side by side. I noticed only a small amount of mildew on the fabric, and the tent didn't smell nearly as rank as I had expected from the aroma of its owner.

"It's a nice tent," I said, emerging. "How much are you asking?"

We bargained him down to a reasonable sum.

"Dude," Lash said, "it's a pretty good tent and all. I just don't understand why you're buying it now. There's, like, a hundred and thirty-five miles left. You can get through that without a tent."

"Isis and I are hiking again," I said.

"Next year?"

"No, we're gonna yo-yo."

"No shit!"

Lash and Tim looked at us, their jaws hanging open. Charlemagne had another laughing fit, ending with the same choking cough. "Well, I'll be damned," he said once he had caught his breath. "That tent's gonna cover more miles than I am this year."

Isis

Lash and Tim hitched into the town of Franklin at Winding Stair Gap, while we hiked three miles farther, to Rock Gap Shelter.

"We're ahead of the guys!" jackrabbit crowed. "Remember when we thought we'd never catch up to them? Oh, and look at this . . ." she ran her finger along the bottom of the map, counting off the miles. "We just pulled a barefoot twenty, and it's not even dark yet! At this rate, we'll reach Georgia in a day and a half."

"And Springer by the end of the week!"

We were still congratulating each other on our newfound speed-hiking abilities as we packed up the next morning.

"I wonder if they'll catch us by lunchtime?" I mused. "I've got some chocolate I've been meaning to share."

"If we hike as fast as we did yesterday, we might have to eat it all ourselves," jackrabbit answered, strapping on her pack.

"No such luck," I told her, and waved at Lash and Tim, who had just stridden into view around a corner of the shelter trail.

Jackrabbit turned and greeted them. "Hey, guys. Bright and early. Either the nightlife in Franklin left something to be desired, or else you missed us terribly."

"Uh, both, I guess." Lash looked more distracted than the early hour could explain. "Hey, did you ladies see the Tree?"

"I've seen a few lately. Why, did you lose one?" I teased him.

"They haven't seen it!" Tim exclaimed, practically dancing with excitement. "Come on, we'll show you. It's just half a mile back . . ."

"Back?" Jackrabbit could hardly have sounded more indignant if Tim had asked her to rinse out his socks for him. But curiosity got the better of her, and a few minutes later, we were both walking north up the trail, following the guys.

They turned onto a side trail marked by a sign we hadn't noticed the day before in our hurry to reach the shelter. *Wasilik Poplar, 0.5*, it read. *Point five off the Trail?* I thought. *We'll have walked two miles this morning before we get anywhere.* But I didn't say anything; to turn back at that point would have meant a mile completely wasted.

The side trail snaked down the ridge for what seemed much longer than its stated distance. Around each bend, I expected to see an unusually large tree, but there was only more of the same second-growth forest. Unbroken by either snow or sunlight, it formed a monotonous, muted tableau of gray and beige.

Then I saw it, at the bottom of a long downhill—a tree that made the forest around it look like a thicket of saplings. A broken-down split-rail fence, circling the tree twenty feet out from the trunk, looked like Tinker Toys beside it. There was nothing beautiful about the Wasilik Poplar; stubby, broken limbs protruded from a trunk shaped like a monstrous wine bottle, as thick at the base as ten of the ordinary trees beside it, and tapering halfway up to only four times their thickness. But the sight of this last giant of the Southern forests, raising its lightning-scarred branches high over the crowns of its neighbors, filled me with such joy and wonder that I forgot all about the long day's hike ahead of us. I wanted to spend hours tracing the fissures in its bark and leaning my head against the trunk, imagining that I could hear the sap rising. I wished I had something to leave with the tree, an offering to this survivor from the ancient forests.

As I stepped through a gap in the fence, into the circle of the Poplar's clearing, something dark and shimmering among the dry leaves by the fence post caught my eye. I brushed the leaves away: a smooth, dry coil of cast-off blacksnake skin, lighter than paper. What a gift, this symbol of renewal when the long winter had left the woods bleached and barren, and no sign of spring yet showed. And what a place to have found it, in the clearing of the Poplar. It would be a powerful talisman to carry with me, pressed in my notebook, for luck on our northbound hike. Or perhaps I would send it home and ask my mother to put it on my altar, between the sculpture of Inanna and the smooth triangle of black stone that I had found on a beach in Alaska.

In the end, I carried it over to the base of the tree and tucked it in a crack between the roots. *May your seedlings grow old as you are*, I prayed, as I clasped hands with my three companions, reaching as far around the trunk as the four of us, together, could.

We reached Carter Gap Shelter just after dark; our visit to the Wasilik Poplar had gotten us off to a very late start. The unmistakable roar of a Dragonfly stove greeted us, and a barrage of headlamp beams fixed on us as we stepped into the shelter. When my eyes adjusted to the light, I saw four men and a woman, all in their early twenties, sitting on the edge of the sleeping platform. They had the fashion sense of winter thru-hikers: shorts worn over long underwear, hooded fleece jackets, and tight knit caps in virulent colors. But none of the men had much in the way of beards, and, even more strangely, I couldn't smell them from where I was standing. They seemed to be able to smell me, though; the two who had been eating put down their spoons.

"Um, hi," said the young woman. "I'm Amy. Are you guys thru-hikers? I don't think we've met before."

"Hi, Amy," said Tim, in his most suave accent. I saw her nose wrinkle a little as he stepped forward, but she shook his proffered hand. "I'm Tiny Tim. This is my pack, Scrooge. And these are my hiking companions, Isis, jackrabbit, and Lash. We're southbounders."

"Southbounders! No way!"

"Through the winter?"

"All the way from Katahdin?"

"How did you get through the Smokies?"

"Man, you guys must be nuts!"

"Southbounders! I'm embarrassed to call myself a thru-hiker in front of y'all."

I was hungry and tired, and I wanted to find the water source before the storm that had been threatening all afternoon broke over us. I remembered, though, how excited we'd been when we met our first nobos in the Wilderness—those gaunt, scraggly men and muscular women whose eyes seemed to gaze into a distance I couldn't fathom. They had reminded me of storybook heroes, Robin Hood's merry men, with staves in their rough, tanned hands. I had wanted to sit all night at their campfires, asking about every detail of their journeys. Thinking back to my own early days on the Trail, I tried to answer these starting northbounders' questions patiently.

"Go ahead, call yourself a thru-hiker," I told the man who'd spoken last. His eager, round face, rimmed in a couple millimeters of fuzzy blond stubble, looked terribly young. "We always did."

When the excitement had died down, Amy told us how to get to the spring. "There's another shelter, too," she said. "The old one—just across the trail. The maintainers who built this one haven't torn it down yet, and it looks like it's still sturdy enough to use. You guys might want to stay there; this shelter's pretty packed with all five of us."

I glanced at the packs, stoves and jackets strewn across the sleeping platform. *These nobos have no idea, yet, how many people could fit in here*, I thought. I thanked Amy for the information, though, before we headed over to the old shelter. No point in foisting our stench on them for the duration of the night, and I was just as glad to be free of questions.

"Sobos sleepin' on the wrong side of the tracks," joked jackrabbit, as we spread our foam pads on the pitted, slanting floor of the old shelter. The whole building tilted slightly to the left, looking as though one good gust of wind would knock it into a heap of kindling.

We were eating dinner when the storm struck: a distant rumble of thunder, a light patter of rain on the tin roof, silence, and then a deluge. Rusted spots on the ceiling darkened and began to drip. We scrambled around, rearranging our sleeping bags to avoid the major leaks, and trying to patch the minor ones with candle wax and duct tape.

By the time we had patched all the leaks that our improvised caulking could handle, finished our suppers, and snuggled into our sleeping bags, the storm was right overhead. Thunder crashed like cymbals, with the simultaneous lightning flashes lending us glimpses of wind-tossed hemlocks, rhodo-dendron leaves rustling and gleaming like the wing covers of hundreds of huge black beetles, and a swaying, iridescent curtain of rain. The darkness between flashes had a velvety thickness to it, like the darkness inside a cave. I took a hand out of my sleeping bag and held it up in front of my face. I couldn't see it. Not the faintest glimmer of pale skin differentiated it from the shelter floor or the clearing beyond.

"This would be a good night for ghost stories," came Lash's voice, from my left.

"Yeah," said Tim. "It's like in those horror movies, where you can't see anything. Then there's a flash of lightning, and a homicidal maniac runs into the clearing with blood dripping from his ax!"

I laughed. "What homicidal maniac would be out on a night like this, ten miles from the nearest town? Besides, it's raining so hard that all the ketchup would wash off his ax before they had time to shoot the scene. He'd have to go back to the makeup tent to get it reslathered."

Tim's voice became quiet and ominous. "This is Eric Rudolph territory, you know. The F.B.I. never caught him." He lowered his voice even more and spoke in a stage whisper. "Maybe he's out there right now."

I laughed again. The infamous clinic bomber was one of the last people I'd like to meet alone in the woods, but it seemed preposterous that anyone who lived in the mountains would choose to venture out on a night like this. Even the bears, I thought, hungry as they were from their long sleep, would retreat to their caves in such weather. And then there was the utter darkness. A moment ago, its strange weight had frightened me, but now I felt it cover me like a protective mantle.

"Come on, Tim," I said. "If I can't see my hand in front of my face, he couldn't see me to attack me, even if he did night-hike all the way over here for the express purpose of terrorizing thru-hikers."

"Night-vision goggles," Tim answered, a note of malicious triumph in his voice. "Imagine Eric Rudolph with night vision goggles. Out there. Right now."

It worked. Adrenaline coursed through my veins like an electric shock. No movies I've ever seen, and few nightmares, have filled me with such intense, irrational panic. It didn't matter that a wanted man wasn't likely to show up in a shelter full of hikers. I didn't stop to wonder how he would have come by the night-vision goggles, either. The idea of a man out there, hunting me, who could see me even when I couldn't see him—wouldn't be able to see him if he were standing a foot away from me—made me feel nauseous with terror. I stifled a scream.

"Stop it Tim! Stop!" I sobbed. I shuffled down in my sleeping bag until the rough logs of the wall pressed into my back. My body shook uncontrollably, and my eyes snapped open wide, as if they could stare hard enough to pierce the darkness. A flash of lightning threw the clearing into dazzling relief. Trees, rain, the slick black leaves of rhododendrons. In the corners of my vision, I saw my friends staring up at me.

"Hey . . . Isis, I was kidding. Okay?" Tim sounded just as dismayed by my reaction as I was. "Listen, night-vision goggles are really expensive. And the good ones are military issue only. There's no way Eric Rudolph would have a pair. So don't worry, okay? Don't worry."

"I'm fine," I told him, trying to control the tremor in my voice. "I don't know what happened. I'll be fine."

I'll be fine. Just fine. I repeated to myself, but the panic took a long time to quell. I lay awake for hours, staring into the blank darkness. When I woke up the next morning, I still had my back pressed hard against the wall. The thunder and lightning had passed, but rain still hammered on the leaky roof. Lash had rolled under a drip in the night; he woke up cursing and left in a hurry. Tim followed close behind him. Jackrabbit and I made hot chocolate and ate a slow breakfast, waiting for the rain to let up. It didn't. Finally, we put on our Gore-Tex, picked up our packs, and stepped out into the downpour.

The day started with a mile of downhill, followed by the gradual, five-mile-long ascent of Standing Indian Mountain. As we began climbing, I noticed that the sleeves of my jacket were sticking to my arms. Was I sweating? I felt too cold. I looked down at my sleeves. Water darkened the cloth, instead of beading up and rolling off it. Somewhere in the course of the winter, my rain jacket had lost its waterproofing. So had my rain pants; I could feel them beginning to cling to my legs. I turned to look at jackrabbit. I took in the dark shade of her coat and the way the fabric stuck to her arms; her rain gear was failing, too. I met her eyes, and I was shocked by their dull, trapped expression.

"Keep going," she said, in a weary monotone. "We need to stay warm."

I walked on, faster, trying to warm myself up. It worked on the uphill, but once we started down the other side of the mountain, I couldn't go fast enough. The soaking Gore-Tex didn't seem to offer any insulation; I felt as if I were swimming in fifty-degree water. *I can't put any more layers on,* I thought. *I need my wool shirt and my fleece to change into at the shelter. I need to keep them dry. There's nothing I can do about the cold.* Halfway down the mountain, stumbling and limping on the sharp gravel trail, I recognized the thought pattern: *hypothermia.* I threw down my pack.

"Let's get our wool shirts on," I said to jackrabbit. "They'll keep us warm even if they're wet. I'm getting hypothermic, and I'll bet anything you are, too."

She responded by bursting into tears.

Oh shit, I said to myself. *Oh fuck. I'm too late; she's a basket case already.* I raised my voice.

"Jackrabbit. Take your pack off and put your wool shirt on."

"That's what I'm doing," she answered, through gritted teeth. She slung her pack to the ground, pulled back the pack cover, and grabbed her wool shirt.

"Okay. Sorry. I was afraid you were too hypothermic to understand me."

"It's the rain. I hate the rain. Fuck it! I hate being wet, the way my fingers and toes shrivel up and turn spongy, like they're rotting."

She continued talking as we stripped our wet jackets off, tugged the sleeves of our wool shirts up our wet arms, and put our jackets back on over them.

"You remember that spring I worked as a gardener, out on the West Coast? I was there four months and I saw the sun maybe three times. It rained all day, every day. I worked outside from eight to five, kneeling in the mud pulling weeds. My rain jacket was a piece of shit and I didn't want to buy a good one—I was trying to save money. I was just out of high school. I thought, is this all there is? Is this what the rest of my life is going to be like? And I guess I could have just quit and gone anywhere, but it was easier to stay there. Stay miserable. That's what being wet all day reminds me of—being seventeen and depressed."

The rain fell steadily all morning and into the afternoon. My shirt kept me warm enough, but I could feel the wet wool chafing my back and armpits. We passed Muskrat Creek Shelter without pausing to check the register; both of us knew that if we stopped in a shelter, we'd stay there.

"We're almost to Georgia," I told jackrabbit. "I think it's only three more miles to Bly Gap."

She sighed. "Isis . . . I don't think I can do it."

"What's wrong? Are you sick? Come on, let's go back to Muskrat Creek—"

"No, I don't want to go back. I'm not sick. It's just . . . I'm so tired. My hip aches. My knees are bothering me again. My toes feel like they're burning, and my hands—look at them—in this rain, they're falling apart."

I balanced my hiking sticks in the crook of one arm, and took her hands in mine. She was right; they felt cold, the skin looked waxy and gray, and it had peeled back around the cuticles so far that it was bleeding in some places.

My own hands had worried me all winter. Most mornings, I woke to find them cramped into the position in which they held my hiking sticks; sometimes it took five minutes to massage them open again. The first three fingers on my right hand turned a bloodless yellow when they got too cold and came back to life, burning, half an hour later. I had exposed them so often in winter, to mend my pack or prepare our lunches, that they seemed to have suffered the same kind of circulatory damage as my toes. Compared to jackrabbit's, though, my hands looked strong and rosy.

"Isis . . ." Her voice sounded almost pleading. "I feel like I've spent all the strength I have, getting this far. There's nothing left in me. I don't think I'll make it to Springer."

"You will. Here, borrow some of my strength if you want it." I gave her hands a gentle squeeze. "You'll make it, and we'll yo-yo. Right?"

"I wish I had your confidence."

"I wish I could give it to you." I squeezed her hands again, then let them go and grabbed my hiking sticks. "Come on, sister, let's go to Georgia. Maybe the weather will be better there."

The rain did let up as we hiked down the last hillside into Bly Gap. I tried to cross my fingers around my hiking sticks. It didn't work very well, so I sent out a prayer to Nuit, the Egyptian sky-goddess, instead. *Enough water. Thank you for the water. Now could we have some sunshine? I know I'm very demanding, but it's for my sister. She needs a little encouragement right now.*

Just then, we came to a clearing. Through the drizzle, I saw a large oak in the middle of the trail, a few hundred yards downhill from us, so gnarled that it looked like a giant bonsai tree. Half the length of its trunk twisted along the ground, then forked into two main branches and a graceful lattice of side limbs, covered in lichen the color of oxidized copper. A white blaze shone from the nearest branch.

"Do you think that's the Georgia Oak?" asked jackrabbit. Seeing my blank look, she explained. "A nobo told me about it. He said there's an oak tree in Bly Gap that marks the Georgia border for thru-hikers. I asked if there was a sign there, telling which tree it was. He just said, 'you'll know it when you see it.'"

"I bet that's it, then. It's a pretty distinctive tree."

By the time we reached the oak, the rain had stopped completely. I took a picture of jackrabbit standing beside the tree. Over her shoulder, far to the south, I could see the clouds breaking up, a few patches of pale blue showing between the tattered bands of gray.

A quarter mile down the trail, we found a small wooden sign that said, simply, *NC/GA*. A little beyond that, we came to a side trail marked *viewpoint*.

"Let's have a look at our new state, shall we?" I said.

We stepped through a thicket of rhododendrons and found ourselves on a small cliff, overlooking a series of low, gray hills. As we stood there, the first rays of sun broke through the clouds, warming our faces and making our jackets steam.

"I think I like Georgia," said jackrabbit, with a wan smile. "Maybe I'll make it after all."

By the time we reached Plum Orchard Gap Shelter, the clouds had vanished completely, and an evening star shone in the clear, pale sky.

As we stepped into the shelter clearing, a large dog came sashaying toward me, head tipped up and lips drawn back in what looked like a ferocious snarl. Close behind her stood a familiar, hulking figure in a plaid flannel shirt.

"Heald? Annie? Oh, wow. This is awesome. I thought you would have finished the Trail by now!"

"We did. Sort of," Heald answered. "Got within forty miles of Springer and decided to turn around. Too crowded down there this time of year. But this fellow," Heald jerked a thumb toward Lash, who stood beside him, grinning, "talked me into turning around again and hiking down to Springer with you guys."

"Oh, Heald! Thank you! It's so great to see you again!"

"Well, don't get too excited. I might change my mind," he answered, but I could see him smiling through the dusk.

We walked over to the shelter, an elegant, three-story building of recent construction, and introduced ourselves to the seven or eight northbounders already there. They seemed less eager to question us than the last group had been; perhaps Tim, Lash, and Heald had already satisfied their curiosity. After a few minutes' conversation with a slender, middle-aged woman who wanted to know how easy it was for vegetarians to find food in Trail towns, we sat down to cook supper with our sobo companions.

"Lash and I have a plan," Tim said, grinning as he stirred his Lipton dinner.

"No more horror stories," said jackrabbit, severely. (I hoped that no one could see my blush in the light of our stoves and candle lanterns.)

"Nothing like that," he said. "Don't worry. The plan is, well, we're only four miles from Dick's Creek Gap—"

"We'll get up really early—" Lash chimed in.

"Get to the gap by eight or nine, and hitch into Hiawassee for breakfast."

"Shoney's," said Lash. "Mmm, greasy town food. All-you-can-eat, man."

"Mmm, breakfast," said jackrabbit, digging her spoon into our instant beans and rice. "I can hardly wait."

After dinner, I rolled out my sleeping bag on the third floor of the shelter, a narrow little attic with windows at either end. I thought I might have the space to myself, since the other sleeping platforms were much larger and easier to reach. Just as I got into my sleeping bag, though, a hugely overweight man, in his late fifties or early sixties, trundled up the ladder to the loft. I racked my brains for his trail name. It was the brand name of some alcoholic beverage. *Heineken? Bacardi? Coors Lite? Johnny Walker would have been clever,* I thought, *but it's not that.* Finally I settled for a sleepy "hullo."

The man walked past me, acknowledging my presence with an unintelligible grunt. He rolled out his sleeping bag at the other end of the loft, got into it, and promptly began to snore. I was tired enough that no amount of noise would have kept me entirely awake, but his raucous, irregular snore woke me many times during the night. When the first light of dawn finally slipped through my window, I was more than ready to leave the shelter.

I sat up and began to brush my hair. From the platform below me, I heard Tim, Lash, and jackrabbit packing as quietly as they could—a soft rustle of plastic, a whispered question and response. At the other end of the loft, Captain Morgan or whatever his name was turned over with an enormous snort. A few minutes later, he sat up.

"I guess it's morning *somewhere* in the world," he said in a loud, testy voice. "You and your friends must be in an awful hurry to get to town."

"I'm sorry we woke you up," I whispered.

"Woke me up?" he roared. "You kept me awake all night with your snoring!" He leaned over the edge of the platform, addressing the hikers below, all of whom were stirring now. "This girl snores like a freight train! Did you people hear her? I didn't sleep a wink!"

We reached Dick's Creek Gap by eight-thirty, but hitching a ride on the small, rural highway proved far more difficult than we'd expected. A car passed every fifteen or twenty minutes, most of them going in the wrong direction. As the sun rose higher, traffic became a little heavier, but no one stopped for us. A few people even sped up when they saw five ragged hikers and a dog beside the road.

"All-you-can-eat breakfast, only ten minutes' drive away, and we're missing it!" moaned Lash. "I'm gonna faint if I don't get some food in my stomach soon."

"You just ate three granola bars," said jackrabbit.

"That was five minutes ago." He gave her a pouty look. "And granola bars don't count, anyway. They're Trail food."

"Lash is right, man," Tim said. "We've been here for two hours, and we haven't had the least prospect of a ride. If we don't do something drastic, soon, we'll be too late for the Shoney's special." He paused dramatically. "Ladies, I have a plan, but I'm going to need your help with it."

Tim, Lash, Heald, and Annie went back across the road and walked about twenty yards into the forest. Jackrabbit and I stayed where we were, our thumbs out. Just for good measure, jackrabbit let her hair down. The first car to pass, a huge silver SUV, skidded to a halt in the trailhead parking lot.

"Thanks so much," I said to the driver, a well-groomed man with short gray hair. I turned around to help jackrabbit load her pack, and waved to the guys over her shoulder.

"Oh, hey," I said, doing my best to sound surprised. "There's some of our friends coming down the trail right now. Do you think you could give them a lift, too?"

When he saw the three smelly, sweaty guys striding toward him, followed by a large orange dog, his smile faltered.

"Hey, ladies, fancy meeting you here!" Tim clapped me on the shoulder. "Looks like you've got yourselves a ride." I scowled at him, but he smiled even more broadly as he turned to the driver. "Mind if we come along?"

"I'm not sure all of y'all will fit . . ." the man answered, sounding despondent. He knew he'd been had.

"Sure we will. Just watch us," Tim said, helping Annie clamber into the back of the vehicle.

We drove down the mountain in silence. I could feel myself blushing, and I was afraid that if I opened my mouth, I'd blurt out something horribly melodramatic. *I'm so sorry I deceived you! I wouldn't have resorted to such tactics . . . but we're so hungry . . ."*

About halfway to town, the driver spoke. "No offense, but . . . y'all could really use a shower." It was the only thing he said to us, before dropping us off in front of the supermarket. We were too late for the Shoney's buffet.

"Well, here we are in Hiawassee," said Lash. "I hope it's a good Trail town, 'cause we may be here a few weeks if the hitching's as bad on the way out."

"We'll worry about that tomorrow," I told him. "Come on, let's get some food!"

Tim and Heald waited in front of the store with Annie, while Lash, jackrabbit, and I went in search of lunch. We brought out a picnic of bread and cheese, cherry tomatoes, carrots, cider, oranges, donuts, apple pie, and a box of dog treats for Annie.

"You're spoilin' her," Heald growled, as we sat down against the warm brick wall of the store, safely upwind of the dirty socks that Tim had spread on the pavement to dry. "She won't be fit to hike."

We wolfed the food down and went back in to buy our resupplies. I was standing in the rice and pasta aisle, comparing the weight-to-calories ratios of two instant dinners, when I felt a light tap on my shoulder. I turned to see a fine-featured woman with short blond hair smiling up at me.

"I'm sorry to bother you, miss, but you wouldn't happen to be an Appalachian Trail hiker, would you?"

"My trail name's Isis," I said, holding out my hand. "I'm hiking southbound with my sister, jackrabbit."

"Southbound! Did y'all hike all winter? Y'all must've had all kinds of adventures! Oh, I'm sorry, I'm forgetting my manners. My name's Dee. Hiking the Trail has been a dream of mine for years and years. My husband Dan and I've been planning to hike it together ever since we got married. You wouldn't mind if I ask you a few questions, would you? I know you're busy, but it's such a treat to meet a real thru-hiker."

By the time jackrabbit showed up, bearing a box of dried milk, a pound of butter, and a dozen candy bars, Dee and I were deep in discussion about different methods of water purification. I introduced my sister, and soon she was telling Dee about the wildlife we'd seen on the Trail, and how we protected our food from bears and mice.

"It's really great talking with y'all," Dee said after about twenty minutes. "I don't want this conversation to end. I hate to keep y'all, though. I know y'all've got some shopping to do."

"No, no, it's been great to meet you," I said. I really had enjoyed talking with someone who was so interested in the Trail. Better still, I could see the light in jackrabbit's eyes and the way her shoulders straightened as she recounted our adventures to Dee.

"Listen," said Dee, "I hesitate to invite y'all, 'cause our cabin's not quite finished, and it's kind of a mess right now . . . but I'd just love it if y'all could stay the night with me and Dan. I'd love for him to meet you, too."

"Thank you so much for the offer," I said. "I'd really like to. But we're hiking with three other people and a dog right now, and I kind of want to stay with them."

"They'd be welcome, too," said Dee. "There's plenty of room, but like I said, it's a bit messy."

"Are you sure? I mean, we smell bad! And there's five of us! Will we even fit in your car?"

"It'll be tight, but we'll manage. Now, what do you want for supper? How about pasta? Is a pound each enough for you? I know hikers have big appetites."

Dee's "unfinished cabin" turned out to be a lovely, spacious timber frame building perched on the bank of the Hiawassee River. In one corner of the living room, the flooring hadn't been laid yet, but there was no mess to speak of. Dan, a tall, powerfully built man with a white crew cut, showed us around the house. He was just as enthusiastic to meet us as Dee had been, asking about every aspect of our gear and our daily schedules.

I helped Dee make spaghetti while the others traded adventure stories with Dan. From the scraps of conversation I overheard, I found out that he had traveled some six thousand miles by canoe, down several rivers and through the Great Lakes system.

"That was my dream," I heard him say, "and I did it, a few years before I met Dee. "Now it's time for her dream to happen—hiking the Appalachian Trail."

I could tell that Dee heard him, too; a soft smile lit her face as she poured the sauce into the frying pan.

We slept on the living room floor in front of the fireplace. In the morning, Dee prepared us huge platters of eggs and toast. I scribbled my address on a scrap of paper and handed it to her as we left the house.

"Thanks for everything," I said. "And best of luck with your thru-hike. We can never repay your kindness, but when you guys get to Maine, please visit."

jackrabbit

Dee's son Jeb drove us to the trailhead. Lash, Tim, Heald, and Annie crowded into the back of his pickup with our packs, and Isis and I sat up front. It was early; mist from the river still filled up the hollows.

"Thanks for the ride, Jeb," I said.

"Oh, it's no big deal. I love to be out in the mountains this time of day." He had a subtle north Georgia drawl. "This is one of the prettiest places on earth."

Watching the cloud-wreathed mountains, their wooded peaks reflecting the early sun, I had to agree.

"A lot of people want to come and live here," Jeb said. "Trouble is, there's just not enough jobs to go around. I'm a building contractor, and I hate to say it, but that's one of the few honest jobs there is in this county."

"So what do the rest of the people do?" I asked him.

"Well, these mountains are a good place for hiding things. Back during Prohibition there was a still on every hillside. These days, everybody and his brother grows pot."

"Well, they say it's the biggest cash crop in just about every state."

"'Round here, it's about the only cash crop." He laughed. "It's so common, people don't hardly try to hide it. The sheriff knows everybody, and knows their business, but he's not the type to rock the boat. That's why he keeps getting reelected. There was just one time folks got in trouble for it."

The road came through a gap, and ahead of us the mountains were gilded with low sunlight. "Y'all hear about Eric Rudolph?" Jeb said.

"Yeah." Isis shuddered. "Wasn't he supposed to be hiding out in the mountains around here?"

"That was the rumor, anyway," Jeb said. "The F.B.I. sent some undercover people to town to check things out. Everybody knew who they were—a bunch of white guys in suits, driving brand-new fancy cars with county plates. Well, they stayed near on two years and didn't find a trace of the man. Guess they figured they had to do something to justify the time they'd spent here. They ended up having a grandscale pot bust." He laughed. "Just about two-thirds of the adults in Hiawassee did time."

The trail climbed steeply out of Dick's Creek Gap, among thickets of rhododendrons and the furrowed trunks of tulip poplars. I thought I heard another car pull into the lot as Jeb's truck left, and voices far below us, but I couldn't be sure. We were walking barefoot, and it took all my concentration; the trail here was rougher than in the Nantahalas, with larger patches of gravel.

I kept expecting Lash and Tim, at least, to pass us, but no one came up the trail behind us. The first people we met, in midmorning, were a pair of northbound women. One was tall and blond, the other shorter and dark-haired. They were impeccably dressed; hardly a speck of mud clung to their boots, and their cotton shirts looked freshly laundered and ironed. They were so new to the Trail that the rank hiker aroma had not yet begun to cling to them. (Suddenly the smallness of the remaining distance appeared in sharp relief. I tried to remember how far along the Trail I'd gotten before the hiker funk caught up with me at Antlers Tentsite—forty miles? Fifty?) I could tell that these women were long-distance hikers only by their heavy packs.

"Good morning," said the blond woman. She had a delightful, slightly British-sounding accent.

"Morning," Isis said. "You guys thru-hiking?"

"Yes, indeed," said the brunette in the same charming accent. "That is, we hope so. It's much harder than I imagined." Dimples showed when she smiled.

"Oh, it gets easier when you've been out here a while," I said. "Where are you guys from?"

"Australia," said the blond.

"Wow. You came a long way," Isis said. "I hope you have a great hike."

"Thanks. We've certainly enjoyed it so far," the blond said. We exchanged a few more pleasantries and continued down the trail.

It was almost noon before the next people caught up with us: Spike and Caveman, slacking.

"Hi, guys," I said. "Where're your packs?"

"We decided to be minimalists for the last sixty-five miles," Caveman said (and once again I had the rushing sense of how short that distance was becoming). "We're just going to breathe air and drink a little water. Then, when we reach Springer, we'll be light enough to simply ascend into the ether."

Spike whooped with laughter. "In the meantime, would you like some chips and hummus?" She dropped her fanny pack beside the trail.

I did my best Black Forest impression. "Do I have an ass?"

We sat at the roots of a huge oak tree and shared our lunches. Isis and I had brought more common Trail fare—crackers and cheese, dried fruit, granola bars—and the chips and hummus tasted great.

"What section are you guys slacking?" I asked.

"Dick's Creek Gap to Unicoi Gap," Caveman said.

Spike nodded. "The guy at our motel, the Hiawassee Inn? He's really hiker-friendly. He doesn't charge for shuttles or anything. Kind of a character, though. He's picking us up at Unicoi Gap tonight." She glanced at her watch. "Tim and Lash met us in the parking lot this morning, and they're coming too." She frowned. "I wonder what's taking them so long."

"I have a fair idea," I said. "Did you meet the Australians?"

"Oh, yeah. I bet you're right."

"Those two'll probably be in town tonight," I said. "It'd be interesting to see how things turn out."

"You guys could come, too," Spike said. "There's lots of room in the van."

"What time are you meeting him?"

"Five."

"If we are where I think we are, we'll have to make, like, three miles an hour to get there on time."

Just then, Tim and Lash came racing up the trail, packless.

"Dude! They *said* they were going into town tonight."

"They were too clean. Maybe we didn't hear right. Maybe they'd just left town." Tim sounded a little mournful. "But if they didn't . . . Oh. Hi, guys," he said as he almost tripped over Caveman's long legs. "Barefoot Sisters! You coming to town?"

"Maybe," Isis said.

"Par-tay in Hiawassee." Tim gyrated his hips. "Come on! We don't wanna be late."

We finished our lunch quickly and laced our boots up. Three miles an hour with full packs was doubtful; barefoot with full packs, it would be almost impossible. I had seen the altitude profile for the next section, and I tried to forget the two steep thousand-foot climbs awaiting us on Tray Mountain and Rocky Mountain.

Dripping with sweat, we came to the trailhead parking lot just a few minutes after five. The sun had sunk below the ridges already, leaving the gap in shadow. A large white van was parked at the edge of the lot. Peeling letters on its side spelled out *Hiawassee Inn*.

The driver, a stocky man with dark hair and a mustache, got out and threw open the back doors. From inside the van, Tim, Lash, Spike, and Caveman called their greetings.

"I was about to leave without youse!" the driver said. He had a flat New Jersey accent, incongruous in this part of the South. "Come on, toss your packs in the back and get on board. One of youse is gonna have to sit in the back here." He indicated a small space among the packs behind the back seat.

"Hey, no problem," I said. "I may not be lightweight, but I'm packable." I climbed into the pile of gear, and he carefully shut the door. It was a tight fit; I hoped the latches would hold.

He jumped into the driver's seat and began a monologue that would last all the way to town. His voice carried over the sound of the engine. "I'm glad youse are staying with us. I'm the manager at the Hiawassee Inn, and I'm happy to say, it's a high-class establishment, not like some *other* places I could mention in town . . . Some motels, all that goes on there is funny business. You know, you see the same woman come in with five different men in a week's time, that's funny business. I don't want none of that in my motel . . . One time, there was this red-headed lady. She kept coming in, over the course of a few weeks, with three different fellows. I says to myself, 'there's some funny business going on.' So you know what I did? I threw her out of the motel. Permanently. *Then* you know what I did? I burned those sheets! I don't want no funny business here. If I get so much as a hint of funny business, I tell you, I burn those sheets! . . . But lemme tell youse about some of the hikers we've had here. There was a young lady come in here not two weeks ago, with two fellows. One of 'em was old enough to be her grandpa. I had to burn those sheets!"

He continued his tales of debauchery and sheet-burning until we reached the motel parking lot. Isis and I decided to share a room with Tim and Lash to save money. The manager looked askance at us, but said nothing. While we unloaded our packs from the van, the two Australian women came out of their room.

"Good evening," said the blond.

"Hi, how are you?" Isis said.

"Quite well, thanks."

"A little tired, but otherwise fine," the brunette added.

I waited for Tim and Lash to proffer a dinner invitation. When I glanced over at them, though, it was clear they were in no condition to do so. They were staring at the Australians as though hypnotized, their mouths hanging open, eyes glassy. I decided I would take matters into my own hands.

"We were gonna go to that Mexican place up the road for dinner," I said. "You guys want to come?"

"Oh, no thank you," the blond woman said demurely. "We've already eaten."

Tim and Lash looked crushed.

"Won't you join us for cocktails, then?" I asked. "I hear they have great margaritas." I had heard nothing about their drinks, one way or the other, but I was determined to have the Australians' company. Tim and Lash were bad enough normally; now, with their libidos raging from this encounter with clean, unhikerly women, I knew they would be insufferable. Hoping Isis and I would not have to deal with their excess of male energy by ourselves, I crossed my fingers behind my back.

"I suppose," the blond woman said.

"Great. We've got to take showers and stuff. I guess we'll call you when we're ready to go."

"All right." The Australians gave us their room number and we parted ways.

Our room was cramped and Spartan, decorated with faded shades of pink and orange, but mostly clean. Isis called first dibs on the shower, and while she washed, Tim and Lash berated me for mishandling the situation.

"Dude! Why did *you* ask them to dinner?"

"Well, it sure didn't look like you guys were about to." I sat down on the faded chenille bedspread. My legs were stiff and tired from the fast hiking.

"We would have," Tim said indignantly. "We were just—"

"Just standing there with your tongues hanging out, from what I saw. Didn't look like you could have strung two words together."

Lash fixed me with a severe look. "Dude. We were being *suave*."

"Yeah." Tim attempted a glare. "That's it. Suave."

By the time we had all showered, it was dark outside. Isis called Spike and Caveman, who appeared in the doorway a few minutes later. Then she dialed the Australians. "Hi, this is Isis. We're ready to go now. Sorry it's taken so long . . . what's that? . . . really? . . . oh, I'm sorry to hear that. Well, good luck with your hike . . . Yeah, you too. Bye." She hung up the phone with a resigned expression. "They're not coming."

"What?" Tim said. His face fell.

"Yeah, they said it was getting late and they'd rather just go to bed."

"What did you say to them?" he demanded.

"You heard what I said to them."

"No, what did you *really* say? You must have been using some kind of female mind control beam." He imitated a computer voice. "*Stay away. These men belong to us.*"

"Mrowr!" Lash added.

Spike laughed. "Men are so weird. It's a wonder we ever get along with them."

"You women are the weird ones," Lash said. "It's like a conspiracy. Using your mysterious wiles and powers to keep your competition away."

"Lashy-Lash," Isis said sweetly. "We don't waste our feminine wiles on other women. It's so much easier to control *men*. We just bombard you with our Female Power Rays until you stand there all moony-eyed with your jaws hanging open."

"Dude," he protested feebly. "We were *being suave*."

The margaritas were excellent, actually, but so huge that I nursed one all evening long and still got slightly drunk. Lash ordered a Dos Equis, which came in a tankard fully the size of his head. He stared at it for a while, gave a shrug and a little smile, and drank the whole thing before the food arrived. He ordered another one as we wolfed down our tacos and plates of rice and soupy refried beans, and a third one shortly afterwards.

"Lash, are you sure that's a good idea?" Spike asked.

"In other stories we're following," Caveman said in his best newscaster voice, "an Appalachian Trail hiker exploded this evening from excessive beer consumption. Friends tried to prevent the man from ordering his third gallon."

Lash gave us an obstinate stare. "You guys're makin' fun of me. If the Australians were here, I bet they wouldn' make fun of me."

"Sure, Lash, drink away your sorrows," Tim said. He was the only one of us who hadn't ordered a drink, I noticed.

"Hey, I tried, man," I said. "They were just tired. Besides, they're nobos. You'd never see them again."

"Feminine mind control beams," Lash said, and stumbled off to the bathroom.

"You're not drinking tonight, Tim?" I asked.

"I don't really feel like it. I feel kind of . . . subdued tonight, you know? Just how close the end of the Trail is. We're in freaking Georgia."

"And those lovely Australians turned you down," Isis said.

"One of life's great missed opportunities." Tim sighed theatrically. "But they were just nobos, after all. And I bet neither of them could've hiked five steps barefoot." Isis and I laughed, but Tim continued. "Seriously, I mean this. You guys have raised my standards. You're pretty, but you're also smart. And tough. I've never met a tougher pair of women. Here's to you." He raised his water glass.

"Thanks, Tim," Isis said. "That's really sweet."

"I want to make a toast to all of you guys," I said. "Southbounders." (Lash came back and sat down quietly.) "We've been through a hell of a winter together. There were so many times when I was just ready to give up and pack it in, ride a Greyhound from the next town. Then I'd look around me and see all of you surviving. More than that. Being *happy* surviving. It takes a rare kind of person to do that. Some of you guys can be a pain in the ass sometimes—" Tim and Lash shrugged and made "who, me?" expressions, "—but one thing I know: I couldn't have done this without you. You guys all rock. I'm so glad to have met you, hiked with you. To the winter sobos of 2000!" I raised my glass high.

"Hear, hear!" The rest of the table followed suit.

Only Lash still looked glum. "What about Heald, man? He hiked back north to see us, but he's stayin' in the woods tonight. Save money, he said. I feel bad for him. Gotta do something to make it up to him." He brightened.

"I know. Gonna get him a fifth of bourbon. Pack it out tomorrow. Yeah." He drained the last of his tankard with an effort.

After the bill was settled, we left the restaurant and ran across the busy four-lane road to a supermarket in the shopping plaza on the far side. The margarita was powerful; I felt the ground swaying underneath us. Isis and I picked up a loaf of French bread and a wedge of Brie to celebrate something—something that was very clear at the time, but would make little sense by morning light. Lash decided against bourbon—"Dude, it all comes in these glass bottles"—and instead, for reasons which made even less sense than our celebration, bought a five-liter box of blush wine.

Isis and I tried to talk him out of it. "Lash, do you know how much that *weighs*?"

"Got to make it up to Heald," he said doggedly, lugging the box to the cash register.

Back at the hotel, Lash took the silver wine bag out of its box and tried to fit it into his pack. No matter how he squashed it down, or how tightly he stuffed in the rest of his gear, it wouldn't quite fit. Finally, with a sigh, he lifted the bag of wine and took a long swig from the spigot.

Isis and I couldn't help laughing.

Lash slumped back in the threadbare armchair. "Isis. Jackrabbit. I wanna tell you somethin'." He raised his index finger as though lecturing and squinted at a point in midair. "You don' know how hard it is to, to hike with you. You're famous. Everybody knows the Barefoot Sisters. I wanna get some credit. I hiked this whole trail, too. But I meet these nobos. They say, 'dude! You know the Barefoot Sisters?' They don' say, 'dude? You're Lash?' They don' even ask about my hike. You don' know how hard it is!"

"I'm sorry," Isis said, though I could tell she was trying not to laugh. He did cut a somewhat ridiculous figure, slouching in an old pink armchair, wagging his finger at us, with the stripe shaved out of the middle of his beard. "But it's not our fault, really."

"We didn't ever want to be famous," I said. "It's no picnic for us, either."

Lash looked skeptical. "You don' know how *hard* it is."

"Seriously, Lash," I said. "You ever think about what it's like to have people come up and ask if they can poke your feet? Have you ever lost count of the number of people that said to you, in one day's time, 'you must be crazy'? Do you think we *like* being treated like freaks of nature, just because we enjoy hiking a little differently than most people?"

He was still sulking. "I jus' wan' some *credit*!"

"Lash, you get credit from me," I said quietly. "You get credit for putting up with us all those miles. For hiking a freaking twenty-five to catch up with us before Grayson. Bringing us wine at N.O.C. Being a gentleman."

"Mostly," Isis interjected.

"You get credit for hiking the whole Trail so far, which is more than I can say I've done. And anybody who doesn't give you credit—well, just send 'em my way and I'll set 'em straight." I cradled my right fist in my left palm.

Lash grinned. "Yeah. Tha's more like it." In a few minutes, he was snoring softly. Tim helped us lift him out of the chair and onto the bed.

The morning looked all too bright. I squinted against the glare in the parking lot, trying to clear the muzziness from my brain. I could only imagine how Lash was feeling. He was on his feet, though, and he and Tim, ever hopeful, scanned the parking lot and the row of curtained windows for signs of the Australians.

The hotel manager helped us load our packs into the van in the morning, energetically tossing the stinking bundles into the back. "There you go! Hup! One more!" He brushed off his hands on his jeans.

"Did those two northbound girls take off?" Tim asked.

"What, the ones with the funny accent? Yeah, I took 'em up to the gap first thing this morning."

Tim and Lash looked crestfallen. Lacking a better target, they turned their attention to Isis and me.

"That was some night, ladies," Tim smirked.

"Ooh, baby," Lash said. He turned to the hotel manager. "Guess you'll be burning *those* sheets."

The man laughed and shook his head. "Naw, those sheets are fine. I went by there twice last night to check. Didn't hear a thing."

Isis

We hiked out late under a gloomy sky. The forest, so recently released from ice, seemed drained of color. All of the views were the same: lifeless ridges that resembled creased piles of dryer lint. I could feel jackrabbit's spirits sink as the clouds darkened. Her shoulders hunched, and she walked with a quick, clipped stride that was almost a limp. When three hours had passed and the rain hadn't started, we sat down in the tangled branches of an enormous fallen tree and got out our lunch: the French bread and Brie. Jackrabbit, somewhat cheered by the prospect of good food, smiled and said,

"All we need is the wine!" Just then, Lash walked up. We hadn't even realized he was behind us.

"You've gotta help me," he groaned, throwing down his top-heavy pack and pulling out the silver bladder of rosé.

"I'd do anything for you, darling," laughed jackrabbit, holding out her tin camping cup.

She drank a few cupfuls and put on her shoes—by then, we knew that walking barefoot under the influence of anything, be it boxed wine or ibuprofen or the emergency aspirin one can get by chewing willow bark, was not worth the risk—and suddenly she was happy, whistling as she struggled up the gray Georgia hills with the sky threatening rain and the thick mud sticking to the soles of her sandals.

jackrabbit

As evening fell, we all assembled at Hogpen Gap—Spike and Caveman, Lash, Tim, Isis, and I. Dusk had begun to gather in the oak woods on either side of the path. Lash was visibly dragging; the added weight of the wine was getting to be too much for him. At the bottom of the gap, we crossed a deserted, winding mountain road and found a flat space of cleared ground with room for all of our tents and tarps. Nearby, a leaf-clotted marshy pool of water reflected the last light.

Heald and Annie came down the trail a few minutes later. "Don't like to camp so close to a road," Heald said by way of greeting.

"It's getting dark, man," Lash said. "And I haven't heard any traffic on that road. Hey, it's good to see you. I'm sorry we went to town without you and all."

"No problem. Me and Annie, we had a good time in the woods. Met some crazy northbounders. Jeez." He shook his head. "Some people, you just gotta wonder. Saw a couple of guys that must've been carrying eighty pounds apiece. One of 'em says to the other, 'where are we?' and the other guy says, 'gee, lemme check.' Then he takes out one of them GPS things. Must've weighed a full pound. He starts reading off numbers. Finally he looks up, and he says, 'Far as I can tell, we're still in Georgia.'"

We all laughed.

"That's a good one, dude," Lash said. "Hey, I got something for you." He reached into his pack and took out the wine bag. It was still mostly full.

Heald's eyes brightened. "Is that what I think it is? You packed that thing all the way out here for me? Lash, you shouldn't've."

I filtered our drinking water from a slow-flowing spring at the edge of the marsh, where a fresh current welled up and made an oily turmoil on the surface in the failing light. As I moved aside a submerged oak leaf, clearing a space for the filter intake, a salamander moved ponderously out of the way. It was dark blue, patterned with tiny white points like stars. I moved another leaf and startled one of a different color—brownish red with a crosshatch pattern on its back. I took a closer look—a multitude of salamanders, large and small, swam between the leaves. The oak woods around me, which had seemed so dead when we arrived, looked suddenly full of secrets, full of hidden life waiting to emerge.

Spike and Caveman turned in early, retiring to their big dome tent. Lash and Tim set up their tarps, but returned to the bank where Isis, Heald, and I sat.

"We should make a fire," Isis said.

Heald shook his head. "Naw, too close to the road."

Instead, we sat around the candle lantern in the gathering dark, passing the bag of wine back and forth. Isis refused categorically—"it came out of a *box*!"—but the rest of us enjoyed it.

"Come on, Isis," Lash said. "This is the kind of wine my *mother* drinks. It's innocuous."

"Big word," Heald grunted.

"Yeah, well, that's what my mom says. Means it won't knock you out."

Heald chuckled. "Pass it over here, then." He took a long swig. "You know, Lash, I think you're much smarter than you want people to think you are."

In the thin candlelight, I couldn't see Lash's face. By the way he laughed, though, a little forced, it seemed that Heald had hit close to the mark. "If you keep people's standards low enough," he finally said, "you can always exceed their expectations."

Heald sat up, alert to some sound I hadn't yet detected. "Car coming," he said in a tense voice. "Cover the light."

Isis blew out the candle lantern. Now I heard the sound of the approaching motor, too, and saw the headlights coming over the crest of the hill.

"I never like to camp this close to a road in the South," Heald said in the sudden dark. "Out on the Trail, you can trust people. But you never know who's coming up the road. Joe Redneck and his buddies looking for somebody to blame for all the shit that's happened to 'em. I heard too many stories. Had a couple close calls myself, when I was too dumb to know better.

Here, I figure we got strength in numbers. Just as good we didn't light a fire, though."

"Yeah," Tim said. "This country around here is where *Deliverance* was set. Wasn't it s'posed to be based on a true story?"

"Tim," Isis said in a warning tone. "If you freak me out again . . ."

"Sorry, Isis." There was little contrition in his tone.

The car slowed a bit as it came through the gap. We all held our breath. I remembered the truck that had nearly run over John and me before we crossed the Roans. Then the car passed, the red taillights receding in the dark, flashing between the tree trunks.

"Jeez," Heald said. "I feel like a bunch of hobos, hiding out in a boxcar when the cops go by."

"Bunch of sobos," I said.

Heald gave a snort of laughter. "Here, pass me that wine again."

The day dawned gray, but the clouds broke up as we packed our tent. I filtered two more liters from the leafy spring. No more salamanders came to light; they must have hidden themselves well for the daylight hours.

In the hazy sunlight, the north Georgia mountains seemed to stretch forever into the purple distance. Our endpoint was somewhere out there, somewhere close, but none of us knew which mountaintop it was. Isis and I paused at the top of the first steep ridge to search for Springer, and Lash and Tim came trotting up behind us.

"I think it's that one," Lash said, indicating a flat-topped ridge in the middle distance.

"That can't be it; too close. We're still, like, thirty-five miles from it," Tim said.

"Thirty-five miles. That's, like, nothing," Lash said. "That's a day and a half."

I looked around. All of us wore the same expression of disbelief.

Tim gave a lewd wink. "A lot can happen in thirty-five miles, eh, ladies?"

Isis rolled her eyes. "Give it up, Tim."

I was pretty tired of his nonstop innuendo, too. "If you haven't gotten laid in the last 2,133 miles, Tim, what makes you think you'll get lucky in the next thirty-five?"

We came to Neel's Gap at midmorning. Sounds of traffic came up through the leafless woods for a long while before we saw the road. The

white blazes of the Trail led through the alcove of a stone and wooden building, the Walasi-Yi Outdoor Center. We'd heard about the place from people
who had hiked in previous years, and from the nobos we had met. Thirty
miles from Springer, Walasi-Yi is the first outfitter's store that nobos reach,
and the first place with a phone and easy access to transportation. Many
people completely overhaul their packs there, buying expensive new gear
to replace things deemed too heavy or bulky in the first few days of hiking.
Others, realizing that thru-hiking is not quite what they thought, leave the
Trail there.

Downstairs, right next to the white-blazed posts of the alcove, was a small
room with washers, dryers, and an overflowing hiker box. Isis rifled through
the hiker box, emerging with two bags of dried fruit—banana chips and
pineapple—and several gourmet freeze-dried meals.

"Sweet! Nice haul," I said.

"Yeah. Look at these dinners—the expensive kind!"

"Who would have left food like that?"

"Maybe they quit the Trail. Can you imagine quitting after thirty miles?"
she said.

"Thirty miles. Where would that have put us sobos, Nesuntabunt?"

"Earlier, I think. That swamp with all the bugs. We had to run over the
bog bridges for about a quarter mile. Remember?"

"Oh, yeah. I did think about quitting there. It wasn't an option, though."

"Maybe that's why sobos have a higher finishing rate," Isis mused. "We
don't really have an out until Monson. We have to be more committed from
the start."

"Or maybe we *ought* to be committed!" I said. "Look at what we've been
through: eaten alive by bugs, icebound, frostbitten, hungry . . . why would anybody in their right mind go sobo?"

"The people," Isis said. "Look at the friends we have."

Lash and Tim came around the corner of the building, each holding a
Snickers bar. "Any chance the exchange rate has gone up?" Lash asked.

Tim made puppy dog eyes. "Time's running out."

We took our packs up to the porch on the side of the building, where
there were picnic tables with another view of countless late winter mountains. The sun bounced off the flagstones and the wall, making a small patch
of warmth. Isis and I bought a couple pints of Ben and Jerry's, that staple of
hiker hangouts all along the Trail, and set to work. Lash and Tim sat at the
next table clad in ratty spandex, mending their shorts with inexpert stitches.

Heald lay on the flagstones, napping, with Annie draped over his midriff. Spike and Caveman came up in a few minutes with their own cartons of ice cream in hand.

A small group of northbounders, looking a little shell-shocked and uncertain, leaned their enormous packs against the railing. I remembered the feeling of the first few days on the Trail—the full-body weariness and disorientation, the perpetual effort of suspending disbelief. *Two thousand miles is just a number to them*, I thought, and I wanted to reassure them that yes, what they were doing was possible.

"You guys thru-hiking?" I asked.

"That's the plan," one of them said. He was a tall, lanky fellow, barely out of his teens.

"Awesome. Enjoy it while it lasts. This trail is a pretty amazing experience." Suddenly I realized my voice echoed the wistful tones of ex-hikers I had met all along the Trail.

"Are you a southbounder?" he asked, incredulous.

I nodded and gestured toward our ragtag group. "All of us, actually."

We enjoyed a few moments of adulation, shaking hands with the new nobos and wishing them luck—all of us except Heald, who squinted up into the bright sunlight and grunted something, but didn't move.

After the ice cream, we settled into a comfortable stupor, leaning against the picnic tables and soaking up the sunlight.

"I don't feel like hiking," Spike said, lolling against Caveman's shoulder. "I feel like . . . slacking. Yeah."

"Sounds good to me," Isis said.

Caveman stirred. "This is a popular place. Chances are we can find somebody to shuttle us to Woody Gap or thereabouts, and hike back."

"And then we could stay at the cabins down the road, and eat town food!" Spike said, getting more excited.

Lash, Heald, and Tim elected to stay on the trail for one more night. Part of me was sorry to be spending our second-to-last night as southbounders without them, but most of me was glad to be away from the deluge of innuendo and double entendre that followed Lash and Tim like a bad smell.

In a short while, we sat in the back of Wes Wisson's van, headed for Woody Gap. A stout man in a plaid shirt and jeans, he regaled us with tales of the hikers he had shuttled. "There's one guy I brought out here this spring, said he was going to hike the Trail eating nothing but power bars. I said, 'good luck, buddy!' Haven't heard anything since. Another guy, couple of years ago, called me from Atlanta wanting a shuttle up to Amicalola. So I went down there, and he had all the gear, you know, brand new pack, new tent, new boots, new rain gear. Musta spent thousands of dollars on it. And then, about five days later, I get a call here at Neel's Gap, from somebody wants to go back to Atlanta. I get here, and it's the same guy! He said hiking wasn't his thing. I thought, jeez, the least you can do is try it out first, before you spend four thousand bucks on it! There's no telling what people will do with their money."

The grass in the valley was beginning to turn green. In a few places, the fragile buds of daffodils peeked up through the mud. I thought how difficult it would be to leave the Trail now, with spring just starting, and I was glad that Isis and I planned to yo-yo. I wondered what lay ahead of us on our return journey. The southbound trip had been one surprise after another, some wonderful, some terrible. I had no idea what to expect or prepare for in our northbound hike.

Wes grew reflective as the countryside rolled past. "The Trail's a wonderful thing for a lot of people. It brings folks together. It's given me opportunities. Before I started this shuttle business, I was just a retired guy on a disability pension. Now I'm famous!"

Spike began to giggle.

"Oh, it's true," Wes told her with a look of severity. "Did you ever hear of a guy named Bill Bryson?"

"Oh, that was you!" Caveman exclaimed. "You're the guy that shuttled Bill Bryson from Atlanta! I remember that part of the book! I kind of pictured you older and crustier, though."

"He did take a few . . . liberties," Wes said, smiling. "But it made me famous. It really did. My wife and I were flying to Paris for our fortieth anniversary, and somebody on the plane knew who I was from that book. He must've said something to the flight attendant, because all of a sudden they announced it over the intercom. They said, 'Ladies and gentlemen—'" he paused, enjoying the memory, "—'we have a famous person on board, Mr. Wes Wisson!' So I stood up, and people were cheering for me! They really were!"

He stopped the van in a gravel parking lot, and in a moment my eyes found the first white blazes and the narrow path winding off into the trees.

"Woody Gap," he said. "I'll see y'all tomorrow, then, at the cabins."

"Can I shake your hand, Wes, since you're famous?" Spike asked, with laughter playing about her face.

"Maybe tomorrow," he answered her, barely suppressing a grin.

We raced along the path in the midday sun, giddy with the sudden freedom of leaving our packs behind, passing droves of northbounders. On one mountaintop, there was a young woman trying to get reception for her cell phone. "Hello? Can you hear me? Hello? I can't hear you. Where are you?" The new hikers seemed to be almost all overburdened and underprepared, looking glum and resentful under huge loads. It was difficult, sometimes, not to laugh at the gear we saw; one man carried a cast iron saucepan that must have weighed ten pounds, and another had an electric coffee-maker strapped to the outside of his pack. I remembered the contemptuous comments of some northbounders we had met in Maine, though, and I tried to be considerate. I knew I must have looked just as foolish when I started southbound.

As evening wore on, we came to the shoulder of Blood Mountain, a place called Slaughter Gap. The sun set in a fierce red light that seemed to ooze between the branches and drip from the trees.

"I feel like Lady Macbeth," Spike said, looking at her hands. Turned palms-up, they looked bloody in the weird light.

"This is freaky!" Isis said.

"Where does the name Blood Mountain come from, anyway?" I asked. "And Slaughter Gap?"

Caveman said, "I think there was a big massacre here, when the settlers were fighting the Cherokees. I can't remember which side got killed."

"Probably the Indians," Spike said. "Whoever it was, a bunch of people died here." She shivered in the diminishing red light. "History's all about people dying, people killing, people taking things that don't belong to them. I want to write a new history."

"I think that hiking the Trail is a step toward it," Caveman said. "You begin to see the continuity of things out here. We're all part of the same community."

"Yeah," I said. "If we could just extend that to society out beyond the Trail."

"It's our mission," Spike said in a mock-heroic tone. "We must keep the Trail spirit alive, to bring freedom, happiness, and ramen to all mankind."

"I love you, guys," Caveman said in a drunk, weepy voice, and we all broke down laughing. The spell of the red hillside dissolved around us.

All day, I had been expecting to cross paths with Lash and Heald. We finally found them at the summit of Blood Mountain, two and a half miles south of Neel's Gap. The Blood Mountain Shelter loomed behind us, a stocky four-sided building of stone and timber that looked like a fortress.

"Hey, guys, you've gotta see this," Lash said. He stood on a rock pile by the shelter. I scrambled up beside him and looked out over the valley. Twilight had stained the sky dark red and purple, with a thin rim of gold along the western edge. The tops of distant mountains reflected the fading light, and the lights of houses in the valleys were just coming on, little enclaves of fireflies here and there among the deep shadows of the hogbacked ridges.

"Isn't that awesome?" he said. "Isn't that the most awesome thing in the world? The lights, man. Look at all the lights. All those people down there. And us up here. Long as I live I'm gonna miss this."

Isis, Spike, Caveman, and I said farewell to Lash and Heald, after exacting a promise that they would meet us at Hawk Mountain (eight miles from Springer) the following night. We galloped down the mountain in the gathering dark, leaping over roots and caroming off the larger rocks. Spike's joyous whinnying laugh echoed through the dusky trees as she ran. Far off in the valleys, more lights began to flicker on, and we ran faster, just for the sheer joy of running, free, packless. I felt as though I had suddenly gained superhuman jumping abilities. We made it from the summit to the road in half an hour, and came to Walasi-Yi just as the Goose Creek Cabins van came into the parking lot.

The driver was a grandfatherly man in his sixties, whose whole face crinkled up when he smiled. "Welcome," he said. "We can go on down to town for dinner if y'all'd like that. It's all-you-can-eat crab legs night at the Riverside."

"Sounds good to me!" Caveman said.

The Riverside Café was a busy diner, set, as the name suggested, on the bank of a rushing river. From our table, we could look almost straight down on the water. The air was thick with the perfume of frying things. The waitress, a petite young woman with permed blond hair and makeup that threatened to overwhelm her features, poured us water and handed menus around.

"Our special tonight," she said in a thick drawl, "is the all-you-can-eat crayubb for ten ninety-nine. For twelve ninety-nine you get crayubb and shriy-ump."

Other than the seafood, everything on the menu was fried: fried trout, fried chicken, chicken-fried steak. Even the vegetable side dishes—turnip, squash, sweet potato, okra—passed through the Fry-o-lator. The food arrived quickly and was plentiful, accompanied by pitcher after pitcher of sweet tea. Isis, Spike, and I got identical-looking plates piled high with breaded, fried things. Trout, turnips, sweet potatoes—it was all indistinguishable in a coating of breadcrumbs, but it tasted heavenly to our trail-whetted appetites.

Caveman's plate was different; a tangle of long, ungainly crab legs draped over a heaping bowl of Gulf shrimp. It looked like a large amount of food, even for a hiker.

"Just what the doctor ordered," he said, smiling, and dug into the plate with abandon.

Caveman surfaced as the three of us were halfway done with our fried platters, and the waitress, frowning slightly, brought him another heaping plate.

There were other tables of hikers in the restaurant, easily recognizable by their lightweight clothes and general scruffiness, but none of them were as scruffy as the four of us, and none nearly as hungry. We drew more than a few stares.

"I guess they must not get too many southbounders here this time of year," Spike said, after the waitress brought out Caveman's third plate of crab legs with an alarmed expression on her face. We ordered some French fries to keep him company.

The restaurant was clearing out by the time Caveman's appetite slowed down. The fourth plate of seafood languished on the table. Caveman picked up half a crab and put it in the end of his sleeve like a red, warty hand. He stirred his water glass with the crab legs, then reached up to scratch his head with a look of stern concentration. Isis and Spike and I clutched our bellies, laughing helplessly. Caveman used the crab legs to wave down the waitress, who approached our table with a certain trepidation.

"Y'all want the check?" she asked, and Caveman shook his head.

"Before you bring it, could I please have a small dish of vanilla ice cream?"

Isis

A series of five or six short, steep hills, where the map's elevation profile showed two nearly level miles, changed our easy twelve-mile day into a grueling march. We doubted our position on the map, wondered aloud whether we'd gotten lost on an older section of trail, as we had in Pennsylvania, and almost went back to look for a place where we might have taken a wrong turn. The iron-gray sky didn't help our moods—now that our Gore-Tex had given out, rain threatened us with hypothermia as well as discomfort.

"If there was a train track right here," jackrabbit growled as we slogged up the fourth unexpected PUD, "I'd hop on the first freight car that came along, and go right home to Maine. If there was a road, I'd hitch out. I'm sick of this."

"Nothing but logging roads between here and Springer, and I doubt we'll see any cars on them," I told her. "I'm afraid we're in it for the long haul."

Twenty minutes later, we came down into Hightower Gap, where the trail crossed the intersection of two logging roads. To my surprise, I noticed a small blue car parked in the V of gravel between the roads. I turned to jackrabbit.

"Hey look, there's your ride! You still wanna hitch out?"

"It'd be hard to hitch a ride from a car with no driver," she said, her lips curving in a faint smile. "I wonder what the driver's doing out here, anyway?"

"Probably taking a hike," I said.

"This time of evening? This time of year? *This* stretch of trail? No one in their right mind . . ."

Her voice trailed off, and we looked at each other, laughing.

The twilight deepened as we hiked the last half-mile up to Hawk Mountain Shelter, where we planned to spend the final night of our southbound hike. *One foot in front of the other*, I told myself, picking my way up the rocky trail in the gathering darkness. *The shelter can't be far from here.* I heard running footsteps and looked up. A handsome, clean-shaven young man with bright blond hair, wearing sneakers, shorts, and about fifty Mardi-Gras necklaces was hurtling down the trail toward us. *My God, he must be crazy!* I thought. *I wonder who on earth he is. Not a northbounder, that's for certain. No one would have that kind of energy after his first day hiking. A sobo? Crazy. Sobo.* Suddenly I had it—Tuba Man.

It was indeed Tuba Man, on his way back down to his car to get his tuba. He had gotten jackrabbit's last e-mail update, calculated the day we'd reach Hawk Mountain, and driven out to the Trail to serenade us on the night before we finished.

"I forgot the pizza, though." He sounded contrite, as though he'd messed up a really important plan. "I was going to bring you a pizza. I could still go back to town and get one . . ."

"Pizza! Forget pizza!" jackrabbit laughed, flinging her arms around his beaded neck. "You brought yourself!"

It was an interesting evening at Hawk Mountain. Spike and Caveman had arrived early. Tim, Lash and Heald came in a little after we did, bringing the total number of Y2K sobos at the shelter to eight. Of the thirty-odd starting nobos camped there, nine were "repeat offenders"—people who had hiked the Trail in previous years and returned to hike it again. There were almost as many of us who had completed, or nearly completed, thru-hikes, as there were beginners who had just hiked their first eight miles of the A.T.

Jackrabbit, Spike, Caveman, and I gathered wood for a campfire, while Tuba Man played an arrangement of "Linus and Lucy" so fast that I wondered how he found time to breathe. An hour later, he was playing something more sedate, when two men dressed in full camouflage, carrying assault rifles and what looked like binoculars on strings around their necks, stepped into the light of our fire. The older one cleared his throat and began speaking.

"We're with the Army Rangers," he said. "We're training a group of R.O.T.C. cadets here tonight, and we're going to simulate a reconnaissance mission. A few of our men will pose as enemy soldiers; they'll build a campfire behind the shelter. At twenty-one hundred hours—forty-five minutes from now—the cadets will move in from the north, circle the shelter in a clover-leaf formation, and take notes on the enemy position. After ten minutes, they'll leave the way they came, and return to the rendezvous point. Thank you for your cooperation."

"Cooperation?" I asked jackrabbit, as the men vanished into the woods. "It doesn't sound like we have any say in the matter."

At ten of nine, I headed to the woods to pee, but stopped halfway there. What if the R.O.T.C. class had arrived early? What if they were out there even now, watching our every move? I could wait to pee until I was sure they had come and gone.

I waited. Nine o'clock came and went, and not the least rustle of a leaf betrayed the presence of the R.O.T.C. class. *Damn, these guys are good*, I thought to myself. *Either that or they're late.* I crossed my legs under the table, and asked the woman sitting across from me, a petite, frail-looking brunette named Abbie, how it felt to be a repeat offender.

"It's a dream come true," she answered. "I've missed the Trail every day since I finished, back in '98."

Around quarter to ten, a loud crashing noise came from the woods down the hill to the north of us. Ten or fifteen yards beyond the shelter clearing, I could see about twenty people, most of whom seemed to have glow-sticks taped to their backs, running back and forth between the rhododendron bushes. They continued dodging from thicket to thicket, occasionally tripping over each other with muffled curses, for the next five minutes. Laughing to myself, I walked a ways into the forest on the other side of the shelter and relieved my aching bladder.

When I returned, I found Tim and Tuba Man telling a story to a rapt audience of hikers, while jackrabbit bandaged a cut on Tuba Man's hand. In the background, the crashing and cursing continued, still concentrated down the hill to the north of us.

"We decided, since they were doing such a lousy job of sneaking up on us," Tim said, "we'd circle around behind *them*, sneak up on them, and show them how it's done."

"The poor kids!" I exclaimed. "You probably gave them the fright of their lives!"

"Naw. The guy I sneaked up on, he just thought I was one of his companions. When he saw I was a hiker, he looked kinda confused, not scared or anything. But Tuba Man—"

"I sneaked right up behind this guy," Tuba Man said with a grin, "and he didn't even notice me. So I jumped up and hollered, 'who brought the beer?' Then he turned around, and I noticed that he wasn't a kid. He was one of the officers. He glared at me for a minute, and then he said, in this really disapproving voice, 'we're on a mission here.'"

An hour or so later, when the R.O.T.C.ers had finally crashed away down the mountain, I lay in my sleeping bag, going over in my mind the evening that had just passed. It seemed so surreal: forty hikers at one shelter, tuba music, Mardi-Gras beads, and the inept soldiers-in-training running around in the bushes with glow-sticks on their backs.

When I thought of the day that lay ahead of us, though, it seemed even less believable. Eight miles to Springer. Eight miles out of two thousand one hundred and sixty-eight. (This was the number the *Data Book* offered—more accurate, I knew, than the mileage on the sign atop Katahdin. The actual length of the A.T. varies each year as sections are relocated.) I'd been hiking toward Springer for eight and a half months, through the White Mountains and the rocks of Pennsylvania and a winter I couldn't have imagined until I found myself in the midst of it. And now it was half a day's journey away. It was too much to contemplate. I closed my eyes and fell asleep.

jackrabbit

M ist hung about the trees in the morning as I packed up the wet tent. For once, I didn't mind the extra weight of it—I knew today's hike would be short. Tuba Man came over as I stuffed the soggy bundle into my pack.

"Hey, thanks for coming out here," I said.

"No prob. I had a good time." In the early morning light, his eyes were a heart-stopping shade of blue.

I wanted to say something, anything, but I found myself tongue-tied. "It's great to see you," I finally blurted.

"Yeah. It's good to be back here. I miss the Trail."

"I hope, I mean, maybe, I'll see you again sometime?" My voice came out high and breathless, and I knew I was blushing.

He didn't seem to notice, though. "You never know where me and Charisma might turn up," he said with a sweet smile that made my knees weak. Then he was gone, walking down the side trail with his sleeping bag and tuba under one arm, waving to everyone with his free hand. I watched him until he disappeared into the thick fog.

Isis and I finished packing and left the shelter only a few minutes behind the other sobos. We walked barefoot in the cool red mud, wearing a few strands of Mardi-Gras beads that Tuba Man had given us. I had expected to feel boundless elation as the destination approached, but the fog-shrouded woods seemed to swallow up my feeling of triumph. Instead, I felt a certain numbness, and something almost like regret. *I'm finishing the Trail, but I haven't even hiked the whole thing. I've spent eight months of my life doing—what?* It seemed like just another day on the Trail. I kept walking. The thick clay underfoot stuck between my toes, staining my feet red.

A few miles into the day, we followed the short side trail to Long Creek Falls. Among the rhododendrons, indistinct in the mist, the rain-swollen stream cascaded over a ten-foot drop. The rush of falling water shut out all other sounds. Isis and I stopped to eat a snack, and I watched the ever-changing shapes of lace in the current. All at once I felt the singularity of time close in around me: *This is the only time I will ever stand here, in this weather, twenty-three years old, thinking exactly these thoughts, my feet exactly here in the dead leaves. Each moment of my life is as unique, as irrevocable, as the patterns in this waterfall.*

Before long, we came to a Forest Service parking lot. It began to rain steadily, long needles of water that shimmered in the open air. We pulled up the hoods of our jackets. I read the wooden trail sign tacked to a tree at the edge of the clearing:

Springer Mtn. Shelter   *0.7*
Springer Mtn.   *0.9*

Less than a mile now. Like the 2,160 miles on the sign at Katahdin's summit (or the 2,168 in the current *Data Book*), it was just a number. But slowly, underneath the numbness in my brain, I could feel joy and amazement gathering. It was March 3, 2001, and a journey of more than eight months was ticking down to its final minutes.

We stopped at the shelter. Tim, Lash, and Heald huddled in their sleeping bags in the loft.

"Did you guys summit yet?" I called.

"No," Tim said, almost wistfully. "I don't want to go up there in the rain. And it's like . . . well, I guess I don't want it to be over, you know?"

Lash peeked out from under his fluorescent orange hat. "Yeah, what he said."

"It's just another mountain," Heald grunted.

"Think we'll go up tomorrow," Lash said.

"Come on, guys," Isis said. "Who's going to take our summit photos?"

Tim intentionally misunderstood. "What'd you say? Naked summit photos?"

"Too cold for that, man," I said. "Come on, somebody's got to take pictures for us."

"Spike and Caveman went up there just a few minutes ago," Heald said. "You could probably catch 'em if you head out now."

"Thanks, man. See you in a few."

We heard Spike's laughter, echoing through the trees in the thickening mist, long before we saw her. She came running down the trail, followed by Caveman, who was grinning from ear to ear.

"Look what I got! Look what he gave me!" Spike said in a breathless voice. She held up her left hand, showing a ring with an enormous glittering diamond.

"Oh, Spike! Congratulations!" I hugged her.

"I carried it for the whole Trail," Caveman said, a little choked-up. "I thought, if we could put up with each other for two thousand miles, it was worth a try—"

"—so he got down on one knee, and he said, 'will you—will you . . .'" tears of happiness streamed down her cheeks.

"That's so sweet. Congratulations," Isis said. "Come back to the summit with us. We'll take pictures for you."

"Thanks," Caveman said. "It's only a couple minutes' hike."

A couple minutes. The sense of joy gathered inside me now, stronger and stronger. We were almost running. The rain picked up, huge chilly drops that dripped from the gray trees and splattered against the hood of my Gore-Tex jacket, but the weather could not mar my happiness. I hardly felt the cold mud and sharp gravel underfoot as we climbed the last few feet of the rise.

And there it was. The low, wooded summit of Springer Mountain in the rain. A brass plaque set in a boulder marked the southern terminus of the Appalachian Trail, and a smaller plaque marked the last blaze. As my fingers touched the cold, wet metal, it finally became real to me—this was the end-point. The destination. This stand of oak trees, this dark rock, this forest around us receding in the mist, was the goal for which we had struggled for so many months. And we had arrived. I found myself laughing and crying at once.

It was too cold to stand still for long. We all took pictures of each other posing by the plaque. Spike showed us where a register was hidden in a cranny under the rock. I wrote a few inane sentences, overcome by emotion, and left a message for the Family from the North. I hoped we would be back on the Trail in time to see them summit. My fingers cramped around the pen in the cold; rain dripped off the hood of my jacket and blurred the letters.

I looked around the clearing one more time, trying to fix it in my memory. The shapes of the trees and rocks seemed to take on meaning, like fragments of a pattern wholly beyond my understanding. I sent a silent prayer of thanks to the overcast, rainy sky. And then we turned to walk down the mountain, back the way we had come.

Isis

We sat in the corner of Springer Mountain Shelter, listening to the rain on the roof.

"My God. We did it. I never really believed we'd make it. And here we are," jackrabbit murmured. I glanced over at her; a radiant smile shone through the tears that still streamed down her face.

I felt buoyant with happiness, but my joy had more to do with Spike and Caveman's engagement and jackrabbit's peace of mind than with any great sense of accomplishment. It was another day on the Trail, no more momentous or heroic than another. We had hiked up to a wooded peak of inconsequential height, important only because its name had been on our tongues for two-thirds of a year. Important because there had been times when we had both thought that we'd never reach it. But why shouldn't we have reached it? We'd reached hundreds of little, wooded mountains, and hiked over most of them without a second thought. Third Mountain. Fourth Mountain. Mount Mist. Bake Oven Knob. Hazeltop. Mount Love. Devil's Tater Patch. Springer. *Springer.* The name still gave me a little shiver of delight, like the name of some magical distant place I'd read about in childhood, Timbuktu or Cairo or Zanzibar; I just couldn't reconcile it to the mountain where we had stood.

I found the shelter register and searched it for the final entries of our other sobo friends. I'd expected poetry and philosophy and heartfelt goodbyes to friends behind, but most of the entries were brief and to the point. *I made it! Can't believe it! Time to hit the nearest town and order the last large pizza I'll be eating by myself for a while.*

The starting northbounders were more prolix, recording their hopes and fears by the paragraph. I wondered if we'd left register entries like that in the Wilderness. Probably. I thought back to our first few weeks on the Trail—no bread, far too many peanuts. Matt sharing his crackers with us at Wadleigh Stream Lean-to. Tenbrooks striding out of a thunderstorm and joining us for tea. Highlander singing in the summer night. Waterfall complimenting jackrabbit on a well-turned Piscataquis Pirouette. Waterfall stealthing with us in the Whites and playing piano with jackrabbit the afternoon before she left Hanover. Waterfall. There had been a time when we thought that we'd finish the Trail together.

"Hey, ya'll! Surprise!" I looked up and she was there, her blue eyes full of laughter, her blond pigtails framing her face under a floppy cotton hat. I had to blink a few times to make sure I hadn't imagined it. Behind her stood a group of other hikers, friends we'd met at the Gathering. They'd all driven out with her to meet us. I sprang to my feet and ran to embrace Waterfall, feeling tears start in the corners of my eyes. Suddenly, I felt like we'd accomplished something. We'd caught up with Waterfall, and here we were, standing on Springer together in the rain.

To be continued . . .